Canada's Population
in a Global Context

Canada's Population in a Global Context

An Introduction to Social Demography

Second Edition   Frank Trovato

OXFORD
UNIVERSITY PRESS

OXFORD
UNIVERSITY PRESS

Oxford University Press is a department of the University of Oxford.
It furthers the University's objective of excellence in research, scholarship, and education
by publishing worldwide. Oxford is a registered trade mark of Oxford University Press in
the UK and in certain other countries.

Published in Canada by
Oxford University Press
8 Sampson Mews, Suite 204,
Don Mills, Ontario M3C 0H5 Canada

www.oupcanada.com

Library and Archives Canada Cataloguing in Publication
Trovato, Frank, 1951-, author
Canada's population in a global context: an introduction
to social demography / Frank Trovato. -- Second edition.

Includes bibliographical references and index.
ISBN 978-0-19-901112-4 (pbk.)

1. Demography--Canada--Textbooks. 2. Canada--Population--
Textbooks. I. Title.

HB3529.T695 2014   304.60971   C2014-904761-4

Cover image: Liz Couldwell & Susan Doyle/Photodisc/Getty Images

Photo Credits: page 1: Sean Kilpatrick / Canadian Press Images;
page 105: Lonely Planet / Getty Images; **page 191:** Erproductions Ltd / Getty Images;
page 339: Stefano Sforza on board the S.S. Italia, 1959. Canadian Museum of Immigration at
Pier 21 (DI2013.1816.2); **page 449:** AFP / Getty Images

Oxford University Press is committed to our environment.
This book is printed on Forest Stewardship Council® certified paper
and comes from responsible sources.

MIX
Paper from
responsible sources
FSC® C103567

Printed and bound in Canada

1 2 3 4 — 18 17 16 15

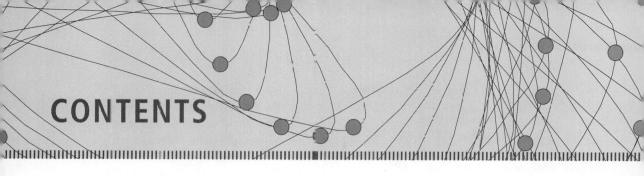

CONTENTS

Part Three
Demographic Processes I: Fertility and Mortality

Part Four
Demographic Processes II: Internal and International Migration

PREFACE

Canada's Population in a Global Context: An Introduction to Social Demography, Second Edition

Since the early 1970s, generations of Canadian college and university students have learned about the demography of this country from a select number of excellent textbooks. Notable among these are the several editions produced by the late Warren Kalbach and his collaborator Wayne McVey (Kalbach and McVey, 1971, 1979; McVey and Kalbach, 1995). The works of Roderic Beaujot and Kevin McQuillan (1982) and of Beaujot and Don Kerr (2004) deserve mention here as well. But although these introductory texts have provided a foundational understanding of the demographic trends and patterns of Canadian society, they give limited attention to the broader global aspects of population as a field of study and as a comparative discipline. This textbook, which shares many features with its predecessors, is designed to complement those excellent textbooks on Canadian population by incorporating a global perspective as well as coverage of the fundamental concepts, theories, and perspectives of demography and population studies.

For a Canadian textbook such as this to adopt an international perspective seems particularly important today, given the intense interest among scholars and the public at large in the phenomenon of globalization. The pervasive diffusion of Western values, ideas, and economic practices has had a homogenizing effect on many countries. Paradoxically, there are also widespread socioeconomic gaps between countries, with poverty an ongoing reality in many parts of the globe. In terms of demographic development, it is clear that while some developing countries have, or nearly have, caught up to the industrialized countries' stage of demographic transition, many others continue to lag far behind. In the light of these divergent demographic and socioeconomic patterns affecting countries worldwide, it seems no longer useful to examine Canadian population in isolation of the broader global context.

This textbook identifies issues at the heart of demography as a scientific field and covers areas of population studies typically included in introductory university courses, including population history and theories of population change; the relationship of population to environment and resources; fertility, mortality, and nuptiality; migration and urbanization; age and sex composition; and population policy. The text's twelve chapters are organized in five parts. Part I deals with the concepts and theories of population studies, including data sources and population history. Part II covers demographic composition, focusing primarily on age and sex structure and nuptiality. Part III is devoted to the central demographic processes of fertility and mortality, while Part IV focuses on the other key demographic process: migration. Finally, Part V examines the interconnection of population with urbanization, the interconnection of population with resources, and the interconnection of population change with policy concerns, each of these treated as a separate chapter. Together, these five parts provide a framework for addressing some fundamental questions:

- What roles do individuals play in the production of demographic phenomena?
- How do culture and social structure influence individual demographic action?
- Why did the human population begin growing at such explosive rates so recently? What important demographic and non-demographic factors are responsible for this?
- Why is the human population distributed unevenly across the world's geographic regions? Why are birth and death rates so low in some parts of the world and relatively high in others?
- Why do some nations discourage population growth and others encourage it?
- How do the demographic histories of Canada and other countries of the industrialized world differ from those of today's developing nations?
- What accounts for the different trajectories of population growth for developing nations versus industrialized societies?

Both reader and instructor will find that this text places strong emphasis on conceptual and theoretical frameworks of demographic phenomena. Wherever possible, figures and schematic representations are offered to clarify key concepts and theories. In over two decades of teaching, I have found illustrations of this kind extremely useful in helping students grasp complex ideas. I have also tried to situate, wherever possible, current and historical Canadian demographic trends as either varying from or conforming to patterns elsewhere in the world, an approach that will help instill in the beginning student a strong appreciation of the universality of demographic concepts, measures, and theories.

Another feature that distinguishes this text from others in the field is its use, where appropriate, of techniques of demographic analysis, which are frequently minimized in or omitted from introductory textbooks. Technical matters are not avoided here, although the techniques featured are kept at an introductory level appropriate for beginning students. I believe it is necessary and beneficial to include technical rudiments of demographic analysis as long as these are presented in an accessible manner. Each chapter, at its conclusion, offers exercises designed to help reinforce substantive and technical material covered in the main text. Instructors are encouraged to incorporate new data as they become available to complement the study questions and the corresponding data laid out in this part of the book. Each chapter also includes a list of additional readings for further exploration.

As with any introductory textbook on population, much of the information used has come from published vital statistics and census materials from Canada and from international statistical agencies, most notably the United Nations and the World Health Organization. Fortunately, there is an abundance of data on population. However, one drawback of this is that new data are always being published, making it virtually impossible for any writer to keep abreast of all the latest statistics. While recognizing this characteristic feature of the field, I have tried to emphasize the enduring and foundational principles of demographic analysis and population studies in the hope that instructors will feel confident relying on the text as a source for the presentation of basic concepts, theories, and methods to their students, in spite of the availability of newer data.

Demographic trends can never occur in isolation of the social, cultural, and institutional contexts of society. The substantive orientation of this textbook is sociological. In particular, I assume that since all societies are, by definition, populations, and since populations are dynamic bodies that are constantly changing, the systematic study of population, to a significant extent, necessarily implies the study of social change. Society cannot be understood in isolation of demography, nor can demography be fully appreciated without knowledge of how sociological structures and processes affect people's actions towards such things as marriage, divorce, children, or moving. Furthermore, demographic change is thought to be both a cause and a consequence of social, institutional, and cultural processes, operating through their effects on individuals' decisions and actions. A systematic appreciation of how populations change in size, distribution, and composition over time, and how these in turn relate to societal processes, is a prerequisite for anyone seriously interested in gaining a fundamental understanding of how societies are structured, how they change, and how they function.

The interconnectedness of demographic and societal change can be illustrated with numerous examples. How is it possible to fully understand the current baby dearth in Canadian society (and in most other industrialized countries today) without first knowing about the baby boom of the postwar years, between 1946 and 1966? How is it possible to properly appreciate the current low fertility pattern without knowing about the successive boom and bust trends in the marriage rate between the 1950s and the early 1980s? On a different note, most readers are acutely aware that over the past three decades or so, Canadian society has been transformed into an increasingly multiracial nation. Is international migration partly or mainly the cause? What has been the role of changing immigration patterns in this phenomenon?

It is my wholehearted belief that such questions are best answered through an interdisciplinary approach. Demography is a field that overlaps greatly with many other disciplines in the natural and social sciences. So, even though the substantive emphasis in this textbook is mainly sociological, many of the theoretical perspectives presented are contributions by scholars from diverse fields, including biology, economics, geography, history, mathematics, anthropology, political science, public health, epidemiology, and statistics, among others. This interdisciplinarity is, in my view, an essential feature of demography as a scientific discipline.

As with the first edition, this version of *Canada's Population in Global Context* places strong emphasis on conceptual and theoretical frameworks in the explanation of demographic phenomena in their cross-national variability and complexity. It is hoped that readers will find this feature of the book both interesting and informative and that it will foster an appreciation of the universality and usefulness of demography as a scientific discipline. The essential structure and conceptual framework underlying the first edition have been maintained. Two main considerations guided my decision to revise. First, it seemed necessary to update the text to take into account the most recent developments in demography and population studies—given the staggering volume of publications in these interrelated fields, this proved to be a challenging, though highly rewarding task. Second, since the publication of the first edition new data on Canadian population has become available based on the 2011 census, it seemed therefore appropriate to update the statistical contents to take into account, where possible, the new census information. At the same time, I have integrated the latest information from the United Nations Population Division on global population trends as well as other major international agencies, including the World Health Organization.

No changes have been made to the notation used in the text. As in the first edition, the subscript x is typically used to denote a given age group or category. For example, in the presentation of the age-specific fertility rate, the formula $f_x = B_x/W_x$ is used. This formula says that the fertility rate (f_x) for women aged x is equal to the number of births to women of that age (B_x) divided by the number of women of that age (W_x). As applied in this textbook, the symbol x can represent either single years of age or grouped age categories, most frequently five-year age groups (e.g., 0–4, 5–9, 10–14, ... or 0, 1–4, 5–9, 10–14, ...). In the formal treatment of grouped age-specific rates, the convention is to represent an age interval symbolically as $x, x + n$, where x is the beginning age in the interval, and n is the number of years in the interval. Demographic rates are typically computed for a specific period of time, most often a calendar year; in such cases, unless otherwise indicated, the population at risk (the denominator) is the mid-year (or more generally, the mid-interval) population. These types of rates are conventionally referred to as "central" demographic rates.

Acknowledgements

In producing this revision I have benefitted from the valuable feedback received from colleagues who teach and conduct research in population studies. Their input has allowed me to refine and expand on certain aspects of the text as to make it more accessible. For this I am especially grateful to Anatole Romaniuk, Rod Beaujot, Ann Gauthier, Teresa Abada, and Alison Yacyshyn. Many students at the University of Alberta offered valuable insights as well, and I am thankful to them. Of course, it goes without saying that responsibility for any inconsistencies or errors rests solely with me.

Oxford University Press provided me invaluable assistance throughout the process of completing this work. Special thanks are due to Tanuja Weerasooriya for her dedicated editorial work and meticulous reading of the chapters, and also Wendy Yano for her excellent copyediting skills. Many thanks to Mark Thompson, Sarah Carmichael, Caroline Starr, Kate Skene, Peter Chambers, and Phyllis Wilson for their involvement at various stages of this project.

My deepest gratitude goes to my family, Frances, Laura, and Cathy, for their patience, continued support and encouragement.

Frank Trovato
Edmonton, 23 July 2014

To the memory of Antonio De Simone.

PART ONE

Population as a Scientific Discipline

1 The Study of Population

Introduction

Demography is commonly perceived by the layperson as a discipline whose principal concern is the rapid growth of human population. This is certainly one aspect of the field. The "population problem" receives much attention in the literature and continues to stimulate important scholarly inquiry. Interest reached a peak during the 1960s and 1970s, when the global population was growing faster than at any other time in history. The threat of "overpopulation," with its dire implications for the future of a world with runaway population growth, became a frequent topic of discussion in the popular media and academic circles, stoked by influential books like Paul Ehrlich's *The Population Bomb* (1968) that warned of looming disaster. This anxiety was also reflected in *The Limits to Growth* (Meadows et al., 1972), a study grounded on a massive simulation model of the world system. It projected, among other things, that the continued exponential growth of humans would have a devastating effect on environmental quality, renewable and non-renewable resources, and industrial output. Pondering the results of their simulation models, the study's authors concluded that if the growth trends in world population, industrialization, pollution, food production, and resource depletion were to

continue unchanged, the limits to growth on the planet would be reached sometime in the twenty-first century, resulting most probably in a sudden, uncontrollable decline in both population and industrial capacity (Meadows et al., 1993: 23).

The population literature today remains concerned with the question of how the world can sustain a growing population that, according to some estimates, will reach 8 billion by 2025 and possibly approach 10 billion by 2050. How will the world cope with environmental and ecological challenges that by most estimations are bound to exacerbate?

The situation concerning population growth is perceived differently, however, depending on which part of the world we examine. For the highly developed industrialized countries the trouble on the horizon may be tied not to explosive growth but to below-replacement birth rates coupled with annual rates of population growth close to zero—into negative figures for some countries. In these countries, population aging and its associated societal implications have surfaced as critical concerns, along with issues surrounding the growing sociocultural diversity of their populations due to increased immigration (Teitelbaum and Winter, 1985). For the developing countries, rates of population growth have also been declining for some time, though clearly not uniformly across all regions. In a subset of countries—the least developed ones—growth rates remain well above the global average, aggravating existing problems of poverty, unemployment, and slow socioeconomic development.

Perhaps less alarmist in tone, scholars remain highly concerned about our collective future given the complex interactions of demographic change with critical dimensions of the human condition—ecological sustainability, climate change, resource scarcity, sociopolitical unrest, and poverty. The world has perhaps escaped the "population bomb," but may not be "out of the woods" (Lam, 2013). A recent work by Jørgen Randers (2012), *2050: A Global Forecast for the Next Forty Years*, is a 40-year follow up to *The Limits to Growth* study (himself a past member of that team). He warns that the world can no longer continue as business as usual. Over the next four decades, the course of the human conditions will be shaped not only by demographic change but also our increasingly fragile capitalist system that is impacted heavily by declining global resources, our ability to maintain democracy in the face of ecosystem decline, rising tensions between the young and older generations, and climate instability.

As concerned individuals, we need to be attentively informed about these important issues facing the planet. Less evident, perhaps, to the beginning student is the fact that the subject matter central to demography is based on some common experiences we all share. Consider this: all of us were born and will someday die, and between these two fateful occurrences we will experience a host of formative events, which might include graduation, a first full-time job, marriage, parenting, divorce, remarriage, widowhood, change of residence, and so forth.

The *timing* and *intensity* of these events—when in life they occur, and how frequently in the population—are important subjects of investigation. *Demographers*—those who study population dynamics—investigate what we call *aggregate manifestations* of such behaviours among broadly defined groups of people.

An example of an aggregate measure is the birth rate. It summarizes the extent to which individual women in the population have given birth during a specified period. Similarly, the death rate can tell us how many members of a particular group, on average, died over a particular time interval. Aggregate measures such as these also mirror aspects of population change. In particular, whether a population will grow, decline, or remain stable in real numbers will depend on shifting rates of *fertility*, *mortality*, and *migration*—the three fundamental variables of demographic analysis.

While fertility, mortality, and migration are central to population change, other factors play an indirect role by acting on these variables. Two examples are age and sex. At the individual level, age and sex are biological facts: every one of us is born male or female, and we measure our age in years. In the aggregate, age and sex are used to characterize the composition of an entire population, so that a population may be described as having a relatively young or relatively old age structure, and a balanced or distorted sex composition. Age and sex are so important in population analysis that they merit their own chapter.

"Population analysis" sounds like an occupation reserved for specialized academic study, yet a look through any of our major daily newspapers reveals that demography is a topic we encounter frequently in the popular press. For example, a headline in the 18 February 2013 edition of the *Globe and Mail* announces, "The baby bust: In a first, the newly retired outnumber the newly hired" (Friesen, 2013). The ensuing story, based on a Statistics Canada report, outlines an unprecedented development in Canada's population: during 2013 the ratio of persons aged 15 to 24 to those aged 55 to 64—a rough measure of the number of new entry-level workers to the number of workers nearing retirement—would fall to below parity (that is, a value of 1:1). Thus, while historically, the number of young Canadians entering the workforce has always exceeded the number nearing retirement, this is no longer the case. Earlier, in the mid-1970s, there were many more young adults to enter the labour force, and this ratio reached a historic maximum at 2.4 to 1. Over the next half-century or so, this ratio is expected to fluctuate, but overall the anticipation is that there will be relatively fewer entry-level workers as compared to older workers. It is important to note that this is not solely a Canadian phenomenon, as many other highly industrialized countries are undergoing a similar demographic change. Common to all these countries is a continuing pattern of below-replacement fertility that began in the early 1970s and therefore accompanying increases in population aging. Among the many possible societal implications of these interrelated trends, Canada is faced by a situation in which the baby boom generation of workers is steamrolling into retirement and soon there will not be enough young people to replace those leaving the workforce. On the other hand, this type of scenario may augur well for young adults' socioeconomic prospects. As they are in short supply, there would be an increased demand for younger workers and consequently a rise in the average wages for entry-level workers. Of course, increased immigration will also figure into this picture as a way to address worker shortages. Clearly, the societal ramifications of an aging population are complex and multidimensional and should be of great interest to both the public at large and especially policy officials.

Another *Globe and Mail* headline warns: "We have seen the future, and it's sprawl and emissions" (Simpson, 2007). This article confirms what many of us know: Canada, the world's second-largest land mass, is a predominantly urban country, with most of its population living in large and expanding metropolitan areas. Urban expansion is gobbling up agricultural land at an alarming rate, with outlying suburban areas growing much faster than urban centres themselves. One consequence of urban sprawl is a greater reliance on automobiles to commute longer distances to work, which results in more greenhouse gas emissions and more pollution. In this case, population growth can be viewed as an indirect contributor to the problems of urban sprawl and increased carbon emissions. With population growth there is increased demand for housing in the less expensive outlying areas surrounding large cities. This in turn generates increased commuting distance to the city and therefore more gas emissions from the increased number of motor vehicles on the road.

In a related *Globe and Mail* story, Dawn Walton (2013) asks: How is the environment on this day? (5 June 2013); 18 facts are reviewed regarding the environment. Population growth is included as a factor in environmental conditions. Walton points out that there are over 7 billion people on the planet, and that 82 per cent of the world's population lives in the developing countries. Moreover, it is stated that in 2012, worldwide births outpaced deaths, with 267 births occurring on average every minute as compared to 107 deaths. Although this net positive natural gain of population bodes well for the continuation of our species, this fact serves to highlight an important point: population growth is an integral part of a complex equation explaining global environmental change—a topic we shall return to later in this book.

A final example is based on a cover story in the 28 May 2007 issue of *Maclean's* magazine: "Hey Lady! What will it take to make you breed?" (George, 2007). This provocative headline speaks to another important population issue facing Canada and most other high-income nations today: baby dearth. Over the last four decades the birth rate has been falling and currently sits at its lowest point in Canadian history. The average Canadian woman in her childbearing years has just 1.6 children; in some countries, this figure is even lower. The demographic implications of very low fertility are far-reaching, and it is the role of the demographer to discover the causes and consequences. We shall discuss this matter in greater detail later in Chapter 6, which deals specifically with fertility.

Newspaper coverage of issues like Canada's aging workforce, urban sprawl, the environment, and baby dearth is proof that these matters are of interest to all Canadians. The importance of population expands beyond Canada, however. Population is a topic of central concern to all citizens of the world. The importance attributed to population issues is highlighted in periodic articles and analyses appearing in influential magazines, including *Science*, *Nature*, *National Geographic*, and the medical journal *Lancet* (see, for example, the story in *National Geographic* [11 July 2013], "On World Population Day, Unpacking 9.6 Billion by 2050," and the feature article in *Nature* by Zlotnik [2013], "Population: Crowd Control," discussing the United Nations' population projections to the year 2050).

Demographers, as we shall see throughout this textbook, play an important role in shedding light on these and other aspects of importance to society.

Population Defined

We have already noted that demography is concerned with the study of population, but before we proceed much further we should clarify that term. Generally, the term *population* refers to a collectivity sharing certain common features. For example, in researching animals in the wild, ecologist Peter Turchin (2003: 19) defines *population* as "a group of individuals of the same species that live together in an area of sufficient size to permit normal dispersal and migration behavior, and in which population changes are largely determined by birth and death processes." In the case of humans one can think of a variety of collectivities: students, workers, physicians, parents—and each one may be considered a population. To a demographer, however, *population* refers specifically to a collectivity of people co-existing within a prescribed geographic territory, such as a country, a province, or a state, at a given point in time (Pressat, 1985: 176); and consistent with Turchin's definition, the collectivity changes as a function of the interplay of migration, birth, and death processes.

Because human populations are constantly changing in size and composition, temporal continuity must also be introduced as another element in our definition. The notion of temporal continuity recognizes that people living today are descendants of many earlier generations (Ricklef, 1990). Norman Ryder (1965) refers to the succession of generations in a population as "demographic metabolism"—a continuing process of societal renewal through the fundamental demographic processes of birth, death, and in- and out-migration. In modern times, the census is the tool that allows us to count the number of persons present in a given area at a specified time (Clarke, 1997: 13–14; Petersen, 2000: 1).

A human population, then, is a dynamic aggregate existing within a defined geographic boundary and continuously changing as a result of the complementary processes of *attrition* (losses through deaths and emigration) and *accession* (gains through births and immigration). A national population exists through time and can be projected using mathematical procedures guided by sound assumptions concerning the anticipated direction and magnitude of changes in fertility, mortality, and migration (Preston, Heuveline, and Guillot, 2001: 1).

Notwithstanding this seemingly straightforward definition, in actuality there are always challenges in delimiting the boundaries of a population. Geoffrey McNicoll (2003a: 731) provides the following example to reinforce this point. "Consider," he writes, "the population of a city. . . . Even if there are agreed physical boundaries, the number of legal residents may differ greatly from the number of *de facto* residents. . . . The actual number of people within a city's defined borders varies greatly by time of day, day of the week, and season." We can add, to this challenge, the fact that for any national population, the census can identify three subsets of the overall population:

the civilian population, the total resident population, and the total population living abroad (including nationals who are military personnel, tourists, professionals of various types, missionaries, students, employees of voluntary organizations, and so forth). As a result, it is seldom possible for the census to trace and enumerate every living citizen of a country, and so there will always be varying degrees of census undercount of population. In Canada, the census undercount has been estimated to be in the range of 2 to 4 per cent (Statistics Canada, *The Daily*, 2003).

Formal Demography and Population Studies

The term *demography* derives from the Greek words *demos*, meaning "people," and *graphia*, meaning "the study of." Demography, then, is the scientific study of population and how population is affected by births, deaths, and migration. Roland Pressat (1985: 54) suggests that most demographic work focuses on three core areas:

1. the size and makeup of populations according to diverse criteria (age, sex, marital status, educational attainment, spatial distribution, etc.)—in short, pictures of a population at a fixed moment;
2. the different processes that bear directly on population composition (fertility, mortality, nuptiality, migration, etc.); and
3. the relationship between these static and dynamic elements and the social, economic, and cultural environment within which they exist.

This last point identifies sociology (and by extension, the social sciences) as an important vehicle towards a proper understanding of population phenomena. Nathan Keyfitz (1996a: 1) is explicit in his acknowledgement of this, calling demography ". . . a branch of sociology [that] uses birth and death rates and related statistics to determine the characteristics of a population, discover patterns of change, and make predictions." The social sciences figure prominently in *population studies*, one of two principal branches of demography customarily recognized in introductory courses. The other branch is commonly known as *formal demography*. While it would be misleading to suggest there is consensus on whether and how to differentiate population studies from formal demography, the division is helpful, particularly in a text of this kind. These two branches are explained in the sections that follow.

Formal Demography

The statistical and mathematical aspects of the field constitute what is commonly called *formal demography*. Formal demography deals with the quantitative study of population in terms of growth, distribution, and development (or change). As David Yaukey (1985: 1) neatly puts it, formal demography is concerned with finding out "how many people, of what kind, are where." The first part of this question, *how many?*, highlights the accounting aspect of demographic analysis involved in determining or estimating, for example, the size of a population and its change over time. The question *of what kind?* draws attention to population composition, the statistical analysis of the distribution of a population in terms of specific demographic characteristics, particularly age, sex, and marital status.

Some of the other characteristics subject to this kind of analysis are racial and ethnic origin, language, religion, employment status, income, and occupation. The final part of the question, *where?*, refers to formal demography's concern with the geographic dimension of population analysis—the distribution and concentration of the population across geographic space, and its mobility across borders.

Achille Guillard, a French political economist, coined the term *demography* in his *Eléments de statistique humaine, ou démographie comparée* (1855). William Petersen (2000: 4) observes that

> earlier writings about birth and deaths, the growth in numbers, and the relation of population to other social processes went by different names: "political arithmetic" (used to denote the pioneer efforts of such mercantilist writers as the English professor of anatomy William Petty, who coined the phrase); "political economy" (the term current at the time of Thomas Robert Malthus to designate the study of population, among other topics); and "human statistics" or simply "statistics" (used particularly by German analysts of the early modern period).

Population Studies

The study of population is an interdisciplinary science. This means that demographers usually expand their analyses beyond the formal methodologies of the discipline to include perspectives, models, and theories drawn from diverse fields, including sociology, economics, geography, history, anthropology, biology, ecology, epidemiology, and medicine. Likewise, specialists from these and other disciplines frequently rely on demography in their work. Economists, for instance, would use demography to study the interrelation of demographic and economic variables across human populations; ecologists study human (and animal) populations to see how they develop and change in the context of varying conditions in their natural environment; sociologists and other social scientists investigate demographic change in terms of underlying social forces; geographers look at spatial dimensions of demographic development; medical scientists and epidemiologists focus on the demographic bases of population health; and so on. In short, scientists from these different fields, though they approach the study of population from the perspectives of their respective disciplines, share a common appreciation of and reliance on formal demographic methods and their proper application to the analysis of population phenomena. The interplay between demography and these other disciplines makes up the bulk of demography's second branch, *population studies* (also known as *social demography*).

Central to population studies is its emphasis on identifying *determinants* and *consequences* (broadly speaking) of demographic change. Whereas formal demography is concerned with statistics and finding out "How many people, of what kind, are where?" population studies has as its core questions "How come?" and "So what?" (Yaukey, 1985: 1). Implicit in the first of these questions is the importance of specifying the causal mechanisms responsible for population change—in other words, the social determinants of demographic change. The term *social* here is used in its broadest sense to encompass environmental and societal factors (political, cultural, psychological, etc.) of potential relevance. The "So what?" question points to the consequences of population change for both the individual and society (for instance, social policy issues that derive from current and projected demographic trends). Table 1.1 reviews the core questions of formal demography and population studies.

The demarcation of formal demography and population studies provides a neat division that helps the beginning student gain a basic understanding of the field, but it should be noted that in actual practice, this distinction is often a matter of degree; the two aspects are seldom separate in true demographic study. The scientific analysis of population usually involves the use of both principles or methods of formal demography and substantive conceptual frameworks of population studies. Seldom does a demographer rely on a formal technique or methodology for purely technical motives. Rather, formal methods are typically developed and applied in the context of some clearly specified theoretical groundwork. This is the case even in applied demography (where formal techniques are typically applied to address practical problems in areas such as in business or urban planning), though in such cases the theoretical context may be subordinate to the technical application.

TABLE 1.1   Typology of the two traditional domains in the scientific study of population

Domain	Central questions	Analytical approaches	Principles implied in the question
Formal demography	How many people, of what kind, are where?	• Quantitative accounting of demographic processes and phenomena • Formulation and application of mathematical and statistical models of population processes and dynamics • Planning and collection of demographic data (census, vital registration, surveys) • Detection and adjustment of errors in demographic data • Estimation and projection of population, and demographic parameters	"How many people?" implies: Population size and its change over time (i.e., growth, stability, decline) "Of what kind?" implies: The distribution (i.e., composition) of the population in accordance with specific characteristics (esp. age, sex, and marital status) and change over time in these distributions "Are where?" implies: The distribution and concentration of population with respect to geographic space (e.g., urban/rural, province/state, etc.), and change over time in distribution and concentration
Population studies	How come? (i.e., why, how, where, when, who) So what? (implications)	• Development and application of substantive theories/models from the social sciences and other sciences to describe and explain systematically micro- and macro- level population phenomena (models-based approach) • Application of multivariate methods for analysis (formal demographic methods and models)	"How come?" implies: How and why population processes occur and change over time; where and when is change occurring? (past, current, future) Who (what part of the population) is/are involved in the phenomenon? (The whole population? One or more subset of the population? etc.) "So what?" implies: What are the sociological implications of population change for the present and the future? What policy interventions, if any, are needed to address the current and projected implications of demographic change?

Source: Adapted from Yaukey (1985).

This text is premised on the view that formal demography and population studies represent complementary rather than separate aspects of population analysis. For this reason, a statistical description of demographic trends is usually complemented by substantive sociological analysis. In fact, it may be argued that many technical quantitative methods thought of as "formal" and thus separate from substantive population analysis are fundamentally theoretical descriptions of demographic processes (Burch, 2002a, 2002b). We may ask questions such as "Is the population increasing or decreasing?," "Is the change in population over some period of time due to a rise or a decline in fertility?," "Is change solely accounted by migration?" But once answered, these questions typically lead us to how-, why-, and *so* what–type queries.

The Nature of Demographic Change

The study of population phenomena may be approached from either a *static* or a *dynamic* perspective. A static analysis would focus on demographic conditions at a fixed point in time. By contrast, a dynamic analysis would study the change in demographic conditions over a period of time. This kind of analysis might emphasize *process variables*—variables that reflect human behavioural processes, such as fertility, mortality, and migration. Fertility can be treated as a process variable because it presupposes the existence of couples, in sexual unions, undergoing sequential stages of the fertility process: conception, gestation, and parturition. Mortality can be described as a process because a variety of causal mechanisms and conditions can operate over a period to cause the death of an individual. Consider, for example, that currently on an annual basis about 36 000 Canadians die of ischemic heart disease (Statistics Canada, 2013a)—a condition caused by a reduced amount of blood supplying the heart muscle due to the presence of thick plaque along the inner walls of arteries formed by the building up of cholesterol or other lipids. This disease typically develops over many years; for some, there

may be a genetic predisposition, while for others, poor diet and a host of lifestyle-related problems (smoking, stress, lack of exercise, and so on) may be responsible. Migration is also a dynamic process. In most cases, geographic relocation involves a conscious decision by an individual, but the move is not instantaneous. The person will have to make arrangements to leave his or her place of residence and arrangements to take up residence elsewhere; all of these aspects of migration presuppose a process of decision making and adjustment on the part of the individual. In the population as a whole, these three demographic processes—fertility, mortality, and migration—take place more or less on a continuous basis.

Change in Population Size

We can measure the change in the size of a population between two points in time by examining the natural processes of fertility and mortality, as well as net migration (the net difference between the number of incoming and outgoing migrants). This principle is illustrated by the *demographic balancing equation*, also known as the *demographic components equation*:

$$P_{t+1} - P_t = (B_{t,t+1} - D_{t,t+1}) + (IN_{t,t+1} - OUT_{t,t+1})$$

P_t and P_{t+1} represent, respectively, the population at the beginning and the population at the end of some specified interval, t to $t+1$. The numerical change in population over the interval $(P_{t+1} - P_t)$ can be expressed as a function of the difference in births and deaths $(B_{t,t+1} - D_{t,t+1})$ plus the net exchange in the numbers of person migrating into the population ($IN_{t,t+1}$) and those leaving ($OUT_{t,t+1}$). The component $B_{t,t+1} - D_{t,t+1}$ is called *natural increase,* and the term $IN_{t,t+1} - OUT_{t,t+1}$ is *net migration.* Therefore, we may summarize the demographic equation as follows:

$$P_{t+1} = P_t + (\text{natural increase}_{t,t+1})$$
$$+ (\text{net migration}_{t,t+1})$$

Figure 1.1 displays the demographic balancing equation in graphic form for Canada for the period 2010–11. During this one-year interval, births in Canada exceeded deaths by a notable margin, and immigrants greatly outnumbered emigrants.

However, as the figure shows, the net effect of migration was greater than the effect of natural increase and therefore played a larger role in population growth. In proportionate terms, natural increase accounted for 37 per cent of population growth, while net migration accounted for 63 per cent. Over recent years *net migration* has surpassed *natural increase* in accounting for Canada's population growth, a phenomenon attributable to a continued pattern of low fertility in conjunction with rising immigration. Table 1.2 presents a conceptual view of how the demographic components interact.

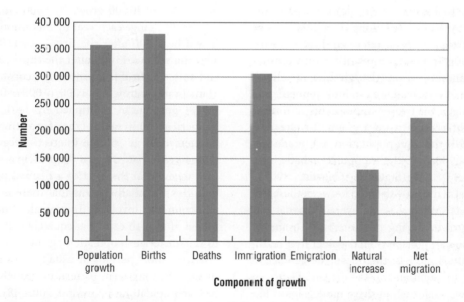

FIGURE 1.1   Demographic components of Canada's population growth between 1 July 2010 and 30 June 2011

Note: Population and components of growth as of 1 July of each year. Immigration derived as follows: (immigrants + net non-permanent residents + returning emigrants). Emigration derived as follows: (emigrants + net temporary emigrants).

Source: Statistics Canada (2013b, 2013c).

TABLE 1.2   The interaction of demographic components in population change

IIIIIIIIIIIIIIIIIIIIIIIIIIIIIIIIIIIIIIIIIIIIIIIIIIIIIIIIIIIIIIIIIIIIIIIIIIIIIIIIIIIIIIIIIIIIIIIIIIIIIIIIIIIIIIIIIIIIIIIIIIIIII

		Net migration is		
Natural increase is		Positive (In > Out)	Negative (In < Out)	Zero (In = Out)
Positive	(B > D)	(1) *I*	(2) *IDS*	(3) *I*
Negative	(B < D)	(4) *IDS*	(5) *D*	(6) *D*
Zero	(B = D)	(7) *I*	(8) *D*	(9) *S*

Note: The letter "*I*" means increase in population size; "*D*" means decrease in population size; and "*S*" indicates stability in population size. "*IDS*" means any one of these three outcomes can occur.

Source: Adapted from Goldscheider (1971): 10.

Linear, Geometric, Exponential, and Logistic Models of Population Growth

We can study variations in population size over time without referring directly to the demographic processes of fertility, mortality, and migration (though these are always implied). Instead, we can look at population change over two or more points in time as might be shown on a graph. To illustrate, in 1901 the total population of Canada was 7 207 000; by 1991, the population had grown to 31 111 000 (Statistics Canada, 2003a). What is the growth trend between these two points? What was the average annual rate of growth during this interval? To answer these questions, we can consider four mathematical models: the linear, the geometric, the exponential, and the logistic. Figure 1.2 shows what each of these models looks like in graphic form and provides a description of each model's elemental characteristics.

The *linear model* (also known as the *arithmetic model*) assumes a straight-line progression of change over time. The population grows by the same amount between time points (e.g., each year) and therefore

the rate of change is constant. So, if an initial population of 10 000 grows by 1 000 annually, it will change each year by this amount: It will be 11 000 after the first year, 12 000 after the second, 13 000 after the third year, and so forth. In this example, the constant annual rate of growth is 1 000/10 000 = 0.10 (or 10 per cent if multiplied by 100). In financial accounting this type of growth rate is referred to as "simple interest" because the interest is paid only on the principal, the sum invested at the start of a defined period. This essentially means that there is no compounding involved. Though the linear model of growth can be adequately applied to characterize population growth over relatively short periods, it usually does not fit well the long-term pattern of growth of human populations (Rowland, 2003: 48). In most cases, the historical trajectory of population growth corresponds more closely to the geometric and exponential models.

Geometric and *exponential models* assume that growth follows a non-linear trend over time. Unlike the linear model, where growth entails constant increments,

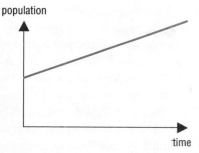

Linear
Trend: (1, 2, 3, 4, 5, 6, . . .); growth through
constant increments at constant intervals
Growth rates: constant
Absolute increments: constant
Ratio of adjacent populations: changing

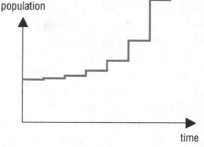

Geometric
Trend: (1, 2, 4, 8, 16, 32, . . .); growth compounding
at constant intervals (e.g., at end of each year)
Growth rates: constant
Absolute increments: changing
Ratio of adjacent populations: constant

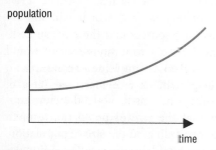

Exponential
Trend: growth compounding continuously
Growth rates: constant
Absolute increments: changing
Ratio of adjacent populations: constant

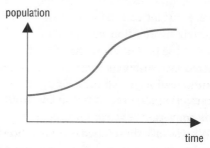

Logistic
Trend: "S"-shaped pattern of growth
Growth rates: changing in relation to population size
Absolute increments: changing
Ratio of adjacent populations: changing

FIGURE 1.2   Graphic representations of linear, geometric, exponential, and logistic population growth

Source: Adapted from Rowland (2003: 47, 50

geometric and exponential growth produce a larger increment of population numbers over time, and this occurs because of compounding. Using a financial analogy, this means that given a fixed rate of interest, the amounts earned on the principal and previously accrued interest amounts are added together, thus generating ever larger absolute gains over time. Yet another

key feature of the geometric model is that it assumes growth occurs at discrete time points, such as at the end of each year. Thus, a person who invests $100 at a fixed 10 per cent annual rate of interest will, at the end of the first year, have $110; by the end of year two, her investment will have grown to $121, and so forth. By the end of year five, she will have $161. With the same interest rate, the linear model would produce a return of $10 each year, such that by end year five she would have $150. What would be the outcome with the exponential growth model? At the end of year one, the investor would have $110.52, at end of year two, $122.14; and at the end of year five, the amount would have grown to $164.87. As can be seen by these examples the exponential yields larger growth over time than the geometric and the linear models. This is the power of continuous compounding.

The geometric and exponential models are actually quite similar. The main difference between them is that the exponential model assumes continuous compounding at every instant of time as opposed to the geometric assumption of compounding at discrete time points. Nevertheless, it should be noted that if time intervals are made sufficiently small (e.g., make the time unit days instead of years), the two models would nearly converge.

Which of these two models best describes human population growth? In practice, both are commonly applied in demographic analysis. In many situations, the geometric model is used because the population data become available only at regular intervals (e.g., once a year or every five years, as in the case of census data) and for this reason the geometric model would seem appropriate, given its inherent assumption of discrete time. The exponential model also receives a great deal of applications, especially in mathematical modelling of population processes, due to its closer approximation to the fact that births, deaths, and migration occur more or less on a continuous basis in the population and therefore population change would also be more or less continuous.

On a global level, indefinite geometric/exponential population growth cannot be sustained without the population at some point exhausting its ecological limits (Coale, 1974). As we shall see later, this was a key concern to Thomas Malthus' (1766–1834) theory of the interrelationship of population and resources. Recognition of the impossibility of indefinite exponential growth led to the development of the *logistic model* of population growth (Pearl and Reed, 1920; Verhulst, 1838). A variation of the exponential model, the logistic model assumes that a human population undergoing prolonged exponential growth will eventually experience insupportable levels of *population density*, which will impose strains on resources and the environment; and under such conditions society would be compelled to implement measures to curtail growth or face increased rates of mortality. The logistic model therefore supposes that the rate of population growth varies depending on the size of population: when the population is small and population density is low, the rate of growth will increase, gradually at first but with greater intensity as population increases; then, as the population approximates a maximum, the growth rate will begin to decline *asymptotically* (i.e., gradually towards zero, though never actually reaching zero). The upper tail of the logistic curve in Figure 1.2 reflects continued population growth at progressively reduced rates of change.

Although the logistic curve would seem to be a more realistic model of long-term population change as compared to linear, geometric, or exponential, there is to date no evidence of any national population having conformed fully to the logistic model of growth (Cowgill, 1971). In the early twentieth century, Raymond Pearl and

Lowell Reed (1920) predicted that the population of the United States would follow a logistic growth pattern. Their extrapolations of the US population to 1940, based on the logistic equation computed with population counts from 1790 to 1910, proved fairly accurate: the model provided a very close fit to the observed population counts obtained from American censuses. However, extensions of the logistic model beyond the 1940s produced population estimates well below the figures observed in the censuses (Ricklef, 1990: 328; Rowland, 2003: 54). As is true of the other models reviewed, the logistic model suffers from an inability to predict the future. Nevertheless, it has wide applicability in many scientific areas, especially the statistical study of disease epidemics. Finally, along with the geometric and exponential models, the logistic model represents a possible picture of long-term future global population growth (Coale, 1974). This point will be discussed further in Chapter 3, which looks at the history and future of the human population.

Compositional Change

Populations are also subject to *compositional change*, or change in the distribution of key population characteristics, such as age, sex, marital status, education, and occupation. *Distribution* here refers to either *absolute* or *relative frequencies* of the number of people across categories of age, sex, marital status, and so on. An example we will consider in Chapter 4 is the *age–sex pyramid*, which is a graphic representation of the distribution of the population in terms of age and sex. As we will see, the age and sex compositions of populations can change as a result of any one of a number of demographic mechanisms. One mechanism is sex-selective

migration, a process in which a large influx or exodus of either men or women alters the gender balance of a population. Sex-selective mortality is another factor that can alter the gender balance of a population (men typically have higher death rates than women do). Significant change in fertility is typically the most significant factor explaining change in the age distribution of a population.

Individual Behaviour and Demographic Processes

Demography is principally interested in aggregate population phenomena. At the same time, however, demographers recognize the importance of studying ways in which individual action helps "produce" phenomena at the population (macro) level. Individual behaviour is strongly conditioned by our perceptions of and responses to situations in the broader social environment. Demographic change at the macro level must therefore arise through the expression of individual behaviours guided by cultural values, norms, and institutional structures. While the study of aggregate phenomena remains the overarching concern of this textbook, we will stop here briefly to touch on a point generally neglected in introductory population texts: the importance of individual action to demographic phenomena.

Individual State Transitions as Demographic Behaviour

Individuals in a population occupy multiple statuses that are socially defined and that carry certain responsibilities and obligations. For example, consider the intersecting statuses of a divorced man, aged 45, who is a father of two children, and who is currently employed as a bank manager. In demographic analysis, the intersection of these statuses constitutes a *multistate classification*. Individuals can move in and out of such states, making what demographers call *interstate transitions*, or simply *state transitions* (Hazelrigg, 1999). Some transitions are *repeatable*. For instance, the move from "employed" to "unemployed" status is a repeatable transition, since one may be re-employed after a spell of unemployment, and so on. Death, as it can occur only once, is a clear example of a *non-repeatable transition* (also referred to as an *absorbing state*).

Hazelrigg (1997: 99) makes an important point regarding the variability of state transitions when he says that "Both the probability of a transition and the duration of a transition may be variably sensitive to the preceding state duration, as well as to other factors." State transitions are probabilistic occurrences, since there is a varying probability attached to any particular movement between given states. The probability varies in accordance with the characteristics of the individual—age, education background, length of time spent in the *exiting state* (the state being left)—as well as a multitude of conditions external to, but which influence, the person (i.e., culture, social structure, environment).

Figure 1.3 sketches four models of state transition. Diagram (a) illustrates the processes of birth, death, and migration from the demographic balancing equation, which we reviewed on page 10. Diagram (b) illustrates a single non-repeatable state transition (alive to dead). Diagram (c) shows one kind of repeatable state transition, becoming a parent. The arrows

pointing to "dead" are there to show the continuous presence of some probability of death, which exists for the person regardless of his or her status as a parent. Finally, diagram (d) displays a multistate situation with respect to marital statuses and mortality. Marital statuses are repeatable states, since a person may become married, divorced, or widowed more than once. Death is a non-repeatable event, but since the probability of death exists regardless of a person's marital state, there are several arrows pointing to death.

Individual state transitions account, in varying degrees, for change in certain compositional characteristics of a larger population. Consider marital status as an example: the greater the number of adults in a population exiting the single state to enter the married state, the greater the proportion of married persons to single persons in the population. Students of population dynamics who are interested in analyzing aggregate measures of demographic processes—including the birth rate, the death rate, the migration rate, and the marriage rate—are wise to keep in mind that such demographic rates are aggregate manifestations of individual state transitions.

Individual State Transitions and Demographic Rates

The concept of *rate* is central to demographic analysis. A rate is a dynamic, quantifiable measure of risk given exposure to some specific event over some specified interval. For example, the death rate is a measure of the risk of death for the average person in the population during a given period (e.g., a year). This example illustrates two related ideas. First, a rate is based in part on the

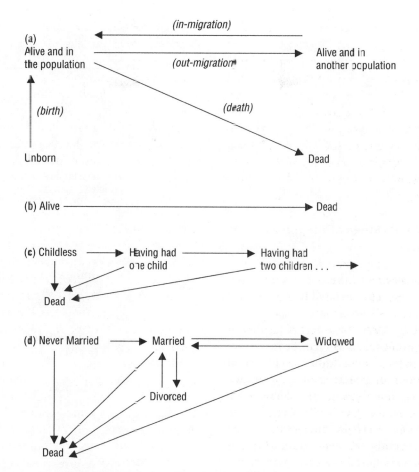

FIGURE 1.3   Four representations of state transitions

(a)   the demographic balancing equation as a multistate classification
(b)   state transition involving a non-repeatable event (death)
(c)   state transitions involving a repeatable event (childbearing)
(d)   multistate transitions involving both repeatable and non-repeatable events

Source: Adapted from Hinde (1998): 2, 3, 78.

sum of a specific event that has actually occurred during a defined interval (this is the numerator). Second, it implies the existence of a population that is exposed to the risk of experiencing the event in question during the specified time period (this is the denominator). Thus,

$$rate = \frac{\text{number of events in a given time interval}}{\text{number of persons in the interval exposed to the risk of experiencing the event}}$$

We can think of the death rate as an aggregate representation of individual

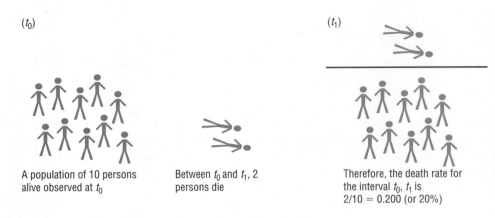

FIGURE 1.4   **Schematic representation of the death rate**

state transitions in the population (from living to dead) as depicted in diagram (b) of Figure 1.3. Thus, generally speaking, a high (or low) rate of a particular demographic event (such as birth or marriage) implies a greater (or lower) incidence of a corresponding state transition among individual members of the population. The concept of rate is sketched out in Figure 1.4. A clear understanding of rate is essential as demographic analyses are often based on the computation and investigation of rates of some type of event.

Ideally, the denominator should be the population at the beginning of the interval. However, this information is often not available. So, it is customary in demographic analysis of rates to make the denominator the midpoint population for a given interval, whether that interval is one year, five years, or some other length of time. In many applications, the time interval is one year, so the exposed population at risk is the population at the midway point of the year. Two examples are the annual crude death and birth rates:

$$\text{crude birth rate (CBR)} = \frac{\text{number of births in given year}}{\text{mid-year population in given year}} \times 1\,000$$

$$\text{crude death rate (CDR)} = \frac{\text{number of deaths in given year}}{\text{mid-year population in given year}} \times 1\,000$$

The numerical value of a rate depends not just on the intensity of the event in question (the frequency with which the event occurs in the population—i.e., the numerator) but also on the size of the population exposed to the risk of experiencing the event (i.e., the denominator). For this reason, a constant number of events in a population compared over two different intervals may result in two different rates because the denominator may change from one point in time to the other: it could increase (owing perhaps to natural increase and/or net migration) or it could decline. In either of these conditions, a constant numerator will derive two different rates. This principle is sketched out in Figure 1.5.

Table 1.3 presents an illustration of how individual action relates to state transitions and to demographic rates. The example makes use of two concepts discussed earlier: the concept of "state" (a status occupied by an individual at a given point in time) and the notion of "state transition" (a change of status between two specific points in time). The hypothetical scenarios concern the childbearing status and pregnancy status of women of childbearing age observed over two points in time. Let us denote t_0 as the start and t_1 as the end point. At the start of the observation period, some women were in the state of "childless," while others were in the state of "mother," meaning they had given

birth to at least one child as of time point t_0. Cells C and D in the table represent two different state transitions: cell C involves women who were childless at time t_0 and who became mothers in the interval between t_0 and t_1; cell D concerns women who were already mothers at time t_0 and who had an additional child during the interval between t_0 and t_1. Cells A and B represent static conditions: the women described in these cells occupied the states of "childless" or "mother" at time t_0 and remained in their separate states over time.

From the information in Table 1.3 we can derive aggregated counts of all the state transitions involving the individual women during the interval t_0 to t_1. For example, by dividing cell H by cell I, we can obtain the birth rate for women of childbearing age (15 to 49) for the interval t_0 to t_1. Alternatively, we could measure the rate of childbearing for first-time mothers—cell C divided by cell I. Though hypothetical, these scenarios reflect a demographic process in real populations. Demographers observe the aggregated sums of state transitions like these and calculate corresponding rates to measure the intensity and extent of the behaviour in question. Observed over time, this kind of data can help establish the occurrence of either upward or downward trends in certain demographic rates.

Reclassification Processes

Another way that a population can experience change in the distribution of some of its characteristics is through *reclassification*. Reclassification is similar to state transition, though, as we shall see, there are some key differences between these two processes. The following example will help to illustrate the meaning of reclassification in the

---

t_0

number of events = 10
population exposed = 100
rate = 0.10 (or 10 per 100 population)

---

t_1(a): the population at risk increases but the numerator remains the same

events = 10
exposures = 200
rate = 0.05 (or 5 per 100 population)

---

t_1(b): the population at risk decreases but numerator remains the same

events = 10
exposures = 75
rate = 0.133 (or 13.3 per 100 population)

FIGURE 1.5 Rate under varying populations at risk but same number of events

TABLE 1.3   Relationship between states, state transitions, and demographic aggregates: example of women of childbearing ages

pregnancy status occupied by women at time t_1	Childbearing status occupied by women at time t_0		
	childless	mother	aggregated totals at time t_1
not pregnant	(A) childless women at t_0 who remained childless between t_0 and t_1	(B) mothers at t_0 who did not bear children between t_0 and t_1	(G) total number of women at t_1 who did not bear children between t_0 and t_1
have given birth	(C) childless women at t_0 who became mothers between t_0 and t_1	(D) mothers at t_0 who gave birth between t_0 and t_1	(H) total number of women at t_1 who gave birth between t_0 and t_1
aggregated totals for time t_0	(E) = (A) + (C) total number of women who were childless at t_0	(F) = (B) + (D) total number of women who were mothers at t_0	(I) = (G) + (H) = (E) + (F) total number of women at t_1 who were either childless or mothers at t_0

Note: Conceptually, t_0 is meant to represent the start of the process, and t_1 the end point.

context of demographic change. In Canada, the census asks people to record their ethnic background and country of birth, as well as a number of other social and economic characteristics; this information tells us how many members of the population identify themselves as belonging to a given ethnicity. A change in distribution of ethnic identification between census periods would imply, among other things, the occurrence of some degree of reclassification in the population. In fact, over the last several censuses in Canada, demographers have noted a great deal of *ethnic mobility*—shifts in the distribution of ethnic self-identification beyond what can be attributed to natural increase and net migration.

The underlying reasons for the phenomenon of ethnic mobility are complex, but one important factor is the high rates of marriage involving persons of varied ethnic origins and the tendency for the children of these "mixed" marriages to vary their ethnic identification from one census to the next (Krotki, 1997; Krotki and Odynak, 1990). For example, the child of an Italian-born mother and a French-Canadian father may identify herself on the census as "French Canadian" or "Italian" or both, or possibly also "Canadian." In a subsequent census, she may or may not list the same ethnic affiliation she identified previously, depending on her sense of ethnic identity at the time of the census. Ethnic mobility is generally more frequent among the second and subsequent generations of immigrants.

A similar phenomenon has been observed among Canadian Aboriginal peoples. Over the last several censuses, the growth rate for Canada's Aboriginal population has been greater than would be expected based on natural increase (birth and death rates) or immigration (there is little international in- or out-migration among Aboriginal peoples). How, then, can we account for the Aboriginal growth rate? One explanation has to do with the increasing tendency among Aboriginal Canadians to declare their First Nations ancestry on the census. Another explanation involves recent changes to the *Indian Act*, which have broadened the definition of "Aboriginal," making the category more inclusive than it was. Thus, the greater-than-expected growth of the Aboriginal population in Canada can be attributed to a significant extent to these reclassification processes (Goldmann and Delic, 2014; Guimond, 1999; Guimond, Robitaille, and Sénecal, 2014).

These examples highlight an important distinction between the concepts of "state transition" and "reclassification": while state transitions involve a behavioural change on the part of an individual (for instance, a person exits the state of singlehood by getting married), reclassification can involve a change in identification by individuals. The example of ethnic mobility reflects this idea.

Demographic Change and Social Change

If demographic rates are aggregate manifestations of individual state transitions, it follows that social change, broadly speaking,

must somehow be associated with demographic change in society. It is not always possible to establish in causal terms where social change originates: does demographic change lead to social change or is demographic change brought about by changes in the social system? In many instances, demographic shifts are conceptualized as "social change." Consider, for instance, the commonly held view that the divorce revolution of recent decades in the industrial nations (a *demographic fact*) represents a radical shift in orientation (a *sociopsychological fact*) about the permanency of the family institution (a *sociological fact*). In fact, this is something of a chicken-and-egg scenario, as it is seldom possible to establish, unambiguously, the temporal order between changes in the demography of a society and change in the social system (Moore, 1974).

The complexities surrounding the study of social change have prompted one sociologist, commenting on the difficulty of defining social change, to wonder, "How much does something have to change to call it change?" (Charon, 1998: 182). Generally, we say that social change has occurred when a social pattern (or structure, or culture, or institution) is significantly different from what it has been in the past. The questions we then need to ask: "What causes social patterns to change and how is demographic change involved?"

In addressing these questions, Joel Charon (1998: 182) lists, among other things, "acts of individuals" and "changes in population" as agents of social change, while recognizing that new technologies can often engender significant changes in society. He also observes that in many cases, "change in one social pattern affects other social patterns" (182). Some social change can be seen as a manifestation of demographic change, and alterations in the social system can, in some cases, influence individual behaviour. Kingsley Davis and Pietronella van den Oever (1982: 495) reflect on this point while discussing the interrelationship between demographic changes and one of the most important social movements in the recent history of the Western world:

> . . . [D]emographic changes in advanced industrial societies— changes such as increased longevity, widening sex differences in mortality, aging populations, and low fertility— . . . give rise to new circumstances between men and women. . . . This in turn brings forth [new] ideological developments such as the feminist movement. It is not that the demographic trends are perceived by each individual and thus consciously adapted to, but rather that they arise spontaneously in advanced societies and alter the conditions of life.

Social change may be brought about by the action of individuals in cases where, for instance, a novel behaviour develops into a widespread social phenomenon. Once widely adopted, the behaviour may become *normative*, meaning that it becomes a standard form of behaviour. The current widespread preference among young Canadian couples to form cohabiting unions may be cited as an example of a demographic development towards a behaviour that in earlier times was thought of as non-normative. Diffusion of new ideas and behaviours such as cohabitation become widespread in society through the process of imitation (people imitating what others are doing), and through the action of the mass media (the transmission of new ideas to the masses via television and other media). Both processes play a crucial role in social change (Carlson, 1966; Kohler, 2000).

The historian David Herlihy (1997) offers a fascinating account of the complex interconnection between demography and social change in *The Black Death and the Transformation of the West*. Herlihy suggests that the Black Death, the epidemic that devastated Europe, parts of Asia, and northern Africa during the fourteenth and fifteenth centuries, was indirectly responsible for the development of European nationalism and the establishment of several national European universities. Herlihy argues that many wealthy Europeans bequeathed their fortunes to new centres of higher learning that were being established as alternatives to the ancient universities of Bologna and Padova in Italy and of Paris in France. Many teachers in the new universities, because they were unfamiliar with Latin—the language of higher learning at the time—used vernacular languages in their teaching. Consequently, Herlihy surmises, instructors and students developed strong nationalistic loyalties. In this way, he argues that a demographic phenomenon—the sustained rise of mortality due to the Black Death—brought significant structural and cultural transformations in European society.

Age, Period, and Cohort: The Mechanisms of Demographic Change

The aggregate actions of individuals in society, we have seen, help produce demographic phenomena. We have also seen that the translation of individual demographic action into aggregate demographic change occurs through individual behaviour (i.e., state transitions) in the context of social and cultural forces. These relationships suggest a series of related facts:

1. Individual action necessarily implies individual reaction to societal forces of significance to the individual.
2. All individuals experience *biological aging,* the passage through life from birth to death.
3. All individuals experience *chronological aging,* the passage through biological and calendar time simultaneously.
4. Individuals in a society who are born during a specified time interval form a unique *birth cohort,* whose members pass through biological and chronological time together.
5. Every member of the population belongs to a distinct birth cohort, whose members generally tend to experience formative life course events and transitions at similar points in time.

These postulates indicate interconnectedness among three key variables: age, calendar time ("period"), and cohort. These three variables are involved in complex ways, in all demographic phenomena (Lutz, 2012; Ryder, 1965, 1972), so it is important to gain an understanding of how they are interrelated. Mathematically, each can be derived from knowledge of the other two: cohort = period – age; period = age – cohort; age = period – cohort. Figure 1.6 sketches how these variables in combination entail the presence of individual lifelines. This type of conceptual device was introduced by the German mathematician Wilhelm Lexis (1837–1914), and is referred to as a *Lexis diagram.*

For illustrative purposes, let us focus on four hypothetical cohorts over a two-year

period. The period dimension (calendar time) is the horizontal axis, indexed by the symbol t. The interval $t-1$ to t encompasses the first year of observation, and t to $t+1$ demarcates year two. (Naturally, we assume that each calendar year starts on 1 January and ends on 31 December.) The vertical axis on the left signifies exact age at last birthday, indexed by x. Thus, $x+1$ is interpreted as the age of a person that is one year older than age x, and $x-1$ would mean one year younger than x. To make this concrete, assume that x = age 30; then $x-1$ = age 29, $x+1$ = age 31, and $x+2$ = age 32. Since age and calendar time are perfectly correlated (i.e., getting older by 1 year = passage of 1 calendar year), their intersection always derives the exact age of a person at a specific point in time. The diagonal areas in Figure 1.6 designate three different birth cohorts whose members would have been born at different points in the past. If we let C be the cohort of focus, then $C-1$ is the neighbouring cohort made up of older individuals born one year earlier than the members of cohort C, and $C+1$ is made up of younger individuals born one year after those in cohort C. The quadrant formed by the letters LNMO captures the intersection of age and period encompassing $x-1$ to $x+2$ and $t-1$ to $t+1$. Within this quadrant a number of parallelograms can be envisioned, each representing a segment of a given birth cohort with respect to age and calendar time. Thus, the parallelogram formed by the points TRUS pertains to cohort C in the intersection of x to $x+1$ with $t-1$ to $t+1$.

Similarly, MUVW intersects $x-1$ to x with $t-1$ to $t+1$ pertaining to cohort $C+1$. The four representative hypothetical lifelines are shown within their respective birth cohort. On 31 December of year one (point t on the period axis), person 0_2 of cohort C was aged exactly $x+0.5$; individual 0_1 of cohort

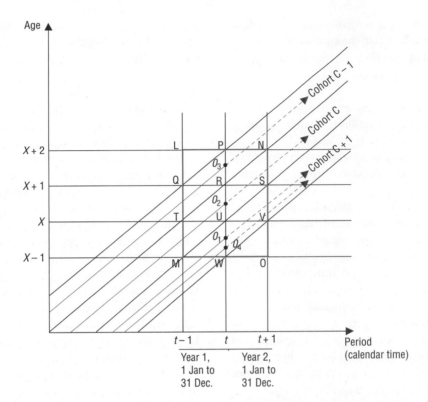

FIGURE 1.6   Schematic representation of the relationship of age, period, and cohort, and the lifeline of individuals extending through age and time

Legend:
0_1 lifeline of a member of cohort $C + 1$
0_2 lifeline of a member of cohort C
0_3 lifeline of a member of cohort $C - 1$
0_4 lifeline of a member of cohort $C + 1$ that is younger than 0_1
LNMO = quadrant encompassing two calendar years, $t - 1$ to $t + 1$, and ages $x - 1$ to $x + 2$
————— = lifeline of an individual from birth to the present, time point t
- - - - - - = projected lifeline of an individual into the future, extending from time point t
x = age of an individual (e.g., x may be age 20; therefore, $x - 1$ would be age 19, age $x + 1$ would be age 21, etc.)

$C+1$ was aged exactly $x-0.5$, and person 0_3, a member of cohort $C-1$, was aged $x+1.5$. It can be seen that person 0_4 in Cohort $C+1$ is slightly younger than 0_1. Finally, for these four hypothetical cases, the solid line represents the portion of life lived, and the hatched line symbolizes future expected life as these individuals progress into the future with respect to age and calendar time. At some point into the future, these individuals will die, though not necessarily at the same time.

This conceptual framework can be generalized by adding more lifelines into the sketch. By doing so, one can easily extrapolate that a population is in fact composed of many lifelines intersecting age and calendar time, each belonging to a unique birth cohort.

The significance of Figure 1.6 for our understanding of demographic processes extends into the sociological realm. As suggested earlier, members of birth cohorts tend to experience similar sets of life conditions and circumstances as they pass through life, including important events such as graduation, entry into the labour force, marriage, home ownership, childbearing, relocation, and family disruption. The *timing* (i.e., the age at which these events occur) and *intensity* (i.e., the number of persons involved) of such events can be ascertained from summary measures specific to a cohort (or across cohorts): the average age at which members of a cohort experience an event, the proportion of the cohort that have experienced an event by a given age, the rate at which the cohort undergoes a specific state transition, and so forth.

As described, all demographic phenomena imply the interrelationship among age, period, and cohort. The conceptual framework in Figure 1.6 dealt with these concepts from the point of view of birth cohorts passing through life all the while aging across calendar time. There is yet another way of looking at the idea of cohort. It is possible to identify in the population various types of cohorts. For example, one can think of a *marriage cohort* consisting of all the people that married in a given year. These cases can be followed over time and age to study various demographic processes occurring to this cohort, including for instance, the proportion of the marriage cohort that dies at a given age, or the percentage of the cohort that experiences

divorce or widowhood at given duration of marriage, and so forth. One could also, for example, think of a cohort of students entering their first year of university; or a cohort of migrants arriving to a country in the same year. Clearly, these demographic categories will include individuals of varying ages from different birth cohorts born at different times. The people that marry in year *t* will not have been born exactly in the same year, nor will the students entering university or the immigrants, necessarily.

Besides taking a cohort approach, demographic phenomena can also be studied from a strictly *period perspective*. This is a common approach in the social sciences. In such types of studies, the emphasis is on some phenomenon occurring at a given point in time or time interval. To give an example, during periods of economic recessions the overall rate of unemployment usually increases. This may result from the loss of many jobs among some cohorts and not others (e.g., young workers with little seniority). Or perhaps the rise in the overall unemployment rate is uniformly a function of all cohorts of workers, young and old. In period analysis, these competing possibilities could be assessed by computing the unemployment rates for each age group in the given period of observation and then seeing the contribution of the different age cohorts to overall unemployment rate. In this way, we would be summarizing the experiences of all cohorts in the working ages in period *t* with respect to unemployment.

Irrespective of whether one takes a cohort or period analytical perspective, it is important to understand that the population of a society at any given point in time is really composed of unique birth cohorts that are at different stages of their lives. At a given time point *t*, for instance, the birth rate results from the contributions of different cohorts of women in the childbearing ages having babies in that specific point in time. Some of the women will belong to younger cohorts and others to relatively older cohorts close to the end of the childbearing years. Thus, differential behaviour of the members of different birth cohorts is what underlies observed aggregate demographic phenomena at any given point in time in society. The effects of periodic shocks in society will therefore be felt differently by cohorts. For example, the occurrence of a severe economic depression will affect more intensely cohorts that are composed of young adults who may have entered the labour force recently as compared to those belonging to older cohorts near the end of their working life (Hardy and Waite, 1997; Ryder, 1965; Winsborough, 1978). This type of variation in how cohorts are affected by and respond to periodic

shocks in society is to a large extent what gives rise to demographic phenomena.

Cohorts and Generations

The conceptual framework in Figure 1.6 can help us to understand another important concept in demography, that of *generation*. Depending on the scholarly discipline, the meaning of this term can vary. Donald Rowland (2003: 138) has provided an instructive summary of the different meanings and aspects of the term (see the accompanying box).

Here, we are primarily concerned with the demographic meaning of generation. We think of generation in the context of the reproduction process, whereby one generation of parents produces a new generation of children, who themselves eventually go

---

WHAT IS A GENERATION?

Meaning	Interpretation
Contemporaries	Generation as people living in a particular historical period.
Lineage	Generation as the line of descent, for example referring to child, parent, and grandparent generations in the same family. Ryder (1972: 546) considers this the appropriate use of the term.
Time	Generation as an interval of time, measured as the average difference in age between mothers and daughters. The time separating them, or the *mean length of a generation,* is typically around 29 years (Pressat, 1985: 87). In demography, it is calculated as the average age of mothers at the birth of their daughters. The average does not vary greatly between populations. This is because childbearing begins at an early age and finishes late where families are large, but starts later and finishes earlier where families are small.
Age	Generation as an age range or life stage. Found in studies comparing "older" and "younger" generations, the focus is on differences between age groups. For example, to describe the aged in Japan as the fastest growing "generation" is to equate generation with an age range.
Cohort	Generation meaning birth cohort. Ryder (1972: 546) recommended that cohort and generation should not be used interchangeably, but it has become common in contemporary usage.

Source: Adapted from Rowland (2003): 138.

on to produce a new generation of children, and so forth. In this sense, we can see that the population of a society consists of co-existing generations that interact with each other: parents, children, parents of the parents (grandparents), and so forth (Golini and Iacoucci, 2006). This view of "generation" is central to demographic analysis because of its inherent connection to reproductivity and population growth. In essence, to say that a population is growing is to mean that each parental generation is having on average more children than needed to just replace itself (more specifically, this concept pertains to mothers replacing themselves by having daughters; this topic is discussed in greater detail in a later section of this book).

Sociologically, a generation typically encompasses different birth cohorts that experience some significant defining societal experience such as living through a war, a prolonged economic depression or economic boom, or some other sociohistorical development of major societal importance (e.g., the fall of the Soviet Union). The birth cohorts comprising a generation identify themselves with such experiences and develop a unique consciousness and outlook on the world that helps to differentiate them from other generations (Mannheim, 1923).

Depending on the historical circumstances generations can also be affected quite differently in terms of life chances and socioeconomic opportunities (Easterlin, 1987; Hardy and Waite, 1997; Ryder, 1965; Winsborough, 1978). For example, one can think of the generation born during the Great Depression, between 1930 and 1939. As children, members of this generation were raised in a context of economic crisis and hardship. This experience had to leave a lasting influence on their view of the world and life in general. They are known as a lucky generation. They were lucky because they were too young to serve in the military during World War II, and also because when they entered the labour force after the war had ended, the post-war economic boom of the 1950s and 1960s provided unprecedented job prospects and security. Under these favourable conditions, this generation produced the post-war baby boom between 1946 and 1966. They felt economically secure, married early in life, and had lots of children (Carlson, 2008; Foot and Stoffman, 1998).

The *baby boom* generation as it passed through childhood and adulthood (and eventually through old age) have experienced very different sociological conditions than predecessor generations. First, the high fertility of the parents means that this is large generation in demographic terms. Second, as children they grew up in an economically prosperous environment. Third, as teens and young adults this large generation would exert major influence on all aspects of the society, ranging from music and fashion (e.g., the countercultural movement of the 1960s and 1970s) to societal attitudes and values. Among other things, this generation has been described as having being highly skeptical towards tradition in general and in particular religion (Lesthaeghe and Surkyn, 1988). As a parental generation themselves, the boomers have produced Generation X, the cohorts of 1965 through 1981, and to a large extent—due to later parenthood—also Generation Y, the cohorts born between 1982 and early 1990s. In contrast to older generations, Generations X and Y share a strong concern for global issues such as poverty eradication and preservation of the environment. Having grown up in the age of the Internet, fast computers, and smartphones, they are technologically savvy and more connected globally.

How Do We Know the Facts of Demography?

In a classic work, Nathan Keyfitz (1975) asked, "How do we know the facts of demography?" Keyfitz was hoping to demonstrate that demographic phenomena, for the most part, could not be fully explained by direct observation of data or statistical relationships among variables. Rather, he argued, observation of statistical relations could only be a starting point to explanation: the analyst must have in mind a model of the causal mechanisms governing the phenomenon he or she is trying to understand. "No model," he wrote, "no explanation." The data by themselves are insufficient basis for causal explanation of phenomena.

Like any scientific discipline, demography places emphasis on describing and explaining phenomena, not just observing and measuring them. We have noted in this chapter that relying solely on quantitative trends provides an insufficient account of *why* and *how* social phenomena develop. An important part of explanation is the formulation of *theory*, a systematic attempt to describe and explain phenomena in a way that clearly sets out, or *predicts*, the conditions under which a phenomenon is expected to occur.

Philosophers of science point out that there are three kinds of models that scientists use or develop in their work: physical scale models, visual (diagrammatic) models, and theoretical models (Giere, 1999: 5). Physical models are concrete representations, such as a small-scale model of a building; visual models are pictorial representations of some abstraction of the real world. Theoretical models are verbal statements, propositions that are logically interconnected, that attempt to explain some aspect of the real world—in Ronald Giere's words, "Abstract objects, imaginary entities whose structure might or might not be similar to aspects of objects and processes in the real world" (5). Throughout this book, we will look at a variety of models and theories (making no real distinction between the two) that help explain population phenomena.

That demography is a purely quantitative discipline devoid of any concern for theory is an antiquated and, frankly, incorrect perception. Demographers and other population scholars, whether their preoccupations may be formal methodologies or substantive analysis, are primarily concerned with explaining real-world situations and how populations behave under different social and ecological conditions. In other words, population scientists are inherently interested in developing and applying models of demographic action or processes in order to gain a better understanding of population dynamics. It should be no surprise, then, that a great deal of material in this book involves theories or models of demographic processes and phenomena.

The models of demographic phenomena presented in this book are mostly visual, since rigorous mathematical models are simply beyond the scope of an introductory text. As a result, mathematical treatment of population dynamics and processes is kept to a minimum, though certainly not avoided when necessary, and, wherever possible, concepts have been illustrated in diagrammatic form. Finally, following the discussion earlier in this chapter, we have left behind the traditional demarcation of "formal" demography and "population studies." Instead, this book is guided by the principle that the scientific study of population involves the development and application of sound models in conjunction with formal methodologies, which are inherently theoretical and should not be treated as different from substantive demographic theory (Burch, 2002a, 2002b).

Micro and Macro Models of Demographic Phenomena

As we have seen, the aim of population studies is to explain aggregate demographic phenomena, which are the products of individual action, or *micro-level phenomena*. Demography, then, relies on *micro-level models*, models of individual decision making and behaviour, as well as *macro-level models*, which examine the behaviour of entire populations.

Micro Models of Human Action: Rational Actor, Normative, and "Drift"

One class of micro models is the *rational actor model* (also called the *microeconomic model*), which describes actors as *maximizing agents*. In this conceptualization, the individual is seen as attempting to minimize perceived costs associated with an intended action (for example, to have a baby) while at the same time attempting to maximize the benefits to be derived from the intended action. Thomas Burch (1979) presented a synthesis of rational actor models that can be summarized under the theme "human decision making (and therefore action) as driven by maximizing principles." Processes such as marriage, divorce, migration, changing residence, and having children can all be explained by elemental microeconomic and sociopsychological principles: an individual

forms rational decisions based on perceived gains (material and psychological) and losses (material and psychological) from some anticipated action.

Rational action seldom occurs in the absence of normative considerations by the individual. This point leads us to a second model of human action: the *normative model*. The fundamental premise of this model is that individual behaviour is conditioned by two sets of factors: rational microeconomic principles, as outlined earlier, and normative considerations. Normative considerations are based on perceptions of how a significant other (or significant others) would react to an intended action. Significant others include spouses, children, extended family members, co-workers, peers, and others who would be expected to exert varying degrees of influence on the individual (Burch, 1979).

The normative and the microeconomic rational models of human action are essentially complementary explanations of behavioural intentions, both based on the premise that behavioural intentions are highly correlated with actual behaviour (Fishbein, 1972). Implicit in this formulation is the idea that the individual is always consciously involved in the decision-making process, fully aware of the motives, goals, and constraints to any intended behaviour. Critics have questioned whether this conceptualization can accurately capture the complex nature of the human decision-making process (e.g., Field, 1984; Leibenstein, 1982). Is human behaviour always rational? Are individuals always perfectly aware of the potential costs and benefits of an intended course of action? Are there some aspects of human behaviour that cannot be fully explained by maximizing principles or normative principles alone?

Questions such as these lie behind an alternative conceptualization proposed by Lincoln Day (1985), who argues that most human action is guided by what he calls "drift principles." Day envisions a continuum of behaviour: at one pole is the microeconomic model, which describes an individual who coolly calculates the gains and losses to be anticipated from available possibilities; at the opposite pole is the normative model, depicting an individual who constantly conforms to normative expectations. Day's drift principles lie somewhere between these poles, governing decisions about a range of important life matters—whether to have a child; when to have a child; whether or not to marry, to divorce, to move out—that are seldom executed in the narrow, calculative, and precise manner dictated by the microeconomic model or in automatic adherence to normative constraints as implied by the normative model.

In reality, people make conscious choices within a broad range of normative options that are themselves under limits imposed by society. Society's broad normative framework sets out what behaviour is considered appropriate under given circumstances and also sets the boundaries for the means one can use to realize certain goals (Field, 1984; Leibenstein, 1982). In this sense, conscious choice exists only if one thinks of conscious choice as being a matter of degree rather than something in absolute terms. The *"drift" model* assumes that behaviour arises almost by accident at one or another point within a limited range of socially allowable choices, and then it is gently (but not necessarily inexorably) guided by underlying influences towards its conclusion in a manner largely imperceptible to the person

doing the acting (Day, 1985: 196). Obviously, not all behaviour is like this, and the degree to which conscious choice governs particular behaviours differs according to the particular psychological and social milieux occupied by individual actors. Nevertheless, argues Day, the "drift" model is an accurate representation of a very high proportion of human behaviour.

While the drift model may not be antagonistic to utility and normative perspectives, Day's central point is that human action is mostly contingent on emergent properties of interaction, habit, and even unconscious motivation (see also Field, 1984; Leibenstein, 1982; Miller and Godwin, 1977). Debra Friedman and colleagues (1994), arguing along these same lines, suggest that certain demographic behaviours—having a child, changing residence, getting divorced, and so on—are often driven by an unconscious need on the part of individuals to reduce uncertainty in life. For example, a teenaged couple's decision to have a child may appear as an irrational and self-defeating outcome, but having a baby will set a predictable—albeit difficult in most cases—pattern in the life of the parents.

Micro models of human action are instructive because they help us to get beyond the macro-level explanations frequently found in demography and population studies. It is important to understand how micro processes relate to phenomena at the societal level. And while it may not always be possible to specify how individual-level models of behaviour apply to observed macro-level phenomena, we can at the very least remind ourselves that there are alternative realities operating at the level of the individual actor, and that aggregate phenomena are manifestations of individual action.

Macro Models of Demographic Change

Macro models of demographic phenomena attempt to describe and explain population change in the context of structural changes in society. A cornerstone of demographic theorizing is the *demographic transition theory*. Though it will be discussed in greater detail later in the text, Dudley Kirk's sketch of the theory (1996: 361) will be helpful here: "stripped to essentials [the theory] states that societies that experience modernization progress from a pre-modern regime of high fertility and high mortality to a post-modern one in which both are low." Thus, the demographic transition is a description of long-term shifts in a society's vital rates, from a primitive stage of high birth and death rates (and thus very low rates of population increase), to an intermediate stage of declining mortality and high fertility (and therefore very high rates of population growth), to a final stage of low fertility and mortality levels (hence, a return to very low growth rates).

Even in this elemental form, it is clear that the demographic transition is but one of several transformations a society may experience as it moves from a pre-industrial type of social organization based on an agrarian or feudal economy to an urban-industrial complex social system (Moore, 1974). Associated with this transformation are radical shifts in other aspects of society:

- *political change,* from disparate monarchic or feudal forms of governance to democratic government;
- *scientific-technological revolution,* as modern science replaces traditional folkways of understanding nature;
- *institutional complexity,* as life becomes increasingly organized and compartmentalized under different sectors of the social system (for example, children's education is taken out of the home and into the academic institutions); and
- *industrialization,* as work shifts away from the family farm and into the urban industrial economy.

Joseph Spengler (1974: 153) identifies a number of structural indicators of modernization: "the fraction of a country's labour force that is engaged in agriculture" (the higher the percentage engaged in non-agricultural work, the greater the degree of modernization); the percentage of the population living in urban, as opposed to rural, areas (a larger percentage of urban dwellers implies greater modernization); and rising incomes, as reflected in the gross national product (GNP).

Beyond structural change, socio-economic modernization implies a socio-psychological transformation of the society, or a cultural shift. As Spengler (1974: 153) explains, "modernization consists of a variety of changes describable as changes in the 'content of the mind.' That is, there occurs a diffusion of secular-rational norms and values in the culture system; there is greater personal freedom of expression." Spengler then cites the six dimensions of individual modernity identified by Alex Inkeles and David Smith (1974):

(1) openness to new experiences; (2) increasing independence from traditional authority figures and a shift of allegiance to public leaders; (3) a belief in the efficacy of science and medicine to solve human problems

as opposed to a belief in non-rational means such as magic and witchcraft; (4) the development of achievement and social mobility aspirations; (5) a strong desire to participate in civic life; (6) a strive to attain general as opposed to localized knowledge about social life and world events. (cited in Spengler, 1974: 153)

This brief, and admittedly incomplete, outline of modernization theory is intended to give only a general overview of what is a very complex and varied literature concerning the historical experiences that socioeconomic modernization implies for a society. Clearly, there are many discontinuities in the process of modernization (Gusfield, 1967; Hoogvelt, 1976). Not all societies pass through the stages of development in exactly the same way or even in the same sequence. For instance, some contemporary societies that are modernizing economically are characterized by non-democratic systems of government (consider, for instance, some of the oil-rich countries in the Middle East). Conversely, some of the relatively recent democracies (for example, countries in Latin America) are lagging in their economic development as compared to the Western industrial societies. In other words, modernization is not necessarily a unilinear process (Gusfield, 1967). Only in the most general sense can one claim that, in the long term, all societies pass through the various stages of social, economic, and cultural change. The conditions and factors that account for modernization can vary from society to society. As part of this large-scale change, societies undergo demographic transition.

As one of the most important conceptual models in population studies, the demographic transition theory receives special attention in parts of this book. Revisions to demographic transition theory have been proposed in recent years, and these will be examined later in the text. In essence, as we have already mentioned, the demographic transition is a theory about fertility change, mortality decline, and population growth in a context of massive societal transformations. In actuality, the demographic transition theory subsumes sub-theories of fertility change and mortality change, as well change in patterns of geographic mobility.

Macro-level theories of demographic change are part and parcel of a larger theoretical framework: modernization theory. These theories range from economic (e.g., population growth and economic development theories) to ideational ones (i.e., the role of ideas and innovations and their diffusion in society). Finally, there are theoretical formulations we shall see that focus on the broader question of the causal relevance of population to environment and resources. In this class of theories, we shall examine the main ideas of Malthus, Marx, and their contemporaries. Though stated in macro terms, these theories have clear implications not just for society as a system but for the individual as well.

Conclusion

A human population is a collectivity—a community of people bound by common beliefs or interests—co-existing within a geographic area at a certain point in time. The concept of population also entails time continuity, as the people who make up a population are descendants of those who made up the population in the past. Populations renew themselves through fundamental demographic processes (births, deaths, in-migration, and out-migration).

The scientific study of population is broadly divided into formal demography and population studies. Formal demography is primarily concerned with the quantitative aspects of the field, while population studies (also called social demography) aims to explain the sociological causes and consequences of demographic change and development. Although the division represents an effective way to examine the field, in reality, formal demography and population studies are inseparable: they are complementary rather than separate aspects of population analysis.

The natural processes of fertility and mortality combined with net migration account for the difference in population size between two points in time. These components of demographic change are represented neatly in the demographic balancing equation. Other mathematical models used to study trends in population growth include the linear, geometric, exponential, and logistic models.

Demographers study numerical changes in population, but they also examine compositional change—shifts in age and sex distributions of a population as well as changing trends associated with other important characteristics, such as marital status, education, and occupation.

A society is necessarily a population organized under the umbrellas of culture and social structure. Individual behaviour is conditioned by these features of the social world. Therefore, aggregate demographic phenomena must, to a large extent, reflect individual behaviours in accordance with the norms, values, and institutional structure of the society. In this regard, it is individual state transitions that help produce many macro-level demographic phenomena. State transitions occur whenever a person undergoes a change in status, from single to married, for example, or even from living to dead. Individual state transitions are reflected in demographic rates for the greater population.

Three important mechanisms of demographic change are age, period, and cohort. These variables are interrelated: it is impossible to extricate any one from the others. The intersection of aging with time is something we all experience as individuals going through life, from birth to death. People who are born at roughly the same time and who advance through the life course together make up a birth cohort. New cohorts are born in the population, and old ones exit through death. Cohorts differ in their social and economic circumstances: for example, some cohorts reach their formative years in prosperous economic times, while others come of age during economic downturns or times of war. Cohorts, as collectivities, are important agents of social as well as demographic change.

It is often stated that the primary concern of population studies is to explain aggregate demographic phenomena. While this is true, understanding micro-level dynamics is also essential in order to gain a complete appreciation of demographic phenomena. Several models of individual action are reviewed in this chapter: the rational actor model, the normative model, and the "drift" model. Of the three, the "drift" model places the greatest emphasis on the less rational features of human behaviour.

Macro models of demographic phenomena attempt to describe and explain population change in the context of structural changes in society. One of the most important macro models of demographic change is the demographic transition theory, which is a useful generalization of the demographic shifts that occur as part of a society's large-scale transformations during socio-economic modernization. One of the most important conceptual models in population studies, the demographic transition theory subsumes sub-theories of changes in fertility, mortality, and geographic mobility.

Exercises

1. Table 1.4 gives data for Canada and Sweden for 1988–89. Use the demographic balancing equation to estimate the values left blank in the table.

TABLE 1.4   **Population data for Canada and Sweden, 1988–89**

	Canada	Sweden
Population at beginning of 1988	26 449 888	8 416 599
Population at end of 1989	26 798 303	8 461 554
Growth during period		
Births during period	384 035	112 080
Deaths during period	188 408	96 756
Natural increase during period		
In-migration during period	178 152	51 092
Out-migration during period	25 364	21 461
Net migration during period		

Sources: Adapted from Preston, Heuveline, and Guillot (2001); and Statistics Canada (2003b): 22–3.

2. From the data in Table 1.4, calculate the crude birth rate (CBR) and the crude death rate (CDR) for Canada and for Sweden, and also the two countries' rates of natural increase (RNI). The population denominators for these rates can be derived by adding the respective population counts for the beginning and the end of the period and then dividing by 2. (This is necessary because these rates require the denominators to be the mid-year populations.) The rate of natural increase (RNI) per capita is:

$$RNI = \frac{births - deaths}{mid\text{-}year\ population}$$
$$= (b - d)$$

where b = the birth rate per capita; d = the death rate per capita.

Alternatively, if the birth and death rates are given as per 1000 population, this measure can be computed as:

$$RNI = \left[\frac{CBR}{1\,000} - \frac{CDR}{1\,000} \right]$$

This gives the rate of natural increase per capita, which can also be expressed as a per cent—i.e., RNI(100).

3. The average annual rate of growth of population can be computed as:

$$r = \frac{\left[\frac{P_1 - P_0}{P_0} \right]}{n}$$

Or alternatively,

$$r = \left[\frac{\frac{P_1}{P_0} - 1}{n} \right]$$

where r = the growth rate, P_1 = population at the end of the interval, P_0 = population at the beginning of the interval, and n = the number of years in the interval. Then, r (100) gives the average annual rate of growth expressed as a per cent. This is a linear (arithmetic) formula for the population growth rate. In Chapter 3, we will look at the geometric and exponential models.

Use the data in Table 1.4 to compute the growth rate for the two populations.

4. Write a short essay explaining how demographic phenomena can be understood as both micro-level and macro-level processes. Use examples from the news media to illustrate your arguments.

Additional Reading

Caselli, Graziella, Jacques Vallin, and Guillaume Wunsch, eds. 2006. *Demography: Analysis and Synthesis: A Treatise in Population Studies,* 4 vols. Amsterdam: Academic Press.

Demeny, Paul, and Geoffrey McNicoll, eds. 2003. *Encyclopedia of Population*, vols. 1 and 2. New York: Macmillan Reference USA/ Thomson Gale.

Heer, David M., and Jill S. Grigsby. 1992. *Society and Population*. Englewood Cliffs, NJ: Prentice Hall.

Kammeyer, Kenneth C.W., and Helen Ginn. 1986. *An Introduction to Population*. Chicago: Dorsey.

LeBras, Hervé. 2008. *The Nature of Demography.* Princeton: Princeton University Press.

Matras, Judah. 1977. *Introduction to Population: A Sociological Approach*. Englewood Cliffs, NJ: Prentice-Hall.

Nam, Charles B. 1994. *Understanding Population Change*. Itasca, IL: F.E. Peacock.

Petersen, William. 1975. *Population*, 3rd edn. New York: Macmillan.

Poston, Dudley L., and Leon F. Bouvier. 2010. *Population and Society: An Introduction to Demography*. Cambridge: Cambridge University Press.

Riley, Nancy E., and James McCarthy. 2003. *Demography in the Age of the Postmodern*. Cambridge: Cambridge University Press.

Stycos, Mayone, ed. 1989. *Demography as an Interdiscipline*. New Brunswick, NJ: Transaction.

Weeks, John R. 2012. *Population: An Introduction to Concepts and Issues*. Belmont, CA: Wadsworth.

Yaukey, David, Douglas L. Anderton, and Jennifer Hickes Lundquist. 2007. *Demography: The Study of Human Population,* 3rd edn. Long Grove, IL: Waveland Press.

2 Population Data: Their Sources and Nature

Introduction

It is generally agreed that *census* and *vital statistics* are the most important data sources for demographic research and analysis. Population surveys and administrative databases (such as health records or tax files) provide additional information that is useful for the study of population. This chapter surveys the two principal systems of data collection: census and vital statistics registration.

The Population Census

The term *census* derives from the Latin verb *censere*, which means "to assess." Since ancient times, societies have been listing and counting the population within their territories. Censuses are said to have been taken as early as 3800 BCE in Babylon and 2000 BCE in ancient China (Statistics Canada Census Operations Division, 1997: 7). But as William Petersen (2000) notes, the counting of population was an uncommon practice until fairly recently. In the distant past, counts of the population were closely connected to the collection of taxes, the recruitment of conscripts for the military, and other state interests. It is doubtful that these early censuses were comprehensive enough to account for all citizens. It was not before the middle part of the eighteenth century that European countries started to undertake regular censuses (Petersen, 2000); prior to that time, listing and counting the population must be assumed to have been not only irregular but also highly inaccurate and incomplete (Coale, 1974: 15; Petersen, 2000: 10).

According to Ansley Coale (1974: 15), the first series of modern censuses taken at regular intervals of no more than 10 years was begun by Sweden in 1750; decennial enumerations were begun in the United States in 1790 and in France and England in 1800, and have been conducted ever since. Yet Coale (1974: 15) also indicates that it was not until the nineteenth century that the census became widespread among the more developed countries, and the practice has spread slowly to other parts of the world. India's population has been enumerated at decennial intervals only since 1871, and a number of Latin American populations have been counted, mostly at irregular intervals, only since the late nineteenth century. The first comprehensive census of Russia was not conducted until 1897, and the population of most of Tropical Africa remained uncounted until after World War II.

A Brief History of the Canadian Census

In 1608, some 70 years after Jacques Cartier travelled up the St. Lawrence River and established France's claim to North America, a small number of French settlers led by Samuel de Champlain set foot in present-day Quebec and thus helped found the colony of New France. Half a century later, Jean Talon was entrusted by the French king Louis XIV to oversee the development of the fledgling colonies and help them become self-sufficient producers of goods required "for the growth of French industry" (Statistics Canada Census Operations Division, 1997: 7). As part of his mandate, Talon in 1666 organized and directed the colony's first census, considered by some the first systematic modern census (Beaujot, 1978: 5). The 1666 count set the total population of New France at 3 215, of which 2 034 were men and 1 181 were women. The census also determined that 1 019 persons were married, and that there were 528 families (Statistics Canada Census Operations Division, 1997: 7). It is important to point out that the tally did not include Aboriginal inhabitants or members of the military stationed in the colony.

Between 1666 and the early part of the twentieth century, periodic censuses were taken in Canada at irregular intervals and with varying degrees of coverage. It was not until the mid-1800s that legislation was passed to provide regular and complete counts of the population in Canada, beginning in 1851, and it was not until 1905 that a permanent Census and Statistics Office was established in Ottawa; this became the Dominion Bureau of Statistics in 1918, and renamed Statistics Canada in 1971 (Wargon, 2002; Statistics Canada, 2013d).

During the French regime, covering the period from 1608 to 1759, no fewer than 36 censuses were conducted. Under British rule, the first census of Canada's population was carried out in 1765. It was during this time that questions concerning race, ethnicity, religion, and place of birth first began to appear in the census questionnaires. During the early 1800s, censuses of the populations of the Atlantic colonies, Lower (Quebec) and Upper (Ontario) Canada, and Manitoba were taken sporadically. With Confederation in 1867, the Constitution Act (formerly the British North American Act) stipulated that an official count of the population would be undertaken every ten years, beginning in 1871 (Wargon, 2002). In 1956 the interval between censuses was changed from ten to five years to make up-to-date information on Canada's rapidly changing population more readily available.

Table 2.1 outlines milestones in the history of the Canadian census. Canada's 2011 census marks 345 years of population counting; over this time, the country has grown from the 3 215 people documented in Jean Talon's 1666 census to a nation of more than 34 million inhabitants, who co-exist in a rapidly changing social, economic, and demographic environment.

Contemporary Population Censuses

A modern census provides a complete account of a country's population at a point in time, including its size and geographic distribution as well as its demographic and socioeconomic characteristics. It is, as some have described it, a "snapshot of the population"—a statistical portrait of a country and its people at one point in time.

TABLE 2.1   Milestones in the history of the Canadian census

1666	First census in New France. The total population was 3 215, excluding Aboriginal people and royal troops.
1739	Last census under French rule.
1767	The Census of Nova Scotia adds religion and ethnic-origin variables.
1817	The Census of Nova Scotia adds place-of-birth variable.
1831	The first census in what would become western Canada is taken in the Assiniboine.
1851	With the enactment of legislation requiring censuses in 1851, 1861, and every tenth year thereafter, the decennial census is born.
1870	First census of British Columbia and Manitoba.
1871	First census of Canada after Confederation. The questionnaire was produced in both English and French, as it has been in every census since.
1905	The census office becomes a permanent part of the government.
1906	A quinquennial census is taken in Manitoba, Saskatchewan, and Alberta.
1911	The census is moved from April to June to avoid poor weather and road conditions and to improve the accuracy of crop acreage data.
1918	The Dominion Bureau of Statistics is established with the enactment of the 1918 Statistics Act.
1941	The census is moved for this year only to 14 June to avoid conflicting with the first Victory Bond campaign. Sampling is used for the first time; the questions concern housing.
1956	The first nationwide quinquennial census is conducted.
1971	For the first time, most respondents complete the questionnaire by themselves (self-enumeration). The Dominion Bureau of Statistics becomes Statistics Canada. A new Statistics Act requires that a census of population and agriculture be conducted every five years.
1986	The census contains a question on activity limitations, which is later used to form a sample for the first postcensal survey on activity limitations.
1991	The question on common-law status is asked for the first time.
1996	For the first time, the census collects information about unpaid housework and mode of transportation to work.
2001	For the first time, the census collects information about common-law couples of the same sex, as well as information on language of work.
2006	For the first time, the census counts same-sex married couples, reflecting the legalization of same-sex marriages in July 2005.
2011	Couples with children can be classified as intact families or stepfamilies. A voluntary National Household Survey replaces the traditional census long form (short form still mandatory).

Sources: Adapted from Statistics Canada (2011a, 2011d); Statistics Canada Census Operations Division (2003a): 27.

Most of the world's countries, except the very poorest ones, have formal statistical agencies responsible for planning and administering demographic data collection and dissemination. Statistics Canada is this country's statistical bureau, in charge of conducting the census and collecting vital statistics, among other responsibilities. Since the registration of births, deaths, marriages, divorces, and fetal deaths is a provincial function, these vital records are collected by provincial government bureaus and then passed on to the central statistical agency for assessment, processing, and dissemination. The same principle applies in the United States, where the US Census Bureau is the organization entrusted with planning and executing the census, while the National Center for Health Statistics (NCHS) oversees the vital registration system with files supplied through state-operated registration systems (Siegel, 2002: 88–9). In other industrial countries, such as France, the United Kingdom, the Netherlands, and Italy, national agencies devoted to census and vital statistics systems perform similar functions.

A national census is very costly and requires extensive preparations and planning. For these reasons, most national governments find it efficient to conduct a complete enumeration of their populations at periodic intervals, usually every five (as in Canada) or ten (as in the US) years. In an effort to help achieve a standard set of practices that would make it easier to compare census data across countries, the United Nations proposed a number of guidelines for population counting, including the following four points:

1. A census should be based on individual responses to predetermined questions regarding specific demographic data, including age, sex, marital status, and a wide array of secondary traits (e.g., education, occupation, income).
2. It should be universal in scope, in order to include all members of the population.
3. It should be conducted throughout a nation's territory on a predetermined date.
4. It should be carried out at regular intervals; those countries taking censuses at ten-year intervals should do so on the years ending in zero. (Shryock and Seigel, 1976)

Taking censuses at regular intervals helps make the results consistent and easier to compare across nations. Encouraging countries to monitor changes in demography at regular intervals also makes computing intercensal estimates of the population easier and more accurate.

Censuses can be conducted on either a *de jure* or a *de facto* basis. With the *de jure* method of enumeration, people are counted at their usual place of residence, not wherever they happen to be living or staying at the time of the census. In the case of *de facto* census, the respondent is counted as a resident of the address where he or she happens to have stayed on the night preceding the day of the census, regardless of whether the respondent is temporarily away from his or her usual residence. In Canada, where the *de jure* census is used, students attending university away from home are enumerated with their parents even though they live elsewhere most of the year (if based on the *de facto* method, a student who usually resides in Halifax but who is studying at the University of Montreal at the time of the census would be counted as a resident of Montreal). Similarly, Canadian residents living temporarily abroad (e.g., army personnel and government representatives posted in another country) receive separate questionnaires and are asked to provide their usual place of residence in Canada. In addition to Canada, the United States and a large number of European countries have adopted the *de jure* method, while

France, the United Kingdom, Greece, and Russia are a few of the countries that still favour *de facto* censuses.

Census data are extremely useful for a wide range of purposes. They can alert governments to demographic shifts that could pose challenges without proper advanced planning. A rapidly growing child population, for example, should signal the need for new schools as well as recruitment and training programs for additional teachers. A central government uses census data as an objective basis for distributing funds to its constituent parts—provinces, territories, states. In Canada, for example, a key criterion for allocating government transfer payments is a province's population size: the larger the province's population, the greater the share of funds it receives to cover the costs of delivering social programs, building new hospitals, maintaining roads, establishing daycare facilities, and improving transit systems. Census counts are also used for establishing and revising electoral boundaries, since the number of government seats allocated to each territory depends on its proportionate share of the total population (Statistics Canada Census Operations Division, 2003a). Of course, it is not just governments that use population figures and other census data. Businesses frequently scrutinize census data to discover population trends that will help them target potential markets.

A national census typically covers a wide array of questions on several key topics. The Canadian census, for example, asks questions on the following categories:

- **demographic characteristics**: e.g., name, relationship of household members to the person filling out the census questionnaire, age and date of birth, sex, marital/common-law status
- **sociocultural characteristics**: e.g., place/ country of birth, citizenship, landed immigrant status, racial and ethnic origin, Aboriginal status, year of immigration, knowledge and use of the two official languages (English and French)
- **socioeconomic characteristics**: e.g., education, occupation, employment status, income, number of hours worked during the previous year, home ownership
- **geographic characteristics**: e.g., place of residence, place of work, mobility status

A national census may introduce new questions on topics of importance to the government of the day. For instance, recent Canadian censuses have covered topics pertaining to health and disability. The Canadian census also includes a section on agriculture.

The Census: A Reflection of Its Time

Over the years some questions have been cropped from the Canadian census and others added. Some items dropped from an earlier census are reinstated in a subsequent census, while certain questions are asked only every tenth year. None of this is as arbitrary as it sounds. Changes to the census questionnaire largely mirror sociological change in the population. As new social trends begin to emerge, questions pertaining to these trends are proposed and then carefully evaluated for inclusion on the census questionnaire. Wayne McVey and Warren Kalbach (1995: 12) identify three general criteria used by census authorities to assess the suitability of new questions:

1. ***practical value to the nation broadly speaking:*** including government departments at all levels, business, industry, the research community, and citizens

2. ***public acceptance of a question:*** the question must be socially acceptable so that people will be willing to answer honestly

3. ***comparability with previous censuses:*** new questions must be similar in wording and presentation to questions asked in previous censuses

Once a question has been screened and assessed, it must be officially approved by the federal government before it is allowed a place on the census questionnaire.

The topics of common-law relationships and same-sex marriages illustrate how sociological changes in the population are reflected in the census. Unions of men and women living together but not legally married had become increasingly common in Canada since the 1970s, and by the 1980s it had become apparent that the trend would continue and needed to be studied systematically. Census planners could not avoid including a question on such an important trend, and finally added the item in the 1991 census. A similar development was the addition in 2001 of a question regarding same-sex unions—a topic that in earlier times would have been viewed as too controversial or socially unacceptable, but by the start of the twenty-first century had sufficient popular support to warrant inclusion. In 2005, same-sex marriages became legalized in Canada. A growing number of countries have been following this same trend.

Space limitations and the costs involved in including and tabulating items in the census often mean that adding a new item to the questionnaire requires the removal of another. From 1941 to 1991, every decennial census included a question about "children ever born." Adult women respondents were asked to declare the number of children they had ever had, including children from previous marriages, children born outside of marriage, and children who were deceased.

When it was introduced in the mid-twentieth century, the question on "children ever born" was seen as an important way to track fertility among Canadian women, and the data it yielded was used in important analytical studies on changing fertility patterns in pre- and post-war Canada (see, for instance, Balakrishnan, Ebanks, and Grindstaff, 1979; Charles, 1948; Henripin, 1972). But by the end of the century, Canadian fertility had stabilized at below-replacement levels, and variations in fertility rates across subgroups—groups from different regions or representing different ethnic backgrounds, for instance—had practically converged to the national level. So a question on completed fertility seemed secondary in importance to emerging issues of greater social and economic significance.

One of the issues demanding greater attention is unpaid work—caring for children and seniors, preparing family meals, doing housework and home maintenance—and how this relates to the rising trend in women's participation in the labour force. As a result of changing priorities, the fertility question was removed and an item on unpaid work was added in the 2001 census.

Ethnicity is another topic that has garnered increasing coverage in recent censuses. In 1981, respondents could for the first time declare more than one ethnic origin, and the 1986 census included detailed instructions to guide respondents in filling out the multiple ethnicity question. Both additions reflect an acknowledgement on the part of Canada's census planners that the country's multicultural makeup and growing ethnic diversity need to be properly studied. In 2001, the census included a question about parents' place of birth, a topic that had been treated in earlier censuses before being removed in 1976. In this case, it was the research community that pressured Statistics Canada to put the item back on the census form. This data, they argued, was key to assessing the socioeconomic progress of first- and second-generation immigrants.

Political changes can also lead to changes in the census. In 1985, the federal government amended provisions of the Indian Act of Canada that caused Native women to relinquish their Indian status if they married a non-Indian. The 1985 amendments allowed these women, as well as their children, to regain their Indian status, which led to a dramatic increase in the population of registered Indians. Between 1985 and 1993, the number of registered status Indians in Canada rose by over half a million (553 559), or 54 per cent. Particularly striking is the growth, over the same period, of the off-reserve Indian population, from 104 455 to 226 872—a change of 117 per cent. In 1991, Statistics Canada added a question about registered Indian status to the census questionnaire. While this addition no doubt reflects growing awareness of and interest in Aboriginal issues, it can almost certainly be tied to the 1985 Indian Act amendments, which were largely responsible for the sudden growth of Canada's Native population.

The Use of Sampling in the Census

In Canada, since 1941, *sampling* has been made an integral part of the census. Although since that time procedures have been modified, the basic idea behind sampling in the census is the same: data are obtained from a representative sample of households from which it is then possible to derive the characteristics of the population. This allows for a cost-efficient manner of collecting the information and also for describing the demographic state and characteristics of the population. For example, in the 2006 census, Statistics Canada distributed to a one-in-five sample of private dwellings in all self-enumerated areas the so-called long-form questionnaire, which contained basic demographic questions and a large number of additional items covering a host of socioeconomic and sociocultural characteristics (e.g., place of birth, ethnic origin, religion, education, occupation, income, etc.). The short-form questionnaire containing only basic demographic questions (age, sex, marital status, common-law status, mother tongue, relationship to the household reference person, type of dwelling) was filled out by all enumerated private dwellings.

In 2011, Canada introduced a significant change. For the first time, the long-form census was replaced by a voluntary survey, the National Household Survey (NHS). Many have decried this move on the grounds that people would opt out of participating in a voluntary survey, and this would compromise the quality, generalizability, and historical comparability of the results. The response rate to the NHS was indeed lower than expected: 68.6 per cent as compared to 94 per cent in the 2006 long-form census. Wide variations have been noted by Statistics Canada across municipalities, with larger centres having substantially higher response rates than smaller ones. Statistics Canada has applied a weighting methodology to the NHS data to compensate statistically for these geographic differences in response rates. For example, for the nation as a whole, the unweighted response rate of 68.6 per cent resulted in a weighted rate of 77.2 per cent; for Ontario, the unweighted and weighted rates were 67.6 and 76.3 per cent, respectively (Statistics Canada, 2014a). In light of this situation, data analyses for small geographic areas must be executed with a great deal of caution. The potential for bias due to variability in response rates is also a concern when analyzing subpopulations (e.g., sociocultural groups) of varying population size, as no all-embracing data quality indicator is available in these cases.

A growing number of countries have been moving in the same direction as Canada in considering alternative ways of collecting census data. According to Paolo Valente (2010), between 2000 and 2010, half of European Union countries surveyed maintained a traditional census; the rest applied a mix of approaches, including the use of register data (an ongoing register of all demographic events in a community) with total enumeration of the population or the use of sample surveys. Also, given the diffusion of computers and the Internet in society, countries are looking at ways to incorporate online participation rather than relying on traditional means of enumerating the population. The main justifications by government for these types of changes hinge on very high cost and complexity of census preparations and the growing reluctance among citizens to participate in a process considered intrusive. Valente (2010: 2) provides additional insight on these matters in the following text box.

THE "TRADITIONAL CENSUS": CHALLENGES AND DRIVERS FOR CHANGE

From Paolo Valente, "Census Taking Europe: How Are Populations Counted in 2010?":

> Respondents are increasingly reluctant to open their doors [to census enumerators], especially when they are older, living alone, or residing in large cities or neighbourhoods where security is a concern. The growing number of singles with mobile lifestyles and multiple residences also make the enumeration very difficult. In addition, the respondents may be reluctant to provide information that is already available from other sources, such as administrative registers. In fact, some countries have specific laws or administrative provisions to prevent the

statistical office from requesting information that is available in registers.

At the same time, there is increasing demand for detailed, high quality data covering new areas and emerging phenomena. Yet, because of the complexity of collecting and processing such large amounts of data, and because censuses are generally organized only once every ten [or five] years, the census results may quickly become out of date for certain purposes or for users needing very recent information. Finally, the range of information collected in the census needs to be continually adjusted and expanded to take account of rapid changes in society. This is only partially possible with the traditional census, not only because of its weight and complexity, but also because of a concern to ensure the historical comparability of results.

Over the last decades, these difficulties and challenges have convinced many countries in Europe and North America to consider alternative methodologies to the traditional census approach. From the 1970s, the use of the long form and short form was adopted in the United States and Canada, while the Scandinavian countries started moving towards the register based census. . . . More recently, several countries have developed alternatives based on different combinations of field enumeration, data from existing registers, ad hoc sample surveys, or existing sample surveys.

Source: Paolo Valente published in *Population & Societies*, 467, May 2010: "Census taking in Europe: how are populations counted in 2010?" Published by Institut National d' Étude Demographiques.

Census Undercoverage

In theory, a national census is supposed to obtain a complete enumeration of the population. In truth, this is seldom the case, as there is always some level of *undercounting*. Generally, census bureaus throughout the world experience varying degrees of difficulty in successfully enumerating marginal sectors of their populations. This may be due to a combination of factors, including limited resources and difficulty in locating certain categories of individuals, such as indigenous populations in remote geographical areas, and persons that wish to remain unnoticed from the authorities such as illegal immigrants, criminals, nomads, and the homeless (McVey and Kalbach, 1995: 16; Petersen, 2000: 11). In the case of Canada, officials take various steps to minimize the problem of undercounting; for instance, census takers are dispatched to remote areas and Native reserves to complete some household questionnaires in person (Statistics Canada Census Operations Division, 2003b). But despite such efforts, the reality is that certain segments of the population are particularly difficult to track; others (e.g., some Native reserves in Canada) may even refuse to participate in the census.

A less frequent complication is that of *overcoverage* due to persons being enumerated more than once. Statistics Canada computes a *net census undercoverage* rate that takes both types of problems into account. A national census is followed by a post-enumeration survey to obtain, from a representative survey of the population, an estimate of the population size that should correspond to the population count obtained through the census. The survey data is used along with the actual census count (and additional information from other sources) to derive estimates of undercoverage, overcoverage, and then net census undercoverage. To this figure, Statistics Canada also takes into account any undercoverage due to non-participation of Native reserves. As shown in Table 2.2 for the 2001 and 2006 censuses, undercoverage rates in Canada are relatively low, at around 3 per cent.

Population Estimates

Knowledge of net census undercoverage helps in the derivation of population estimates for non-census years. There are two types of *population estimates:* postcensal, and intercensal. *Postcensal estimates* are produced by using data from the most recent census (adjusted for census undercoverage) and estimates of the components of demographic change (births, deaths, net migration) since that last census. *Intercensal estimates* are produced every five years and reconcile previous postcensal estimates with the latest census counts (Statistics Canada Demography Division, 2007a: 8–9).

Population estimates make it possible to track population trends over regular intervals and also facilitate the preparation of population projections. *Population projections* are a series of population estimates, typically by age and sex, derived from the application of assumptions regarding change in the demographic components over the course of a defined time horizon. In other words, projections are conditional estimates of population at future dates

TABLE 2.2 **Estimated census net undercoverage, Canada, provinces and territories, 2001 and 2006 Censuses**

Census	Census population	Census net undercount	Incompletely enumerated Indian reserves	Adjusted population count	Undercoverage rate (%)
	(A)	(B)	(C)	(D)	= (B+C)/D*100
2001	30 007 094	924 430	34 539	30 966 063	3.10
2006	31 612 897	868 658	40 115	32 521 670	2.79

Source: Statistics Canada Demography Division (2013a): 88, Table 1.

(Bryan, 2004a: 523). The latest projections for Canada have been calculated to the year 2061. The starting point for these projections is the 1 July 2009 postcensal population estimates (Statistics Canada Demography Division, 2010).

Specialized Population Surveys

National statistical agencies frequently conduct sample surveys of the population to obtain demographic information that is not typically asked for in a census. In Canada and the United States, for example, surveys of the labour force are taken routinely to monitor employment and unemployment trends and other economic indicators. The US Census Bureau, on behalf of the Bureau of Labor Statistics, carries out a monthly survey of around 50 000 households; known as the Current Population Survey (CPS), it is designed to obtain information about the employment status of respondents and their families (Anderson, 2003 122). Two important surveys conducted by Statistics Canada are the Aboriginal Peoples' Survey and the National Population Health Survey. Both are typically taken shortly after a census.

Vital Statistics

In the Western world, vital statistics were first compiled by churches (Petersen, 2000: 10). In England, the clergy was required as early as the sixteenth century to keep records of christenings, marriages, and burials; similar records began to be kept by the clergies of France, Italy, and Spain during the seventeenth century. As a result, many historical records about early modern populations come from the parish registers, which, especially in the case of the earliest records, suffer serious deficiencies concerning their accuracy and completeness.

In North America, the clergy and government officials in the colonies began to record vital statistics in the seventeenth century. On a national level, the US government started publishing annual records of deaths in 1900 and of births in 1915 (*Columbia Encyclopedia*, 2003). In Canada, the publication of annual vital statistics for the country and the provinces began in 1921, although, as we have seen, the history of census taking in what would become Canada dates back to the early seventeenth century (see Table 2.3).

Early Investigations of Vital Records and the Origins of Population Studies

The modern foundations of population studies as a discipline are closely connected to a number of scholars who conducted early investigations of one form of vital statistics: mortality. The English economist and clergyman Thomas Malthus (1766–1834) is often cited as the "father of modern demography." It is certainly fair to say that he was one of the founding fathers but perhaps not the only one. Others who, along with Malthus, contributed to the early development of the discipline include pioneer demographers John Graunt (1620–74) and William Petty (1623–87). Graunt is credited with having produced, in 1662, the first known (though very crude) life table based on the death records of the city of London, known as the Bills of Mortality. Donald Rowland (2003: 14) neatly summarizes the historical context surrounding Graunt's work:

TABLE 2.3	Highlights of the development of national vital statistics in Canada, 1605–1945
1605	Priests enumerate 44 settlers in the colony of New France.
1608	Quebec City is founded by Samuel de Champlain.
1617	Louis Hébert and his family, the first colonists, settle in Quebec.
1665–6	Jean Talon enumerates 3 215 inhabitants in the first census of the colony of New France.
1847	The Census and the Statistics Act of 1847 is passed, providing for a decennial census and the registration of births and deaths in the United Provinces of Upper and Lower Canada.
1867	The British North American Act creates the Dominion of Canada through the union of Ontario, Quebec, Nova Scotia, and New Brunswick.
1871	The first census of the Dominion of Canada is conducted. Published results include the compilation of vital statistics on the French Roman Catholic population of Quebec from 1608 to 1871.
1879	The Dominion of Canada's first Census and Statistics Act provides for the decennial census of 1881, and for the collection, abstraction, and tabulation of vital, agricultural, commercial, and other statistics.
1881	Census takers are required to take an oath of secrecy.
1898	An American Public Health Association meeting in Ottawa recommends the adoption of the *International Classification of Causes of Death* by registrars of Canada, the United States, and Mexico.
1905	Canada's first permanent Census and Statistics office is established.
1915	The office of the Dominion Statistician is created.
1918	The Statistics Act of 1918 is passed, creating the Dominion Bureau of Statistics (DBS).
1919	An order-in-council detailing the establishment of a national system of vital statistics is approved by the dominion government.
1921	The first detailed report on vital statistics is published by DBS, covering eight provinces.
1926	A national vital statistics report covering all of Canada (i.e., nine provinces plus the Yukon and Northwest Territories) is published.
1935	Improvements are made to registration techniques and procedures (e.g., revision of the medical certificate of death).
1938	The fifth revision of the *International List of Causes of Death* is adopted.
1940	The *Vital Statistics Handbook* and *Physician's Pocket Reference* are prepared.
1944	National tabulations on births and deaths begin to be reported by place of residence in addition to place of event.
1945	The national scheme of Family Allowances is implemented on 1 July.

Source: Statistics Canada, 'The Development of National Vital Statistics in Canada: Part I, From 1605 to 1945' by Marth Fair in Health Reports 6 (3), February 27, 1995. Reproduced and distributed on an 'as is basis with the permission of Statistics Canada.

After the fourteenth century Black Death killed at least a quarter of the population of Europe, and around 50 million in Europe and Asia overall, there followed centuries with further devastating epidemics of bubonic plague. Early in the sixteenth century, an ordinance required parish priests in London to compile weekly lists of deaths from plague, called the Bills of Mortality. These were intended initially to identify outbreaks and areas for quarantine. Later, other causes of death were included, as well as weddings and christenings and the collection was extended to cover all English parishes. Disastrous plagues struck London in 1603 and again in 1625. In the latter year an estimated one quarter of the population of London died. Interest in population at the time centred on the effects of epidemics on population numbers, together with the new field of "political arithmetic" concerned with estimating national wealth.

This context of epidemic mortality may have influenced Graunt to write his *Natural and Political Observations Made upon the Bills of Mortality*.[1] In assessing this work and its impact on the study of population, Philip Kreager (2003: 472) describes Graunt as "the author of the first quantitative analysis of human populations." Graunt explored some of the essential measures of demographic analysis—simple ratios, proportions, odds, and rates—and calculated basic measures of mortality, including rates of infant and child mortality, sex ratios, and crude death and birth rates. But his most enduring legacy was his invention of the life table. According to Kreager (2003: 473),

Graunt's estimate of the "number of fighting men" (i.e., for London's defence) relied on a hypothetical table of mortality by age. Mathematicians interested in the nascent calculus of probabilities,

such as . . . Christian Huygens, astronomer Edmund Halley, and philosopher and mathematician Gottfried Leibnitz (1646–1716), quickly recognized in his reasoning a more general logic for calculating life expectancy. Although Graunt had not employed his table for that purpose, their analyses gave rise to the first abstract model of population: the life table.

William Petty, a contemporary and close acquaintance of Graunt's, is considered the originator of national accounting systems. Petty regarded population dynamics 'as an integral part of social accounting" (McNicoll, 2003b: 729). He made important contributions to population analysis with his early (and crude) estimates of mortality and population size for major cities. Petty presented his ideas on population in his book *Political Arithmetic*. Geoffrey McNicoll (2003a: 729) points to Petty's early survey of Ireland as the basis for that country's first census, in 1659. Petty's work helped lay the foundations for the more systematic analyses of social and economic statistics by subsequent scholars such as Gregory King (1648–1712) and Edmond Halley (1656–1742), both of whom went on to expand on the work of Graunt by refining the life table as a mathematical construct (Rowland, 2003: 267). Halley, like Graunt, based his work on his analysis of the Bills of Mortality, but in his case for the city of Breslau, Germany. His contribution in this area, argues Rowland, is especially noteworthy, as it is a "foreshadowing [of] methods used today" (Rowland, 2003: 267).

Another early demographer who is worth mentioning here is Antoine Deparcieux (1703–68), whose importance is outlined by Roland Pressat (1985: 55–6). Like Halley, Deparcieux was an astronomer who developed further extensions of the life table. He is responsible for introducing the concept of "exposure to risk" in mortality analysis, in addition to helping refine the process for computing life expectancy. Deparcieux published one of the earliest modern studies on the life table, *Essay on the Probabilities of the Length of Human Life*, in 1746.

THE DEVELOPMENT OF POPULATION STUDIES IN CANADA—A BRIEF OVERVIEW

A great deal of what we know about the history of Canadian demography as a discipline is owed to Sylvia Wargon's (2002) authoritative analysis, *Demography in Canada in the Twentieth Century*. In a real sense, the establishment of Dominion Bureau of Statistics in 1918 (Statistics Canada since 1971) marks the beginning of Canadian demography as we know it today. This agency would not only systematically collect census and vital statistics data on the Canadian population but would also undertake and publish analytical studies of the demographic trends, a tradition that continues today. Among the works issued by this agency are ten monographs based on the 1931 census, two from the 1941 census, eight from the 1961 census, and ten based on the data from the 1971 census. Many of these monographs have been written by academics from various Canadian universities. But pioneering analyses have also come from non-academics, one notable example from the journalist Georges Langlois, who in 1935 published *Histoire de la population canadienne-française*. Enid Charles from the Dominion Bureau of Statistics issued in 1948 *The Changing Size of the Family in Canada*, a study based on the data from the 1941 census.

Around this time, several researchers, including two internationally renowned Canadian scholars, Nathan Keyfitz and Norman B. Ryder, began to produce outstanding works in demography that to this day remain essential reading for students of population.

From the beginning of the twentieth century to about 1950, there were no programs for demography at Canadian universities, even though some scholars taught courses and conducted research on population topics within university departments. Nonetheless, the 1950s proved to be the "incubation" period for Canadian academic demography; and by the late 1960s, several university departments had established programs devoted to research and training in demography and population studies, including the formation of the only department of demography in Canada at the University of Montreal.

In Quebec, there has developed a strong emphasis on historical demography, and many studies have been based on the extensive genealogical records of the French-Canadian population, as reflected in Hubert Charbonneau's *Vie et mort de nos ancétres*, published in 1975. Considerable attention in Quebec has been devoted to the linguistic dimension of population change. No doubt, this interest is grounded in the province's unique sociopolitical history and its ongoing concerns with preserving the French language and culture. The precipitous fall of the birth rate in Quebec since the early 1960s following the Quiet Revolution represents yet another area of importance to Quebec demographers. Emblematic of this research tradition are the works of Jacques Henripin (1926–2013), including his 1961 census monograph, *Trends and Factors of Fertility in Canada*, and the 1974 collaborative study, *La Fin de la revanche des berceaux: qu'en pensent les Quebecoises?* An ongoing research focus today concerns the social and demographic dimensions of immigration and population diversity in Quebec.

Immigration and immigrant adaptation has also occupied a central focus of research in the rest of Canada. Within the large body of work accumulated in this area is the 1961 census monograph of Warren Kalbach (1922–2005), *The Impact of Immigration on Canada's Population*, and Anthony Richmond's *Postwar Immigrants in Canada*, which appeared in 1967, the year of Canada's centennial. In the area of fertility and family is the significant contribution of T.R. Balakrishnan from the University of Western Ontario, and colleagues Karol Krotki (1922–2007; University of Alberta) and Evelyne Lapierre-Adamcyk (University of Montreal): *Family and Childbearing in Canada*. An ongoing focus of research today in Canada is demographic aging and public policy, as exemplified by the knowledge mobilization cluster on Population Change and Lifecourse, at the University of Western Ontario.

Many academic demographers in Canada teach and do research within departments of sociology, which is consistent with the American tradition of treating demography as a sub-field of sociological analysis. From the 1970s onward, the departments of sociology at the University of Western Ontario (now Western University) and University of Alberta have offered specialized training in population studies. The Population Research Laboratory at the University of Alberta conducts research on a wide range of population topics, including an annual survey of the population of Alberta; at McGill and at the University of Lethbridge, new population programs have been recently established; across other Canadian universities, population courses are being taught in departments of sociology, economics, and geography, including at the University of Toronto, Carleton, and the University of Victoria. Many professional demographers are employed at Statistics Canada and by municipal governments across the country.

Canada has two professional demographic associations, the Canadian Population Society (CPS) and Association des démographes du Québec (ADQ), which are both constituents of the Federation of Canadian Demographers (FCD). The two associations publish their own professional journals, *Canadian Studies in Population* (CPS) and *Cahier québécois de démographie* (ADQ).

Modern Vital Statistics Systems

Unlike the census, which is a periodic undertaking, the registration of vital events is a continuous activity. The main purpose of a national *vital statistics system* is to collect, compile, and process statistical information on all vital events that take place in the population on a daily basis. Carl Grindstaff summarizes these events as "the entrance to and exit from life, and the civil statuses that are acquired along the way" (1981: 47). Like the census, vital registration systems are institutionalized legal administrative institutions that form an integral part of the governmental bureaucracy.

As indicated by the United Nations Statistics Division (2002) in its *Handbook on Training in Civil Registration and Vital Statistics Systems,* a vital statistics system must be continuous and complete. It must also satisfy a number of additional requirements:

1. Vital events must be officially recorded within a short period of time, as specified by the legal authorities.
2. Events must be recorded at the geographic place (the city, town, municipality, and so on) where they occur, but the legal form must ask for the inclusion of usual residence of a case being registered (e.g., usual residence of the mother if registering a birth; or if a death, the informant gives the usual residence of the decedent), as well as the actual place of occurrence.
3. The registration of a vital event should be free, or only a nominal cost.
4. Registration is compulsory.

As members of a population, we are all part of a vital statistics system, and as we go through life, we are at times required to register vital events. Each of us has a birth certificate; each of us will also, someday, have a death certificate. Many of us will at some point submit a marriage certificate to the vital statistics registry, and if we should dissolve that marriage, we would be bound to declare the divorce with the registration system. From birth to death, we are involved in the legal observance and recording of many such facts of life, or vital events.

The list of vital events that must be reported by law varies from country to country. For example, according to the United Nations Department of Economic and Social Affairs Population Division (2002: 6), in some countries and territories, only births and deaths are registered, and with varying degrees of accuracy and completeness. In Canada, the following information must be reported by law:

- live birth
- death
- fetal death
- therapeutic abortion
- marriage
- divorce
- legal separation
- annulment
- adoption

Annually published vital statistics usually include births, deaths, fetal deaths, marriages, and divorces.[2]

In an effort to collect information on vital events for each country, the UN established a set of standard definitions for vital events (United Nations Department of Economic and Social Affairs Population Division, 2002: 7) (see text box, page 54).

Unfortunately, these definitions are not applied uniformly across all countries. For example, in some countries an infant must survive for at least 24 hours before it can be inscribed in the live-birth register; in other jurisdictions, an infant born alive who dies before registration is considered a late fetal death. Such cases might not be counted either as births or as deaths, and without proper adjustments, accurate comparative studies of birth and death rates are difficult to achieve.

Marriage and divorce can pose even greater difficulties, for as the UN points out, "Unlike birth and death, which are biological events, marriage and divorce are defined only in terms of laws and custom and as such are less amenable to universally applicable statistical definitions" (United Nations Department of Economic and Social Affairs Population Division, 2002: 7). Marriage laws in particular vary widely. The most broadly applied requirement is a minimum legal age, but there are often other requirements that must be met (for instance, in some countries, parental consent may be required for a marriage to be official). Divorce is also highly regulated. In some countries, the dissolution of marriage is strictly prohibited, while in many others there are many grounds for the granting of divorce. Again, to the extent that such practices and customs vary from society to society, there will be a varying degree of discrepancy in the statistics.

One obstacle faced by vital statistics systems is how to address the *underregistration* of vital events. Underregistration may happen for a number of reasons. Rural and isolated areas may not possess the infrastructure required to monitor and enforce prompt reporting, while some countries are home to nomadic

populations that are constantly mobile. The result, in either of these cases, can be a considerable lag between the time an event occurs and the time it is registered, if it is registered at all. In varying degrees, some level of underregistration can occur even in the industrialized countries of the world, including Canada (Statistics Canada Health Statistics Division, 1999: xiv).

Population Registers

Some countries maintain what is called a *population register*, in which change of residence, in addition to births, deaths, marriages, and divorces, must be declared to the authorities. This kind of continuous registration system exists in 27 EU countries, including the initial three that pioneered this type of accounting in the eighteenth and nineteenth centuries: Sweden (1749), Belgium (1847), and the Netherlands (1850) (Valente, 2010). Population registers are also common in certain Asian countries, including Taiwan, Israel, Japan, and China (Shryock and Siegel, 1976: 23–4).

Monitoring Migratory Movements

The discussion of population registers brings us to an important question: If in many countries there is no system to keep track of the movements of it citizens, how is migration studied?

With regard to immigration, most countries have established procedures for processing foreigners crossing their borders, and migration into a country is monitored and recorded systematically by appropriate government agencies. Counting the number of people leaving

UNITED NATIONS STANDARD DEFINITIONS FOR VITAL EVENTS

Live birth is complete expulsion or extraction from its mother of a product of conception, irrespective of the duration of pregnancy, which after such separation breathes or shows any other evidence of life such as beating of the heart, pulsation of the umbilical cord, or definite movement of voluntary muscles, whether or not the umbilical cord has been cut or the placenta is attached; each product of such a birth is considered live-born regardless of gestational age.

Death is the permanent disappearance of all evidence of life at any time after live birth has taken place (postnatal cessation of vital functions without capability of resuscitation). This definition therefore excludes fetal deaths.

Fetal death is death prior to the complete expulsion or extraction from its mother of a product of conception, irrespective of the duration of pregnancy; the death is indicated by the fact that after such separation the fetus does not breathe or show any other evidence of life, such as beating of the heart, pulsation of the umbilical cord, or definite movement of voluntary muscles. Late fetal deaths are those of 28 or more completed weeks of gestation. These are synonymous with the events reported under the pre-1950 term stillbirth.

Abortion is defined, with reference to the woman, as any interruption of pregnancy before 28 weeks of gestation with a dead fetus. There are two major categories of abortion: spontaneous and induced. Induced abortions are those initiated by deliberate action undertaken with the intention of terminating pregnancy; all other abortions are considered as spontaneous.

Marriage is the act, ceremony, or process by which the legal relationship of husband and wife is constituted. The legality of the union may be established by civil, religious, or other means as recognized by the laws of each country.

Divorce is a final legal dissolution of a marriage, that is, that separation of husband and wife which confers on the parties the right to remarriage under civil, religious, and/or other provisions, according to the laws of each country.

Source: United Nations Department of Economic and Social Affairs Population Division (2002). Reprinted by permission of United Nations Publications.

a country is a much more difficult task, however. Normally this aspect of population counting is incomplete and must be estimated using various methods and data sources, including census and administrative data bases to arrive at proper estimates of emigration. Some countries have official agreements to share data collected from travellers using their airports. Canada, for example, has an official agreement with the United States, the United Kingdom, and some other countries to record and exchange information about individuals travelling between these partner nations. Clearly, not every country is involved in these types of arrangements. The estimation of emigration is a complex subject. More will be said on this topic in Chapter 9 on international migration.

What about the movement of people *within* a country where a continuous recording of changes of residence is not kept? In such cases, internal migration is monitored using administrative databases. In Canada, this kind of monitoring is done through such data sources as tax files, which all adults must submit to the government at the end of each taxation year. Since the respondent must indicate his or her address on the tax return, migration between cities or provinces, signified by change in address from one year to the next, is easily discovered. The census is another valuable source of migration statistics. Usually, one or more questions on the census will ask about residential moves during the previous five years; this information gives a reliable indication of the extent of internal migration during a five-year interval. Recent Canadian censuses, as well as the 2011 National Household Survey, have also included a question on one-year mobility to get information on moves made in the year preceding the census.

Indirect Estimation of Vital Events

In some poor countries, censuses are rarely taken and vital statistics collected only sporadically. Typically the problem is a lack of both the necessary infrastructure and the funds to support institutions responsible for continuous registration of vital events. For settings in which a census is not possible and where registration systems are lacking or are deficient, demographic parameters such as births and deaths must be estimated. Often these estimates are based on incomplete information. Demographers have developed specialized techniques to handle such problems (see, e.g., Marks, Seltzer and Krotki, 1974; United Nations Department of International and Social Affairs, 1983).

Canadian Vital Statistics: Background and Overview

Prior to 1921, when the Canadian vital statistics system was launched, each province ran its own registration of vital events. Although church authorities in Quebec had been registering baptisms, burials, and marriages since 1610, there was little standardization across the provinces in the way the data were collected and processed. It was with an eye to correcting these inconsistencies that the federal government initiated the national registration system.

Founded in 1918, the Dominion Bureau of Statistics (known by its current name,

Statistics Canada, since 1971) organized two planning conferences to discuss the establishment of a standardized system of registration and reporting. Under the legislative purview of the Canada Vital Statistics Act, the Bureau would supply all provinces with standard forms for recording vital events, and the provinces would forward to the Bureau transcripts of their vital statistics certificates each year. The Bureau would check and then process the data, which would be published in an annual report. The practice is very much the same today. The provinces and territories supply electronic copies of registration forms to Statistics Canada in Ottawa.

The first vital statistics report, issued in 1923, reported on data taken in 1921 on births, deaths, and marriages for Canada and the eight provinces (Canada Dominion Bureau of Statistics, 1923).[3] Quebec joined the system in 1926, and Newfoundland joined in 1949. Data for the Yukon and the Northwest Territories were first included in the annual publications in 1950 (Statistics Canada Health Statistics Division, 1999: x), and Nunavut was added to the annual publications in 2000.

Officially, the mandate of the Canadian vital statistics system is "to obtain and preserve such documentary evidence as is necessary to protect the legal rights of the individual" (Statistics Canada, 1990: iv). The data is available to the public, so that at any time after registration, an individual may refer to his or her own family's records to verify facts concerning a birth, marriage, or death. However, the data are also used extensively by researchers and health professionals. At the national level, the data is used for population estimates and projections, demographic trend analyses, health surveillance, and epidemiological research (Statistics Canada, 1990: v–vi). The process involved in reporting vital statistics is outlined in Figure 2.1, which is based on an earlier sketch by McVey and Kalbach (1995: 19).

The Use of Census and Vital Statistics Data in Population Analysis

Researchers interested in computing basic demographic measures for a population typically draw the data for these computations from vital statistics and the census. Consider, for example, the computation of crude birth and death rates for a census year. This would be quite straightforward because we could easily obtain the number of births or deaths (numerator) that occurred in that year from the vital statistics database. And we would use the population at mid-year from the census (properly adjusted for net census undercoverage) as the denominator to get the rates.

How, then, are such rates computed for non-census years? The numerator for this kind of calculation would be available annually from the vital statistics system, since it is continuous. To obtain the denominator (i.e., the mid-year population) for a year in which a census is not taken researchers would have to rely on a *population estimate,* typically available from publications produced national statistical agencies. Many other demographic measures are calculated the same way, using vital statistics data as numerators and population data (actual or estimated) as denominators. Various such computations will be introduced throughout this book.

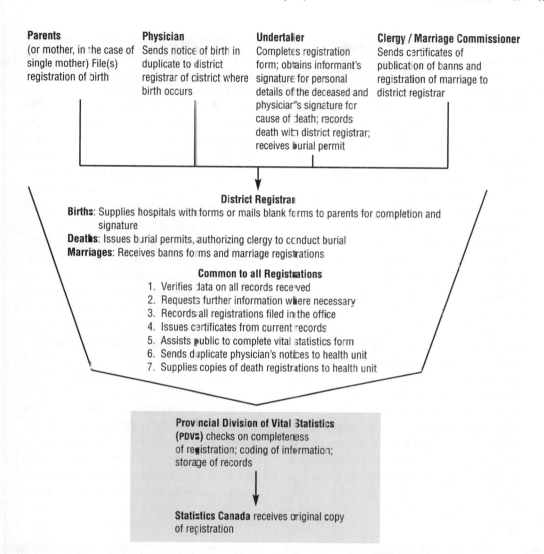

FIGURE 2.1   General overview of the Canadian vital Registration Process

Source: Adapted from McVey and Kalbach (1995): 19.

Conclusion

This chapter looked at the two principal sources of data for demographic analysis: the census and vital statistics. The census is a one-point-in-time accounting of the population with respect to a variety of demographic, geographic, social, and economic characteristics. It provides a realistic indication of the demographic, social, and economic state of the population at a point in time. The vital statistics registration system is an ongoing process in which citizens of a country are required by law to register births, deaths, marriages, and divorces. In some countries, there are population registers, where change of residence is recorded on a continual basis in addition to these other vital occurrences. In countries that do not have population registers, such as Canada and the United States, data on migration are obtained from other sources, including administrative records and censuses.

Other sources of population data include postcensal surveys and special demographic sample surveys. Several of these surveys are taken routinely in Canada; examples include the Labour Force Survey, the General Social Survey, the National Population Health Survey, and the National Longitudinal Survey of Children and Youth. All modern societies have similar types of surveys to supplement data gathered from their censuses and vital statistics systems. One important function of a postcensal survey is that it allows for an estimate of the degree of census undercoverage, which in Canada has generally ranged from 2 to 4 per cent.

The history of population studies is closely connected to early studies of vital statistics. The study of death records for the city of London by John Graunt in 1662 is considered the first systematic analysis in demography. His work based on the Bills of Mortality set the foundations for the life table, a staple of demographic analysis. While population counting of various sorts and extensiveness has been practised since antiquity, the census is a fairly recent invention, initiated by the Scandinavian countries in the mid-1700s. In recent years, a growing number of countries are considering new approaches to collecting census data, including online participation as a way to reduce the costs and complexities of preparing and conducting a traditional census. Some countries are adopting the principle of voluntary participation, as is the case with the recently introduced National Household Survey by Statistics Canada.

Many demographic measures require the use of vital statistics and census population. Vital statistics data are usually used as the numerators and census population as the basis for estimating the denominators for the computation of demographic rates.

Exercises

1. Locate the United Nations' latest *Demographic Yearbook*. Read the "Introduction" of this publication (http://unstats.un.org/unsd/demographic/products/dyb/default.htm). Also visit the Population Reference Bureau website (www.prb.org) and download their latest *World Population Data Sheet*. Read the "Notes, Sources, and Definitions" section of the data sheet. What problems can you identify in these two sources with respect to definition and measurement of demographic variables across different countries?

2. Write a short essay to describe how information obtained from the census could be used for academic and applied purposes. In addressing this question it may be instructive to examine the 2011 Canadian census forms (www12.statcan.gc.ca/census-recensement/2011/ref/about-apropos/questions_guides-eng.cfm) and also the list of questions included in the National Household Survey (www12.statcan.gc.ca/nhs-enm/2011/ref/nhs-enm_guide/guide_6-eng.cfm#A_7_1).

3. Sample copies of vital statistics forms for birth, death, and marriage for Alberta are provided in the Appendix online. In these forms, some questions are asked consistently throughout, while others are not. Identify the "common" questions. Why do you think these common questions are necessary?

Additional Reading

Bernstein, Peter L. 1996. *Against the Gods: The Remarkable Story of Risk*. New York: John Wiley & Sons.

Curtis, Bruce. 2001. *The Politics of Population: State Formation, Statistics, and the Census of Canada, 1840–1875*. Toronto: University of Toronto Press.

Le Bras, Hervé. 2008. *The Nature of Demography*. Princeton Princeton University Press.

Petersen, William. 2000. *From Birth to Death: A Consumer's Guide to Population Studies*. New Brunswick: Transaction Publishers.

Pressat, Roland. 1985. *The Dictionary of Demography*. Christopher Wilson, ed. Oxford: Basil Blackwell.

Stigler, Stephen M. 1986. *The History of Statistics: The Measurement of Uncertainty before 1900*. Cambridge, MA: The Belknap Press of Harvard University Press.

United Nations. 2001. *Principles and Recommendations for a Vital Statistics System—Revision 2*. E.01.XVII.10. New York: United Nations.

———. 1998. *Draft Principles and Recommendations for Population and Housing Censuses—Revision 1*. E.98.XVII.8. New York: United Nations.

Wargon, Sylvia T. 2002. *Demography in Canada in the Twentieth Century*. Vancouver: UBC Press.

Worton, David A. 1998. *The Dominion Bureau of Statistics: A History of Canada's Central Statistical Office and Its Antecedents, 1841–1972*. Montreal and Kingston: McGill-Queen's University Press.

Notes

1. The full and unwieldy title of Graunt's book is *Natural and Political Observations Mentioned in a Following Index, and Made upon the Bills of Mortality, with Reference to the Government, Religion, Trade, Growth, Air, Diseases and the Several Changes of the Said City*.

2. Statistics Canada has recently decided to no longer publish marriage and divorce statistics beyond the year 2008. However, the provinces may continue to make these data available through their own annual vital statistics reports. Divorces are compiled by the Central Registry of Divorce Proceedings (CRDP) at the Department of Justice Canada. Regarding therapeutic abortions, Statistics Canada stopped collecting these data in 1995. This information is now collected and published by the Canadian Institute for Health Information (CIHI).

3. Specifically, the table of contents of the 1921 *Vital Statistics of Canada* lists the following items: births, infant mortality, general mortality, mortality by causes of death, and marriages. Divorces were not included in the publications until 1944, and it was not until 1969, after the passage of the Divorce Act, that statistics on divorce for Canada and the provinces and territories began to appear regularly in vital statistics publications (though as indicated in the preceding footnote, as of 2008, marriages and divorces are no longer included in Statistics Canada annual vital statistics reports).

3

Population: Past, Present, and Futures

Introduction

This chapter is divided into two parts. The first part begins with an examination of the world population situation in 2012, and then looks at the historical growth of the human population from ancient times to the present before turning to future projections for both industrialized and developing countries. The second part provides an overview of the demographic history of Canada and some of the more important social demographic transformations that have taken place in this country over the past 150 years or so.

Population History

World Population Today

Midway in 2014, the population of the world stood at 7.238 billion people, up to this point, the largest ever recorded in the history of humanity. It can be expected that this figure will increase substantially over the course of the 21st century. The difference between the crude birth and death rates—20 and 8 per 1000 population, respectively—produces an annual rate of natural increase of 1.2 per cent (Population Reference Bureau, 2014). If this rate of growth were to remain constant, the world's population would grow by approximately 87 million persons annually and

double in roughly 58 years. However, population growth is not uniform throughout the regions. As Table 3.1 shows, the more developed countries have an overall rate of natural increase of only 0.1 per cent, while the rest of the world is growing substantially faster, with rates somewhere between 1.4 and 2.6 per cent. Growth rates in some industrialized nations (e.g., Germany, Italy, and Japan) and a number of populations in Eastern Europe (e.g., Hungary, Bulgaria, and Romania) have fallen below zero in recent years; by contrast, countries such as Niger, Nigeria, Ethiopia, Congo, and Guatemala, among others, are growing at rates well above 2 per cent (Population Reference Bureau, 1995, 2001, 2006, 2012, 2014).

Together, the *less developed countries* today account for roughly 82 per cent of the world's total population; if China is excluded, this proportion falls to 63 per cent. The vast majority of the earth's people endure a standard of living far below that enjoyed in the developed countries. Indeed, the average income in the *more developed countries* is almost six times greater than that in the less developed world. Compounding this disparity is the high population density in the less developed world. This discrepancy is even greater for the least developed countries whose average income per capita is 2010 was only $1 444 in comparison to the $33 460 of the more developed countries.

Table 3.1 also shows regional patterns of population size, variability in growth

TABLE 3.1   Demographic data for the world and more developed and less developed regions, 2012

Area	Population mid-2012 (millions)	% of world total Population	Births per 1 000 population	Deaths per 1 000 population	Rate of natural increase	Population doubling time (years)	GNI PPP per capita 2010 (US$)	Population per square area kilometre
World	7 058	100.0	20	8	1.2	58	10 760	52
MDCs[1]	1 243	17.6	11	10	0.1	700	33 460	27
LDCs[2]	5 814	82.4	22	8	1.4	50	5 900	70
LDCs (excl. China)	4 464	63.2	25	8	1.7	41	5 380	61
Least Developed	876	12.4	35	10	2.4	29	1 444	43
Africa	1 072	15.2	36	11	2.5	28	2 630	35
Sub-Saharan	902	12.8	38	12	2.6	27	1 970	38
Northern	213	3.0	26	6	2.0	35	5 760	25
Western	324	4.6	40	13	2.7	26	1 810	53
Eastern	342	4.8	38	11	2.7	26	1 150	54
Middle	134	1.9	43	15	2.8	25	1 890	20
Southern	59	0.8	22	12	1.0	70	9 890	22
North America	349	4.9	13	8	0.5	140	46 400	16
Latin America/Carib.	599	8.5	19	6	1.3	54	10 760	29
Central	160	2.3	21	5	1.6	54	12 050	65
Caribbean	42	0.6	18	8	1.1	64	—[3]	179
South	397	5.8	18	6	1.2	58	10 930	22
Asia	4 260	60.4	18	7	1.1	64	6 860	134
Asia (excl. China)	2 910	41.2	21	7	1.4	50	6 500	130
Western	244	3.5	24	5	1.9	37	12 620	50
South central	1 823	25.8	23	7	1.6	54	3 560	169
Southeast	608	8.6	19	7	1.2	58	5 140	135
East	1 585	22.5	12	7	0.4	175	10 430	135
Europe	740	10.5	11	11	0.0	—[4]	27 080	32
European Union	502	7.1	10	10	0.1	700	31 730	116
Northern	101	1.4	13	9	0.3	233	36 290	56
Western	190	2.7	10	9	0.1	700	37 940	172

Area	Population mid-2012 (millions)	% of world total Population	Births per 1000 population	Deaths per 1000 population	Rate of natural increase	Population doubling time (years)	GNI PPP per capita 2010 (US$)	Population per square Area kilometre
Eastern	295	4.2	11	13	-0.2	-350[4]	16 590	16
Southern	154	2.2	10	9	0.0	—[4]	27 760	117
Oceania	37	0.5	18	7	1.1	64	26 560	4

Note: GNI PPP per capita 2010 (US$) is gross national income in purchasing power parity (PPP) divided by mid-year population. This measure makes it possible to compare the quantities of goods and services that the average person in each country could afford to buy, based on that country's GNP.

[1] more developed countries (all of Europe and North America plus Australia, Japan, and New Zealand).

[2] less developed countries (all other regions and countries).

[3] data not available.

[4] the doubling time is undefined given a 0 rate of natural increase.

Source: Population Reference Bureau (2012).

rates, birth and death rates, income, and population density. The highest birth rates in the world are found in Africa—especially the sub-Saharan region, where the crude birth rate of 38 per 1000 population is substantially higher than in western and south central Asia, the regions with the next highest birth rates (24 and 23 per 1000, respectively). Europe, North America, and east Asia have the lowest birth rates, ranging between 10 and 13 per 1000. Crude death rates show little variation across regions but are highest in Africa, reflecting to a significant extent the devastating impact of HIV/AIDS in recent decades. The combination of rapid population growth, relatively low income, and high population density suggests that socioeconomic conditions for the average citizen in the poorer countries of the world may not improve appreciably as compared to other parts of the world with more favourable demographic and economic conditions.

The regional gaps in birth and death rates determine regional differences in natural increase. One way to determine how fast a population is growing is to compute its *doubling time*—the number of years it would take for the population to double if its current rate of growth were to remain unchanged. With few exceptions, African countries have natural growth rates of 2 per cent or above. In such cases, the doubling time would be relatively short. (See the Notes for Further Study, page 97 for a detailed discussion of doubling time.) With a growth rate of 2.8 per cent in 2012, middle Africa would experience a doubling time of only 24 years. This is currently the highest rate of natural increase in any of the world's major regions.

In sharp contrast, European natural growth rates are very low. In fact, a number of European countries have been experiencing negative rates of increase (e.g., Czech Republic, Hungary, Serbia, Croatia) on the order of –0.1 to –0.5 per cent; if the negative growth rates were to remain constant, in the absence of migration those populations would eventually become extinct. On the other hand, with a rate of natural increase of zero, Europe as a whole is in a steady-state-type situation—i.e., not growing nor declining. In this case, immigration plays a pivotal role in determining future population growth. Natural increase in the regions of North America and east Asia, at around 0.5 or 0.4 per cent, are also well below the world average of 1.2 per cent. The situation in Asia depends on whether China is included in the computations: 1.4 per cent with China, 1.1 per cent without. Within Asia, the western sub-region is the fastest-growing area, at 1.9 per cent. Oceania (which includes Australia and New Zealand) had a growth rate of 1.1 per cent in 2012.

From Gradual to Explosive Growth

To understand the current and possible future state of the world's population, it is necessary to look at the broader context of human history. The farther back we go, however, the less certain our estimates are; before about 1750 we are essentially reduced to making educated guesses (Coale, 1974; Trewartha, 1969). Long-term future projections suffer from uncertainty as well. The reasonableness of our estimates regarding the distant past depends on the quality of the assumptions we introduce into our calculations regarding mortality and fertility. The same is true of future projections:

informed assumptions can produce reasonable projections, especially over the short term (less than 25 years into the future), but the picture becomes increasingly uncertain over longer periods.

Ansley Coale (1974) divides population history into two broad segments: the first, from the beginning of humanity to around 1750 CE, was a very long era of slow population growth; the second—extremely brief in historical terms, from *c.* 1750 to the present—is one of explosive increases. The estimated average annual growth rate between 8000 BCE and 1 CE was only 0.036 per cent per year. Between 1 CE and 1750, the average rate rose to 0.056 per cent; from 1750 to 1800, it increased to 0.44 per cent. By the 1950s,

growth rates had reached approximately 1.5 per cent per year. And during the 1960s and early 1970s, they soared to their historic maximum of just over 2 per cent (Coale, 1974). Figure 3.1 offers a long-view perspective on human population from prehistory to the present. As it shows, the growth since roughly 1750 CE has been exponential.

Although the graph suggests a smooth progression over the millions of years leading up to 1750, in fact population change has been irregular through most of human history. Until the advent of the *Agricultural Revolution*, also known as the *Neolithic Revolution* (between the tenth and fifth centuries BCE), and throughout the medieval and modern periods, cycles of population

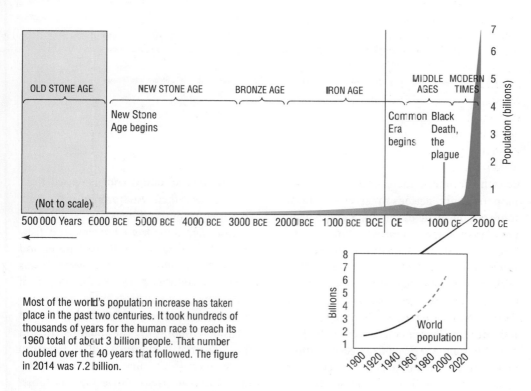

Most of the world's population increase has taken place in the past two centuries. It took hundreds of thousands of years for the human race to reach its 1960 total of about 3 billion people. That number doubled over the 40 years that followed. The figure in 2014 was 7.2 billion.

FIGURE 3.1   **Population of the world through history**

World population growth through broad historical periods and projections

IIIIIIIIIIIIIIIIIIIIIIIIIIIIIIIIIIIIIIIIIIIIIIIIIIIIIIIIIIIIIIIIIIIIIIIIIIIIIIIIIIIIIIIIIIIIIIIIIIIIIIIIIIIIIIIIIII

	Estimated population	Estimated average annual growth rate (%)	Years to add 1 billion
1 million–8000 BCE	8 million	0.010[1]	
8000 BCE–1 CE	300 million	0.036[1]	
1 CE–1750	800 million	0.056[1]	
1804	1 billion	0.400[1]	all of human history
1927	2 billion	0.540[1]	123
1950	2.5 billion	0.800[1]	—
1960	3 billion	1.7–2.0[2]	33
1974	4 billion	2.0–1.8[2]	14
1987	5 billion	1.8–1.6[2]	13
1999	6 billion	1.6–1.4[2]	12
2011	7 billion	1.4-1.2[2]	12
2025 (projected)[3]	8 billion	0.88[3]	14
2043 (projected)[3]	9 billion	0.51[3]	18

[1] Estimated average rate of growth at the end of the period.
[2] Range of growth rates between specified periods.
[3] Population projections for 2025 and 2043 are estimated based on the 2012 revision of the UN's *World Population Prospects*, medium variant (United Nations Department of Economic and Social Affairs, Population Division, 2013a).

Sources: Figure adapted from Trewartha (1969): 29. Table based on Coale (1974); Trewartha (1969); Bongaarts and Bulatao (2000); Population Reference Bureau (various years).

growth, decline, and recovery were common, reflecting periods of "crisis" mortality followed by birth deficits and subsequent population surges (Biraben, 2006; Cipolla, 1962; Coale, 1974; Diamond, 1999; Herlihy, 1997; Livi-Bacci, 2012; Wrigley, 1969; Wrigley and Schofield, 1981).

The evidence also suggests that the human population has gone through periods of abrupt increases (see Figure 3.2). Jean Noel Biraben (1979, 2003a, 2003b, 2006) counts three great population surges, each associated with a major technological revolution that made humans less vulnerable to the vagaries of nature and increased their control over their environment. The first of these revolutions was the acquisition of clothing, along with hunting and fishing tools, in the Upper Paleolithic period (*c.* 30 000–10 000 BCE). The second was sedentarization and the development of agriculture, animal husbandry, and maritime navigation in the Neolithic period (*c.* 8 000–5 000 BCE). The most recent was the Industrial Revolution, which began in the eighteenth century and is now coming to its end as we move into the post-industrial era.

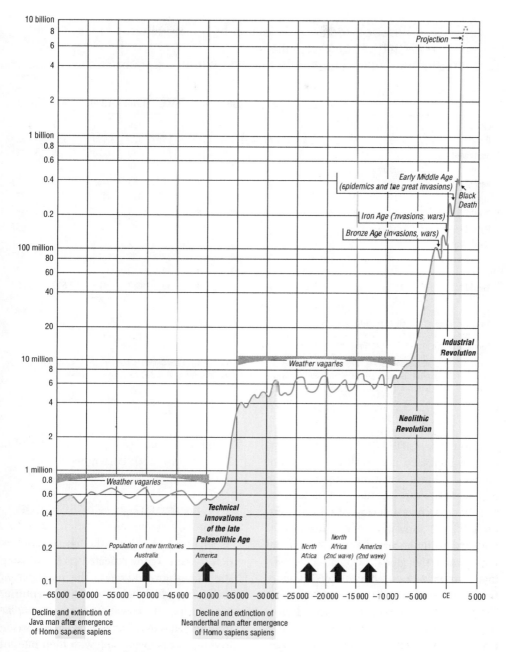

FIGURE 3.2   Population growth over 65 000 years

Source: Biraben, Jean Noel. 2003a. 'The Rising Numbers of Humankind', Population and Societies 394 (October): p. 3. Copyright Institut national d'études démographiques. Reprinted with permission

TABLE 3.2   World population estimates, by region, selected dates, 400 BCE–2000 CE (millions)

Region	400 BCE	0	500 CE	1000	1300	1400	1500	1700	1800	1900	2000
China[1]	19	70	32	56	83	70	84	150	330	415	1 273
India[2]	30	46	33	40	100	74	95	175	190	290	1 320
Southwest Asia	42	47	45	33	21	19	23	30	28	38	259
Japan	0.1	0.3	2	7	7	8	8	28	30	44	126
Rest of Asia	3	5	8	19	29	29	33	53	68	115	653
Europe[3]	32	43	41	43	86	65	84	125	195	422	782
North Africa	10	13	12	10	9	8	8	9	9	23	143
Rest of Africa	7	12	20	30	60	60	78	97	92	95	657
North America	1	2	2	2	3	3	3	2	5	90	307
Latin America[4]	7	10	13	16	29	36	39	10	19	75	512
Oceania	1	1	1	1	2	2	3	3	2	6	30
World total	**152**	**250**	**205**	**257**	**429**	**374**	**458**	**682**	**968**	**1 613**	**6 062**

[1] China includes the Korean Peninsula.
[2] India includes Pakistan, Bangladesh, and Sri Lanka.
[3] Europe includes the former Soviet Union.
[4] Latin America includes the Caribbean.

Source: Biraben, "World Population Growth," in *Encyclopedia of Population*, 2nd edn., by Paul George Demeny and Geoffrey McNicoll (eds.), 2003. Republished with permission of Cengage Learning from Encyclopedia of Population, 2/e by Paul George Demeny and Geoffrey McNicoll (Eds), 2003. Permission conveyed through Copyright Clearance Center, Inc.

From 400 BCE to 1 CE, population seems to have increased across all the regions of the world. Since that time, however, some regions have experienced cycles of depopulation and recovery during certain periods. As Table 3.2 shows, a notable instance of crisis mortality occurred between 1300 and 1400, when the global population is estimated to have been reduced by 65 million, from roughly 429 million in 1300 to about 364 million a century later. The decline seems to have been especially marked in China, India, and Europe. The plague, which spread throughout continental Europe between 1347 and 1351 (and re-appeared intermittently over the next three centuries), killed between one-quarter and one-third of the European population (between 20 and 35 million people) (Alchon, 2003: 21; Cohn, 2003; Herlihy, 1997; Porter, 1997: 123).

The Demographic Transition

As we noted previously, the human population has undergone repeated cycles of rising and falling growth rates. The most recent such cycle, which began about two centuries ago, is generally known as the *demographic transition*. It is usually described as occurring in three stages, beginning with high rates of both births and deaths, moving through a transitional phase of high birth and declining death rates, and concluding with low rates of both fertility and mortality. (Some authors divide the second stage into two periods; for

THE NEOLITHIC DEMOGRAPHIC TRANSITION

The Neolithic Revolution—the transition from foraging to farming—represents one of the most significant fundamental structural processes of human history. This transition is responsible for a significant growth spurt of human numbers referred to as the Neolithic demographic transition. As noted by Jean-Pierre Bocquet-Appel (2011), after the members of the genus *Homo* had been living as foragers for at least 2.4 million years, agriculture began to emerge in seven or eight regions across the world, almost simultaneously at the beginning of the Holocene: in the Levant (Mesopotamia), in North and South China, in New Guinea and Ethiopia, and in eastern North America, Mesoamerica, and South America—all during the chronological window from 11500 to 3500 years ago. Bocquet-Appel's (2011) research (see also Bocquet-Appel and Bar-Yosef, 2008), based on world archaeological sequences, shows that the emergence of agriculture coincides with a considerable increase in artefact remains, which was long interpreted as indicating a spurt in demographic growth. A key signal of this is an abrupt increase in the proportion of juvenile skeletons found across excavated cemeteries in the northern hemisphere. The population explosion of the Neolithic demographic transition, detectable in cemeteries, was unprecedented in the history of *Homo sapiens*. The world's population on the eve of the emergence of agriculture is estimated to have been around 6 million individuals as against 7 billion today, multiplying by 1200 in just 11000 years.

instance, Trewartha [1969] identifies "early expanding" and "late expanding" phases within stage two; see Figure 3.3. It was only about two centuries ago that developments in public health, sanitation, and nutrition began to achieve significant increases in human life expectancy. Until that time, mortality rates were very high. The same was true of fertility rates in the days before the development of modern contraceptive techniques. Since both rates were high, however, rates of natural increase remained very low until fairly recently in human history.

In the pre-transition decades around 1700, total fertility rates in Europe were between 4 and 6.5; life expectancy at birth ranged from 20 to 35; and population growth remained near zero (Coale, 1974, 1986: 23). Today, long after the completion of the transition, fertility rates in Western Europe are quite low by historical standards, averaging about 1.6 births per woman; life expectancy at birth has surpassed 80 years; and rates of population growth are once again close to zero. The change from pre- to post-transitional status is clear in the second part of Figure 3.4, which shows how fertility and life expectancy in European societies have changed since the pre-modern period.

During the second stage of the demographic transition, death rates typically decline first, while fertility rates remain high

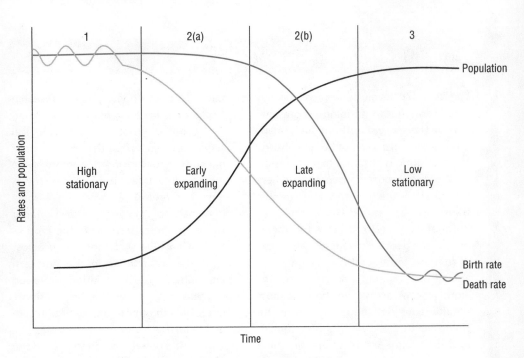

FIGURE 3.3 **The classic demographic transition model**

Stage	Fertility	Mortality	Population growth	Economy
1. Pre-industrial	High, fluctuating	High, fluctuating (low life expectancy)	Static to very low	Primitive or agrarian
2. Early industrial	High	Falling	High, explosive	Mixed
3. Modern urban industrial	Controlled: low to moderate to sub-replacement levels	Low (high life expectancy)	Low to moderate to negative	Urban industrial to post-industrial

Source: Adapted from Trewartha (1969): 45, 47.

for some time. Various hypotheses have been proposed for the early mortality declines in Western Europe, from changing climatic conditions that helped reduce the lethality of some infectious microbes, to improvements in general hygiene and the introduction of the vaccine against smallpox, to improved standards of living and nutrition (Galloway, 1986; McKeown, 1976; McKeown, Brown, and Record, 1972; Mercer, 1990; Omran, 1971; Razzel, 1974; Schofield, Reher, and Bideau, 1991). This subject is discussed in greater

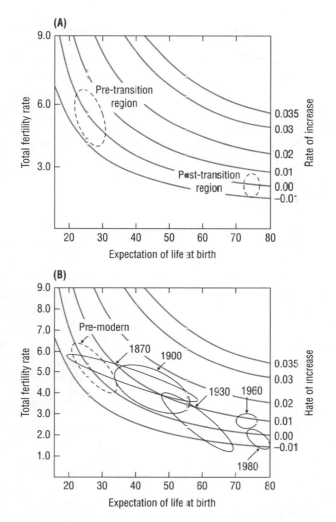

FIGURE 3.4 **Expected trajectory of fertility, mortality, and natural increase for societies moving from pre- to post-demographic transition regimes (A), and actual trajectory of European populations across the stages of the demographic transition (B)**

Note: The ellipses represent groups of countries.

Source: Adapted from Coale (1986): 23, 27.

detail in Chapter 7. In Europe, this period of imbalance in the two vital rates extended from the mid-1700s through the early 1900s. According to Thomas McKeown (1976), the unprecedented rates of natural increase caused by this demographic imbalance in

Europe (and in other regions) were responsible for the modern rise of population. Gradually, as European societies attained greater levels of modernization and socioeconomic development, birth rates began to fall, and by 1930, both mortality and fertility in most Western nations were the lowest they had ever been. As a consequence, the rate of natural increase once again fell. This time, the decline in population growth rates was attributable to humans' increasing control over nature: industrialization, urbanization, economic growth, modern science and medicine, and widespread use of contraception to regulate family size—all of which helped to bring down the death rate to historically low levels.

Extensive research into the fertility component of the transition across Europe led Coale (1973, 1986) to conclude that the timing and the societal preconditions for long-term fertility decline varied widely. He therefore argued that an all-encompassing theory was not possible. However, his observations suggested three general preconditions for fertility decline (Coale, 1973):

1. Fertility must be within the "calculus of conscious choice." Potential parents must consider it acceptable to balance advantages and disadvantages before deciding to have another child—unlike, for example, most present-day Hutterites or Amish, who do not practise birth control and would consider any such calculation immoral.
2. Social and economic circumstances must be such that individual couples will perceive reduced fertility as advantageous in some way.
3. Effective techniques of fertility reduction must be available. Techniques that will in fact prevent conception or birth must be known, and there must be sufficient communication between spouses to use those techniques successfully.

Unless all three of these preconditions are present, fertility is likely to remain high or decline slowly. This is the case in some contemporary developing countries, where family planning may not be readily available or accessible by many. In others, where family planning is available, traditional norms may work against the widespread adoption of birth control. Moreover, in highly insecure socioeconomic environments, children represent a form of security for parents, and large families are therefore highly desirable.

There has been some debate over whether the demographic transition model qualifies as a "theory" (Kirk, 1996). Strictly speaking, a theory should both explain and predict phenomena in the real world. But while the demographic transition account explains in a general sense the historical shifts in birth and death rates in the context of socioeconomic modernization, it has had some difficulty specifying what conditions must prevail in a society, and at what intensity, in order to provoke sustained mortality and fertility declines. Prediction is another area of admitted weakness. In the case of the Western countries, for example, the model could not have predicted the baby boom that followed World War II. These weaknesses notwithstanding, the demographic transition still offers a solid account of macro-level change across societies, and it should be regarded as one of the mainstays in demographic theorizing and research. See, for example, Cleland and Wilson (1987); Coale (1969, 1973); Coale and Watkins (1986); Davis (1945); Landry (1934, 1945); Notestein (1945, 1953); Thompson (1929, 1944).

The Demographic Transition in the Industrialized Countries

Although the classical formulation of the demographic transition theory suggests that all societies will experience this transition in much the same way, the timing and intensity of mortality and fertility declines have in fact varied widely. Figure 3.5 charts the demographic transitions of England and Wales, France, Sweden, Finland, and Japan. The graphs depicting England and Wales and Sweden show the classic pattern, with mortality beginning its decline first (Chesnais, 1992) and the birth rate rising before it starts to fall. A pre-decline rise in fertility has characterized virtually every case of demographic transition, Western or otherwise (Dyson and Murphy, 1985). The mechanisms responsible for this rise are changes associated with modernization. First, as the living standard improves, so does the health of the population, causing natural fertility levels to rise; then fertility rates increase accordingly until the practice of contraception becomes widespread (Romaniuk, 1980). As the graph for France shows, however, the increase in fertility is not always large. Another respect in which the French experience differed from the British was that French birth and death rates declined at a similar pace, with the result that the rate of natural increase did not rise substantially.

Both Sweden and Finland experienced several intense temporary rises in mortality during their pre-transitional stages, reflecting periods of famine, epidemic disease, and wars. In fact, all five of the graphs in Figure 3.5 clearly show the patterns associated with major crises such as wars and epidemics: a rise in mortality and a decline in fertility, followed by a fertility surge and a

return to low mortality soon after the cessation of conflict. Finally, Japan's demographic transition closely resembles the classic Western European type, with the important exception that it took place over a much shorter period of time. The same is true of some contemporary developing countries, where first mortality and then fertility have declined rapidly.

Mechanisms of Transition: Western and Japanese Experiences

Different societies have followed different combinations of social, cultural, economic, and demographic paths towards completion of their demographic transitions (Caldwell, 1976, 2001; Caldwell and Caldwell, 1997; Casterline, 2001; Cleland, 2001; Matras, 1965). Focusing mostly on the fertility side of the equation, and drawing on examples from both Europe and Japan, Kingsley Davis (1963) has proposed a *multiphasic response theory*. This theory assumes that widespread fertility declines in a society occur in a context of rising socioeconomic opportunities, coupled with sustained high rates of natural increase (as during stage two of the European demographic transition) due to declining death rates, especially in infancy and childhood. Under such conditions, individual members of the population will eventually recognize that a large family is an impediment to upward mobility, but how they respond will depend on the types of responses available, some of which are dependent on the culture. In Ireland, for example, population pressure during the second stage of demographic transition meant that family land had to be subdivided into smaller and smaller plots for the increasing number of adult children. Meanwhile, as parents lived longer, the children had to wait longer to inherit family property. The Irish

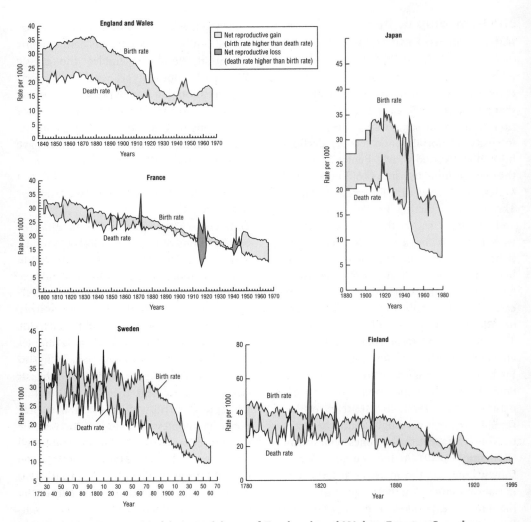

FIGURE 3.5 **Demographic transitions of England and Wales, France, Sweden, Finland, and Japan**

Sources: For Sweden: Bogue (1969): 59; reprinted by permission of the author. For England/Wales and France: Kosinski (1970): 26, 28 (Figures 9 and 10); copyright © Pearson Education Limited. For Finland: Kannisto, Nieminen, and Turpeinen (1999): 22 (Figure 1); reprinted by permission of the authors. For Japan: Chesnais (1992): 246 (Figure 8.4); reprinted by permission of Oxford University Press.

responded in various ways to these conditions: mass migration from the rural areas to the cities, out-migration to the Americas, delayed marriage, and increased celibacy. These responses had the effect of relieving population pressure and also reducing fertility. Japan experienced similar conditions and responses; and generally, populations will adopt the responses that are least inconvenient and least threatening to their cultures. And so, although abortion would not have been an "available" response to the

Catholic Irish, it was widely "available" and adopted by the Japanese as a way of controlling family size (Davis, 1963).

Demographic Transition of Developing Countries

Michael Teitelbaum (1975) has pointed out a number of important differences in the demographic histories of the West and the developing countries:

1. *The pace and sources of mortality decline.* In Europe, mortality declined gradually, whereas in developing nations the pace of decline has been quite rapid. Furthermore, whereas the technologies and public health measures responsible for the improvements in the West were largely endogenous (developed within the society), in the developing countries they have been mainly exogenous (imported from outside—e.g., public health and family planning programs).
2. *Fertility levels before the decline.* In contemporary developing nations, fertility rates are generally higher to begin with than they were at the corresponding point in Western Europe.
3. *Rate of population growth.* European nations undergoing the demographic transition rarely experienced doubling times of less than 50 years. In contrast, doubling times in some developing nations can be as low as 30 years. At no point in their transitions did European nations experience the growth rates found in many contemporary developing countries, which can reach 3 per cent or more.
4. *Momentum for further growth.* As a result of the relatively high fertility and youthful age structures in developing

nations, the potential for further significant population growth exceeds that of the industrialized nations by a wide margin.

5. *International migration as an outlet to relieve population pressure.* Western Europe was able to export tens of millions of its citizens to colonies in the Americas, Oceania, and elsewhere. Such outlets are extremely limited for the contemporary developing countries.

These observations are clearly reflected in Figure 3.6, which highlights the contrasting situations of Sweden (representative of the Western classical model) and Mexico (representative of many contemporary developing countries). Notice the considerably higher levels of birth and death rates for Mexico in the early stage of its transition as compared to Sweden between 1750 and 1800. The vital rates in Mexico in 1900—at the time of stage one—were between 35 and 45 per 1000 population. Also clear in this graph is how much more precipitous the crop in Mexico's death rate was compared to Sweden's. A third point to note is the relatively short time span in which Mexico moved from the first to the later part of the second stage of the demographic transition. In Sweden, it took roughly 120 years—from about 1810 to 1930—to move from stage one to late stage two. In Mexico, the same developments have taken only about 75 years. Perhaps even more striking is the rapid pace of Mexico's mortality decline; the crude death rate dropped from over 40 per 1000 population in 1925 to below 20 per 1000 in 1950; and by 2000 it had declined to about 5 per 1000—below that of Sweden's rate. Finally, the difference in the rate of natural increase between Sweden and Mexico at similar stages of demographic evolution

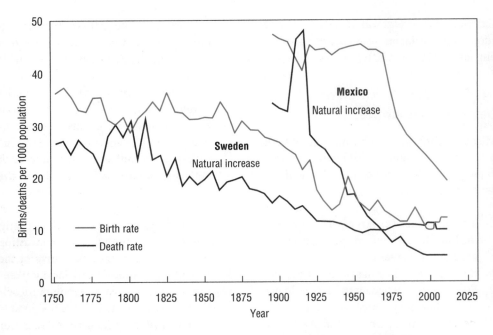

FIGURE 3.6   Demographic transition in Sweden and Mexico, 1750–2012

Sources: Adapted from 'World Population Beyond Six Billion', by Alene Gelbard and Carl Haub, p. 6, figure 2. In Population Bulletin 54, 1. © 1999 Popoulation Reference Bureau. Reprinted with permission.

is significant: historically, Mexico's natural growth rate has been notably higher; this is symptomatic of the very different demographic experiences of Western and non-Western countries (see also Figures 3.7 and 3.8 on pages 78 and 79).

Transitional and Delayed Transition Societies

Developing countries can be distinguished by the progress they have made towards completion of the demographic transition. In broad terms, there are two sets of developing countries: those that have recently completed or are approaching the end of the demographic transition (*transitional populations*), and those where this process has only recently begun (*delayed transition populations*). Since in most cases mortality

has been declining since the 1950s or earlier, the crucial factor determining how far a society has progressed into its demographic transition would appear to be the pace of fertility decline. Among the places that began their fertility transitions relatively early, in the 1960s and 1970s, are Singapore, Taiwan, Thailand, Hong Kong, Malaysia, South Korea, Mexico, and many countries in Latin America and the Caribbean (the exceptions are Bolivia, Nicaragua, Honduras, and Haiti, which are in the delayed transition group). Between the 1950s and the late 1970s, fertility rates in Singapore, Taiwan, China, Hong Kong, and South Korea had dropped by between 50 and 70 per cent (Coale, 1983). The 1990s saw further significant fertility and also mortality declines in these populations. These countries now have birth and death rates that approximate those of the highly industrialized countries, and have in essence completed the demographic transition (McNicoll, 2006).

China's birth rate was about 46 per 1000 in 1951. By 1971, it had declined by 27 per cent to 33 per 1000; and by 2001 it had fallen to 21.5—a drop of 35 per cent since 1971. In 2012, China's birth rate was 13.4. A large part of the decline in China's birth rate since the early 1980s can be attributed to the vigorous family planning regime, the one-child policy, put in place in 1978. But the initiation of the fertility decline in China started earlier, and may be attributable to other factors, notably rapid urbanization, increased education, and industrialization (Cai, 2010; Coale, 1983; Lavely and Freedman, 1990). The death rate has fallen from 22.2 per 1000 in 1951 to about 6 per 1000 in 2012, the sharpest drop occurring between 1971 and 1981. Consistent with these changes, China's rates of natural increase have dropped considerably, from over 2 per cent in 1951 to just 0.63 per cent in 2012. The disastrous Great Leap Forward experiment of the late 1950s initiated by Chairman Mao resulted in temporary increases in the death rate and declines in fertility between 1951 and 1961.

India too has joined the transitional countries. Its birth and death rates have been declining steadily over time. In 1951, India recorded a birth rate of 44 per 1000 and a crude death rate of 28.1 per 1000. By 1981, these rates had declined to 34.7 and 12.1, respectively. This fall in the birth rate represents a 21 per cent reduction; for mortality, the improvement over this same period has been nearly 57 per cent. In 2012, India's birth and death rates had dropped to 20.4 and 7.9 respectively.

Egypt and other parts of northern Africa (e.g., Morocco) and some areas of the Middle East (e.g., Turkey) have also experienced significant mortality and fertility declines since the 1980s. However, irrespective of this general phenomenon, rates of natural increase in these countries may not necessarily fall to uniformly low levels because—as is typically the case in transitional populations—death rates fall faster than do birth rates, which accounts for rapid population growth as part of the transition.

An important generalization based on the experience of many developing countries is that those that have made significant headway in the demographic transition have had vigorous family planning programs in place for some time (Bongaarts, Mauldin, and Philips, 1990; Bongaarts and Sinding, 2009; Potts, 2006; Robey, Rutestein, and Morris, 1993). Another important factor is female education. Birth rates are lower in countries where female literacy is relatively high, because education serves to delay age at marriage and also allows women greater freedom to access effective contraceptives and greater control over reproductive decisions (Cleland and Hobcraft, 1985; Robey, Rutestein, and Morris, 1993; Westoff, 1990).

As Figures 3.7 and 3.8 show, the latecomers to the demographic transition—the *delayed transition populations*—typically have high rates of natural increase (2 per cent or more). Most of them are located in sub-Saharan Africa. Although birth rates in this region have declined over the past two decades, the rates of natural increase remain well above the world average, which in 2012 was 1.2 per cent. Meanwhile, many of these same countries have experienced stalls in their fertility transitions and also setbacks in their mortality declines; some have seen rising death rates as a result of the HIV/AIDS epidemic (Bongaarts, 2008). South central Asia is another region that includes a number of delayed transition countries with high rates of natural population growth (e.g., Afghanistan, Iraq, the State of Palestine, and Pakistan). A few countries in Central and South America (e.g., Haiti, Belize, Guatemala, Honduras, Bolivia, and French Guiana) also show high rates of natural increase, thus indicative of being in a state of delayed demographic transition.

What Accounts for Delayed Development?

One of the most fundamental puzzles in economics was posed by Adam Smith: "What determines some nations to be wealthy and others poor?" (1776 [1904]). A long list of economic historians, including Karl Marx and Max Weber, and more recently Fernand Braudel and Immanuel Wallerstein, among others, have wrestled

with the same question. To be sure, economic success is closely connected to the ability to industrialize and innovate technologically (Kuznets, 1955; Easterlin, 1999). In these respects, the West has been quite successful. According to David Landes (1999) in his *The Wealth and Poverty of Nations*, Western society developed institutional structures conducive to innovation and technological advancement, supported by a culture of openness towards discovery, freedom (i.e., democracy), and enterprise, all of which set the stage for economic dominance (see also Acemoglu and Robinson, 2013; Ferguson, 2011; Galor, 2011; McNeill, 1963; Morris, 2010, 2013; Williamson, 2006).

Jeffrey Sachs, Andrew Mellinger, and John Gallup (2001) attribute international differences in wealth to complex interrelationships among geography and climate. For instance, nations in tropical zones are vulnerable to higher rates of infectious diseases such as malaria. Consequently, these nations

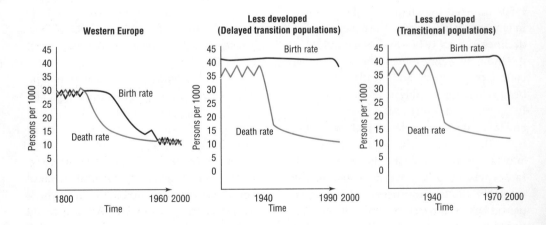

FIGURE 3.7   Schematic representation of demographic transition: Western, delayed, and transitional models

Source: Adapted from Trewartha (1969): 45, 47.

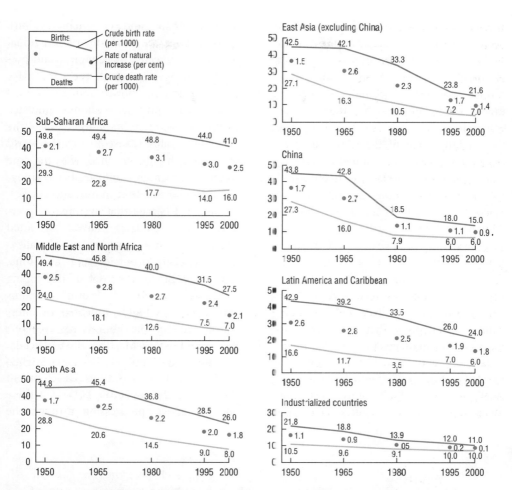

FIGURE 3.8   Rates of birth, death, and natural increase by region, 1950, 1965, 1980, 1995, and 2000

Note: In each case, the upper line shows the crude birth rate per 1000 and the lower line the crude death rate per 1000, the numbers in the middle of each graph show the percentage rate of natural increase.

Sources: Donaldson (1991): 12 (Figure 1.1); Population Reference Bureau World Population Data Sheets (1995, 2000).

experience more sickness and lower levels of economic productivity than countries in temperate zones. Moreover, according to these authors, the very poorest regions in the world are typically burdened by not only a tropical or desert environment but also lack easy access to maritime transport routes, which affects their ability to export goods.

Important as they are, culture and geography cannot fully explain the Western world's economic advantage in relation to the developing countries. An important part of Western success is due to its history of imperialistic exploitation and colonization of underdeveloped regions from 1500 onward after the discovery of the New

World. Colonialism enabled the European powers to gain economically and to enjoy significant advantage in world affairs. Decolonization over the past half-century has allowed former colonies to become independent countries, but the effects of colonialism on these countries have been far reaching. One of the most important consequences of their colonial experiences has been their relative lateness to industrialize and develop economically (Davis, 2000; Harvey, 1975; Held et al., 1999; Hoogvelt, 2001; Myrdal, 1957; Skartein, 1997).

Marxist-oriented writers such as Andre Gunder Frank (1969, 1984, 1991) link the impoverishment of some countries to the ongoing unequal exchange relations between the industrialized and developing countries, relations that inevitably promote the underdevelopment of the less advantaged countries. Similarly, following the early studies of Fernard Braudel (1966, 1979), Immanuel Wallerstein (1974, 1980) looks at the world as consisting of core,

semi-peripheral, and peripheral regions. These regions are made up of individual countries connected by economic and political exchanges in which the core states exercise *hegemonic* power (indirect domination through political/economic influence and/or threat of military force) over the dependent states. Consequently, the world economy is highly stratified, with the core countries (i.e., highly industrialized) enjoying disproportionate economic success.

While it is true that over recent years developing countries have benefitted significantly from economic globalization, especially countries such as China, India, and Brazil, a subset of developing countries—the "Third World"—remains very poor and highly indebted to international lending institutions (Barro, 1997; Barro and Sala-i-Martin, 2004; Dicken, 2011; Firebaugh, 2003; Fischer, 2003; Stiglitz, 2002, 2003; United Nations Development Programme, 2003a, 2003b, 2013). For these poor countries, progression through the

The damage done by European colonialism around the world is undeniable. Nevertheless, colonialism does not explain all the problems that developing countries face (Ferguson, 2011). For instance, a UN-sponsored report on human development in the Arab world (United Nations Development Programme, 2002), drafted by a group of Middle Eastern intellectuals, acknowledges that many of the socioeconomic problems facing the Arab world have been largely self-created. Among the factors cited by the report are the subjugation of women; political autocracy that ensures censorship, stifles creativity, and promotes corruption; limited use of the Internet; high rates of emigration among talented scientists; high population growth; and a general "freedom deficit" for a large segment of the region's population.

In a significant number of developing countries, social and economic development is constrained by corrupt regimes and weak adherence to the rule of law (Bhagwati, 2000, 2002; Buhaug, 2010; Burke et al., 2009; *The Economist*, 2011a, 2003a, 2003b; *Foreign Policy*, 2005; Lamarchand, 2009; Lindstrom and Berhanu, 1999; Weil, 2009).

demographic transition can potentially help facilitate economic progress and possibly break the *poverty trap*, wherein high rates of natural increase and poverty feedback on each other, resulting in a vicious cycle of suffering and deprivation (Bloom and Canning, 2001; Dyson, 2010; Easterly, 2002, 2006; Lee, 2003; Moyo, 2009; Sachs, 2005, 2007; Werlin, 2009).

Mechanisms of Demographic Transition: Western and Non-Western Cases

The forces that sparked the demographic transition in Western Europe were mainly *endogenous* to European society, the cumulative effects of innovations and structural changes that—by improving living conditions over a long period of time—served to gradually reduce mortality (i.e., increased food supply, better nutrition, urbanization and industrialization, improvements in hygiene, public health, and modern medicine). For developing countries, rapid mortality declines early in the demographic transition came for the most part in the absence of major economic development, a point articulated by Davis in 1956 and more recently by John Caldwell (1986). The statistical analyses of Samuel Preston (1975, 1980, 1986a) reinforce these observations. Widespread mortality declines in the developing countries between the 1930s and 1960s can be attributed to a variety of factors that are largely independent of economic development—the diffusion of medical technology and medicines to the developing countries, improved provision of public health services, better nutrition and vaccination programs, and to a lesser extent also aid and assistance from the industrialized countries (e.g., anti-malarial and immunization

programs). However, as shown by Preston (1986a), during the mid-1960s to 1979, mortality fell at a more sluggish pace in the developing countries; and this time variables related to economic development (such as improved national income), explained a good portion of the decline in death rates (see also Pritchett and Summers, 1996).

A multitude of social, cultural, and economic factors contributed to the massive downturn in Western Europe's fertility rates between the mid-1800s and the first three decades of the 1900s. Some scholars—*innovation theorists*—have emphasized the role played by new contraceptive technologies and new ideas emphasizing small families (Bulatao, 2001; Carlson, 1966; Cleland and Wilson, 1987; Caldwell, 1976; Lesthaeghe, 1983). Others—known as *adjustment theorists*—have suggested that new socioeconomic opportunities in a context of industrialization and urbanization made large families less desirable than they had been in the past (Becker, 1960; Davis, 1963; Friedlander, 1969).

According to innovation theorists, the idea of limiting family size was foreign to most people before the mid-1800s and spread only gradually, beginning with the upper classes and the urban population. Etienne van de Walle (1992: 490) has suggested that "the perception of a particular family size as a goal" was generally non-existent prior to the nineteenth century. The invention of modern birth control, then, can be seen as a product of growing demand for an effective way of achieving the desired family size. Philippe Ariès (1980) has argued that the emergence of the small-family ideal reflected the desire of parents in the nineteenth century to do all they could to ensure that their progeny would have the best possible life. Having fewer children made it possible to devote more time, care, and resources to each child.

Adjustment theorists, on the other hand, maintain that different methods of family limitation, most notably *coitus interruptus*, have been known throughout human history; what was lacking until the nineteenth century was the motivation for most couples to apply that knowledge. With socioeconomic modernization, however, couples began to see the advantages of curtailing their fertility through whatever means might be available, including the use of modern contraceptives. According to this theory, then, the fertility transition in Western Europe emanated not from a novel idea or technology (i.e., modern birth control), but from an adjustment process, whereby adults began to see tangible advantages in having fewer children.

As demonstrated by John Knodel (1977), it is entirely possible that both innovation- and adjustment-type processes contributed to the European fertility transition.

Explanations for the fertility transition in developing countries also point to a wide range of factors: cultural, social, economic, and demographic (Caldwell, 1976; Cleland and Wilson, 1987; Easterlin, 1983; Hirschman, 1994; Mason, 1997a). The central factors, however, appear to be the rapid spread of Western ideas and a change in the way parents and society think about children; the implementation of vigorous *family planning* programs backed by governments; declines in infant and childhood mortality; and improvements in education and literacy, especially among women. With socioeconomic modernization, the nuclear family takes priority over the extended family; couples move away from the larger family constellation and set up independent households (Caldwell, 1976). In the course of this nucleation process, the child in particular becomes the focus of attention in the family. Compulsory education further elevates children's status in the society, and the intergenerational flow of wealth (i.e., money, time, and resources) shifts so that children are no longer seen primarily in terms of their economic contributions to the family; rather, parents come to see them as persons in whom it is worth investing time and resources to promote their well-being and development. Eventually, as in the West, this change in the way children are perceived leads parents to desire fewer children. For Caldwell, these structural and ideational shifts in developing societies are necessary conditions for the fertility transition to begin.

With rising levels socioeconomic modernization, there follows a decline in infant and child mortality. As childhood survival rates improve, couples adjust their ideal family size to favour fewer children. And as traditional norms and values erode, couples will increasingly resort to modern contraceptives and family planning methods. Improvements in the status of women through education and increased access to economic independence can also contribute to rapid changes in fertility rates (Robey, Rutestein, and Morris, 1993). The transitional societies undergoing these types of changes tend to enjoy greater access to health and family planning programs, and have governments strongly committed to family planning (Berelson et al., 1990; Ross and Mauldin, 1996).

Demographic Transition and World Population Growth

A number of generalizations about population history can now be laid out. First, the prime cause of the *world population explosion* was the dramatic decline in death rates starting in the mid-eighteenth century, at a time when fertility rates remained high. Declining mortality coupled with persistently high fertility fuelled a "population explosion" that began around 1750 and intensified over the following century and a half. Second, now that the Western nations, Japan, and other industrialized countries are well into the post-transition stage, they are experiencing very low growth—with the result that the developing countries now account for most of the world's population growth.

World Population Futures

The global population growth rate has been declining steadily for over four decades. This trend is expected to continue into the foreseeable future. By 2050, the rate may even fall below 0.5 per cent (Bongaarts and Bulatao, 2000: 20; Eberstad, 1997; Lutz, 1994; United Nations Department of Economic and Social Affairs Population Division, 2013a, 2013b). This remarkable reduction will come about as a result of anticipated declines in fertility and mortality over the next half-century. In the not-so-distant future, as more countries complete the demographic transition, the world as a whole will enter a *post-transitional regime* characterized by low fertility, high life expectancy, low rates of natural increase, and high levels of demographic aging. The highly developed countries are already there; the *transitional countries* will soon join them; and the *delayed transitional countries* will in time, by the end of this century, enter this new stage. The world seems to be moving in this direction (Lee and Reher, 2011; McNicoll, 2012; Wilson, 2011, 2013).

World Population Projections

As discussed in Chapter 2, a *population projection* is a computational exercise intended to determine a future population's size and age–sex distribution (Haub, 1987: 7), based on anticipated changes over a specified period in rates of birth, death, and, where appropriate, migration (projections for a specific country or region would consider migration, whereas projections for the world as a whole would not). The recent UN projections (United Nations Department of Economic and Social Affairs Population Division, 2013a, 2013b) projections of the world's population to 2050 were based on low, medium, and high variant assumptions regarding the timing, degree, and direction of change in fertility and mortality over the projection period. The *medium variant* is the scenario considered to be the most likely to occur. The base population for the projections is usually obtained from the latest census or population estimates. What is considered a "low," "medium," or "high" scenario depends on the analyst's own understanding of why and how fertility and mortality rates change historically. Much also depends on the ability to anticipate circumstances or conditions in society between the present and the future that could cause fertility and mortality (and migration where applicable) to increase or decrease. Thus, the calculation of population projections requires historical data analysis as well as a strong appreciation of demographic theory. Although demographers take great care in determining the assumptions they will use, projections are very sensitive to changes in fertility, which can be an unpredictable variable. Even small changes in fertility can have dramatic effects on the projected population.

According to the UN projection in Table 3.3, the world's population in 2050 will *likely* reach about 9.6 billion. But the high variant scenario might produces a total of more than 10 billion, and the "constant" model—which assumes that fertility will remain at its present level—projects a population of more than 11 billion in 2050.

Figure 3.9 depicts these possible futures in graphic form. Of particular note is the "low variant" possibility of a gradual downswing beginning around 2060. But the 8.3 billion in 2060 under this scenario would still represent a gain of approximately 1.2 billion over the 2012 total of 7.1 billion. Continuing growth until about midway into this century seems unavoidable. Why?

Population Momentum

As a legacy of past high fertility, the proportion of the world's population in the reproductive ages today is still growing and will continue to grow over the next several decades. What makes this inevitable is *population momentum* (Bongaarts, 2009; Bongaarts and Bulatao, 2000; Cohen, 2003; Lutz, 1994). Underlying the concept of population momentum (to be discussed in greater detail in Chapters 4 and 6) is the fact that to a significant extent for any population the demography of the future is inseparable from the demography of the past. As an illustration, suppose that fertility rates around the world were to fall overnight to replacement level—2.1 children per woman (the extra ".1" allows for low to moderate mortality among women of childbearing age)—while mortality remained constant: despite this new fertility regime, the total population would ultimately number more than the current population. The difference between the two population sizes would reflect population momentum: the amount of unavoidable growth that is built into the current age structure of the population. The reason for this effect is that high fertility levels in the past have produced a largely young population that has yet to reach the childbearing years. As this population gradually progresses through the childbearing years, it will produce many offspring and, as a result, the population will expand beyond its current size.

Population momentum can also operate in the opposite direction (negative momentum). For example, if a population experienced a prolonged period of below-replacement fertility—say three or more decades—and then suddenly saw an increase to the replacement level of 2.1 children per woman, the "ultimate" population would be smaller than the current actual population. So, in this case, momentum translates into population decline despite a fertility increase. The reason for this effect is the prolonged period of below-replacement fertility in the past, which has produced a population made up largely of older people, with relatively few people in the younger age groups. As these smaller cohorts pass through their childbearing years, they will produce relatively few children and, ultimately, a smaller population.

Some Demographic Certainties for the Future

However uncertain population projections may be, beyond the growth associated with

TABLE 3.3   Population estimates for the world and regions in 1950 and 2013, and projected population in 2050 based on different variants

||||||||||||||||||||||||||||||||||||||||||||||||||||||||||||||||||||||||||||||||||||||||||||||||||||||||||||||||||||||

Region	Estimated population (millions)		Projected population (millions) in 2050, by type of variant			
	1950	2013	Low	Medium	High	Constant
World	**2 526 (100)**	**7 162 (100)**	**8 342 (100)**	**9 551 (100)**	**10 863 (100)**	**11 089 (100)**
More developed regions	813 (32.2)	1 253 (17.5)	1 149 (13.8)	1 303 (13.8)	1 470 (13.5)	1 268 (11.4)
Less developed regions	1 713 (67.8)	5 909 (82.5)	7 193 (86.2)	8 248 (86.2)	9 398 (86.5)	9 821 (88.6)
Least developed countries	195	898	1 594	1 811	2 043	2 552
Other less developed countries	1 518	5 011	5 599	6 437	7 355	7 269
Africa	229 (9.1)	1 111 (15.5)	2 119 (25.4)	2 393 (25.4)	2 686 (24.7)	3 210 (28.9)
Asia	1 396 (55.3)	4 299 (60.0)	4 482 (53.7)	5 164 (53.7)	5 912 (54.4)	5 805 (52.3)
Europe	549 (21.7)	742 (10.4)	622 (7.5)	709 (7.5)	804 (7.4)	673 (6.1)
Latin America/ Caribbean	168 (6.6)	617 (8.6)	674 (8.1)	782 (8.1)	902 (8.3)	885 (8.0)
North America	172 (6.8)	355 (5.0)	395 (4.7)	446 (4.7)	500 (4.6)	453 (4.1)
Oceania	13 (0.5)	38 (0.5)	50 (0.6)	57 (0.6)	64 (0.6)	62 (0.6)

Notes: Numbers in parentheses are percentages. The sum of least developed and other less developed countries is the total population for the less developed countries. The sum of the six regions is the overall world total population.

The United Nations Statistics Division (http://unstats.un.org/unsd/methods/m49/m49regin.htm) counts as "more developed" regions Australia/New Zealand, Europe, North America, and Japan. "Less developed regions" are Africa, Asia (excluding Japan), Latin America and the Caribbean, as well as Melanesia, Micronesia, and Polynesia. The "least developed" countries are 49 nations: Afghanistan, Angola, Bangladesh, Benin, Bhutan, Burkina Faso, Burundi, Cambodia, Cape Verde, Central African Republic, Chad, Comoros, Democratic Republic of the Congo, Djibouti, Equatorial Guinea, Eritrea, Ethiopia, Gambia, Guinea, Guinea–Bissau, Haiti, Kiribati, Lao People's Democratic Republic, Lesotho, Liberia, Madagascar, Malawi, Maldives, Mali, Mauritania, Mozambique, Myanmar, Nepal, Niger, Rwanda, Samoa, Sao Tome and Principe, Senegal, Sierra Leone, Solomon Islands, Somalia, Sudan, Togo, Tuvalu, Uganda, United Republic of Tanzania, Vanuatu, Yemen, and Zambia.

Source: From World Population Prospects: The 2012 Revision, vol. 1 http://esa.un.org/wpp/Documentation/pdf/WPP2012_Volume-I_Comprehensive-Tables.pdf, United Nations Department of Economic and Social Affairs Population Division. Copyright © 2013. United Nations. Used by permission of the United Nations.

population momentum there are some demographic trends that seem beyond doubt. In some of the industrialized countries, sustained sub-replacement fertility rates coupled with demographic aging will produce very slow growth, and in some cases—including Japan, Russian Federation, Germany, Italy, among

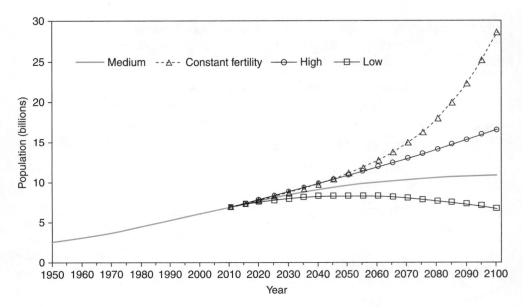

FIGURE 3.9   Estimated and projected population of the world by projection variant, 1950–2100

Source: From World Population Prospects: The 2012 Revision, vol. 1 http://esa.un.org/wpp/Documentation/pdf/WPP2012_Volume-I_Comprehensive-Tables.pdf, United Nations Department of Economic and Social Affairs Population Division. Copyright © 2013. United Nations. Used by permission of the United Nations.

others—population declines. Of particular interest is also the projected decline of China's population by approximately 590 million (United Nations Department of Economic and Social Affairs Population Division, 2013a).

Most population growth over the next half-century will take place in the developing countries, especially among the least developed, where, on the whole, rates of natural increase today remain well above the world average. Africa's share of the world's population will increase despite the ravages of HIV/AIDS; in fact, the region that has been hit hardest could still see its population more than double over the next 50 years (see Table 3.3, page 85).

Over the course of this century, all populations will become older, but the effect will be most pronounced in the countries where fertility has been low for a long time, and where recent reductions have been most rapid. Under the UN medium population projection assumptions, about 21 per cent of the world's population in 2050 will be over the age of 60 (just over 2 billion people). This segment of the population will likely account for 32 per cent of the population in the industrial countries, and nearly 20 per cent in the developing world as a whole.

All this implies that the proportion of children aged 0–14 in the world will decline from 26 per cent today to about 21 per cent in 2050. The decline will be especially pronounced in the more developed countries, where the number of older people has already surpassed the number of children; by 2050, the number of older people is anticipated to represent nearly twice the number of children (United Nations Department of Economic and Social Affairs Population Division, 2013a).

Finally, only one industrialized country (USA) is expected to be among the top 10 populations in 2050. The most populous countries will likely be the following (in order of projected population): India (1.62 billion); China (1.39 billion); Nigeria (440 million); the United States (401 million); Indonesia (321 million); Pakistan (271 million); Brazil (231 million); Bangladesh (202 million); Ethiopia (188 million); Philippines (157 million) (United Nations Department of Economic and Social Affairs Population Division, 2013a).

The Distant Future

According to the UN projections, in 2100 the constant fertility scenario would produce a global population of nearly 29 billion! The high fertility model suggests a population of about 17 billion. The medium-range projection points to a population of just below 11 billion. Under the low growth assumption, world population would possibly start a very gradual decline after about 2050, eventually arriving at nearly 7 billion by 2100. This scenario, if it were to materialize, would take us back to the global population size of 2009.

The United Nations has published a series of long-term highly speculative projections for the world and its regions to the year 2300, using a variety of assumptions (United Nations Department of Economic and Social Affairs Population Division, 2004a). In 2300, the global population could number anywhere from 2.31 (low variant) to 36.44 billion (high variant). The medium variant projection works out to 8.97 billion.

Canadian Population History: An Overview

As one of the world's most advanced nations, Canada enjoys exceptionally favourable natural, social, economic, and demographic conditions. Birth and death rates are among the lowest in the world, and the annual rate of natural increase is currently less than 1 per cent. Its 35 million people (as of 2014) are concentrated in a relatively narrow strip of the geographic landmass: along the Atlantic seaboard, down the St Lawrence River system to the Great Lakes region, then along the 49th parallel to the Pacific coast (see Figure 3.10). Only a small proportion of Canadians (mainly Aboriginal) live in the northern regions of Nunavut, Yukon, and the Northwest Territories. The ten provinces are predominantly urban: more than two-thirds of Canadians live in the three largest census metropolitan areas (Toronto, Montreal, and Vancouver), and as a whole, 80 per cent of the population lives in urban areas. Low rates of fertility since the early 1970s have caused the average age of the population to climb steadily, from 22 in 1921 to 37.3 in 2001, and 39.9 in 2011 (Statistics Canada *The Daily*, 2011). Today, Canada's population growth depends more largely on immigration and than on natural increase.

Figure 3.11 shows the contributions of natural increase and net migration to population growth. Until very recently, natural increase was the driving force behind Canada's population growth, contributing most of the total gains between census periods. Before the mid-1980s, the effect of net migration on overall population growth was, in general, substantially lower than that of natural increase. The only exception was during the decade

FIGURE 3.10   Canada: Population density by geographic area, 2011

Source: Source: Statistics Canada, Canada at a Glance 2013. Reproduced and distributed on an "as is" basis with the permission of Statistics Canada.

from 1901 to 1911, when more than 1.5 million newcomers, mainly from eastern and northwestern Europe, took up the Laurier government's offer of free land in the Prairie West. To this day, that wave of immigration remains the largest in Canada's history. The contribution of net migration to total population growth was negative between 1851 and 1901, largely as a result of heavy emigration to the United States, where economic opportunities were greater. A period of very low immigration was 1931–41, when the Great Depression brought immigration to almost a halt.

Since the end of World War II—and particularly from the middle part of the 1960s onward—immigration has accounted for an increasing share of population growth: from almost 29 per cent of the total in 1951–6 to more than 60 per cent in 2006–11. The importance of immigration to the maintenance of Canada's population over the long-term future is underlined by the fact that, overall, the average annual rates of population increase have been falling ever since the mid-1950s, when the post-war baby boom reached its height.

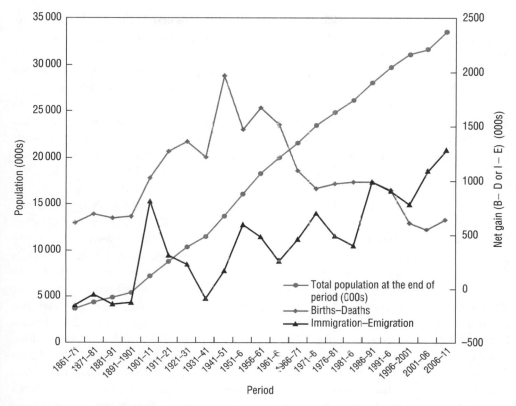

FIGURE 3.11   Population growth, natural increase, and net migration, Canada, 1861–2011

Note: Before 1971 to 1976, the population at the end of a period represents census counts. Starting with 1971 to 1976, it represents population estimates adjusted for census net undercoverage as of 1 July.

Sources: Based on data available at Statistics Canada, (2012a, 2013c); Statistics Canada Communications Division (2012), "Chart 1: Population Growth."

Demographic Conditions in the Frontier Society

The demography of Canada has changed significantly over the past century and a half. At the time of Confederation, in 1867, the country consisted of Lower Canada (Quebec), Upper Canada (Ontario), Nova Scotia, and New Brunswick. Although demographic data for Quebec is available as far back as 1608, and the populations of the Maritime provinces and Upper Canada

were enumerated at various times before Confederation, the country did not establish a national statistics system until 1921, and it is only since 1949, when Newfoundland entered Confederation, that we have had a full demographic account of Canada as it exists today.

The Demographic Transition in Quebec and Canada

From the founding of Quebec in 1608 through the end of the French regime in

1760, detailed records of marriages, baptisms, and burials were kept both by the French authorities and by local parish priests. Demographers at the University of Montreal have used these records to construct a picture of the demographic realities of the frontier society (Charbonneau, 1975; Charbonneau et al., 2000; Gauvreau, 1991; Henripin, 1954; Henripin and Péron, 1972; Pelletier, Lérgaré, and Bourbeau, 1997; Trudel, 1973).

From estimates provided by Hubert Charbonneau (1975: 30) at the founding of Quebec in 1608, Champlain and his companions numbered a mere 28. Only 8 of these individuals survived the first winter in the new colony. Notwithstanding the harsh conditions in the new land, this small group of settlers and periodic arrivals from France would contribute to phenomenal population growth in the new colony, such that by 1666 the population had grown to 3 216. One year after the English conquest in 1759, when New France comprised Quebec, Montreal, and Trois-Rivières, the population had reached 70 000. And by the end of the nineteenth century, it had multiplied to 200 000 (Charbonneau et al., 2000). Remarkably, most of this growth was the result of natural increase. Charbonneau and colleagues (2000: 106–11) estimate that between its founding and 1650, New France received about 25 000 immigrants, though only about 15 000 settled permanently. Of these settlers, 10 000 left descendants in the colony. The overwhelming majority of the early migrants—originating mainly from Normandy, the area around Paris and central western France—were men: soldiers, indentured workers, clerics, even some prisoners. During the 1660s, however, the French Crown subsidized the immigration of hundreds of young women of marriageable age. Known as the *filles du roi* (the king's daughters), they helped to balance the sex ratio.

The demographic success of New France can be attributed to three key factors: (1) high marriage rates and early entry into marriage, (2) exceptionally high fertility, and (3) death rates that were somewhat lower than might be expected for a frontier society (Henripin, 1994; Livi-Bacci, 1997: 63; McVey and Kalbach, 1995: 36). Data assembled by Jacques Henripin and Yves Péron (1972) suggest that from 1711 to 1760, crude death rates generally fluctuated between about 20 and 27 per 1 000 population. By the end of this period, however, the death rate had risen to almost 40 per 1 000. From around 30 per 1 000 in the mid-1760s, the crude death rate then began a gradual—if irregular—descent that continued through the early 1800s, when a more precipitous and sustained drop began (see Figure 3.12). By 1951, crude death rates in Quebec had reached modern levels (8 to 10 per 1 000 population); birth rates, however, stayed in the vicinity of 30 per 1 000. Infant mortality in the first half of the eighteenth century remained very high, perhaps reaching 246 per 1 000 births (Henripin and Péron, 1972: 225), and did not fall below 100 per 1 000 births until the early 1920s (Beaujot, 2000: 211). The crude birth rate in New France was always considerably higher than the crude death rate, ranging between 51 and 56 per 1 000 population between the periods of 1711–15 and 1756–60. At that point it began to decline, picking up speed after the 1820s and reaching a low of about 30 births per 1 000 population by the early 1950s. The large difference in the two vital rates between the late 1770s and 1951 produced very high rates of natural increase—in the range of 2.5 per cent per annum on average (Charbonneau et al., 2000: 131).

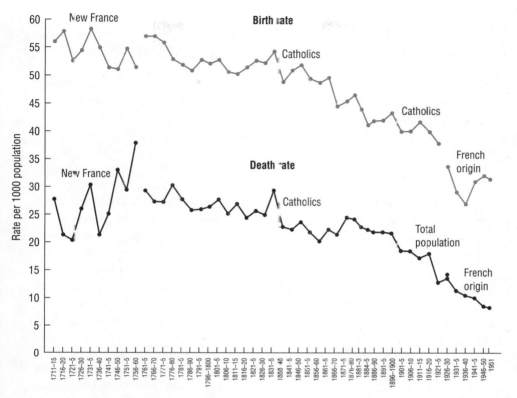

FIGURE 3.12   Crude birth and death rates for New France–Quebec, 1711–1951

Note: Due to limited availability of data, the series pertain to different sections of Quebec's population at different points in history.

Source: Henripin, Jacques and Yves Péron. 1972. 'The Demographic Transition of the Province of Quebec', in D.V. Glass and Roger Revelle, eds, Population and Social Change. London: Edward Arnold: p. 224.

Marriage was practically universal in colonial French Canada. Charbonneau and colleagues (2000: 116) calculated that in the 1600s the average age at marriage was 28 for men and 19 for women. In about 13 per cent of all cases, a single male married a widow (large numbers of widows reflecting the higher mortality of males). Under the prevailing mortality conditions, widowhood occurred on the average around age 51 for men and 47 for women. Roughly 60 per cent of marriages in the colony of the St Lawrence Valley would have been broken by the death of the husband; about 36 per cent

of widows, and 50 per cent of widowers, would remarry. These figures improved slightly in the following century, when fewer marriages were ended by the death of the husband and fewer weddings involved a single man and a widowed woman (see Table 3.4).

As women married relatively early in life, most were probably in their late teens or early twenties when they first gave birth. Children must have been closely spaced; and limits on fertility were factors such as natural sterility, postpartum amenorrhea, and fetal mortality. In a context of

THE ABORIGINAL POPULATION: FROM NEAR-EXTINCTION TO RECOVERY

Beginning in the sixteenth century, the demographic history of Canada's Aboriginal peoples was profoundly affected by the arrival of Europeans. We know that Aboriginal populations were devastated over the centuries that followed by (among other things) exposure to new diseases against which they had no natural immunity; warfare with Europeans and European-inspired conflict among themselves; European weaponry; and famines resulting from the Europeans' appropriation of their lands (Dobyns, 1983). Determining the extent of that devastation, however, remains a challenge because it is so difficult to estimate the size of pre-contact populations.

According to John Dickinson and Brian Young (2003: 5), at the beginning of the sixteenth century (c. 1500) the main Aboriginal groups in the eastern part of what is now Canada and the northeast United States were the Algonquin and the Iroquois. These authors estimate their combined population to have been about 270000: 170000 Algonquin (70000 in central and eastern Canada and 100000 in New England) and 100000 Iroquois (in the Chesapeake Bay area, the Lower Great Lakes, and along the upper St Lawrence Valley). To the north, the Inuit numbered perhaps 25000 in total, of whom 3000 were settled in Quebec and Labrador. In the region of French settlement along the St Lawrence, the Aboriginal population fell so dramatically that the Europeans were in the majority by 1650 (Dickinson and Young, 2003: 20).

On the broader scale, Russell Thornton (2000: 11) suggests that the Aboriginal population of the western hemisphere as a whole at the time of first contact was probably about 75 million. The population decline that began at that time continued for roughly four centuries. Figure 3.13 shows the birth rate trajectories for the Aboriginal population and New France–Canada from 1650 to 2006. The drop in Aboriginal birth rates following European contact is clear, starting in the early 1700s and reaching its lowest point in the 1820s and 1830s. Aboriginal population numbers began to recover around the turn of the twentieth century, and the recovery continues to this day. High rates of natural increase in the Aboriginal population reflect both persistently high fertility— attributable to social isolation, poverty, and possibly also a pronatalist culture— and substantial declines in death rates. A number of factors associated with socioeconomic modernization helped to delay the peak of the baby boom among Canada's Aboriginal peoples by roughly a decade (Jaffe, 1992; Romaniuk, 1980, 2008). One such factor was the decision of many Aboriginal mothers to abandon breastfeeding for bottle-feeding. Since breastfeeding serves as a natural contraceptive, this change meant that many became pregnant again sooner than they would have in the past. Consequently, Aboriginal fertility increased in the early 1960s. Fertility eventually began to decline as modern contraception became widely available to Aboriginal women (Romaniuk, 1980).

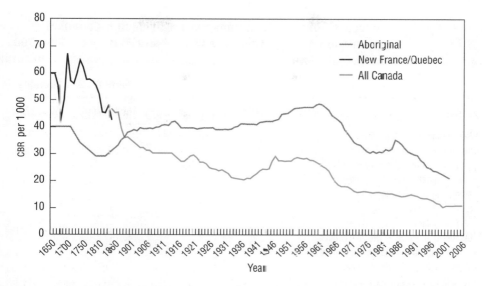

FIGURE 3.13   Crude birth rates, Aboriginal population and New France/Quebec–Canada, 1650–2006

Source: *Canadian Studies in Population* Volume 35, No. 1. "History-based Explanatory Framework for Procreative Behaviour of Aboriginal People of Canada" by Anatole Romaniuk. Reproduced under the Creative Commons License Deed http://creativecommons.org/licenses/by/3.0/.

"natural fertility" conditions—i.e., a general absence of conscious family limitation (Bongaarts, 1978)—childbearing would have continued until fairly late in a woman's life (Charbonneau et al., 2000: 118–19). Henripin and Péron (1972: 220) estimated that for the period from 1711 to 1886 French Canadian women had an average fertility of 7.1 children.

Birth rates in Quebec remained well above the Canadian average until the early 1960s, when in the context of rapid industrialization and urbanization, in a period known as the "Quiet Revolution," Quebec society experienced massive fertility declines. The "revenge of the cradle" strategy—by which the francophone minority historically had sought to maintain itself by sheer force of numbers—gave way to a new ethos of individualism and secularism in an environment of newly emerging

socioeconomic opportunities for the people of Quebec (Dickinson and Young, 2003).

The Nineteenth Century Onward: From Rural to Urban Industrial Society

Demographic conditions in the rest of Canada have also changed considerably since the days of the frontier. Before the mid-1800s, birth and death rates here, as elsewhere, would have risen and fallen in response to unpredictable social and environmental conditions, although the crude death rate when the decline began was only about 15 per 1000 population—a rate that in Europe was not generally seen until well into the twentieth century. The mortality decline that began in the 1850s has continued ever since and, except during the baby boom period (1946–66), has been

TABLE 3.4   Selected demographic parameters for the French-Canadian population of the St Lawrence Valley (New France), c. 1608–1760

Variable	Nuptiality 17th century	Nuptiality 18th century	Fertility 1608–1760	Mortality 1608–1760
Average age at marriage: Male	28.1	27.0		
Average age at marriage: Female	18.9	22.2		
% marriages broken by death of husband	61.8	54.8		
Average age at widowhood: Males	50.8	50.0		
Average age at widowhood: Females	47.3	49.8		
Fertility rate at age 30 (per 1 000, all ages at marriage)			479	
Duration of the interval (average number of months) between marriage and the first birth (women married at age 20–24)			14.3	
Average age at birth of last child (women married before age 20)			40.1	
Completed fertility for women married before age 20 (average number of children)			11.8	
Infant mortality rate (per 1 000 births)				225
Life expectancy at birth (both sexes)				35.5

Source: Adapted from Charbonneau et al. (2000): 116, 123, 126.

accompanied by a parallel decline in the birth rate.

As a result of large-scale reductions in mortality and fertility over the last century, life course events that were "expected" in early Canadian society, such as the early loss of a spouse or the death of a child, are now relatively rare (see Table 3.5). Life has become more "predictable" for the average person, and death has become increasingly removed from day-to-day personal experience. In 1851, some 20 per cent of infants would fail to reach their first birthday; today, infant mortality is just below 5 per 1000 births. Parents today can be almost certain that their offspring will survive to adulthood. Consequently, the typical couple

has only one or two closely spaced children (Grindstaff, 1995, 1994; 1975; Ram and Rahim, 1993).

Ellen Gee (1994) has constructed a statistical portrait of the typical life course for different birth cohorts of Canadian women. Women born between 1831 and 1840 married for the first time around the age of 25 and bore their first and last children at ages 27 and 41, respectively. Women born in the decade before 1900 tended to marry slightly earlier, at age 23.4; they bore their first and last children earlier as well, at ages 25.4 and 33.9. Among more recent cohorts, these formative events have generally been "compressed" into fewer years. Thus, women born between 1951 and 1960 typically married

TABLE 3.5   Demographic parameters for Canada, selected periods, 1851–2011

Variable	1851	1891	1901	1921	1931	1946	1951	1981	1991	2001	2011
% married, age 30–54: Males				77.7	78.2		83.4	85.9	73.3	71.5	55.0
% married, age 30–54: Females				80.5	80.9	78.6	82.7	84.5	74.0	74.9	57.0
% married population 15+	54.8	53.0		62.0	59.0		64.2			59.5	46.4
Average age at marriage: Brides		23.8	24.6	25.5		24.1	23.8	25.7	28.8	31.2	29.6
Marriage rate per 1 000 population				7.9	6.4	10.9	9.2	7.8	6.4	5.1	4.4*
Common-law unions as % of all unions								5.6	9.9	16.0	19.9
Crude birth rate	46.2		29.8		23.2	27.2	15.3	15.3	14.0	10.7	11.3
Crude death rate	22.2		14.4	11.6	10.5	9.4	10.1	7.0	6.9	7.3	7.4
Total fertility rate	7.03		4.009		3.2	3.36	3.503	1.704	1.71	1.51	1.61
Life expectancy at birth (both sexes)	41.1	45.2	50.2	59.7	62.1	66.8	70.8	77.8	79.0	79.7	80.9
Infant mortality rate (per 1 000 births)			139.0	102.2	86.0	47.3	39.0	9.0	6.4	5.3	4.9
Median age of mother at first birth						24.2	23.5	24.7	25.8	27.4	30.2

Note: *estimated

Sources: Basavarajappa and Ram (1983): A110–153; Beaujot (1995): 38; Beaujot and McQuillan (1982); Bélanger (2002): 16–19; McInnis (2000a): 547, 596–9; McVey and Kalbach (1995): 225, 245; Péron and Strohmenger (1985): 115, 202; Statistics Canada website and various reports.

on average at age 22.5, bore their first child at age 25.4, and completed their childbearing by age 26.3, according to Gee (1994). The median age of mothers at the birth of their first child has changed significantly since 1946, when it was 24.2; by 1981 it was to 24.7, and by 2011 it had risen to 30.2.

Gee's (1994) analysis of female cohorts at the end of their childbearing years indicates that the percentage of ever-married women without children declined from 12.8 per cent for the cohort born between 1861 and 1876 to just 7.2 per cent for the 1932–6 cohort. Among more recent cohorts, particularly those born after 1945, the percentage of women still childless at the end of their childbearing years (age 50) may increase above this level as a function of voluntary decisions and in some cases infertility due to more women delaying motherhood to older ages.

Future Outlook

What will the demographic future hold for Canada? The population dynamics of highly industrialized countries such as Canada, the United States, the United Kingdom, France,

Australia, and New Zealand have converged significantly since the early 1950s. But despite their similarities in fertility and mortality, they show substantial differences in their age distributions (Keyfitz, 1987). Part of the variation can be attributed to differences in immigration patterns, and part to the different trajectories that the declines in their birth rates have followed. Historical events such as wars also help to explain differences in age distribution and associated birth deficits among certain age cohorts. In 1987, Nathan Keyfitz predicted that by the second decade of the twenty-first century Canada would see a near doubling of its population aged 50 and older, and a decline of 10 per cent or more in its population around the age of 20. Consistent with this prediction, the 2006 and 2011 censuses confirmed that the senior population (aged 65 and older) has been increasing steadily since 1951, and the population aged 15 and under has been declining since 1966. For the first time, in 2013 the number of 15- to 24-year-olds fell below the number of 55- to 64-year-olds (Friesen, 2013). Owing to population aging, and especially the arrival of baby boomers at age 65, the proportion of elderly could reach double that of children towards the middle of the twenty-first century (Statistics Canada, 2008a).

The long-term demographic destiny of any population is largely a function of its fertility levels and trends. Today, however, the future for countries like Canada also depends heavily on international migration. If Canada's current low fertility rates remain stable, the median age of the population will continue to rise and the crude death rate will increase. It would seem that future growth will depend increasingly on the contribution of immigration in the context of an increasingly aging population.

Medium variant projections released by Statistics Canada Demography Division (2010) suggest that Canada's population could reach 43.8 million by 2036 and 52.6 million by 2061. Although natural increase would remain positive over the whole projection period, immigration will continue to be the main factor in population growth. Finally, beside a continuation of low fertility and increasing levels of population aging, seven social demographic trends seem destined to intensify as we approach the first quarter of the twenty-first century:

1. continued reliance on immigration from non-European countries;
2. increase of ethnic diversity and multiculturalism;
3. concentration of the population, especially immigrants, in the largest cities;
4. increase of Canadians reporting two or more ethnicities in the census;
5. growth of the Aboriginal population;
6. growth of the female labour force; and
7. increase of diversity of family configurations.

Conclusion

In addition to surveying the overall growth of the human population from ancient times to the present, this chapter has looked at projections for the near-term future. Much of the discussion centred on the demographic transition as a generalized pattern of change in vital rates that all societies can expect to undergo as they move into the modern industrial age. Particular attention was directed to the social, cultural, and economic factors that have typically delayed the onset of the demographic transition in the developing world. Countries described as transitional have made significant economic and demographic progress in recent decades and are now either very close to completing their transitions or have recently completed the transition. By contrast, a number of countries—mostly in sub-Saharan Africa and parts of Asia—have experienced significant delays in their demographic transitions and have only recently begun to show sustained fertility declines. While death rates have been reduced over time, some of these countries have been severely affected by HIV/AIDS, with the result that in some cases mortality rates have once again started to rise. Nevertheless, a significant portion of the anticipated growth in human numbers to the year 2050 will take place in the poorest regions of the world. Meanwhile, the industrialized countries that have completed their transitions are now experiencing significant demographic aging. Eventually, as birth rates everywhere decline, the average age of the entire world's people will inevitably rise.

The second part of this chapter looked at Canada's demographic history, with a particular focus on Quebec. The demographic transitions of Quebec and Canada were also examined and compared to the typical Western European pattern.

Four years after Confederation, the 1871 census counted a total population of roughly 3.7 million people. As recently as 1931, Canadian society was still predominantly rural. Today, by contrast, Canada is an overwhelmingly urban, industrial—some would say post-modern—society of more than 35 million people. Though its birth rate is now one of the lowest in the world, the population is expected to continue growing as immigrants continue to arrive from all over the world.

Notes for Further Study

Population Growth Models and Doubling Time

Given a rate of change of the population r we can calculate the *doubling time* of population. The greater the value of r, the shorter the time it will take a population to double its size—assuming that this growth rate remains constant. The lower the value of r, the longer the doubling time. A simple formula for calculating doubling time is the *law of seventy*. It can be illustrated by assuming the growth rates shown in the following table: doubling time = $70/r$. Thus, if r is 2 per cent, the doubling time will be approximately $70/2.0 = 35$ years. If r is 1.5 per cent, the doubling time will be approximately 47 years. When r is negative, we can expect population to decline. As the following table shows, there is an inverse non-linear relationship between the growth rate and the doubling time.

r (100)	Doubling time (years)
0.5	140
1.0	70
2.0	35
3.0	23
4.0	17
5.0	14
7.0	10
10.0	7

Linear Growth Model

If we observe two population counts at the beginning (P_0) and the end (P_1) of some interval n, the *linear* (arithmetic) *growth rate r*, in population over this interval, is:

$$r = \left[\frac{P_1}{P_0} - 1 \right] / n$$

This formula gives r, the average annual rate of change of the population over the interval denoted by n.

Letting P_0 represent population size at some initial point in time; P_1 population size at some later point; n the interval of time in years between these two populations; and r the rate of growth, as defined previously, the population at the end of the interval will be:

$$P_1 = P_0 (1 + rn)$$

This formula represents the *linear growth model*. Let us work out a hypothetical example using this model. Let
$P_0 = 100\,000$, the population at the beginning of the interval
$P_1 =$ population size at the end of the interval
$r = 0.02$ (i.e., 2 per cent annual rate of growth) during the interval
$n = 5$ (an interval of 5 years)
Then:
$P_1 = 100\,000 (1 + 0.02(5))$
$\quad = 100\,000 (1.10)$
$\quad = 110\,000$

Assuming linear growth of 2 per cent per year over this five-year interval, the population would grow to 110 000.

Geometric Growth Model

As described in Chapter 1, the linear model assumes growth occurs at constant increments; that is, the population grows by a constant amount across time intervals. This model does not consider the effect of compounding on population growth. The *geometric growth model* assumes compounding.

Under this model, the compounding is assumed to occur at discrete time points. For example, compounding may take place halfway through the interval, or perhaps at the beginning or at the end. The formula for the geometric model is:

$$P_1 = P_0 (1 + r)^n$$

Let us work out a hypothetical example using this model with the same information as applied in the preceding example. Let
$P_0 = 100\,000$, the population at the beginning of the interval
$P_1 =$ population size at the end of the interval
$r = 0.02$ (i.e., 2 per cent annual rate of growth) during the interval
$n = 5$ (an interval of 5 years)
Then:
$P_1 = 100\,000 (1 + 0.02)^5$
$\quad = 100\,000 (1.02)^5$
$\quad = 100\,000 (1.10408080)$
$\quad = 110\,408$

Assuming geometric growth of 2 per cent per year over this five-year interval, the population would grow to 110 408.

The geometric formula can be rearranged to determine initial population size P_0, given knowledge of P_1, the length of the time interval n, and the rate of growth r:

$$P_0 = \frac{P_1}{(1 + r)^n}$$

And if we wanted to find the interval of time n, between two population counts, the formula can be written as:

$$n = \frac{\log \frac{P_1}{P_0}}{\log (1 + r)}$$

where "log" means base 10 logarithm.

Assuming geometric growth, the *doubling time* of the population, defined here as n, is obtained by

$$n = \frac{\log 2}{\log(1 + r)}$$

To see how this formula works, let us use it to calculate the doubling time of a hypothetical population whose growth rate is 1.33 per cent per year (i.e., $r = 0.0133$). Assuming that this rate of growth remained constant, how many years would it take the population to double? We need to find n, such that

$$\frac{P_1}{P_0} = 2P_0.$$

Therefore:

$$n = \frac{\log 2}{\log(1 + 0.0133)}$$

$$= \frac{0.30103}{\log 1.0133}$$

$$= \frac{0.30103}{0.005738}$$

$$= 52.5 \, \text{years}$$

The "law of seventy" formula gives: 70/1.33 = 52.6 years. Note that we do not need to know the actual populations to work this out.

Exponential Growth Model

Population growth can be viewed as a continuous process. At any given moment, there are some people being born and others dying; and there are people entering and leaving the population through immigration and emigration. *The exponential model* accounts for this important feature of population change. The exponential growth formula is:

$$P_1 = P_0 \, e^{rn}$$

where e is the base of the system of natural logarithms, having the approximate numerical value of 2.71828 . . . ; r is the growth rate; and n is the time variable (e.g., number of years). Let us work out a hypothetical example using this model. Let

$P_0 = 100\,000$, the population at the beginning of the interval

$P_1 =$ population size at the end of the interval

$r = 0.02$ (i.e., 2 per cent annual rate of growth) during the interval

$n = 5$ (an interval of 5 years)

Given this information, under the exponential model of growth, the population at the end of five years will be 110 517:

$$P_1 = 100\,000 \, e^{(0.02)(5)}$$

$$= 100\,000 \, (1.10517)$$

$$= 110\,517$$

Geometric and Exponential Rate of Growth

Both the geometric and exponential models can be applied to determine the rate of population growth between any two points in time. The *geometric growth rate* over some interval n can be computed by:

$$1 + r = \left[\frac{P_1}{P_0}\right]^{1/n}$$

Therefore, r is solved as:

$$r = \left[\frac{P_1}{P_0}\right]^{1/n} - 1$$

Let us apply this formula. Suppose:

$P_1 = 150\,000$

$P_0 = 109\,000$

$n = 10$ years (the time interval between t_0 and t_1)

Then the geometric rate of growth is:

$$r = \left[\frac{150\,000}{109\,000}\right]^{1/10} - 1$$

$$= (1.37614679)^{1/10} - 1$$
$$= 1.032443 - 1$$
$$= 0.032443$$

The average rate of growth under the geometric model is about 3.24 per cent per year during this ten-year interval.

Another way to solve for r using the geometric model is to apply base 10 logarithms as follows:

$$r = exp \left[\frac{\log P_1 - \log P_0}{n} \right] - 1$$

where exp means to take the exponent (i.e., the antilog) of the quantity in the brackets.

Let us apply this formula using the same assumed figures as before. Then:

$$r = exp \left[\frac{\log 150000 - \log 109000}{10} \right] - 1$$
$$= exp \left[\frac{5.176091 - 5.037426}{10} \right] - 1$$
$$= exp(0.013866) - 1$$
$$= 1.032443 - 1$$
$$= 0.032443$$
$$= 3.24\%$$

The result is identical to the one found before (i.e., 3.24 per cent growth rate).

As we have already noted, the *geometric growth formula* assumes that population change occurs at discrete points in time. If one assumes *continuous change*, the *exponential formula* should be used to compute the rate of growth:

$$r = \frac{\ln \left[\dfrac{P_0}{P_0} \right]}{n}$$

or alternatively,

$$r = \left[\frac{\ln P_1 - \ln P_0}{n} \right]$$

where ln means "natural logarithm."

Applied to the same data used in the previous example, the exponential model gives an average rate of growth of 3.19 per cent per year:

$$r = \left[\frac{\ln 150\,000 - \ln 109\,000}{10} \right]$$
$$= \left[\frac{11.91839 - 11.599103}{10} \right]$$
$$= \frac{0.319287}{10}$$
$$= 0.031929$$
$$= 3.193\%$$

Table 3.6 shows computations based on data from selected countries over different time intervals. Notice the differences and similarities in the results. In comparing columns (7) and (8), for instance, the exponential model requires a slightly lower rate of growth than the geometric to attain the same amount of growth over an equal time interval. The difference reflects the power of continuous compounding in the exponential model.

As for computing *doubling time* with the exponential model, we may use the same example as applied earlier in the case of the geometric model, which assumed that $r = 0.0133$. As before, the question is this: assuming that this rate of growth remained constant, how many years would it take the population to double its size? The formula in this case is:

$$n = \frac{\ln 2}{r}$$

TABLE 3.6   Measures of population change for selected countries over two points in time

Country (periods in parentheses)	Population at t_0	Population at t_n	Number of years between t_0 and t_n	% change between t_0 and t_n	Average annual % change between t_0 and t_n	Average annual % rate of growth between t_0 and t_n, Geometric Model	Average annual % rate of growth between t_0 and t_n, Exponential Model
(1)	(2)	(3)	(4)	(5)	(6)	(7)	(8)
China (1982, 1990)	1 003 913 927	1 130 510 638	8	12.61	1.580	1.496	1.485
Benin (1975, 1995)	3 112 000	5 408 463	20	73.79	3.690	2.800	2.764
Canada (1971, 1991)	21 568 310	27 296 860	20	26.56	1.330	1.185	1.177
Mexico (1979, 1990)	69 381 104	81 249 645	11	17.11	1.560	1.450	1.440
Sweden (1980, 1993)	8 310 473	8 745 109	13	5.23	0.402	0.393	0.392
Bulgaria (1980, 1992)	8 761 535	8 540 272	12	−2.53	−0.210	−0.213	−0.213
Japan (1975, 1995)	111 933 800	125 570 246	20	12.18	0.609	0.576	0.575
Italy (1974, 1998)	55 179 995	57 563 354	24	4.32	0.180	0.176	0.176

Note: The time intervals are all different; therefore the more general notation "t_n" is used here to denote the end point of an interval.

Source: *United Nations Demographic Yearbook* (various years).

where n is the number of years for the population to double; ln means natural logarithm; and r is the rate of natural increase.

Therefore

$$n = \frac{0.693}{0.0133}$$

$$= 52.1 \text{ years}$$

What if the value of r is negative? How would this change our calculation of doubling time? In actuality, a negative r would imply population decline, and in such cases we speak not of the doubling time but rather of the number of years for the population to decline to half its current size. Using the exponential model, the formula to compute the number of years it would take for a population experiencing a constant negative rate of growth to reach half its current size would be:

$$n = \frac{\ln 0.5}{-r}$$

Here, we take the natural logarithm of 0.5, because instead of doubling we are concerned with halving the population (i.e., $(\frac{1}{2})P_0 = (0.5)P_0$). Let us assume $r = -0.0133$. The formula says to take the natural logarithm of 0.5, which is -0.69315. Dividing this by -0.0133 gives a halving time of approximately 52.1 years. The "law of seventy" formula gives 52.6 years. The two results are very close.

Exercises

1. Table 3.7 contains populations for selected countries over two points in time, 2000 and 2012. For each country, calculate the average annual population growth rate over this period using the linear, geometric, and exponential formulas, respectively.

TABLE 3.7   Population in 2000 and 2012 of selected countries

Country	Mid-year population (millions)		Growth rate, 2000–12			Population projection to 2050 (2012 as base and 2000–12 growth rate)		
	2000	2012	Linear	Geometric	Exponential	Linear	Geometric	Exponential
Egypt	68.3	82.3						
Niger	10.1	16.3						
Nigeria	123.3	170.1						
Congo Dem. Rep.	52.0	69.1						
South Africa	43.4	51.1						
Canada	30.8	34.9						
USA	275.6	313.9						
Mexico	99.6	116.1						
Brazil	170.1	194.3						
Afghanistan	26.7	33.4						
India	1 002.1	1 259.7						
Pakistan	150.6	180.4						
Indonesia	212.2	241.0						
China	1 264.5	1 350.4						
Japan	126.9	127.6						
Sweden	8.9	9.5						
UK	59.8	63.2						
France	59.4	63.6						
Germany	82.1	81.8						
Russian Fed	145.2	143.2						

Sources: Population Reference Bureau, 2000 and 2012 *World Population Data Sheets*.

2. Use the three growth models and the respective growth rates computed in Question 1 to project for each country the population in 2050. Use the population in 2012 as the base for the projections.
3. Interpret your results. Do the three models produce different results?

Additional Reading

Brown, Craig, ed. 2002. *The Illustrated History of Canada*. Toronto: Key Porter.

Chew, Sing C., and Robert A. Denemark, eds. 1996. *The Underdevelopment of Development: Essays in Honor of Andre Gunder Frank*. Thousand Oaks, CA: Sage.

Glass, D.V., and Roger Revelle, eds. 1972. *Population and Social Change*. London: Edward Arnold.

Hart, Michael H. 2007. *Understanding Human History: An Analysis Including the Effects of Geography and Differential Evolution*. Augusta, GA: Washington Summit Publishers. A National Policy Institute Book.

Innis, Harold A. 1930. *The Fur Trade in Canada: An Introduction to Canadian Economic History*, revised edn. Toronto: University of Toronto Press.

McEvedy, C., and R. Jones. 1985. *Atlas of World Population History*. London: Penguin, Harmondsworth.

Trebilcock, Michael J., and Mariana Mota Prado. 2011. *What Makes Poor Countries Poor? Institutional Determinants of Development*. Cheltenham, UK: Edward Elgar.

Wade, Mason. 1968. *The French Canadians, 1760–1967*. Toronto: Macmillan.

Weil, David N. 2013. *Economic Growth*, 3rd edn. Boston: Addison Wesley.

Wenke, Robert J. 1990. *Patterns in Prehistory: Humankind's First Three Million Years*, 3rd edn. New York: Oxford University Press.

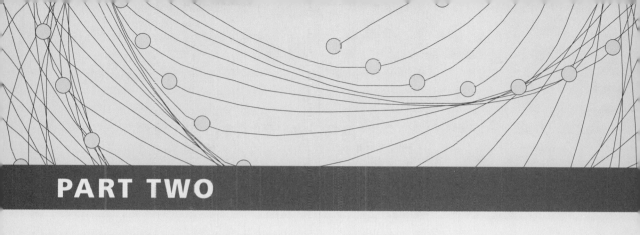

PART TWO

Demographic Composition

4 Age and Sex Structure

Introduction

All demographic phenomena are either directly or indirectly determined in some respect by *age*. The processes of birth, death, and migration—the three key demographic processes—are all age-dependent. The probability of experiencing these demographic events varies strongly with age (though not in a simple linear fashion). Age is also a determining factor in the incidence of other demographic events, including cohabitation, marriage, divorce, remarriage, widowhood, labour-force activity, and unemployment.

Another recognizable feature of all demographic phenomena is that they are in various ways related to *sex* and *gender*. For instance, females enjoy lower death rates than males in most circumstances; the chances of long-distance relocation are usually greater for males than for females; widowhood is more prevalent among females than among males; men are generally more likely than women to remarry; and so forth. The survival advantage of women over men, for example, is nearly universal. This may be a function of not only some biological factors favouring females but may also involve a multitude of sociological determinants (i.e., gender) that are inherently linked to differential

socialization of men and women that serve to explain behavioural differences between the sexes. The sociological importance of these two demographic characteristics explains our society's preoccupation with the collection of information on the basis of people's age and sex. Not only are age and sex data important markers of social and legal status for individuals in society but they are highly relevant in the occurrence of various types of social and demographic behaviour (Clarke, 2000; Riley, 1987). It is difficult, if not impossible, to envision any behavioural phenomenon in the social world that is not related, directly or indirectly, to age and sex.

This chapter will examine age and sex composition in the context of demographic analysis, specifically with regard to fertility, mortality, and migration. The term *composition* in this case refers to the distribution of the population in accordance with the intersecting characteristics of age and sex. Thus, in some contexts age and sex characteristics will be discussed together, as when we speak of the age–sex distribution of a population. In other contexts, the focus will be on one of the two, without any direct reference to the other. Wherever the main emphasis falls, however, the underlying assumption is that the two are highly interrelated.

Principles of Age and Sex Composition

Population Age Distribution

In demographic analysis, population data are usually arrayed according to age and sex. Regarding age, demographers are typically (though not exclusively) interested in three segments of the population: those under 15, those aged 15–64, and those aged 65 and older. These broad age groups represent, respectively: youth, who typically are not engaged in full-time economic activity and consequently require basic services such as education from the society; those of working age, who make up most of the labour force and therefore are the ones who pay the taxes that the government uses for societal maintenance and the post-retirement component of society.

These designations are only rough approximations of the realities they purport to reflect. Not all persons aged 65 and older, for example, are retired from the labour force. Nor are all individuals aged 15–64 working full-time; some may be unemployed or out of the labour force altogether. Similarly, in some countries many children and youth do not attend school but participate virtually full-time in family work activities. What, then, is the usefulness of these three broad age categories? By looking closely at these three demographic sectors, social scientists can get a sense of the economic "dependency" burden in a given society. By taking the ratio of youth plus old-age dependents to the working-age population, we obtain a measure of a society's overall dependency on the workers, who must provide for those not in the labour force. This is the *total dependency ratio*, which is expressed as follows:

$$\text{total dependency ratio} = \frac{P_{0-14} + P_{65}}{P_{15-64}} \times 100$$

This ratio can be broken down into two component parts:

$$\text{youth dependency ratio} = \frac{P_{0-14}}{P_{15-64}} \times 100$$

$$\text{old-age dependency ratio} = \frac{P_{65+}}{P_{15-64}} \times 100$$

A dependency ratio greater than 100 would indicate the presence of more dependents than workers in the population: the higher the ratio, the greater the dependency "burden" on the working population. And a ratio below 100 would signify the opposite situation. The overall dependency ratio is the sum of the youth and old-age dependency ratios.[1] Typically, if a population has a high youth dependency ratio, its old-age dependency ratio will be relatively low, and vice versa. In some situations, however, the youth and old-age components of the dependency ratio can be roughly equal. These three measures are shown in Table 4.1 for a number of selected countries and for the world as a whole, the more developed countries, and the less developed countries obtained from the United Nations (United Nations Department of Economic and Social Affairs Population Division, 2013b). The ratios are expressed as per 100. The table also shows the percentage distributions for three age categories: <15, 15–59, and 65+.

The values of the dependency ratios in Table 4.1 are closely related to a population's age distribution; they reflect the percentage distribution of the population by age. In Niger, for instance, almost half (49.8 per cent) of the total population consists of youths below age 15, and only 2.6 per cent is aged 65 and older. The situation is similar in

Nigeria and the State of Palestine, where the proportion of the population below age 15 approaches 45 per cent. Given these large youth components, we would expect the youth dependency ratios to be high as well, and they are: 104.7 per 100 in Niger, 82.7 in Nigeria, and 76.3 in the State of Palestine. In the case of Niger, there are more youths than there are working-age persons; in the other two cases, the situation is not as extreme but the ratio of youth to workers is still very high, nearing a situation of there being almost as many youths as persons of working age. Unsurprisingly, the old-age dependency ratios in these populations are quite low, all about 5 per 100. By contrast, countries like Japan and Sweden have relatively high old-age dependency and low youth dependency ratios. In these populations, the youth components account for only between 21 and 22 per cent of the total population, while the old-age components—in the range of 25 to 36 per cent—are among the largest in the world.

Finally, from the last column in Table 4.1, we see that *median age of population* corresponds closely to the population distribution of youth and elderly: Populations with relatively large old-age components tend to have relatively small youth components, and have a relatively high median age.

Of course, it is also possible to examine population distribution across a more detailed age classification. This usually involves observing absolute and relative frequencies of population by age and sex. As an illustration, the age–sex distribution of Canada in 2011 is shown in Table 4.2. Note that the distribution starts with the age group 0–4, followed by 5–9, 10–14, and so forth, up to 100+. Population frequencies are given for males and females separately as well as the total age-specific counts summed across sex. Age–sex-specific relative frequencies (percentages) are shown in the table, expressed on the basis of the total population. These relative frequencies (or absolute counts themselves) can be graphed to create a population age pyramid.

| TABLE 4.1 | Distribution of population by age, dependency ratios, and median age in 2010; the world, regions, and selected countries |

||||||||||||||||||||||||||||||||||||||||||||||||||||||||||||||||||||||||||||||||||||||||||||||||||||||||||||||||||||||||||||||||

Geographic area	Age group (%)			Dependency ratio (per 100)			Median age (years)
	<15	15–64	65+	Youth	Old age	Total	
World	26.6	65.7	7.7	40.5	11.7	52.2	28.5
More developed regions	16.4	67.5	16.1	24.3	23.8	48.1	39.9
Less developed regions	28.9	65.3	5.8	44.2	8.9	53.2	26.4
Least developed countries	40.9	55.7	3.5	73.4	6.2	79.6	19.3
Less developed regions, excl. least developed countries	26.8	67.0	6.2	40.0	9.3	49.3	27.8
Less developed regions, excl. China	32.4	62.6	5.0	51.7	8.0	59.7	24.2
Specific Regions							
Sub-Saharan Africa	43.4	53.5	3.1	81.2	5.8	86.9	18.1
Africa	41.1	55.4	3.4	74.2	6.2	80.4	19.2
Eastern Africa	44.6	52.4	3.0	85.1	5.8	90.8	17.5
Middle Africa	45.4	51.7	2.9	87.8	5.6	93.4	17.1

TABLE 4.1   (continued)

Geographic area	Age group (%)			Dependency ratio (per 100)			Median age (years)
	<15	15–64	65+	Youth	Old age	Total	
Northern Africa	31.5	63.6	4.9	49.6	7.7	57.3	24.3
Southern Africa	30.6	64.4	5.0	47.6	7.8	55.4	24.6
Western Africa	43.8	53.4	2.9	82.1	5.3	87.4	18.0
Asia	25.4	67.7	6.8	37.6	10.1	47.6	28.8
Eastern Asia	17.7	72.6	9.7	24.4	13.3	37.7	35.5
South central Asia	30.9	64.2	4.9	48.1	7.7	55.7	24.8
Central Asia	29.3	65.9	4.8	44.4	7.3	51.7	24.8
Southern Asia	30.9	64.1	4.9	48.2	7.7	55.9	24.8
Southeastern Asia	28.2	66.3	5.5	42.5	8.3	50.8	27.2
Western Asia	30.8	64.1	5.0	48.1	7.8	55.9	25.1
Europe	15.4	68.3	16.3	22.6	23.9	46.5	40.3
Eastern Europe	14.7	71.2	14.0	20.7	19.7	40.4	38.5
Northern Europe	17.5	66.0	16.5	26.5	24.9	51.4	39.7
Southern Europe	15.0	67.0	18.1	22.3	26.9	49.3	41.3
Western Europe	15.7	65.8	18.5	23.9	28.1	52.0	42.3
Latin America and the Caribbean	28.1	65.1	6.8	43.2	10.4	53.6	27.3
Caribbean	26.6	64.9	8.5	41.0	13.1	54.0	28.9
Central America	31.5	62.7	5.8	50.2	9.2	59.4	24.8
South America	26.9	66.1	7.0	40.7	10.6	51.3	28.1
North America	19.5	67.3	13.2	29.0	19.6	48.5	37.3
Oceania	24.0	65.3	10.7	36.7	16.4	53.1	32.2
Australia/New Zealand	19.2	67.4	13.4	28.5	19.8	48.3	36.8
Melanesia	37.7	59.1	3.2	63.9	5.5	69.3	21.3
Micronesia	30.9	64.0	5.0	48.3	7.8	56.1	25.7
Polynesia	31.3	62.7	6.0	49.9	9.5	59.4	25.2
Selected Countries							
China	18.1	73.5	8.4	24.7	11.4	36.0	34.6
State of Palestine	42.1	55.2	2.8	76.3	5.0	81.3	18.2
Niger	49.8	47.6	2.6	104.7	5.4	110.1	15.1
Nigeria	44.0	53.2	2.7	82.7	5.1	87.8	17.9
Brazil	25.5	67.6	6.9	37.7	10.2	47.9	29.0
India	30.2	64.8	5.1	46.6	7.8	54.4	25.5
Mexico	30.0	64.0	6.0	47.0	9.4	56.3	26.0
United States of America	19.8	67.1	13.1	29.6	19.5	49.0	37.1
Canada	16.5	69.4	14.2	23.7	20.4	44.1	39.7
Sweden	16.5	65.3	18.2	25.3	27.9	53.2	40.7
Russian Federation	14.9	72.0	13.1	20.7	18.2	38.9	38.0
Japan	13.3	63.8	23.0	20.8	36.0	56.9	44.9
United Kingdom	17.6	65.9	16.6	26.7	25.2	51.9	39.8

Source: United Nations Department of Economic and Social Affairs Population Division (2013b), File POP/15-1: Annual total population (both sexes combined) by five-year age group, major area, region and country, 1950–2100 (thousands); File POP/5: Median age by major area, region and country, 1950–2100 (years). From *World Population Prospects*: The 2012 Revision, United Nations, Department of Economic and Social Affairs, Population Division © 2013 United Nations. Used by permission of the United Nations.

TABLE 4.2   Age and sex distribution and associated summary measures, Canada 2011

Age	Number of persons			%		
	Males	Females	Total	Males	Females	Total
0–4	978 594	930 730	1 909 324	2.8	2.7	5.5
5–9	939 635	885 964	1 825 599	2.7	2.6	5.3
10–14	975 941	924 042	1 899 983	2.8	2.7	5.5
15–19	1 123 671	1 072 690	2 196 361	3.3	3.1	6.4
20–24	1 235 040	1 169 125	2 404 165	3.6	3.4	7.0
25–29	1 229 320	1 193 839	2 423 159	3.6	3.5	7.0
30–34	1 174 227	1 174 738	2 348 965	3.4	3.4	6.8
35–39	1 147 820	1 140 405	2 288 225	3.3	3.3	6.6
40–44	1 204 909	1 189 542	2 394 451	3.5	3.4	6.9
45–49	1 384 027	1 364 982	2 749 009	4.0	4.0	8.0
50–54	1 332 972	1 334 698	2 667 670	3.9	3.9	7.7
55–59	1 161 092	1 193 134	2 354 226	3.4	3.5	6.8
60–64	999 079	1 040 397	2 039 476	2.9	3.0	5.9
65–69	744 848	790 722	1 535 570	2.2	2.3	4.5
70–74	539 839	603 581	1 143 420	1.6	1.8	3.3
75–79	416 404	503 049	919 453	1.2	1.5	2.7
80–84	294 403	410 181	704 584	0.9	1.2	2.0
85–89	158 379	283 023	441 402	0.5	0.8	1.3
90–94	53 203	128 349	181 552	0.2	0.4	0.5
95–99	11 758	37 533	49 291	0.0	0.1	0.1
100+	1 796	6 294	8 090	0.0	0.0	0.0
Total	**17 106 957**	**17 377 018**	**34 483 975**	**49.6**	**50.4**	**100.0**
<15	2 894 170	2 740 736	5 634 906	8.4	7.9	16.3
15–64	11 992 157	11 873 550	23 865 707	34.8	34.4	69.2
65+	2 220 630	2 762 732	4 983 362	6.4	8.0	14.5
Total	**17 106 957**	**17 377 018**	**34 483 975**	**49.6**	**50.4**	**100.0**
YDR			23.6			
ODR			20.9			
TDR			44.5			
Population sex ratio			98.4			
Population median age			39.9			

Note: YDR = youth dependency ratio; ODR = old-age dependency ratio; TDR = total dependency ratio.

Source: Author's computations based on data from Statistics Canada Demography Division (2012).

Age Pyramids

Age–sex percentages can be plotted on graph paper to produce an *age–sex pyramid*: a pictorial representation of the age and sex composition of the population. A population pyramid displays the percentage distributions of males and females separately on opposite sides of the graph. For each age–sex intersection, we compute a corresponding percentage by using the total population size as the denominator. To illustrate, Table 4.2 indicates that there were 975 941 males aged 10–14 in Canada in 2011, and that the total population was 34 483 975. The corresponding percentage for males aged 10–14 is therefore 975 941/34 483 975 × 100 = 2.8 per cent. There were 924 042 females aged 10–14; and the corresponding percentage is 924 042/34 483 975 × 100 = 2.6 per cent. These computations are executed independently for all the age–sex groups in the population, starting with age 0–4 through 95–99 and finally 100+. Thus:

$$\% \text{ males in age group } x = \frac{\text{number of males in age group } x}{\text{total population}} \times 100$$

$$\% \text{ females in age group } x = \frac{\text{number of females in age group } x}{\text{total population}} \times 100$$

Using the information in Table 4.2, the dependency ratios for Canada in 2011 have been worked out as 23.6 (youth) and 20.9 (old age). The overall dependency ratio is the sum of these two values (44.5). This table includes another important statistic computable from the age distribution: the *median age*. This is the age that divides the distribution in half, so that half the population is above the median and half is below it (see Notes for Further Study on page 143).

Typology of Age Pyramids

With each stage of the demographic transition, the age distribution of the population changes in significant ways. Figure 4.1 adapted from Herwig Birg (1995) illustrates this point. In the early stages of the transition, the age pyramid can be described as 'pagoda'-like, with a very wide base and dramatic narrowing of the structure at ages beyond childhood. In the most explosive growth stage, the triangular shape emerges, brought on by the combined effects of high fertility and rapidly declining mortality. As the population passes through the late expanding stage, the combination of falling birth and death rates produce a 'bell'-shaped distribution, characterized by a noticeable narrowing of the bottom and a bulging middle, reflecting high fertility in the past, coupled with increased survivorship in the population. The post-transitional phase of the demographic transition can generate a number of different scenarios with respect to age composition. The "urn"-shaped pyramid is characterized by a narrow bottom and a large bulge of in the middle to old-age segments, with a sharp narrowing at the very top. These changes in age composition through the different stages of demographic transition result from the interplay of change in the two vital rates, births and deaths, and importantly, the rate of natural increase. Figure 4.2 highlights the important point that in concert with the demographic transition, societies pass through an *aging transition*, from an initially young to an eventual aging structure. Countries today are at different stages of the aging transition because of national variations in the onset and speed of fertility and mortality declines (Mason and Lee, 2011; Preston and Stokes, 2012).

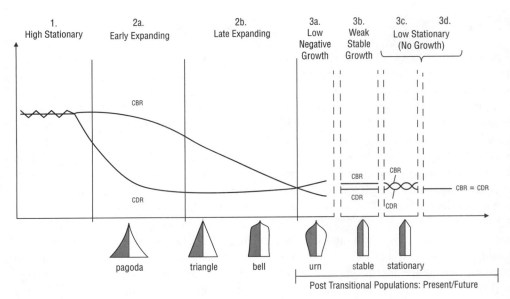

FIGURE 4.1   Typology of change of population age composition by phase of demographic transition (ideal-type scenarios)

Source: Adapted from Birg (1995:47).

Rapidly growing populations passing through the demographic transition ("pagoda" and "triangle" types) can have natural growth rates in the range of 2 per cent or more. Some developing countries have been gradually moving away from the "pagoda"-type form and into the more triangular shape, as the part of the distribution corresponding to the reproductive ages, roughly 15 to 50 grows wider. This type of age composition can be seen in transitional populations in which both mortality and fertility are declining steadily, but the difference between these vital rates remains substantial. Another set of developing countries includes China, Brazil, Thailand, Venezuela, and Indonesia. In these populations, the bottom of the age pyramid is visibly narrowing as a result of sustained declines in fertility in recent years. Eventually, these countries

would be expected to approximate the "bell" shape, as natural growth rates fall. Many of the post-transitional populations are now in the "urn"-type scenario, some of which are experiencing small negative rates of natural growth annually (e.g., Japan, Italy, Germany, Bulgaria, Hungary, Romania, Russian Federation, and Ukraine, among others).

Canada's current age structure (Figure 4.2) fits closely the "urn" type of pyramid. The base is narrow, there is a noticeable bulge in the ages between 35 and 65, and the top—representing those over the age of 65—is fairly wide. This age pyramid contrasts sharply with that of contemporary developing countries (see Figure 4.3).

A number of interesting features may be outlined in regard to Canada's age composition in 2011. The most obvious feature in this pyramid is the bulge associated with

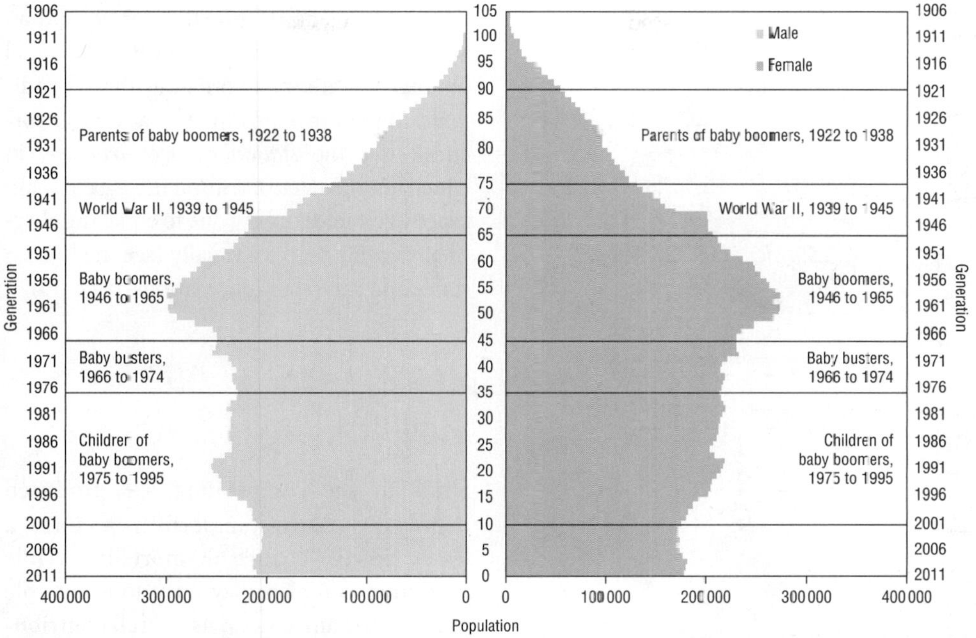

FIGURE 4.2   The age pyramid of the Canadian population in 2011, showing different generations

Source: Author's computation with data from Statistics Canada (2013e).

the baby boom generation, born between 1946 and 1955, who in 2011 were aged 46 to 65. This is the largest segment of the population, accounting for nearly one in three Canadians. Near the top of the age pyramid are the parents of the baby boomers, aged 73 to 89 in 2011, who were born between 1922 and 1938. This older generation has been gradually losing its members (in 2011, it accounted for less than 10 per cent of Canadians). Near the bottom of the age structure are the boomers' children, born between 1975 and 1995 and who were aged 16 to 36 in 2011. There is a slight bulge in this part of the age pyramid—a reflection of an "echo" effect of the baby boom and the impact of higher fertility in the early part of the 1990s. In 2011, this cohort represented about 27 per cent of Canadians. Those

who were born between 1966 and 1974 and who in 2011 were aged between 37 and 45 are the baby bust generation; this is a relatively small set of birth cohorts due to the sharp drop in fertility during this period, the end of the baby boom. The Second World War cohort, born between 1939 and 1945 and who in 2011 were between 66 and 72, is another relatively small generation. Reduced fertility during the war explains this feature, but given the age range of this generation, mortality has also played a role in reducing the number of survivors in these cohorts.

Theoretically, post-transitional populations could evolve into a *stable population* structure with very low constant rates of natural growth. Others can experience very low but fluctuating birth and death rates

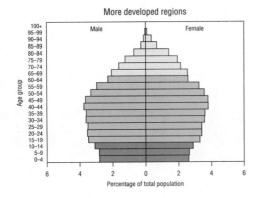

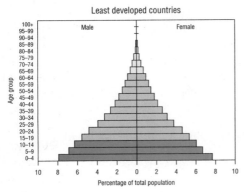

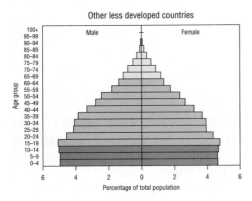

FIGURE 4.3   Population pyramids of more developed regions, the least developed countries, and other less developed countries, 2005

Source: United Nations Department of Economic and Social Affairs Population Division (2006a): 23 (Figure II.1). From World Population Prospects: The 2004 Revision (2006e), United Nations Department of Economic and Social Affairs Population Division. © 2006 United Nations. Used by permission of the United Nations.

that produce annual growth rates around an average value of zero. Many post-transitional populations are approximating these conditions. Yet another possibility—at least theoretically—is the *stationary age structure*, in which annual rates of natural increase remain exactly zero indefinitely due to equal numbers of births and deaths annually (see the box on stable and stationary populations, page 115).

Determinants of Age Composition

Shifts in age composition are produced mainly by changes in fertility and (to a lesser degree) change in mortality. While migration can also play an important role in some circumstances, its overall contribution is in general relatively minor (Preston, Heuveline, and Guillot, 2001). A comprehensive account of the demographic dynamics that determine whether a population is aging or growing younger was developed by Ansley Coale (1957a, 1957b, 1964, 1972), who found fertility to be the major determinant of changes in age composition. A young population is produced by increasing fertility rates, and an old population by declining fertility. Under sustained high fertility conditions, there will be a relatively high proportion of people under the age of 15, and the median age of the population will be relatively young compared to that of a population with a smaller proportion under 15. Declining fertility rates produce an aging population, with a smaller proportion of people under 15 and a growing proportion over 65. As we shall see, as compared to fertility, mortality decline plays a lesser role in changing the age distribution of a population, though under some conditions it can be become increasingly important.

STABLE AND STATIONARY POPULATIONS

What would happen to the age structure of a population if its age-specific birth and death rates remained constant over a long period—say, 70 years or more? This is the fundamental question that underlies one of the most important constructs in demographic analysis: the stable age distribution. Under such conditions, both the age distribution of the population and its rate of growth would be constant. Despite its name, a *stable population* can be either increasing or decreasing in size, as long as the rate of change remains constant; what is "stable" is the shape of the age distribution (Newell, 1988: 120) A special kind of stable population is known as the *stationary population*. In this model, the rate of growth is zero: neither the size of the population nor its age structure changes from year to year (Pollard, Yusuf, and Pollard, 1981: 102–3). This is the only case in which the total number of people in the population and the number and percentage of the population within each of the age categories all remain constant.

At present, no population in the world actually fulfills all the restrictive criteria of the stable population model, though (as we have seen) some countries are moving in that direction. Nevertheless, the stable population model is useful because it allows analysts to develop "what if" scenarios. For example, a researcher might want to assume constant age-specific birth and death rates in a real population over a specified number of years into the future so as to ascertain how this situation would affect the age distribution. Other possible uses of the model would be to hold current age-specific fertility rates constant while varying the age-specific death rates (i.e., raising or lowering them) or to hold mortality rates constant while altering fertility rates. Such experiments can help researchers anticipate future scenarios in actual populations.

The origin of stable population theory can be traced back to Leonhard Euler (1707–83), who first proposed that a set of constant age-specific death rates and a constant number of births per unit time in all generations would produce a stable population. More than a century later, Alfred Lotka (1880–1949) developed an equation (the "renewal equation") that made it possible to calculate "the rate of increase implied by a [given] regime of birth and death rates" (Keyfitz, 2003: 322; Véron, 2008). Lotka also formulated equations for the *intrinsic birth rate* (the rate at which mothers bear their daughters in a stable population, determined by a set of constant age-specific birth rates) and the *intrinsic death rate* (the death rate in the stable population, determined by a set of constant age-specific death rates): the difference between these two rates determines the *intrinsic growth rate* (*intrinsic rate of natural increase*) of the stable population, which can be positive, negative, or even zero (as in the case of a stationary population). The stable population therefore will also have a corresponding life table and life expectancy function.

The Relative Importance of Fertility and Mortality

The relative importance of fertility and mortality in determining age composition can be illustrated with a simulation based on stable population models (see box, page 115). Table 4.3 shows stable age distributions derived by combining different fertility and mortality levels. The indicator of mortality is life expectancy at birth—a measure of survival determined by a population's age-specific mortality rates; the higher the life expectancy, the better the survival probabilities. The index of fertility is the gross reproduction rate (GRR), which measures the average number of daughters born to a woman, given a prevailing schedule of age-specific fertility rates; the greater the GRR, the higher the fertility. The table shows six panels, each reflecting a certain level of mortality (expectation of life at birth, e_0) and fertility (the gross reproduction rate, GRR). The percentages of the population across three broad age categories are shown in each panel.

It should be noted that varying mortality while holding fertility constant has a relatively small effect on age distribution. For example, in level 1 of the table, life expectancy is just 20, whereas in level 6, it is 70. Yet when fertility is kept constant at GRR = 1.00, the proportion aged <15 changes by only 4 percentage points: from 15 per cent in level 1 to 19 per cent in level 6. By contrast, the proportions within each age class change dramatically as fertility varies from a GRR of 1.00 to a GRR of 4.00. These results, based on stable population distributions derived by varying the combination of fertility and mortality rates, are consistent with Coale's (1964) calculations showing that change in fertility is the key determinant of change in the age composition, and that mortality change plays a smaller role.

Even so, it is important to point out that declining mortality generally contributes to make the age distribution younger. This may seem paradoxical at first because the common assumption is that a reduction in the death rate should have the effect of raising the average age of death and therefore more old people in the population. But as explained by Coale (1964: 49–50), the effect of falling death rates serve to make the population younger because there would be more young people and also more births:

"It is true that as death rates fall, the average age at which people die is increased. But the average age of a population is the average age of living persons, not their average age at death. It is also true . . . that as death rates fall the number of old persons in a population increases. What we do not so readily realize is that reduced mortality increases the number of young persons as well. More persons survive from birth to ages 1, 10, 20, and 40, as well as more living to old age. Because more persons survive to be parents, more births occur".

In the early stages of the demographic transition when societies are beginning to undergo socioeconomic modernization and fertility rates are high, mortality improvements do not generally take place uniformly throughout the age structure. Improvements tend to occur first among infants, children, and women of reproductive age (Omran, 1971). These mortality reductions help to increase the numbers of children and young persons who will eventually go on to bear children when they reach parental age, and as Coale (1964) described, this helps to maintain a young age structure.

TABLE 4.3   Stable population age distributions derived by varying combinations of mortality and fertility rates

Mortality	Fertility	% distribution in the stable population			Mortality	Fertility	% distribution in the stable population		
		0–14	15–59	60+			0–14	15–59	60+
Level 1. $e_0 = 20$	GRR				Level 4. $e_0 = 50$	GRR			
	1.0	14.8	68.3	16.9		1.0	17.8	60.7	21.5
	2.0	28.9	64.0	7.1		2.0	34.2	57.2	8.6
	3.0	38.5	57.6	3.9		3.0	44.6	50.9	4.5
	4.0	45.2	52.4	2.4		4.0	51.5	45.8	2.7
Level 2. $e_0 = 30$	GRR				Level 5. $e_0 = 60.4$	GRR			
	1.0	16.3	65.0	18.7		1.0	18.7	59.4	21.9
	2.0	31.4	60.9	7.7		2.0	35.6	55.8	8.6
	3.0	41.3	54.5	4.1		3.0	46.0	49.6	4.4
	4.0	48.2	49.2	2.6		4.0	52.9	44.4	2.7
Level 3. $e_0 = 40$	GRR				Level 6. $e_0 = 70.2$	GRR			
	1.0	17.0	62.6	20.4		1.0	19.5	58.6	21.9
	2.0	32.9	58.8	8.3		2.0	36.8	54.7	8.5
	3.0	43.1	52.5	4.4		3.0	47.3	48.4	4.3
	4.0	50.0	47.3	2.7		4.0	54.1	43.3	2.6

Source: Adapted from United Nations Department of Economic and Social Affairs Population Division (1973): 274. Reprinted with the permission of the United Nations.

An important question is whether there may be a point in the demographic experience of populations that have completed the demographic transition when further mortality reductions begin to amplify population aging—that is, when the pattern of age structure shifts from fertility-dominated aging to mortality-dominated aging (Caselli and Vallin, 1990; Horiuchi, 1991). Based on the studies of Coale (1957a, 1957b, 1972) and others, it has been shown using stable population models that, in general, when mortality declines are concentrated in infancy and early childhood,

the effect will be to make the population younger. If, on the other hand, survival improvements are concentrated in the ages above 45—as is the case for highly advanced societies today—the effect will be to age the population (Preston, Heuveline, and Guillot, 2001: 160–1).

In post-transitional populations with high levels of socioeconomic development and advanced health systems, mortality rates in infancy, childhood, and the reproductive ages have fallen to very low levels. In these societies, mortality improvements on an annual basis tend to be increasingly concentrated in the over-60 age segment (Manton, 1991; Olshansky and Ault, 1986), and this amplifies demographic aging.

Effects of Migration on Age–Sex Structure

The effects of migration on age structure at the national level tend to be negligible compared to the effects of fertility and mortality change (Preston, Heuveline, and Guillot, 2001). Nevertheless, there are cases in which migration can have a visible impact on the age composition. Migratory effects are more likely to be noticeable in small national populations or perhaps at lower levels of aggregation such as a city. In large national populations such as China and India, and also Canada, any amount of migration—in or out—will have only a minor impact in the age distribution.

Immigration's effects on a host population's age structure will largely depend on the size of the age categories into which immigrants are moving, the numbers of immigrants entering those age categories, the gender composition of the immigrants, and the intensity of immigration over time. As immigration is a highly selective process, the age composition of an immigrant group is generally quite different from that of the host population. For example, in the Canadian case, the age pyramid of the foreign-born population is shaped more like a diamond than a pyramid: there are relatively few immigrants below the age of 15, and relatively few over 65. This means that most immigrants are concentrated in the prime labour-force ages of 20 to 64 (Bélanger and Dumas, 1998: 94). The impact of immigration on Canada's median age is minor because the average age on arrival is around 30, after which immigrants

age along with the rest of the population (Statistics Canada, 2007a).

Age Distribution as Demographic Memory

A fundamental principle of stable population theory is that two populations with radically different age structures will converge to identical age compositions if the two populations have identical age-specific birth and death rates over 70 years or more (Coale, 1972: 3; Lopez, 1961). Age distributions gradually "forget" their past. Consider two populations with very different age compositions in 1960: Sweden and Sri Lanka. Sweden's age distribution in 1960 was typical of an industrialized post-transitional population, while Sri Lanka's reflected a young, rapidly growing population that had not yet completed its demographic transition. Alfred Pollard and colleagues (1981) conducted a simulation in which they used Sweden's age-specific birth and death rates from 1960 as the set of constant age-specific rates to be applied to these two different populations over a period of ten decades—1960 to 2060 (migration was not considered). As Figure 4.4 shows, these two age structures start out very differently—as would be expected—but eventually converge, assuming identical shapes in the last decade. This principle of stable population theory has been called the *ergodic property* of populations: the tendency to eventually "forget" their initial age distributions (Coale, 1972: 3; Keyfitz, 1968: 90).

It takes roughly a century for a population's age structure to change completely (Preston, Heuveline, and Guillot, 2001: 1). During this time, significant sociological

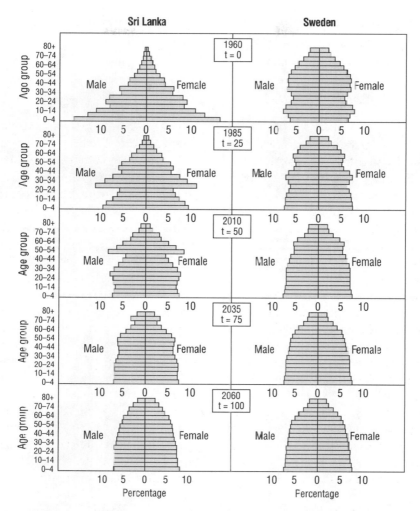

FIGURE 4.4 Hypothetical evolution of Sri Lankan and Swedish age pyramids over a century, given Sweden's (1960) fertility and mortality rates (t = years after 1960)

Source: Pollard, Yusuf and Pollard (1981): 102 (Figure 7.1). From: *Demographic Techniques*, 2nd edition, © 1981 Pergamon Press. Reprinted with permission of Farhat Yusuf and Geoff N. Pollard.

information remains visible in the shape of the population's age pyramid. For instance, extreme irregularities in a population's age structure can sometimes be traced to major historical events that have affected birth and death rates over the long term, and are reflected in the shape of its current age pyramid. In Figure 4.5, for example, the French and German pyramids are typical of the European nations that endured two world wars (Pison, 2014), while the distortions apparent in the Chinese pyramid can be linked directly to government policies (Yongping and Peng, 2000).

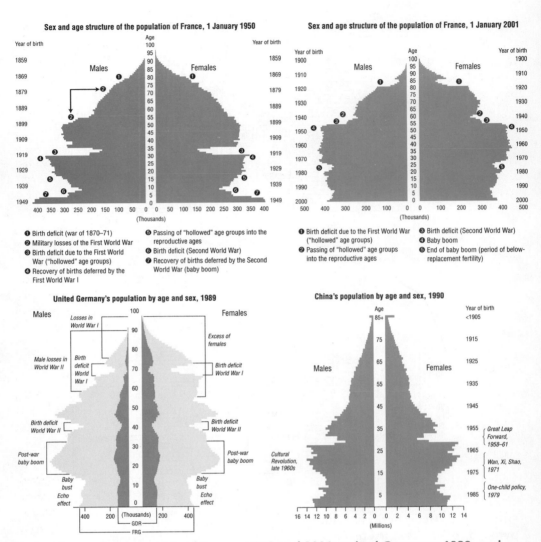

FIGURE 4.5   Age pyramids of France, 1950 and 2001; united Germany, 1989; and China, 1990

Sources: France 2001 and 1950: Pison, Giles. 2001. 'The Population of France in 2000', *Population and Societies* 366 (March): 3. Copyright Institut national d'études démographique (INED); Germany: Heilig, Gerhand, Thomas Buttner, and Wolfgang Lutz. 'Germany's Population: Turbulent Past, Uncertain Future', *Population Bulletin* vol. 45, issue 4. ©1990 Population Reference Bureau. Reprinted with permission; China: from Peng, Dr. Xizhe and Li Yongping, *The Changing Population of China*, p. 65.© 2000 Wiley Blackwell. Reprinted with permission: From The Determinants and Consequences of Population Trends, vol. 1, United Nations Department of Economic and Social Affairs Division, ©1973 United Nations. Used by permission of the United Nations.

Population Momentum

As we saw in Chapter 3, a certain amount of growth is built into the current age structure of any population. The basic question behind the concept of *population momentum* is this: If a country could reduce its fertility rate to replacement level immediately, by how much would its population continue to grow before growth actually stopped? Assuming this change in fertility and if mortality remains constant and there is no in- or out-migration, such a population will in the long run reach a stationary state with an unchanging age distribution and zero growth rate (see the box on pages 122-23). Various ways of estimating population momentum have been proposed by authors including Nathan Keyfitz (1985), Nan Li and S. Tuljapurkar (1999), and Samuel Preston, Patrick Heuveline, and Michel Guillot (2001). The basic approach is to estimate the ratio of the stationary population that will eventually be produced under the new fertility regime (i.e., constant fertility at the replacement level of 2.1 children per woman) to the population size when the fall in fertility occurs:

$$M = \frac{\text{size of the stationary population}}{\text{size of the initial population}}$$

Appropriate population projection methods are applied to determine the size of the stationary population. A country's population is projected for 100 years assuming replacement fertility, constant mortality at the level for the initial year, and no migration (Rowland, 2003: 331).

A value of M greater than 1 would indicate that the population would grow as a result of momentum generated by the youthful age structure of the population. A value of 1 would imply no momentum (i.e., stationary population), while a value below 1 would mean population decline (i.e., negative momentum).

Values of M calculated by Preston, Heuveline, and Guillot (2001: 164) illustrate the range of variation in population momentum across regions and countries in 1997:

Nathan Keyfitz (1985) devised a formula for deriving the growth factor that represents population momentum:

$$M = \frac{be_0}{1\,000\sqrt{NRR}}$$

where M is momentum, b is the population's crude birth rate, e_0 is its life expectancy at birth, and NRR is the *net reproduction rate* of the population before the drop in fertility to the replacement level. Thus, if a population has a crude birth rate of 35, a life expectancy at birth of 65, and a net reproduction rate of 2.5, it would grow by a factor of 1.439

before it levelled off following an immediate drop in fertility:

$$M = \frac{35 \times 65}{1\,000\sqrt{2.5}} = 1.439$$

Applied to Canada, this formula shows that momentum has fallen significantly over time, from 47 per cent in 1951 to just 1 per cent in 2010. This confirms recent calculations by Barry Edmonston (2014), indicating that population momentum in Canada will likely remain modest in future years. By comparison, Niger's M factor in 2010 was 1.62!

	b	e_0	NRR	M
1951	27.24	68.5	1.61	1.47
1985	14.82	76.4	0.83	1.27
2010	11.20	80.9	0.80	1.01

If, in 1997, fertility had declined to the replacement level and mortality remained constant, the population of the world would still grow by a factor of 1.35 (i.e., 35 per cent); and Africa and western Asia would grow the most—by a factor of 1.56—because of their youthful age compositions. In sharp contrast, the population of Europe as a whole would decline by 2 per cent. The populations of Austria, Russia, Italy, and Germany would also decline, as their momentum factors were below 1. These cases demonstrate that there can be a momentum to population decline (*negative population momentum*) as well as to population growth (Preston, Heuveline, and Guillot, 2001: 164). The eventual stationary populations in these cases would be smaller than the populations at the time at which replacement fertility is imposed.

The analysis of population momentum is useful for planning purposes. If a society with a rapidly growing population wishes to reduce its rate of growth, it must be prepared to look far into the future. The magnitude of population momentum will depend on whether a population decides to stop growing now or at some point in the future (Bongaarts, 2009). The difference can be quite significant. A growing population that abruptly reduces its fertility to replacement level and maintains it there will still grow for two generations or so. This residual growth will be even larger if the decline to replacement fertility takes place gradually (as is the case in reality) rather than instantaneously (Blue and Espanshade, 2011; Li and Tuljapurkar, 1999).

> Net reproduction rate (NRR) is a measure of population reproductivity—that is, the extent to which mothers replace themselves by bearing daughters, taking into account mortality to women in the reproductive ages (this measure does not consider migration). Thus, a NRR of 1 is consistent with zero natural population growth in the long run.

POPULATION MOMENTUM

The impact of population momentum on future population levels can be illustrated by the following example of two families. The first generation of each family consists of one man and one woman. Each woman has four children over her reproductive life. This second generation includes four females and four males.

PERIOD ONE
Fertility above Replacement Level; Total Population, 12

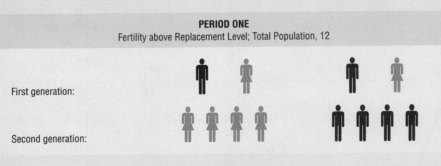

First generation:

Second generation:

POPULATION MOMENTUM

In period two, the first generation dies and everyone in the second generation marries. Each woman in the four resulting couples has two children, producing a third generation of four males and four females. Even though the second generation reaches replacement levels of fertility, population momentum causes a 33 per cent increase in total population, from 12 to 16, between period one and period two.

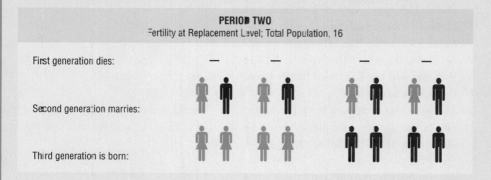

PERIOD TWO
Fertility at Replacement Level; Total Population, 16

First generation dies:

Second generation marries:

Third generation is born:

The process is repeated in period three. The second generation dies; the third generation marries and produces a fourth generation. If the third generation remains at replacement levels of fertility, the total population stabilizes. The size of the steady-state population in the final period is the result not only of the fertility decisions of the second and third generations, but of those of the first generation as well.

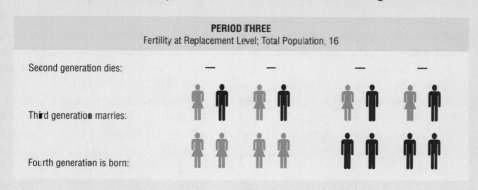

PERIOD THREE
Fertility at Replacement Level; Total Population, 16

Second generation dies:

Third generation marries:

Fourth generation is born:

Population momentum also can work in reverse. If subsequent generations have lower than replacement fertility, the decline in total population could be rapid, reflecting the fertility decisions of both current and previous generations.

Source: Box 7.2, "Population Momentum," from *Economics of Development*, 6th edn, by Dwight H. Perkins, Steven Radelet, and David L. Lindauer. Copyright © 2006, 2001, 1996, 1992, 1987, 1983 by W.W. Norton & Company, Inc. Used by permission of W.W. Norton & Company, Inc.

Generalizations about Age Structure

The preceding paragraphs suggest several important generalizations:

1. Rapidly growing populations typically have high fertility rates, which manifest themselves in broad-based age pyramids. The age group 0–4 reflects the births that have occurred between years t and $t - 5$ years ago. The more babies are born, the wider the base of the age pyramid will be. The fewer babies born, the narrower the base.

2. The proportion of people at the upper end of the age pyramid diminishes with advancing age. The higher the age, the fewer the people still living. The increasing intensity of mortality translates into a narrowing of the age pyramid with advancing age.

3. Since the sum of the percentages across age and sex must be 100, a pyramid with a wide base will necessarily have a narrow middle and top. Populations with a relatively low (i.e., young) median age characteristically have a larger proportion under 15 and a relatively small proportion over 65.

4. Populations age as a function of sustained low fertility (i.e., "aging at the bottom"); however, post-transitional populations are also "aging at the top" as a result of increased longevity among seniors.

5. As a population experiences sustained low fertility, the base of its age pyramid will constrict. If this condition persists over a long time, the result will be a transformation in shape, towards an inverted or "urn" shape: narrow at the base and wide at the middle and upper parts. In this case, a large percentage of the population will be older than 65 and the population will be declining. Contemporary post-transitional populations appear to be evolving toward a more or less stable age structure, characterized by fluctuating low rates of positive and negative natural increase around an average value of zero.

Sex Ratios

Basic Principles

The *sex ratio* reflects the numerical balance between males and females in a population:

$$\text{sex ratio} = \frac{\text{number of males}}{\text{number of females}} \times 100$$

The computation of this measure can be easily illustrated with the data for Canada in Table 4.2 (page 110). There were 17 309 143 males and 17 571 348 females. Thus, the sex ratio was 98.4 males for every 100 females. This indicates the presence of about 1.6 per cent more women than men. All things being equal (in reality they are not), the sex ratio of a population should be close to 100 males per 100 females (i.e., equal proportions of males and females).

Globally, this expectation is confirmed. In 2010, the population comprised 3 478 million males and 3 418 million females, resulting in a sex ratio of 101.7—an almost equal balance. However, if this ratio is derived for smaller units such as regions or countries, it can deviate considerably from 100. Dyson (2012: 444) calculated that sex ratios are well above 100 in East Asia (106.2) and South Asia (105.7); ratios are close to 100 in North Africa (100.5), sub-Saharan Africa (99.9), and Southeast Asia (99.0); but for

Latin America (97.6) and North America (97.5), the ratios indicate slightly more females than males. Even more pronounced is the situation in Western Europe, with a sex ratio of 93.0. The three most "feminine" countries appear to be Ukraine, Estonia, and Latvia, with sex ratios around 85; and the most "masculine," Qatar (311), United Arab Emirates (228), and Bahrain (166).

Why are these ratio not exactly 100? In order to answer this question, we need to distinguish between three types of sex ratios. The *primary sex ratio* is the ratio of males to females at conception; the *secondary sex ratio* is the ratio at birth; and the *tertiary sex ratio* is the ratio at ages beyond infancy.

Sex Ratio at Conception

Obtaining a precise measurement of the human sex ratio of conceptions (primary sex ratio) is not so straightforward. Some estimates are available based on medical studies on the sex ratio of spontaneous abortions. It been suggested that the human sex ratio at conception lies somewhere in the range of 115 to 130 males for every 100 females (Chahnazarian, 1988; Ciocco, 1938; Clarke, 2000, 2003; Hassold, Quillen, and Yamane, 1983; McMillen, 1979; Perls and Fretts, 2002; Teitelbaum, 1972). What accounts for the preponderance of male conceptions remains unclear. Biological/hormonal mechanisms are thought to be involved (James, 1987a, 1987b, 1996, 2004, 2012). The phenomenon may represent an evolutionary human adjustment to males' greater vulnerability as compared to females (Mealey, 2000). Barring interventions such as sex-selective abortion of female fetuses or female infanticide, males are at greater risk of death than females throughout the entire lifecycle (Kramer, 2000). Perhaps, then, as suggested by Ronald Fisher (1890–1962) in *The Genetical Theory of Natural Selection*, the tendency to conceive more males and for the sex ratio at birth to be just nearly balanced in favour of males is a way of compensating for their greater innate vulnerability.

Sex Ratios at Birth and in Early Childhood

In principle, the secondary sex ratio (i.e., at birth) depends on two factors: (1) the sex ratio at conception; and (2) sex-selective loss during pregnancy (James, 2012: 183). We know that across human populations, on average roughly 105 boys are born for every 100 girls, and the normal range is between 103 and 107; in percentage terms, these proportions mean that on average about 49 per cent of all births in a given year will be girls and about 51 per cent will be boys. But as noted, the imbalance at this stage is much smaller than it was at conception. Even though in general more boys are conceived, substantially more male than female fetuses are lost to spontaneous abortion or stillbirth; as a result, the sex ratio at birth is reduced to its average level of about 105 (Clarke, 2000, 2003; Leridon, 1976; McMillen, 1979). This average value of the secondary sex ratio is usually applied in theoretical demography to model population processes. This appears to be a good approximation of reality (see, for example, Table 4.4 and Figure 4.6).

Variations around this average have been observed, and a host of factors presented to explain these variations (see Clarke, 2000; Chahnazarian, 1988; James, 2012; and Teitlebaum, 1972 for reviews). Among the list of factors are birth order, race, maternal and paternal age, age gap between parents, frequency of sexual intercourse, the timing

TABLE 4.4   **Sex ratios at birth and at age 0–4, and percentages of male and female births for selected countries and periods**

Country	Period	Sex ratio at birth	% Male births	% Female births	Sex ratio at age 0–4[1]	Period
Egypt	1998	1.065	0.516	0.484	1.050	1996
Canada	1997	1.055	0.513	0.487	1.052	1998
USA	1991	1.046	0.511	0.489	1.046	1998
China[2]	1996	1.162	0.537	0.463	1.200	1996
Hong Kong	1999	1.087	0.521	0.479	1.068	2000
Japan	1999	1.056	0.514	0.486	1.052	1999
South Korea	1999	1.096	0.523	0.477	1.134	1995
Malaysia	1998	1.071	0.517	0.483	1.061	1991
Pakistan	1997	1.077	0.519	0.481	1.040	1998
Singapore	2000	1.092	0.522	0.478	1.072	2000
Belgium	1992	1.049	0.512	0.488	1.045	1999
Bulgaria	1997	1.081	0.519	0.481	1.054	1997
Denmark	1999	1.048	0.512	0.488	1.055	2000
France	1997	1.055	0.513	0.487	1.048	1998
Germany	1997	1.055	0.513	0.487	1.055	1999
Italy	1995	1.064	0.516	0.484	1.059	1999
Sweden	1999	1.053	0.513	0.487	1.052	1999
United Kingdom	1999	1.056	0.514	0.486	1.052	1999
Australia	1999	1.048	0.512	0.488	1.054	1999
Average of these countries		*1.069*	*0.517*	*0.483*	*1.066*	

[1] Sex ratios for age group 0–4 based on population estimates or actual census counts for this age category.
[2] Sex ratios for infancy and corresponding proportions based on population estimate (rather than vital statistics) for ages 0–1 and 1–4, respectively.

Source: United Nations Department of Economic and Social Affairs Population Division (2002). Reprinted with the permission of the United Nations. From the 2000 Demographic Yearbook, United Nations Department of Economic and Social Affairs Population Division. © 2002 United Nations. Used by permission of the United Nations.

of conception during the menstrual cycle, the season in which conception occurs, and even the effects of war and post-war periods.

However, irrespective of whether these variables are associated with increase or decrease of sex ratio at birth, they cannot explain the proximate causes of variability in the ratio because all these effects must in some way operate through biochemical/biologic pathways. The hypothesis advanced by William James (1987a,

1987b, 1996, 2004, 2012) is that beside sex-differential fetal mortality, the sex ratio at birth is controlled by parental hormone levels at the time of conception. If conception takes place early or late in the menstrual cycle, there is a higher chance of conceiving a boy than if conception occurs in the middle of the cycle. The reason, according to James, is that these points in the menstrual cycle are associated with increased concentration of parental hormones, testosterone

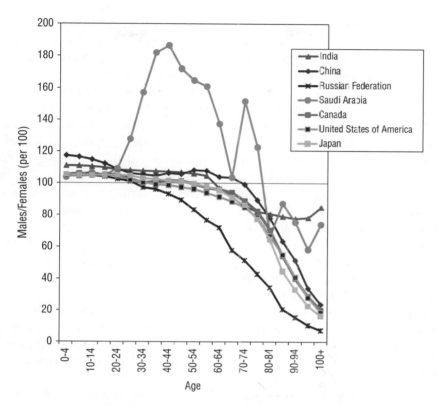

FIGURE 4.6   Age-specific sex ratios for selected countries, 2010

Sources: Author's computation with data obtained from the United Nations Population Division, available at http://esa.un.org/wpp/;
United Nations Department of Economic and Social Affairs Population Division (2013b).

and estrogen. In contrast, in mid-cycle, there is a high concentration of gonadotrophins and progesterone, which raises the probability of conceiving a girl: "high concentrations of testosterone and estrogen increase the probability of a son; and high concentration of gonadotrophins and progesterone increase the probability of a daughter" (James, 2004: 1250).

In line with James's thesis, variations in secondary sex ratio away from near parity must result from exposure to external conditions that somehow affect the proximal hormonal mechanisms at the time of conception, or possibly affect the mother during pregnancy. One factor thought

to play a significant role in this respect is mother's exposed to severe stress during the periconceptional period or early in the pregnancy. This situation has been hypothesized to result in a lower sex ratio at birth (i.e., more baby girls). A number of studies give some support for this interpretation based on highly traumatic events including the September 11 terrorist attacks in New York City (Catalano et al., 2006, 2009, 2010; Fukuda et al., 1998; Hansen, Møller, and Olsen, 1999; Torche and Kleinhaus, 2012). One explanation for these effects on the sex ratio at birth relies on evolutionary biology theory, which posits that in the animal kingdom pregnant females when faced by severe stressors preferentially abort frail male fetuses (Catalano et al., 2012a, 2012b; Catalano, Yorifuji, and Kawachi, 2013; Mealey, 2000; Trivers and Willard, 1973). However, no one has directly proven this biological mechanism in humans.

The fact that sex ratios in some regions of the world—notably parts of South Asia, East Asia, the Middle East, and North Africa and certain areas of the Caucasus region—are highly distorted in favour of boys in early childhood reflects a combination of cultural and social structural factors (e.g., level of economic development, differences in family form, rules of primogeniture and inheritance, rules for the care of the elderly, and marriage customs) that predispose parents to desire sons over daughters (Attané, 2013; Bhat and Halli, 1999; Goody, 1996; Hesketh and Xing, 2006; Lavely, Li, and Li, 2001; Leone, Matthews, and Dalla Zuanna, 2003; Michael et al., 2013; Sen, 2003). Now that screening technologies make it possible to determine sex before birth, some parents will choose to abort a fetus of the "wrong" sex (Banister and Coale, 1994; Coale, 1991; Croll, 2000; Goodkind, 1996; Junhong, 2001; Klasen, 2003; Yount, 2001). Throughout history, however, many human societies have probably practised sex-selective infanticide, neglect, or abandonment under certain circumstances (e.g., conditions of severe food scarcity) (Hrdy, 1999; Johnson, 1996; Scrimshaw, 1978, 1984).

In China especially, son preference and the recent widespread reliance on sex-selective abortion has resulted in a serious shortage of women (Eberstadt, 2011; *The Economist*, 2011b; Tuljapurkar, Li, and Feldman, 1995). This problem is also quite severe in certain parts of India—another country where son preference is especially strong. Worldwide, John Bongaarts (2013: 186) has estimated there are over 1.4 million missing girl births, all determined by son preference and the practice of sex-selective abortion. It appears that "son preference is more widespread than commonly acknowledged," and people want more sons than they are actually having. As fertility rates decline across the developing world and sex-selective technologies become widely accessible, further increases in the sex ratio of birth are likely in countries where son preference is strong.

Sex Ratios in Adulthood and Old Age

Age-specific sex ratios in adulthood are almost entirely determined by gender-based differences in mortality, though migration can also play an important role in some circumstances. In virtually all societies, females have lower age-specific death rates than males, and on average they live longer than men (Lopez and Rucyka, 1983; Perls and Fretts, 2002). On the basis of the sex mortality differential alone, we could expect the ratio of males to females in the population to decline gradually with age. Indeed, in the industrialized countries, the balance in the numbers of males to females begins to approach parity around the age of 30 or 35, but typically the ratio will not fall below 100 until about age 60 or so, at which point it begins to favours females disproportionately. In the advanced ages beyond 80, the ratio drops quite dramatically, in some cases falling to fewer than 25 males for every 100 females.

In Russia, a country with relatively high adult death rates especially among men, the age group in which the number of women in the population begins to exceed the number of men is 30–34, whereas by comparison, in the United States it is 45–49. In India and China, the crossover point has been observed to occur at ages 60–64. The common underlying factor in these two countries is the relatively high mortality among females in the ages below 40, and especially in early childhood (Dyson, 2012: 448). Some Middle Eastern countries, such as Qatar, United Arab Emirates, and Saudi Arabia, exhibit a peculiar age pattern of sex ratios due to the high volume of immigration to these societies of male workers in the labour-force ages (Dyson, 2012). Age misreporting may also be a contributing factor; and this may explain in part, the highly irregular pattern for Saudi Arabia in Figure 4.6.

Societal Ramifications of Change in Age–Sex Composition

Sex Ratio Effects

Severely skewed sex ratios can have a variety of important sociological effects. One illustration is given by Steven Messner and Robert Sampson (1991), who conducted a study of 153 large cities in the United States in order to ascertain how unbalanced sex ratios might affect the incidence of violent crime and family disruption for black and white populations. Their statistical results showed that for both black and white populations a surplus of males between the ages of 15 and 59 was correlated with relatively low levels of family disruption (as measured by the percentage of households headed by a female) and high rates of violent crime (as indexed by robbery and

homicide rates). Not surprisingly, they also found that higher rates of family disruption were strongly correlated with higher rates of violent crime (the higher the percentage of female-headed families, the higher the violent crime rate in cities). By contrast, in cities characterized by low sex ratios (i.e., where there was a deficit of males in relation to women in the ages of 15–59), the level of violent crime was relatively low, but family disruption levels were high. These relationships held after controls for a number of relevant variables had been introduced into the multivariate analysis. Messner and Sampson (1991: 705–7) concluded that their results generally support a "model of countervailing direct positive effects of the sex ratio on rates of criminal violence and negative indirect effects via family disruption." Thus, distorted sex ratios can produce two separate structural problems. First, a high sex ratio (more men than women) generates a large demographic group that is at risk of committing violent offences; second, a low sex ratio (fewer men than women) is associated with reduced commitment to family and marriage by young men and women alike, and therefore higher levels of family instability.

Research based on *The Sex Ratio Question* (Guttentag and Secord, 1983) has shown that in certain contexts an increased risk of divorce can be partly explained by sex ratio imbalances in the prime marriageable ages (Lichter et al., 1992; Messner and Sampson, 1991; South and Lloyd, 1992). One such study, by Scott South and K.M. Lloyd (1992), found that the risk of marital dissolution was highest where either wives or husbands encountered an abundance of spousal alternatives—for instance, in places with high rates of labour-force participation among unmarried women. In other words, areas with a surplus of either gender in the young adult age groups are likely to have higher rates of divorce than areas with a more balanced gender distribution. "In this sense, marital dissolution is, in part, a product of the demographic opportunities embedded in the social structure" (South and Lloyd, 1992: 33).

Imbalanced sex ratios may interact with social structure and culture to cause a *marriage squeeze* affecting either men or women in the prime marriageable ages (Guttentag and Secord, 1983; Schoen, 1983; Veevers, 1994). One such example is the case of China, where state policy has combined with culture to create a severe shortage of marriageable young women. In combination with a strong cultural preference for sons, the one-child policy introduced in the late 1970s has led to the widespread practice of sex-selective termination of female pregnancies. Over time, this situation has created a severe distortion in the balance of the sexes for the male cohorts in the prime marriageable ages of 18 to 34 (Attané, 2013; Tucker and Van Hook, 2013; Tuljapurkar, Li, and Feldman, 1995).

India is faced with a similar situation. Through a series of simulations, Christophe Guilmoto (2012) determined that in both China and India the number of prospective grooms will exceed that of prospective brides by more than 50 per cent for three decades into this century. Under the most favourable of scenario considered, rates of male bachelorhood will not peak before 2050, and the squeeze conditions will be felt several decades thereafter. On the other hand, if the sex ratio at birth is allowed to return to normalcy by 2020, the proportion of men unmarried at age 50 would likely rise to only 15 per cent in China by 2055 and to 10 per cent in India by 2065.

Demographic Aging: Crisis or Opportunity

Among the anticipated effects of population aging are labour-force shortages and increasing pressures on health care and public pension systems (Bongaarts, 2004; Day, 1978, 1992; Kotlikoff and Burns, 2012; Lee, 2007; Mason and Lee, 2011; Teitelbaum and Winter, 1985). Other ramifications of population aging may include changes in popular ideas about what it means to be "old," and possibly even rethinking of intergenerational obligations within families. Increased longevity in general, and among the elderly in particular, means that interaction among children, parents, grandparents, and related family members has the potential to continue over a considerably longer stretch of time than was the case in the past (Day, 1992; Uhlenberg, 1980, 1996; Watkins, Menken, and Bongaarts, 1987). As a consequence, new intergenerational living arrangements may be needed to help young families cope with the increasing costs of looking after aging parents as well as their own growing households. At the same time, as aging societies must increasingly depend on immigration to supplement their dwindling supply of native-born labour, their social fabric is likely to become increasingly multicultural and multiracial (Lutz, Kritzinger, and Skirbekk, 2006).

Being the oldest country in the world, Japan perhaps faces these challenges more imminently. Its total population—127.1 million in 2014—has changed hardly at all in recent years. On an annual basis, the number of births has been declining while the number of deaths has reached unprecedented levels since the end of World War II. In fact, these two trend lines crossed in 2005 and the population started to shrink (*The*

Economist, 2004). Today, Japan has both the highest average age on the planet (44.9 in 2010) and the highest proportion of elderly people, with 23 per cent of its population over the age of 65.

Industrialized countries around the world are looking for ways to reduce the risk of a social security crisis. For countries like Canada and the United States, which experienced large baby booms in the two decades following the end of World War II, the pressure on the public pension system is expected to grow between 2011 and 2036, when the baby boom generation reaches retirement age. In fact, according to Bongaarts (2004), all the G-7 nations (Canada, United States, Britain, Italy, France, Germany, and Japan) will see a

THE GLOBAL WAR AGAINST BABY GIRLS

For 2005 to 2010, the United Nations estimated the world sex ratio at birth as 107 boys to 100 girls. Assuming 105 is natural, this translates into a global "girl deficit" of at least 32 million, according to Nicholas Eberstadt. He writes this is an ominous and entirely new form of gender discrimination: sex-selective feticide, implemented through the practice of surgical abortion with the assistance of information gained through prenatal gender-determination technology. All around the world, the victims of this new practice are overwhelmingly female—in fact, almost universally female. The practice has become so ruthlessly routine in many contemporary societies that it has impacted their very population structures, warping the balance between male and female births and consequently skewing the sex ratios for the rising generation towards a biologically unnatural excess of males. This is sufficiently severe that it has come to alter the overall sex ratio at birth of the entire planet, resulting in millions upon millions of new "missing baby girls"

each year. In terms of its sheer toll in human numbers, sex-selective abortion has assumed a scale tantamount to a global war against baby girls.

Can policy be implemented to solve the war against girls? Sex-selective abortion is illegal in virtually all countries. The situation in two very different settings, China and India, leaves little hope for the effectiveness of policy. China's draconian one-child policy is a sharp contrast to India's voluntary approach to family planning, and yet in both cases there is widespread practice of sex-selective abortion. The solution may lie in the social realm. The experience of South Korea provides hope for positive change. In the 1990s, South Korea's sex ratio at birth had reached a high of 115, but has since fallen to 107. Eberstadt attributes this change to the power of a social movement in South Korean society honouring, protecting, and prizing daughters. Could such a movement evolve in China and India?

Source: Eberstadt (2011).

substantial rise in old-age dependency ratios between 2000 and 2050, with Japan and Italy facing the most severe increases and the United States the least.

As the pensioner-to-worker ratio increases, the average value of public pension benefits declines. The severity of the public pension crisis may be mitigated if governments can persuade older workers to delay retirement; continuing labour-force activity on the part of the elderly would increase the government revenues available to fund the system. First, though, governments will have to ensure not only that jobs are available but that they are sufficiently attractive in terms of salary, hours, and so on. The latter may not be easy, given the options (travel, hobbies, etc.) available to retirees today.

Any solution is also likely to entail reducing the benefits that pensioners will receive. Bongaarts (2004) suggests that even though OECD countries have been trying to reform their public pension systems so as to avert impending difficulties, it is likely that "today's workers will have to save more, work longer, retire later, receive less generous benefits, and perhaps pay more taxes" (21).

Alternative solutions are possible: governments could increase the legal retirement age, or require workers to make larger contributions to the pension plan. But persuading voters to accept these solutions could be difficult. The immigration solution to dealing with labour-force shrinkages is deeply problematic for countries such as Japan, which—unlike Canada, the United States, and Australia—has never seen itself as a country of immigrants.

Concerning health care, in the industrialized countries recent generations of elderly people tend to be healthier than previous generations of seniors and therefore to live longer on the average (Chen and Millar, 2000; Christensen et al., 2009). However, even though most seniors can expect to enjoy relatively good health for some time, a longer life for more people must ultimately mean a rise in serious chronic disabilities in the advanced ages beyond 85 (Manton, 1982; Olshansky and Ault, 1986). Therefore, population aging can be expected to increase the costs of health care in most societies because older age groups tend to need more care (Kinsella and Vlekoff, 2001: 45; Schneider, 1999).

Not all views on these matters are so pessimistic. One emerging perspective maintains that population aging in itself is not the main factor in many of the future "crises" envisioned by some analysts. Proponents of the *anti-apocalyptic demography* perspective (Chappell et al., 2003; Day, 1992; Gee and Gutman, 2000; Zimmer and McDaniel, 2013) assume that demographic aging is inextricably connected to the socioeconomic situation in which it occurs and cannot be understood apart from the broader social context. Thus, they argue, for example, that diseases associated with aging (e.g., Alzheimer's) may be over-diagnosed, and that governments may use the aging paradigm to justify policy changes (e.g., increases in immigration levels or cutbacks to education) that may in fact be made for other reasons. The society creates images and ideas of aging, then scientists and policy makers work towards solving the "problems" of an aging society within the paradigms established by these images. In this way, the aging paradigm takes on a reality of its own, as a self-fulfilling prophecy—a prophecy that comes true not because it was true all along but because people acted as if it were true. Furthermore, when we invoke population aging as the cause of shifting markets, the aged welfare burden, and increased health care costs, we may miss the mark as to the real causes of the problem. For example, politicians may erroneously attribute the depletion of pension funds to population aging, when in fact the pension system itself is poorly designed or badly managed. Similarly, overemphasis on the demographics of aging encourages us to think of the health care burden as an unsolvable problem rather than one that can be managed through the development of appropriate policies.

A balanced perspective between these contrasting paradigms—the demographic crisis and the "anti-apocalyptic"—would incorporate elements of both schools of thought in the assessment and implementation of policies associated with population aging. The demographic crisis perspective hinges on the premise that population projections have a reality of their own. The "anti-apocalyptic" perspective suggests that the demographic weight of seniors on society, though real, is blown out of proportion by governments and certain sectors of academe. Perhaps the truth lies somewhere in between. We can expect an aging population to raise challenges and to put significant demographic pressures on a society, but the severity of its impact will depend on other conditions, such as the nation's economic health and its ability to absorb increasing costs. If the rate of economic growth exceeds the rate of cost increases incurred by population aging, the problems posed by the latter may not be as severe as many have predicted. The costs of providing health care to a growing senior population may be offset to some extent by a decline in the youth dependency ratio resulting from low fertility (Denton and Spencer, 1975).

The Developing Countries: Demographic Windfall versus Poverty Trap

Today, in about half of the countries of the world—concentrated in Africa, Latin America, and South Asia—the working age population is growing faster than other age groups; and these are still relatively young populations. The other half of the world—countries in Europe, North America, and East Asia—has long completed the demographic transition, and the proportion of population in the working ages is either falling or will soon decline, as the share of the elder population grows (Mason and Lee, 2011). For the first set of countries, the age structure is favourable for economic growth. However, as Figure 4.7 suggests, success will depend not only on a favourable conjunction of demographic conditions but also on whether governments will seize the opportunity to capitalize on the *demographic dividend*—in other words, the presence of more workers per dependent and more saving out of income—by assiduously investing in education, training, health care, and capital generation to promote a healthy youthful expanding labour force (Ahlburg, Kelley, and Oppenheim Mason, 1996; Birdsall, Kelly, and Sinding, 2001; Birdsall and Sinding, 2001; Bloom, Canning, and Sevilla, 2003; Cincotta and Engelman, 1997; Mason and Lee, 2011).

Developing economies today, especially those in sub-Saharan Africa, whose populations are growing most rapidly (Eastwood and Lipton, 2011), may learn from the experience of the "Asian Miracle" countries (South Korea, Taiwan, Singapore, Indonesia, Malaysia, and the former Hong Kong Territory), which in the 1990s attained significant economic success because they

AGING POPULATIONS AND GENERATIONAL ACCOUNTING

Societies share an implicit *intergenerational contract* because we all pass through life and experience sequential stages of dependency (childhood), productivity (labour-force years), and again dependency (old age). We all take our turn through these different stages. However, looked at from an aggregate perspective, changes in age composition affect the size of the population giving and receiving assistance. This means that populations will experience different support burdens.

Andrew Mason and Ronald Lee (2011) have developed aggregate measures of consumption and production flows and their net balance for a large number of countries. One such measure is the *support ratio* (SR), the ratio of the effective numbers of producers to the effective numbers of consumers in a society. As explained by these authors, an intuitive interpretation of SR is that "it measures the effect on consumption of changes in population age structure while holding constant other factors—work effort, interest rates, assets, saving, and net transfers from the rest of the world. So, each percentage-point increase in the SR allows a percentage-point increase in consumption at every age, all other things being equal. An increase in the SR is essentially a demographic dividend.

A decrease in the SR leads to a decrease in consumption, all other things being equal" (13).

With the exception of Japan, SR declined in all the countries for at least 15 years between 1950 and 1975. It began to increase at different times and for varying durations, but every economy has experienced or is experiencing a prolonged increase in its SR. The industrialized economies have all peaked—most of them during the 1990s and some, such as the United States and Spain, more recently. Most East and Southeast Asian economies, Japan aside, have just reached their peak or will soon do so. Many Latin American economies will peak within the next 10 or 15 years. India's SR will not peak until 2040; and the Philippines, Nigeria, and Kenya will have rising support ratios through 2050. The two African economies are projected to experience very substantial gains in their support ratios between 2010 and 2050. SR declines will be most precipitous in South Korea, Taiwan, and Japan as well as in Spain, Austria, Germany, and Slovenia. In the United States, SR is projected to decline by 10 per cent (which is quite lower than these other countries but still highly significant).

were able to capitalize on the "demographic bonus." The governments of these countries understood the importance of investing in all the crucial areas for the promotion of economic growth in a context of a rapidly growing youthful labour-force population: education, training, attracting foreign investments, as well as technological innovation

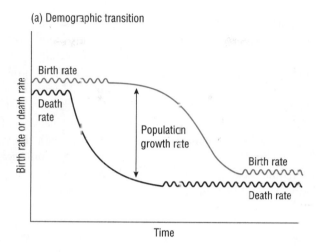

(a) Demographic transition

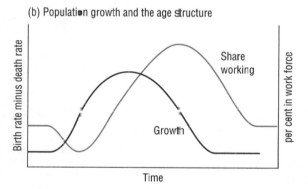

(b) Population growth and the age structure

FIGURE 4.7   Demographic transition stage, population growth rate, and the lagged growth and decline of the working-age population

Source: Bloom and Williamson (1998). Copyright © by The World Bank. Reprinted with permission.

and research in the industrial and manufacturing sectors. All these structural conditions helped to increase prosperity, savings, and consumer spending, which in turn helped boost further economic growth (Bloom and Canning, 2001; Crenshaw, Ameen, and Christenson, 1997; World Bank, 1993).

China's huge economic success recently has been aided by a favourable combination of demographic and structural changes over the past several decades: a large labour force due to high fertility in the past accompanied by declining population growth rates today; significant government success in attracting foreign investment; and economic globalization (Choudhry and Elhorst, 2010). As a result, millions of Chinese have found productive work in the country's growing cites, representing one of the most significant economic phenomena of the past half-century (Gomez and Lamb, 2013; Ogawa and Chen, 2013).

India—the other demographic giant—is positioned to take advantage of the demographic window of opportunity. But there is concern that it may squander its "dividend" because the structural conditions in the country are mostly unfavourable: rampant government corruption run by gerontocrats slow to fully liberalize the economy; generally low confidence among the people in the banking system and some other institutions, especially the police; very high inflation rates; too many bureaucratic hurdles for entrepreneurs to overcome seeking to create businesses and jobs; a plethora of India's young who are ill-prepared even for the most rudimentary of jobs; over-reliance by some large manufacturers on technological rather than human labour power, thus denying many potential jobs to workers. Most disconcerting is the fact that these conditions have created a great deal of disenchantment and discontent with the system among the youth, many of whom leave country to gain employment in China and elsewhere where labour is in demand (*The Economist*, 2013a).

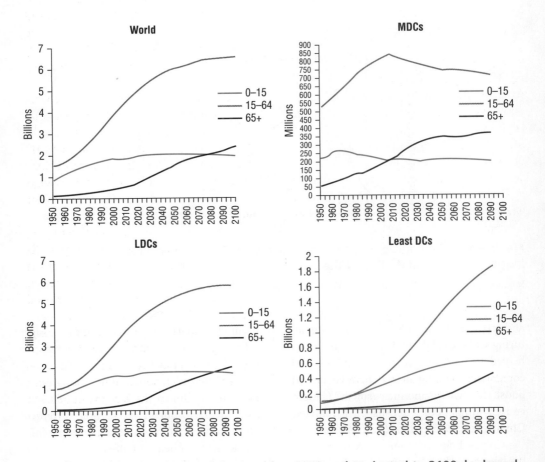

FIGURE 4.8   The population of the world to 2010 and projected to 2100, by broad age groups and development region

Source: Author's computations based on data from United Nations Department of Economic and Social Affairs Population Division (2013b), File POP/15-2: Annual male population by five-year age group, major area, region and country, 1950–2100 (thousands).

The Future: The Population Will Be Older

Over the course of the twenty-first century, the population of the world will continue to age, in some areas more than others. According to Wolfgang Lutz and colleagues (2008), the speed of this process will likely accelerate during the first part of the century, and then around mid-century start to decelerate, accompanied by lower rates of global population growth.

The data from the 2012 UN World Population Prospects revision (medium variant assumptions) confirms this general picture, though the regional outlook is far from uniform (see Figure 4.8). An interesting feature of these projections is the crossover point at which seniors outnumber children. In developed countries, this phenomenon occurred in 2012, which is an unprecedented event in history. In the developing countries, this turning point is not expected to take place until late in the century.

Canada's Age–Sex Composition: Change and Challenges

Populations pass through the demographic transition and experience simultaneously an aging transition, from youth to maturity. Canada has passed through all the stages.

From the late nineteenth century until about the third decade of the twentieth, Canada's age structure reflected the youth of the country. In 1881, the median age was only 20.1 years (McVey and Kalbach, 1995: 60), and this figure rose only gradually over the following decades. Not until the 1950s did the median age rise to just over 27. The fertility surge that followed World War II—caused by a combination of economic prosperity and a host of sociological conditions that together boosted marriage rates among young Canadian men and women—pulled the median age back to 25.4 by 1966. As shown here, it started rising again as fertility rates dropped after the baby boom:

The effect of the large boomer generation born between 1946 and 1966 is clearly visible in the Canadian age pyramids beginning in 1951 (see Figure 4.2 on page 113 and Figure 4.9). With the passage of time, the bulge in the age pyramid that reflects the boomer generation shifts upward as its members grow older.

As we saw in our earlier discussion, a population will eventually "forget" its past. In other words, disturbances in the age pyramid resulting from past increases or decreases in vital events (e.g., increased mortality, fertility deficits, and recoveries associated with war) eventually dissipate as the generations affected by such events die off. But this takes a long time. In Canada's case, the boomer bulge will likely be visible in the age pyramid until 2060 or so, when most of the boomers will have died. Thus, the social demographic

Year	1956	1961	1966	1971	1976	1981	1986	1991	1996	2001	2006	2011
Median	27.2	26.3	25.4	26.2	27.8	29.6	31.6	33.5	35.3	37.6	39.5	39.9

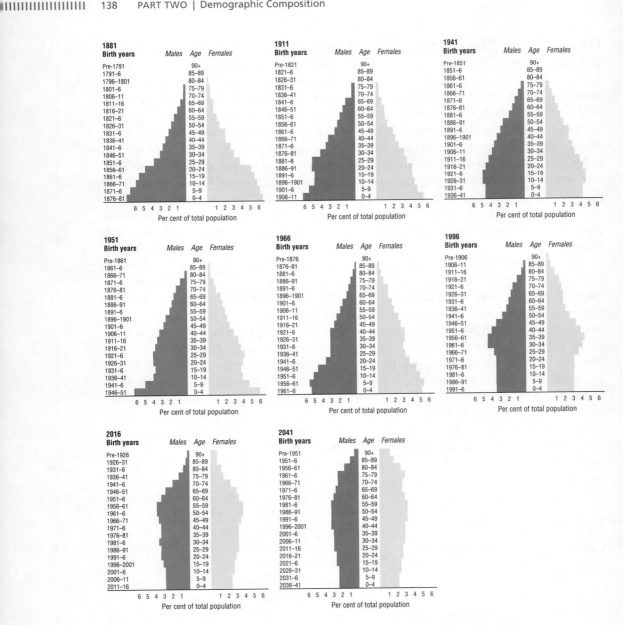

FIGURE 4.9   Age–sex pyramids for the populations of Canada at different points in history and projected to the future

Sources: Adapted from Grindstaff (1981): 134–5 (Figure 6); George et al. (2001): 179, 181 (Table A3); Denton, Feaver, and Spencer (2000): 48–9 (Figure 3.1).

impacts of the boom generation on Canadian society will be felt for decades to come (Foot and Stoffman, 1998; Kettle, 1980; Owram, 1996).

Looked at over time, dependency ratios can help us predict changes in the dependency burden facing the working-age population. Historically, the dependency ratio values indicate that even though our population is aging, until very recently in Canadian history the youth component has represented a greater dependency burden than has the older population.

Wayne McVey and Warren Kalbach (1995: 73) have calculated these three measures for Canada as far back as 1881.

As Figure 4.10 shows, the youth dependency ratio declined from 67.7 per 100 in 1881 to 42.4 in 1941. It increased during the baby boom period, peaking at 57.6 in 1961, and then, as fertility rates fell, declined to 25.7 in 2006, falling further to 23.6 in 2011. The old-age dependency ratio rose gradually for the most part, from 7.2 in the late 1800s to 17.3 in 1991 and 20.0 in 2006. By 2011, its value had reached 20.6. An eventual crossover of the youth and old-age dependency ratios can be expected in the future.

The overall sex ratio in Canada favoured males (Figure 4.11) from 1881 until the early 1970s, when the ratio of

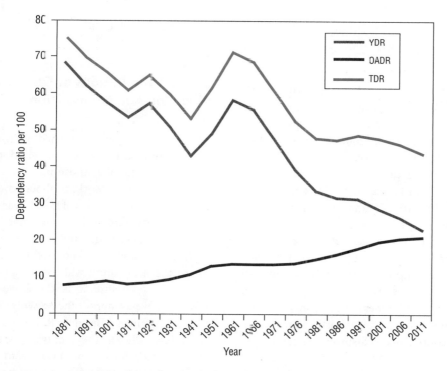

FIGURE 4.10   Youth, old-age, and total dependency ratios for Canada, 1881–2011

Sources: McVey and Kalbach (1995): 73; Statistics Canada (2002a); Statistics Canada (2007b).

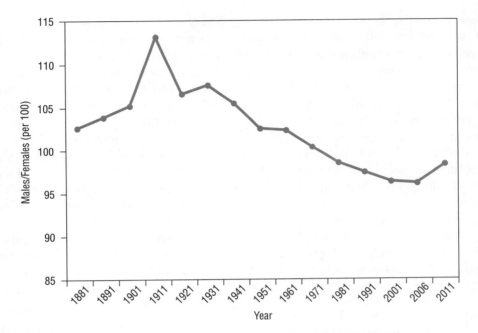

FIGURE 4.11 **Change in overall sex ratios, Canada, 1881–2011**

Sources: McVey and Kalbach (1995), 57; Statistics Canada (2002a); Statistics Canada (2007b).

males to females fell to just about 100; its peak was 112.9, in 1911. Since 1971, the ratio declined from 98.3 in 1981 to 97.2 in 1991 and 95.9 in 2006, but rose slightly in 2011 to 98.4 (Statistics Canada, 2007a). The high sex ratios around the turn of the century can be explained by sex-selective migration to Canada, which was pre-dominantly male. The declines in recent decades may in part reflect the increase in female migration to Canada. However, the more important factor is the survival advantage of women over men. Because of the much higher death rates of males in old age, the sex ratio in the age groups above 65 favours females disproportionately. The recent increase in the sex ratio (though still below 100) reflects, in part, improvements in male mortality.

Societal Implications of Canada's Changing Age Composition

The first of the boomers turned 65 in 2011, and before long those over 65 will, for the first time, outnumber those under 15—the next generation of workers about to enter the labour force. The ratio of 15–24-year-olds to 55–64-year-olds has been declining since 1970 (Statistics Canada, 2007a). The fact that there will be fewer workers paying income tax in the near future will have important implications because it is those workers who will have to support the growing popu-lation of retirees (Beaujot, Ravanera, and McQuillan, 2007). The reality is that the effects of the baby boom on Canadian soci-ety will continue to be felt over the twenty-first century. However, unlike the past, this

POPULATION AGING AND PUBLIC PENSIONS

Frank Denton and Byron Spencer (1999, 2011) have observed that Canadians are living longer and retiring younger from the labour force. Continued gains in life expectancy when not accompanied by an extension of working life result in increasingly large percentage of the human lifespan spent in retirement. Therefore, as the large baby boom generation retires over the next two decades, there will be a sharp increase in the fraction of the population eligible to receive public pension benefits. Based on these observations, Denton and Spencer (2011) modelled the impact of continued future gains in life expectancy on the size of the population that receives public pension benefits and the resulting *support ratios* (i.e., the ratio of labour force to age-eligible for pension population).

In their simulations and projections to the year 2036, they pay special attention to possible increases in the age of eligibility and the pension contribution rate that would maintain the publicly financed component of the retirement income security system. Various scenarios were considered regarding possible change to the age at retirement (AE) in determining the size of the pension-eligible population:

- AE0: age of eligibility remains at 65
- AE1: age of eligibility increases by one month each year from 2011 to 2035

- AE2: age of eligibility increases by one month each year from 2016 to 2035
- AE3: age of eligibility increases by three months each year from 2011 to 2030
- AE4: age of eligibility increases by three months each year from 2016 to 2035
- AE5: age of eligibility increases adjust fully to gains in life expectancy at birth, from 2011

The projections for the year 2035, shown here, are broken down into two separate assumptions about the rate of contribution to the pensions system given the labour-force participation rates of those aged 55 and older: (a) rates constant at 2009 levels (base year); (b) rates changing to reflect adjustments in age at pension entitlements (i.e., adjust rates to reflect increases in age of eligibility; that is, assume a shift of the age pattern of labour-force participation for those aged 55 and older, such that a one-year increase in the age of eligibility results in those aged 56 having participation rates previously associated with those 55, and in those 57 having rates previously associated with those 56, and so forth).

Under the "no change" assumption (AE0), the labour-force population would increase from 18.6 million in 2010 to just over 20 million by 2035, and the support ratio would decline from 3.9 to only 2.0 over this same period. The

(continued)

other scenarios all show varying levels of increase of the labour force, though adjusting the rate of participation to be consistent with the changes in age at eligibility would result in larger labour-force populations as opposed to no change in participation rates. Nonetheless, among the five scenarios, the combination of AE3 and AE4 would seem to produce the most desirable outcomes in the sense that they would derive the largest gains in the size of the labour force and consequently a relatively larger support ratio, from 3.9 in 2010 to 3.0 in 2035 if participation rates are allowed to adjust. The combined scenario is noteworthy in that the support ratio is highest throughout the projection period because of a rapid and early starting increase in the age of eligibility (see the previous assumptions).

Labour-force population (000s)	AE0	AE1	AE2	AE3–4	AE5
1966	7 609	7 609	7 609	7 609	7 609
2010	18 679	18 679	18 679	18 679	18 679
2035 participation rates constant	20 255	20 255	20 255	20 255	20 255
2035 participation rates adjust	20 255	21 339	21 122	22 866	22 129

Ratio, labour-force population/age-eligible population (support ratio)

	AE0	AE1	AE2	AE3–4	AE5
1966	4.9	4.9	4.9	4.9	4.9
2010	3.9	3.9	3.9	3.9	3.9
2035 participation rates constant	2.0	2.3	2.2	2.7	2.4
2035 participation rates adjust	2.0	2.4	2.3	3.0	2.7

Source: Denton, Frank T. and Byron G. Spencer. 2011. "Age of Pension Eligibility, Gains in Life Expectancy, and Social Policy." *Canadian Public Policy* 37 (2): 183-199. Reprinted with permission.

The results of Denton and Spencer (2011) illustrate that modest increases in the age of eligibility for the benefits that are available from public pension plans would moderate the inevitable decline in the size of the labour force relative to the size of the retired population, while making "possible a reduction in the contribution rate (more generally, the rate of taxation, broadly defined) that would be needed to maintain the public component of the retirement income system" (197).

time the impact of this generation on society will be by its retirement patterns and eventually, death (Beaujot, 2012). Chapter 12 will discuss in greater detail some of the policy issues and concerns arising from this demographic reality over the course of the twenty-first century, especially in regard to retirement patterns, pensions, health care, and jobs for younger generations of Canadians following the boomer cohorts.

Conclusion

This chapter has looked at the demographic determinants of age and sex composition, with special attention to the societal ramifications of changes in that composition and the contrasting situations of the developed and the developing countries with regard to the process of demographic transition Population aging is a worldwide phenomenon that has been going on for a long time and will continue as fertility rates continue to fall worldwide. As we proceed through the twenty-first century, among the many challenges facing the industrial societies are the following:

- growing pressures on the public pension system;
- the need for health care reform to take into account the additional needs of a growing elderly population, especially the "old-old" population 85 and older;
- increasing economic demands on a shrinking working-age population;
- rising immigration pressures as the proportion of native-born workers in the prime working ages shrinks; and
- adequate opportunities for the younger generations to have productive work.

As for the developing countries, progression through the demographic and aging transitions should bring substantial economic benefits. Some countries have taken advantage of the "demographic bonus" associated with past changes in fertility, and currently favourable age structures and have prospered economically as a consequence. Unfortunately, some developing countries may find it difficult to break out of the "poverty trap"; others that have the opportunity to take full advantage of a demographic dividend may be squandering their chances and thereby possibly experience sociopolitical unrest due to the large numbers of young adults without adequate work opportunities (Cincotta and Doces, 2012; Urdal, 2012).

Notes for Further Study

There are various indices for studying age composition beside those noted in this chapter (see for example, Lee and Mason, 2011; Lutz et al., 2008; Sanderson and Scherbov, 2010). Below are five other basic measures:

$$\% \ elderly = \frac{Population \ 65+}{Total \ population} \times 100$$

$$\% \ youth = \frac{Population < 15}{Total \ population} \times 100$$

$$aging \ index = \frac{Population \ 65+}{Population < 15} \times 100$$

$$\begin{array}{l} caretaker \\ ratio \end{array} = \frac{Population \ \ 80+}{\begin{array}{c} Female \\ population \ 50-64 \end{array}} \times 100$$

$$support \ ratio = \frac{Population \ 15-64}{Population \ 65+} \times 100$$

In notational form, the median age (M_d) of population is:

$$M_d = l_{Md} + \frac{\frac{P}{2} - \sum P_x}{P_{Md}} \ i$$

where l_{Md} = the lower limit of the age group containing the median;

P = total population;

ΣP_x = the population in all age groups preceding the age group containing the median;

P_{Md} = population in the age group containing the median; and

i = the width of the age interval containing the median.

To construct a population pyramid with Excel (2007 version), follow the following steps:

1. Compute male and female % columns.
2. Place negative (−) sign next to female %s (this is necessary for Excel to work).
3. Highlight %male and %female columns.
4. Go to INSERT; click on "Bar Graph."
5. Point to pyramid bars and right-click mouse.
6. Select "Format Data Series" for Series Options.

7. Set "Series Overlap" at 100%; "Gap Width" at 0%.
8. Point to blank space on graph and right-click mouse; click "Select Data".
9. Click "Edit" on Horizontal (Category) Axis; then click on "Select Range"; select data (age group); click OK.
10. Go to "Layout" in Chart Tools; Click on "Chart Title"; select chart title "Above Chart Option"; give a title.
11. Now go to "Axis Titles" in Layout; first go through "Primary Horizontal Axis Title"; then click on "Title Below Axis"; write title (%).
12. Again go to "Axis Titles" in Layout; now go to "Primary Vertical Axis Title"; then click on "Rotated Title"; write title (age).
13. Go to "Gridlines" in Layout; click on "Primary Vertical Gridlines"; select "None."
14. To change colour, if desired, go to FORMAT in chart tools and click on "Shape Fill"; Choose your desired colour.

Exercises

1. Visit the World Population Prospects page at the United Nations Population Division website[2] and choose two countries. Compute the corresponding age–sex pyramids for two points in time: 1970 and the most recent year available. Use a spreadsheet program such as Microsoft Excel to plot the four age–sex pyramids for the two countries at two points in time (see previous instructions).
2. Use the information provided by the UN website to conduct a comparative analysis of the two countries with respect to the following demographic measures:

   a) the median age of population
   b) the youth dependency ratio
   c) the old-age dependency ratio
   d) the overall dependency ratio

e) the support ratio
f) the sex ratio
g) the annual exponential growth rate of population between the two periods corresponding to your computed age–sex pyramids

3. Analyze the results based on of the computations in Questions 1 and 2. Describe how your chosen populations have changed demographically between the two points of observation.

Additional Reading

Attané, Isabelle, and Christophe Z. Guilmoto, eds. 2007. *Watering Thy Neighbour's Garden: The Growing Demographic Female Deficit in Asia*. Paris: Committee for International Cooperation in National Research in Demography.

Brian, Éric, and Marie Jasson. 2007. *The Descent of Human Sex Ratio at Birth: A Dialogue between Mathematics, Biology and Sociology*. Dordrecht: Springer.

Clark, Robert L., Naohiro Ogawa, and Andrew Mason, eds. 2006. *Population Aging, Intergenerational Transfers and the Macroeconomy*. Cheltenham, UK: Elgar.

Hardy, Ian C.W., ed. 2002. *Sex Ratios: Concepts and Research Methods*. Cambridge: Cambridge University Press.

Hvistendhal, Mara. 2011. *Unnatural Selection: Choosing Boys over Girls*. Jackson, TN: Public Affairs.

Kotlikoff, Laurence J., and Scott Burns. 2012. *The Clash of Generations: Savings Ourselves, Our Kids and Our Economy*. Cambridge: MIT Press.

Laslett, Peter. 1996. *A Fresh Map of Life: The Emergence of the Third Age*, 2nd edn. Houndsmills and London: Macmillan.

Low, Bobbi S. 2000. *Why Sex Matters*. Princeton: Princeton University Press.

Potts, Malcolm, and Thomas Hayden. 2008. *Sex and War: How Biology Explains Warfare and Terrorism and Offers a Path to a Safer World*. Dallas, TX: Ben Bella Books.

Uhlenberg, Peter, ed. 2009. *International Handbook of Population Aging*. Dordrecht: Springer.

Notes

1. In some calculations, the youth dependent population is considered to be 0–19.
2. Go to http://esa.un.org/unpd/wpp/index.htm and click on "Population" under the "Data" options. Then select "population by five-year age group" for males and females, separately. By clicking on these icons, you can download the Excel spreadsheets containing the age-specific population counts for males and females, respectively, for the countries of the world.

5 Nuptiality

Introduction

Strictly speaking, "nuptiality" refers to the frequency or incidence of marriage in a population. The social demographic study of nuptiality, however, encompasses all aspects of family formation and dissolution, including divorce, widowhood, and remarriage, as well as alternatives to traditional marriage, such as common-law cohabitation and same-sex marriage, and even singlehood. These nuptiality processes are of crucial importance to the sociological study of population change because of their close connection to the family as a social institution. Changes in nuptiality patterns reflect fundamental changes in society, and in this sense they serve as a barometer of social change. To the extent that marriage rates increase or decline, they do so in response to structural (e.g., economic) and ideational (values) changes in society. And the degree to which couples dissolve their unions—be it marriage or some other form of conjugal relationship—will in turn affect reproductive levels in society. A clear understanding of nuptiality dynamics therefore allows for a better understanding of demographic processes, most notably fertility—although as we shall see in subsequent chapters, nuptiality and family processes are also linked to migration, health, and mortality.

Nuptiality in Social Demographic Analysis

As a demographic factor, nuptiality does not directly affect population numbers in the way that mortality, fertility, and migration do. Yet marriage and its equivalents are highly relevant to these demographic processes. For instance, in the case of fertility, even though *cohabitation* without marriage (also known as common-law or consensual union) has become common in the industrialized countries, many children (if not the majority) are born to married couples. However, there are important cross-national variations: while 45 to 65 per cent of all births in Denmark, Norway, Sweden, and Iceland take place within non-marital unions, in Japan, Greece, and Italy this is true in only 1 to 9 per cent of cases (Wolfe, 2003).

Whether birth rates rise or fall is in many ways determined by the average age at which women marry or enter a similarly socially accepted form of conjugal relationship, whatever the society (Davis and Blake, 1956). Thus, demographic analysis has focused mainly on marriage and other forms of conjugal unions with particular emphasis on the timing of first marriage or similar unions, since subsequent unions (e.g., remarriage) have much less impact on fertility from a societal perspective (Pressat,

1985: 165). A case can be made that marriage is also a factor in mortality and health (see, for example, Gove, 1973) as well as migration (see, for example, Bielby and Bielby, 1992).

Since demographic phenomena mirror sociological processes, trends in family formation and dissolution can serve as indicators of socioeconomic conditions in society. Historically, marriage rates have risen during periods of prosperity and fallen in periods of economic decline (Kirk, 1960). There is additional evidence that during times of war or other major social disruption, couples tend to postpone marriage (Easterlin, 1969; Ermisch, 1981). Finally, it can be argued that to a significant extent nuptiality trends reflect a society's orientation towards the institutions of marriage and family (Cherlin, 2003, 2004; Westoff, 1978). In the Western world, marriage rates have been falling and cohabitation is on the rise. Do these divergent trends not reflect that something fundamental has changed about how people think about marriage and more broadly the family as an institution? We find a range of views on this question. Many have welcomed the shift away from traditional marriage as it allows greater personal freedoms and flexibility, especially for women because they can now combine family and career much more readily than they could in earlier times (Heuveline and Timberlake, 2004; Lapierre-Adamcyk and Charvet, 2000). Others, however, fear that these changes may be detrimental, especially to children growing up in non-traditional family structures (Blankenhorn, 2007; Cherlin, 2003).

Nuptiality as a Demographic Process

Nuptiality can be understood as the demographic process in which individuals move between various marital states (Cherlin, 1981). Figure 5.1 illustrates the relationships between marital statuses and possible transitions between them. From birth to young adulthood, people are in the *never married* state (i.e., single). Then, at some point, most young adults will enter formal marriage or some other socially recognized equivalent such as cohabitation, and the first such union can be either *first marriage* or *first cohabitation*. Eventually, every union will come to an end, whether through separation, divorce, or the death of one partner (i.e., widowhood). Clearly, as Figure 5.1 shows, there are a number of possible transitions—back and forth—between the various conjugal states. The chance that any one of these events will occur depends on many factors, including age, gender, education, income, and the duration of the union. In the event of divorce, either or both parties may re-enter the married state (i.e., remarry); those who are widowed may also remarry.

Note that because of the possibility of transitions between states in both directions (back and forth) it is also possible to conceive of broader marital status categories beyond those shown in Figure 5.1. For instance, the *married* state would contain those who are married for the first time and those who have remarried. In this case, demographers would speak of such individuals as being in the *currently married* state. Similarly, the *non-married* category would include those who have never married as well as those who have been divorced or widowed. *Formerly married* would cover both divorced and widowed people, while *ever married* would include the currently married, plus the divorced and widowed. Finally, the term *marital dissolution* is often used to describe the breakup of families due to separation, divorce, or death of a spouse/partner.

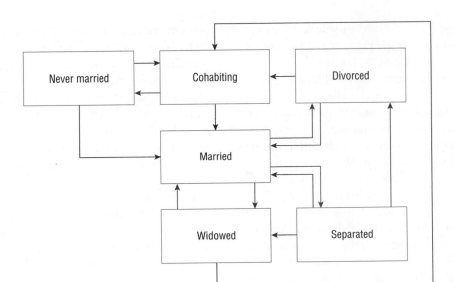

FIGURE 5.1   Schematic structure of marital states and transitions

Source: Hinde (1998): 258. From *Demographic Methods*, Andrew Hinde, Copyright © 1998 Edward Arnold, reproduced by permission of Taylor & Francis Books UK.

Measures of Nuptiality

A fundamental measure of nuptiality for a given population is the *crude marriage rate*:

$$\text{crude marriage rate} = \frac{M}{P} \times 1\,000$$

where M represents the total number of marriages (including both first marriages and remarriages) that take place in a given interval (usually one year; and this is assumed in the presentation below), and P is the mid-interval population (i.e., at mid-year).

Similarly, the *crude divorce rate* is defined as

$$\text{crude divorce rate} = \frac{D}{P} \times 1\,000$$

where D stands for the number of divorces, and P is the population.

To illustrate, Table 5.1 shows crude marriage and divorce rates for Canada in 2008, as well as the total numbers of marriages and divorces that year, and the mid-year population used in the computation of rates.

Even though they are used widely in the literature, these two measures are not completely satisfactory. The main problem is that the denominator (P) in each case includes some people who by definition do not belong to the relevant risk set: that is, persons under the age of 15 (too young to marry) and, in the case of divorce, people who have never been married in the first place, as well as those who have been widowed. Sometimes, if the appropriate data are available, it is possible to refine the denominator first by narrowing the risk set to the mid-year population aged 15 years of age and older and then by specifying

TABLE 5.1	Marriages, divorces, and corresponding crude rates, Canada, 2008			
Mid-year population	Marriages	Divorces	Crude marriage rate per 1 000 population	Crude divorce rate per 1 000 population
33 317 662	147 288	70 226	4.421	2.108

Source: Author's computations with data from Statistics Canada CANSIM database, Tables 101-6501 and 101-1004; and population data from Statistics Canada (2013f).

the sex of that population (typically the denominator consists of females 15 and over). Thus, the *general marriage rate* and the *general divorce rate* can be expressed as follows:

$$\text{general marriage rate} = \frac{M}{P^f_{15+}} \times 1\,000$$

$$\text{general divorce rate} = \frac{D}{P^f_{15+}} \times 1\,000$$

where $P^f_{15}+$ is the number of females aged 15 and older at mid-year.

These two general rates are usually expressed "per 1000" population and give a more meaningful indication of the extent of marriage or divorce in the adult population over a specified time interval, usually one year. Table 5.2 displays these rates for Canada in 2008.

Further refinements can be achieved by including in the denominator the female population at mid-year that is married (for the divorce rate) or single, widowed, or divorced (for the marriage rate). The *refined marriage rate* and

TABLE 5.2	Marriages, divorces, and corresponding general rates by sex and overall, Canada, 2008				
Sex	Mid-year population 15+	Marriages	Divorces	General marriage rate per 1 000 population	General divorce rate per 1 000 population
Male	13 639 958	147 288	70 226	10.798	5.149
Female	14 066 766	147 288	70 226	10.471	4.992
Overall	27 706 724	147 288	70 226	5.316	2.535

Source: Author's computations with data from Statistics Canada CANSIM database, Table 101-6501 and 101-1004; and population data from Statistics Canada (2013f).

refined divorce rate would be determined as follows:

$$\text{refined marriage rate} = \frac{M}{P_{s,d,w}^{f}} \times 1\,000$$

$$\text{refined divorce rate} = \frac{D}{P_{mar}^{f}} \times 1\,000$$

where $P_{s,d,w}^{f}$ is the single, divorced, and widowed female population at mid-year, and P_{mar}^{f} is the married female population at mid-year.

Although these more precise measures are obviously preferable to the less refined ones, the information required to compute them may not be readily available. Table 5.3 shows the refined marriage and divorce rates for Canada in 2008.

First-Marriage Rate

Order-specific marriage rates are of particular interest for demographic analysis because, in general, first marriages are more strongly correlated with the birth rate than are second or higher-order marriages (Faust, 2004). The *first-marriage rate* is defined as the number of first marriages divided by the mid-year never-married (single) population:

$$\text{first - marriage rate} = \frac{M_1}{P_{15+_{nm}}} \times 1\,000$$

where M_1 is marriages of order 1 (i.e., first marriages), and P_{15+nm} is the mid-year never-married population aged 15 and older.

Second-order marriage rates can be computed in the same way, by making the numerator the number of second marriages, and the denominator the population aged 15 and older that is widowed or divorced. Table 5.4 shows the first-marriage rates for men and women and for Canada overall in 2007. The first-marriage rate for single men in 2007 was 22.91 per 1 000 population aged 15 years or older, and for single women it

---

TABLE 5.3	Marriages, divorces, and corresponding refined rates by sex and overall, Canada, 2008				
Denominator	**Mid-year population 15+**	**Marriages**	**Divorces**	**Refined marriage rate per 1 000 population**	**Refined divorce rate per 1 000 population**
Males (S+W+D)	7 123 269	147 288	70 226	20.677	
Males (Mar)	6 516 689	147 288	70 226		10.776
Females (S+W+D)	7 598 271	147 288	70 226	19.384	
Females (Mar)	6 468 495	147 288	70 226		10.857
Overall (S+W+D)	14 721 540	147 288	70 226	10.005	
Overall (Mar)	12 985 184	147 288	70 226		5.408

Note: S = single; W = widowed; D = divorced; Mar = married.

Source: Author's computations with data from Statistics Canada CANSIM database, Tables 101-6501 and 101-1004; and population data from Statistics Canada (2013f).

TABLE 5.4 First marriages and corresponding first-marriage rates for males and females, Canada, 2007

Sex	Mid-year single population 15+	Number of men and women who married for the first time	First-marriage rate per 1 000
Males	4 819 894	11 404	22.91
Females	4 047 526	11 311	27.50
Overall	8 867 420	22 715	25.00

Note: Single population includes single never-married plus single living in common-law (legal marital status definition). The number of first-time marriages in 2007 to men and women were estimated by applying the age-specific first-marriage rates for males and females to the corresponding age-sex-specific single never-married populations in 2007.

Source: Author's computations with data from Statistics Canada CANSIM database (Tables 01-1007 and 101-1008); population counts from Statistics Canada (2013g).

was 27.50 per 1000. Obviously, the number of single men getting married was not identical to the number of single women entering marriage for the first time. If we combine the men and the women marrying for the first time, the rate turns out to be 25.00 per 1000.

Additional measures of marriage and divorce incidence are possible. We shall outline four important ones here: the *age-specific marriage rate*, the *age-specific divorce rate*, the *total marriage rate*, and the *total divorce rate*.

Age-Specific Marriage and Divorce Rates

As in the cases of mortality and fertility, the age composition of a population can affect the incidence of marriage and divorce within it. Computing age-specific rates makes it possible to focus on trends within each specific age category while controlling for the size of the population in each age group. Age-specific rates in general can be computed for either single years of age

categories or five-year age groups. The general form of the *age-specific marriage rate* for a given age x, can be expressed as

$$\text{marriage rate for age group } x = \frac{M_x}{Px_{nm}} \times 1\,000$$

where x can signify either single years of age or grouped age categories, M_x is the number of marriages to those in the age category x occurring in a given year, and Px_{nm} is the number of never-married persons aged x at mid-year.

This measure can be computed for males and females separately by altering the numerator and denominator accordingly. Analogous age-specific rates can be computed for divorce—that is to say, *age-specific divorce rates*:

$$\text{divorce rate for age group } x = \frac{D_x}{Px_m} \times 1\,000$$

where, D_x is the number of divorces in a given year to persons in age category x, and Px_m is the number of married persons aged x at mid-year.

This measure as well can be computed for males and females separately by altering the numerator and denominator accordingly.

Figure 5.2 shows age-specific marriage (for 2007) and divorce rates (for 2008) for males and females in Canada. Each set of rates follows a distinct pattern. Although marriage rates are higher for females than males at ages 15–19, in both cases the rates are exceptionally low. They rise sharply thereafter, however, peaking in the 25–29 age category for females and 30–34 for males. Beyond these points they fall off precipitously, although in the case of males, there is a slight incline in ages beyond 50, which is not noticeable for females. As for divorce, the rates increase for both males and females from age 15 to about age 40. Thereafter, they drop sharply, with the male rates being slight higher at ages beyond 44.

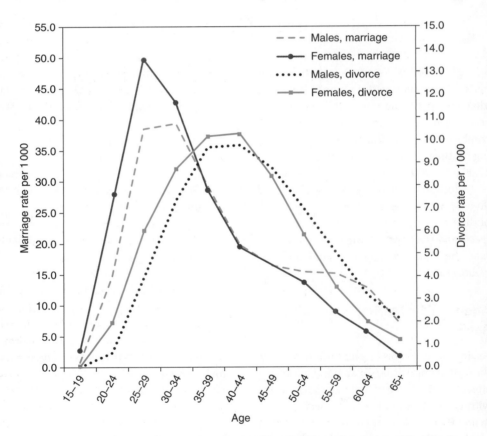

FIGURE 5.2   Age-specific marriage rates (for 2007) and age-specific divorce rates (for 2008) for men and women, Canada

Sources: Author's computations with data from Statistics Canada CANSIM database (Tables 101-1007; 101-1008; 101-6507); and age-specific population counts from Statistics Canada Demography Division (2012): 48; and Statistics Canada (2013g).

Total Marriage Rate

The age-specific marriage rates in a given period can be summed to obtain a total marriage rate (TMR) for the period. Typically, this measure is computed for the age range of 15 to 50, which are the prime marriageable ages. Conceptually, this is a synthetic measure, as it speaks to a hypothetical type of situation based on period specific information. It can be interpreted as the number of marriages that would occur on average to a hypothetical cohort as it passes through life from age 15 to 50. This measure can be computed for males or females separately (the chance of marriage is different for the sexes: men tend to marry at an older age than do females). For illustrative purposes, let us focus on the female rate. The symbol TMR^f signifies the total marriage rate for females.

$$TMR^f = \sum_{x=15}^{\omega} \frac{M_x^f}{P_x^f} \times 1\,000$$

(multiply by 5 if age is in 5-year age categories)

where M_x^f is the number of marriages in a given year to females aged x, and P_x^f is the female population at age x at midyear. (The Greek letter Σ, "sigma," is the symbol for summation—in this case, summation of all the age-specific rates beginning with age 15 to the last age category, denoted by the Greek symbol ω, omega, which in this case is age 50.)

Once computed, the interpretation of TMR^f is as follows: if a hypothetical cohort of 1 000 women aged 15 at time t were followed though life to age 50 and they experienced the prevailing age-specific marriage rates at time t, they would end up having the marriage rate computed with the formula. Since this formula is based on age-specific rates, it gives a sense of what the marriage rate is in the prime marriageable ages at a given point in time. Looked at over time, it gives additional information on the trends, whether increasing or declining. Although it is hypothetical, it provides an indication of what the future marriage rate might be *if* the current age-specific rates in this age range continued indefinitely. It is also possible to compute the same measure for first marriages—that is to say, the *total first-marriage rate* (see Table 5.5).

The total divorce rate can be computed in a similar way. In this case, age-specific divorce rates in the population for a given year t are calculated first, and then these rates are summed to obtain the total divorce rate. The *total divorce rate* for females (TDR^f) is

$$TDR^f = \sum_{x=15}^{\omega} \frac{D_x^f}{P_x^f} \times 1\,000$$

(multiply by 5 if age is in 5-year age categories)

where D_x^f is the number of divorces in a given year to women aged x, and P_x^f is the mid-year population of women aged x. (In this formula, ω can be greater than age 50.)

The total divorce rate parallels the total marriage rate in two ways. First, it is a period measure of the average number of divorces per 1 000 females aged 15 and older in the population at time t. Second, it can be interpreted as the divorce rate that would be obtained in a hypothetical cohort of women who married at age 15 and throughout their lives were exposed to the age-specific divorce rates prevailing in the population at time t. Table 5.5 displays computed total first-marriage rate

TABLE 5.5   Age-specific male and female first-marriage rates (2007) and divorce rates (2008) in Canada (rates per 1000 population)

Age	Marriage		Divorce	
	Males	**Females**	**Males**	**Females**
15–19	0.8	2.6	0.01	0.02
20–24	14.1	23.6	0.65	1.96
25–29	31.1	35.9	3.99	6.01
30–34	23.0	19.4	7.35	8.72
35–39	11.3	8.0	9.70	10.17
40–44	5.1	3.6	9.78	10.29
45–49	2.6	1.9	8.78	8.37
50–54			6.98	5.82
55–59			5.04	3.50
60–64			3.14	1.96
65+			2.10	1.18
Sum of rates	88.0	94.1	57.5	58.0
TFMR$_{15-49}$ (= sum of rates × 5)	439.8	470.7		
TDR$_{15-65+}$ (= sum of rates × 5)			287.6	290.0

Source: Author's computations with data from Statistics Canada CANSIM database (Tables 101-1011; 101-1012; 101-6507); and age-specific population counts from Statistics Canada Demography Division (2012: 48); and Statistics Canada (2013g).

(for 2007) and the total divorce rate (for 2008) for men and women in Canada.

When looked at over time, the different measures described should all point to similar trends. The actual values of the indices will vary, but their overall direction should be consistent (McVey and Kalbach, 1995).

Nuptiality Trends: Cross-national Overview

Crude Marriage Rates

Figure 5.3 shows crude marriage rates for 33 countries between 1970 and 2010. The most immediate impression is that over this period there has been a generalized decline in marriage. This is clearly evident for Western European countries, including the United Kingdom; southern European societies; and the Western offshoot countries of Canada, the USA, Australia, and New Zealand. The United States stands out among the latter group for its notably higher marriage rates, even though its trend is unmistakably downward. Marriage rates among the five Nordic European countries of Denmark, Finland, Iceland, Norway, and Sweden have fallen sharply over time but have risen slightly since about the mid-1980s. By 2010, however, these countries had nearly converged around a rate of about five or six marriages per 1000 population. Among the Eastern European countries, Russia and Poland have seen recent upturns in marriage, though both rates remain substantially below the levels witnessed in the early 1970s. Although following an irregular pattern, Japan and South Korea have seen definite declines in marriage rates since the early 1970s. The two middle-income economies—Mexico and Turkey—show a similar pattern of change until about the year 2000, at which point the two rates diverged, with Mexico continuing its downward trend and Turkey showing some increases.

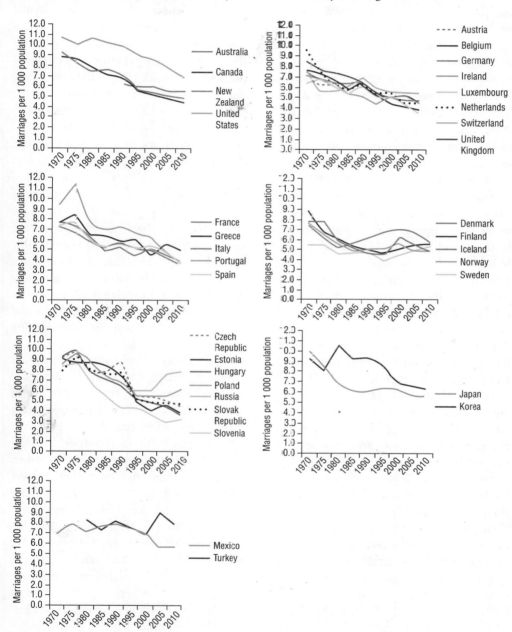

FIGURE 5.3   Crude marriage rates for selected countries, 1970 to 2010

Sources: Organisation for Economic Co-operation and Development (OECD) (2009): Ch. 4, G 4.2; United Nations, *UN Demographic Yearbook* (various years).

First-Marriage Rates

Crude marriage rates do not consider the fact that some marriages may be of second or higher order (remarriages). For this reason it is desirable to examine the first-marriage rate. Table 5.6 shows first-marriage rates per 1000 females across a number of industrialized countries between 1960 and 2010. Although there is limited data beyond 2000, one can evince the general trend in the rates. Across countries, with a few exceptions, marriage rates have been falling from the highs recorded in 1960 and 1970. In fact, the 1960 and 1970 rates in some cases exceeded 1000, because of high volumes of marriages combined with a decline in the age at marriage. This combination of demographic conditions can produce a total marriage rate greater than 1000. The trend towards declining marriage rates across countries did not occur uniformly, of course. The first signs of decline in northern and Western Europe appeared after 1965–70; in southern Europe after 1975; and in Eastern Europe after 1990 (United Nations Department of Economic and Social Affairs Population Division, 2003). The decline was quite abrupt in Western Europe, where the rate fell from around 900 per 1000 females to only about 600 in a matter of 20 to 25 years. The fall was particularly steep in southern Europe (Greece, Italy, Portugal, and Spain), where it started about a decade later. In Eastern Europe, the decline between 1960 and 1980 was slight, but it increased considerably by 2000; today total first-marriage rates in this region tend to be somewhat lower than anywhere else in Europe (though as noted earlier, some countries in this region have seen a slight upturn in marriage recently, e.g., Czech Republic).

Some of the decline in total first-marriage rates can be attributed to the tendency to postpone marriage until later in life, and some to the rejection of formal marriage; unfortunately, it is not possible to separate these two explanations. Whatever the cause, the same pattern can be observed not only in Europe (Eastern and Western) but also in Japan, South Korea, and the United States, as well as in countries such as Mexico and Turkey to a lesser extent.

While statistics on total first-marriage rates for years past 2000 are limited, it is possible to gain a wider sense of nuptiality trends by examining the proportions of women aged 20–24 and 25–29 who have never married. The larger the percentage of singles in these two prime marriageable ages, the lower the incidence of marriage. The information in Table 5.7 is generally consistent with an earlier United Nations report published in 2003 (*Partnership and Reproductive Behaviour in Low-Fertility Countries* [United Nations Department of Economic and Social Affairs Population Division, 2003]), which documented significant increases in the proportions of single women in the two age groups across most countries between the early 1970s and 2000 in industrialized countries. The figures indicate that the proportion of women in the countries with established market economies who had not married by the age of 30 increased from roughly one-quarter in 1975 to more than half in 2000. In some societies where cohabitation is still relatively rare (e.g., southern Europe and East Asia), the postponement of marriage became "really extreme, pushing age at marriage beyond prime reproductive ages" (34). Eastern Europe has also seen increases in the proportions of single women between the ages of 24 and 29, especially since 1990,

| TABLE 5.6 | Total first-marriage rates per 1 000 females by country, 1960, 1980, 2000, and 2010 |

|||||||||||||||||||||||||||||||||||||||||||||||||||||||||||||||||||||||||||||||||||||||||||||||||||||||||||||||||||||

	Period				% change		
Country	1960	1980	2000	2010	1960–80	1980–2000	2000–10
Austria	1 030	675	538	—	−34.5	−20.3	
Belgium	983	772	518	—	−21.5	−32.9	
Denmark	1 010	534	727	664	−47.1	36.1	−8.7
Finland	960	672	621	—	−30.0	−7.6	
France	1 030	707	624	—	−31.4	−11.7	
Germany	1 060	693	582	—	−34.6	−16.0	
Iceland	—	552	698	—		26.4	
Ireland	1 075	839	—	—	−22.0		
Luxembourg	—	661	551	378		−16.6	−31.4
Netherlands	1 050	676	594	550	−35.6	−12.1	−7.4
Norway	1 040	651	—	—	−37.4		
Sweden	950	525	528	—	−44.7	0.6	
Switzerland	960	662	641	642	−31.0	−3.2	0.2
United Kingdom	1 040	761	—	—	−26.8		
Greece	790	867	521	—	9.7	−39.9	
Italy	980	779	—	—	−20.5		
Portugal	940	889	725	—	−5.4	−18.4	
Spain	1 056	763	612	489	−27.7	−19.8	−20.1
Bulgaria	1 050	970	516	—	−7.6	−46.8	
Czech Rep.	1 040	899	497	616	−13.6	−44.7	23.9
Hungary	1 000	894	491	—	−10.6	−45.1	
Poland	908	903	628	—	−0.06	−30.5	
Romania	1 140	1 016	638	—	−10.9	−37.2	
Slovakia	1 010	874	518	—	−13.5	−40.7	
Russia	1 180	959	—	—	−18.7		
Estonia	1 040	940	639	380	−9.6	−32.0	−40.5
Canada	915	685	546	470.7	−25.1	−20.3	−13.8
United States	—	808	—				
Australia	—	696	—				
New Zealand	1 019	724	—		−28.9		

Note: "—" denotes data not available. For the following countries the rate listed in 1960 is actually for 1970 (no prior information): Belgium, Ireland, Poland, Estonia, and New Zealand.

Sources: Institut national d'études démographiques (2013); Sardon (2002): 111–56, (2006): 248–9; Statistics Canada Health Statistics Division (2003): 24; United Nations Department of Economic and Social Affairs Population Division (2003): 3 ; Wadhera and Strachan (1992): 30.

though to a lesser extent. Nevertheless, the average proportion of never-married women in the 25–29 age group is more than 30 percentage points lower in Eastern Europe than in the West. This means that women in Eastern Europe have tended to marry in large numbers before reaching age 30. Indeed, for the countries that made up the former USSR, nuptiality levels were relatively high and stable until very recently.

TABLE 5.7   Percent single females aged 20–24 and 25–29; selected countries, early 1970s and around 2010

Country	Period	Age 20–24	Age 25–29
Australia	1971	35.8	11.6
	2006	89.6	60.3
Canada	1971	43.5	15.4
	2006	75.6	42.0
Czech Rep.	1970	32.4	9.3
	2011	93.0	65.7
France	1970	46.1	16.5
	2009	92.9	70.8
Germany	1990	74.3	36.6
	2011	92.9	70.9
Hungary	1970	32.3	10.4
	2010	93.4	69.6
Italy	1971	56.5	23.2
	2010	91.2	68.3
Japan	1970	71.7	18.1
	2010	89.6	60.3
Mexico	1970	38.5	17.4
	2010	50.4	28.1
Rep. Korea	1970	57.2	9.7
	2005	93.7	59.1
Russia	1979	36.0	12.0
	2010	57.2	26.3
Sweden	1970	60.0	23.0
	2010	92.3	75.2
Turkey	1970	13.0	13.0
	2008	54.4	22.7
UK	1971	40.3	13.9
	2009	93.3	71.9
USA	1970	88.1	36.3
	2009	97.2	77.4

Source: United Nations Department of Economic and Social Affairs Population Division (2013c). From *World Marriage Data 2012*, United Nations Department of Economic and Social Affairs Population Division. © 2013 United Nations. Used by permission of the United Nations.

Divorce and Cohabitation

Divorce

It has been estimated that between one-third and one-half of all first marriages in the United States, Australia, Canada, and most of Europe today will end in divorce (see Table 5.8). The highest probability—in the range of 55 per cent—has been recorded in the United States (Locoh, 2006). Divorce is still relatively uncommon in southern Europe and East Asia, but its incidence has been rising lately. Much of the variation in divorce rates across societies can be traced to differences in the laws governing the legal dissolution of marriages and how long it has been since those laws were liberalized. In Italy, for example, divorce became legal only in 1971. For this reason, Italy's divorce rate remains one of the lowest in the industrialized world. Divorce has also been relatively uncommon in Greece, Portugal, and Spain, but as shown in Figure 5.4, the rates in all four countries have been going up and moving closer towards convergence with other Western European countries.

In some countries, divorce rates appear to have peaked in the 1980s and 1990s and have since stabilized or declined. For instance, the crude divorce rate in the United States rose to just over 5 per 1000 population in 1980 and has since then dropped to about 3.5 in 2010. Although at lower levels than that of the United States, rates in Canada, Australia, and New Zealand have also followed a declining pattern since 1990. In some Western European countries—including Austria, Belgium, Germany, and the United Kingdom—divorce rates today seem to have reached a more or less stable level after several decades of increase. In Denmark, Finland, Iceland, Norway, and Sweden, the rates have tended to flatten after the 1980s to levels in the range of 2 to 3 divorces per 1000 population. The recent slowdown in divorce rates across a number of countries may be attributed—at least in part—to the decline in formal marriage and a concomitant rise in cohabitation (or common-law) unions. Couples who are not married in the first place do not need a divorce in order to dissolve their union.

Across Eastern Europe, the situation with divorce varies considerably. On the one hand is the case of Russia, whose rates in 2010 approached 5 per 1000—the level experienced by the United States in the early 1980s. On the other hand, one finds relatively low incidence of divorce in countries such as Slovenia and Poland, but intermediate in Hungary and Czech Republic. In some cases, the rates are trending upward (e.g., Slovak Republic), while in others they are declining (e.g., Estonia). As might be expected, these variations reflect national differences in the restrictiveness of divorce laws and variability in the extent of marriage, though clearly national culture may also play a role, in some contexts more than others perhaps (for instance, in Poland, which is a predominantly Catholic country).

An interesting hypothesis for the levelling off or fall in divorce incidence across some countries pertains to the tendency for people to marry at older ages. Diane Rotz (2011) has posed the argument that the critical variable is the rising age at marriage of women. Older brides are more aware of their options since they have spent more time in the marriage market and thus are better informed about their optimal mate. Waiting longer to marry may lessen a woman's incentive to search for a new partner during marriage, as a wife's outside options might deteriorate with age. Other factors must contribute to this phenomenon: for example, the rising trend among women to be employed and thus more financially independent (Becker, Landes, and Michael, 1977; Leherer, 2008). However, such effects should operate through age at marriage, not independently. For instance, increased female education and labour-force participation would serve to delay marriage timing for women. Another possible factor, as already indicated, is the rising incidence of cohabitation. Although such unions can be highly unstable, for many couples cohabitation may serve as a trial marriage that helps to prevent incompatible couples from marrying; meanwhile, it allows those that do eventually marry to form stable unions that

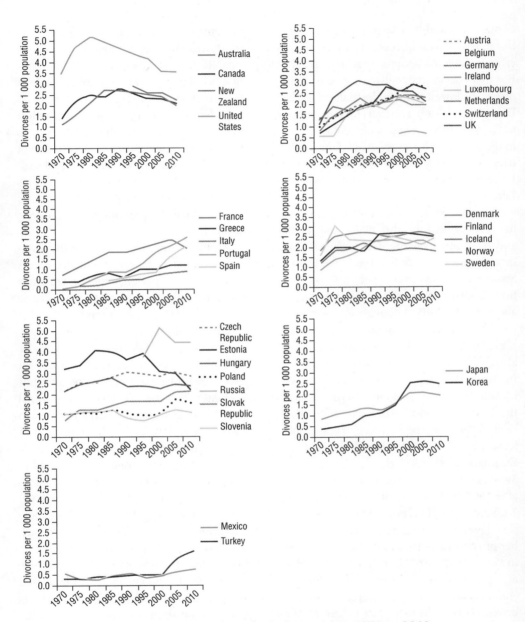

FIGURE 5.4 Crude divorce rates for selected countries, 1970 to 2010

Sources: OECD (2009): Ch. 4, GE4.2; United Nations, *UN Demographic Yearbook* (various years), Divorces and crude divorce rates by urban/rural residence.

are less inclined to divorce (Balakrishnan et al., 1987; Bumpass, 1990; Bumpass, Sweet, and Cherlin, 1991; Liefbroer and Dourleijn, 2006; Rindfuss and Vandenheuvel, 1990).

For the two Asian countries included in Figure 5.4—Japan and South Korea—the level of divorce today is relatively low; however, their overall trend is clearly upward. This

TABLE 5.8 Total divorce rate (per 1 000 marriages); selected countries, 1970, 1980, 2000, and 2010

Country	Period				% change		
	1970	1980	2000	2010	1970–80	1980–2000	2000–10
Austria	182	262	434	434	44.0	65.6	0.0
Belgium	97	207	450	—	113.4	117.4	
Denmark	251	399	445	402	59.0	11.5	−9.7
Finland	169	277	512	—	63.9	84.8	
France	121	223	378	—	84.3	69.5	
Germany	148	252	380	—	70.3	50.8	
Iceland	179	282	395	—	57.5	40.1	
Luxembourg	96	258	474	504	168.8	83.7	6.3
Netherlands	110	253	383	343	130.0	51.4	−10.4
Norway	133	250	447	—	88.0	78.8	
Sweden	233	424	549	—	82.0	29.5	
Switzerland	153	273	255	544	78.4	−6.6	113.3
United Kingdom	150	349	422	—	118.1	20.9	
Greece	54	97	181	—	79.6	86.6	
Italy	50	32	80	—	−36.0	150.0	
Portugal	7	75	262	—	971.4	249.3	
Spain	—	75	123	—		64.0	
Bulgaria	140	180	211	—	28.6	17.2	
Czech Rep.	261	310	433	500	18.8	39.7	15.5
Hungary	216	290	375	—	34.3	29.3	
Poland	140	140	173	—	0.0	23.6	
Romania	45	196	191	—	335.6	-2.6	
Slovakia	108	175	269	—	62.0	53.7	
Russia	337	424	503	—	25.8	18.6	
Estonia	—	500	529	—		5.8	
Canada	293	328	373	376	11.9	13.7	0.8
United States	548	589	—	480	7.5		
Japan	9	12	16	20.5	33.3	33.3	28.1

Note: — means no data available. For 2010 USA and Japan, rates are estimated. Japan rate assumes average exponential rate of growth 1970–2000 applies to 2000–10. USA rate for 2010 is taken from Copen et al. (2012: 16), based on 1- probability of a first marriage to American women remaining intact after 20 years, as derived for the interval 2006–10.

Sources: Copen et al. (2012): 16; Institut national d'études démographiques (2013); Milan (2013a): 14; Sardon (2002): 111–56, (2006): 197–266; United Nations Department of Economic and Social Affairs Population Division (2003): 31.

situation parallels closely the experience of the southern European countries, whose levels of family dissolution were very low in the 1960s and 1970s but rose substantially thereafter. In the two middle-income countries included in our analysis—Mexico and Turkey—divorce remains relatively rare, but this seems destined to change in the near future, as in both these cases the time trend of the divorce rate is inexorably upward. These two societies appear to be in the early stages of the divorce transition, moving away from a traditional pattern of low rates of family dissolution.

Cohabitation

Sociologists interpret the "destandardization" of family forms as a reflection of the increasing emphasis on personal choice among the younger generations with respect to sexuality, mate selection, and conjugal relationships: "Cohabitation can thus be seen as one component in the process in which individual behavior is becoming less determined by tradition and institutional arrangements and more open to individual choice" (Bernhardt, 2003: 154). In her analysis of European trends, France Prioux (2006) observed that fewer and fewer persons are marrying and more and more are living together without being married; and people are also separating and divorcing more frequently, often to form a second or even a third union. She uncovered five trends concerning cohabitation in Europe:

1. premarital cohabitation is more common in the north than in the south;
2. cohabitation leads less often to marriage;
3. fewer men and women are marrying;
4. unions are more short-lived; and
5. increasingly, people are experiencing several unions in a lifetime.

Cohabitation is still relatively rare in southern and Eastern Europe but very common in Nordic countries, particularly Sweden, Denmark, Norway, Finland, and Iceland; although Estonia and Latvia are culturally similar to their Scandinavian neighbours, their cohabitation rates are closer to those found in northern and Western Europe. This suggests that attitudes towards cohabitation are rooted in different cultural, sociohistorical, and legal traditions. The early wide acceptance of cohabitation in the Scandinavian countries, for instance, has been facilitated by the region's historical tendency to see marriage as a contract between two individuals; by contrast, cohabitation is generally discouraged in societies that have traditionally seen marriage primarily as a contract between families, as is the case in southern Europe (and also in non-European societies such as Japan, for example). Thus, in some countries policies are in place that make cohabitation similar to marriage (e.g., Netherlands, Sweden), while in others the laws are less explicit (Austria, Germany, Switzerland)—for example, in regard to such things as the obligation to pay alimony to an ex-partner and the division of property and household goods after separation (Perelli-Harris and Sánchez Gassen, 2012; United Nations Department of Economics and Social Affairs Population Division, 2003: 23).

Kairi Kaserau and Dagmar Kutsar (2011) confirm that some countries are in the early stages of the diffusion process where cohabitation is mainly confined to young adults. In other countries, cohabitation has become normative, serving as a type of trial marriage or as an alternative to formal marriage. In yet another set of countries, cohabitation and formal marriage have become indistinguishable, and a significant proportion of children are born to cohabiting couples. Such countries are thought to have reached the final stage of the cohabitation transition as exemplified by Sweden and Denmark. And in some societies, cohabitation involves growing numbers of formally married (divorced) individuals for whom it serves an alternative to a second marriage. Finally, there is cross-national variability in degree of union stability. Cohabiting unions can be highly unstable, but they appear to be least fragile where the aggregate level of cohabitation approaches 50 per cent. Presumably in such settings, the characteristics of cohabitors and of those who marry are similar. Cohabiting unions appear to be most unstable in national settings at either extremes of the cohabitation transition (Liefbroer and Dourleijn, 2006).

Patterns of cohabitation can be gauged through a variety of indices, including the proportions of women who by age 25 have entered a cohabiting union as their first conjugal relationship. The data in Table 5.9 are arranged according to the respondent's birth cohort. A number of conclusions are possible from this data, but the most glaring trend is that in all the countries selected, younger generations have been much more likely than their predecessors to cohabit without marriage. The bastions of cohabitation are Sweden, where the level was roughly 75 per cent across cohorts, and Norway, which started at only 9 per cent

among the 1945–50 cohort but has seen significant increases with subsequent cohorts.

An unambiguous indicator of how far a population has progressed through the cohabitation transition is the extent to which births occur outside of traditional marriage. As shown in Figure 5.5, the Scandinavian countries, especially Sweden, Denmark, and Iceland, have led the way in non-traditional forms of family formation and therefore in the extent of childbearing that takes place outside of traditional marriage. This trend has diffused beyond the Scandinavian countries. Currently, about 40 per cent of all births in the European Union (EU) occur extramaritally (i.e., outside of traditional marriage); and in Belgium, Bulgaria, Estonia, France, Iceland, Slovenia, Norway, and Sweden, this figure exceeds 50 per cent. Iceland holds the top spot at 65 percent.

TABLE 5.9   **Percentages of females, by birth cohort, reporting cohabitation as their first conjugal relationship by age 25, selected countries**

| Country | Birth cohort | | | | | % change |
	1945–50 %	1950–5 %	1955–60 %	1960–5 %	1965–70 %	1950–5 to 1960–5
Austria	22	38	45	55	58	44.7
Estonia	29	47	49	61	64	29.8
France	15	21	35	46	60	119.0
Hungary	—	7	15	18	—	157.1
Italy	1	3	3	5	5	66.7
Latvia	16	24	25	29	40	20.8
Netherlands	—	18	28	45	50	150.0
Norway	9	26	44	58	—	123.1
Poland	3	3	4	4	—	33.3
Spain	2	3	5	7	10	133.3
Sweden	68	74	76	74	—	0.0
Switzerland	18	33	45	51	51	54.5
Canada	7	20	32	42	—	110.0

Note: — denotes data not available.

Source: Adapted from United Nations Department of Economic and Social Affairs Population Division (2003): 24–5.

SIX DEGREES OF COHABITATION

Countries can be classified along a continuum with respect to their stage of cohabitation transition. Patrick Heuveline and Jeffrey Timberlake (2004) classified countries according to six distinct types of cohabiting regime:

1. *Marginal cohabitation*   This is the arrangement in countries where cohabitation is rare and socially discouraged (e.g., Italy, Spain, Poland). In these countries, the incidence and duration of adult cohabitation is low, and children's exposure to this kind of living arrangement is even lower.

2. *Prelude to marriage*   In countries including Belgium, the Czech Republic, Hungary, and Switzerland, cohabitation tends to be a prelude to marriage, akin to a trial marriage. The period of unmarried cohabitation in these societies is typically short, and relatively few children are born into cohabiting unions of this kind.

3. *Stage in the marriage process*   In countries like Austria, Finland, Germany, Latvia, and Slovenia, cohabitation is seen not as a prelude to marriage but as a stage in the marriage process. Cohabiting couples in these countries typically do not feel strongly about the order and timing of childbearing and marriage, and children are often born before the marriage is formalized. However, since the period of this kind of cohabitation tends to be brief, children's exposure to cohabitation is also short.

4. *Alternative to living single*   Partners who wish to postpone getting married but would rather live together than separately during courtship belong to this model of cohabitation, which is typical of New Zealand and the United States. The commitment of these partners is more characteristic of a dating relationship; the period of cohabitation is usually brief and often ends in separation rather than marriage.

5. *Alternative to marriage*   In some societies, such as those of Canada (particularly Quebec) and France, couples choose to cohabit instead of marrying, and form families as married couples would.

6. *Indistinguishable from marriage*   In societies like Sweden where cohabitation is widely accepted, with plenty of institutional supports for unmarried parents, couples may opt for cohabitation not because they view it as an alternative to marriage but because they are simply indifferent to the idea of marriage, which offers no tangible benefits. Compared with countries where cohabitation is seen as an alternative to marriage, this societal context—where there is cultural approval and institutional support for children born out of wedlock—will see a greater number of children born to cohabiting parents. However, the duration of cohabitation is still fairly short (with or without children) because many of these unions eventually transition to formal marriage.

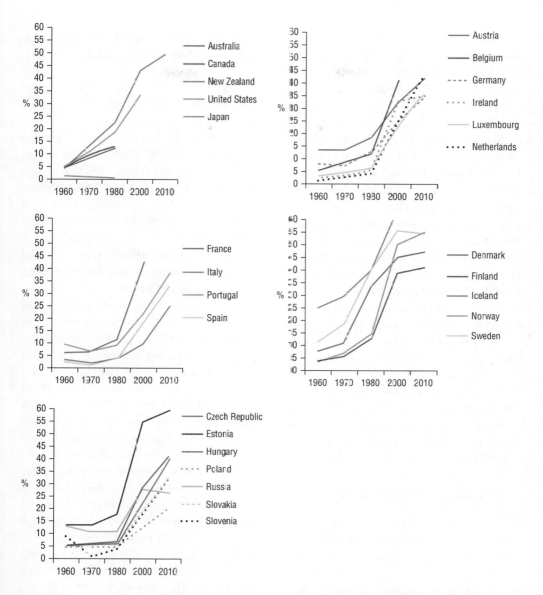

FIGURE 5.5   Proportion of all births that are extramarital; selected countries, 1960 to 2010.

Note: Incomplete data for some countries.

Source: Compiled with data available at Institut national d'études démographiques (2013).

The rising trend in extramarital births is also evident in Eastern Europe—especially in Estonia, whose trend seems to emulate closely those of Iceland and Sweden. The phenomenon is evident for Canada and the United States, though at much lower levels than Iceland and the other Scandinavian countries. For some countries in southern Europe, namely France, Italy, Spain, and Portugal—though also Ireland—the rising trend in extramarital births may seem surprising given the predominantly Catholic culture of these countries. Diffusion of this phenomenon to these societies suggests that traditional norms regarding family and reproduction have been broken.

However, Japan stands out for its very low levels of extramarital births. This feature of Japanese society seems unique because many of the same sociological changes that have evolved in the other industrialized countries over the last six decades have also permeated Japanese society (Rindfuss et al., 2010). It appears that aspects of Japanese traditional culture work against the widespread occurrence of extramarital births.

Developing Countries: Nuptiality Patterns

The developing countries have seen some change in nuptiality patterns in recent decades. The changes are not uniform, of course, and there are regional variations in the prevalence of different conjugal forms. Polygyny, for example, is common in Africa but relatively rare elsewhere, while in other regions—such as parts of Latin American and the Caribbean—consensual unions of various forms and formal marriage have co-existed since long before the rise of cohabitation in the industrialized world. This section will provide an overview of

nuptiality trends in the developing world, specifically Africa, Asia, and Latin America.

Africa

Judging from Table 5.10, marriage or some similar form of conjugal union is widespread in Africa. The percentage of women married or cohabiting with a man ranges between 41 and 84 per cent, with the average approximately 65 per cent. Although this table does not differentiate between marital and non-marital unions, Charles Westoff's (2003) analysis of Demographic Health Survey countries found that informal non-marital cohabitation is quite prevalent in some regions of Africa.

Early marriage is most prevalent in sub-Saharan Africa and least common in North Africa (Singh and Samara, 1996). Across the continent, the median age at first marriage (see Table 5.10) is still relatively low (about 19); only in Namibia and South Africa is the median over 20. Even so, that age has been rising in recent years: Westoff (2003) reports that this trend can be seen in 21 of the 30 countries surveyed in sub-Saharan Africa. Thus, a major nuptiality transition seems to be underway. After a long period of no real change in the age at first marriage for women, sub-Saharan Africa is now experiencing notable increases in this indicator. Westoff's (2003) analysis indicates that the proportion of women married for the first time before the age of 20 has declined in Niger, Nigeria, Malawi, Senegal, Mauritania, Gabon, Eritrea, Zimbabwe, and Kenya, among others; however, no such trend is evident in Burkina Faso, Uganda, Mozambique, the Central African Republic, Togo, or Guinea.

Among the cultural factors that help to explain regional variations in marriage in Africa are differences in the rules governing

TABLE 5.10	Nuptiality statistics for developing countries included in Demographic Health Surveys in the 1990s and early 2000s

Country/region	% never married	% married/ cohabiting	% divorced/ separated	Median age at first marriage, women 25–49
Sub-Saharan Africa				
Benin 2001	21.7	73.4	3.1	18.8
Burkina Faso 1998–9	16.9	80.4	1.0	17.6
Cameroon 1998	23.4	66.9	6.6	17.4
Central African Republic 1994–5	19.5	69.4	9.1	17.3
Chad 1996–7	13.7	78.2	5.0	15.8
Comoros 1996	39.0	53.6	6.3	18.5
Côte d'Ivoire 1998–9	30.4	61.3	6.2	18.7
Eritrea 2002	23.3	65.5	7.4	18.3
Ethiopia 2000	24.0	63.7	8.7	16.0
Gabon 2000	32.6	54.1	12.1	19.7
Ghana 1998	23.7	64.6	9.9	19.1
Guinea 1999	13.9	82.4	2.2	16.4
Kenya 1998	30.1	61.4	4.9	19.2
Madagascar 1997	23.4	62.8	11.6	18.5
Malawi 2000	17.0	71.5	8.0	17.8
Mali 2001	13.5	83.5	1.8	16.5
Mauritania 2000–1	28.6	58.8	10.8	17.1
Mozambique 1997	15.1	74.4	9.3	17.1
Namibia 1992	51.3	41.6	5.5	24.8
Niger 1998	11.2	84.2	3.1	15.1
Nigeria 1999	26.0	70.1	2.2	17.9
Rwanda 2000	34.1	48.5	9.5	20.7
Senegal 1997	26.9	68.1	4.1	17.4
South Africa 1998	48.3	43.2	6.1	24.2
Sudan 1990	39.8	55.5	2.7	17.8
Tanzania 1999	23.4	65.8	7.6	18.1
Togo 1998	24.9	67.9	4.8	18.8
Uganda 2000–1	20.1	67.4	9.2	17.8
Zambia 2001–2	24.8	61.3	9.3	17.8
Zimbabwe 1999	27.7	61.1	7.0	19.3
North Africa/West Asia/Europe				
Armenia 2000	28.8	64.1	3.8	20.5
Egypt 2000	31.9	62.8	1.8	19.5
Jordan 2002	45.6	51.7	1.2	21.8
Morocco 1995	42.4	52.2	3.4	20.2
Turkey 1998	27.7	69.0	1.5	19.5
Yemen 1997	28.3	67.4	2.4	16.0
Central Asia				
Kazakhstan 1999	25.3	62.9	8.8	21.2
Kyrgyz Republic 1997	21.5	69.5	6.5	20.4
Turkmenistan 2000	32.4	61.7	3.6	21.5
Uzbekistan 1996	24.9	70.2	3.0	20.1

(continued)

TABLE 5.10   (continued)

IIIIIIIIIIIIIIIIIIIIIIIIIIIIIIIIIIIIIIIIIIIIIIIIIIIIIIIIIIIIIIIIIIIIIIIIIIIIIIIIIIIIIIIIIIIIIIIIIIIIIIIIIIIIIIIIIIIIIIIIIIII

Country/region	% never married	% married/ cohabiting	% divorced/ separated	Median age at first marriage, women 25–49
South/Southeast Asia				
Bangladesh 1999–2000	17.3	76.2	2.9	14.7
Cambodia 2000	31.8	59.1	3.1	20.0
India 1998–9	19.9	75.1	1.6	16.9
Indonesia 1997	25.3	69.7	2.5	18.6
Nepal 2001	17.9	78.5	1.2	16.7
Pakistan 1991–5	24.2	74.2	0.4	18.6
Philippines 1998	36.4	59.6	2.3	22.1
Vietnam 1997	33.5	62.7	2.0	21.3
Latin America/Caribbean				
Bolivia 1998	33.4	59.4	5.7	20.9
Brazil 1996	30.6	60.1	7.7	21.1
Colombia 2000	34.0	51.2	12.7	21.5
Dominican Republic 2002	23.0	59.8	16.6	19.0
Ecuador 1999	32.1	58.0	8.5	—
El Salvador 1998	29.6	55.8	—	—
Guatemala 1998–9	26.2	65.8	6.5	19.3
Haiti 2000	31.4	58.7	8.3	20.5
Nicaragua 2001	25.8	56.8	16.5	18.2
Paraguay 1995–6	30.1	62.3	6.7	20.9
Peru 2000	35.8	56.1	6.6	21.4

Note: — means data not available.

Source: Adapted from Westoff (2003): 2–3, 25.

things like property succession and dowry, and the norms aimed at controlling female sexuality. These cultural traditions tend to erode with increasing urbanization and all the other social, psychological, and economic changes typically associated with socioeconomic modernization and the global diffusion of Western ideas and values (Caldwell, 1982; Caldwell et al., 1998; Singh and Samara, 1996; Zuberi et al., 2003). One of the most powerful agents of change in marriage timing in Africa and other developing countries is formal schooling for girls, because education opens up options that otherwise are not readily available (Mason, 1993).

Asia

Asia is not only vast but highly diverse, both demographically and culturally. Although marriage remains almost universal, there are notable cross-country variations. At one extreme, women in the Indian subcontinent have historically married very early (Hajnal, 1965). Thus, the median age at first marriage for Indian women is estimated to be roughly 17, and the figures are similar for Pakistan, Bangladesh, and Nepal. At the other extreme, marriage patterns in Japan, South Korea, Taiwan, and China are closer to the Western European pattern of late average entry into marriage. With a few exceptions (e.g., Kazakhstan, the Kyrgyz

Republic, and Uzbekistan), the median age at first marriage has been rising in the Middle East and West Asia, and there has been a corresponding general decline in the proportions of women marrying before the age of 20 (Westoff, 2003).

Latin America

In their overview of nuptiality patterns in Latin America between 1950 and 2000, Elizabeth Fussell and Alberto Palloni (2004) draw attention to three noteworthy trends in the region:

1. Marriage or the equivalent consensual union is nearly universal and still occurs relatively early in life for women (between the ages of 20 and 25).
2. The proportion of the population entering into marriages or consensual unions increased over the 50-year period from already very high levels (in 2000, the proportion of women aged 45–49 who were single ranged between only 1 and 15 per cent).
3. Rates of divorce and separation, though increasing slightly, are still low.

According to these authors, consensual (i.e., non-marital) unions constitute a large proportion of all unions in Central America and the Caribbean (e.g., in El Salvador, Guatemala, Honduras, Nicaragua, Panama, and the Dominican Republic), but are relatively rare in the more economically advanced countries (Argentina, Brazil, Chile, Costa Rica, Mexico, and Uruguay). The Andean countries (Bolivia, Colombia, Ecuador, Paraguay, Peru, and Venezuela) are in the middle range. Countries where consensual unions were common in the past tend to follow the same pattern today. Countries where consensual unions were less common have seen some increases in this type of union.

Explanations of Nuptiality Change: Industrialized Countries

This section will examine a variety of perspectives on the question of how the Western world's current nuptiality patterns became established over the past half century or so (for a longer term historical analysis, see Hajnal, 1965).

The "Flight from Marriage": Theoretical Explanations

No single explanation can account for the "flight from marriage" since the early 1970s: the sociological causes are complex and multifaceted. It is widely accepted, however, that contemporary family patterns in the West are at least in part the result of profound changes set in motion by the Industrial Revolution. In the agrarian economy, the family was the primary unit of economic production: all family members contributed their labour to the growing of food, the making of tools, and so on. At the same time, the family was the primary social institution, responsible for everything from the education and socialization of children to the care of the elderly. With modernization, the family was gradually displaced from many of these traditional functions. In the process of shifting the locus of economic production from the farm to the factory, industrialization created the *"male breadwinner" system*, in which the man of the family became the sole earner and provider and the woman specialized in domestic affairs. Meanwhile, the introduction of mandatory formal schooling displaced the family from its educational function, and in time the care of the infirm and elderly was increasingly delegated to external institutions as well. Today, the nuclear family may still be the primary unit for (1) reproduction, (2) common residence, (3) economic co-operation, (4) the socialization of children, and (5) the satisfaction of adults' sexual needs (Leslie and Korman, 1989: 14). But it is certainly not the only setting for the performance of these functions.

Although economic co-operation remains an important feature of the modern nuclear family, the nature of that co-operation has changed radically since industrialization made women economically dependent on male breadwinners. The options available to women expanded briefly during World War II, when their productive activity was crucial to the war effort. But those options quickly contracted again once the war ended and the baby boom began. This was the period described by Betty Friedan in her book *The Feminine Mystique* (1963), in which women were generally expected to devote themselves exclusively to family life and their husbands' economic success.

The decline of the male breadwinner system began gradually in the 1950s and early 1960s, when women started seeking alternatives to marriage and total commitment to reproduction and childrearing (Davis, 1984). Entry into the labour force has meant that women no longer need to rely on matrimony for economic security. For many scholars, this shift was a primary cause of family change in the industrialized countries (Davis and van den Oever, 1982; Goldscheider and Waite, 1986, 1991; Westoff,

1983). Indeed, as early as 1978, Westoff (70) proclaimed that the steady decline since 1960 in the proportion of women marrying at ages 20–24 marked the beginning of a radical change in the family. Today, the median age at first marriage continues to rise, and increasing numbers of people are choosing not to marry at all.

The "Second Demographic Transition" Perspective

The structural changes associated with socioeconomic modernization have been accompanied by changes in societal values regarding marriage and the family. Some scholars have described this phenomenon as a "second demographic transition." At the core of this perspective is the idea that in post-modern societies tradition has largely ceased to function as a guiding principle in people's lives: in its place an ethos of individualism, complemented by secularism and materialism, is leading growing numbers of young people to choose alternative lifestyles, especially in the areas of sexuality and conjugal behaviour (Lesthaeghe, 1995; van de Kaa, 1987). According to Louis Roussel (1985: 233), the two distinguishing features of the current system are high "marital mobility" (resulting from the increasing prevalence of divorce) and growing diversity of household models. For the second demographic transition theorists, all these trends—late marriage, divorce, cohabitation, same-sex unions—are part of the same shift in values away from the family and towards the individual. According to Dirk van de Kaa (1987: 6–7), these tendencies—pervasive among young people in post-modern societies—stem from two sources: a personal desire for greater self-fulfillment, and a growing tolerance of diversity in other individuals' lifestyles.

Some of the leading theorists in the second demographic transition school (e.g., Lesthaeghe, 1995, 2010; Lesthaeghe and Neels, 2002; Lesthaeghe and Surkyn, 1988; van de Kaa, 1987) have identified a *"post-materialist"* tendency among young people to reject the conventional, materialistic aspirations of the bourgeoisie in favour of emotional intimacy, or what Anthony Giddens (1992) refers to as the *"pure relationship."* In relationships of this kind, external criteria (i.e., traditional norms) are irrelevant: the relationship exists purely for the sake of what it can give emotionally the persons involved. As Giddens points out, such a relationship is by nature unstable and impermanent, since it can be terminated more or less at will by either party at any time. To the extent that the "pure relationship" has come to represent the primary model of intimacy for young people, it serves to undermine traditional marriage by promoting non-traditional alternatives (i.e., living together without marriage) and encouraging a mindset in which impermanence is the norm. Proponents of the "second demographic transition" theory would argue that the "pure relationship" is a reflection of the growing importance of post-material values in a society where traditional conventions are increasingly relegated to secondary status (see also Simons, 1980; Thornton and Philipov, 2009).

Demographic Theory

In the early 1970s, Ruth Dixon (1971) proposed that the timing and extent of marriage in society are determined by three factors:

1. the availability of potential mates (i.e., sex ratios in the prime marriageable ages);
2. the feasibility of marriage (i.e., young adults' economic circumstances); and

3. the desirability of marriage (i.e., social attitudes and orientation towards marriage).

With respect to the first factor, Dixon (1971: 22) hypothesized that *masculinity ratios* (i.e., the ratio of males to females) "should be positively correlated with marital delays among men and with bachelorhood, and negatively correlated with marital delays among women and with spinsterhood." In other words, an oversupply of males would mean, on average, longer waits for men and shorter waits for women before marriage, while an oversupply of females would mean the reverse.

There is a cultural preference in the West for women to marry men who are a little older than themselves; the difference is usually about two or three years. This *mating gradient* can therefore play an additional role in the way sex ratios can affect marriage markets (Akers, 1967; Davis and van den Oever, 1982; Veevers, 1994). A more complex theory regarding the consequences of skewed sex ratios has been proposed by Marcia Guttentag and Paul Secord (1983), who argued that discrepancies in the numbers of men and women in the prime marriageable ages at the macro level can lead to profound changes in what they call "dyadic power" between the sexes at the micro level. According to these authors, a surplus of males would typically result in intense competition for female partners. Under these conditions, gender roles would be governed by "traditional" norms and expectations, and the sexual division of labour would conform to the male breadwinner pattern. In this context, women might lack "structural power" (i.e., economic and social power), but they would enjoy significant influence with their male partners. The family in this social context would be stable, divorce rates would be low, and no significant alternatives to traditional marriage would be available. Pioneer societies of the past conformed to this pattern. By contrast, a surplus of females would mean a wider selection of partners for young men to choose from. Women under these conditions would be less highly valued, and therefore their dyadic power would be reduced. In this scenario, marriage rates would be low, since men would not need to commit to matrimony in order to find sexual partners, and rates of family dissolution would be high.

Both of these scenarios have prevailed at different times in history. The contemporary situation in the industrialized world does not conform to either pattern, however. Through formal education and large-scale participation in the labour force, women have for the first time in history acquired both structural power and economic independence from men. Under these conditions, imbalanced sex ratios no longer matter, because women now see marriage as just one among a number of possible options. Thus, Guttentag and Secord would suggest that the decline of marriage and the rise both of divorce and of common-law relationships in the advanced societies lately is mainly attributable to changes in the status of women.

The Economic Opportunities Thesis

Not all scholars agree with the emphasis on women as the principal actors in family change. Richard Easterlin (1980, 1969), for example, proposed that the decline in marriage in the West is primarily a function of the economic opportunities available to young men rather than women's reduced desire for matrimony. Valerie Oppenheimer (1988, 1994, 1997) concurs, remarking that the social demographic literature must "bring men back" into the explanation of family change. For Easterlin and Oppenheimer, both the post-war marriage boom and the marriage bust of the period since the 1970s can be best understood as reflections of the economic prospects that different cohorts of young adult men have faced and hence their ability to afford marriage and family building.

From this perspective, the increase in marriage rates after World War II was a function not only of economic prosperity but also of the fact that opportunities for young male workers were relatively numerous because the cohorts entering the labour force after the war had been born in the 1930s—the time when birth rates had reached their lowest level in history. According to Easterlin (1980), members of small cohorts generally enjoy several advantages over members of larger cohorts, including less competition for entry-level jobs, easier advancement in the workplace, and higher average wages.

In the same way, these scholars interpret the marriage bust that began in the mid- to late 1970s as a reflection of the relative economic deprivation faced by the large cohorts of young male baby boomers, beginning with increased competition for entry-level positions. These structural conditions are seen as discouraging to early marriage, and may have led some men to avoid matrimony altogether. To make matters worse, the world has seen several recessions since the 1973 oil crisis, and in recent years economic globalization has intensified competition for consumer markets and profits. The need to cut costs has led to job losses as a result of restructuring, and many manufacturing jobs have been lost to the developing countries where labour costs are lower.

More recent entry-level cohorts, born in the low-fertility regimes of the 1980s and 1990s, have certainly been smaller in size, but they too have faced less-than-optimal labour market conditions, which have been reflected in declining marriage rates. In short, the key problem, for Easterlin and Oppenheimer, is the erosion of economic security among young men.

Rising divorce rates and the rise of alternative family forms can also be interpreted as consequences of the declining socioeconomic fortunes of young men, since economic instability leading to financial difficulties would tend to intensify marital tensions and ultimately increase the likelihood of divorce. The trend towards cohabitation can also be viewed as a consequence of economic insecurity, on the assumption that young men might see common-law arrangements as less costly than marriage.

The "Gains to Marriage" Thesis

As we have seen, Dixon (1971) proposed that marriage propensities in a society are affected not only by the feasibility of marriage and the supply of potential partners, but also by the extent to which young adults consider marriage desirable. The more alternatives to traditional matrimony become available, the less desirable marriage itself will become. The economist Gary Becker (1973, 1974, 1991) has developed a thesis that elaborates on this proposition. His *gains to marriage* thesis explains how the gains associated with traditional marriage have waned since 1960, especially for women. In the past, under the male breadwinner system, the husband specialized in market work and the wife in home production. The wife traded domestic services, including childbearing and childraising, to the husband in exchange for economic security provided through his income. Today, however, women who have gained economic independence are less accepting of a traditional division of labour in the home. The decline in the "gain" associated with marriage is reflected not only in rising divorce rates and growing numbers of unmarried couples living together, but in the increasing numbers of families headed by women, and to some degree also the trend towards childbearing outside of traditional marriage.

From Becker's perspective, women are the principal agents of family change in contemporary industrial society. Similarly, Becker attributes the rise of divorce as a further manifestation of women's rising status in society. In general, marriages dissolve because the gains that women today can expect from divorce outweigh the gains they can expect from staying married (Becker, Landes, and Michael, 1977; Grossbard-Schechtman, 1995; Hess, 2004). In other words, women who are capable of economic self-sufficiency have little reason to stay in an unrewarding marital relationship. Together, therefore, rising wages and labour-force participation among women, especially married women, have probably also contributed significantly to the growth in divorce rates.

A number of other studies in the context of European and American societies are consistent with these ideas (Booth et al., 1984; Ermisch, 1981; Hiedemann, Suhomlinova, and O'Rand, 1998; Preston and Richards, 1975). Some research, however, has shown lower divorce probabilities are associated with wives having greater economic resources, or when the two partners' resources are similar (Coltrane, 1996; Ono, 1998; Risman and Johnson-Sumerford, 1998). Nonetheless, the chance of divorce would ultimately depend on the quality of the marriage—i.e., how happy each spouse is with the marriage and the extent to which a dissatisfied partner would be able to absorb the economic consequences of divorce (Rogers, 2004).

Towards a Synthesis of Explanations

There is no overarching theory that can explain completely the causes of the changes in nuptiality observed over the last half-century or so in the West and more generally in the industrialized countries (Seltzer et al., 2005). In Dixon's (1971) cross-national analysis, the sex ratio thesis showed the weakest correlation with marriage rates, leading her to conclude that "Overall, delayed marriage and celibacy are most highly correlated with indicators of the desirability of marriage, less so with feasibility, and least with availability" (225). Sex ratio imbalances in the prime marriageable age groups obviously affect the availability of eligible partners, but culture and social structure seem to have more influence on nuptiality change. The Easterlin/ Oppenheimer thesis focuses on how men's socioeconomic prospects affect their marriage probabilities and divorce. Becker's "gains to marriage" explanation emphasizes changes in the status of women as the central factor in marriage and family change. On the other hand, it is possible that declines in marriage may not indicate that women are abandoning marriage altogether: many women may simply be postponing marriage to older ages, and this process may involve cohabitation as a precursor to marriage.

A complete explanation of nuptiality change would likely have to take into account not only changes in the status of women in society but also changes in the lives of men, broadly speaking. It is true that the behaviour of both young men and young women today is conditioned to some extent by their economic prospects, but other factors are also important—among them value shifts, or ideational change; the breakdown of tradition and the rise of secular society; the diminished desirability of traditional marriage among the younger generations; the trend towards greater symmetry in gender roles; the multiplicity of lifestyles available to people; and increasing societal acceptance of alternatives to traditional marriage including cohabitation and same-sex marriage (Chamie and Myrkin, 2011; Goldscheider and Waite, 1986, 1991; Lesthaeghe, 2010).

Explanations of Nuptiality Change: Developing Countries

Explanations of nuptiality change beyond the Western world, and in particular the developing countries, encompass structural and ideational factors as outlined for the industrialized societies. Some theories give prominence to the role of structural change such as increasing levels of urbanization and economic development under the general rubric of socioeconomic modernization; others give special weight to the importance of ideational change (i.e., shifts in value systems) as prime movers of change. Of course, structural and ideational factors do not act independently and most often interact in complex ways. The theoretical literature on global patterns of family change is extensive, extending far back, for example, to the early study of Edward Westermarck (1891) on *The History of Human Marriage*. For our purposes, we will focus on a few recent influential works in this area.

Convergence Thesis

In *World Revolution and Family Patterns*, William Goode (1963) emphasized the centrality of the conjugal family in modern industrial society. By "conjugal," Goode essentially meant the nuclear Western family. His main point was that urban industrial society relies heavily on a geographically and socially mobile educated population; individuals must be free to relocate to where their skills are in demand, unencumbered by a traditional family type that restricts movement. The family type that seems most suitable for market economies is the Western conjugal system because its principal foundations are personal independence and freedom to pursue socioeconomic opportunities in the market economy, as well as the following three other features that make the nuclear family highly suitable for urban industrial society:

1. young adults have personal autonomy in selecting their own partner to marry based on mutual attraction (love) not on the basis of an alliance between families;
2. couples establish their own independent households and are focused exclusively on their own and their children's well-being; and
3. the conjugal unit operates independently economically, and also in day-to-day decisions.

For Goode, the Western conjugal family seemed to represent the system that is most consistent with socioeconomic development. From this idea, Goode surmised an eventual global convergence of family forms to that of the Western conjugal family.

Divergence Thesis

In *Between Sex and Power: Family in the World, 1900–2000*, Göran Therborn (2004) shows that in actuality there is considerable heterogeneity of family systems across the world's regions, all shaped by complex interactions of cultural, religious, economic, and historical factors. Therborn observes that the world's family systems derive from the great world religions and the cultural history of civilizations, and therefore five fundamental family systems can be identified—those of East, South, and West Asia (with North Africa), sub-Saharan Africa, and Europe—together with two important interstitial or hybrid systems—of Creole America (i.e., Caribbean and other parts of Latin America, and blacks in the USA), and of Southeast Asia—each with significant subvariants.

His comparative overview of these seven family systems looks at their internal power relations, their marriage patterns, and regulation of sexuality and fertility patterns. He finds that although changes tend to move in the same direction across the world regions—e.g., the spread of birth control, falling fertility rates, rising age at first union, etc.—these changes do not imply convergence to a common family form. For example, Hindu and Muslim family practices in north India have been similar but markedly distinct from Hindu practices in south India. In Africa, Christianity has had to accommodate to African *polygyny*. In the former, the rigid patriarchies of Confucianism, Islam, and

Catholicism were mellowed by Buddhist indifference in family matters. In the case of the Creole family system, European conquest created a combination of rigid *patriarchy* among rulers, mass *miscegenation*, and an uprooted non-marital family pattern among the conquered indigenous and the imported slave populations. Thus, the imperial conquest of the western hemisphere produced the first sudden transformation of family structure before the twentieth century.

Up until the twentieth century, the great majority of family systems have been *patriarchal* systems, resting on the power of older males over the young of both sexes and on the institutionalized superiority of men over women, even though in general Europe, Southeast Asia, and Africa proved less unfavourable to women (in Africa, for example, polygyny and matriarchal systems have been present and there has been less rigidity towards sexual mores). According to Therborn, of all the family systems, that of the West has been the least patriarchal, as women have had comparatively more freedoms.

While family systems of the world have changed over the course of the twentieth century, they are still showing signs of diversity and the vestiges of their traditional cultures in varying degrees. For instance, as already noted, today in the West, one finds much complexity in the types of family forms available, as reflected by the variety of living arrangements. These are partly driven by increased divorce rates and partly by the erosion of traditionalism supplanted by an ethos of individualism—i.e., cohabitation, same-sex unions, non-marital births, lone families, step-families, empty-nesters, and so forth, along with formal marriage and dual-earner families. The apparently relatively novel phenomenon of cohabitation in Europe, it turns out, is not at all a new invention. We are told by Therborn that this type of union arrangement in fact had long existed in Western Europe itself and also in Creole America (e.g., Jamaica, other Caribbean islands, and other parts of Central and Latin America).

In some regions, there exist family systems that continue to practise arranged marriages, especially where there is strict control over female sexuality, and consequently in these societies there is also widespread practice of early marriage of daughters (e.g., India, Pakistan, Bangladesh, Nepal). In some societies, divorce is widely accessible (e.g., Malaysia and Indonesia, and some Arabic states); in others, it is highly discouraged (e.g., South Asian societies including India). In many of these geographic areas (rural especially), families are more likely to be dissolved by the death of a father or a mother than by divorce, and cohabitation and extramarital births are very rare.

In certain parts of Africa, such as in the western region, around half of all married women have a co-wife; yet in others, such as Zimbabwe in the south, this is much less prevalent. Burundi, a predominantly Catholic country, has much more polygamy than any Muslim country outside sub-Saharan Africa. And due to the ravages of the AIDS epidemic, families in parts of Africa have been forced to change as more adults succumb to the disease. Consequently, many elderly grandmothers now find themselves having to raise the children of their adult daughters or sons who have fallen victim to AIDS.

Diffusion of the Second Demographic Transition

Ron Lesthaeghe (2010) has proposed that the *second demographic transition* should be unfolding beyond the West and Eastern Europe. Thus, across non-Western countries four key features should be emerging, though not necessarily simultaneously:

1. widespread fertility postponement (later parenthood) accounting for low overall period fertility rates;
2. growing prominence of free partner choice and female autonomy
3. premarital cohabitation must become more common and more widely acceptable; and
4. at both the macro level and the individual level, connections must exist between demographic features and value orientations (i.e., in countries where the second demographic transition is more advanced one should find more people exhibiting post-modern values consistent with greater openness to autonomy and greater skepticism towards traditional sources of authority).

Lesthaeghe's own analysis of Japan, Hong Kong, Thailand, South Korea, Philippines, and Indonesia, among other Asian countries, does indeed show these non-Western countries are following nuptial patterns now prevalent in some European countries that are in the early to intermediate stages of a second demographic transition. He finds there is widespread fertility postponement; the proportion of never-married women in the prime marriageable ages has been rising; and there is a definite trend towards later marriage and younger cohorts remaining single longer (see also Jones, 2007). Even in Japan—a country often described as having very low rates of cohabitation and premarital childbearing—a fifth of women and men aged 25–29, regardless of their current status, reported that they had ever experienced cohabitation. Finally, cross-national surveys reveal a close connection between individuals holding post-modern values (i.e., values that reflect greater openness to diversity and gender equality and that challenge traditional systems) and these emerging nuptiality features. There is further evidence that the second demographic transition has spread to Latin American countries, where cohabitation has risen significantly, in some cases reaching levels in excess of 50 per cent among women aged 25–29 (Esteve, Lesthaeghe, and Lopez-Gay, 2012).

Towards the Future

Taken together, these perspectives suggest patterns of continuity and change in regard to nuptiality and family across countries. Cultures in their diversity interpret and reinterpret newly introduced ideas to their societies but never recede completely. Societies adapt and accommodate to ideas that may threaten the established order of pre-existing family systems and structures by forging hybrid solutions consistent with their cultural history and, in many instances, religious norms. Where marriages have been traditionally arranged by parents, young adults may have gained the autonomy to independently select a marriage partner but at the same time seek parental approval before proceeding to matrimony. In other cases, there may be a return to more traditional nuptial forms. In some countries where cohabitation is widespread, the more educated and economically successful are increasingly opting for traditional marriage, while the less educated tend to rely on cohabitation. This seems to be taking hold in the United States lately, according to Andrew Cherlin (2012); this is also occurring in some Western European countries (Kalmijn, 2007, 2013; Ohlsson-Wijk, 2011).

Such ebbs and flows between continuity and change in both developed and developing countries are not inconsistent with the postulates of the second demographic transition. In the developing countries its unfolding coincides with the widespread diffusion of modern contraception and family planning, rising age at marriage, greater levels of autonomy among young adults—especially women—and greater acceptance of diversity of conjugal unions. A common feature underlying all this is the gradual erosion of patriarchy (Therborn, 2004, 2006; Lesthaeghe, 2010).

ON THE ORIGINS OF SOCIAL MONOGAMY

The question of how the institution of social monogamy and patriarchy have evolved has preoccupied scholars from diverse disciplinary backgrounds for a long time (see for example, Engels, 1884[1964]; Kanazawa and Still, 1999; Kappeler, 2013; McDonald, 2001; Potts and Campbell, 2008; Smuts, 1995; Todd, 1985). Here, we review three recent works in this area.

1. Opie et al. Thesis

For Christopher Opie and associates (2013), the most compelling reason for the development of social monogamy in primates, and potentially in humans, is male infanticide. In their extensive analysis of 230 species, the presence of infanticide was found to correlate strongly for the appearance of monogamy. Thus, social monogamy in primates may have resulted from a number of interrelated conditions, most notably the long lactation periods of infants caused by altriciality (requiring nourishment), which makes them particularly vulnerable to infanticidal males. Biparental care shortens lactation length, thereby reducing infanticide risk and increasing reproductive rates.

Opie and colleagues suggest that the development of human pair bonding originated during human evolutionary history as a response to the pressures that long infant dependency places on females to find effective protection for their young. The transition to social monogamy in humans has resulted from females choosing to stay faithful to males, even when of lower quality; and once in place, "these pair bonds would facilitate paternal care in the form of male protection and provisioning. Male infanticide could thus have been the pressure that drove females as well as males to stay in long-term consortships or bonds" (13330).

2. Lukas and Clutton-Brock Thesis

D. Lukas and T.H. Clutton-Brock (2013) sought an explanation to the fact that paternal care characterizes most socially monogamous species today. They suggest that this feature of monogamous species has actually evolved after—not before—pair bonding had formed, thus challenging the Opie et al. idea that the risk of male infanticide was the prime cause of the evolution of pair bonding.

3. Henrich, Boyd, and Richerson Thesis

Joseph Henrich and colleagues (2011) proposed a normative explanation of social monogamy in human societies grounded on *cultural evolutionary principles*. Although polygyny has been widespread in history, monogamous marriage emerged as the most preferred marriage system. The reason for its widespread diffusion, they write, is because the norms and institutions that compose the modern package of monogamous marriage have been favoured by cultural evolution; that is, monogamy thrives because it provides significant benefits to society.

As an institution, monogamy suppresses intrasexual competition and reduces the size of the pool of unmarried men, which in turn reduces rates of crime, including rape, murder, assault, robbery, and fraud, as well as personal abuses. By assuaging the competition for young brides, normative monogamy decreases the spousal age gap as well as fertility and gender inequality. Further, by shifting male efforts from seeking wives to paternal investment, the aggregate normative monogamy increases savings, economic productivity, and greater investments in children. At the level of the family, monogamy increases relatedness among immediate and extended family members, thus reducing intrahousehold conflict, and lowering rates of child neglect, abuse, accidental death, and homicide. Finally, monogamy may have served as the basis for the development of democracy in the Western world. In this sense, "the peculiar institutions of monogamous marriage may help explain why democratic ideals and notions of equality and human rights first emerged in the West" (667).

Canadian Nuptiality Trends and Patterns

From the Early 1920s Onwards

The Canadian vital statistics system was not established until 1921; hence, our knowledge of nuptiality trends before that time is limited. However, it seems that marriage rates in Canada in the second half of the nineteenth century were somewhat higher than was the case in Western Europe (McInnis, 2000a, 2000b; Mertens, 1976).

Change in the Marriage Rate

Industrialized countries became fully urban and completed the demographic transition in the first half of the twentieth century—a period that also included two major world wars and the Great Depression. As might be expected, the Canadian marriage rate declined in response to these events, but in each case it recovered once the disruption came to an end. Figure 5.6 shows the long-term trends in crude marriage and divorce rates in Canada from 1921 to 2006, while Figures 5.7 and 5.8 show provincial variations in marriage and divorce rates. The marriage rate in 1921 stood at 7.9 per 1000; eleven years later, in 1932, it had declined to 5.9—one of the lowest levels ever recorded in Canadian history. Such a low rate would not be seen again in Canada until the early 1990s. Higher marriage rates in the early to mid-1940s, according to McVey and Kalbach (1995: 228), were stimulated by a combination of social, economic, and demographic influences, especially (1) the economic recovery sparked by Canada's involvement in World War II; (2) the increased employment levels and rising prosperity that continued into the post-war period; and (3) the fact that people

who had had to postpone marriage because of the Depression of the 1930s or the war were finally able to wed. As a consequence of these developments, Canada reached its peak crude marriage rates of 10.6 and 10.9 per 1000 in 1942 and 1946, respectively.

The marriage rate then began a prolonged decline that lasted until 1963, when it reached 6.9 per 1000. The main reason for this trend was the fact that the cohorts born during the Depression and reaching marriageable age in the 1950s were unusually small. In fact, the proportion of people aged 15–25 who were marrying for the first time actually increased between 1941 and 1961, as did the married proportion of the total population 15 years of age and older. But these increases were insufficient to overcome the negative effects on overall marriage rates of the small Depression-era cohorts. The fact

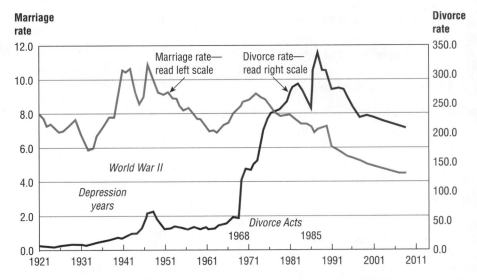

FIGURE 5.6 Crude marriage and divorce rates, Canada, 1921–2008

Note: Rates are per 1000 population in the case of marriage; per 100000 in the case of divorce.

Sources: Adapted from McVey and Kalbach (1995): 230. Additional sources for years after 1991: Bélanger (2006): 64, 69; Statistics Canada (2002b): 2, (2003c): 4. Marriage rates for 2003–6 were calculated with data from Statistics Canada (2007c, 2007d: 20); for 2007 and 2008, Statistics Canada CANSIM database (Tables 101-1004; 101-6501).

that Canada was experiencing an economic recession in the early 1960s may also have contributed to the decline in the crude marriage rate (McVey and Kalbach, 1995: 229).

After 1963, the marriage rate began to rise again, peaking in the early 1970s, but it never again reached the heights attained immediately after 1945. This more recent marriage surge can be attributed mainly to the coming of age of the cohorts born during the early years of the baby boom. As Figure 5.7 clearly shows, marriage rates fell precipitously after 1972, reaching 4.4 in 2008. This is the lowest level recorded in Canadian history. No doubt part of the reason for these low marriage rates is the demographic effect of declining fertility beginning in the early 1960s and the consequent declines over the course of the last several decades in the size of cohorts of young men and women of marriageable age (McVey and Kalbach, 1995: 229). Among the other factors that could be mentioned are changes in the economy and the impact of such changes on the economic prospects of young people. For instance, the additional education and training demanded of entry-level workers by today's economy means that many young men and women are staying in school longer and therefore marrying later than earlier generations did. But this is not the whole story. Values have changed as well. For many people today, marriage does not appear to be the central institution it once was, and society is much more tolerant of alternative living arrangements.

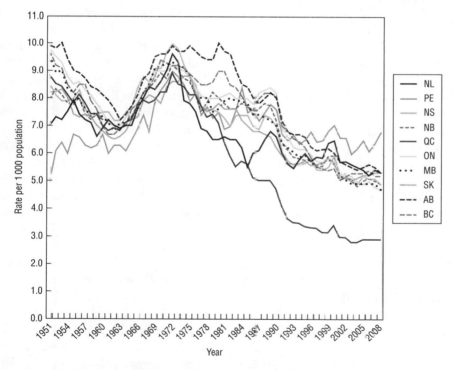

FIGURE 5.7   Crude marriage rates per 1000 population, by province, 1951–2008

Sources: Bélanger (2003): 106, (2006): 64; Statistics Canada CANSIM database (Table 101-1004); Wadhera and Strachan (1992): 17–18.

Change in the Divorce Rate

Before 1968, when the laws were liberalized, a Canadian couple wishing to dissolve their marriage required a Private Act of Parliament in order to obtain a divorce decree (McVey and Kalbach, 1995: 231). For this reason, Canadian divorce rates until the late 1960s remained quite low. We can identify three distinct waves of divorce in Canada since the end of World War II. The first, between 1946 and 1951, largely reflected the disruptive effects of separation during the war. The dramatic spike that began in the late 1960s and continued until 1982 was the result of the liberalizing reforms that passed into law in 1968. Having peaked in 1982 at 285.9 divorces per 100 000 population, the rate declined slightly and then rose again, reaching an all-time high of 345.2 per 100 000 in 1987 (McVey and Kalbach, 1995: 232). This third wave followed the passage of the 1985 Divorce Act, which further relaxed the legal restrictions. Under the revised act, the evidence required to support a claim of marriage breakdown was reduced considerably, making a divorce even easier to obtain than had been the cases under the 1968 act. Consequently, there was a spike in the divorce rate in 1987. Since then, however, the rate of marital dissolution has actually been declining, both in the country as a whole and across the provinces (see Figure 5.8). The rate in 2003—roughly 223 per 100 000—was close to the rates recorded in the early 1970s. The declining trend through the 1990s was in part a reflection of the decline in marriage rates beginning around the early 1970s. As marriage rates have continued their downward trend, divorce rates have also continued to decline as the risk set of potential divorcees has become progressively smaller over time.

But demographic changes are not the only factors that may help to explain the recent reductions in the incidence of divorce. Canadian society in the 1960s witnessed radical sociological shifts, two of the most relevant were the counterculture movement's rejection of traditional values, including marriage, and the social changes that made it easier for women to enter (or re-enter) the labour force. These shifts allowed many unhappily married women to make the transition to divorced status with greater ease and confidence than before (McVey and Kalbach, 1995: 232).

It may be argued that in addition to the recent gains made by women, the divorce revolution of the 1970s reflected a general shift in social attitudes regarding the permanency of the marital institution. Since the early 1960s, society has come to take a much more relaxed view of family break-up. In the past, people who had been divorced might well have faced social ostracism. Today, by contrast, the individuals involved can return to the life of singlehood without facing any social penalty. And if singlehood is unsatisfactory, they can find new partners either to marry or to live with. Perhaps the most fundamental change in regard to both marriage and divorce since the early 1970s, then, has been a change in mentality whereby a growing proportion of the society has come to regard marriage as less important than it once was.

Over time, marriage and divorce rates alike have shown a fair degree of uniformity across the provinces (see Figures 5.7 and 5.8). In 2008, the highest and lowest marriage rates were recorded by Prince Edward Island and Quebec, respectively; the highest and lowest divorce rates, by Alberta and Newfoundland. The general similarity of these trends across the country suggests similar underlying conditions (Goyder, 1993). One common factor in the decline of divorce, for example, is the demographic effect of the growing tendency to choose cohabitation rather than formal marriage: the more couples opt for cohabitation, the lower the marriage rate; and fewer marriages mean fewer divorces.

Trends in Remarriage and Common-Law Unions

For individual people, remarriage represents a quest to re-establish a marital bond. For a society, a trend towards remarriage could indicate that marriage as an institution is in better shape than high divorce rates would

suggest. In recent years, approximately one-third of Canadian marriages have involved at least one previously divorced or widowed spouse (Bélanger, 2006: 62). The proportion of remarriages in which both spouses had been previously married has actually increased since the early 1980s, from almost 4 per cent in 1981 to nearly 46 per cent in 2002 (more recent data not available). In fact, estimates indicate that between two-thirds and three-quarters of divorced Canadians do eventually remarry (Wu and Schimmele, 2005). One possible interpretation of these trends in remarriage is that the high rates of divorce seen in Canada have less to do with declining respect for

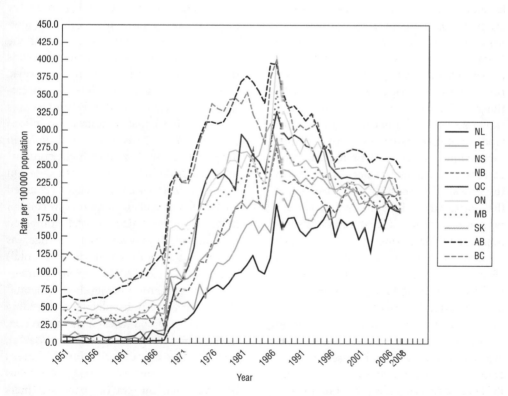

FIGURE 5.8   Crude divorce rates per 100 000 population, by province, 1951–2008

Sources: Bélanger (2003): 28; Statistics Canada (1979, 1984); Statistics Canada CANSIM database, Table 101-6501.

marriage as an institution than with desire for a "good" marriage and low tolerance for one that is unhappy and unrewarding.

On the other hand, remarriage rates do not necessarily tell us a complete story because it seems likely that a large proportion of the divorced people who do not remarry still form new common-law relationships, which account for a rising proportion of relationships in recent decades.

Data on common-law couples were available for the first time from the 1981 census. At that time, they represented 5.6 per cent of all census families. Since then, the proportion of common-law couples has grown to 16.7 per cent of all census families in 2011 (Statistics Canada 2012b). Common-law unions are most prevalent among those aged 25–29, though all age groups have seen increases over time. Young Canadians today are significantly more likely than earlier generations to report that their first conjugal union was a common-law relationship (as opposed to matrimony). In a recent survey, when never-married or previously married people were asked if they were willing to live in a common-law union, there was a clear age gradient in affirmative responses: the younger the respondent, the greater the willingness to accept this type of relationship (Milan, 2003). On the other hand, in comparison to marriages, common-law unions in Canada are not very stable (Budinski and Trovato, 2005; Hall and Zhao, 1995; Le Bourdais, Neill, and Turcotte, 2000; Wu, 2000). And even though many common-law relationships eventually end up as marriages, such unions experience very high rate of separation as compared to marital unions; in some cases, the separation rates can exceed 60 per cent by the fifteenth year of union (Cooke and Baxter, 2010; Eichler and Pedersen, 2013).

The instability of all types of conjugal unions—marital and common-law—in Canada today suggests that increasing proportions of adults may be spending a significant part of their lives living alone or in short-term relationships. This is particularly likely to be the case among younger cohorts, where break-up rates tend to be high (Le Bourdais, Neill, and Turcotte, 2000; Milan, 2000; Statistics Canada, 2002c).

The Case of Quebec

The nuptiality patterns of Quebec differ from the rest of Canada. Until the Quiet Revolution of the late 1950s and early 1960s, marriage rates in Quebec were generally high and people tended to marry early. Today, Quebec has both the lowest marriage rate in the country and the highest incidence of non-marital unions (Le Bourdais and Lapierre-Adamczyk, 2004). This is true across all broad age categories (see Figure 5.9). The latest census of 2011 showed that common-law unions accounted for 31.5 per cent of all couples in the province. This is a much higher proportion than any other province in Canada. On a national level, in 2011, Quebec accounted for 44.3 per cent of all common-law couples in the country, which in total numbered 1.57 million. The closest other province was Ontario (25.2 per cent of the national total) (Statistics Canada 2012c). Even by international standards, the level of cohabitation in Quebec is unusually high, exceeding the figures for countries such as Sweden, Finland, and Denmark (Cooke and Baxter, 2010: 521; Statistics Canada, 2007e).

Jacques Henripin (2003: 185) has observed that the era of "paperless marriage" in Quebec began in the 1970s, and all the relevant indicators—declining marriage

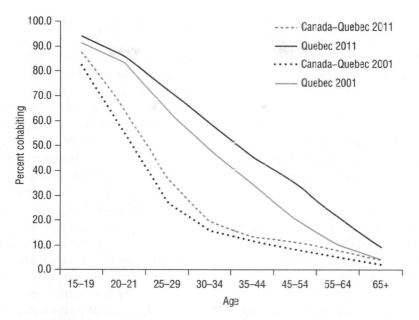

FIGURE 5.9   Percentage of couples in common-law unions by age of woman in Canada (less Quebec), and in Quebec, 2001 and 2011.

Note: The age-specific percentages are based on the number of cohabiting females in each age category divided by the total of cohabiting females plus married females in the same age group. Thus, the figures represent the percentage of females in cohabitation in relation to females in couple unions.

Source: Author's computation with data from Statistics Canada (2011b, 2011c).

rates, rising age at first marriage, high rates of both divorce and cohabitation—suggest that it is now well established. In the rest of Canada, cohabitation is usually a precursor to marriage, but this is not the case in Quebec: the chance that cohabiting women will eventually marry is 33 per cent lower in Quebec than in other provinces (Wu, 2000). As Henripin (2003: 187) notes, it appears that cohabitation in Quebec is not primarily a kind of trial marriage for young couples, or even an alternative to traditional marriage: rather, it appears to be evolving into a new type of family form that increasingly includes a growing proportion of all children born in the province. In Canada, the proportion of children aged 14 and under who

lived with common-law parents increased from 12.8 per cent in 2001 to 16.3 per cent in 2011. In Quebec, the corresponding figure for 2011 was 37.8 per cent (Statistics Canada, 2012c).

Future Outlook

By the end of the twenty-first century, the Canadian family could look quite different than it does today. Data gathered from the last several censuses show that traditional marriage is in decline while common-law unions and single-parenthood are on the rise. The number of married couples counted in 2011 was nearly 6.3 million, but although this constituted the largest group of all census families, the proportion of married couples has been sliding steadily since the 1960s. Between 2006 and 2011, the number of married couples increased by just 3.1 per cent; by comparison, over the same period the total number of common-law unions (nearly 1.6 million in 2011) grew by nearly 14 per cent. Another indication that the traditional Canadian family is changing is the diminishing proportion of couples with children (47 per cent in 2011); the continued rise in the numbers of single mothers (over 1.2 million in 2011) and single fathers (nearly 327 545); the decline in families with five or more members; and the rising trend of one-person households (see box).

The Canadian family is continuing to evolve as we move further into the twenty-first century. While the majority of Canadians today still marry, this is a less frequent occasion compared to earlier times. For those that do marry, nuptial vows occur at older ages. Divorce has increased significantly in response to legislative changes that made dissolution of marriages easier. Meanwhile, Canadian society has increasingly become accepting of diverse non-traditional forms of conjugal arrangements. The widespread acceptance of common-law relationships and more recently legalization of same-sex marriages are clear reflections of a definitive shift in value orientations—away from rigid traditionalism and towards greater acceptance of post-modern values. Taken together, these trends strongly suggest that Canadian society is unlikely to return to the more traditional family models of earlier times, as the momentum behind these trends seems much too strong.

Conclusion

In this chapter, we examined the basic concepts and measures of nuptiality and looked at the trends in marriage, divorce, and cohabitation across the developed and the developing regions of the world. Our broad overview suggests that in the developed countries marriage has been declining, and cohabitation without marriage increasing, since the 1970s. This pattern reflects profound changes in the way young adults think about marriage and the institution of the family in general. In the developing countries, age at first marriage has generally increased since the early 1970s. In time, with increasing levels of urbanization and especially improvements in the status of women, age at first marriage can be expected to increase further. As urbanization, globalization of the economy, and the spread of Western values continue throughout the world, nuptiality patterns may become increasingly similar across the regions, though it seems unlikely that full convergence is possible.

In the Western world, the social barriers to diversity in family form have weakened considerably and are likely to weaken further. People now have a plethora of options: they can remain single; marry or cohabit; divorce and form new relationships, with or without marriage; bear and raise children with or without a partner of either sex. In one sense, these trends can be viewed as a challenge to traditional notions of the family; on the other hand, they can be thought of as welcoming new options to people, irrespective of the uncertainty they may pose.

CENSUS HIGHLIGHTS ON CANADIAN UNIONS AND FAMILIES

1. Married couples families are becoming less common

   Married couple families in 2001: 70.5%; in 2011: 67% (6.29 million of 9.39 million total families including lone-parent families).

2. Common-law unions increasing, and more children live with common-law parents

   In 2011, common-law couples (1.6 million) surpassed single-parent families (1.53 million). Common-law families in 2011 comprised 19.9% of total couple families; in 1981, this was 6.3%. The proportion of children aged 14 and under who live with common-law parents increased from 12.8% in 2001 to 16.3% in 2011.

3. Canadian households getting smaller

   Average number of children per family in 1961 was 2.7; in 2011, this was 1.9. The average family size of one-family households was 3.9 in 1961 and 2.9 in 2011.

4. Declining percentage of married couples with children

   In 2011, 54% of married couple families had children; in 2006, this was 56%.

5. More young adults (age 20–29) live with parents (i.e., never left or have returned)

   In 2011, the percentage of this age group living with parents was 42%; in 1981, it was 26%.

6. More people are living alone

   In 2006, one-person households comprised 26.8% of all private households. In 2011, this was 27.6%. Couple households with children aged 24 or under comprised nearly the same proportion in 2011 (26.5%).

7. Women aged 65 and over most likely to live alone

   In 2011, among those aged 65 and older, 31.5% of women lived alone as compared to 16% of men in this age group.

8. Same-sex couples on the increase

   In 2006, the census counted 45 345 same-sex couples; in 2011 the number was 64 575 (of which 21 015 were married and 43 560 were common-law: male couples, 54.5%; female couples, 45.5%). Of same-sex couples with children, 80% were female couples.

9. Step-families counted for the first time

   Of all couples with children (3.7 million), 87.7% were *intact families* (biological/adopted children of both parents); and 557 950 (12.6%) were *step-families*, of which 5.2% were *complex* type (one child of both parents as well as one child of one parent only) and 7.4% *simple* type (all children are the children of one of the parents).

10. More lone-parent families

    In 2011, there were 1.53 million lone parent families (80% lone mothers; 20% lone fathers). The number of lone-parent families in 2001 was 1.31 million.

Source: Adapted, data obtained from various census tabulations, Statistics Canada website.

Notes for Further Study

Singulate Mean Age at Marriage (SMAM)

From the age distribution of the proportion single, it is possible to derive a measure of first marriage timing proposed by Hajnal in 1953, the singulate mean age at marriage (SMAM). SMAM gives the average length of single life in years among those who marry before age 50. It is relatively straightforward to compute, as it requires only census data on age-specific proportions of single persons between the ages of 0 and 50. Below are some selected SMAM for females and males across selected countries covering the early 1970s and the period around 2010. The data (taken from the United Nations Department of Economic and Social Affairs Population Division [2013c]) suggest a general increase over time in the average age at first marriage for both men and women. Although men are typically older than their female partners, the age gap (f-m) has been shrinking over time.

Country	Period	SMAM female	SMAM male	f − m
Canada	1971	22.0	24.4	−2.4
	2006	26.6	28.6	−2.0
USA	1970	21.5	23.5	−2.0
	2009	26.9	28.8	−1.9
Japan	1970	24.7	27.5	−2.8
	2010	29.7	31.2	−1.5
Mexico	1970	21.2	24.4	−3.2
	2010	24.3	26.5	−2.2
Rep. Korea	1970	23.3	27.2	−3.9
	2005	28.8	32.0	−3.2

Exercises

1. Discuss the sociological causes of declining marriage rates and increased divorce in the Western world since the early 1970s.
2. Evaluate the proposition that cohabitation is replacing marriage in Western countries today. To what extent is cohabitation a precursor to marriage rather than an alternative to it? Is there an education gradient in marriage and cohabitation? If so, what explains this gradient?
3. Describe how the family institution is changing in the developing countries. How widespread is the Western family ideal across developing countries?

Additional Reading

Dabhoiwala, Faramerz. 2012. *The Origins of Sex: A History of the First Sexual Revolution*. Oxford: Allen Lane/Oxford University Press.

Esping-Andersen, Gosta. 2009. *The Incomplete Revolution: Adapting to Women's New Roles*. Cambridge, UK: Polity Press.

Inglehart, Ronald. 1990. *Culture Shift in Advanced Industrial Society*. Princeton, NJ: Princeton University Press.

Linerberg, Eric. 2012. *Going Solo: The Extraordinary Rise and Surprising Appeal of Living Alone*. New York: The Penguin Press.

McQuillan, Kevin, and Zenaida R. Ravanera, eds. 2006. *Canada's Changing Families: Implications for Individuals and Society*. Toronto: University of Toronto Press.

Ridley, Matt. 1993. *The Red Queen: Sex and the Evolution of Human Nature*. New York: Penguin Books.

Shorter, Edward. 1975. *The Making of the Modern Family*. New York: Basic Books.

Stone, Lawrence. 1977. *The Family, Sex and Marriage in England 1500–1800*. New York: Harper and Row.

Van den Berghe, Pierre L. 1979. *Human Family Systems: An Evolutionary View*. New York: Elsevier.

Wright, Robert. 1994. *The Moral Animal: Why We Are the Way We Are: The New Science of Evolutionary Psychology*. New York: Vintage Books.

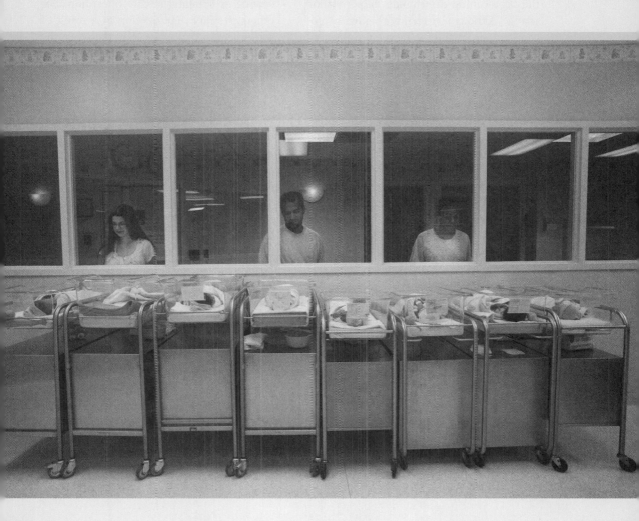

PART THREE

Demographic Processes I:
Fertility and Mortality

6 Fertility

Introduction

Along with mortality and migration, fertility is a central determinant of population change. Although inherently a biological process, human fertility is strongly influenced by societal and cultural factors that make it a collective as well as an individual matter. A society's continuity depends on its fertility, and for this reason all societies possess elements of culture that promote and encourage some level of reproduction. A population's fertility is therefore the product of biological, social, and behavioural factors.

Basic Concepts and Measures

Fecundity and Fertility

Fecundity describes the physiological ability of a woman, a man, or a couple to reproduce. Logically, fecundity depends on a sequence of events: the female must produce an egg capable of being fertilized; the male must produce sperm that can fertilize the egg; fertilization must occur; the fertilized egg must survive to implant in the uterus; and, once implantation has occurred, the pregnancy must result in a live birth (Trussell, 2003: 397). The opposite of fecundity is *infecundity*—the total inability to reproduce (in other words, *sterility*).

For some individuals, infecundity may be the result of a lifelong genetic or biological condition that prevents them from conceiving or bringing about conception. For others, sterility may develop as a result of some acquired disease that damages the reproductive system (McFalls, 1979: 4). We can distinguish sterility as either *primary sterility* or *secondary sterility*. Primary sterility are cases where sterility is present before the individual has had a child; the latter are cases that have had at least one child prior to becoming sterile (see Figure 6.1).

Sub-fecundity (often also referred to as *infertility*) is the term used to describe the reduced ability of couples to have children because of impairments in any of the biological aspects of reproduction. These impairments include the following:

- *coital inability*, the temporary or permanent inability to perform normal heterosexual intercourse because of physical or psychological disease;
- *conceptive failure*, the diminished ability to conceive or to bring about conception; and
- *pregnancy loss*, the involuntary termination of a pregnancy before a live birth, including spontaneous abortion, late fetal death, and stillbirth (but does not include either induced abortion or neonatal mortality). (McFalls, 1979, 1990)

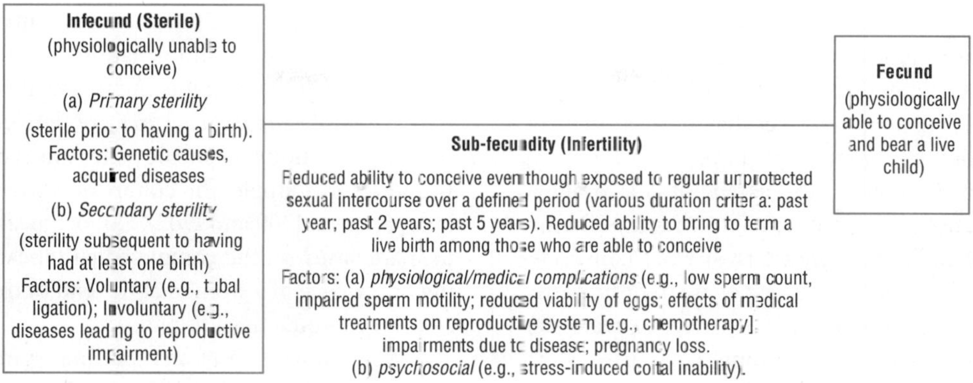

FIGURE 6.1   Sterility–fecundity continuum

The extent of sub-fecundity can vary, from situations where both partners have chronic reproductive impairments to cases in which one partner suffers from an impairment that is medically treatable.

The realization of fecundity is referred to as *fertility*. Fertility is the actual reproductive output of a woman, a man, or a couple, as measured by the number of offspring. At the aggregate level, this term implies some summary measure of reproduction for a population.

Deriving a precise estimate of the level of sub-fecundity and sterility in contemporary populations is not a straightforward matter, as many couples rely on contraception and even voluntarily sterilization—e.g., tubal ligation, vasectomy (Menken, 1985; Menken, Trussell, and Larsen, 1986). Some estimates of sterility have been obtained based on studies of historical populations in which contraception was absent. Such studies indicate there is an aging effect, in that fecundity in women reduces with increasing age but most notably after age 40; and lifetime childlessness, as an indirect measure of sterility, ranged between 3 and 7 per cent (Trussell and Wilson, 1985).

A recent analysis by Maya Mascarenhas and colleagues (2012) based on 53 Demographic Health Surveys shows that among contemporary populations primary sterility falls in the range of 0.6 and 3.4 per cent.

In regard to secondary sterility, these authors estimated a much wider range: between 8.7 and 32.6 per cent. Undoubtedly, a major reason for this high degree of variability has to do with differential exposure to diseases—especially sexually transmitted diseases—that impair the reproductive system. In some poor developing countries, secondary sterility can be quite high by modern standards due to poor socioeconomic and generally unsanitary conditions (see, e.g., Romaniuk, 2011 in regard to Tropical Africa). In more developed countries, the level of secondary sterility would be expected to be comparatively lower (Menken, Trussell, and Larsen, 1986).

As for sub-fecundity, this problem is likely also quite extensive in poor countries with high levels of secondary sterility. In such countries, one would expect to find a strong correlation between the high prevalence of secondary sterility and the level of reproductive impairments. In more developed countries, where we have more information, sub-fecundity seems to be on the increase. There appears to be a growing proportion of couples that desire a child and wish to conceive but have problems doing so. Of course, the extent of this problem can vary from country to country. The use of different definitions of what constitutes sub-fecundity (i.e., exposure to unprotected sex over one year, two years, five years) can also make cross-national comparisons difficult (Gurunath et al., 2011). Nonetheless, there is some convergence in the estimates. For instance, in Canada and the United States, the estimated levels of sub-fecundity are between 11 and 16 per cent of couples (McFalls, 1979, 1990; Mascarenhas et al., 2012; Bushnik et al., 2012). Sub-fecund couples can access a variety of medical procedures that have varying degrees of success to help them conceive. These range from *in vitro* fertilization to fertility drugs, diagnostic tests, donor eggs, surrogate carriers, and donor sperm (Nelson, Telfer and Anderson, 2013; Sartorius and Nieschlag, 2010; Schmidt et al., 2012; Spaar, 2006). Some couples can elect to adopt.

The rising trend in sub-fecundity in more developed countries is mainly related to the tendency towards later parenthood, as older women, especially beyond age 30, are more likely to experience varying degrees of reproductive impairment (Menken, Trussell, and Larsen, 1986). At the same time, for some couples, it contributes to an increasing rate of involuntary childlessness and thus smaller families than desired.

Measures of Fertility

Generally speaking, the study of aggregate fertility for populations is based on two types of measures: period and cohort.

Period measures of fertility are computed on the basis of current information, usually for a given year or some other specified interval, while *cohort measures* are derived from information on specific generations of women (for example, the cohort of women born between 1900 and 1905). Cohort measures are based on the completed childbearing experience of a woman at the end of the cohort's reproductive lifespan.

The following sections outline some common period and cohort measures of fertility. As we will see, some of the period measures, like the total fertility rate and the gross and net reproduction rates, can also be computed for cohorts. However, while the methods of calculating period and cohort measures are essentially the same, their data requirements and the implications of their results will, of course, differ.

Crude Birth Rate

The crude birth rate (CBR) measures the number of births over a specified period per 1000 population:

$$\text{CBR} = \frac{B}{P} \times 1000$$

where *B* represents the number of births in a given time period (usually one- or five-year interval), and *P* is the corresponding mid-interval population.

In 2014, the world's crude birth rate was 20 per 1000 population. In the more developed countries, the CBR was only 11 per 1000 population, while in the less developed countries, it was 22, or about 10 per cent above the world rate. Africa stands out for its high birth rates (middle Africa, for instance, has a rate of 45 per 1000), while the lowest CBRs are in Europe. Over recent times, the rates for southern, Western, and Eastern Europe seldom exceed 10 per 1 000.

Although very useful in many technical and substantive applications, the CBR has a number of drawbacks that may make it impractical for comparative analysis of fertility differentials. First, it overlooks the effect of age on fertility. As we shall see later, women's fertility varies with age; the CBR does not account for age differences. Second, the population used in the denominator includes not just women of childbearing age but also children, the elderly, and men— segments of the population that have no direct relationship to the risk of childbearing. For these reasons in particular, analysts will often compute other period measures that are based on age-specific data for women in the reproductive ages.

General Fertility Rate

The simplest age-limited measure of fertility is the general fertility rate (GFR), which represents the number of births per 1 000 women between the ages of 15 and 49 (which is generally considered the reproductive age span for women):

$$\text{GFR} = \frac{B}{P^f_{15-49}} \times 1000$$

The numerator is the total number of births in a given period in the population, and the denominator corresponds to the mid-interval population of females (signified by the superscript f) aged 15–49. Note that in some applications of this formula for industrialized countries, the upper age is set at 44, since relatively few women in these societies bear children past this age (even though late childbearing has become more common recently).

Table 6.1 shows Canada's GFR for 2011 computed separately based on the

two denominators, 15–49 and 15–44. The derived figure of 52.19 based on the first of these denominators indicates that in 2011 there were roughly 52 births for every 1 000 women of childbearing age (15–49). The second computation, based on the shorter childbearing span typically used for industrialized countries (15–44), gives a higher rate of 54.28. We may gain a sense of how Canadian fertility rates have changed over time by comparing these two calculations with rates from earlier in the twentieth century. In 1957, the Canadian GFR$_{(15-49)}$ was 118.0, and the GFR$_{(15-44)}$ was 129.8. These are the highest recorded GFRs for Canada since 1921.

Age-Specific Fertility Rates

Age-specific fertility rates get around some of the problems associated with the crude birth rate. The formula for an age-specific fertility rate can be written as follows:

$$f_x = \frac{B_x}{W_x} \times 1000$$

where f_x symbolizes the age-specific fertility rate for a given period, B_x is the number of births in the period to women aged x, and W_x is the mid-interval female population aged x.

Thus, this formula calculates the number of births to women of a given age group in a given period for every 1 000 women in the same age group.

If we were to plot age-specific fertility rates on a graph, we would notice a distinct pattern across age: rates tend to be relatively low for women aged 15–19 but rise steeply for those aged 20–24 and 25–29 before levelling off and declining. In populations with high overall fertility, birth rates

TABLE 6.1   Number of live births by age of mother, female population, and calculated age-specific fertility rates and general fertility rate, Canada 2011

Age of mother	Number of live births	Female population	Fertility rate per 1 000 women
15–19	13 436	1 072 690	12.53
20–24	53 478	1 169 125	45.74
25–29	113 628	1 193 839	95.18
30–34	124 349	1 174 738	105.85
35–39	59 656	1 140 405	52.31
40–44	12 207	1 189 542	10.26
45–49	708	1 364 982	0.52
Total	377 462	7 232 631	
GFR_{15-49}			52.19
GFR_{15-44}			54.28

Source: Author's computations using data from Statistics Canada (2013b, h).

are usually highest in the age group 20–24. In the developed countries, where women are more inclined to have children later in life, the peak age group is usually 25–29 or (especially in recent years) 30–34. In general, fertility rates fall precipitously after the mid-thirties, approaching very low values as women reach their mid- to late forties. Figure 6.2 illustrates the age-specific fertility pattern of American Hutterite women in the early 1920s in comparison with the rates for women from other populations. The Hutterites are thought to be the most fertile group in history (Coale, 1969; Eaton and Meyer, 1953; Henry, 1961).

Total Fertility Rate

An advantage of age-specific fertility rates is that they can be used to compute other important population indexes of reproduction. One of these is the *total fertility rate* (TFR), which is a summary measure of the total reproductive output for a given population during a specific interval (usually a year). As a single index of fertility, the TFR has the advantage of being easily computable and interpretable. It is a pure fertility measure that is not affected by age composition, and it is one of the few aggregate-level period measures of fertility that can be interpreted in terms of the number of children expected to be born to an individual woman over the course of her childbearing years. In other words, the TFR represents the expected average number of children ever born to a randomly selected woman who survives to the end of her reproductive span (usually menopause or some suitably advanced age, such as 50 years), given that the current age-specific fertility rates in the population remain constant (Wood, 1994: 27). Similarly, we can think of a hypothetical cohort of 1 000 women who start reproducing at age 15, and who will eventually end their childbearing once they reach age 50. If this hypothetical cohort were to bear children in accordance

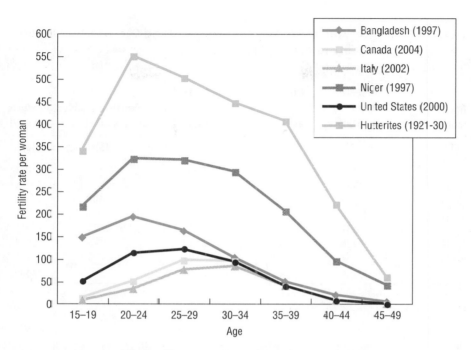

FIGURE 6.2   Age-specific fertility rates for selected countries, late 1990s–early 2000s, and of Hutterite women from South Dakota married between 1921 and 1930

Sources: Henry (1961); Statistics Canada (2006a); United Nations Department of Economic and Social Affairs Population Division (2005).

with the age-specific fertility rates of a real population, then at the end of their childbearing years these hypothetical women would end up with a certain average number of children. That eventual average is the TFR.

In terms of how it is calculated, the TFR is the sum of age-specific fertility rates for women aged 15 to 49, and can be expressed as follows:

$$TFR = \sum_{15}^{49} f_x$$

where f_x represents age-specific fertility rate *per woman.*

In many applications, the data are grouped into five-year age categories and the formula is expressed slightly differently than shown above. The sum of the rates must be multiplied by 5 to take into account the five-year age interval, so the formula becomes:

$$TFR = 5 \times \sum_{15-19}^{45-49} f_x$$

In Table 6.2, the sum of age-specific fertility rates per 1000 women is 322.39. Multiplying this value by 5 gives a TFR of 1612 children per 1000 women of reproductive age, or approximately 1.61 children *per woman.* Another way of stating this is to say that a hypothetical woman aged 15 in 2011, if she were exposed to the age-specific fertility rates of Canada in 2011, would by the age of 50 have borne 1.61 children

TABLE 6.2   Computation of TFR, GRR, and NRR using Canada's age-specific fertility rates for 2011

Age of mother	Age-specific fertility rate per 1 000	Age-specific fertility rate per woman	Age-specific female birth rate per woman	Female life table survival ratio	Products (4) × (5)
(1)	(2)	(3)	(4)	(5)	(6)
15–19	12.53	0.0125	0.0061	4.9657	0.0303
20–24	45.74	0.0457	0.0223	4.9584	0.1104
25–29	95.18	0.0952	0.0463	4.9509	0.2294
30–34	105.85	0.1059	0.0515	4.9416	0.2547
35–39	52.31	0.0523	0.0255	4.9278	0.1255
40–44	10.26	0.0103	0.0050	4.9067	0.0245
45–49	0.52	0.0005	0.0003	4.8745	0.0012
Sums	322.39	0.3224	0.1570		0.7761
TFR	1612.0	1.6120			
GRR			0.7850		
NRR					0.7761

Notes: Column (4) assumes the proportion of newborns that are female within each age category of mothers is 0.4869, which corresponds to a sex ratio at birth of 1.0538 (the ratio for Canada in 2011).

Sources: Author's computations using data from Statistics Canada (2013b, 2013g). The life table survival ratios for females were derived from the 2007–09 Canadian female life table (Statistics Canada, 2013i).

(keeping in mind that this is an average figure).

Demographers frequently attempt to determine whether a population is growing fast enough to replace itself, and the total fertility rate is useful in this regard. The fertility level required for a population to replace itself varies depending on mortality conditions up to the end of the childbearing ages. It has been calculated that if a population has a life expectancy at birth of 25 years, the TFR needed for replacement is 5.21 children per woman. With a life expectancy at birth of 45 years, a population would require a TFR of 3.08 for replacement. A TFR of 2.1 coincides with a life expectancy at birth of 75 years. Since many countries have attained this life expectancy, a TFR of 2.1 is usually regarded as replacement-level fertility (Coale and Demeny, 1983).

Some countries have fertility levels well above the 2.1 replacement level. A notable case is Niger, where in 2013 women had on average nearly eight children. Age-specific fertility rates in this country are unusually high by today's standards, especially among 15- to 19-year-olds which suggests that, relatively speaking, women in Niger enter sexual unions and start reproducing earlier than women in other parts of the world, and consequently have large families.

A measure related to the TFR is the *total marital fertility rate* (TMFR). It is identical to the TFR except that it relates specifically to *married* women of childbearing age. The difference between the TMFR and the TFR for a given population provides a measure of the effect of marriage on overall fertility.

Gross Reproduction Rate

It is important to understand, however, that *replacement fertility* really has to do with the average number of *female* offspring that women produce. The measure that addresses this important feature of a population's reproductivity is the *gross reproduction rate* (GRR).

The formula for GRR indicates to sum the age-specific female birth rates (i.e., based on the births that are female as the numerators) and then multiply this sum by 5, the width of the age intervals, where f_x^F represents the age-specific female birth rate:

$$GRR = \sum_{15-19}^{45-49} f_x^F \times 5$$

The information in Table 6.2 can be used to illustrate the computation of GRR. Column (4), the age-specific female birth rates, were derived by multiplying the corresponding age-specific fertility rates in column (3) by 0.4869. This was done because the specific actual numbers of female births to mothers in each age were not available. The error in using this indirect approach should not be significant because in most populations the proportion of female to male newborns does not vary significantly from one year to the next, and typically fluctuates around a proportion value of 0.49, which corresponds to a sex ratio at birth of 105 baby boys to every 100 baby girls. Over recent years in Canada, the proportion has been in the range of 0.4869, and this was applied to derive the age-specific female birth rates in the table.

Another way to derive the GRR would be to multiply the computed TFR based on the general age-specific fertility rates by the overall proportion of newborns that are female, below represented by the symbol π:

$$GRR = TFR \times \pi$$

In Table 6.2, the computed TFR per woman is 1.612, and the gross reproduction rate works out to 0.7850. This is the expected number of female children a woman will have assuming that she survives through the childbearing ages and has children according to the age-specific fertility rates prevailing in the population in 2011. If the computed GRR is below 1—as it is in this case—it means that on average, mothers are having fewer than one daughter. Over the long term, this level of reproductivity is insufficient to ensure that the population will replace itself; any value greater than 1 is considered to be above-replacement fertility (but see below for further clarification on this point). Gross reproduction rate of 1 would be consistent with zero population growth in the long run, meaning that each woman in the population would essentially be replacing herself with one daughter.

Net Reproduction Rate

The gross reproduction rate does not account for the possibility that some of the women of childbearing age who are exposed to the chance of giving birth may not survive through the childbearing ages. The *net reproduction rate* (NRR) represents the average number of female births to women after the effect of mortality to women in the reproductive ages has been taken into account. Stated differently, the NRR is in actuality the gross reproduction rate (GRR) adjusted for mortality to women in the childbearing ages. So if, for instance, the GRR is computed to be exactly 1, we would expect the NRR to be somewhat lower than 1 because of the effect of mortality to women in their childbearing years. In fact, the NRR will always be smaller than the computed GRR because in any population it can be expected that there will be some level of mortality, however low, to women in the childbearing years.

In order to derive the NRR, we need the age-specific survival ratios for women between the ages of 15 and 50, which can be obtained from an appropriate female *life table*. Life tables will be explained in detail in Chapter 7. At this point, it suffices to say that a life table reflects the mortality experience of a hypothetical cohort of newborns, followed through life as the cohort ages. At each age, there will be deaths and survivors according to a schedule of age-specific mortality rates taken from an actual population. Male and female life tables are calculated separately because men's and women's mortality rates differ substantially. In our case here, our objective is to use the female life table to derive age-specific survival ratios for women in each age group, from 15–19 to 45–49. Since the life table begins with a hypothetical cohort of 100 000 newborns, the age-specific survival ratios will be calculated by dividing the number of person-years lived by the cohort at a given age by 100 000. So, the female age-specific *survival ratios* (SR_x) would be computed as follows:

$$SR_x^F = \frac{L_x^F}{100\,000}$$

where L_x^F represents the number of person-years lived by the life table cohort of females in age group x. The value of 100 000 is a constant (i.e., the size of the female life table cohort at birth).

According to the Canadian female life table for 2007–9, women aged 15–19 together lived a total of 496 570 person-years. The survival ratio (SR_x) for this age category is therefore 496 570/100 000 or 4.9657. In practical terms, this tells us that a woman in this age category would live almost the full number of years of the age interval (i.e., very low mortality risk).

Once we have the survival ratios for each age category, we can apply them to the corresponding age-specific female birth rates shown in column (4) in Table 6.2. The survival ratios are shown in column (5). The products of these two columns are listed in column (6). The sum of these products gives the net reproduction rate (NRR):

$$NRR = \sum_{15-19}^{45-49} f_x^F \cdot SR_x^F$$

The net reproduction rate is a key indicator of long-term potential population growth in the absence of migration. A net reproduction rate greater than 1 means population growth without limit in the long run. A net reproduction rate less than 1 will lead, in the long run, to the population becoming extinct. Turning to Canada, the computations in Table 6.2 (page 198) indicate that current fertility is substantially below replacement. Not taking into account the possibility of international migration, this level of fertility would be insufficient to maintain long-term population growth.

NRR is fundamentally a period measure since it is computed with current age-specific fertility rates. Thus, it must be interpreted with some degree of caution. Since populations do not have stable population growth rates over very long periods of time, the NRR cannot be used as a definitive predictor of a population's ultimate fate. Rather, the NRR provides an *indication* of where a population is headed with respect to long-term growth or decline based on its current net level of reproductivity. The qualifier "in the long run" is very important. To reiterate, a net reproduction rate equal to 1 will lead to zero population growth only if it should prevail *in the long run*. Moreover, the possibility of migration as a factor in population growth should be kept in mind. The conventional concept of "replacement-level fertility" hinges on the idea that we have a closed population with no in- or out-migration. As immigration is becoming an increasingly important component of population growth in many low fertility countries, the TFR needed to avoid eventual population decline can be somewhat lower than the commonly assumed 2.1 children per woman (Wilson et al., 2013).

Cohort Fertility Rate

Since fundamentally, the period TFR reflects fertility only for the period for which it is calculated, it would be risky to interpret this measure as the fertility rate of the future since period TFR can fluctuate considerably from one year to the next. For this reason, it also useful to examine cohort fertility rates to gain a better sense of future fertility.

We can assemble retroactive data for cohorts of women who as of current year have already passed through their reproductive lifespans. With this information, we compute the average completed family size for the cohorts. The input data for this would be period age-specific fertility rates over many years, beginning as far back as data are available and ending with the most recent year for which the data are available. For instance in Canada, vital statistics data

are available from 1921. The age-specific fertility rates for each of the years since 1921 can be assembled into a matrix that juxtaposes age and calendar year. The diagonal elements in this matrix would represent the age-specific fertility rates of different cohorts of women born at different points in time. For each cohort, we would compute the average completed fertility in the same manner we calculated the period TFR.

To illustrate, Table 6.3 is a matrix of age-specific fertility rates for Canadian women from 1960 to 2010. These observations are spaced in five-year intervals (single-year data are preferable but are not readily available). There is complete information for just five cohorts: those for 1941–5, 1946–50, 1951–5, 1956–60, and 1961–6 (see also Table 6.8 in the Exercises, page 253). For ease of identification, the diagonals for the corresponding age-specific fertility rates have been bolded. The shaded bottom triangle of the matrix is truncated, as it contains incomplete information for cohorts born before 1941. The shaded triangle at the upper left-hand corner pertains to younger cohorts born after 1965, for which there is insufficient data at present to compute a cohort completed average family size. Period TFRs for 1960 through 2010 are also shown in this table to help clarify the difference between cohort and period fertility. It is clear that cohort completed fertility rates (CCFs) have been falling across different generations of women (from 2.413 for those born in 1941–5 to 1.915 for the cohort of 1961–5). Also note that CCFs for the women that completed their childbearing in 1990, 1995, 2000, 2005, and 2010 differ from the period TFRs for these years. In fact, period and cohort rates are rarely the same.

TABLE 6.3   Age-specific fertility rates (per 1 000) by period (1960–2010) for Canadian women, showing period TFR, cohort completed fertility, and the period of birth of completed cohorts

Year (t)	Age of women							Period TFR year (t)	Cohort completed fertility year (t)	Period of birth of cohort completing in year (t)
	15–19	20–24	25–29	30–34	35–39	40–44	45–49			
2010	13.5	48.0	96.4	105.7	51.6	9.9	0.4	1.628	1.915	1961–1965
2005	13.4	50.4	97.3	97.4	42.1	7.1	0.3	1.540	1.930	1956–1960
2000	16.3	56.1	97.9	89.9	35.5	6.1	0.3	1.552	1.966	1951–1955
1995	24.5	70.6	109.7	86.8	31.3	4.8	0.2	1.640	2.095	1946–1950
1990	26.9	85.4	140.2	87.5	28.6	3.9	0.1	1.863	2.413	1941–1945
1985	23.7	85.3	125.3	74.6	21.8	3.0	0.1	1.669		
1980	27.6	100.1	129.4	69.3	19.4	3.1	0.2	1.746		
1975	35.3	112.7	131.2	64.4	21.6	4.8	0.4	1.852		
1970	42.8	143.3	147.2	81.8	39.0	11.3	0.9	2.332		
1965	49.3	188.6	181.9	119.4	65.9	22.0	2.0	3.146		
1960	59.8	233.5	224.4	146.2	84.2	28.5	2.4	3.895		

Sources: Statistics Canada (1997, 2002d, 2013j); Wadhera and Strachan (1993).

The formula for the average completed fertility rate for cohort k (CCF_k) is:

$$CCF_k = \sum_{15-19}^{45-49} f_x$$

The formula indicates to sum all the age-specific fertility rates for women in cohort k.

It is interesting to note that on the basis of the period TFRs alone, it would appear that fertility in Canada has been below replacement since the mid-1970s. However, values for cohort completed fertility declined below 2.1 starting with the post-war cohort of 1951–5. The generations of women born before had completed family sizes above 2.1. As this example shows, period and cohort rates can provide very different—and equally important—perspectives on the reproductive patterns of a population.

Mean Age at Childbearing

Closely connected to both period and cohort fertility is the mean age at childbearing (MAC), a measure of the average age at which women bear children. An increasing trend in the MAC reflects a postponement effect, which sees women putting off childbirth until later in life, and correlates closely with total fertility: a greater degree of postponement translates into a higher MAC and a lower period TFR. This principle applies to cohorts as well: to the extent that generations postpone having children, the average age at maternity for the cohort will increase.

We can derive MAC from age-specific fertility rates:

$$MAC = \frac{\sum\limits_{15-19}^{45-49} f_x \cdot m_i}{\sum\limits_{15-19}^{45-49} f_x}$$

where m_i is the midpoint for a given age group (here, age is grouped into five-year age categories) and f_x is the age-specific fertility rate.

Using this formula, the mean age at childbearing for Canadian women in 2000 was 29.02, which is comparable to countries such as the Netherlands, Sweden, and Japan (Schmidt et al., 2012: 31).

When considering the relationship between period total fertility rate (TFR), cohort completed fertility (CCF), and mean age at childbearing (MAC), it is important to bear in mind that situations that are unfavourable to early childbearing—war, economic depression, and so on—would be reflected in an older average age at childbearing, while comparatively favourable socioeconomic conditions might have the opposite effect. These factors would have a bearing on period TFR and possibly also on cohort completed fertility rates.

Postponed fertility in today's low-fertility populations mostly reflects planned behaviour by young couples striving to establish themselves economically as they pass through their prime childbearing years. This translates into low period TFRs, producing what Norman Ryder (1965, 1980) would call a *tempo effect*.

Tempo effects can serve to either increase or decrease period fertility rates. An acceleration of fertility towards younger ages would raise the period TFR (this type of effect occurred during the baby boom years in Canada and some other industrialized countries following World War II). On the other hand, as is the case today in the industrialized countries, postponement of childbearing towards older ages would have the effect of lowering the period TFR.

Recently, demographers have begun to make adjustments to the period TFR for tempo distortions caused by delayed childbearing (Billari and Kohler, 2004; Bongaarts and Feeney, 1998; Bongaarts and Sobotka, 2012; Frejka and Sardon, 2004). The studies in this area, based on highly developed countries, indicate that once adjustments are introduced for tempo distortions caused by fertility postponement, the period TFR typically increases, though in most cases it remains well below 2.1. For example, in Japan the TFR in 2006 was 1.29, but after adjustment for postponement effects it rose to 1.44 (Schmidt et al., 2012: 33).

Ryder also described a *quantum effect* on the period TFR, which concerns the quantity of childbearing as reflected in the average number of children born to cohorts (i.e., cohort completed family size).

As is true of tempo effects, changes in quantum can either serve to increase or decrease period TFR. The former type of situation arises when cohorts have more children than expected and consequently have the effect of boosting the numbers of children born in a given period. The latter occurrence is when cohorts have fewer children than expected, thereby contributing fewer numbers of children in a given period.

The period TFR in a given year is thus a function of tempo and quantum. That is, change in the number of births in year t is due to (a) *tempo*—the change in the number of births in year t as a result of change in cohort timing (i.e., change in mean age at childbearing); and (b) *quantum*—the change in the number of births in year t due to change in cohort completed fertility.

In a relative sense, quantum effects seem to have played a relatively small role in explaining TFR fluctuations in the industrialized countries over recent decades (Bongaarts and Sobotka, 2012). This suggests that cohorts over this period have tended to behave in a more or less homogeneous manner in regard to completed fertility targets (i.e., completed fertility does not change much from cohort to cohort), even though some variability does exist across countries. For example, as noted by Mikko Myrskyla, Joshua Goldstein, and Yen-Hsin Cheng (2013: 38), in East Asian, Mediterranean, and Eastern European countries, the range of average cohort completed fertility among those cohorts that have recently completed their childbearing (i.e., cohorts completing in the years between 1975 and 1979) is around 1.5 children per woman; on the other hand, among the English-speaking countries (UK, Canada, USA, Australia, New Zealand) as well as Nordic and Baltic countries, the average tends to be somewhat higher (Myrskyla, Goldstein, and Cheng, 2013: 38). Finally, as noted earlier for Canada, in comparing older and more recent cohorts, there has been a general declining trend in average completed fertility across successive cohorts of women (Myrskyla, Goldstein, and Cheng, 2013).

Very recently, some European countries experienced unexpected increases in total fertility rates, this after a long period of low—in some cases very low—fertility that started in the early 1970s. This recent phenomenon can be explained mainly by the effect of diminished postponement among cohorts. Many of these European populations have reached (or have nearly reached) the end of the "postponement transition," meaning that there is now little change from year to year in the mean age at childbearing. At the same time there seems to be no convincing evidence that these TFR increases have resulted from fertility recuperation of previously postponed fertility (Bongaarts and Sobotka, 2012; Goldstein, Sobotka, and Jasilioniene 2009).

Finally, it should be pointed out that quantum effects on the period TFR are not necessarily independent of tempo effects. This is so because the average age at first birth for women (whether relatively late or relatively early) ultimately affects the total number of children for a cohort. The longer women wait to have their first child, the less time left to have subsequent children, whereas early age at childbearing would have the opposite implication.

Society and Fertility: Social–Biological Interactions

Human fertility can be understood as a product of interactions between biological and societal factors, broadly speaking. This can be illustrated with a number of examples that we will review in the sections that follow.

Age at Menarche and Age at First Birth

In a cross-national study, Richard Udry and R.L. Cliquet (1982) found that variation in age at menarche, or first menstruation, influences the timing of first sexual intercourse, first marriage, and first birth among women. Early onset of menstruation in girls is highly correlated with early sexual intercourse and a young age at first marriage, both of which in turn correlate strongly with having a first birth relatively early in life.

The main biological factor at play in this causal relationship is the production of hormones that affect the timing of puberty and increase "readiness" for early sexual intercourse: the earlier a woman enters puberty,

the greater the probability of early sexual experience, marriage, and of conceiving a child. The sociocultural aspect of this phenomenon is the way the development of secondary sexual characteristics increases attractiveness to males: girls who develop early are more likely to attract boys at an earlier age and hence experience first sexual intercourse earlier than late-maturing women. Another important societal factor to consider is the set of norms surrounding female sexual behaviour and the ideal timing of marriage for women, which varies from culture to culture.

Moral Codes towards Sexuality, Contraception, and Abortion

One of the most influential modern scholars to fully examine the interplay of biological and societal factors affecting human sexuality and fertility was Sigmund Freud. In *Civilization and Its Discontents* (1930 [2005]), Freud argued that our collective unhappiness is connected to the way society controls our lives, including our sexual instincts. The individual, in Freud's view, is caught in an irreparable conflict between natural instincts and the social institutions that inexorably seek to suppress or regulate them. Because sex is such a powerful natural instinct, society must constantly control it through mores and legal proscriptions. This is an inherent feature of civilization. More recently, David Barash and Judith Lipton, in *The Myth of Monogamy* (2001), have supported Freud's view in arguing that monogamy is but a social invention designed to control our natural sexual urges. Noting that "extra-pair" sex is the most common form of sexual arrangement in the animal kingdom, they argue that monogamy does not truly exist even among humans.

THE DEMOGRAPHIC STUDY OF SEXUAL INTERCOURSE

Surprisingly, sexual intercourse has received little systematic attention in the demographic literature. Recently, though, demographers have been exploring the question of gender differences in the initiation of sexual intercourse. This is an important topic because early sexual initiation can often lead to early pregnancy and, possibly, early entry into marriage or cohabitation.

Michel Bozon (2003) looked at cross-country variations in the median age at first sexual intercourse for men and women born around 1950 and around 1970–5. He uncovered three models of sexual initiation in the cohorts born in 1950:

1. Societies where women and girls are pressured by family to enter into sexual relationships and conjugal unions—typically with much older men—as close to puberty as possible. This model characterizes countries of sub-Saharan Africa (e.g., Mali, Senegal, Ethiopia) and the Indian subcontinent (e.g., Nepal). Men in these societies are free to engage in premarital sexual activity without any real social sanctions.

2. Societies where social controls are exerted to delay young women's union formation and sexual activity. In these societies, a woman is under considerable pressure to preserve her virginity as long as possible to avoid dishonouring herself, her family, and her prospective spouse. Young men, on the other hand, are encouraged to prove their manhood early, either with prostitutes or with older women, so they experience sexual initiation at a younger age than women do. Societies fitting this model include countries of southern Europe (e.g., Greece, Portugal, Italy, Spain), Latin America (e.g., Brazil, Chile), and Asia (e.g., Thailand).

3. Societies in which the timing of first sexual intercourse is similar for men and women. Examples include Singapore, Sri Lanka, China, and Vietnam. In these societies, there is usually later marriage and strict supervision of the conduct of young people. In fact, some countries in this category—Poland and Lithuania, for example—are seeing a trend towards later sexual initiation for both men and women. In contrast, in many European countries—notably those of Scandinavia, but also Germany and the Czech Republic—sexual initiation occurs at a comparatively young age, though it remains "gender-equal" in its timing.

Among the younger cohorts—those born in the 1970s—Bozon (2003) observed a narrowing of the gap in timing for men's and women's sexual initiation. In general, almost all men and a lower, though growing, number of women in this cohort experienced sexual initiation before first union (i.e., marriage, or cohabitation), reflecting an increasing level of personal freedom among young people worldwide.

Bozon (2003: 4) concluded that for women in societies where contraception is not widely used, the traditional connection between first sexual intercourse and entry into reproductive and conjugal life still exists. However, even in societies where contraception is prevalent, sexual initiation is still a gender-differential event: men view it as a relatively non-committal experience, but women place much importance on the choice of first partner—typically older and more experienced—with whom they will likely form a relationship.

Throughout much of history, the key agent of social control over sexuality and fertility has been organized religion. In the Christian church, sexuality is associated with the "original sin" of Adam and Eve. Malcolm Potts and Roger Short (1999: 296–7) contend that the early religious leaders erred in viewing the sexual act as a sin rather than the basis of adult love: "[B]y claiming that sexual intercourse was licit only if it was associated with the possibility of procreation, they categorized women as dogs, where copulation does indeed coincide with ovulation and sex is limited to procreation." This contempt for sex except for procreation helps to explain the Church's position against abortion and contraception. Saint Augustine (354–430) and Thomas Aquinas (1225–74) are among the early theologians whose writings served as the moral basis for state-implemented penal codes with severe punishments for those resorting to contraception or abortion (Potts and Short, 1999: 296).

In recent times, there have been many challenges to religiously based codes, and the idea that sexual intercourse is sinful—justifiable only to conceive a baby—is no longer a widely held view. Laws about sexuality, contraception, and abortion have been liberalized to allow greater freedom to the individual in such matters, and

contraception today is accepted widely in the developed countries and increasingly in the developing world (Bongaarts, 2003; Spinelli et al., 2000). Similarly, the prevalence of abortion today is widespread (Dalla Zuanna, 2006; David and Skilogianis, 1999; Henshaw, 2003). The relaxing of these societal controls over contraception and abortion has had a significant depressing effect on fertility rates. Couples have greater means to prevent or abort an unplanned and unwanted pregnancy. But with this "freedom" comes a certain responsibility: the onus lies squarely on the individual to make important decisions about the proper timing of childbearing based on personal socioeconomic considerations.

Seasonality of Conceptions and Births

While humans, unlike other mammals, are sexually active throughout the year and do not have a defined breeding season, there is evidence of seasonal patterns of conceptions among different human populations. This seasonality may have biological (i.e., hormonal), ecological, social, and even behavioural dimensions to it (Campbell and Wood, 1994; Potts and Selman, 1978; Wood, 1994).

CONTRACEPTION IN HISTORY

In his *Medical History of Contraception,* Himes (1936 [1963]) outlined the many, often bizarre, customs, and practices tried by people through the ages in order to avoid conception—all of them highly ineffective until the advent of modern birth control! The study of Himes is a sweeping investigation into the ever-present quest among humans to find effective means of controlling their fertility. As described in his own words,

> The persistence of the folk practices detailed . . . suggests . . . that the human race has in all ages and in all geographical locations desired to control its own fertility; that while women

have always wanted babies, they have wanted them when they wanted them. And they have wanted neither too few nor too many. This is the great "paradox" of the biological history of man. In reality, however, it is no paradox at all. It is merely one phase of the dialectic of history. What is new is not the desire for prevention, but effective, harmless means of achieving it on a grand scale. (Himes, 1936 [1963]: 185)

Below are a few of Himes' illustrative accounts based on various literature sources of the past:

Item indicated to avoid conception	Source
• Application of *alum* into the vagina or on the penis before coitus; dries and narrows the vagina, and prevents the seed from reaching the uterus	Cheikh Nefzaoui, *The Perfumed Garden* (16th century)
• The widespread practice of *coitus interruptus* in the royal courts of Europe	Abbé de Brantome, *Les Dames Galantes* (1614)
• The use of a "sheath" (primitive condom) to avoid getting syphilis and also to prevent conception	Gabriele Fallopio, *De Morbo Gallico: Liber Absolutissimus* (1564)
• To prevent conception, the use of a gold ball intravaginally; the use of a sheath; the application of half a small lemon from which the juice has been extracted as an efficacious cervical cap	Giacomo Casanova, *Memoirs* (1725–1798)

Historical demographers have studied the seasonality of births and deaths across a variety of populations of the past. E.A. Wrigley and R.S. Schofield (1981), after

examining reconstituted parish records for England dating back to the 1500s, discovered a distinct seasonal pattern that appeared fairly consistently from the sixteenth century though the late eighteenth century. They found that the number of conceptions was highest in the late spring and early summer (April to July) and lowest in the late summer and autumn (August to November). According to the two authors, the annual seasonal pattern of conceptions reflected biological and social factors (Wrigley and Schofield, 1981: 291–2). The fall in conceptions between August and November occurred during the crop-gathering months for northwestern Europe. Whether the people recognized it or not, their sexual activity appears to have been conditioned by the agricultural cycle.

More recently, researchers have reported a preponderance of births occurring during the spring and early summer (March to July), with a secondary peak in births for the month of September. This pattern has been identified in the United States (Seiver, 1985), in Canada (Trovato and Odynak, 1993), and in a number of other national settings (Lam and Miron, 1991; Wood, 1994). In general, there is a trough in births during the late fall and the winter months (coinciding with conceptions in January through May). And although the intensity of the spring effect in births varies considerably from country to country, in virtually all settings examined there is unmistakable evidence of a secondary peak in births occurring in September, a trend that has been observed in both northern and southern hemispheres (Lam and Miron, 1991, 1996).

There are many interpretations of the spring/summer rise in birth probabilities. Scholars have identified factors ranging from the biological (seasonal fluctuations in sex hormones) to the sociological (preference for having children in the spring and summer) and the cultural (the influence of seasonal customs on birth timing motivation) (Bobak and Gjonca, 2001; Cummings, 2003; Greksa, 2003; Lam and Miron, 1996; Panter-Brick, 1996; Rojansky, Brzezinski, and Schenker, 1992; Seiver, 1985; Trovato and Odynak, 1993; Wood, 1994). The current tendency for many couples in Canada and many other industrialized countries to have children in the spring and summer likely reflects the conscious decision to avoid giving birth during the harsh winter months; most couples would prefer to have a child in the spring and summer, when mother and baby can enjoy the warmth and comfort of milder weather. To this end, couples discontinue the use of birth control at the appropriate time in the year as to effect the desired timing of their baby nine months later. Miller and colleagues refer to this type behaviour as "*proception*" (Miller, 1986; Miller, Severy, and Pasta, 2004). It would appear that most couples "procept" during the peak summer months, resulting in the large number of births between May and July. On the other hand, the September spike in births may reflect the influence of winter holidays—particularly Christmas/New Year's—on rates of sexual activity (Cesario, 2002; Lam and Miron, 1991; Seiver, 1985; Trovato and Odynak, 1993). Wrigley and Schofield (1981: 293) recognized this phenomenon for the historical populations in Europe: "[t]he greater conviviality of this time of year may have led to an increase in the frequency of sexual activity, producing a surge of births in the following September." Notably, the historical seasonal variation in Canadian births seems to have also followed the rhythm of life as governed to a large extent by such factors as the agricultural cycle early in Canadian history (Trovato and Odynak, 1993).

Natural and Human-made Disasters and Fertility

Demographers have identified several links between traumatic events—such as war, terrorism, or natural disasters—and fertility. We know that the fertility rate usually drops significantly during major wars, famines, and epidemics, partly because such events prevent large numbers of couples from marrying, but also because they are associated with conditions that can adversely affect *fecundability*, including poor nutrition and health, increased rates of involuntary fetal loss, forced separation of couples, and reduced coital rates (Agadjanian and Prata, 2002; Cai and Feng, 2005; Hill, 2004; Lindstrom and Berhanu, 1999; Mamelund, 2004).

However, a period of devastation can also engender a temporary surge in the birth rate, once the disruption has ended and "normal life" resumes. A notable instance of this phenomenon, which has been observed in a number of historical and contemporary contexts, is the baby boom that occurred throughout Europe, North America, and Australia and New Zealand following the end of World War II. Although the causes of the baby boom are multivariate and complex, one possible causal mechanism may have been a strong unconscious impulse to celebrate life in the wake of such a devastating event. Having children is, after all, a natural way to recognize the value of human life. A similar baby boom occurred in Sarajevo following the civil war that shattered the former Yugoslavia in the 1990s. Between the end of hostilities in 1993 and Christmas 1994, there was reportedly a 50 per cent rise in the number of births in the city (*Il Nuovo Mondo*, 1995).

War can also spark a less celebratory, more pragmatic approach to fertility. In the Chechen Republic, which has been embroiled in a costly military conflict with Russia since declaring its independence in 1991, many Chechens have expressed the feeling that "they have to replace all the men that are dying" (Canadian Broadcasting Corporation, 2004). Traumatic acts of terrorism may have a similar effect on fertility. Joseph Rodgers, Craig St John, and Ronnie Coleman (2005) studied fertility rates in the state of Oklahoma following the Oklahoma City bombing that claimed 195 lives—many of them children—in April 1995. They discovered that in the ten-year period following the event, fertility rose in Oklahoma County (though not in the state's other nine counties). In attempting to explain this change, they suggested that there had been an unconscious motivation among the people of the community most affected by the bombing to replace the children and other loved ones who had perished in the tragedy.

Devastating acts of nature may engender a similar effect. A *Globe and Mail* report with the headline "Indonesia Prepares for Baby Boom" (Oziewicz, 2005) described the anticipated rise in the country's birth levels in the wake of the December 2004 tsunami. The article quoted an aid worker who speculated, based on her experience with similar situations, that Aceh province, which had been particularly hard hit by the tsunami, would experience an unusual rise in births by the end of the year. "[W]hat we know from a lot of other emergencies where there are a lot of deaths is that populations right themselves, they get themselves sorted out again. . . . We have to be prepared for a lot of pregnancies."

Proximate Determinants of Fertility

Davis and Blake Framework

According to Kingsley Davis and Judith Blake (1956), social structure and culture affect fertility indirectly through a series of *intermediate variables*. These variables fall into three sets of factors:

1. variables that affect exposure to intercourse;
2. variables that affect exposure to conception; and
3. variables that affect gestation and successful parturition of pregnancies (see Figure 6.3).

The premise of the Davis and Blake framework is that change in the level of fertility observed for a population is the result of change in one or more of the intermediate variables. For example, an increase in the use of contraceptives (an intermediate variable that affects exposure to conception) will cause a decrease in fertility, assuming that the other intermediate variables remain constant.

This principle of a direct effect on fertility does not apply to background societal

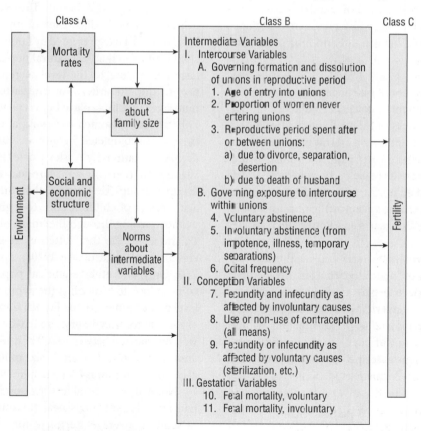

FIGURE 6.3   The Davis and Blake intermediate framework of fertility analysis

Source: Springer US, *The American Sociologist*, 'Theorizing about Fertility', vol. 4, May 1969, pp. 100-104, David Yaukey © The American Sociologist. With kind permission of Springer Science + Business Media.

factors. For example, if there has been an overall increase in income in a society, any impact of this change on fertility will be made indirectly through one or more of the intermediate variables. Therefore, any difference in fertility rates within and across populations can always be traced to variations in one or more of the intermediate variables (Bongaarts, 2003: 412).

Bongaarts' Proximate Determinants

John Bongaarts (1978) reformulated the Davis and Blake model to make it quantifiable. He began by showing that virtually all fluctuations in fertility rates across populations could be attributed to four proximate variables:

1. the extent of marriage;
2. the extent of contraceptive use;
3. the extent of induced abortion; and
4. the extent and duration of breast-feeding (a proxy for postpartum amenorrhea—i.e., postpartum infecundability, as breastfeeding acts as a natural contraceptive) (Bongaarts, 1975, 1978; Bongaarts and Potter, 1983).

Other proximate variables, listed under the category of "natural marital fertility factors," were shown to play a relatively minor role in explaining fertility variations (Bongaarts, 2003; Leridon, 2006). These factors include the frequency of intercourse, sterility, spontaneous intrauterine mortality, and duration of the fertile period.

Natural Fertility Populations

Louis Henry (1961) coined the term *natural fertility* to describe the behaviour of couples in earlier populations who did not plan their

family size or alter their reproduction habits depending on how many children they already had. This type of procreative pattern differs radically from that of contemporary developed societies, where contraception is widely practised and where couples adjust their childbearing to achieve the desired family size, the desired spacing of children, and even the desired timing of each birth.

The most prolific of the various natural fertility populations are the Hutterites, an Anabaptist religious sect, originally from Europe, that in the 1880s settled in parts of the United States (South Dakota and Montana) and Canada (Manitoba, Saskatchewan, and Alberta). The Hutterite belief system prohibits the use of any kind of birth control. Data presented by Louis Henry (1961) indicates that few natural populations have come close to the level of reproduction of the Hutterites. For Hutterites with marriages that took place between 1921 and 1930 involving women marrying at age 20, the average completed fertility was 10.9 children. Calculations by Ansley Coale (1969: 4) suggest an even higher reproductive rate for this group. He showed that the average number of children born to a group of women passing through life, married at age 15, and subject to the Hutterite age-specific childbearing rates of the 1920s, would be 12.6. Only one other historical population comes close to matching the reproductive level of the Hutterites: the French Canadians of the eighteenth century. French-Canadian women married between 1700 and 1730 had an average completed family size of 10.8 (see also Charbonneau, 1977; Henripin, 1954).

None of the natural fertility populations had reproductive levels near the estimated maximum average fertility for human populations. The estimated maximum average fertility (i.e., *total fecundity*) for a population is 15.3 births per woman (Bongaarts,

1975, 1978; Bongaarts and Potter, 1983). This level of fertility can be achieved only by a rare combination of conditions:

1. There is continuous exposure to the risk of conception between menarche and menopause, meaning that a woman is in a steady sexual relationship throughout her entire reproductive lifespan.
2. There is complete avoidance of any method of birth control, including natural methods of avoiding conception, during a woman's entire reproductive lifespan.
3. There is no reliance on abortion or any action that could cause a spontaneous miscarriage.
4. There is no practice of breastfeeding. (Hill, 1990: 146)

Women in natural fertility societies (i.e., populations that do not consciously practise any form of family limitation) could not achieve this maximum average fertility because they would be pregnant for only about one-sixth of their reproductive years; they would spend the remainder of these potential childbearing years in states that do not produce children, such as the unmarried state, the sterile state for those who are infecund, and postpartum anovulatory periods after a birth (Bongaarts and Potter, 1983).

Bongaarts (1978) concluded that the gap between maximum potential fertility (total fecundity) and actual fertility achieved by "high fertility" populations today arises from the inhibiting effects of the proximate determinants on total fecundity. Thus, for example, high fertility populations such as Niger, where total fertility is in the range of 7.5 children per woman, do not come close to the estimated maximum value of 15.3. This is because none of the four conditions listed above can prevail fully in Niger—or in any other population for that matter. In actuality, all populations, even

high fertility ones, will experience fertility rates well below 15.3. The difference between this standard value and the observed fertility rate in a population is due to the inhibiting effects of the proximate determinants. Bongaarts' (1978) formula below helps us to understand this principle by breaking down the observed TFR of a population into the contributions of what he determined to be the four principal *proximate determinants of fertility* that explain virtually all of the gap between total fecundity and observed fertility rates. Each of the indices in the formula below range in values between 0 and 1:

$$\text{TFR} = C_m \times C_c \times C_a \times C_i \times T_F$$

where C_m is the *index of nuptiality* (1 = all women of reproductive age are married or are in a similar type of sexual union; 0 = no woman of reproductive age is in a marital or similar type of sexual union);

C_c is the *index of noncontraception*. (1 = no contraception; 0 = all fertile women use a method that is 100 per cent effective);

C_a is the *index of nonabortion*. (1 = no abortion; 0 = all pregnancies are aborted);

C_i is the *index of postpartum infecundability*. (1 = no woman breastfeeds and there is no abstinence from coitus; 0 = the duration of infecundability is infinite—i.e., all women breastfeed and there is complete abstinence from sexual intercourse after a birth); and

T_F is total fecundity (i.e., maximum total fertility), which is fixed at an average value of 15.3 children per woman.

A population that scores exactly 1 on all four proximate determinants will end up with a total fertility rate of 15.3 (i.e., $1 \times 1 \times 1 \times 1 \times 15.3 = 15.3$). However, depending on the extent to which the values of the proximate determinants deviate from 1, the observed TFR will be below 15.3. Thus, the effect of the proximate determinants is to inhibit total fecundity, bringing this maximum rate down to the observed TFR.

We can illustrate how the proximate framework is applied by drawing on Mazharul Islam and colleagues' (2003) analysis of Bangladesh, where between 1975 and 1999 the total fertility rate fell from just over six to roughly three children per woman. Over the same period, total fecundity actually increased, due to improved socioeconomic conditions and health in the population. Therefore, the drop in the TFR between these two time periods must have been caused by the inhibiting effects on total fecundity of the proximate determinants, a conclusion supported by the evidence. The index of nuptiality had a 15 per cent inhibiting effect on fertility in 1975 but just 14.2 per cent in 1999; in other words, there was little change in the proportion of unmarried women, and the inhibiting effect of non-marriage on fertility changed only slightly. The inhibiting effect of contraceptive use rose from nearly 10 per cent in 1975 (i.e., an index value of 0.90) to over 58 per cent in 1999 (i.e., an index value of 0.42), contributing greatly to the reduction in TFR during this time interval. The inhibiting effect of *postpartum infecundability* (i.e., postpartum amenorrhea) was relatively minor in 1975 but by 1999 had become more pronounced, with the value of this index falling from nearly 0.75 to just under 0.28 over the period. This suggests that the interval between births widened, contributing to a modest inhibiting effect on total fecundity. Islam and associates (2003) did not calculate the index of abortion because the relevant data was not available (the implicit assumption is that due to cultural prohibitions induced abortion in Bangladesh is non-existent).

The proximate determinants can also be analyzed for a specific point in time or time interval. If we look at 1999 only, early marriage is found to be the most important proximate variable accounting for high fertility in Bangladesh, since the inhibiting effect of nuptiality on total fecundity is relatively small (only 0.14). Contraceptive use, on the other hand, is the strongest inhibiting variable, with an effect on total fecundity of around 0.42. Postpartum infecundability, which relates to the spacing of births, accounted for an almost 28 per cent inhibiting effect on total fecundity. So Bangladesh's 1999 TFR of about 3 can be explained by examining the countervailing effects of these three proximate determinants: the high marriage rate and relatively young age at which women were entering into sexual unions (which, together, raise potential fertility) versus increasing contraceptive use and widening birth intervals (both of which act to reduce fertility). Given the relative importance of nuptiality and contraception, we can conclude that if more women were to marry later and adopt modern contraceptives, Bangladeshi fertility would be substantially lower than it is today.

Fertility Transition

European Fertility Transition

The low fertility in the developed world today is the culmination of a century-long period of change that demographers have called the *fertility transition*. In the past, when people did not have knowledge of or recourse to effective measures of family limitation, fertility was largely a matter of

PROXIMATE DETERMINANTS OF FERTILITY IN CANADA

Figure 6.4, taken from Henripin (2003), indicates that in Quebec in 1896 the maximum fertility rate of 15 was reduced by 2 to a value of 13 due to the inhibiting effect of temporary sterility. Relatively short marriage duration due to early death of a husband further inhibited this level by 6 points, bringing the fertility rate to 7, which was the total fertility observed in Quebec in 1896. For Canada as a whole, the diagram shows that between 1900 and 2000, the observed TFR dropped from 4.2 children per woman to 1.7. Over time the inhibiting effect of contraceptive use has gained strength (from

an effect of 2.4 in 1900 to 4.5 in 2000). By comparison, the effect of temporary sterility was stronger in 1900, and today this variable plays a relatively minor role in explaining Canada's observed TFR. The inhibiting effect of marriage duration has intensified over time, from an impact of 7.2 in 1900 to 8 in 2000. Stated differently, today's relatively low TFR is explained primarily by the inhibiting effects on maximum fertility of marriage duration (shorter duration due to later entry into marriage) and the widespread use of contraception. Abortion and sterility play smaller roles compared to these other two variables.

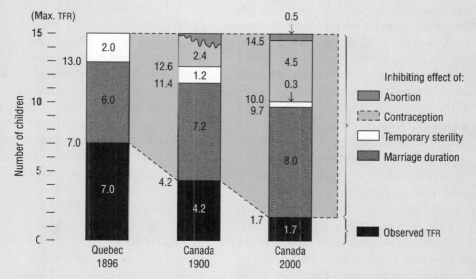

FIGURE 6.4   Average number of births averted due to the inhibiting effects on maximum biological fertility of four proximate determinants for three points in time in Canada

Source: Jacques Henripin (2003), *La métamorphose de la population canadienne*. Montreal: Les Éditions Varia, 168; reprinted by permission of the publisher

chance (Watkins, 1989). As Western society became more modern and standards of living improved, death rates declined and, some time later, birth rates also fell. In the period between the fall in death and birth rates, there were unprecedented increases in natural population growth. A third stage followed, characterized by low birth rates as well as low death rates, which brought the low rates of natural increase we see today.

The trouble with the sweeping picture of birth rate movement in Western Europe as presented by the classical version of the demographic transition theory (Davis, 1945; Notestein, 1945, 1953; Thompson, 1929) is that it overlooks many national and sub-national variations and the fact that fertility declines took place under a wide variety of social, economic, and demographic conditions (Ariès, 1960; Carlson, 1966; Cleland and Wilson, 1987; Coale, 1973; Davis, 1963; Dyson and Murphy, 1985; Friedlander, 1969; Kirk, 1996; Knodel, 1977; Lesthaeghe and Wilson, 1986; Mosher, 1980; van de Walle, 1992). As already noted in Chapter 3, the impossibility of incorporating the varied historical experiences of European countries into a coherent overarching theory of fertility transition led Coale (1973) to propose the following three preconditions for a fertility transition:

1. Fertility decisions must be within the calculus of conscious choice; that is, beliefs and norms should not forbid family planning, nor should they favour large families.
2. Reduced fertility must be viewed by couples as economically advantageous.
3. Effective methods of fertility control must be known and be available to couples.

The State of Fertility Transition Today

While Japan and countries of the West have already passed through the fertility transition (interrupted briefly by the post–World War II rise in the birth rate), most of the world's populations have begun to undergo fertility transition only since the end of World War II. Today, birth rates remain high in sub-Saharan Africa and in certain less developed countries such as Bangladesh and Afghanistan. On the other hand, since the early 1970s, there have been rapid fertility declines in some developing countries, including South Korea, Tunisia, Hong Kong, Iran, Mongolia, Albania, Kuwait, Vietnam, and China (United Nations Department of Economic and Social Affairs Population Division (2006a: 43).

The UN's recent *World Fertility Report* (United Nations Department of Economic and Social Affairs Population Division, 2011a) notes that the period from 1970 and the first decade of the twenty-first century was characterized by significant fertility reductions worldwide. Total fertility fell in all but 3 of the 185 countries or areas for which data are available, and by 2005–10, 75 countries or areas had a total fertility below 2.1 children per woman. On a broad regional scale prior to 1970, there was no significant downward trend in total fertility across the main development groups. On a country-by-country basis, the only exceptions were the economically advanced nations in East Asia and Latin America, whose TFRs started declining in the 1960s (Wilson, 2011).

The fertility gap between the developed world and the "other developing countries" group has narrowed considerably over time: In the early 1950s, the difference was in the order of 3.3 children per woman; by 2005–10, this had reduced to about 0.7 of a child. This is an important phenomenon for the world because these two sets of countries together hold approximately nine-tenths of the globe's population today. Therefore, the vast majority of people today live in countries where birth rates have dropped significantly, reaching current total fertility of about 2.1 children per woman. It has been estimated by Chris Wilson (2011) that if this trend continues, the gap between other developing countries and the developed world will converge sometime early in the second decade of the twenty-first century.

Africa, particularly the sub-Saharan countries comprising this region, stands out as the area showing the highest total fertility in the world. The TFR there has hovered around a range of 5 to 6 children per woman from 1950 to the late 1980s. It was only after this point that fertility has started to fall noticeably. By today's standards, its fertility rate is still very high, standing at 5.3 in 2005–10. Indeed, the vast majority of high-fertility countries today (35 out of 39) are in this regional category. According to Wilson's estimation, the pace of fertility decline for this region from 1990 onward has not differed appreciably from that of the other regions. Therefore, assuming this condition holds it would seem likely that in about 50 years this part of the world will see its total fertility rate reach the level currently observed in the developed world.

As of 2005, a number of countries showed no sign of even beginning the fertility transition, and only recently have some of these countries experienced TFR declines of at least 10 per cent from their maximum recorded levels (see Table 6.4).

These 13 countries represented almost 25 per cent of the population living in the least developed areas of the world. According to the United Nations, the majority of the developing world's population lives in 70 countries where total fertility levels range from 2.1 to 4 children per woman; and these countries make up over 40 per cent of the world's total population (United Nations Department of Economic and Social Affairs Population Division, 2006a).

All together, more than 42 per cent of the population in Asia, three-quarters of the population in Oceania, and nearly all of the population of Europe and North America live in countries where fertility levels are below replacement. Finally, of particular interest is the fact that almost 30 per cent of the population in the less developed regions has achieved below-replacement fertility levels similar to those in more developed countries (United Nations Department of Economic and Social Affairs Population Division, 2006a).

Theories of Fertility Change

The significant declines in reproductive levels worldwide since the 1970s require some explanation. Why is fertility below replacement levels in some countries and close to eight children per woman in others? Why has fertility fallen rapidly in certain cases and very little in others? Charles Hirschman (1994) observed that although the demographic literature contains an abundance of theories aimed at explaining the fertility transition of Europe and most of the developing countries, not one has really provided a single exhaustive explanation of the causes. The theories span a host of causative mechanisms,

Although Africa is recognized as a high-fertility region, its countries can be classified under four different transition stages.

Transition stage	Range of TFR in 2005–10	Countries
Early	<3	Algeria, Libya, Morocco, Tunisia, South Africa, Reunion
Recent	3–4	Egypt, Botswana, Namibia, Swaziland, Zimbabwe, Ghana, Cote d'Ivoire, Djibouti, Sao Tome and Principe
Slow/irregular	About 5	Nigeria, Togo, Benin, Burkina Faso, Cameroon, Congo, Madagascar, Mauritania, Sudan, Kenya, Tanzania, Rwanda, Zambia, Guinea-Bissau, Mayotte
Very slow/incipient	5–7	Angola, Burundi, Chad, Mali, Gambia, Gabon, Uganda, Sierra Leone, Liberia, Niger, Ethiopia, Somalia, Eritrea, Democratic Republic of Congo, Tanzania, Malawi, Mozambique

Source: Adapted from Guengant and May (2009).

from the Malthusian idea that fertility levels are determined by sexual passion and the moral restraints imposed to control them (an idea we will examine at length in Chapter 11) to the notion that mortality declines and growing socioeconomic pressures prompt individuals at the household level to adopt means of reducing their family size (Davis, 1963; Hirschman, 1994).

Theories of fertility change fall under a number of different headings—economic, sociological, sociopsychological, anthropological, and even evolutionary. Some fertility theories are macro-level explanations, while others are aimed at explaining micro processes at the household or individual level. We will focus here on several macro-level theories that have gained widespread attention in the demographic literature. Some of these theories apply to fertility change strictly in the industrial countries, while others consider developing societies now undergoing socioeconomic modernization. In spite of the many different angles on fertility change, there is a certain amount of overlap among the various perspectives.

We begin our review with the theory of Gary Becker, who specified the economic conditions for a fertility transition from a traditional regime of high birth rates to modern low birth rates, based largely on the experience of the United States and other high-income countries.

TABLE 6.4   Countries where the fertility transition had not begun by 2000–5, showing TFR in 2012 and its change from the maximum level

Country	TFR 1950–5	TFR 2000–5	Maximum level during 1950–2005	2000–5 per cent decline from maximum	Reference period of maximum level	TFR 2012	2012 per cent decline from maximum
Niger	7.7	7.91	8.2	3.6	1975–2000	7.1	13.4
Uganda	6.9	7.1	7.1	—	1965–2005	6.2	12.7
Guinea-Bissau	5.58	7.1	7.1	—	1970–2005	5.1	28.2
Mali	7.11	6.92	7.56	8.4	1970–85	6.3	16.7
Burundi	6.8	6.8	6.8	—	1950–2005	6.4	5.9
Liberia	6.45	6.8	6.9	1.4	1965–95	5.4	21.7
Angola	7.0	6.75	7.4	8.8	1950–70	6.3	14.9
Dem. Rep. Congo	6.0	6.7	6.7	—	1980–2005	6.3	6.0
Chad	5.77	6.65	6.66	0.1	1970–2005	6.0	9.9
Sierra Leone	6.09	6.5	6.5	—	1975–2005	5.0	23.1
Congo	5.68	6.29	6.29	—	1970–2005	5.1	18.9
Equatorial Guinea	5.5	5.89	5.89	—	1985–2005	5.2	11.7
Afghanistan	7.7	7.48	8.0	6.5	1990–2000	6.2	22.5

Note: Countries are ordered by total fertility in 2000–5 and, where that is equal, by total fertility in 1950–5.

Sources: United Nations Department of Economics and Social Affairs Population Division (2006a): 39. Reprinted with the permission of the United Nations. For 2012, Population Reference Bureau (2012), *World Population Data Sheet, 2012.*

Becker's Economic Theory

Central to economic theories of the family are the rising material and non-material costs of parenting in contemporary society. Here, the concepts of supply and demand take centre stage. Prices in the market are based on the supply and demand of consumer goods: if demand is high and supply is limited, prices for a given good will be high; if demand is low and supply is plentiful, prices will be low. Becker's (1960, 1991) idea about fertility is in essence a demand-based theory. The "demand" for children—that is, the number of children desired by parents—is a rational evaluation. Parents desire the best-quality goods subject to their ability to afford them. Becker's theory treats children as a special type of consumer durable for which quality considerations figure prominently.

Becker made the important observation that during the process of socioeconomic modernization, fertility falls as income increases (see Figure 6.5). He found this counterintuitive, since it suggested that

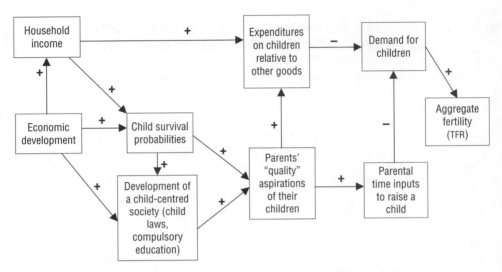

FIGURE 6.5   A rendition of Becker's economic theory of fertility change

Note: The positive sign means the relationship between variables is positive (as X increases, Y increases), whereas a negative sign means the opposite. In this model, the total effect of household income on the demand for children is negative because its effects through the intervening variables are always negative.

children are an inferior "good," purchased only when, in relation to other goods, they are less costly; as a result, it would seem, parents would "acquire" more children only if their income were to fall. He reasoned that, on the contrary, based on basic economic principles, rising income should produce a corresponding increase in the number of children born to parents, since children, like consumer goods, become more affordable (Becker, 1960). According to Becker (1991), child quality is attained through parental investments of time and money in the child's human capital, especially through the provision of education, and the nurturing of the child's talents and skills. Parents today will therefore opt for smaller families and invest more of their time and resources in each child.

For Becker, and others in the tradition of the New Household Economics school,

this substitution of child quality for child quantity (i.e., a quality-quantity tradeoff) explains the usually observed inverse association between income and fertility in the empirical literature (Becker and Lewis, 1973; Becker, Murphy, and Tamura, 1990; Ermisch, 2003: 110; Robinson, 1997; Willis, 1973a, 1973b;). Parents will try to "produce" the best possible child, given the household's budgetary and time constraints. Children who have more resources spent on them and more time devoted to them by parents are considered "higher-quality" children (though Becker was quick to caution that "higher quality" in no way implies "morally better," as morality is a completely different matter). In short, if parents voluntarily spend more on a child, it is because they obtain additional satisfaction (utility) through the child from the additional expenditure (it is this additional satisfaction that represents higher quality); thus, parents choose the best combination of the number of children, their desired quality, and the parents' own standard of living subject to the lifetime income of the parents and the prices that they face in life towards maintaining a household.

Should the parents' income increase, there would be an increase in both the quantity and the quality of children; however, in view of the tendency for parents to increase the quality of most consumer durable goods proportionately much more than the quantity of such goods when their income increases, Becker (1960: 212) argued that this is also likely to be the case for children: "an increase in income should increase both the quantity and quality of children, but the quantity elasticity should be small compared to the quality elasticity."

Commenting on Becker's theory, Bernard Okun (1960: 240) expanded this idea more broadly to describe the historical change in fertility from a high regime of the past to the current low fertility regime of the present: "The secular rise in income causes an increase in the quality of children, and therefore expenditures per child rise. This tends to diminish the quantity of children demanded, and the well-known empirical inverse relation between income and the birth rate reasserts itself." Ronald Lee and Andrew Mason (2010) provide recent cross-national support for this proposition, as do Larry Jones and Michéle Tertilt (2008) in the context of the United States, who found the negative association between income and fertility surprisingly stable over time for American cohorts born between 1880 and 1960.

Applied to today's industrialized societies, Becker's theory would imply that low fertility is the result of parents investing in fewer children of greater quality. In the modern context, children are no longer economic assets as they were in the past—in fact, they are, for the most part, economic liabilities for their parents. Instead, their utility to parents is primarily of an inherently non-material nature (i.e., *psychic utility*), manifest in such intangible benefits as self-fulfillment, pleasure, prestige, extension of the self (Fawcett, 1983; Hoffman and Hoffman, 1973; Morgan and King, 2001).

Easterlin's Cyclical Theory

The economist Richard Easterlin (1961b, 1969) has noted that, based on the historical experience of the United States over the twentieth century, increases and declines in birth rates have followed a cyclical pattern, whereby periods of low fertility are followed by periods of high fertility and so forth. After the end of World War II, birth rates in Canada, the United States, Australia, New Zealand, Japan, and also some European countries rose unexpectedly, following a period of low fertility that had lasted through the 1930s. In fact, recent evidence presented by Jan Van Bavel and David Reher (2013) indicates in some countries the recovery of fertility actually started late in the 1930s and continued into World War II (USA, Australia, Sweden, Norway); in others, recovery began during the war itself (Belgium, France, England, Wales). In the countries with the most pronounced baby booms (USA, Canada, Australia, New Zealand), the surge in births lasted approximately two decades, from 1946 through the mid-1960s, and was followed by a protracted "baby bust," characterized by long-term fertility declines that have culminated in the sub-replacement birth rates characteristic of most high-income nations today. This pattern can be seen in Table 6.5, which includes data on the 13 countries that experienced a post-war baby boom. The peak birth rates occurred at different times for the 13 countries, all between 1957 and 1964 (1957 for USA, 1959 for Canada, and between 1961 and 1964 for the others), but by 1975, fertility had plummeted across all of the nations. Even so, there are some notable variations. For instance, Australia showed a TFR of 2.20 in 1975, while the other 12 countries had by this time seen their birth rates fall to below replacement levels, with West Germany showing the lowest rate at 1.45 births per woman. By 1995, fertility rates had declined beyond 1975 levels in all countries except for the United States, whose TFR in 1995 was just above 2.0.

The fall of the birth rate during the 1930s (the Great Depression) followed by the post-war rise and then decline since the mid-1960s represents a cyclical pattern of change. Easterlin (1969, 1980, 1987) attributes this pattern to the combined influences of demographic, sociological, and economic factors:

- the state of the economy and how well young adults have been able to realize their material aspirations (i.e., their income relative to their material aspirations);
- the proportion of young workers to older workers (i.e., relative cohort size and its impact on the opportunity structures of cohort members); and
- the type of socialization that cohorts experienced during their childhood and adolescence (i.e., differential socialization of preferences for children and material aspirations).

Easterlin's thesis implies that the post-war boom in fertility can be attributed to the generations of adults born in the 1920s and 1930s, whose childhood and adolescent socialization took place in the hard days of the Great Depression when the economy had collapsed. Moreover, their social values were strongly shaped by tradition and adherence to strong family norms. Given this combination of social and economic conditions, the generations of the 1930s developed strong preferences for early marriage and family building.

Moreover, during the 1950s and 1960s, in the aftermath of World War II, the economies of industrialized countries underwent a period of rapid growth, and the demand for workers was intense. For young men entering the labour force, this situation presented a fortuitous combination of circumstances: jobs were plentiful, and opportunities for advancement in the workplace were better than ever. The favourable state of the economy, combined with this generation's traditional childhood socialization experience and its small numerical size, produced a setting highly conducive to early matrimony and parenting. These young adults could realize their material aspirations while at the same time conforming to traditional expectations to marry young and have plenty of children.

For Easterlin, the drop in birth rates across industrialized countries after the 1960s can be explained by the same sets of forces attributed to the baby boom period. In this instance, however, the socioeconomic conditions for young adults entering the labour force during the 1970s, 1980s, and 1990s were less favourable to early marriage and childbearing. These young adults had been raised in the very prosperous socioeconomic environment of

TABLE 6.5 Total fertility rates for selected low-fertility countries, 1930s–2012

Country	Pre-WWII (1930s)	Post-WWII (early 1950s)	Baby boom peak	Baby bust (1975)	1985	1995	2005	2012
Australia	2.16 (1933)	3.09 (1950–2)	3.51 (1961)	2.2	1.89	1.83	1.8	1.9
Austria	1.65 (1933–4)	2.07 (1950–2)	2.81 (1963)	1.83	1.47	1.4	1.4	1.4
Belgium	1.96 (1933–7)	2.37 (1948–52)	2.69 (1964)	1.74	1.51	1.55	1.6	1.8
Canada	2.69 (1936–40)	3.53 (1950–2)	3.93 (1959)	1.83	1.64	1.65	1.5	1.7
Denmark	2.13 (1936)	2.53 (1950–2)	2.63 (1963)	1.92	1.45	1.8	1.8	1.8
United Kingdom	1.83 (1933)	2.15 (1950–2)	2.88 (1964)	1.81	1.8	1.71	1.8	2.0
Germany[1]	2.03 (1934)	2.06 (1951–3)	2.54 (1964)	1.45	1.28	1.34	1.30	1.4
France	2.07 (1934–8)	2.85 (1949–53)	2.86 (1964)	1.93	1.82	1.7	1.9	2.0
Netherlands	2.63 (1933–7)	3.17 (1948–52)	3.19 (1961)	1.66	1.51	1.53	1.7	1.7
Norway	1.84 (1934–5)	2.60 (1951–5)	2.96 (1964)	1.98	1.68	1.87	1.8	1.9
Sweden	1.70 (1933–7)	2.31 (1948–52)	2.49 (1964)	1.78	1.74	1.74	1.8	1.9
Switzerland	1.75 (1937)	2.34 (1950–2)	2.66 (1964)	1.61	1.52	1.48	1.4	1.5
United States	2.04 (1934–6)	3.08 (1949–51)	3.76 (1957)	1.78	1.84	2.03	2.0	1.9

[1] 2005 and 2012 figures are for united Germany.

Sources: Adapted from Morgan (2003); Population Reference Bureau (2006, 2012).

the 1950s and 1960s, which helped instill strong materialistic aspirations. The factors affecting the fertility rate among the "baby boomers" of this generation—especially the large cohorts born at the peak of the baby boom (the late 1950s to mid-1960s)—can be summarized as follows:

- These cohorts, born during a period of very high fertility, are numerically large.
- The material aspirations of this generation are very strong, because as children these individuals were raised in a context of economic prosperity.
- The new economy since the 1970s has made job and career prospects for young adults more tenuous than was the case for the generations that preceded them.

This unfavourable conjunction of demographic, sociological, and economic conditions, according to Easterlin, has fostered a sense of socioeconomic insecurity in today's young adults, especially young men (see also Macunovich, 2002; Oppenheimer, 1994, 1997). Under such conditions, young people are reluctant to commit to matrimony, and among those who are married, the insecurity generated by this set of precarious economic circumstances has led many couples to postpone having children and perhaps avoid having children altogether.

The cyclical theory does not rule out a possible return to above-replacement fertility in the future, but it would depend on two important conditions. The first of these— that the current "baby bust" generation be relatively small numerically—has been satisfied already. The product of low fertility since the early 1970s, this generation should experience a relatively favourable labour-force situation on the basis of this factor

alone (Kohler, Billari, and Ortega, 2002). But in order for fertility rates to rise, the economic prospects for these young adults would have to improve appreciably in order for them to gain a strong sense of security and confidence about long-term socio-economic prospects. Unfortunately, this latter condition may be difficult to satisfy.

To review briefly the two fertility change theories we've seen so far, Easterlin argued that today's low fertility stems from young adults' struggles to satisfy their material aspirations because of economic insecurity, which is compounded by the large size of their generation; these factors lead to a general flight from marriage on the one hand and to postponed parenthood on the other. Becker, in contrast, emphasized the declining desire by parents to have large families because they prefer to meet the increasing costs of raising children by investing in quality over quantity. Unlike Easterlin's theory, which allows for the possibility of a return to higher fertility in the future, Becker's view suggests that low fertility is likely to persist, since the cost—in time and money—of raising high-quality children continues to rise, together with parents" preference for quality over quantity.

The Countercyclical Thesis

William Butz and Michael Ward (1979a, 1979b), following many of Becker's postulates, proposed a countercyclical explanation of fertility change, which challenges Easterlin's view of a possible return to higher fertility levels. In particular, Butz and Ward take aim at what they view as important limitations in Easterlin's formulation, most notably the changing role and status of women in society since the 1960s, the consequent rise of women's economic independence, and the expanded range of role options women now enjoy beyond marriage and motherhood.

Unlike Easterlin, whose theory focuses mainly on how the economic prospects of young men affect marriage and procreation, Butz and Ward (1979a, 1979b) make a distinction between men's and women's incomes and how each of these in turn affects fertility. They suggest that, all other things being equal, a rise in men's income would have the effect of increasing the number of children a couple would have, which is consistent with the postulates of the New Household Economics school. Thus, the baby boom can be understood as a response to rising male income after the war. However, since the 1960s, women have improved their economic situation significantly through increased levels of education and labour-force participation. In their empirical analysis, Butz and Ward (1979a, 1979b) determined that a rise in women's earnings would have a reducing effect on fertility. Any increase in a woman's average wage would raise the household income but would simultaneously raise the cost of having children by the amount of earnings lost while an employed woman takes time off work to have and raise children. While showing that increased male income raises a couple's fertility, Butz and Ward determined that the negative impact of women's opportunity costs on fertility is significantly stronger, thus producing a negative net effect on fertility.

Bearing children affects working women's *opportunity costs* in at least three ways:

1. There is an immediate effect on women's employment.
2. There are long-term effects on earning power.

3. There will be, as a result, a loss in terms of future pension coverage.

Although many women today combine childrearing and employment, the estimated loss of gross earnings associated with motherhood remains substantial in most cases (Davis, Joshi, and Peronacci, 2000)—and this is expected to remain an important factor in explaining low fertility (Ermisch, 2003; Jones, Schoonbroodt, and Tertilt, 2011). There are also important non-material costs associated with having children, including the stress associated with having to take care of children while maintaining a job or career and the restriction on personal freedom as a consequence of being a parent. As noted, Butz and Ward conclude that low fertility in the industrialized world is largely a function of women's rising opportunity costs associated with motherhood, and they predict that as long as women's roles in society do not change radically from what they are today, birth rates are bound to remain low.

Notwithstanding this prediction, it is interesting to note that recent evidence based on countries where female labour-force participation rates are generally high shows that total fertility rates have unexpectedly increased—though not necessarily to replacement levels (Brewster and Rindfuss, 2000; Myrskyla et al., 2009a, 2009b). This new development likely reflects a combination of relatively recent structural alterations in these highly advanced societies, including change in the institutional structure that serve to reduce the incompatibility between employment and childrearing for women (e.g., subsidized daycare, more flexible parental leaves from work); greater acceptance of women working; greater support of families even if childbearing occurs outside of traditional marriage (family-friendly policies); and more egalitarian gender roles (Brewster and Rindfuss, 2000; Engelhardt, Kogel, and Prskawetz, 2004; Fernández, 2013; McDonald, 2000; Rindfuss, Guzzo, and Morgan, 2003). The new trend does not necessarily invalidate the prediction of Butz and Ward; it does, however, lead to a more nuanced perspective on the question of future of fertility in highly advanced countries.

Sociological Theories

Sociological theories of fertility change typically consider macro-structural changes in society as the key agents of value shifts and behavioural changes. For many sociological theorists, the root cause of today's low birth rate is the inherent nature of postmodern society. In such societies, contemporary values, attitudes, and lifestyles seem incompatible with marrying early and raising large families. The traditional sources of authority in matters of family and procreation—religion, community, extended family—have weakened considerably, and have been supplanted by an ethos of individualism. Consequently, many of the pronatal forces of the past have receded to near insignificance.

In explaining low fertility, sociological theorists point to the traditional family form's apparent loss of centrality as a source of self-fulfillment for young men and women, as alternative family forms are increasingly accepted (Ariès, 1980; Keyfitz, 1986; Preston, 1986b; Simons, 1980; Westoff, 1986). In this general context, it is no longer seen as unusual for young couples to consciously avoid having children or for individuals to forgo matrimony in favour of less committed conjugal relationships, such as cohabitation

(Bourgeois-Pichat, 1986; Rindfuss, 1991). We can also note the breakdown of the traditional "breadwinner system" of gender roles, its obsolescence hastened by the rise of female participation in the paid economy (Davis, 1984, 1986; Davis and van der Oever, 1982). Such changes, when combined with modern contraceptive technology and legalized abortion, make it easy to understand today's low fertility rates (Westoff, 1983: 101). For the sociological school, the prognosis is quite clear: since none of these changes seems likely to be reversed, a continuation of low fertility should be expected.

Second Demographic Transition Perspective

We have already discussed this perspective in Chapter 5 in connection with nuptiality change. This perspective also covers important elements towards explaining fertility change. Broadly speaking, the *second demographic transition* refers to a situation in countries that have long passed through the first demographic transition and are now experiencing significant change in several key social demographic dimensions. These changes include:

- a pluralization of living arrangements among young adults, accompanied by a pervasive tendency to postpone marriage in favour of cohabiting unions;
- declining marriage rates;
- increased divorce probabilities;
- very high levels of contraceptive use;
- very low fertility rates;
- increased proportion of couples remaining childless; and
- an increasing tendency among couples for childbearing outside of traditional marriage.

Proponents of this theoretical school view this configuration of social demographic trends as fuelled by a completely separate set of factors than those involved in the first demographic transition of the nineteenth and early twentieth centuries. The earlier transition was sparked by an enormous sentimental and financial investment in the child by parents; in this context, smaller families were much better suited to enhancing parents' ability to properly look after their children (Ariès, 1960, 1980). In contrast, the contemporary "birth dearth" has been provoked by a diametrically opposed attitude: the days of the "child king" as the central purpose of marriage and family has given way to the self-actualization of the individual, or the "queen couple." Theorists in this school of thought (e.g., Inglehart, 1997; Lesthaeghe, 1995, 2010; Lesthaeghe and Surkyn, 1988; van de Kaa, 1987, 1999, 2003, 2004a, 2004b) point to the importance of post-modernity, post-materialism, and associated values that centre on the ethos of individualism—freedom, self-expression, personal search for a better way of life (self-actualization), and detachment from traditional values, institutional authority, and group ethics enshrined in religion.

For Dirk van de Kaa (1999: 31), this shift in value orientation provides a perfect explanation for the many demographic changes in the Western world beginning in the second half of the twentieth century. It is consistent with an individualistic lifestyle in which people feel free to have children within or outside marriage, alone or with a partner, early or late in life; a lifestyle where it is understood that sex and marriage are no longer closely related, and that contraception is interrupted only to have a self-fulfilling conception. Also common to post-modern societies is the reflexive nature of the individuation

process—a process of self-questioning and self-confrontation by prospective parents. Couples typically ask themselves if having children will enrich their lives. In many cases today, the answer appears to be "no." But once a couple decide that they do want a child, they will do everything possible to realize their desire, even if it means seeking medical assistance through such means as *in vitro* fertilization, surrogate motherhood, and adoption (van de Kaa, 2004b).

The Individuation Thesis of Lesthaeghe and Surkyn

Ron Lesthaeghe and Johan Surkyn (1988) proposed a sociological theory that incorporates the kinds of changes described by the second demographic transition perspective with some elements of Easterlin's theory. In essence, they argue that when a generation feels satisfied with the institutions of family, economy, government, and religion, young adults tend to marry and raise families fairly early in life, and marriage and fertility rates are generally high. However, under conditions of widespread disenchantment with the major social institutions, young people see marriage and family formation as less desirable, and they look for alternative family forms that are incompatible with high fertility.

Each generation comes equipped with values acquired through the experience of childhood and adolescent socialization in the parental home. But these values are not immutable, and each new generation of young adults invariably challenges established values. A generation's unique socio-historical experiences of events such as war, economic depression, or technological revolution can cause value shifts on a large scale by provoking new attitudes and ideas (i.e., autonomous value change).

An example of this, described by Philippe Ariès (1980), is the countercultural movement of the 1960s and 1970s (often referred to as the "hippie movement"). While questioning and rejecting many traditional values, the youthful members of this movement also introduced new ideas—free love, communal living, rock music, mod fashions, and so forth. The countercultural movement was inherently skeptical of tradition as a guide to life, and questioned and rejected many traditional sources of regulation and authority in personal matters, especially institutionalized religion. It also instilled alternative conceptions of family, intimacy, sexuality, and commitment to marriage; indeed, it may be argued that the rise of cohabitation and the generalized rejection of traditional marriage so widespread among today's young adults had its genesis in the counter movement of the 1960s.

Lesthaeghe and Surkyn suggest that the generations born after World War II are characterized by high levels of disenchantment with established social institutions, and this has provoked the diffusion of "post-material values" (made easier by the spread over this period of communication technologies—radio, television, film, the Internet). The profusion of post-material and post-modern values reflects an increasingly individualistic orientation to life, which can only mean a continuation of low marriage and fertility rates—the legacy of ideational shifts brought on by the "rebellious" generations of the 1960s and 1970s. Not all social demographic change should be ascribed to the rebellious generations, however. The generation that preceded the baby boomers themselves questioned certain entrenched traditional values. The divorce boom of the early 1970s, for instance, was mainly a product of that generation's growing disenchantment with marriage and the family institution.

Wealth Flow Theory

The theories of fertility change that we have seen so far have all been based on the experience of industrialized countries. John Caldwell (1976, 1982, 2006) presented a theory that attempts to describe the process of fertility transition in developing countries as they undergo socioeconomic modernization. Caldwell's theory hinges on the fundamental assumption that individual reproductive behaviour is economically rational but modified by non-economic factors—particularly physiological, social, and cultural factors—to produce the level and pattern of fertility that is observed in a society.

Caldwell distinguished two types of societies: one of stable high fertility, where there would be no net economic gain accruing to the family from lowered fertility levels, and one in which economic rationality alone would dictate a low level of reproduction. The former is characterized by a "net wealth flow" from younger to older generations—i.e., from children to parents—and the latter by "flows" in the opposite direction—i.e., from parents to children. By "wealth flow," Caldwell means monetary and other benefits and services that one family member provides for another. In traditional societies, the predominant flow of wealth is from children to parents. Examples of monetary and other benefits provided by children to their parents include the following:

- the provision by working children to their parents of a portion or most of their wages;

- care for aging parents;
- continuation of the family name through childbearing;
- performance of necessary religious services for deceased ancestors;
- help and security given to the immediate and extended family in times of need or devastation (e.g., famine, natural disasters, war); and
- the provision of labour, so that an aging parent may be relieved of a workload.

In societies where wealth flows predominantly from the parents to the children (as is the case in contemporary advanced societies), children can expect to benefit from a range of material and non-material goods and services: protection, care, and the provision of education and other necessities until the child reaches adulthood. As noted earlier with Becker's theory, in such societies children are costly and parents demand fewer children, while at the same time emphasizing quality of children subject to the parents' income.

According to Caldwell, the divide between high- and low-fertility regimes will be bridged by a modernizing country when

1. there is a sustained infusion of Western values into the society (which, Caldwell maintains, can occur even in relatively underdeveloped countries); and
2. there is a shift in the intergenerational flow of wealth, from a traditional regime characterized by wealth flowing from child to parents, to an arrangement in which wealth flows primarily from parents to the children.

Figure 6.6 shows that the two main conditions hastening these developments are the "Westernization" of values and ideas (especially through Western mass media and education) and the increasing recognition by parents and society at large of the integrity and uniqueness of the child, leading to the establishment of child-protection laws guaranteeing mandatory education and freedom from abuse and exploitation.

Central to the change in how children are viewed in developing countries undergoing socioeconomic modernization is a process known as the *nucleation* (both economic and emotional) of the family. In the economically nucleated family, parents direct their resources to their immediate household in the same manner that nuclear families of the industrialized countries do. The parents' principal financial obligation is to their children and then to themselves and their household; the financial needs of the extended family are a secondary priority. As a result, the material value of children to parents declines, and the material costs of raising children increase significantly. The child becomes the focal point of the family, and the primary force that binds family members is love and affection (i.e., emotional nucleation). In an argument reminiscent of Becker's (1960), Caldwell correctly theorizes that in this type of social context, it is rational for parents to opt for small families, because as the parental aspirations for child quality increase, the material costs of having and raising children rise significantly.

Applied to sub-Saharan Africa, where fertility transition lags behind trends of other modernizing countries, Caldwell's wealth flow thesis would suggest that the economic and emotional nucleation of families has not yet occurred on a grand scale. There are many social forces unique to Africa that promote high fertility and

FIGURE 6.6   A rendition of Caldwell's wealth flow theory of fertility transition for developing countries

Source: From John C. Caldwell, "The Globalization of Fertility Behavior," from Rodolfo A. Bulatao and John B. Casterline, eds, *Global Fertility Transition*, supplement to vol. 27 of *Population and Development Review* (New York: Population Council, 2001): 95. Published by Wiley. Reprinted with permission.

therefore slow or delay the course of fertility transition. These include the importance of family lineage and the cultural adherence to ancestor worship, polygyny, and cultural views regarding sexuality (see Caldwell and Caldwell, 1990). As well, many parts of Africa are plagued by crisis, from widespread famine to civil wars, economic meltdowns, and the devastating HIV/AIDS epidemic (Zuberi et al., 2003). In spite of these factors that operate against fertility transition in sub-Saharan Africa, there is evidence of very recent fertility declines, which suggest that the changes Caldwell outlined may have begun to take hold.

Some critics have raised questions about the general applicability of Caldwell's wealth flow theory (see Cain, 1982, 1983; Thandani, 1978). Caldwell (2006) has recently updated his theory along four specific areas:

1. the role of children's labour inputs and consumption in farming communities in the years preceding fertility transition;
2. the mode of production that defines the different cultures of work in traditional society;
3. the role of children as "insurance" to parents; and
4. the conditions necessary for fertility transition.

For the most part, Caldwell's interpretation of the new evidence confirms the wealth flow theory, though placed in a broader framework that includes a host of interrelated factors. Caldwell (2006: 103–4) neatly summarizes his argument thus:

[F]ertility transition began when a series of conditions were met by, in succession, colonial governments, preparing for independence and newly independent governments enthusiastically preparing for the future by a huge increase in educational capacity; the replacement of colonial officials by indigenous ones, usually with a significant growth in the bureaucracy; the realization by parents that they could safely invest in the education of children in contrast to simply in their number; a steep decline in infant and child mortality led by international efforts; urbanization providing new jobs in the private sector; a continuing rise in per capita incomes (except recently in sub-Saharan Africa); and independent governments being in a better position than colonial ones to urge and offer family planning. Cumulatively, these changes finally reversed the wealth flow, and fertility fell.

The Synthesis Framework

In addition to his cyclical theory describing fertility change in industrialized countries, Easterlin (1975, 1978, 1983) posited his synthesis framework of fertility transition in the context of societies undergoing socioeconomic modernization. The Easterlin framework is called "synthesis" because it incorporates elements of economic theory, sociological theory, and the proximate determinants of fertility into a unified explanation of fertility change. In this framework, the concepts of *supply of children* and *demand for children* are of central importance. Supply of children refers to the number of children that parents would

have if they made no attempt at controlling fertility; demand for children refers to the number of surviving children that parents would want if fertility control were costless. Another important factor is *regulation costs*, or the costs to parents (monetary and psychological) of intentionally limiting family size.

Part (a) of Figure 6.7 outlines the synthesis framework, in which background modernization factors (such as improved education and health and living standards, urbanization, and the introduction of new goods into society) and cultural factors that promote traditional norms (especially ethnicity and religion) affect regulation costs (Rc), the demand for children (Cd), and the supply of children (Cn). These three factors in turn influence the proximate determinants of fertility, including deliberate fertility control variables (such as the use of modern contraception). Ultimately, in this three-stage model, the number of children born is a direct function of the proximate determinants, themselves affected by societal factors.

Part (b) of Figure 6.7 lays out the temporal process of change in Cn, Cd, and actual family size (C), as society passes through the modernization process. On balance, over time, modernization should have the effect of lowering the demand for children as well as reducing the psychological and material costs of fertility regulation due to the gradual erosion of tradition on the one hand, and an increase in income on the other. At the same time, however, the supply of children rises with increasing levels of modernization because the health of the population generally improves accompanied by falling death rates. In the early stages of socioeconomic modernization, these conditions can contribute to an

Part (a) The synthesis framework

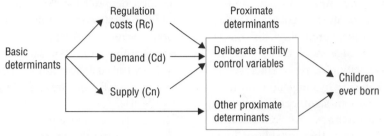

Note: The basic determinants comprise modernization variables (education, urbanization, etc.), cultural factors (ethnicity, religion, etc.), and other determinants.

Part (b) Modernization and fertility change

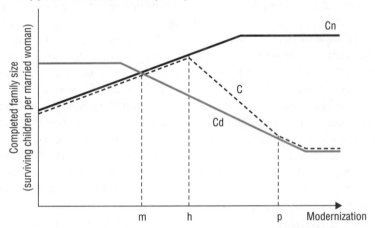

Hypothetical trends in supply (Cn), demand (Cd), and actual family size (C) associated with modernization

FIGURE 6.7   Easterlin's synthesis framework of fertility change for countries undergoing socioeconomic modernization

Source: Reprinted from *Determinants of Fertility in Developing Countries*, Vol.2, Rodolfo A. Bulato and Ronald D. Lee, "Modernization of Fertility" by Richard Easterlin (1983) pp. 582-586 Figure reprinted by permission of the author.

increase in the potential number of children couples can have as a result of improved infant and childhood survival probabilities. Therefore, early in the modernization process, natural fertility (i.e., Cn), can increase and cause a temporary rise in the birth rate. Eventually, as the modernization process unfolds, there will be a gradual acceptance and widespread diffusion of birth control in the population, and at that point fertility rates will embark on a long term declining trend, consistent with the fall in parents' demand for children.

Easterlin (1983: 573–6) explains that as socioeconomic modernization unfolds and the excess of supply over demand grows, the prospective number of unwanted children increases, generating a corresponding growth in couples' motivation to limit family size. Moreover, regulation costs and thus the obstacles to limiting family size decline, and at some point the balance between the motivation for and cost of regulation tips in favour of the former. At this point, couples take deliberate actions to limit family size, and actual family size starts to fall below potential supply, though it still exceeds demand. Motivation for regulation continues to rise and the costs of regulation continue to fall until eventually the population reaches a point at which actual family size corresponds to demand.

Easterlins synthesis thesis attempts to show that countries that have passed through the fertility transition did so because they successfully promoted a shift in motivation from traditional rejection of fertility control to its eventual acceptance in a context of rising potential fertility brought forth by declining rates of infant and childhood mortality. It also helps us understand how a region such as sub-Saharan Africa has been delayed in its fertility transition. In this case, the psychic costs of fertility regulation remain high for couples because of strong traditional norms that encourage the demand for children while at the same time discouraging widespread adoption of family limitation.

Social Interaction Perspective on Contemporary Fertility Transitions

John Bongaarts and Susan Watkins (1996) offer an explanation of fertility transition that relies heavily on the concept of social interactions. Their thesis attempts to shed light on why fertility is high in pre-transitional settings, why it declines with the onset of socioeconomic modernization, and why the timing and onset of fertility transition vary across societies.

After observing statistical correlations between the United Nations' Human Development Index (HDI) and the total fertility rate for 69 developing countries between 1960 and 1990, Bongaarts and Watkins (1996) discovered a number of trends. Among their findings are the following:

- In pre-transition societies, fertility is at first unresponsive to the level of socio-economic development, so that there are significant delays in the onset of fertility transition.
- Once a few countries in a macro-region embark on the fertility transition, other countries in the same region tend to follow sooner than expected.
- As time passes, the onset of fertility transition occurs at ever lower levels of socioeconomic development.
- Once a fertility transition is underway, fertility changes more rapidly than expected as a result of changes in socio-economic development alone.
- The pace of fertility decline is not related to the pace of socioeconomic development, but to the level of socio-economic development when the transition began.

Bongaarts and Watkins' social interaction explanation of fertility change keys in on the role of personal networks in transmitting new ideas about fertility control and family planning throughout the territorial communities, the nation, and groups of nations. For instance, at the local level individuals transmit new knowledge to others in their social networks, and behaviour within those networks is conditioned by social influence—people are more likely to follow network figures that have status and prestige. At the broader level, people from neighbouring communities would exchange information about new methods of family limitation, their interactions facilitated by such communication channels as transportation routes and new communication technologies. To the extent that people have access to radios and televisions, they are also connected to the global community and are thus influenced by what they hear and see in other parts of the world, which could lead to the adoption of innovative behaviours and their subsequent diffusion to others. The process of adopting family planning often spreads through family members, relatives, friends and acquaintances, and eventually the society at large.

By implication, the social interaction thesis suggests that as globalization (economic and ideational) spreads rapidly throughout the developing regions, there will be an opening up of global channels of interaction (e.g., the Internet and television), and that as a result, very few developing countries will fail to undergo the fertility transition over the next few decades.

Women's Autonomy and Fertility Transition in Developing Countries

Throughout the chapter, we have touched on the role of gender structure, and the difficulty women face in balancing family and work responsibilities has been mentioned on several occasions. Theories of fertility transition in the developing countries implicitly recognize gender relations. Caldwell, for instance, in his wealth flow theory, suggests that in a high-fertility regime, the patriarchal extended family is inherently pronatalist. Senior men have power over women and children, and they benefit from their labour; therefore, high fertility is advantageous to the patriarch in the extended family system. The shift to a low-fertility regime occurs when this traditional family system is undermined and the balance of power within nucleated families becomes more equitable. In the emotionally nucleated family, women's control over reproduction is a fundamental force behind fertility transition because they are the ones who are best able to actualize their fertility desires (Mason, 1988).

Mead Cain (1982, 1983, 1993) has written about women's economic dependence on male family members in poor countries like Bangladesh. For women in these harsh and unpredictable settings, having many children is a strategy to enhance their survival and well-being in the face of an institutionalized patriarchal system that promotes male control of women. Unable to own property or gain economic independence, women have children as a form of security or, as Cain would argue, as a form of risk insurance and support in old age. In this situation, sons are preferred over daughters, since sons afford greater security. (Men, too, may be motivated to have sons because daughters typically do not contribute economically to the household.) Thus, this gender role structure promotes high fertility. Presumably, fertility decline occurs only when this gender role regime is destabilized and women gain greater economic independence from males.

Economic theories of fertility and the family tend to depict the household as a partnership in which husbands and wives have equal interests and are bound by a single utility function. This view of the family and household power relations has been challenged by feminist social scientists, including Nancy Folbre (1983, 1988) and Karen Mason (1988, 1993, 1997b), among others (e.g., Jeffery and Jeffery, 1997; Riley, 1999, 2005; Watkins, 1993). Folbre (1983) in particular advocated the need to "bring in" women as active agents in theories of family change, in order to frame a more realistic perspective of how families and households behave, given the differential power and gender role hierarchies that usually exist in families. An influential study of gender and fertility was carried out by Mason (1993); some of her findings are outlined in the box on page 236

Search for Underlying Uniformities

Low Fertility in Industrialized Countries

Based on their comprehensive analysis of fertility patterns across industrialized countries, Tomas Frejka and Jean-Paul Sardon (2004: 2) have concluded that it will be highly unlikely that there will be a return to replacement-level fertility in these countries, some of which have reached what has been defined as "lowest-low" fertility levels (Billari and Kohler, 2004; Bongaarts

EVALUATING DEMOGRAPHIC, ECONOMIC, AND SOCIAL INTERACTION PERSPECTIVES OF FERTILITY

Mary Shenk and colleagues (2013) looked into the causes of the decline in the number of children being born in a developing country setting: Matlab, Bangaldesh. The theories on fertility transition in developing countries emphasize the importance of the role of (i) changing mortality and extrinsic risks to children, (ii) the economic costs and benefits of investing in self and in children, and (iii) the cultural transmission or diffusion of low-fertility social norms.

The findings by these scholars suggest strong support for the importance of economic motivations for parental investment. The economic-and-investment model predicted fertility rates much better than either of the other two models. Child mortality variables do have a strong influence on the number of births. It is well known that parents try to replace babies who have died by having more births, but these variables seem less relevant in explaining what determines the final family size of surviving children. Correlates of cultural norms did not seem to be very predictive either. What did emerge as highly important in the statistical analysis was the ownership of farmland, along with several other factors associated with the costs of spreading parental investment among many offspring. The authors' results also indicate that education is very important, and is one of the things that comprise parental investment.

MASON ON WOMEN'S ROLE IN FERTILITY TRANSITION

In her review and critique of the established demographic literature on matters regarding gender and fertility, Karen Mason (1993) concluded that regular demographic survey approaches could not possibly provide sufficient insight into the ways in which gender relations and power imbalances between men and women affect fertility. She recommended the use of multi-level comparative studies of how women's position affects fertility, to be carried out at both the community and the national level. From her review of the literature, Mason (1993: 30–1) identified seven key ideas that bear on women's role in fertility transition.

1. An increase in women's autonomy will facilitate the postponement of marriage and hence the decline of fertility by reducing the need to control unmarried women's sexuality through early marriage.

2. In family systems that give all rights of women's labour to the husband's family, women's economic independence will facilitate the postponement of marriage and hence the decline of fertility; in other family systems, the effects of women's economic independence on marriage are indeterminate.

3. Because it channels the rewards of children disproportionately to men and the costs of rearing them disproportionately to women, patriarchal family structure encourages high fertility; egalitarian family structure facilitates fertility decline.

4. Women's economic dependency on men produces strong son-preferences among both women and men, and hence relatively high fertility desires for purposes of risk insurance and old-age security; in conjugally oriented family systems, women's economic independence facilitates fertility decline.

5. The extent of women's autonomy and economic dependency determine women's dependency on the maternal role for legitimacy, security, and satisfaction, and hence the opportunity costs of having children and the motivation to limit fertility.

6. Women's autonomy influences their access to modern knowledge and modes of action and hence their propensity to engage in innovative behaviour, including fertility limitation within marriage.

7. Social equality and emotional intimacy between husbands and wives tend to influence fertility by affecting the role that the wife's health and well-being plays in fertility decision making, and by influencing the likelihood or effectiveness of contraceptive use. (Mason, 1993: 30–1)

These ideas are interrelated in that they concern the impact of women's autonomy on their age at entry into marriage and on their motivation to limit fertility within marriage. Mason (1993, 1997b) notes that although the empirical evidence in support of these propositions is often indirect, the literature is generally consistent with them.

Source: Based on WOMEN'S POSITION AND DEMOGRAPHIC CHANGE edited by Nora Federici, Karen Oppenheim Mason & Solvi Sogner (1993) Ch. 1 "The Impact of Women's Position on Demographic Change During the Course of Development" by Karen Oppenheim Mason pp. 19-42, 346 words from pp. 30-31. Reprinted by permission of Oxford University Press, USA.

and Sobotka, 2012; Kohler, Billari, and Ortega, 2002).

It is worth asking if there are some underlying uniformities that characterize low-fertility societies Caldwell and Thomas Schindlmayr (2003) have addressed this question. They have argued that a common underlying force behind all fertility transitions is "the creation of a world economic system where children are of no immediate economic value to their parents" (257). Society rewards women who work outside the home, and this, coupled with the many temptations of the modern consumer society, promotes a desire for material possessions that is stronger than the desire for children.

As a general explanation this covers a great deal of ground, but some critics argue that it may be too sweeping. Van de Kaa (2004b) asserts that the global pattern of fertility decline identified by Caldwell and Schindlmayr is less uniform than these authors maintain. Japan and countries in Eastern Europe, for example, began to achieve low fertility before modern contraception became widely available, and well before globalization became a significant movement. Fertility was already declining when modern methods of family limitation became available.

An interesting alternative explanation for low fertility is Lonnie Aarssen's (2005) suggestion that it is the manifest outcome of evolutionary principles, stemming from a relaxation of innate selective processes for high fertility. Specifically, Aarssen argues that the empowerment of women that leads to reduced fertility is an evolutionary consequence of selection that reflects an inherent preference for lower fertility in females. This has allowed random genetic drift to take place, producing an increased frequency of innate behaviours that at the same time promote low fertility and a discontentment with large families. On the other hand, while low fertility seems a permanent condition in many societies, it is unlikely that birth rates will drop to levels much below what they are today because social norms ensure that the majority of women will want to bear at least one child (Foster, 2000).

Peter McDonald (2000) has advanced an explanation emphasizing the gender system of advanced societies as a central force in fertility change, which may at the same time explain why some industrialized countries are seeing a rise in fertility while others are not. McDonald (2000) distinguishes between "gender equity in individual-oriented institutions" and "gender equity within the family and family-oriented institutions." These two types of gender equity may not necessarily coincide. A society may have a high degree of gender equity in individual-oriented institutions (translating into equal access to higher education and careers in the paid economy) but low equity in the family-oriented institutions. This is the case even in some advanced societies, where in spite of the gains women have made in individual-oriented institutions, the family institution still maintains a relatively traditional gender role structure, where women are expected to take care of the children and perform the usual household chores of cooking, cleaning, and so forth, even while holding full- or part-time jobs (Fuwa, 2004; Torr and Short, 2004).

According to McDonald, this disjuncture between the two types of gender equity systems, which is especially characteristic of Mediterranean countries, is likely to lead to very low fertility because women are less able to cope with the dual demands of work and family. In societies where family-oriented institutions as well as individually based institutions are equitable, fertility rates are typically higher (though they might still fall short of replacement level). Examples of societies that meet both gender equity conditions are the Scandinavian countries and, to some extent, the United States (Engelhardt, Kogel, and Prskawetz, 2004; Frejka, 2004). The key factor in ensuring equity in family-oriented institutions seems to be family-friendly state policies that support and ease parenthood for couples. This implies that if institutions were made to be more family-friendly, birth rates would likely rise (Gauthier and Hatzius, 1997; Hobcroft, 2004; Thévenon, 2011).

Generalizations about Fertility Transition in Developing Countries

During the 1970s and 1980s many developing nations—Taiwan, Indonesia, Thailand, China, and several Latin American and Caribbean countries, to name just a few—embarked on a period of sustained fertility decline; others have recently begun their fertility transitions. But the pattern of fertility transition experienced in these developing countries is different from the changes experienced in Western Europe, where declining birth rates followed long-term economic growth and improvements in living conditions. Important findings from surveys carried out in developing nations indicate that access to methods of birth control, changes in cultural values favouring the small-family ideal, and rising female education and independence—all in conjunction with socioeconomic development—have been some of the key driving forces behind fertility decline (Caldwell, 2001; Robey, Rutstein, and Morris, 1993). As we have seen, theories of fertility transition in the developing countries encompass these factors as well as additional ones. Rodolfo Bulatao (2001: 2–3) provides a useful summary of some of the most important propositions concerning fertility decline associated with fertility transition in developing countries. These propositions, which have received substantial support in the literature, emphasize the interaction of cultural, economic, sociological, and demographic factors in fertility transition. They are outlined in the box on page 240.

Canadian Fertility Trends and Patterns

Back when Canada was a frontier society, the fertility of its people was much higher than what it is today. We know that in the mid-1800s, for instance, the Canadian crude birth rate was around 45 per 1000 (Wadhera and Strachan, 1993). Before that time, it must have been even higher. If we were to look at the long-term trend in the crude birth and death rates for French Canada and Canada, taken together, from the early 1700s all the way to the present (Figure 6.8), we would notice six broad stages of fertility change in Canada:

- **Stage One** (1711–15 to 1756–60) is characterized by fairly stable high fertility and rising death rates, with rates of natural increase fluctuating between 1.4 and 3.6 per cent per year.
- **Stage Two** (1761–5 to 1831–5) is marked by sustained declines in both fertility and mortality, with the death rate

declining somewhat faster than fertility. In this stage, average annual growth rates never declined below 2 per cent and in some cases went up as far as 3 per cent.

- **Stage Three** (1836–40 to 1891–1900) saw fertility decline rapidly. Mortality, despite being on a declining trend overall, showed some increase between 1871 and 1881. The rates of natural increase during Stage Three were still high by most standards, but towards the start of the twentieth century, they began to decline from almost 3 per cent to about 1.6 per cent on average (with some exceptions).

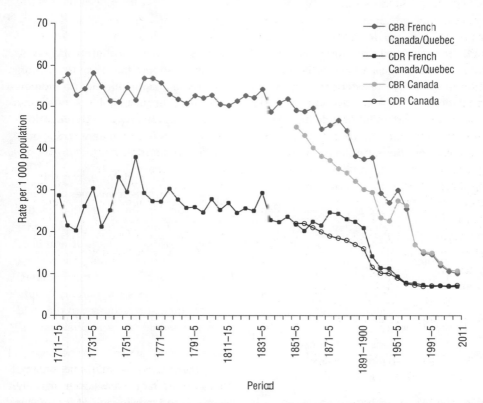

FIGURE 6.8   Historical evolution of crude birth and death rates for French Canada/ Quebec (1711–15 to 2004) and Canada (1851–5 to 2011)

Sources: Bureau de la Statistique du Québec (1997): 149, 132, 135; Henripin (1972): 18; Henripin and Peron (1972): 230; McVey and Kalbach (1995): 184; Nagnur (1986a): 45; Pelletier, Legare, and Bourbeau (1997): 95; Statistics Canada (2006b): 218, (1993): 9, 15, 32–3, 39–40, (2013h, 2013j); Urquhart (1983): A1–14.

Jacques Henripin's (1954: 39) data for French Canada between 1661 and 1770 show crude birth rates fluctuating between 50 and 65 births per 1000 population. These early French-Canadian birth rates exceed crude birth rates found in most developing countries today.

1661–70	50.6	1721–30	54.2
1671–80	52.5	1931–40	58.1
1681–90	47.3	1741–50	59.0
1691–1700	54.2	1751–60	61.8
1701–10	56.4	1761–70	65.2
1711–20	56.9		

BULATAO'S PROPOSITIONS ON FERTILITY CHANGE IN DEVELOPING COUNTRIES

1. In virtually all cases, long-run declines in mortality eventually instill a lagged response for long-term fertility reductions. This is so because reducing infant and childhood deaths lowers the need among parents to produce a given desired number of surviving children.

2. In modernizing societies, once children are viewed as economic burdens, fewer children are desired by parents. In other words, fertility is high when children earn income or contribute materially to the household, and it is low when they do not. Related to this, the introduction of institutionalized social security systems should lower fertility by reducing the need for parents to depend on their children for support in old age.

3. As rearing children interferes with adult activities, the opportunity costs of having children increases. Fertility should fall when there is an increase in opportunities for women to work in jobs that are relatively incompatible with childbearing, which essentially means work outside the home.

4. As societies modernize, the shift to fewer births accompanies a transformation in the institution of the family, from a multigenerational concern with clear lines of authority to a small conjugal unit, focused on the individual needs of the members. In such contexts the parents devote more time and resources to the child as compared to a traditional regime.

5. As societies undergo socioeconomic modernization, traditional norms favouring large families eventually erode, and individuals opt for smaller families.

6. Greater access to modern contraceptives through family-planning programs greatly accelerates the fertility transition.

7. As women increasingly obtain education and participate more in the labour force, there occurs significant delays in marriage among women, and this helps fertility to decline.

8. The diffusion of contraceptive knowledge through the mass media, the education system, other communication systems, and through personal interactions of the small-family ideal, facilitates a widespread process of fertility decline.

Source: Rodolfo A. Bulatao and Jon B. Casterline, eds, "Introduction" in *Global Fertility Transitions*, supplement to vol. 27 of Population and Development Review. Published by Wiley. Reprinted with permission.

- *Stage Four* (1901 to 1941) is characterized by very rapid declines in both vital rates, with rates of natural increase in the vicinity of 2 per cent.
- *Stage Five* (1941 to 1966) saw both Quebec and Canada experience a general upturn in fertility following World War II.
- *Stage Six* (1966 to today) is characterized by a general convergence in birth and death rates. In both Quebec and Canada as a whole, very low crude birth and death rates have produced very low rates of natural increase.

From Baby Boom to Baby Bust

By the early 1930s, the period of fertility transition in Canada had pretty much come to an end, with the birth rate reaching historic lows of about 20 per 1000. As we have already seen, the low fertility of the 1930s was a common phenomenon in the industrial nations of Western Europe and the United States. As the Great Depression of the 1930s unfolded, fertility rates, while

remaining low, increased gradually leading up to World War II. The outbreak of war helped to end the economic depression and at the same time stimulated a surge in the marriage rate, and consequently also the birth rate. By 1943, the crude birth rate had risen to 24 per 1000 (McInnis, 2000a). This increase turned out to be a prelude to what would be an unprecedented surge in the Canadian birth rate immediately after World War II.

The trend in Canada's total fertility rate through the twentieth century and into the twenty-first is shown in Table 6.6. From the Depression until the eve of World War II, the TFR declined, falling to below 3 children per woman for 1936 and 1941. The decline can actually be traced to 1933, when the recorded rate was 2.86. These values remained below 3 until 1943, when the fertility rate reached 3.04 children per woman, and in the ensuing 19-year period, from 1946 to 1965, the total fertility rate remained above 3. In fact, some of the highest-ever Canadian fertility rates were recorded during that period, including the 1952 TFR of 3.64, which was then

TABLE 6.6   Number of live births, and total fertility rates, Canada, 1921–2011

Year	Number of live births	Total fertility rate
1921	264 879	3.536
1926	240 015	3.357
1931	247 205	3.200
1936	227 980	2.696
1941	263 993	2.832
1946	343 504	3.374
1951	381 092	3.503
1956	450 739	3.858
1961	475 700	3.840
1966	387 710	2.813
1971	362 187	2.187
1976	359 987	1.825
1981	371 346	1.704
1986	372 913	1.672
1991	402 533	1.799
1996	366 200	1.630
2001	333 744	1.540
2006	354 617	1.610
2011	377 636	1.610

Sources: Bélanger (2006): 31; McVey and Kalbach (1995): 270; Statistics Canada (2006a, 2013h, 2013j).

the highest birth rate achieved since 1921. This level would ultimately be surpassed when, in 1959, the country recorded a total fertility rate of almost 4 (3.93), marking the apex of the baby boom. In that year, 479 275 children were born in Canada, setting a record yet unmatched in the country's history.

The year 1966 marked the end of the baby boom (Foot and Stoffman, 1998) and the start of the precipitous decline in the birth rate known as the "baby bust" (Grindstaff, 1975, 1985; Romaniuk, 1984). In 1972, Canada saw its total fertility rate fall below the 2.1 replacement level, and the trend since then has been, on the whole, downward. There have been minor upward perturbations, but the rate has not reestablished itself at replacement level.

Explanations for the Baby Boom and Baby Bust in Canada

The rise and fall of fertility in Canada after World War II can be attributed to social, cultural, demographic, and economic factors. The end of hostilities in 1945 brought unprecedented economic prosperity to Canada, stimulating a marriage boom. Jobs were abundant, and Canadian men and women married at younger ages than they had in earlier generations. As a result, couples started their families earlier and had more children on average (Romaniuk,

1984). All of this was facilitated by the abundance of jobs available to young men following the war, as Easterlin (1969, 1980) has argued. Low fertility in the 1930s meant that roughly two decades later, in the 1950s and 1960s, there were fewer entry-level workers seeking jobs. The small cohorts of the 1930s could gain employment relatively easily and enjoy a sense of security and excellent prospects for the future thanks to the booming economic conditions of the time. For that generation of Canadians material aspirations could be actualized even with a household of three or more children. At the same time, governments were enhancing the welfare state in order to provide better social and economic security for Canadians by means of universal health care and education, employment insurance, and so on. Once these developments are considered together, it seems unsurprising that young couples would commit fairly early to the institution of marriage and family.

Against this socioeconomic backdrop, the traditional gender role system that prevailed until the 1960s, which cast the man of the house as the "breadwinner," helped promote higher fertility. This system would later be displaced by a more egalitarian arrangement of gender roles, brought on to a large extent by the efforts of the women's emancipation movement of the 1960s. But before this time, traditional values about family and marriage were strong, and the Church exercised considerable influence in people's lives. In this social context, young people saw value in the institutions of marriage and family, reinforced by religion and society at large, and married in large numbers. Moreover, for many young people in the 1950s, early marriage was seen as a route to personal freedom from the authority of parents; for older couples, especially those

whose family-building desires had been frustrated by the war, this was an opportunity to have children and raise a family. All of this, again, contributed to higher rates of marriage and fertility.

In many respects, the same factors responsible for the baby boom were also involved in the baby bust. If the high fertility of the baby boom period was partly attributable to the traditional system of gender roles, then declining birth rates during the baby bust were also determined by gender roles, but in this case it was the breakdown of the traditional breadwinner system that mattered. The traditional values that had encouraged couples to marry early and have many children became supplanted by new modern ideas about the desirability of small families. The centrality of marriage in people's lives began to wane in the 1960s, and the new generations of Canadians born during the baby boom would eventually explore alternative family arrangements, first noticeable with the rise of cohabitation and common-law unions beginning in the early 1970s. The legacy of these new ideas is in evidence today, as Canada and other post-industrial societies are now in the midst of the "second demographic transition" (Lesthaeghe, 1995; van de Kaa, 1987, 1999, 2003, 2004a, 2004b).

Today, late marriage and non-marriage are the most important proximate determinants of Canada's low birth rate, with contraceptive use a distant second (Henripin, 2003: 168). The probability of a Canadian woman experiencing marriage as her first union has fallen significantly, a trend that is more pronounced among the younger cohorts of Canadian women (Wu, 2000). Rates of remarriage have been on a downward trend since the late 1960s (Wu and Schimmele, 2005: 223), and the rise of cohabitation has not translated into any major sustained increases in fertility rates.

As a result of their growing involvement in the paid labour force and enhanced education and occupational training, an increasing number of women today draw earnings equal to or exceeding those of their husbands. During the early 1970s, this distribution of household income was evident in just 6 per cent of working couples. By the late 1990s, the number of couples in which the wife earned the same as or more than the husband had grown to 25 per cent (Grindstaff and Trovato, 1990; Gunderson, 1998; Little, 2000). This means that working women today must consider the "opportunity costs" of having children, including delayed advancement in the workplace and forgone earnings (Drolet, 2003; Grindstaff, Balakrishnan, and Dewit, 1992). These opportunity costs increase with women's education and professional status. This must be considered an important factor in the recent downturn in fertility in Canada, as young couples adjust to the demands of modern living by having children later in life in order to accommodate career and work aspirations with family goals (Ram and Rahim, 1993).

It is also important to recognize the growing difficulty young people face in getting a start in today's labour market. There have been several recessions in recent decades, the most recent one being the 2008 financial crisis (Larochelle-Côté and Gilmore, 2009). Employment rates for young workers have not been especially favourable it seems, even among those with postsecondary schooling (Marshall, 2010). The earnings of young men have tended to fall behind those of older workers. These conditions facing young adults cannot

Between the early 1980s and 2009, the proportion of babies born outside of marital unions in Canada increased from about 13 per cent to about 39 per cent. This increasing trend is largely attributable to babies born in common-law unions. Among the provinces, this trend is especially pronounced in Quebec, where currently over 63 per cent of all births are non-marital births. In the rest of Canada, the proportions in 2009 ranged between 28 per cent in Ontario, and 49 per cent in Newfoundland and Labrador. In the three territories, the levels are very high, exceeding 70 per cent (Barbieri and Ouellette, 2012: 256; Kerr, Moyser, and Beaujot, 2006).

possibly foster in them a strong desire for marriage and family building (Bélanger and Ouellet, 2002; Romaniuk, 1984: 80).

Differential Fertility

Regional

The long-term trend in the TFR of Canada as a whole and its constituent regions has been fairly uniform over the twentieth century. Following the low fertility of the 1930s, all parts of Canada witnessed the post-war baby boom and subsequent baby bust. In general, the past three decades have seen the TFRs for the provinces move increasingly towards convergence around 1.6, with some relatively minor annual fluctuations (see Figure 6.9). In 2011, provincial TFRs ranged from 1.45 (Newfoundland and Labrador) to 1.99 (Saskatchewan). The regions that stand out are Nunavut and the Northwest Territories, the former having a TFR of 2.97 in 2011, the

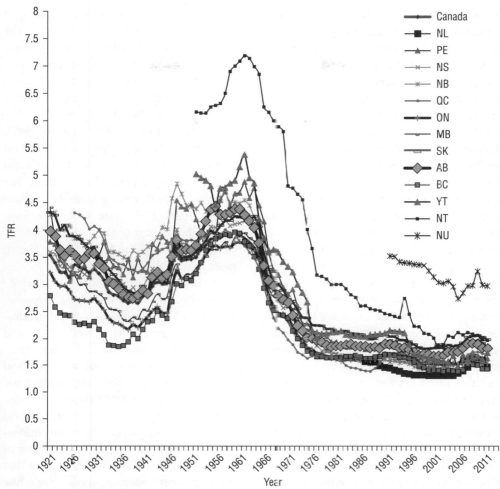

FIGURE 6.9 Historical evolution of total fertility rate for Canada and its provinces and territories, 1921–2011

Note: Data for Newfoundland and Labrador (NL) available only after 1981. Nunavut (NU) came into being in 1989.

Sources: Statistics Canada (1997, 2006a, 1993, 2013j); Statistics Canada: *Births 1991* and *1992* (Cat. 84-210 Annual, Table 17); *Births and Deaths, 1994* (Cat. 84-210. XPD, Table 3.4); *Births and Deaths, 1995* (Cat. 84-210.XPD, Table 3.5); *The Daily* (1998). Data for 1921–82: Romaniuk (1984); data for 1986–99: Bélanger (2002): Table A6; data for 2000–3: Bélanger (2006): 31.

highest in Canada. Geographic isolation, regional underdevelopment, and, perhaps most important, the large percentage of Aboriginal inhabitants in these regions are factors that all help to account for the high fertility of the two geographic areas.

Religion and Ethnicity

Religion and ethnicity have long been of interest to demographers who study fertility trends and differentials in Canada (e.g., Burch, 1966; Charles, 1948; Henripin, 1972; Hurd, 1965; Tracey, 1941). Until midway through the 1970s, Catholics had higher birth rates than did Protestants, and some variability in fertility by urban/rural residence and by ethnic origin were still noticeable (Balakrishnan, Ebanks, and Grindstaff, 1979; Beaujot, Krotki, and Krishnan, 1978; Halli, 1990; Trovato and Grindstaff, 1980). However, by the 1990s, ethnic and religious differences in fertility had receded almost to insignificance (Balakrishnan, Krotki, and Lapierre-Adamczyk, 1993; Henripin, 1972, 2003), except among a few numerically small religious groups (Mormons, Mennonites, Hutterites), Aboriginal peoples, and some immigrant visible minorities (Arabs, West Asians, South Asians) (Malenfant and Bélanger, 2006).

Among Canada's Aboriginal peoples, fertility rates have been declining for some time, though they are not likely to converge with rates for the rest of the country until the mid-twenty-first century. It is interesting that the long-term fertility decline among Canadian Aboriginal peoples, which began in the early 1960s, coincides with fertility transitions among other indigenous populations, including those of the United States, Australia, and New Zealand (Caldwell, 2001: 95). As of the late 1990s and early 2000s, the total fertility rate for Canada's Native people as a whole was about 70 per cent above the national average (see Table 6.7). The TFR is highest for the Inuit, reaching an estimated rate of 3.21 in 1996–2001. The Métis have the lowest TFR, at around 2.15. In many respects, these variations reflect differences in geographic and socioeconomic marginalization from the mainstream Canadian society.

Among the various theories proposed to explain the divergent trends in fertility among disadvantaged subpopulations is *the characteristics assimilation thesis*, which states that minority groups have high fertility because of their disadvantaged socioeconomic position in relation to the larger society. Lower education levels, lower income, and greater rates of unemployment in relation to others all contribute to diminished socioeconomic status, which is believed to contribute to relatively high fertility rates (Johnson, 1979; Trovato, 1987). Another explanation suggests that certain minority groups possess a *particularized ideology* that promotes high fertility. For example, fertility among Catholics at one time surpassed the rate for Protestants, presumably in part because of the Catholic Church's opposition to birth control (Burch, 1966; Day, 1968; Van Heek, 1956).

Certain minority populations, including North Americans of Chinese, Japanese, and Jewish background, also manifest below-average fertility levels (Chui and Trovato, 1989; Johnson and Lean, 1985; Tang, 2006). Calvin Goldscheider and Peter Uhlenberg (1969), articulating the *minority status insecurity thesis*, suggested that these groups suffer sociopsychological insecurities associated with their minority status, which is the underlying cause of their low fertility. They further explain that these minority groups typically have a history of prejudice and discrimination, and share strong aspirations for socioeconomic assimilation. They typically have no particularized ideology prohibiting the use of birth control, so having a small family may be viewed as part of a conscious strategy by minority couples to achieve and maintain socioeconomic success.

If we were to apply these theories to Canada's Aboriginal population, we might conclude that high Aboriginal fertility results from the marginalizing effects of discrimination and prejudice this group has experienced for centuries, and their difficulty achieving

TABLE 6.7   Three perspectives on Canadian Aboriginal fertility: TFR by year, 1974–2001; age-specific fertility rates by age, 1966–2001; and age-specific fertility rates by Aboriginal subgroup, 1996–2001

Year	TFR Registered Indians	TFR All Canadians	Ratio Registered Indians/Canada
1974	4.42	1.88	2.35
1975	4.16	1.81	2.30
1976	3.95	1.79	2.21
1977	3.74	1.76	2.13
1978	3.62	1.71	2.12
1979	3.52	1.70	2.07
1980	3.41	1.69	2.02
1981	3.33	1.66	2.01
1982	3.33	1.64	2.03
1983	3.29	1.62	2.03
1984	3.27	1.62	2.02
1985	3.24	1.61	2.01
1986	3.18	1.59	2.00
1987	3.03	1.57	1.93
1988	2.92	1.60	1.83
1989	2.86	1.65	1.73
1990	2.83	1.71	1.65
1991	2.85	1.71	1.67
1992	2.87	1.71	1.68
1993	2.86	1.68	1.70
1994	2.80	1.68	1.67
1995	2.76	1.67	1.65
1996	2.73	1.62	1.69
1996–2001	2.60	1.56	1.67

Age-specific fertility rates (all Aboriginal peoples) by period

Age group	1966–71	1976–81	1986–91	1991–6	1996–2001
15–19	120.4	112.3	115.5	116.2	99.9
20–24	297.5	203.9	183.1	181.7	168.4
25–29	251.6	160.7	143.8	145.5	131.4
30–34	189.6	85.3	89.3	81.6	74.2
35–39	153.3	51.4	54.3	35.2	33.3
40–44	79.2	24.4	10.5	10.2	11.6
45–49	11.9	2.7	1.3	1.7	1.0

(continued)

TABLE 6.7   (continued)

||||||||||||||||||||||||||||||||||||||||||||||||||||||||||||||||||||||||||||||||||||||||||||||||||||||||||||||||||||||||||||

Age-specific fertility rates (Canada and Aboriginal subgroups), 1996–2001

Age group	Canada	North American Indian	Registered Indian	Métis	Inuit
15–19	20.3	114.2	110.3	72.5	100.0
20–24	64.2	182.3	173.6	142.3	179.0
25–29	103.7	136.7	128.5	119.6	156.9
30–34	85.5	78.5	73.9	63.1	101.0
35–39	32.9	36.8	35.7	25.4	57.4
40–44	5.3	13.7	13.6	5.5	41.0
45–49	0.2	1.0	1.0	0.7	6.6
TFR	1.5605	2.816	2.683	2.1455	3.2095

Sources: Adapted from Loh and George (2003): 122; Ram (2004): 191.

The long-term fertility decline among Canada's Aboriginal populations began in the early 1960s. This point also marks the onset of fertility transition among indigenous populations of the United States, Australia, and New Zealand. Caldwell (2001: 95) prepared the table below to show the similar timing of fertility transition among these indigenous groups.

Indigenous minority	Onset of decline	+5% decline	+10% decline
American Indians	1960	1961	1962
Canadian Indians	1962	1964	1966
New Zealand Maoris	1963	1964	1966
Australian Aborigines	1971	1972	1973

Source: John C. Caldwell, 'The Globalization of Fertility Behavior', from Rodolfo A. Bulatao and John B. Casterline, eds, *Global Fertility Transition*, supplement to vol. 27 of Population and Development Review. Published by Wiley. Reprinted with permission.

socioeconomic parity with the larger society. In empirical analyses, such demographic variables as education and income explain in large part the variation in birth rates between Aboriginal peoples and others. This suggests that socioeconomic improvements could indeed lead to significantly lower birth rates in this group. However, empirical evidence shows that these variables do not completely account for the fertility differential between Aboriginal peoples and others. This suggests (but cannot prove) that there may be a particularized ideology in the Native population promoting high fertility (Trovato, 1981, 1987).

Other Differentials

In the general Canadian population today, the most influential of the variables that differentiate between above- and below-average fertility are women's education and labour-force status, each exerting strong negative effects on fertility (Balakrishnan, Ebanks, and Grindstaff, 1979; Balakrishnan, Krotki, and Lapierre-Adamczyk, 1993; McVey and Kalbach, 1995). Higher income has in the past been shown to have negative effects on fertility (Charles, 1948; Tracey, 1941), but more recent analyses indicate that once social demographic factors such as residence, education, and labour-force status are taken into account, the net influence of income on number of children born is weak (Balakrishnan, Krotki, and Lapierre-Adamczyk, 1993). McVey and Kalbach (1995: 290) have pointed out that over time the relationship "has been shifting to a positive one in which fertility increases with increasing income" beyond middle levels of family income. It would not be surprising if new data showed low-income and upper-income couples with above-average fertility, and middle-income Canadians with below-average fertility. High-income couples may have larger families than the average because they are able to afford children without compromising their household's overall living standards. The low fertility of the middle classes, which are most heavily burdened by taxes and general household expenses, can be explained by their greater degree of economic insecurity. Higher fertility among low-income couples may be explained in part by lack of knowledge about (and ability to purchase) effective birth control, though clearly other factors must also be involved.

Future Prospects

Cohort fertility trends can help us to visualize other dimensions of the changes in the Canadian birth rate in a historical context. As we have already noted, the period TFR measures period fertility as it changes from year to year, while cohort fertility considers the completed family size of generations of women who, in each given calendar year, have reached the end of their reproductive lifespan. Cohort information allows us to discover the average number of children different cohorts of women have borne during their reproductive lives. Figure 6.10, provided by Anne Milan (2011:8) shows, that the total fertility rate (TFR) was higher than the completed fertility rate (CCF) during the 1940 to 1965 period (the baby boom). The last time the total fertility rate was higher than the cohort completed fertility rate was 1965, for the 1937 birth cohort. In that year the TFR was 3.16 and the CCF was 2.92. Since 1966, the completed fertility rate has exceeded that of the total fertility rate. Although since 2003 the total fertility has been inching upward, the cohort completed fertility rate has changed only slightly since 2000.

The time trend in completed fertility for the most recent cohorts is based on incomplete data, since women born after the mid-1970s have yet to reach the end of their childbearing years. Nonetheless, the indication from Figure 6.10 is quite clear: the trend in completed family size has been downward for some time, and seems to have reached a more or less stable plateau at a level under two children per woman.

Even though more recent generations of women tend to show a tendency towards higher fertility rates at ages above 30, this may be insufficient to make up for their substantially lower fertility between ages 15 and 29. Frejka and Sardon (2004) reached this same conclusion after an

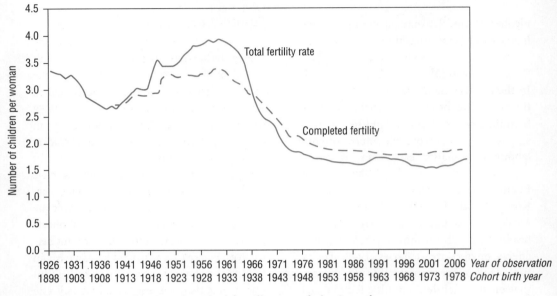

FIGURE 6.10   Cohort and period fertility trends in Canada

Note: The cohort completed fertility rates have been shifted forward from the cohort birth year by 28 years. This assumes that the average age of maternity across the cohorts is 28 years.

Source: Milan (2013b: 8). Statistics Canada, *Report on the Demographic Situation in Canada*, 2013. Reproduced and distributed on an "as is" basis with the permission of Statistics Canada.

extensive study of period and cohort completed fertility in industrialized countries, including Canada: Young Canadian female cohorts cannot make up for the lag established during their twenties with increased fertility in their thirties and forties.

We may at this point offer a concluding assessment about the reasons behind the reduced childbearing of the post–baby boom years and then speculate on possible future trends in Canadian fertility. As we have seen with our overview of theories, lower fertility has resulted from a combination of sociological, economic, and cultural factors. We also saw that ultimately these types of effects must operate through the proximate determinants of fertility.

Let us first examine what factors might serve to maintain fertility rates below replacement levels:

- the increasing secularization of society and the concomitant decreasing importance of tradition, especially in the areas of family and reproduction;
- the tendency for many to postpone or forgo marriage, and a growing preference among recent generations of young adults for cohabitation over traditional marriage, the latter being generally less prolific;
- the tendency for young people to stay in school longer in order to secure a job or career, thus having to wait longer to establish themselves economically and to therefore consider having children;
- the growing economic insecurity among young adults, especially young men, in an uncertain labour market;
- the tendency for young adults aged 18–34 to delay their transition into full adulthood (i.e., leaving school, leaving

their parents' home, having full-year full-time work, entering conjugal relationships, and having children [Clark, 2007; Côté and Bynner, 2008; Mitchell, 2006; Ravanera, Rajulton, and Burch, 1998]) largely due to their precarious socioeconomic circumstances;

- the widespread movement of women into the paid labour force (which has increased the opportunity costs of bearing and raising children);

- higher household living standards and material aspirations that compete with childbearing;

- the postponement of childbearing as women juggle the demands of work, career, and family;

- the ever-increasing cost of living and raising children, and the insufficient access to affordable childcare for many working mothers;

- the increased acceptability of a child-free lifestyle of married and cohabiting couples (during the high-fertility period of the 1950s, less than 10 per cent of married women in Canada were without children; by 1981, the percentage was close to 20 per cent, and this is likely to be even higher today) (McInnis, 2000a: 581; O'Connor, 2012; Ram, 2000); and

- the widespread availability of safe and effective birth control methods, surgical sterilization, and abortion that help reduce the number of unplanned births. The birth control pill is the most widely used method of birth control among women aged 15–29; women past age 30 increasingly opt for surgical sterilization (Bélanger, 2002: 123). Abortion rates have increased steadily since the mid-1970s; there are more than 100 000 per year (Statistics Canada, *The Daily*, 2005a); and nearly

a third of Canadian women experience an abortion during their reproductive years (Norman, 2012).

Can we point to any factors that may in the future exert upward pressure on aggregate fertility rates in Canada? A number of possibilities seem worthy of consideration:

- *The higher fertility of some socio-cultural groups:* Canadian Aboriginal peoples and some immigrant groups (South Asia, Central-Western Asia, and the Middle East) tend to have higher than average fertility in Canada. Many immigrants have their first child in Canada; this can help boost period fertility rates (Bélanger and Gilbert, 2003; Woldemicael and Beaujot, 2010).

- *The higher fertility of some geographic areas:* Fertility rates remain relatively high in Nunavut and Northwest Territories. Across the provinces, those in the Prairies—Saskatchewan, Alberta, and Manitoba—have been showing total fertility rates above the other provinces for about the past decade.

- *The positive effects of economic booms on fertility:* Prior to the financial crisis of 2008, fertility rates had been inching upward (Trovato, 2010); future periods of sustained economic growth could perhaps increase fertility levels by reducing the amount of fertility postponement and possibly induces some recuperation of previously postponed fertility.

- *The end of the postponement transition:* A number of European populations have recently entered the end of the postponement transition (Goldstein, Sobotka, and Jasilioniene, 2009). Could this occur in Canada soon? If so, it would help raise period fertility.

- *The possible "return" to marriage among young adults:* A return to the marriage boom years of the 1960s and 1970s would have a significant impact on fertility rates. There is recent evince that marriage may be "coming back" in vogue in some European countries and in the United States (Cherlin, 2012; Kalmijn, 2007, 2013; Ohlsson-Wijk, 2011). Will this trend also spread to Canada?
- *The introduction of more family-friendly policies offering greater support to working mothers, and fathers:* Such polices have been instrumental in boosting fertility to some extent in some European contexts. Could this also happen in Canada?

In considering these varied possibilities, the crucial question is which set of factors might prevail in the future? The factors thought to exert downward pressure may outweigh those posited to pose upward pressure on fertility. Possibly, the two sets may cancel each other out. These remain important questions for further study.

Conclusion

In this chapter, we examined the basic concepts and measures of fertility before discussing the social/biological determinants of fertility. We also looked at various theories of fertility change to try to discover why the secular pattern of fertility over the past two centuries has followed its observed trajectory. Economic theories of fertility transition emphasize changes in the value of time for parents and the rising costs of raising children. Sociological theories tend to focus on the declining influence of tradition and the increasing secularization that usually accompanies urbanization and socioeconomic modernization. Demographers have attempted to explain how modernization in developing societies produces a fertility transition though various complementary theories that focus on the importance of parents' lowered demand for children with increasing levels of socioeconomic modernization.

The economic theory advanced by Becker and other economists from the University of Chicago assumes that the decision to have a child is a rational choice. Parents weigh the perceived costs and values of having a child in the context of their budgetary constraints. Parents will usually have the number of children they believe they can afford, given their income, their preferences for material comfort, and how much they feel they must invest in the "quality" of children they raise. For most couples in industrialized countries today, this typically means opting for no more than one or two children on average.

We concluded our examination of fertility by taking a close look at the fertility trends and patterns in Canada, with particular attention to the long-term decline in the birth rate, the interruption of this pattern by the post-war baby boom, and the resumption of low fertility that continues to this day. Changes in the proximate determinants, particularly the flight from traditional marriage and the increased reliance on birth control and abortion, together with the postponement of childbearing to older ages explains virtually all of the drop in the TFR to its current below-replacement levels. We note, however, that sociological factors—particularly value-shifts away from traditionalism in favour of post-materialism—have had considerable bearing in affecting the proximate determinants of fertility.

Exercises

1. Table 6.8 contains age-specific fertility rates for Canadian women spanning quinquennial intervals from 1895–9 to 2005–10. Use the data in this table to complete the following.

   a) Compute all period TFRs.

   b) For each period, compute all gross reproduction rates (assume the proportion of baby girls at birth is 0.4860).

   c) For each period, compute the corresponding net reproduction rates. Assume the age-specific female survival ratios (SRs) provided in Table 6.9. For the period 1895–1915, apply the SR values for 1891–1911.

   d) Interpret the computed values of TFR, GRR, and NRR.

   e) Compute all possible cohort completed fertility rates.

   f) Graph the cohort completed fertility rates and the period TFRs.

   g) Explain why cohort completed fertility and period TFRs differ.

TABLE 6.8   Age-specific fertility rates per 1 000 women, 1895–99 to 2005–10

Year t	15–19	20–24	25–29	30–34	35–39	40–44	45–49	Period of birth of cohort
2020								1971–5
2015								1966–70
2010	13.5	48.0	96.4	105.7	51.6	9.9	0.4	1961–5
2005	13.7	51.0	97.4	95.8	40.1	6.9	0.3	1956–60
2000	16.3	56.1	97.9	89.9	35.5	6.1	0.3	1951–5
1995	24.5	70.6	109.7	86.8	31.3	4.8	0.2	1946–50
1990	26.9	85.4	140.2	87.5	28.6	3.9	0.1	1941–5
1985	23.7	85.3	125.3	74.6	21.8	3.0	0.1	1936–40
1980	27.6	100.1	129.4	69.3	19.4	3.1	0.2	1931–5
1975	35.3	112.7	131.2	64.4	21.6	4.8	0.4	1926–30
1970	42.8	143.3	147.2	81.8	39.0	11.3	0.9	1921–5
1965	49.3	188.6	131.9	119.4	65.9	22.0	2.0	1916–20
1960	59.8	233.5	224.4	146.2	84.2	28.5	2.4	1911–15
1955	54.2	218.3	215.1	153.8	89.8	32.3	2.9	1906–10
1950	46.0	181.3	200.6	141.3	87.9	30.8	3.0	1901–5
1945	31.6	143.3	156.8	134.3	90.3	33.5	3.7	1896–1900
1940	29.3	130.3	152.6	122.8	81.7	32.7	3.7	1891–5
1935	26.5	112.5	148.5	128.6	92.6	37.3	4.9	1886–90

(continued)

TABLE 6.8   (continued)

Year t	| 15–19	20–24	25–29	30–34	35–39	40–44	45–49	Period of birth of cohort
1930	30.5	143.0	176.0	148.0	106.7	46.6	5.5	1881–5
1925	33.6	138.8	167.5	139.6	99.3	42.5	5.5	1876–80
1920	38.0	165.4	186.0	154.6	112.3	55.5	6.6	
1915	38.2	180.3	225.3	190.3	150.1	68.4	9.0	
1910	37.3	195.2	255.0	215.3	165.7	71.5	10.0	
1905	31.5	190.1	260.1	230.3	170.7	73.2	10.5	
1900	27.0	175.0	270.4	235.3	175.5	78.3	11.1	
1895	26.0	170.4	285.9	270.2	180.3	80.4	12.2	

Note: The fertility rates shown for 1920 are actually those for 1921, and the fertility rates for 2005 are actually for 2004. The diagonal elements represent age-specific fertility rates for a specific birth cohort of women; the row elements are age-specific fertility rates for a given period. Figures up to and including 1985 exclude Newfoundland and Labrador. Age-specific fertility rates for 1895, 1900, 1905, 1910, and 1915 are estimates.

Sources: Henripin (1972): 27, Figure 2.5; Statistics Canada (1997, 2002d, 2006c, 2013j); Wadhera and Strachan (1993). 1891-1911: Source: Statistics Canada, *New Birth Cohort Life Tables for Canada and Quebec, 1801-1901. 1997.*

1920-1981: Source: Statistics Canada, *Longevity and Historical Life Tables: 1921-1981* (abridged): Canada and the Provinces. 1986.

1981-2000: Source: Statistics Canada, *Canadian Life Female Table for 2007-2009.* Statistics Canada data reproduced and distributed on an "as is" basis with the permission of Statistics Canada.

2. Why have some developing countries advanced through the fertility transition fairly quickly and others more slowly? Under what social structural and demographic conditions are long-term fertility declines most likely to occur? Discuss the role of family-planning programs in fertility transition in developing countries. What other factors are important?

3. In the early stages of socioeconomic modernization, the proximate determinants of fertility operate to increase rather than to decrease fertility. Explain this seemingly puzzling relationship. Also explain why in general modernization should be associated with declining fertility.

4. For about four decades, fertility in many Western societies and Japan has been at below-replacement level. Explain the social, cultural, and demographic factors underlying this phenomenon. Are there any uniform explanations? Are there any countries in the developed world that are experiencing fertility rates at around the replacement level? What is different about such societies? What is the future of fertility in Western societies?

TABLE E.9   Age-specific female life table survival ratios, 1891-2010

Period	SR$_{15-19}$	SR$_{20-24}$	SR$_{25-29}$	SR$_{30-34}$	SR$_{35-39}$	SR$_{40-44}$	SR$_{45-49}$
2010	4.96570	4.95842	4.95089	4.94163	4.92778	4.90671	4.87454
2005	4.96570	4.95842	4.95089	4.94163	4.92778	4.90671	4.87454
2000	4.96455	4.95651	4.94828	4.93893	4.92505	4.90384	4.87100
1995	4.95814	4.94995	4.94135	4.93054	4.91527	4.89142	4.85382
1990	4.95419	4.94528	4.93571	4.92419	4.90792	4.88380	4.84477
1985	4.94567	4.93555	4.92529	4.91279	4.89700	4.87177	4.82934
1980	4.93283	4.92141	4.90922	4.89513	4.87557	4.84430	4.79499
1975	4.91044	4.89714	4.88396	4.86821	4.84498	4.80942	4.75166
1970	4.88610	4.87219	4.85776	4.83942	4.81303	4.77290	4.71275
1965	4.86059	4.84761	4.83329	4.81518	4.78929	4.74996	4.68806
1960	4.84208	4.82907	4.81389	4.79535	4.76378	4.72839	4.66534
1955	4.81279	4.79868	4.78108	4.75895	4.72957	4.68538	4.61490
1950	4.76163	4.74081	4.71638	4.68676	4.64647	4.58867	4.50338
1945	4.69453	4.65983	4.61953	4.57454	4.51971	4.45083	4.35638
1940	4.62030	4.58022	4.52878	4.47018	4.40177	4.31824	4.21233
1935	4.41604	4.36386	4.30412	4.23838	4.16149	4.06313	3.94650
1930	4.44672	4.38412	4.30609	4.22133	4.12888	4.02497	3.90412
1925	4.43176	4.36540	4.28809	4.20880	4.11797	4.01507	3.89812
1920	4.38358	4.31338	4.22852	4.13778	4.03470	3.92058	3.79327
1911	4.07329	3.98891	3.88645	3.77469	3.65787	3.53371	3.39365
1901	3.85443	3.75676	3.64004	3.51483	3.38635	3.25283	3.10602
1891	3.53690	3.53690	3.40946	3.27470	3.13853	2.99955	2.84977

Note: The survival ratios for 2005 and 2010 are assumed to be the same.

Sources: For 1891–1911, Bourbeau, Légaré, and Émond (1997); for 1920–81, Nagnur (1986a); for 1981–2000, Statistics Canada (various years), Canadian life female table for 2007–09 applied to 2005 and 2010 (Cat. no. 84-537-X).

Additional Reading

Andorka, Rudolf. 1978. *Determinants of Fertility in Advanced Societies.* London: Methuen.

Balakrishnan, T.R., Evelyne LaPierre-Adamczyk, and Karol J. Krotki. 1993. *Family and Childbearing in Canada: A Demographic Analysis.* Toronto: University of Toronto Press.

Derosas, Renzo, and Frans van Poppel, eds. 2006. *Religion and the Decline of Fertility in the Western World.* Dortrecht: Springer.

Gauvreau, Danielle, Diane Gervais, and Peter Gossage. 2007. *La Fécondité des Québécoises 1870–1970: D'Une Exception á l'Autre.* Montreal: Les Editions Boreal.

Hawkes, Kristen, and Richard R. Paine, eds. 2006. *The Evolution of Human Life History.* Santa Fe, New Mexico: School of American Research Press.

Henripin, Jacques, Paul-Marie Hout, Evelyne Lapierre-Adamcyk, and Nicole Marcil-Gratton. 1981. *Les Enfants qu'on n'a Plus au Québéc.* Montreal: Les Presses de l'Université de Montréal.

Last, Jonathan V. 2013. *What to Expect When No One Is Expecting: America's Coming Demographic Disaster.* New York: Encounter Books.

Leridon, Henri, and Jane Menken, eds. 1977. *Natural Fertility: Patterns and Determinants of Natural Fertility.* Proceedings of a Seminar on Natural Fertility. International Union for the Scientific Study of Population (IUSSP). Liege, Belgium: Ordina Editions.

Overall, Christine. 2012. *Why Have Children? The Ethical Debate.* Cambridge, Massachusetts: MIT Press.

Potts, Malcolm, and Peter Selman. 1979. *Society and Fertility.* Estover: Macdonald and Evans.

Wilcox, Alan J. 2010. *Fertility and Pregnancy: An Epidemiologic Perspective.* Oxford: Oxford University Press.

7 Mortality and Population Health

Introduction

This chapter is concerned with the main concepts, basic measures, and theories of the demographic study of mortality and offers a survey of health and mortality conditions in developed and developing countries. In the most advanced countries, mortality has fallen to such low levels that newborns can expect to live well into their eighth decade of life. Mortality rates for children and for adults under 60 are so low that further significant improvements in life expectancy are dependent almost completely on improvement of survival probabilities at older ages.

These low rates of mortality are all the more significant when we consider how recent it was in the broad spectrum of human history that the average person would not live much beyond his or her twenty-fifth or thirtieth birthday, and that it was not until the fourth decade of the twentieth century that life expectancy reached 65 years (Acsádi and Nemeskéri, 1970; Coale, 1974; Vallin, 2006). The widespread declines in mortality worldwide since the start of the twentieth century must be considered one of humankind's most important accomplishments. Yet paradoxically, under the generally favourable mortality conditions of today, a portion of the world's population has struggled to keep up in the fight against early death, and in some regions the gains in life expectancy have stagnated or even reversed as a result of massive epidemics of infectious disease exacerbated by widespread poverty and deteriorating living conditions.

Determinants of Population Health

Much of the discussion in this chapter implies a *population health perspective*. The population health perspective recognizes the complex interactions of individual and societal factors in determining health, including the interplay of individual characteristics (including genetics) with social and economic factors (including culture) and physical environments (family, neighbourhood, work, the community, and other important spheres of life). The determinants of population health do not exist in isolation from each other. Therefore, strategies to improve the overall health must address a wide range of social and economic factors that determine health, encompassing such crucial challenges as the reduction of extreme disparities in income and wealth, and improving access to health care among the most disadvantaged sectors of society.

Figure 7.1 represents a conceptual sketch of the determinants of population health as consisting of both structural (i.e., societal) and individual-level factors. Even though the sketch implies a neatly organized causal structure, where variables are seen as acting on population health, it embodies the idea that determinants are in reality highly interconnected and operate in interaction with each other at individual and societal scales. Many of the factors are closely interconnected with socioeconomic inequality. For example, people living in poverty are more likely to experience chronic stress in their lives because they may not have

access to the most basic necessities, from not having adequate housing to the inability to afford a proper diet. These conditions most often foster difficult life experiences for the individual that can culminate in poor physical and mental health, seriously impeding one's ability to get out of poverty. Complex set of circumstances can lead to a vicious circle whereby poverty and poor health feedback on each other (Marmot and Wilkinson, 2006).

In fact, one of the most important findings in the population health literature is that

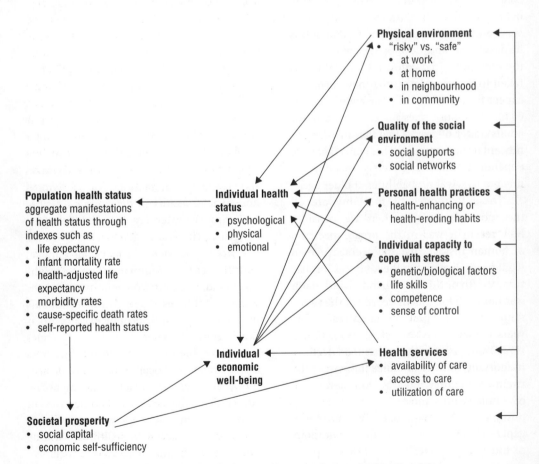

FIGURE 7.1   A framework of the determinants of population health

Note: Arrows at the right-hand side of the model indicate that all factors are highly correlated.

socioeconomic status is a major determinant of conditions that ultimately impact well-being, including the quality of the of the social and physical environments in which one conducts his daily life (at work, at home, in one's neighbourhood, etc.); the extent to which a person has access to social support in times of need; the lifestyle choices one makes (whether they be health-enhancing or health-eroding); and the capacity to cope with stress and adversity in life (Berkman, 2005; Berkman and Breslow, 1983; Berkman and Syme, 1979; Egolf et al., 1992; Feinstein, 1993; House et al., 1988; Hummer et al., 1999; Marmot, 2005a; Marmot and Wilkinson, 2006; Smith and Christakis, 2008; Syme and Berkman, 1976; Wilkinson, 2005; Yen and Syme, 1999).

The effects of these types of influences on health operate through physiological pathways that link an individual's adverse socioeconomic experience to the risk of vascular and other types of chronic diseases over the course of a lifetime, beginning as early as infancy and childhood (Umberson, Crosnoe, and Reczek, 2010). Research on the fetal origins of adult disease (see box, page 260) suggests the problem of poor health in adulthood may actually start in the womb, before one is born (Barker, 1998, 2012; Barker and Osmond, 1986; Caspi et al., 1998; Dong et al., 2004; Duncan et al., 1998; Feinstein, 1993; Finch, 2003; Gortmaker and Wise, 1997; Hayward and Gorman, 2004; Paul, 2011; Power, Kuh, and Morton, 2013).

As suggested by Figure 7.1, from a societal perspective it makes perfect sense to place emphasis on the reduction of socioeconomic inequalities and poverty. Doing so would enhance not only the overall health of a population, but also help increase well-being.

A population's state of health is a crucial determinant of economic prosperity and overall standard of living. Better health translates into a more productive workforce and thus higher levels of affluence. Societal affluence in turn is the key to a society's ability to maintain good health (Bloom and Canning, 2000; Filmer and Pritchett, 1999; Stuckler and Siegel, 2011). Having greater access to economic resources means that governments are in a better position to turn wealth into social services like education and health care (i.e., *social capital*). Services designed to maintain and promote good health, prevent disease, and restore health in all sectors of the population (including infants, children, and adults) are essential to the overall health of a population. A robust health care system is at its best when it operates in tandem with a broader framework of health determinants, such as environmental conditions conducive to good health and individual responsibility for limiting risky lifestyle choices (Evans and Stoddart, 1990: 41–5).

An affluent society should be better equipped to provide its citizens with work and opportunities, through which it fosters well-being and better health for the average citizen. However, this is contingent on government policy and the political willingness to invest in human capital. Countries differ in this regard; consequently, there are wide cross-national disparities in levels of population health (Marmot et al., 2008; Stuckler and Siegel, 2011; Wilkinson, 1996; Wilkinson and Pickett, 2009).

Although they are not shown in Figure 7.1, culture and gender are important factors that may condition many of the interrelationships shown in this conceptual model. Gender encompasses biological and sociological dimensions closely linked to variations in health, morbidity, and mortality risks between males and females (Umberson, 1987; Verbrugge, 1976, 1982;

FETAL ORIGINS OF ADULT DISEASE: INTERACTIONS OF BIOLOGY AND SOCIOECONOMIC ENVIRONMENT

Prenatal conditions can affect later health in adulthood. This idea, now widely accepted by medical experts, originated with David Barker in the 1980s (Barker, 1998, 2004, 2012; Barker and Osmond, 1986). Barker's early mapping of mortality trends in England and Wales led to the observation that geographic areas with the highest infant mortality in 1910 had the highest rate of cardiovascular deaths in the 1970s. This suggested to Barker that an adverse environment in the womb, and during infancy, was causally linked to chronic-disease risk later in life. Subsequent research has indicated that mother's exposure to certain conditions, especially the experience of undernutrition, can affect the structure and function of organs, tissues, and body systems of the developing fetus, and this in turn can affect disease risk in adulthood. The interaction of the prenatal environment with the postnatal environment is of crucial importance in the development of disease in adulthood because the fetal environment and early infant health permanently program the body's metabolism and growth, and thus determine pathologies later in life, including cardiovascular disease, hypertension, and diabetes in middle age (Bateson et al., 2004; Gluckman and Hanson, 2004; de Rooij et al., 2010; Paul, 2011; Sargent, 2010; Schultz, 2010).

All of this hinges on the fact that the human fetus is highly plastic in how it responds to its environment: "Plasticity during intra-uterine life enables animals and humans to receive a 'weather forecast' from their mothers that prepares them for the type of world in which they will have to live" (Barker, 2004: 598S). A mismatch between fetal expectation of its postnatal environment and actual postnatal environment contributes to the development of later adult disease (Gluckman, Hanson, and Pinal, 2005). For instance, in nutritionally adverse circumstances, small size and slow metabolism can facilitate survival, whereas larger size and more rapid metabolism have advantages for health and reproductive success when resources are more abundant. It appears from the research in this area that infants adapted to one environment are at greater risk of developing chronic diseases if exposed to another when they are older (Bateson et al., 2004; Gluckman, Hanson, and Pinal, 2005).

It has also been shown that prenatal exposure to adversity (e.g., significant trauma experienced by the expectant mother) can affect different organ systems in the developing fetus depending on the stage of gestation when the adverse exposure takes place (Catalano et al., 2006; de Rooij et al., 2010). For instance, central nervous system structures are formed in the first trimester of pregnancy; therefore, environmental shocks during this time might result in epigenetic alterations (i.e., environmental factors that influence the expression of genes) to the central nervous system of the fetus that can later lead to a higher risk of mental illness in adulthood.

Waldron, 1983; Wingard, 1982). Like gender, culture can be a predisposing factor in differential health, morbidity, and mortality because it may influence behaviours and orientations that can either compromise or promote health through the life course (MacLachlan, 1997; Masi, 1995; Moore et al., 1987).

Demographic and Sociological Dimensions of Mortality

In demographic terms, mortality refers to the number of events ("deaths") taking place in a given interval in a specific population. The medical definition of "death" is quite specific: it is the postnatal cessation of vital functions without possibility of resuscitation. Since death can occur only after a live birth, it does not encompass miscarriage, stillbirth, or abortion. Demographers operationally define death as the event described in the medical definition previously and verified in writing by a death certificate signed by a licensed physician or medical examiner (or coroner). This means that a person on life-support systems is considered to be alive. Moreover, a person who is missing is assumed to be alive until his or her death has been confirmed (Pressat, 1985: 15).

Sociologically, the long-term decline of the death rate has engendered profound changes across all spheres of the social world. In fact, many of us might not be alive today were it not for novel developments in public health, medicine, and standards of living that were introduced at the start of the twentieth century. Kevin White and Samuel Preston (1996) determined that about half of the current population of the United States would never have been born were it not for significant progress in health and disease prevention made in the early 1900s.

It has been suggested that the nearness and frequency of death in pre-modern societies contributed to religious belief and fascination with ghosts and communities of the dead. Conversely, the reduced social significance of death in modern society has led to the "disappearance" of ghosts and belief in an afterlife (Blauner, 1966).

Socially, too, life today would be vastly different had mortality remained at the high levels of the past. For many of us living in post-industrial societies, death is often viewed as something that occurs only among those in advanced old age, and the experience of losing intimate family members early in one's life is a relatively uncommon occurrence (Uhlenberg, 1980). Try to imagine how, in the past, family life would have been disrupted frequently by the death of an infant, a child, or other loved ones (Ariès, 1974; Gottlieb, 1993; Preston and Haines, 1991). From an individual point of view, the expectation of a long life encourages us to plan for the future, especially for our old age (Preston, 1977). On the other hand, it also often engenders unrealistic feelings of that somehow, with today's medical advances we can defy death. As Philippe Ariès (1974) explains,

> The certainty of death and the fragility of life are foreign to our existential pessimism. On the contrary, the man of the late Middle Ages was very acutely conscious that he had merely been granted a stay of execution, that this delay would be a brief one, and that death was always

WHY ARE YOU ALIVE?

You have a better chance of living longer today than ever before in human history. It's a fact of modern life that we all take for granted. But have you ever considered your chances of never having been born? What if Mom had died of typhoid as a baby? What if Dad had never been born because *his* father had died young?

Researchers have made great advances in medicine over the past 100 years. It has been estimated that about half of us owe our very lives to one big breakthrough: the acceptance of the germ theory of disease and the changes it brought to the practice of medicine, the handling of food, and the treatment of water. Simple sanitation was the innovation with the greatest impact on human life in the past century—indeed, the past 1000 years. Knowledge of germ theory is the mighty lever that opened a new philosophy of life for most of us. We can expect to live. We can expect our children to live. The instruments of that optimism are all around us.

Source: Adapted from Fleischman (1999): 230–1.

present within him, shattering his ambitions and poisoning his pleasures. And that man felt a love of life which we today can scarcely understand, perhaps because of our increased longevity. . . . [Today], [t]echnically, we admit that we might die; we take out insurance on our lives to protect our families from poverty. But really, at heart we feel we are non-mortals. (44–5, 106)

Basic Measures of Mortality

Crude Death Rate

The crude death rate (CDR) is defined as the number of deaths in a given interval, usually a year, divided by the midpoint population (or an estimate of the mid-interval population for non-census years); it is typically expressed per 1000 population:

$$\text{CDR} = \frac{D}{P} \times 1000$$

where D is the number of deaths observed in the interval, and P refers to the mid-interval population.

Demographers commonly compute an average crude death rate by combining several years of deaths in the numerator. This ensures greater stability in the measure as it averages out any unusual yearly fluctuations in the number of deaths. A commonly applied measure is the three-year average crude death rate:

$$CDR = \left(\frac{\frac{1}{3}(D_1 + D_2 + D_3)}{P_2} \right) \times 1000$$

where D_1, D_2, and D_3 represent the number of deaths in three successive years, with year two being the central year. The population at risk is P_2, the mid-year population for the central year.

To illustrate the range of CDRs, the Canadian rate of 7 per 1000 population tells us that in 2012 in Canada, there were 7 deaths for every 1000 people. Countries like Canada, Japan, the United Kingdom, Sweden, and other highly industrialized countries have relatively low rates. The highest crude death rates are found in very poor countries such as Sierra Leone and Zambia (16 per 1000) in sub-Saharan Africa, and Afghanistan in Asia.

An interesting fact is that some of the CDRs of the developed countries are actually higher than those of some of the developing countries. For example, Canada's CDR of 7 is higher than Mexico's CDR of 4. This may be surprising, given the vast difference in the two countries' socioeconomic conditions. What this tells us is that these comparisons cannot be taken as a definitive indication of each country's level of mortality. CDR simply measures the total number of deaths divided by the total population; it does not explicitly take into account the fact that mortality varies by age. Therefore, some developing countries have lower crude death rates because their age compositions are younger than those of more developed countries. Age structure must be taken into account if we are to compare death rates across populations

of interest, and this leads us to the age-specific death rate.

Age-Specific Death Rate

The age-specific death rate is defined as the number of deaths in a given interval to persons of a given age divided by the mid-interval population at risk in that same age category. Age-specific death rates are calculated for separate age categories. The general formula takes the following form:

$$M_x = \frac{D_x}{P_x} \times 1000$$

where M_x stands for age-specific death rate, the letter x indexes a given age category, and the terms D_x and P_x correspond to the deaths and the mid-interval population for age category x, respectively.

It is customary to multiply the age-specific death rates by 1000. If left without the constant, the rate is simply interpreted as *death rate per person*.

Age Pattern of Mortality

If plotted on a graph, the age-specific death rates will form a distinct pattern that is general across all human populations. This age pattern of mortality indeed is so universal that it may be considered a "law-like phenomenon." According to this age pattern, the risk of death is high in the first month after birth but declines during the rest of infancy and childhood and remains low throughout adolescence; it rises in young adulthood but then stabilizes, increasing only slightly until past middle age, when the risk of death begins to intensify with advancing age. These fluctuations in mortality over the lifespan reflect to a large extent changes in human physiological conditions and the organism's resistance to the force of mortality (i.e., biological aging) as well as exposure to external risks including accidents and violence (see box on page 265).

Age-specific death rates for pre-transitional societies reflect very high early life mortality, especially in infancy. With socioeconomic modernization, the incidence of infant mortality declines. This helps to produce the *J-shape pattern of mortality* that is common in the more developed countries (Horiuchi, 2003: 649; Livi-Bacci, 2012: 16; Petersen, 2000: 82, 1995; Levitis and Martinez, 2013). Figure 7.2a displays the pattern of age specific mortality for Canadian men and women. Although they follow a similar pattern over age, mortality probabilities for men are higher than those

for women. On the arithmetic scale, this is difficult to distinguish in the ages between early childhood and middle age; for this reason, it is often useful to plot the data on the logarithmic scale (Figure 7.2b).

It is important to recognize the difference between the *age pattern* of mortality and the *level* of mortality for a population. The former refers to the shape of the pattern of death rates over age, while the latter corresponds to the overall death rate of a population (or some other indicator of mortality, such as life expectancy at birth). The level of mortality is generally lower for advanced countries than it is for poorer nations. This means that if we were to plot the age-specific death rates of an industrialized population and those of a developing country, the former would show relatively low age-specific death rates compared to the latter, though the graphs may have the same basic shape.

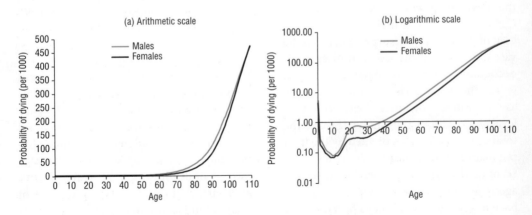

FIGURE 7.2 Probability of dying conditional on age for Canadian males and females in 2010, expressed on the (a) arithmetic scale and (b) on the logarithmic scale".

Source: Statistics Canada Demography Division (2013b): 4–11.

Abraham DeMoivre (1667–1754), in his *Treatise of Annuities on Lives* (1752), was the first to propose a mathematical "law" of mortality. His work, according to Robert Henderson (1915), was a starting point for Benjamin Gompertz (1825), who developed a mathematical model to trace the physiological process of aging. Observing that the same age patterns of mortality were found in all subgroups of the human population, Gompertz proposed a common underlying biological force. His formula assumed that past the age of 15 mortality increases in geometric progression with advancing age, in effect implying that there is an exponential increase in the probability of dying with age. This relationship, Gompertz reasoned, corresponds to the organism's growing "inability to withstand destruction" as it ages. Gompertz specified his formula as $q_x = Bc^x$, where q_x is the probability of dying at age x, and B and c are constants to be estimated empirically.

William Makeham (1860, 1867) took this formula a step further by adding a constant term to represent causes of death that were not dependent on physiological aging. Thus, $q_x = A + Bc^x$, where A is the risk of dying from "external" causes of death, such as accidents and violence. Makeham suggested that the term A was especially dominant among wild animal populations and in primitive human societies (Caughley, 1966; Emlen, 1970; Fries and Crapo, 1981: 149; Kormoncy, 1969).

Infant Mortality Rate and Its Components

Infant mortality is defined as death occurring between birth and the end of the first year of life. For analytical purposes, infant deaths are often subdivided into three categories:

1. *Early neonatal mortality* includes deaths that occur between birth and the end of the first week of life.
2. *Late neonatal mortality* includes deaths that occur from the eighth day after birth to the end of the twenty-seventh day after birth.
3. *Post-neonatal mortality* includes deaths from the twenty-eighth day after birth to the end of the first year.

Early neonatal and late neonatal deaths are sometimes combined under the heading *neonatal mortality*. When calculating infant mortality, it is customary to include late fetal deaths (explained later) with early neonatal deaths to form a fourth category of infant mortality: *perinatal mortality*.

Vital statistics agencies in developed countries also collect information on *fetal deaths*. Fetal death is the death of a fetus (or "product of conception") prior to its complete removal or expulsion from the mother, regardless of the length of the pregnancy—i.e., miscarriages, abortions, and stillbirths. The term *late fetal death* refers to a death that occurs late in a pregnancy, usually in the twenty-eighth week of gestation or later. (*Early fetal deaths* is another category of fetal deaths; in Canada, it is defined as fetal deaths occurring between the twentieth and the twenty-eighth week of gestation.) *Miscarriage* is the spontaneous or accidental termination of fetal life early in pregnancy. *Abortion* is any termination of pregnancy—spontaneous or induced (McGehee, 2004: 266). The World Health Organization (WHO), recognizing that the spontaneous loss of a fetus can occur prior to the twenty-eighth week of gestation, recommends that fetal deaths be classified according to the period of gestation during which they occur:

- *Early fetal mortality* occurs prior to the twentieth week of gestation.

- *Intermediate fetal mortality* occurs between the twentieth and twenty-seventh week of gestation.
- *Late fetal mortality* occurs in the twenty-eighth week of gestation or later. (Gourbin, 2006: 435–6)

Figure 7.3 displays the components of infant mortality. While all of this may sound excessively specific, it is worth noting that not all countries apply a uniform definition of fetal death, and this can cause problems when infant mortality rates are compared (see Chase, 1969; Frisbie, 2005; Gourbin, 2006; Lamb and Siegel, 2004).

The infant mortality rate (IMR) is calculated as the number of infant deaths in

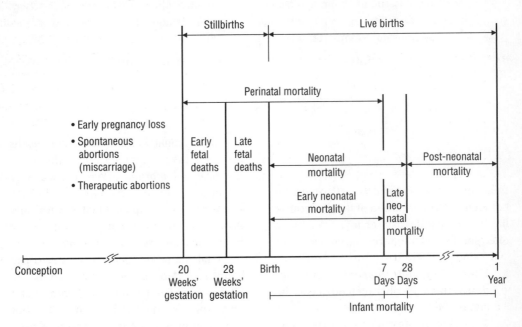

FIGURE 7.3   Infant mortality and its components

Note: In Canada, stillbirths are fetal deaths that occur after at least 20 weeks of gestation or after attaining a weight of 500 grams. In developed countries, there are generally about as many stillbirths as infant deaths, with perinatal mortality (through the first week of life) accounting for about three-quarters of all stillbirths and infant deaths. Among live births, about one-half of all deaths in the first year occur in the first week (one-third in the first day, and 10 per cent in the first hour) (Wilcox, 2010: 169).

Source: Adapted from Péron and Strohmenger (1985): 195; Wilcox (2010): 169.

a given year divided by the number of live births in the same year; it is usually multiplied by 1 000. The formula is expressed as follows:

$$\text{IMR} = \frac{D_0}{B} \times 1\,000$$

where D_0 is the number of infant deaths, and B is the number of live births.

A drawback of this formula is that it overlooks the fact that a proportion of the infant deaths that occur during a given year are deaths of infants who were born during the preceding year and hence are not part of the same "universe" of births used to compute the rate. It is possible to make adjustments for this problem (see Barkley, 1958; Shryock and Siegel, 1976). One adjustment relies on having complete information on the number of live births occurring over three calendar years around a central year (i.e., y_{-1}, y, and y_{+1}, where y is the central year) as well as data on all infant deaths taking place over these same three years in accordance with their year of birth (i.e., y_{-1}, y, and y_{+1}). This data layout makes it possible to separate the different infant deaths occurring in the central year y into two parts: those deaths that belong to the birth cohort of one year ago (i.e., y_{-1}), and those that belong to the birth cohort of the current year y. Infants born in year y who die in the next year, y_{+1}, can then be linked to the birth cohort of year y. Typically, if the numbers of infant deaths and births are not changing radically from one year to the next, the infant mortality rates computed with the usual and the more refined methods give very similar results.

Today, there are wide variations in IMRs across the world, ranging from 116 in

Component-specific infant mortality rates can also be computed. The *early neonatal death rate* can be obtained by dividing the infant deaths that occur in the first week of life by the total number of live births in the year. The *late neonatal death rate* is derived by dividing the infant deaths that occur between the end of the first week of life and the end of the first month of life by the total number of live births in the year. The *post-neonatal mortality rate* is obtained by dividing the number of infant deaths between the end of the first month of life and the end of the first year of life by the total number of live births in the year. The *perinatal mortality rate* is the number of early neonatal infant deaths plus late fetal deaths, divided by the combined sum of live births and late fetal deaths. An alternative measure is the *perinatal mortality ratio*: late fetal deaths plus early neonatal deaths, divided by the number of live births.

Central African Republic to just over 2 for Japan and Sweden. Barring some notable exceptions, the developing countries as a whole have higher rates of infant mortality than do the more developed countries. Worldwide, the IMR for 2013 was 38 per 1 000. Among the more developed countries, the rate was just 5 infant deaths per 1 000 live births; among the less developed countries as a whole, the IMRs are nearly ten times greater on average; the gap is much more pronounced for the least developed countries, where on average infant mortality in 2013 was 64 infant deaths per 1 000 live births (Population Reference Bureau, 2014).

Causes of Death in Infancy

Jean Bourgeois-Pichat (1981 [1951], 1952) proposed that infant deaths could be classified into two major categories, depending on whether they are *endogenous* or *exogenous*. *Endogenous* infant deaths are related to genetic makeup (e.g., chromosomal abnormalities) or internal physiological processes in the fetus (e.g., congenital malformations of the heart and central nervous system, deformities of the musculoskeletal system, etc.), as well as perinatal conditions such as respiratory problems and complications during delivery (Kalter, 1991). Because endogenous deaths stem from complications with the newborn's constitution, they are less amenable to control, though advances in medicine are helping significantly to reduce these rates.

While endogenous infant deaths are heavily concentrated in the perinatal and neonatal periods, *exogenous* deaths occur mainly in the post-neonatal stage of infancy. They are strongly associated with external factors or situations in the socioeconomic environment of the infant, such as exposure to cold or excessive heat, infection, inadequate care, and even injury (Antonovsky and Bernstein, 1977). *Exogenous mortality* also accounts for a significant number of deaths to children between the ages of one and four, especially in the developing countries (Pebley, 2003).

Although this dual classification of infant deaths is sensible, Dudley Poston and Richard Rogers (1985) have shown that some deaths in the post-neonatal period are actually endogenous in nature. This suggests that a proportion of infants born with serious congenital problems can survive past the neonatal period but die before completing the first year of life (see also Galley and Woods, 1999; Sowards, 1997; Woods, 2009).

Aaron Antonovsky and Judith Bernstein (1977) have observed that for populations undergoing socioeconomic modernization, declining mortality rates in the general population are typically accompanied by major improvements in mortality rates for post-neonatal infants and for children aged one–four, yet not for infants in the neonatal period. This differential pattern of mortality decline indicates that improvements to public health, which tend to occur with modernization, have a greater bearing on the causes of post-neonatal and early childhood mortality than on neonatal causes of death, which as we have seen, are mostly endogenous in nature (Gortmaker and Wise, 1997; Kliegman, 1995; Klinger, 1985; Wise, 2003). However, once the infant mortality rate in a population falls to the range of about 20 deaths per 1000 live births, infant mortality tends to become less clustered in the neonatal period as a result of improved care in the prenatal, delivery, and postnatal stages (Pebley, 2003).

One of the major causes of deaths in neonates is *low birth weight*, which is usually associated with prematurity. These problems are especially acute in low- and middle-income countries (Katz et al., 2013). There are different categories of low birth weight:

- *Low birth weight infants* are those whose weight at birth falls between 500 and 2499 grams.
- *Very low birth weight infants* are those whose weight at birth is less than 1500 grams.
- *Extremely low birth weight infants* are those whose weight at birth is less than 1000 grams. (Philip, 1995)

Over the past several decades there have been great improvements in the survival rates for low birth weight babies in the industrialized countries, mainly owing to medical advancements and the institution of neonatal intensive care units in hospitals. Of particular importance has been the application of *exogenous surfactant therapy*, which helps restore normal pulmonary activity in infants with pulmonary functioning complications, a potentially lethal condition in premature or low birth weight babies (*Dorland's Pocket Medical Dictionary*, 1977: 641).

Despite these very positive outcomes, our success in lowering the mortality probabilities of neonates in advanced societies may be reaching a limit. For any dramatic reduction in neonatal mortality rates to occur, it would be necessary to lower even further the death rate for very low and extremely low birth weight babies. This remains an important challenge for medical scientists (Howson et al., 2012; Kliegman, 1995; Philip, 1995).

Cause-Specific Death Rate

A very wide range of diseases and conditions contribute to mortality. In industrialized nations, for instance, two of the deadliest killers are heart disease and cancer, although a large portion of all deaths in these countries can also be attributed to injuries and poisonings. This kind of information is usually made public by central statistical agencies of individual countries. Globally, WHO regularly collects and publishes mortality statistics by cause of death for each country. The cause of death listed in the published statistics is the *underlying cause of death*—that is, the initial cause (or the manner of death, e.g., suicide) of the morbid process leading to death. In reality, there can be more than one cause of death on the death certificate (see Appendices

online). Notwithstanding, the cause given in the published statistics is the underlying cause of death.

These tabulations are based on a classification system called the *International Classification of Diseases* (ICD), which involves a detailed listing of all known diseases and medical conditions that can result in death. Each disease or condition is assigned a letter and a numerical code. For example, under the latest ICD revision (ICD-10), the code for breast cancer is C50, for prostate cancer C61. Unlike cancers and other chronic/degenerative types of diseases that have a physiological organic basis, suicide, homicide, and accidents are considered external causes as they are not the result of physiological pathologies. In any case, these types of external mortality also have ICD codes. For example, because suicide can be committed by several different means, it encompasses a range of codes, from X61 to X88. For all causes of death, the letter in front of the code represents a "chapter," representing different classes of diseases or conditions. The first chapter in the ICD-10 is "Certain Infectious and Parasitic Diseases," which covers cholera, typhoid fever, and many other related viral and bacterial illnesses that can cause death. The second chapter covers all the various cancers (neoplasms); chapter 9 contains diseases of the circulatory system, and so forth. In all, the ICD-10 revision comprises 22 chapters.

The general form of the *cause-specific death rate* is:

$$\text{cause-specific death rate} = \frac{D_c}{P} \times 100000$$

where D_c is deaths due to a particular disease or "cause" c, occurring in the population during a specified interval, and P is the mid-interval population exposed to the risk of dying from disease or condition c in the interval. These rates are usually multiplied by 100 000.

In some circumstances it may be necessary to compute a *cause-specific death ratio* in the form:

$$\frac{D_c}{D} \times 100$$

where the numerator is the number of deaths from a given cause, and the denominator is the total number of deaths.

Unlike the cause-specific death rate, which is a measure of incidence (how many deaths from cause c occur per 100 000 population over a specified period), the cause-specific death ratio tells us what percentage of all deaths in the population are attributable to cause c. For instance, in Canada, about 37 per cent of all deaths in a given year are due to diseases of the circulatory system, and another 27 per cent are caused by cancer; this means that the remaining causes account for about 36 per cent of all deaths.

The cause-specific death rate is really just a crude death rate for a given cause of death. It can easily be expanded to include age, sex, and other characteristics. Since mortality data are usually tabulated by age and sex, it is possible to compute not just cause-specific death rates but also age–sex–cause-specific death rates. To illustrate, in Canada in 1995, the number of people aged 55–64 who died from suicide and self-inflicted injury was 378, including 284 men and 94 women. The total mid-year population for this age group was 2 510 000,

including 1 240 000 men and 1 270 000 women. So the suicide-specific death rates for men and women separately and for the age category overall would be as follows: 22.90 per 100 000 (men); 7.40 (women); 15.06 (overall).

The age pattern of mortality varies by cause of death, reflecting differential types of mortality risks based on age. For instance, the incidence of death due to cancer and circulatory diseases is quite low in the ages below 15 but rises substantially with increasing age, especially at ages beyond 60. Motor vehicle accidents, suicides, and homicides peak in the young adult years and taper off thereafter.

The Life Table

Basic Description of the Life Table

Life tables are used frequently in the biological and social sciences and in many applied industrial situations. For demographers, the life table is a tool for describing a population's mortality using period cross-sectional, age-specific death rates. In this sense, the life table describes the survival experience of a fictional (or *synthetic*) cohort subjected to the current age-specific death rates of an actual population over the cohort's imagined lifetime. This is generally referred to as the *period life table*. A *cohort* (or *generational*) *life table* is computed from historical data for an actual birth cohort that was born many years ago and is now extinct (see, for example, Bourbeau, Legaré, and Émond, 1997).

In technical terms, a period life table is a hypothetical population of 100 000 newborn babies, exposed to the prevailing age-specific mortality schedule of an actual population. We can trace the lives of the 100 000 from birth to death, and in this way we are able to see how the hypothetical population experiences age-specific probabilities of death and survival as it passes through age and calendar time. Table 7.1 contains *single years of age life tables* for men and women in Canada in 2009–11. It is also possible to compute *abridged life tables*, which divide the population into five-year age groups, except for infants, those aged 1–4, and those in the terminal open-ended age group (95+). (Abridged life tables are featured in the exercise section at the end of this chapter.) As a period life table, Table 7.1 applies only to the period from which the age-specific death rates were taken (i.e., 2009 to 2011).

One of the most frequently used measures derived from the life table is *life expectancy*. Life expectancy is the average number of years of life remaining for someone aged *x*, where *x* may represent any age category in the life table, from birth to some upper limit (for example, 110). Let's suppose we wanted to determine the life expectancy of a newborn baby boy. Using Canada's death rates for 2012, we would first compute the 2012 age-specific death rates for males, and then from these rates generate the corresponding life table. We could then consult the life table for the life expectancy figure corresponding to male infants. We might find that, on the basis of 2012 death rates, the life expectancy for a newborn baby boy in Canada is 79 years (Population Reference Bureau, 2012). This tells us that on the average, a male born in 2012 can expect to live 79 years, assuming that 2012 death rates remain unchanged.

It is important to note that although it is an artificial construct, the period life table tells us something very useful about the population upon which it is based. Life

The life table was introduced by John Graunt (1620–74) in his *Natural and Political Observations Made upon the Bills of Mortality*, published in 1662. Early refinements of Graunt's model—made by Gottfried Leibniz (1646–1716), Edmund Halley (1656–1742), William Kersseboom (1691–1771), Nicolaas Struyck (1685–1769), and Antonie Déparcieux (1703–68), among others—were all based simply on the numbers of deaths by age, as the total population at risk was not known. The first modern life table using age-specific death rates was devised by Peter Wargentin (1717–83) in 1766 (Guillot, 2003: 601).

tables are particularly useful for comparing mortality across populations or subgroups within a population having different age–sex compositions. In fact, because all life tables start out with the same number of hypothetical babies (i.e., 100 000), the life table standardizes for age-compositional differences, which allows for better cross-population comparison of mortality and survival probabilities.

Life Table Functions

As we have seen, age-specific death rates are used to generate the life table. Once we have computed age-specific death rates for a population (usually denoted as m_x), we can derive a number of life table functions (i.e., columns) mathematically:

- q_x, the conditional probability of dying within a given age interval, or the proportion of persons alive at the beginning

TABLE 7.1 Life tables for Canadian males and females, 2009–11

Age (x)	Proportion of persons alive at beginning of age interval dying during interval q(x) Male	Female	Of 100,000 born alive: Number living at beginning of age interval l(x) Male	Female	Number dying during interval d(x) Male	Female	Stationary population (person-years lived): In the age interval L(x) Male	Female	In this and subsequent age intervals T(x) Male	Female	Average number of years of life remaining at beginning of age interval (e⁰ₓ) Male	Female
0	0.00522	0.00449	100 000	100 000	522	449	99 531	99 596	7 933 442	8 359 982	79.33	83.60
1	0.00030	0.00021	99 478	99 551	30	21	99 463	99 541	7 833 911	8 260 386	78.75	82.98
2	0.00022	0.00016	99 449	99 531	22	16	99 438	99 523	7 734 448	8 160 846	77.77	81.99
3	0.00017	0.00013	99 427	99 515	16	13	99 418	99 509	7 635 010	8 061 323	76.79	81.01
4	0.00013	0.00010	99 411	99 502	13	10	99 405	99 497	7 535 591	7 961 814	75.80	80.02
5	0.00011	0.00009	99 398	99 492	11	9	99 392	99 488	7 436 187	7 862 316	74.81	79.02
6	0.00010	0.00008	99 387	99 483	10	8	99 382	99 479	7 336 795	7 762 829	73.82	78.03
7	0.00009	0.00007	99 377	99 475	9	7	99 373	99 471	7 237 413	7 663 350	72.83	77.04
8	0.00008	0.00007	99 369	99 468	8	7	99 364	99 464	7 138 040	7 563 878	71.83	76.04
9	0.00008	0.00007	99 360	99 461	8	7	99 356	99 457	7 038 675	7 464 414	70.84	75.05
10	0.00009	0.00008	99 352	99 453	9	8	99 348	99 450	6 939 319	7 364 957	69.85	74.05
11	0.00010	0.00008	99 343	99 446	10	8	99 339	99 442	6 839 971	7 265 507	68.85	73.06
12	0.00012	0.00009	99 334	99 438	12	9	99 328	99 433	6 740 633	7 166 066	67.86	72.07
13	0.00015	0.00011	99 322	99 428	15	11	99 315	99 423	6 641 305	7 066 633	66.87	71.07
14	0.00020	0.00014	99 308	99 417	20	14	99 298	99 410	6 541 990	6 967 210	65.88	70.08
15	0.00028	0.00018	99 288	99 404	28	17	99 274	99 395	6 442 692	6 867 800	64.89	69.09
16	0.00039	0.00022	99 260	99 386	39	22	99 241	99 375	6 343 418	6 768 405	63.91	68.10
17	0.00051	0.00026	99 221	99 364	50	26	99 196	99 351	6 244 177	6 669 030	62.93	67.12
18	0.00059	0.00028	99 171	99 339	59	28	99 141	99 325	6 144 982	6 569 679	61.96	66.13
19	0.00066	0.00029	99 112	99 311	65	29	99 079	99 296	6 045 840	6 470 354	61.00	65.15
20	0.00071	0.00030	99 047	99 282	70	30	99 011	99 267	5 946 761	6 371 057	60.04	64.17
21	0.00075	0.00030	98 976	99 252	74	30	98 939	99 237	5 847 750	6 271 790	59.08	63.19
22	0.00076	0.00031	98 902	99 222	76	30	98 864	99 207	5 748 810	6 172 553	58.13	62.21

(continued)

TABLE 7.1 (continued)

Age (x)	Proportion of persons alive at beginning of age interval dying during interval q(x)		Of 100,000 born alive: Number living at beginning of age interval l(x)		Number dying during interval d(x)		Stationary population (person-years lived): In the age interval (Lx)		In this and subsequent age intervals T(x)		Average number of years of life remaining at beginning of age interval (e_x)	
	Male	Female	Male	Female	Male	Female	Male	Female	Male	Female	Male	Female
23	0.00076	0.00031	98 827	99 192	75	30	98 789	99 177	5 649 946	6 073 346	57.17	61.23
24	0.00074	0.00030	98 752	99 161	73	30	98 715	99 146	5 551 157	5 974 169	56.21	60.25
25	0.00071	0.00030	98 679	99 131	70	30	98 644	99 117	5 452 442	5 875 023	55.25	59.26
26	0.00070	0.00030	98 609	99 102	69	30	98 574	99 087	5 353 798	5 775 906	54.29	58.28
27	0.00069	0.00031	98 540	99 072	68	31	98 506	99 056	5 255 223	5 676 819	53.33	57.30
28	0.00070	0.00032	98 472	99 041	69	32	98 438	99 025	5 156 717	5 577 763	52.37	56.32
29	0.00071	0.00034	98 404	99 009	70	34	98 369	98 992	5 058 279	5 478 738	51.40	55.34
30	0.00074	0.00037	98 333	98 975	73	36	98 297	98 957	4 959 911	5 379 746	50.44	54.35
31	0.00078	0.00040	98 261	98 939	76	39	98 223	98 919	4 861 614	5 280 789	49.48	53.37
32	0.00082	0.00043	98 184	98 899	80	43	98 144	98 878	4 763 391	5 181 870	48.51	52.40
33	0.00086	0.00047	98 104	98 857	84	47	98 062	98 833	4 665 247	5 082 992	47.55	51.42
34	0.00091	0.00051	98 020	98 810	89	50	97 976	98 785	4 567 184	4 984 158	46.59	50.44
35	0.00096	0.00056	97 931	98 759	94	55	97 884	98 732	4 469 209	4 885 374	45.64	49.47
36	0.00102	0.00060	97 837	98 705	100	60	97 788	98 675	4 371 324	4 786 642	44.68	48.49
37	0.00108	0.00066	97 738	98 645	106	65	97 685	98 613	4 273 537	4 687 967	43.72	47.52
38	0.00115	0.00071	97 632	98 580	113	70	97 576	98 545	4 175 852	4 589 354	42.77	46.55
39	0.00123	0.00077	97 519	98 510	120	76	97 459	98 472	4 078 276	4 490 809	41.82	45.59
40	0.00132	0.00084	97 399	98 434	129	83	97 335	98 392	3 980 817	4 392 337	40.87	44.62
41	0.00142	0.00092	97 270	98 351	138	90	97 201	98 306	3 883 482	4 293 944	39.92	43.66
42	0.00153	0.00100	97 132	98 261	148	98	97 058	98 212	3 786 281	4 195 639	38.98	42.70
43	0.00165	0.00109	96 984	98 163	160	107	96 904	98 109	3 689 223	4 097 427	38.04	41.74
44	0.00179	0.00118	96 824	98 056	173	116	96 737	97 998	3 592 320	3 999 317	37.10	40.79
45	0.00194	0.00129	96 651	97 940	187	126	96 557	97 877	3 495 582	3 901 319	36.17	39.83

TABLE 7.1 (continued)

Age (x)	Proportion of persons alive at beginning of age interval dying during interval q(x) Male	Female	Of 100,000 born alive: Number living at beginning of age interval l(x) Male	Female	Number dying during interval d(x) Male	Female	Stationary population (person-years lived): In the age interval (Lx) Male	Female	In this and subsequent age intervals T(x) Male	Female	Average number of years of life remaining at beginning of age interval (e°x) Male	Female
46	0.00211	0.00140	96 464	97 814	203	137	96 362	97 746	3 399 025	3 803 442	35.24	38.88
47	0.00229	0.00153	96 261	97 677	221	149	96 150	97 603	3 302 663	3 705 696	34.31	37.94
48	0.00251	0.00166	96 040	97 528	241	162	95 919	97 447	3 206 513	3 608 094	33.39	37.00
49	0.00275	0.00181	95 799	97 366	263	176	95 667	97 278	3 110 594	3 510 646	32.47	36.06
50	0.00301	0.00197	95 536	97 190	288	192	95 392	97 094	3 014 926	3 413 369	31.56	35.12
51	0.00331	0.00215	95 248	96 998	316	209	95 090	96 893	2 919 535	3 316 275	30.65	34.19
52	0.00364	0.00235	94 932	96 789	346	227	94 759	96 675	2 824 445	3 219 382	29.75	33.26
53	0.00401	0.00257	94 586	96 561	379	248	94 397	96 438	2 729 685	3 122 707	28.86	32.34
54	0.00441	0.00280	94 207	96 314	415	270	94 000	96 179	2 635 288	3 026 269	27.97	31.42
55	0.00484	0.00307	93 792	96 043	454	295	93 565	95 896	2 541 289	2 930 090	27.09	30.51
56	0.00533	0.00336	93 338	95 749	497	321	93 089	95 588	2 447 723	2 834 194	26.22	29.60
57	0.00586	0.00368	92 841	95 427	544	351	92 569	95 252	2 354 634	2 738 606	25.36	28.70
58	0.00645	0.00403	92 297	95 077	595	383	91 999	94 885	2 262 065	2 643 354	24.51	27.80
59	0.00709	0.00442	91 701	94 693	650	419	91 376	94 484	2 170 066	2 548 469	23.66	26.91
60	0.00780	0.00485	91 051	94 275	711	458	90 696	94 046	2 078 690	2 453 985	22.83	26.03
61	0.00859	0.00533	90 340	93 817	776	500	89 952	93 567	1 987 995	2 359 939	22.01	25.15
62	0.00945	0.00586	89 565	93 317	846	547	89 141	93 044	1 898 042	2 266 372	21.19	24.29
63	0.01040	0.00645	88 718	92 770	923	598	88 257	92 471	1 808 901	2 173 329	20.39	23.43
64	0.01145	0.00710	87 795	92 172	1 005	654	87 293	91 845	1 720 644	2 080 857	19.60	22.58
65	0.01260	0.00782	86 790	91 518	1 094	716	86 243	91 160	1 633 351	1 989 013	18.82	21.73
66	0.01387	0.00862	85 696	90 802	1 189	783	85 102	90 411	1 547 108	1 897 853	18.05	20.90
67	0.01528	0.00951	84 507	90 019	1 291	856	83 862	89 591	1 462 006	1 807 442	17.30	20.08

(continued)

TABLE 7.1 (continued)

Age (x)	Proportion of persons alive at beginning of age interval dying during interval q(x) Male	Female	Of 100,000 born alive: Number living at beginning of age interval l(x) Male	Female	Number dying during interval d(x) Male	Female	Stationary population (person-years lived): In the age interval (Lx) Male	Female	In this and subsequent age intervals T(x) Male	Female	Average number of years of life remaining at beginning of age interval (e°x) Male	Female
68	0.01682	0.01051	83 217	89 163	1400	937	82 517	88 694	1 378 144	1 717 851	16.56	19.27
69	0.01852	0.01161	81 817	88 226	1515	1024	81 059	87 714	1 295 627	1 629 157	15.84	18.47
70	0.02040	0.01284	80 301	87 202	1638	1119	79 482	86 642	1 214 568	1 541 443	15.13	17.68
71	0.02247	0.01420	78 663	86 083	1767	1223	77 780	85 471	1 135 086	1 454 801	14.43	16.90
72	0.02475	0.01573	76 896	84 860	1903	1335	75 944	84 192	1 057 306	1 369 330	13.75	16.14
73	0.02726	0.01743	74 993	83 525	2045	1456	73 971	82 797	981 362	1 285 137	13.09	15.39
74	0.03004	0.01934	72 948	82 069	2191	1587	71 853	81 275	907 391	1 202 341	12.44	14.65
75	0.03310	0.02146	70 757	80 482	2342	1727	69 586	79 618	835 539	1 171 065	11.81	13.93
76	0.03647	0.02384	68 415	78 755	2495	1877	67 167	77 816	765 953	1 041 447	11.20	13.22
77	0.04019	0.02649	65 920	76 878	2650	2037	64 595	75 859	698 785	963 631	10.60	12.53
78	0.04430	0.02947	63 270	74 841	2803	2206	61 869	73 738	634 190	887 772	10.02	11.86
79	0.04883	0.03280	60 467	72 635	2953	2383	58 991	71 444	572 321	814 034	9.46	11.21
80	0.05383	0.03654	57 515	70 253	3096	2567	55 967	68 969	513 330	742 590	8.93	10.57
81	0.05935	0.04074	54 419	67 685	3230	2757	52 804	66 307	457 364	673 621	8.40	9.95
82	0.06543	0.04545	51 189	64 928	3349	2951	49 514	63 453	404 560	607 314	7.90	9.35
83	0.07215	0.05074	47 840	61 977	3452	3145	46 114	60 405	355 045	543 861	7.42	8.78
84	0.07957	0.05669	44 388	58 833	3532	3335	42 622	57 165	308 931	483 456	6.96	8.22
85	0.08776	0.06338	40 856	55 498	3585	3517	39 063	53 739	266 309	426 291	6.52	7.68
86	0.09680	0.07091	37 271	51 981	3608	3686	35 467	50 138	227 246	372 551	6.10	7.17
87	0.10678	0.07940	33 663	48 294	3594	3835	31 866	46 377	191 779	322 414	5.70	6.68
88	0.11780	0.08897	30 068	44 460	3542	3956	28 297	42 482	159 914	276 037	5.32	6.21
89	0.12997	0.09977	26 526	40 504	3448	4041	24 803	38 484	131 616	233 555	4.96	5.77
90	0.14341	0.11196	23 079	36 463	3310	4082	21 424	34 422	106 813	195 071	4.63	5.35

TABLE 7.1 (continued)

Age (x)	Proportion of persons alive at beginning of age interval dying during interval q(x)		Of 100,000 born alive: Number living at beginning of age interval l(x)		Number dying during interval d(x)		Stationary population (person-years lived): In the age interval L(x)		In this and subsequent age intervals T(x)		Average number of years of life remaining at beginning of age interval e(x)	
	Male	Female	Male	Female	Male	Female	Male	Female	Male	Female	Male	Female
91	0.15794	0.12542	19 769	32 381	3 122	4 061	18 208	30 350	85 389	160 649	4.32	4.96
92	0.17326	0.13991	16 647	28 319	2 884	3 962	15 205	26 338	67 182	130 299	4.04	4.60
93	0.18931	0.15541	13 763	24 357	2 605	3 785	12 460	22 465	51 977	103 961	3.78	4.27
94	0.20604	0.17190	11 157	20 572	2 299	3 536	10 008	18 804	39 517	81 496	3.54	3.96
95	0.21839	0.18849	8 858	17 036	1 935	3 211	7 891	15 430	29 509	62 692	3.33	3.68
96	0.23536	0.20653	6 924	13 825	1 630	2 855	6 109	12 397	21 618	47 262	3.12	3.42
97	0.25290	0.22549	5 294	10 969	1 339	2 473	4 625	9 733	15 509	34 865	2.93	3.18
98	0.27092	0.24526	3 955	8 496	1 072	2 084	3 420	7 454	10 884	25 133	2.75	2.96
99	0.28933	0.26571	2 884	6 412	834	1 704	2 467	5 560	7 465	17 679	2.59	2.76
100	0.30802	0.28671	2 049	4 708	631	1 350	1 734	4 033	4 998	12 118	2.44	2.57
101	0.32687	0.30810	1 418	3 358	464	1 035	1 186	2 841	3 264	8 085	2.30	2.41
102	0.34576	0.32970	955	2 324	330	766	790	1 941	2 078	5 244	2.18	2.26
103	0.36457	0.35132	625	1 558	228	547	511	1 284	1 288	3 303	2.06	2.12
104	0.38319	0.37280	397	1 010	152	377	321	822	778	2 019	1.96	2.00
105	0.40149	0.39395	245	634	98	250	196	509	457	1 197	1.87	1.89
106	0.41937	0.41461	147	384	61	159	116	304	261	688	1.78	1.79
107	0.43673	0.43462	85	225	37	98	66	176	145	384	1.71	1.71
108	0.45350	0.45386	48	127	22	58	37	98	79	208	1.64	1.63
109	0.46960	0.47222	26	69	12	33	20	53	42	110	1.59	1.58
110+	1.00000	1.00000	14	37	14	37	22	57	22	57	1.56	1.54

Note: The function p_x is not shown because it is easily derivable from the q_x column by taking $1-q_x$ for each age category.

Source: Statistics Canada Demography Division (2013b): 4–11. From Statistics Canada, Life tables, Canada, Provinces and Territories 2009 to 2011. 2013. Reproduced and distributed on an "as is" basis with the permission of Statistics Canada.

ASSUMPTIONS OF THE LIFE TABLE

There are five inherent assumptions underlying life tables:

1. The life table is a hypothetical population that is closed to migration; as a result, births and deaths are the only demographic processes in this population.

2. Because the life table does not take migration into account, the crude death rate and the crude birth rate are identical in this population, and therefore the rate of natural increase will always be zero (because 100 000 people are born, and the same 100 000 people will eventually die). The life table is thus a *stationary population*, meaning that it has stable, unchanging annual age-specific mortality rates, with unchanging numbers of births (i.e., 100 000).

3. The number of births in the life table population is conventionally set at 100 000; this is called the *radix* of the life table.

4. The birth cohort of 100 000 dies according to a predetermined schedule of age-specific death rates taken from an actual population.

5. In most practical cases, it is assumed that the distribution of deaths is uniform within every age category except for infancy, early childhood, and very old age, where the distribution of deaths is clearly not uniform.

Source: Chiang (1984); Shryock and Siegel (1976).

---

of an age interval who will die during the interval before attaining the next birthday;

- p_x, the probability of those at age x surviving to their next birthday (i.e., $1 - q_x$);
- l_x, the number, out of 100 000 hypothetical people born alive, of persons alive at the beginning of age interval x (this column of the life table is called the *survivorship function*);
- d_x, the number, out of 100 000 hypothetical people born alive, of deaths during age interval x;
- L_x, the combined number, out of 100 000 hypothetical people born alive, of person-years lived in the age interval x;
- T_x, the number, out of 100 000 hypothetical people born alive, of person-years lived in the age interval x and subsequent age intervals (this essentially measures the number of person-years left to be lived by the cohort, given its current age, x); and
- e_x^o, expectation of life, or the average number of years of life remaining at the beginning of age interval x (i.e., T_x/l_x).

Figure 7.4 illustrates four stylized life table functions for populations with different levels of mortality: q_x, l_x, e_x^o, and d_x. Note the shift in the age pattern of these functions as life expectancy increases.

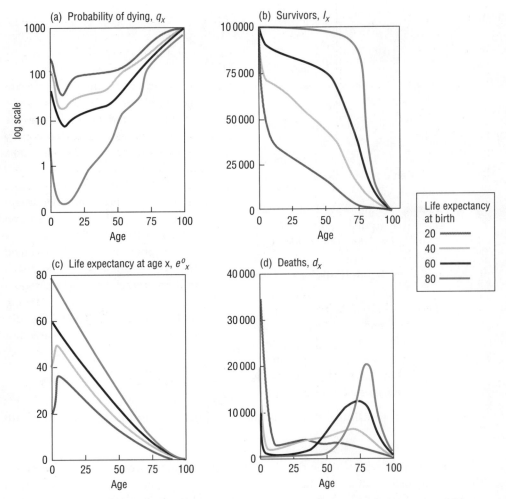

FIGURE 7.4 **Stylized shape of four life table functions at varying levels of life expectancy at birth**

Note: Values are plotted for four life tables from the Coale-Demeny series (region West) for females with life expectancies at birth of 20, 40, 60, and 80 years (see Coale and Demeny, 1983).

Source: Pressat (1985): 127. From *The Dictionary of Demography* by WILSON, CHRISTOPHER; PRESSAT, ROLAND. Reproduced with permission of BASIL BLACKWELL in the format Republish in a book via Copyright Clearance Center.

Mortality Change through History

For much of human history, life was punctuated by famine, war, and repeated waves of epidemic diseases that kept life expectancy low (Galloway, 1986; Schofield, Reher, and Bideau, 1991; Vallin, 2006). Only relatively recently in human history has life expectancy increased significantly. The dramatic increases in life expectancy over the course of the twentieth century can be attributed to the fact that degenerative causes of death have largely replaced deaths caused by infectious and pathogenic diseases (Acsádi and Nemeskéri, 1970: 97; Fogel, 2004a; Preston, 1977: 165; Schultz, 1993).

Epidemiological Transition

In 1971, Abdel Omran presented a systematic account of the shifting historical pattern of disease and mortality experienced in the West. His theory described the complex change in patterns of health and disease, and focused on the interactions between these patterns and their demographic, economic, and sociological determinants and consequences (Omran, 1971: 510). According to Omran's theory, societies as they modernize experience a gradual change in their patterns of disease and mortality. Typically, they move from a long period in which infectious and parasitic diseases (such as cholera, typhus, and smallpox) along with famine, pestilence, violence, and war are the dominant agents of premature death, to a stage in which chronic and degenerative diseases (such as cancer and heart disease) become the leading killers. Omran (1971) identified three stages of epidemiological change, outlined in Figure 7.5 and described in the following sections.

The Age of Famine and Pestilence (Prehistory to c.1750)

From prehistory until roughly the mid 1700s, the pattern of population growth was

Demographic Transition   **Epidemiological Transition**

Stage 1: Age of Pestilence and Famine

High death rate   (a) High and fluctuating mortality
High birth rate   (b) Dominance of infectious and
Low growth rate   parasitic diseases as causes
                                        of mortality
                                    (c) Low life expectancy

Stage 2: Age of Receding Pandemics

Low death rate   (a) Accelerated declines in mortality
High birth rate   (b) Shifts from infectious and parasitic
High growth rate   diseases mortality to degenerative
                                        disease mortality
                                    (c) Rising life expectancy

Stage 3: Age of Degenerative and Man-Made Diseases

Low death rate   (a) Continuation of mortality declines
Low birth rate   and its eventual approach to
Low growth rate   stability at low levels
                                    (b) Dominance of degenerative disease
                                        mortality, caused by aging, changing
                                        lifestyle, and deteriorating environment
                                    (c) Further rise in life expectancy

FIGURE 7.5   Demographic-epidemiological transitions: A brief description of the stages

Source: Nagnur and Nagrodski (1990). From *Canadian Studies in Population*, Volume 17, No. 1. "Epidemiological Transition in the Context of Demographic Change: The Evolution of Canadian Mortality Patterns" by Dhruva Nagnur and M. Nagrodski.

cyclic, with minute net increases. Mortality and fertility rates, fluctuating radically from year to year, were both very high, accounting for very little natural increase. The population during this period was predominantly rural, with a "few crowded, unsanitary, war-famine-epidemic ridden cities of small and medium size" (Omran, 1971). Society was traditional, with a fatalistic orientation sustained by rigid, hierarchical sociopolitical structures. The economy, based on an agrarian system, was heavily dependent on manual-labour production that was susceptible to interruptions caused by debilitative diseases. The standards of living were very low. Public and private spaces were fouled by grossly unsanitary conditions, and most of the population depended on food of poor quality and frequently in very short supply.

Children and women in the fertility years were most adversely affected by these conditions. Life expectancy at birth fluctuated between 20 and 35 years (Acsádi and Nemeskéri, 1970: 256), and infant and childhood mortality was very high (200–300 infant deaths per 1000 births). Women in their adolescent and reproductive years were at higher risk of death than were men, but at lower risk in older ages. Mortality was higher in urban than in rural areas, and the leading causes of death were wars; epidemic scourges; endemic, parasitic, and deficiency diseases; pneumonia-diarrhea-malnutrition complex in children; and tuberculosis-puerperal-malnutrition complex in females. Widespread famine and severe malnutrition underlay disease and death from most other causes. The primary community health problems—epidemics, famine, malnutrition, childhood diseases, and maternal death (death as a consequence of pregnancy and/or childbirth)—were all aggravated by

environmental problems, including contaminated water and food, poor housing, disease-carrying insects and rodents, and lack of personal hygiene. There was no health care system and few decisive therapies; people relied mainly on indigenous healing and witchcraft.

The Age of Receding Pandemics (c.1750 to the early 1920s)

Omran (1971) saw the second stage, characterized by receding pandemics, divided into early and late phases. The early phase ushered in the preconditions for mortality decline and improved health in society. Improvements in agriculture and land use were coupled with modest developments in transportation and communication networks, which encouraged the process of early industrialization. Standards of living remained quite low but began to improve as more effective agricultural methods (e.g., crop rotation and new technology to enhance yields) contributed to better nutrition and reduced death from starvation. Mortality remained high but showed signs of declining as fluctuations became less pronounced. Overall, over this long period life expectancy rose, from a low of 23 in France in 1795, to 48 in the United States in 1900 (Acsádi and Nemeskéri, 1970: 258; Wilmoth, 2003: 655). Women were still at high risk of dying in the adolescent and fertile years. Infant and childhood mortality were also still high, and urban mortality remained higher than rural. The leading causes of death were epidemic scourges, childhood and maternal complexes (especially smallpox in children), and endemic, parasitic, and deficiency diseases. Tuberculosis peaked with industrialization and was especially virulent in young women. Heart disease remained low. There was still no proper health care system, and hospitals were seen as "death traps." However, people began to benefit from gradual improvements in personal hygiene and nutrition.

The late part of this period was marked by explosive population growth due to a sustained pattern of mortality decline coupled with high fertility and a predominantly young population concentrated more and more in cities. Continued improvement in agriculture practices meant greater availability of food and better nutrition, while advances in sanitation and hygiene (including water filtration and garbage removal) and recognition of the importance of workers' health created healthier conditions everywhere except in city slums. As life expectancy at birth gradually rose, mortality declined in children under 15 and women in the reproductive ages, and infant mortality dropped below 150 per 1000 births. Eventually, pandemics of infection, malnutrition, and childhood diseases receded, and plagues largely disappeared, in spite of repeated outbreaks of cholera. Vaccination against smallpox—a leading killer through history—would also play a role in reducing premature mortality from the mid-1800s onward. Infection remained the leading cause of death, but non-infectious diseases, including heart disease and cancer, began to become more significant.

The Age of Human-Made and Degenerative Causes of Death (early 1920s to the 1960s)

In sharp contrast to earlier stages, populations in the third stage of the epidemiological transition enjoyed significant increases in life expectancy such that by the 1960s average length of life would be in the range of 70 years or more. By this period, infant mortality rates had fallen to below 25 per 1000 live births. Maternal death rates also fell significantly. Crude death rates declined to below 20 per 1000 population.

This stage saw cancer, heart disease, and stroke emerge as the leading killers, as infectious and parasitic diseases accounted for relatively few deaths (though pneumonia, bronchitis, influenza, and some viral diseases continued to be significant problems). Polio rose and then tapered off, and scarlet fever began to disappear. Tuberculosis remained low but persistent, especially in slum populations and among older, disadvantaged individuals, particularly men. Smallpox was now rare.

The population during this phase had become predominantly urban, with excessive growth of cities due to rural-to-urban migration, international migration, and urban natural increase. Economically, scientific progress and technology helped produce substantial growth and a consumerist society. Public welfare and leisure spending rose, and society became organized according to rational bureaucratic principles. Large segments of the population enjoyed progressive rises in living conditions, and the nuclear family became the dominant family form. Smaller families allowed women to strive for more options in their social roles, including higher education and careers.

In this societal context, people became extremely conscious of nutrition, especially that of children and mothers. However, increasing consumption of rich and high-fat foods heightened the risk of heart and metabolic diseases. *Morbidity*—rates of disease—began to overshadow mortality as an index of health, as degenerative and chronic illnesses became more prominent, along with mental illness, addiction, accidents, radiation hazards, and environmental conditions. Health systems gradually became oriented to preventive care, in spite of high medical costs. Improvements in survival selectively began to favour the young more than the old, women more than men, and the privileged more than the poor (Omran and Roudi, 1993).

Opinions vary about the causes of Western Europe's epidemiological transition. For instance, what caused the plague to virtually disappear by the start of the twentieth century?[1] One school of thought focuses on the introduction of the Smallpox vaccine in the mid-1800s and the role of improved hygiene (Mercer, 1985, 1986, 1990; Razzel, 1974). Another hypothesis attributes the remarkable declines in Europe's death rate to the recession of virulent epidemic diseases, thanks to major improvements in standards of living and improved nutrition, which enabled people to withstand infections and live longer. This hypothesis, known as the *standards of living thesis* (McKeown, 1976; McKeown, Brown, and Record, 1972), appears to be a plausible explanation, though not a complete account of epidemiological change.

The historical evidence as presented by Thomas McKeown suggests that perhaps beyond the role of the Smallpox vaccine, modern medicine could not have had a major impact on mortality declines until well into the first half of the twentieth century, when germ theory was advanced, leading to the invention of antibacterial drugs (e.g., sulfanomides in 1935, penicillin in 1941, and streptomycin in 1944). Other scholars give specific primacy to the role of incremental public health innovations around the turn of the twentieth century as mainly responsible for mortality declines: water purification (filtration, chlorination); waste disposal systems; midwifery; and massive vaccination programs (Cutler and Miller, 2005; Porter, 1997; Sreter, 1988, 2002).

Extensions to Epidemiological Transition Theory

The Age of Delayed Degenerative Diseases

After the 1960s, the industrialized countries witnessed major declines in mortality from cardiovascular disease, thus heralding a new epidemiological stage. For example, in the United States, death rates from heart disease declined by more than 30 per cent between 1968 and 1982. Most of this decline had occurred among middle-aged and older segments of the population. Researchers have observed this same trend in other industrialized countries (Caselli, Meslé, and Vallin, 2002; Mackenzie, 1987; Ouellette, Barbieri, and Wilmoth, 2014; Salomon and Murray, 2002; Vallin, 2006; White, 2002).

Based on these observations, Jay Olshansky and Brian Ault (1986) have suggested that advanced society has entered a fourth stage of epidemiological transition, the *age of delayed degenerative diseases*. This fourth stage is characterized by continuing slow and often fluctuating mortality declines, which are increasingly concentrated in the later stages of life, and a variable pattern of change in the average onset and duration of major chronic ailments, notably cardiovascular diseases and, to a lesser degree, cancer. In other words, chronic and degenerative diseases continue to dominate, but the onset of major disability from these diseases is occurring later in life as compared to earlier times; and people with these types of diseases now live longer due to widespread access to advanced medical therapies (e.g., cholesterol-lowering medication, advanced cardiac surgery techniques).

The Hybristic Stage

In addition to the trends identified by Olshansky and Ault (1986), Richard Rogers and Robert Hackenberg (1987) identified a number of epidemiological features of post-industrial societies, mostly linked to lifestyle and health behaviours, including smoking, alcohol and drug use, diet, exercise, and so on. Societies in the fourth stage have also seen, particularly among disadvantaged subgroups of the population, a resurgence of some lethal infectious diseases thought to have been long conquered, including new antibiotic-resistant strains of tuberculosis. HIV is among the deadliest and most widely known of these lethal new viruses, which, Rogers and Hackenberg (1987) argue, are partly related to behavioural factors (e.g., profligate sexual behaviours and intravenous drug use). For Rogers and Hackenberg (1987), post-industrial societies have entered a *hybristic* epidemiological stage, characterized by a prominence of both chronic and

LIVE FAST, DIE YOUNG

What do Elvis Presley, Otis Redding, Buddy Holly, Sid Vicious, Freddie Mercury, Brian Jones, Kurt Kobain, and Joe Ramone have in common? They were all famous rock stars who died young. In fact, according to research by Mark Bellis and colleagues (2007), early death is not uncommon among famous rock stars. The study shows that rock stars are three times more likely to die young than the rest of the population. Of over 1000 European and American musicians who had their first chart success between 1956 and 1999, 100 are dead. Forty per cent of the Americans and 28 per cent of the Europeans died from overdoses, accidents, or chronic diseases related to the use of alcohol and illegal drugs. The average age at death for the Americans was 42, and for the Europeans just 35.

Notwithstanding these dire statistics, it must be mentioned that there are honourable exceptions of European and North American rock stars still performing today in their 60s. Notable examples include Mick Jagger and Keith Richards of the Rolling Stones, the Guess Who's Burton Cummings and Randy Bachman, and Bob Dylan.

Cause of death	American rock stars (% deaths)	European rock stars (% deaths)
Suicide	2.8	3.6
Violence	6.9	3.6
Drug/alcohol overdose	15.3	28.6
Accident (drug/alcohol-related)	2.8	7.1
Chronic disorder (drug/alcohol)	9.7	3.6
Cancer	19.4	21.4
Cardiovascular disease	18.0	3.6
Other accident	13.9	21.4
Other	11.1	7.1
Total	100.0	100.0

Source: Bellis et al. (2007). Reproduced from *Journal of Epidemiology and Community Health* vol. 61, issue 10, pp. 896–901. Bellis, Mark A., Tom Hennell, Clare Lushey, et al. "'Elvis to Eminem: Quantifying the Price of Fame Through Early Mortality of European and North American Rock and Pop Stars.'"

communicable disease mortality, as well as many premature deaths associated with unhealthy lifestyles and behaviours, which in combination account for an increasing portion of deaths.

Empirical evidence is consistent with these theories. Ali Mokdad and colleagues (2004) determined that the "real" causes of death today are related mainly to lifestyle behaviours that compromise good health and longevity, specifically smoking, overeating, maintaining an unhealthy diet, and avoiding exercise. In the United States, tobacco use accounts for 18 per cent of all deaths, poor diet and physical inactivity are responsible for 16.6 per cent of all deaths, and alcohol use contributes 3.5 per cent to the total (World Health Organization, 2005a).

A number of other causes of death can be linked to the lifestyle behaviours Mokdad and colleagues (2004) identified. Many deaths are caused each year by unsafe driving, the misuse of firearms, risky sexual behaviours, and illegal drug use. Suicide and homicide remain significant causes of premature death, particularly among young and middle-aged adults (Stack, 2000a, 2000b).

The extensions of epidemiological transition theory presented by Olshansky and Ault (1986) and by Rogers and Hackenberg (1987) may be viewed as complementary descriptions of the epidemiological context of post-industrial societies.

Exceptions to Epidemiological Transition Theory

Although we might expect the developments outlined in the classical form of the epidemiological transition theory to apply generally across all populations, the empirical evidence shows some notable exceptions.

Studies by John Caldwell (1986), among others (Gauri and Khaleghian, 2002; Gjonca, 2001; Gjonca, Wilson, and Falkingham, 1997; Heuveline, Guillot, and Gwatkin, 2002), cast doubt on the generality of a central tenet of the epidemiological theory: that decreased mortality results from socioeconomic advancement, because modernization paves the way to better health care and public health systems. These studies have found that in some poor countries major health improvements are possible without large-scale economic growth. Veijo Notkola, Ian Timaeus, and Harri Siiskonen (2000) studied mortality change in the Ovamboland region of Namibia in southern Africa, where they found the main agent of health transition was not economic change or sociopolitical intervention but the Church. After analyzing parish registers of Namibia's Evangelical Lutheran Church from 1930 to 1990, the authors of the study discovered that between the early 1950s and the early 1960s, adult mortality fell at a rate far greater than one would predict from life table models. Among many developments that contributed to Ovamboland's overall decline in mortality, the most important factor was the establishment of a Western system of health care by Lutheran missionaries from Finland. Regrettably, the recent surge of the HIV/AIDS epidemic in Namibia (and other parts of the African continent) has reversed the favourable trends achieved decades earlier.

Another weakness in the epidemiological theory is its implicit assumption of a linear—and irreversible—progression through the various stages. Graziella Caselli and colleagues (2002) have identified a number of cases of retrogressions in mortality improvements. Among the examples they cite are some of the former Soviet Bloc countries, which have seen reductions in life expectancy over recent decades, a situation not at all envisioned by the classical version of the epidemiological theory. In Russia, life expectancy gains achieved between 1965 and the late 1990s have fluctuated between periods of decline, stagnation, and partial recovery (Anderson, 2003; Anderson and Silver, 1989; Kucera et al., 2000; Mackenbach, 2013; Nierenberg, 2005: 94; Vallin, Meslé, and Valkonen, 2001: 137). These drops in life expectancy are driven largely by a high incidence of premature death among middle-aged adults, particularly males, mainly from cardiovascular diseases, poisonings, and injuries (Zaridze et al., 2009; Zatonski and Bhala, 2012). Key contributing factors to these trends are excessive use of alcohol and tobacco and poor diet (Haynes and Husan, 2003). The former Soviet Bloc countries' rapid turn to mass privatization, poor government involvement in health planning and widening income inequality, are implicated as additional sources underlying their poor health profile (Stuckler, King, and McKee, 2009).

According to Omran's theory, infectious diseases are supposed to play a minor role in mortality during the most advanced stages of epidemiological transition. Yet in recent years, the world has seen the emergence of lethal new viruses that pose serious threats to population health. The appearance of HIV/AIDS in the developed countries in the early 1980s is a clear case in point. Recent threats such as H5N1 and H7N9 avian flu viruses can potentially cause the next major world pandemic, perhaps far deadlier than the Spanish influenza of 1918–19, if these viruses acquire the ability to transmit efficiently from person to person (Chen et al., 2013; Steinhauer, 2013). The return of some old infectious diseases, like antibiotic-resistant strains of tuberculosis, also attests to the inability of the theory to anticipate new epidemiological developments in modern industrial society (Fauci and Morens, 2012).

A final problem is that the theory is essentially silent in regard to health and mortality inequalities among disadvantaged sectors of national populations. Canada's First Nations are just one example of a population whose epidemiological condition is much worse than that of other Canadians; the cases of indigenous populations in the United States and Australia are similar (Gracey and King, 2009; King, Smith, and Gracey, 2009; Kunitz, 1990, 1994; Trovato, 2001; Young, 1994).

Health Transition

Recent demographic literature has broadened in scope to examine ideas surrounding *health transition*. As a theoretical perspective, health transition describes the improvements in life expectancy and overall health of populations over the historical spectrum, going beyond the scope covered by epidemiological transition theory. Health transition theorists concentrate on explaining how the health of a population changes as a result of change in social organization, environment, health care institutions, and prevention systems, as well as genetic and biological factors, lifestyles and behaviour, and culture (Caldwell, 1991; Cutler and Miller, 2005; Frenk et al., 1991; Johansson, 1991; Nathanson, 1996; Riley, 2001, 2005a, 2005b). In particular, they focus on several interacting sets of factors viewed as playing a role in the health of populations:

- *systemic factors*, including those related to the environment and social organization;
- *societal factors*, including cultural and structural determinants such as stratification and inequality in the population;
- *institutional/household-level factors*, including proximate factors like working conditions, living conditions, health care systems, and lifestyles; and
- *individual factors*, such as health status and behavioural risk factors.

Health transition theory examines the role that these determinants of health play in the rising life expectancy at birth (the mortality transition) and the decreasing proportion of deaths caused by infectious diseases (the epidemiological transition). Health transition theorists also point to the contributions of the state and its health care system in health and disease change, adding that economic development is not the only factor—nor necessarily the most important—in the epidemiological change. These theorists emphasize the exceptional experience of poor countries in attaining relatively good health at relatively low levels of economic development, a point elaborated in greater detail later.

Aging and Health Dynamics in Advanced Societies

Life Expectancy Change—Historical Overview

Jacques Vallin and France Meslé (2009, 2010) have identified four distinct trends between 1750 and 2005 based on a compilation of maximum female life expectancies at birth for today's highly developed countries (see Figure 7.6).

1. *1750–1790:* Female life expectancy at birth fluctuated around an average of about 38 years, as represented by Sweden, England, and Finland. In this phase of history there was hardly any progress in population health.
2. *1790–1885:* At the end of this period, life expectation rose to about 50 years. The starting point, 1790, coincides with Jenner's breakthrough in finding a vaccine against Smallpox. But the rise of life expectancy in this period can also be attributed to progress in agriculture and in the production and distribution of food for the population, which helped to reduce famine and thereby vulnerability to epidemic diseases. The country with the best expectancy was Denmark, though Sweden and Finland were close behind.
3. *1886–1960*: After 1886, life expectancy rose more steeply to reach the mid-70s by 1960. This represents a gain of about four months of life expectancy per year over the period. Here, the improvements coincide with major medical discoveries—antiseptics, vaccination, sulfamides, antibiotics. The record during this time alternated between Australia and Norway, the latter taking the lead after World War II up until the early 1970s, at which point it was overtaken by Iceland.
4. *1960–2005:* In this phase, the leader in life expectancy has been Japan since 1983, with current female life expectancy in the range of 85 years. What explains these most recent improvements are widespread reductions in the death rate from cardiovascular-related diseases.

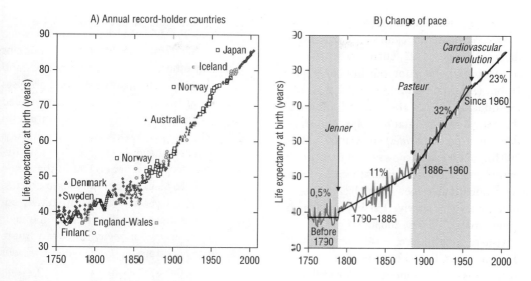

FIGURE 7.6   Highest observed national female life expectancies at a given moment in the world (1750–2005)

Note: Graph A shows the different countries which, in turn, held the life expectancy record for the year. Graph B illustrates the changes of pace as measured by the gradient (in %) of the fitted lines. A 10 per cent gradient signifies that life expectancy increases annually by one-tenth of a year; 20 per cent by one-fifth of a year; 33 per cent by one-third of a year.

Source: Vallin and Meslé (2010): 1. Vallin, Jaques and France Meslé. 2010. "Will Life Expectancy Increase Indefinitely by Three Months Every Year?" *Population and Societies* 473 (December). Copyright Institut national d'études démographiques. Reprinted with permission.

Given this pattern of change among highly advanced countries, early in the twenty-first century, one of the questions being debated is what *maximum average human lifespan* could be attained. Scientific work in this area is wide-ranging and includes laboratory molecular studies on mice and other organisms, computer simulations of the effects of cause-of-death elimination or life expectancy improvements, and epidemiological follow-up studies of cohorts as they pass through life (e.g., Allard et al., 1998; Carey and Judge, 2001; Fontana, Partridge, and Longo, 2010; Gems and Partridge, 2013; Hekimi and Guarente, 2003; Jones et al., 2014 Newman and Murabito, 2013; Olshansky, Carnes, and Cassel, 1990; Partridge, Thornton, and Bates, 2011; Weindruch et al., 1986). In the section that follows, we will look at the concept of lifespan and how it has generated speculations on the future course of longevity in societies of the world that are at the most advanced stages of epidemiological transition.

The Concept of Lifespan

Lifespan is a characteristic of life history that is the product of evolution. For an individual, it refers to the period between birth and death. At the cohort level (as represented in a life table), it is the average age at death, or the life expectancy at birth; thus, it may be called *average human lifespan*. Biologists refer to the highest verified age at death in a particular population, cohort, or species as the *maximum observed lifespan*, and the overall highest verified age for a species is its *record lifespan*. Jeanne Calment, who died at the age of 122, currently represents the record lifespan for the human population (Allard et al., 1998). All sexually reproducing species are assumed to have a theoretical highest attainable age, known as *maximum potential lifespan* (Carey, 2003a, 2003b), but it is not known what that "maximum" might be for humans, because there is no "identifiable age for which some select individuals can survive but beyond which none can live" (Carey, 2003b: 1).

There is evidence, based on Swedish death records, that the record age at death in humans has been increasing for well over a century (Carey, 2003a, 2003b; Wilmoth et al., 2002). The rise of maximum human lifespan to over 120 years is believed to have been brought about by two phenomena. The first is Darwinian natural selection, which is thought to have extended the human lifespan to somewhere in the range of 72 to 90 years. The second, a

Two variables that have strong positive correlations with lifespan for humans and other primates are body mass and relative brain size. Regression analyses using these two variables have yielded predicted lifespans for humans through different periods in evolutionary history. Scientists have estimated that the lifespan for *Homo habilis* was in the range of 52 to 56 years, and for *Homo erectus*, 60 to 63 years. From such studies scientists have concluded that a major increase in longevity between these two ancestors of *Homo sapiens sapiens* must have occurred some 1.7 to 2 million years ago (Carey, 2003a, 2003b). Of course, for much of human history, to live as long or longer than the predicted lifespan must have been extremely rare.

post-Darwinian phenomenon, may be described as "artifactual" growth resulting from improved living conditions of modern society. This second aspect of human longevity improvement may have created a self-perpetuating system of longevity extension through incremental societal improvements that have translated into better health and increased longevity (Burger, Baudisch, and Vaupel, 2012). Robert Fogel and Dora Costa (1997) have referred to this phenomenon as a *technophysio evolution*.

Rectangularization of Survival

For populations in the advanced stages of epidemiological and health transitions, the survival curve in the life table has become increasingly rectangular, reflecting gradual improvements in age-specific survival probabilities (Cheung et al., 2005; Horiuchi and

Born in Arles, France, on 21 February 1875, Jeanne Calment was 122 years and 164 days old when she died in a French nursing home on 4 August 1997. Her total lifespan of an astonishing 44 724 days is the longest confirmed human lifespan in history. She led a remarkable life that spanned the rule of 20 French presidents. As a child, she met Vincent Van Gogh, who often frequented her father's art supply store in Arles. Among the many tributes to her life is a CD titled *Time's Mistress*, which features her voice set to funk-rap, techno, and dance music. For more on Jeanne Calment, see Allard et al. (1998).

Wilmoth, 1998; Robine, 2001). The increasing *rectangularization of the survival curve* in the life table has resulted from two important changes in mortality and survival probabilities by age over time. The first is the significant improvement in survival rates for infants, then children, and later young adults, over the course of the twentieth century. The second is the continued improvement in survival chances for these same age groups in conjunction with significant mortality declines late in the century among those in the older ages. As survival probabilities among the younger ages have tended to level off, survival rates for the elderly have been improving faster, producing a greater degree of rectangularization in the life table curve for the population 65 and over, beginning in the last quarter of the twentieth century (Nagnur, 1986b; Nagnur and Nagrodski, 1990).

Canada's rectangularization trends can be observed in the life table survival curves shown in Figure 7.7. As the figure shows, conditional survival probabilities have improved substantially since the late nineteenth century; however, between successive periods, the survival curves have become less distant from each other. This suggests that further improvements in mortality are not likely to produce the kinds of shifts in the survival curves as obtained in earlier periods. The term *entropy of the life table* describes the tendency for the survival probabilities in the life table to attenuate once a population reaches a high level of life expectancy.[2]

Compression of Morbidity and Mortality

In 1980, James Fries proposed a theory that relies in part on the concept of survival

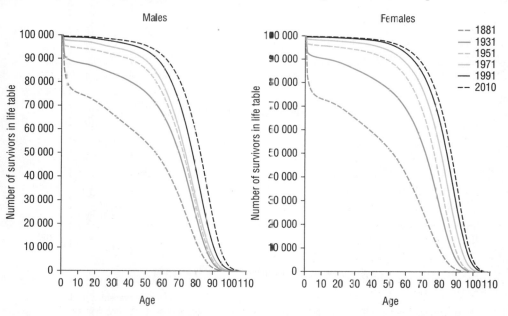

FIGURE 7.7   Life table survival curves for Canadian males and females, 1881, 1931, 1951, 1971, 1996, and 2010.

Sources: Robert Bourbeau (personal communication, October 28, 2014; 1881 single years of age life tables); Dominion Bureau of Statistics (1947) Life Tables for Canada and Regions 1941 and 1931. Ottawa: Minister of Trade and Commerce; Dominion Bureau of Statistics (1953) Canadian Life Table 1951. Ottawa: Minister of Trade and Commerce; Statistics Canada (1979) Life Tables, Canada and Provinces, 1970-1972. Ottawa: Minister of Supply and Services Canada (Cat. No. 84-532); Statistics Canada (1995) Life Tables, Canada and Provinces, 1990-1992. Ottawa: Minister of Industry (Cat. No. 84-537); Statistics Canada Demography Division (2013b).

rectangularization. He reasoned that the future pattern of mortality and morbidity in advanced societies would be affected by a "compression" phenomenon, in which major disability and sickness would be increasingly "compressed" into fewer and fewer years occurring in advanced age, close to the time of "natural death." Fries (1980, 1983) argued that the rectangularization of survival probabilities in the life table over the past century is a reflection of the tendency for each new generation to be generally healthier than the preceding one. Fries (1980) projected a future in which most individuals would remain relatively healthy for most of their lives; only once they approach the maximum average age at death—i.e., life expectancy (which, Fries estimated, would

reach 85 by about 2050) would individuals experience the onset of major disability and illness, soon followed by natural death.[3] Thus, under Fries' scenario, the onset of major disability would occur later and later in life, and the period of debilitating infirmity would be relatively short for the average citizen—compressed, as it were, into a few years, close to the time of death (see Figure 7.8).

There is some research to support the view that a life expectancy much beyond age 85 may not be feasible—at least given current medical and technological knowledge (see Olshansky and Carnes, 2001; Olshansky, Carnes, and Cassel, 1990; Olshansky, Carnes, and Hayflick, 2004). It has been estimated, for example, that

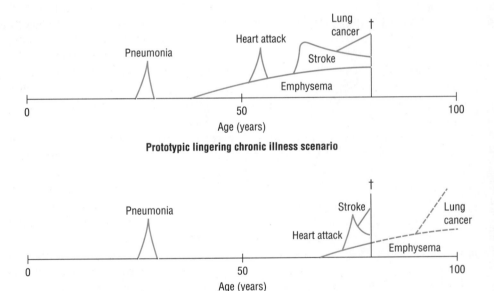

Prototypic lingering chronic illness scenario

Compression of morbidity and mortality scenario

The ability to postpone chronic disease, taken together with the biological limit represented by the lifespan, results in the ability to shorten the period between the clinical onset of chronic disease and the end of life. Infirmity (morbidity) is compressed into a shorter and shorter period near the end of the lifespan.

FIGURE 7.8   Stylized form of the compression of morbidity and mortality concept

Source: Fries and Crapo (1981): 92. Copyright © 1982 Wiley-Liss, Inc., A Wiley Company. *Vitality and Aging: Implications of the Rectangular Curve* by Hames F. Fries and Lawrence M. Crapo. Copyright © W.H. Freeman 1981.

in order for life expectancy in the United States to surpass 85 years, adults late in life would need to attain the mortality profile of teens—in other words, a 55-year-old man would have to have the death rate of a 15-year-old boy (Olshansky, Carnes, and Cassel, 1990). If we accept 85 as the average age at death, with the standard deviation of ten years around this parameter and a more or less normal distribution of deaths, then most people would die between the ages of 75 and 95, and only about 2.5 per cent of the population would cross this upper limit, with very few surviving past 100.

Fries' assumption that each generation is generally healthier than the preceding one has received substantial support in the literature based on high-income countries.

SENESCENCE IN EVOLUTIONARY BIOLOGICAL PERSPECTIVE

Evolutionary biology theory posits that in sexually reproducing species *senescence* (biological aging) is the result of nature's disposability of the organism beyond the reproductive ages (Kirkwood, 2010a). The force of natural selection is strongest early in life, and traits that are beneficial to enhance survival to reproductive age or reproductive output are selected for despite later life costs to the organism (e.g., the process of cell self-destruction is a normal physiological process that eliminates DNA-damaged cells; this same process is a major part of why we get cancer later in life). Hence, harmful late-acting genes can remain in a population if they have a beneficial effect early in life by increasing fitness at early ages or increasing reproductive success. So, the decline in the force of selection with age is viewed by evolutionary theory as the fundamental cause of aging. Starting at reproductive maturity senescence is thought to be inevitable in humans and in all other multicellular species capable of repeated breeding. Thus, as we move past the reproductive phase of life, the force of selection weakens, and with advancing age we get increasingly frail and fall prey to chronic diseases. This further suggests that there are biological constraints that keep us from surpassing longevity beyond certain limits, as the organism must always balance allocating resources to growth and repair on the one hand, and reproduction on the other. Too much of one over the other entails costs either to reproduction or to longevity. Highly reproducing species have short lives because they allocate lots of energy to reproduction; low reproducing species—such as humans—are long-lived because greater energetic resources are allocated to living longer. This process of energy allocation and repair is responsible for limits on how long we live (Kirkwood, 2010a).

Limits notwithstanding, it is important to indicate that evolutionary theory does not say that we should stop trying to improve health and vitality to the fullest extent possible. This goal should always be pursued, regardless.

In general, even though adult obesity may be a growing concern (Olshansky et al., 2005; Wister, 2005), it appears that the typical 65-year-old of today is "younger," in terms of vitality and health, than was the typical 65-year-old a century or even as recently as a quarter-century ago (Burger, Baudisch and Vaupel, 2012; Christensen et al., 2009; Fogel, 2004b; Fogel and Costa, 1997; Fries, 2012; Fries, Bruce, and Chakravarty, 2011; Fries and Crapo, 1981; Rice and Fineman, 2004; Unal et al., 2005; Vaupel, 2010).

Life table analyses of *disability-free life expectancy* (the years of life when an individual's health does not affect the ability to perform normal activities) for Canada and other highly industrialized countries indicate that the average number of years people now spend in a state of disability and infirmity in old age diminished over the course of the twentieth century, especially since the early 1970s (Cambois, Robine, and Hayward, 2002; Costa, 2000; Crimmins et al., 2006; Fogel, 2004b; Manton, Gu, and Lamb, 2006; Manton and Singer, 1994; Martel and Bélanger, 2000; Wolfson, 1996). Kenneth Manton, Xi Liang Gu, and Vicky Lamb (2006) show that between 1982 and 1999 in the United States, *active life expectancy* (i.e., life expectancy free of major disability) increased among those aged 65 and older, and also among those aged 85 and older. Canadian data over the period 2000–2 to 2005–7 show a similar improving trend for both life expectancy and health-adjusted life expectancy at ages 0 and 65 (see Table 7.2).

Expansion of Survival

Many researchers today do not agrees with Fries' assertion that the maximum average age at death (life expectancy) for human populations is 85 (e.g., Barbi,

TABLE 7.2   Life expectancy and health-adjusted life expectancy; Canada 2000–2 and 2005–7

Age group	Sex	Measure	2000–2	2005–7	Change
At birth	Males	Health-adjusted life expectancy	67.5	68.9	1.4
		Life expectancy	77.0	78.3	1.3
	Females	Health-adjusted life expectancy	69.9	71.2	1.3
		Life expectancy	82.0	83.0	1.0
At age 65	Males	Health-adjusted life expectancy	12.6	13.8	1.2
		Life expectancy	17.0	18.1	1.1
	Females	Health-adjusted life expectancy	14.1	15.0	0.9
		Life expectancy	20.5	21.3	0.8

Source: Statistics Canada (2014b). From Statistics Canada, "Health-Adjusted Life Expectancy, at Birth and at Age 65, by Sex and Income, Canada and Provinces," Table 102-0122, CANSIM (database) 2014b. Reproduced and distributed on an "as is" basis with permission of Statistics Canada.

Demographers use four measures of disability:

1. **Prevalence** tells us how many cases of physical disability there are at a given time.

2. **Disability-free life expectancy** tells us how many years an average person is expected to live without major disability.

3. **Disability-free life expectancy with different levels of severity** is essentially disability-free life expectancy computed for varying degrees of disability.

4. **Disability-adjusted life expectancy** assigns weights to the different levels of severity to provide more detail about the influence of these disabilities on personal functioning; it estimates the number of years of good health a person is expected to experience. (Perenboom et al., 2004)

Bongaarts, and Vaupel, 2008; Bongaarts, 2006; Burger, Baudisch, and Vaupel, 2012; Christensen, Doblhammer, Rau, and Vaupel, 2009; Kannisto, 1996; Kannisto et al., 1994; Manton, 1982; Manton and Vaupel, 1995; Oeppen and Vaupel, 2002; Vallin, Meslé, and Valkonen, 2001; Vaupel, 2010; Vaupel et al., 1998; Wilmoth et al., 2002). In fact, there are indicators to suggest that survival probabilities in the older ages have been expanding over time, and that this trend is likely to continue into the foreseeable future. John Bongaarts (2006, 2009) has confirmed that gains in *senescent mortality* (mortality associated with aging) since the mid-twentieth century have outpaced improvements in both juvenile mortality and background mortality (i.e., deaths caused by accidents, violence, and infectious/parasitic diseases). The slowing of senescent mortality translates into longer life expectancy; therefore, there is growing consensus in the literature that further improvements in senescent life expectancy should be forthcoming (Goldstein and Cassidy,

2012; Gurven and Kaplan, 2007; Horiuchi and Wilmoth, 1998; Lynch and Brown, 2001; Manton and Yashin, 2006; Vaupel et al., 1998). Bongaarts (2006) estimated an average increase of about 7.5 years over the next half-century.

Consistent with this prediction, active life expectancy in actuality keeps improving, and there has been a significant growth in the number of centenarians—hundred-year-olds—worldwide. The number of *supercentenarians*—those surpassing age 110—is also on the rise (Maier et al., 2010). In the 14 developed countries with the most reliable statistics, the proportion of centenarians has risen from 5 per million inhabitants in 1960 to 50 per million inhabitants in 1990 (Jeune and Skytthe, 2001: 75). Given these trends, gerontologists now speak of a *healthy aging paradigm*, its principal aim being to promote health and vitality in the elderly (Andersen et al., 2012; Perls and Silver, 1999; Wilmoth and Ferraro, 2007).

As for the future, the two perspectives lead to somewhat different predictions. Fries

MORTALITY: HUMANS, HUNTER-GATHERERS, AND WILD CHIMPANZEES

According to James Vaupel (2010), death is being delayed because successive generations of people are reaching higher ages in better health. Oskar Burger, Annette Baudisch, and Vaupel (2012) add that human mortality has decreased so substantially that the difference between hunter-gatherers and today's lowest mortality populations is greater than the difference between hunter-gatherers and wild chimpanzees (see also Gurven and Kaplan, 2007). The bulk of this mortality reduction has occurred since 1900, which means that it has been experienced by only about 4 of the roughly 8000 human generations that have ever lived. These mortality improvements are on par with or greater than the reductions in mortality in other species achieved by laboratory selection experiments and endocrine pathway mutations. Conventional theories of aging cannot explain this apparent feature of humans, to experience such significant gains in senescent mortality (Burger, Baudisch, and Vaupel 2012; Jones et al., 2014).

and colleagues would maintain that the postponement of morbidity is a factual process and that more improvement is possible in compressing the onset of major disability to older ages; this goal seems more achievable than the postponement of mortality. Theorists subscribing to the *expansion of survival* perspective assume both types of postponement—those of morbidity and of mortality—are possible. So, while few of us could expect to attain the 122-year longevity of Jeanne Calment, the average human lifespan in the future could surpass the presumed upper limit to human average life span suggested by Fries and associates. An intermediate position sees the future as being dependent on the interplay of biological constraints on longevity on the one hand, and the society's ability to innovate further to enhance population health and thereby extend longevity to the extent possible.

Health Patterns in Low- and Middle-Income Countries

Life Expectancy Trends: 1950 Onwards

Across the developing world, the overall picture regarding life expectancy is one of general improvements since 1950. The *UN World Mortality Report* (United Nations Department of Economic and Social Affairs Population Division, 2012a:4) gives estimated trends for the world and its broad development regions (see chart on page 295).

Beyond these broad regional categories, the picture is complex, because, as noted by Meslé and Vallin (2011), one finds both divergent and convergent trends across countries. Some developing countries have been doing better than others and

	1950–5	2010–15	% Change
World	47.7	69.3	+45.3
More developed countries	65.9	78.0	+18.4
Less developed countries	42.3	67.5	+59.6
Least developed countries	37.2	58.8	+58.1
Other less developed countries	43.0	69.4	+61.4

Source: From *World Mortality Report 2011*, United Nations Department of Economic and Social Affairs Population Division. © 2012 United Nations. Reprinted by permission of the United Nations.

are moving closer to completing the epidemiological and health transitions; others have passed through periods of gains and setbacks in the fight against early death. A full picture of all the developing countries' trajectories of change in life expectancy across time is not feasible, given the large number of countries involved. However, we provide an overview based on Meslé and Vallin (2011).

Figure 7.9 shows that judged against Sweden, some developing countries have fared relatively well. For example, Argentina, Chile, and Puerto Rico had by 2010 reached a level of life expectancy not far removed from Sweden's; this, after a long process that started with very low levels well below those of more developed "pioneer" countries that were first to move through the epidemiologic transition.

Egypt has since the early 1990s crossed above the trend of the more developed pioneer countries though it remains far removed from the levels prevailing in Sweden and even in the three South American countries. India has made steady progress since the late 1940s, showing a superior performance since then in relation to the overall trend for more developed latecomers (mainly the former Soviet countries). Yemen too, has seen a rising trend, moving above more developed latecomers since 1970.

Afghanistan's case is emblematic of developing countries plagued by serious sociopolitical and socioeconomic problems and that have consequently passed through periods of steady improvement and setbacks. This applies to the experience of some sub-Saharan countries that have been devastated by HIV/AIDS—for example, South Africa, Zimbabwe, and Zambia. These countries have not yet recovered the losses in life expectancy they experienced since the 1990s. Some other developing countries have seen setbacks in life expectancy due to the effects of economic crises, such as Congo Democratic Republic, Nigeria, and Angola after the 1980 world economic recession. In other cases, the main culprit has been civil war. Cambodia is a clear example of this. In Africa, Somalia and Rwanda both underwent devastating wars that led to severe falls in life expectancy between the late 1980s and late 1990s.

Significant divergence is also seen across Eastern European countries. On one hand, there are cases where the upheaval associated with the fall of the Soviet empire in the early 1990s appears to have been less devastating (e.g., Czech Republic, Poland). On the other, there are the dramatic shifts in life expectancy that have evolved in Russia and Ukraine. In 2005, a Russian baby boy could expect to live only 58 years; a Ukrainian boy 62 years. The recent study of Pavel Grigoriev and colleagues (2014) indicates that Russia has seen an upward trend in life expectancy since 2003. It is cautioned however, that given past experience in Russia, a possible return to mortality stagnation cannot be ruled out.

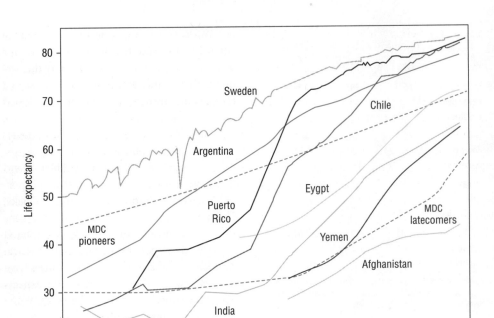

FIGURE 7.9   Long-term trends in female life expectancy for selected developing countries

Note: The two *dotted lines* border an over-simplified range for real life expectancies of all industrialized countries. In *light grey*, Sweden stands for a benchmark of the best levels currently achieved by MDCs.

Source: Meslé and Vallin (2011): 8. From Springer Science-Business Media, *International Handbook of Adult Mortality*, Meslé, France and Jacques Vallin, "Historical Trends in Mortality" Figures 2.8 ©2011. With kind permission from Springer Science and Business Media.

Health-Achieving Poor Nations

The term *low- and middle-income countries* (LMICs) has come into vogue recently as a synonym for "developing countries." By implication, this terminology signifies the existence of a global stratification system (Ebrahim and Smeeth, 2005), in which variations in national wealth are linked to cross-national differences in population health and well-being. Given their limited resources, an ongoing concern for low- and middle-income countries is how to improve the health of their populations at relatively low cost. This

question links to another more fundamental query: How much income growth must a nation experience in order to achieve superior health?

In an extensive cross-national study, Samuel Preston (1975, 1986a) observed for the 1930s and 1960s a positive non-linear association between countries' level of income per capita (a measure of the level of economic development) and life expectancy (an index of population health). In both periods, the curve rises steeply up to about an income level of $400 per head and attenuates thereafter, flattening out at higher income levels beyond $600 per capita. This relationship is known as the *Preston curve*. Figure 7.10 displays updated versions of this curve (Cutler, Deaton, and Lleras-Muney, 2006; Wilkinson, 1996). The consistency of the relationship across time points is noticeable in the graphs.

The early analysis by Preston (1975) suggested that within each period the net effect of change in national income *per se* to gains in life expectancy is actually not very strong. Moreover, it was observed that between the 1930s and 1960s, the curve of life expectancy and national income shifted upwards, and that this upward shift accounted for more of the change in life expectancy than within-period changes in national income. For example, the upward shift of the curve amounted to 10–12 years of life expectancy gain for countries whose incomes were in the range of $100 and $500 per capita. On the other hand, within each period, a change in national income produced a much smaller gain in life expectancy.

Thus, significant improvement in life expectation for countries over the two periods was associated more with the upward shift of the curve than with within-period changes in national income. Stated differently, only 10–15 per cent of increase in a country's life expectancy comes from moving along the curve whereas 85–90 per cent comes from the curve shifting upwards (Wilkinson, 1996).

Therefore, other factors above and beyond a country's current level of income must play important roles in explaining life expectancy improvements. Preston surmised that these other factors are primarily social in nature, such as improvements in public health and the diffusion of health knowledge. Consistent with this view, Richard Easterlin (2004: 87; 113–16) affirms that major mortality declines in some areas of the Third World occurred before World War II under conditions of little or no economic growth. He also notes that the improvement in life expectancy in

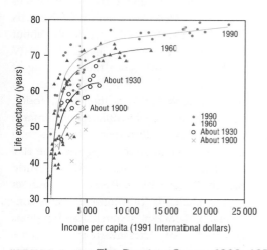
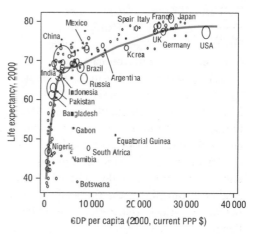

FIGURE 7.10   The Preston Curve, 1900, 1930, 1960, 1990, and 2000

Note: In the graph for 2000, circles denote relative size of population of countries.

Sources: Cutler, Deaton, and Lleras-Muney (2006): 116; Wilkinson (1996). Cutler graph: Cutler, David, A. Deaton and A. Lleras-Muney, "The Determinants of Mortality." Journal of Economic Literature Vol. 41 no. 1 (March 2003), p. 116. Wilkinson graph: Based on Richard G. Wilkinson, Unhealthy Societies, p. 34 'Life Expectancy and Income Per Capita for Selected Countries and Periods." Published by Routledge, 1996.

developing countries has been accomplished by the introduction of essentially the same techniques of infectious disease control as were used in the developed countries: campaigns to eradicate malaria; immunization against Smallpox; improvements in water purification and sewage disposal; better education; and successful social implementation of health knowledge and behavioural changes (e.g., personal hygiene).

All this suggests that it is possible for relatively poor countries with modest national incomes to achieve superior levels of population health. The literature is consistent with this notion.

John Caldwell (1986) showed that health-achieving poor nations share a number of common features. Their societies afford women a relatively high status, which entitles them to enjoy high levels of education and autonomy, and there is a determination on the part of these governments to intervene in the areas of education, public health, and nutrition for the benefit of the population.

Randall Kuhn (2010) has discovered an even larger number of superior and poor health-achieving countries than did Caldwell. The superior category include some countries in Latin America (Jamaica, Costa Rica), Asia (Sri Lanka, China, Myanmar, India, Thailand), and in Africa (Congo, Tanzania, Kenya, and Ghana). A common feature of poor health-achieving countries is that they are predominantly Muslim countries—Oman, Saudi Arabia, Iran, Libya, Algeria, Iraq, Yemen, Morocco, Ivory Coast, Senegal, and Sierra Leone.

Poor nations can learn from the examples of the low-income superior health achievers and hasten their own health transitions in spite of having modest levels of per capita income. The poor health achievers, some of which are relatively wealthy, must come to the realization that it takes more than high national income to attain superior levels of population health. The importance of political will cannot be underestimated. National leaders must be willing to devote a significant portion of national wealth for the betterment of its citizens.

Burden of Disease

The Continuing Threat of HIV/AIDS

Acquired immunodeficiency syndrome, more commonly known as AIDS, is caused by the human immunodeficiency virus (HIV), which is spread through blood, semen, vaginal secretions, and breast milk. Many experts have called HIV/AIDS the most deadly epidemic of our time (Bongaarts, Pelletier, and Gerland, 2011; Lamptey, Johnson, and Khan, 2006; Moore, 2004; Pepin, 2011). According to the 2012 UNAIDS *Report on the Global AIDS Epidemic* (UNAIDS, 2012), globally, about 34 million people were living with HIV at the end of 2011. Since the beginning of the epidemic in the early 1980s, nearly 36 million people have lost their lives. Today, many of the people afflicted are infants and children. In 2011, there were in a total of 3.3 million children living with the HIV infection, with 3.1 million in Africa (World Health Organization, 2013). The burden of the epidemic continues to vary considerably between countries and regions (see Table 7.3). After nearly three decades since HIV's emergence, the annual number of people dying from AIDS-related causes worldwide has been steadily decreasing since the mid-2000s: In 2011, 1.7 million

TABLE 7.3   Regional HIV and AIDS statistics by region, 2001 and 2011

Region and Year	Number of adults and children living with HIV	Adults and children newly infected with HIV
Sub-Saharan Africa		
2011	23.5 million	1.8 million
2001	20.9 million	2.4 million
Middle East and North Africa		
2011	300 000	37 000
2001	210 000	27 000
South and South East Asia		
2011	4.0 million	280 000
2001	3.7 million	370 000
East Asia		
2011	830 000	89 000
2001	390 000	75 000
Oceania		
2011	53 000	2 900
2001	38 000	3 700
Latin America		
2011	1.4 million	83 000
2001	1.2 million	93 000
Caribbean		
2011	230 000	13 000
2001	240 000	22 000
Eastern Europe and Central Asia		
2011	1.4 million	140 000
2001	970 000	130 000
Western and Central Europe		
2011	900 000	30 000
2001	640 000	29 000
North America		
2011	1.4 million	51 000
2001	1.1 million	50 000
Global		
2011	34.0 million	2.5 million
2001	29.4 million	3.2 million

Note: Estimates represent the midpoint of a range.

Source: UNAIDS. 2012. *Report on the Global AIDS Epidemic 2012*. New York: UN Joint United Nations Programme on HIV/AIDS (UNAIDS), page 14. Reprinted by permission of the United Nations.

people died from AIDS-related causes world-wide, representing a 24 per cent drop from the estimated 2.3 million deaths in 2005 (UNAIDS, 2012: 11). This decline is driven by the fall in AIDS-related mortality in the most heavily hit regions—most especially sub-Saharan Africa and the Caribbean. According to UNAIDS (2012: 11–13), some of the hardest hit countries have seen a 50 per cent reduction in deaths between 2005 and 2011 (Botswana, Burundi, Côte d'Ivoire, Dominican Republic, Ethiopia, Guyana, Kenya, Namibia, Rwanda, Suriname, Zambia, and Zimbabwe).

What lies behind this welcome trend are a number of interrelated developments. Most important is the increased availability of *antiretroviral therapy* for those that are living with HIV. And this encompasses significant reductions in mother-to-infant transmission of HIV at birth and during breastfeeding. As well, there have been large-scale behavioural changes that have helped to reduce the spread of HIV (e.g., safe-sex practices and use of condoms). Of course, the fight against HIV is far from over. Medical experts are still trying to find a definitive cure.

Medical scientists Anthony Fauci and David Morens (2012) write that great pandemics and local epidemics of infectious diseases have influenced the course of wars, determined the fates of nations and empires, and affected the progress of civilization—making infections compelling actors in the drama of human history. They identify three types of infectious diseases: (1) *established infectious diseases;* (2) *newly emerging infectious diseases;* and (3) *re-emerging infectious diseases.* Below are ten unique features that make infectious diseases different from other types of diseases:

1. potential for unpredictable and explosive global impact;

2. frequent acquisition by host of durable immunity against re-infection after recovery;

3. reliance of disease on single agent without requirement for multiple cofactors;

4. transmissibility;

5. potential for becoming preventable;

6. potential for eradication;

7. evolutionary advantage over human host because of replicative and mutational capacities of pathogens that render them highly adaptable;

8. close dependence on the nature and complexity of human behaviour;

9. frequent derivation from or co-evolution in other animal species; and

10. possibility of treatment for having multiplying effects on preventing infection in contacts and the community and on microbial and animal ecosystems.

Source: Fauci and Morens (2012).

The Growing Burden of Non-communicable Diseases

The 2010 *Global Burden of Disease Study* by Rafael Lozano and colleagues (2012) shows that worldwide in 2010 there were 52.8 million deaths. At the most aggregate level, *communicable diseases*, maternal, neonatal, and nutritional causes accounted for nearly 25 per cent of the total. Regional variations in leading causes of death were substantial. These disease categories, for instance, accounted for 76 per cent of premature mortality in sub-Saharan Africa alone. The authors of the report also indicated that demographic shifts, along with changing incidence of cause-specific mortality rates by age and sex combined to drive a broad shift from communicable, maternal, neonatal, and nutritional causes towards *non-communicable diseases*. Indeed, the two leading causes of death in 2010 worldwide were of this type: ischemic heart disease and stroke. This shifting epidemiological pattern towards an increasing prevalence of non-communicable diseases is noticeable across all the regions in varying degrees, including those in the low- and middle-income categories.

Within this broad configuration of epidemiological change, some of the world's poorest countries, while fighting rising epidemics of infectious diseases such as HIV, malaria, and tuberculosis, are also facing increasing levels of non-infectious illnesses, such as heart disease, diabetes, and cancer, creating a sort of double-punch (Ebrahim and Smeeth, 2005; Stuckler, 2008). On a national scale, rising levels of chronic disease combined with high levels of communicable illnesses can mean huge economic setbacks (Sachs, Mellinger, and Gallup, 2001; Stuckler, 2008) while overstressing health care systems of countries that cannot cope with the rising burden of disease.

Why are rates of chronic disease growing in the developing countries? On a broad level, this is what would be expected based on the postulates of the epidemiologic and health transition theories. But there are many interrelated causes, ranging from demographic aging to the failure of governments to promote appropriate economic and social policies and make health care more available to their rapidly growing populations. Also, with increasing globalization, the traditional diets of the developing countries, like other aspects of life, have been changing. People are now consuming more energy-dense foods high in sugar, saturated fats, and salt, as well as more processed foods. Compounding the problem are falling rates of physical activity (World Health Organization, 2005b) and growing rates of tobacco use. Without vigorous education and public health campaigns aimed at discouraging unhealthy practices, the increase in chronic disease is likely to continue (Ezzati and Riboli, 2012).

Canadian Mortality: Trends, Patterns, and Differentials

Mortality Trends before 1921

Most of the mortality statistics for Canada are available dating back to 1921, when the Canadian vital statistics registration system came into effect. Estimates for earlier periods are available but are typically based on regional data. Francois Pelletier and colleagues (1997), for instance, prepared an estimate of Quebec mortality in the early nineteenth century, calculating a crude death rate of 26.43 per 1000 population for the year 1810. Surinder Wadhera and Jill Strachan (1994) estimated early mortality statistics for Canada as a whole. Their estimated crude death rate for the mid-1800s was in the range of 22 per 1000 population, declining slightly to 21 for the decade 1861–71. From this point until close to the time of vital registration, the crude death rate dropped steadily to around 12 per 1000 in 1921. In a comparative sense, the level of mortality in Canada during this time is thought to have been lower than that of the United States (McInnis, 2000b).

In general, mortality during the nineteenth century was higher in the towns and cities than in rural areas. It would not be until after the late 1800s—and especially after the start of the twentieth century, as cities adopted sanitation systems and better ways of treating the water supply—that urban and rural death rates would begin to converge (Pelletier, Legaré, and Bourbeau, 1997). Concerning infant mortality, Pelletier and colleagues (1997) estimated that in Quebec in 1851–2 the rate ranged between 93 infant deaths per 1000 live births for the province as a whole to 197 in Quebec City and 232 in Montreal.

Prior to the start of the twentieth century, tuberculosis was the leading killer in Canada. In 1880–1, when the population of Canada was just over 4 million, some 6695 people perished from this disease (McVey and Kalbach, 1995: 204). Marvin McInnis (2000b: 570) has estimated that the death rate from tuberculosis was likely around 180 per 100 000 at that time.

Mortality Trends since 1921

With vital registration data from 1921 on, we are in a more secure position to outline the broad contours of Canadian mortality over the last eight decades.

In 1921, Canada's crude death rate of 11.9 per 1000 population was already low by global standards, and well below the current rates of many of today's developing countries. Then, as Table 7.4 shows, large declines in mortality took place until midway through the twentieth century, with the age-standardized death rate dropping from 12.9 per 1000 in 1921 to 9.0 in 1951. Since then, the decline in overall mortality has been steady, with notable improvements during the 1960s and 1970s, though on the whole less dramatic than the declines of earlier periods.

Early in the twentieth century, infectious and parasitic diseases—especially influenza and pneumonia—were the dominant killers (see Table 7.5), although diabetes (a chronic disease) and violence also accounted for a significant share of deaths. Over time, particularly since the early 1950s, influenza and pneumonia have receded and have become relatively minor forces in Canadian mortality trends. The leading causes of death today are not infectious and parasitic diseases but chronic degenerative ailments, especially heart and other vascular diseases, and cancer. About 60 per cent of all deaths annually are attributable to cardiovascular diseases and cancer combined. Significant reductions in accidental mortalities did not occur until the mid-twentieth century, and even today this category of premature death, which includes automobile fatalities, remains a serious public health problem.

Infant Mortality

Infant mortality in Canada had declined considerably by the second decade of the twentieth century (see Figure 7.11). In 1926, just over 100 of every 1000 babies born

TABLE 7.4   Total number of deaths, crude death rates, and standardized death rates (per 1 000 population), Canada, 1921–2011

|||||||||||||||||||||||||||||||||||||||||||||||||||||||||||||||||||||||||||||||||||||||||||||||||||||||||||||||||||||||||

Period	Deaths	Male death rate**	Female death rate**	Total crude death rate	Male standard-ized death rate***	Female standard-ized death rate***	Total standard-ized death rate***	% change standardized death rate from previous period
1921	104 531*	11.9	11.2	11.6	13.3	12.4	12.9	—
1931	108 446	10.5	9.6	10.2	12.7	11.7	12.8	–0.8
1941	118 797	10.9	9.1	10.1	12.0	10.2	11.2	–12.5
1951	125 823	10.1	7.8	9.0	10.0	8.0	9.0	–19.6
1961	140 985	9.0	6.5	7.7	9.0	6.3	7.6	–15.6
1971	157 272	8.5	6.1	7.3	8.4	5.2	6.7	–11.8
1981	171 029	8.0	6.0	7.0	7.2	4.3	5.8	–13.4
1991	195 568	7.8	6.5	7.2	6.8	4.1	5.4	–6.9
2001	219 114	7.3	6.8	7.0	6.6	4.0	5.1	–5.6
2011	247 608	7.2	6.9	7.1	6.2	3.9	5.0	-2.0

Note: Rates standardized to Canada's 1956 population. Standardized rates shown for 2011 are estimates.
*Excludes the Yukon and Northwest Territories.
**Excludes Newfoundland prior to 1949 and the Yukon and Northwest Territories prior to 1928.
***Excludes Quebec prior to 1926, Newfoundland prior to 1949, and the Yukon and Northwest Territories prior to 1950.

Sources: Adapted from McVey and Kalbach (1995): 188; Statistics Canada (2013k); Statistics Canada Health Statistics Division (1999); Trovato (1994): 22–64; World Health Organization (2006a).

TABLE 7.5   Distribution of selected causes of death, Canada, 1921 and 2000

|||||||||||||||||||||||||||||||||||||||||||||||||||||||||||||||||||||||||||||||||||||||||||||||||||||||||||||||||||||||||

Causes of death	1921		2000	
	Number	%	Number	%
Infectious and parasitic diseases	9 346	13.8	3 112	1.4
Diseases of the circulatory system	9 142	13.5	76 426	35.0
Diseases of the respiratory system	8 668	12.8	17 744	8.1
Diseases of the digestive system	6 840	10.1	8 148	3.7
Perinatal diseases	6 230	9.0	898	0.4
Malignant neoplasms	5 011	7.4	62 672	28.7
External causes of death	4 199	6.2	8 758	4.0
Subtotal	49 436	72.8	177 758	81.3
All causes of death	67 722	100.0	218 061	100.0

Note: Data for 1921 excludes Newfoundland.

Sources: McVey and Kalbach (1995): 206; World Health Organization Mortality Data Base, www3.who.int/whosis/mort/table1.cfm?path=whosis,mort,mort_table1&language=english (accessed 28 June 2006).

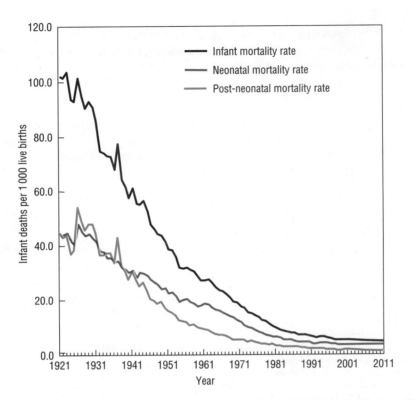

FIGURE 7.11 Infant, neonatal, and post-neonatal mortality rates in Canada, 1921–2011

Source: Wadhera and Strachan (1993): 22–3; Statistics Canada Health Statistics Division (1999); Statistics Canada Health Statistics Division, *Deaths* (various years). Statistics Canada, *Mortality: Overview 2010 and 2011, Component of the Report on the Demographic Situation in Canada, 2013*. Reproduced and distributed on an "as is" basis with the permission of Statistics Canada.

in Canada would perish before reaching their first birthday. By midway through the century, this rate had dropped to 38.5, falling even further to 17.6 by 1971. By the beginning of the 1980s, infant mortality had decreased to below 10 per 1000 live births, and in 2012, the rate stood at 5.1 per 1000 (Population Reference Bureau, 2012). Another way to illustrate the dramatic decline of infant mortality is to compare the actual number of infant deaths earlier in the century with the figure today. In 1921, there were 27 051 infant deaths. By 1951, this number had been cut by almost half, to 14 673. In 2009, the number of infant deaths was just 1872 (Statistics Canada, 2013l).

In the past, tuberculosis (TB) and influenza headed a list of infectious diseases that figured prominently in infant and early childhood mortality. Measles, mumps, chicken pox, whooping cough, and scarlet fever, though not quite as deadly as TB and influenza, all contributed to high rates of death among infants and children (King, Gartrell, and Trovato, 1994). Mothers were also at high risk of dying from infectious diseases. But by the middle of the century, there had been significant improvements in the areas of obstetric medicine and pre- and postnatal care of infants. After 1930, new and effective medical therapies, most notably blood transfusion and antibiotics, greatly improved the survival chances of infants and mothers (Berry, 1977; Mitchinson, 2002). Early-age mortality from communicable diseases dropped considerably after the third decade of the twentieth century, when water chlorination and pasteurization of milk were added to the list of important public health developments (Beaver, 1975). Infectious diseases today are responsible for less than 1 per cent of infant deaths.

The pattern of change in neonatal and post-neonatal mortality rates over the twentieth century parallels the pattern noted for infant mortality in general. Early in the century, neonatal and post-neonatal rates fluctuated very closely together, from approximately 43 deaths per 1000 live births in 1921 to close to 58 per 1 000 in the mid-1920s. From that point, both rates have followed a generalized pattern of decline. The two rates began to diverge in the early 1940s, and since then neonatal death rates have been consistently higher than post-neonatal rates, which have for the most part fallen faster. By 2000, the neonatal and post-neonatal death rates had fallen to 3.64 and 1.7 per 1000 live births, respectively. Thus, the significant reductions in early-life mortality in Canada have been accompanied by a gradual shift in the preponderance of deaths from the post-neonatal to the neonatal phase. While approximately 27 per cent of all infant deaths in 1921 were neonatal, this proportion has risen to about 70 per cent in recent years.

By far, the most prevalent causes of premature death among infants today—accounting for nearly three-quarters of all infant deaths in Canada—are *congenital anomalies* and complications originating in the perinatal period, including low birth weight. Early in the twentieth century, such problems also represented important causes of infant mortality, though proportionately less as compared to today.

Further reductions in perinatal, neonatal, and post-neonatal mortality are possible through a combination of medical and behavioural interventions. Ongoing research is aimed towards perfecting therapies and surgical techniques to help reduce mortality at both the perinatal and neonatal stages. Growing attention is also being given to the prenatal environment as a risk factor in perinatal and neonatal mortality risk (Barker, 1998; Priest and Harding, 2006). Increased education and public health knowledge can help expectant mothers avoid certain risks that compromise the well-being of the fetus, most importantly smoking, alcohol, substance abuse, and excessive distress during pregnancy.

Childhood Mortality

Children Aged 1–4

By today's standards, the probability of death for a child between the ages of 1 and 4 at the start of the twentieth century was exceptionally high—79 per cent for boys and 76 per cent for girls (Bourbeau, Légaré, and Émond, 1997). By 1921, these conditional death probabilities had declined to 39 and 36 per cent, respectively. By the end of the century, the chance of death for children aged one to four was approaching zero, with estimated rates of 1.26 per cent for boys and 0.95 per cent for girls in 1996 (Bourbeau, Légaré, and Émond, 1997). The largest improvements in death probabilities for boys and girls took place around the halfway mark of the century, when mortality from infectious diseases like influenza, bronchitis, pneumonia, tuberculosis, diarrhea, diphtheria, whooping cough, and meningitis receded significantly (King, Gartrell, and Trovato, 1994).

Children Aged 5–14

Large-scale mortality improvements since the 1930s have also been recorded for Canadian children between the ages of 5 and 14. From 1931 to 1951, the death rate for boys dropped from 185 to 89 per 100 000, while the death rate for girls declined from 162 to 59 per 100 000. Reductions since 1951, though modest by comparison with those of the earlier two decades, continue to be significant. Success in reducing child death rates can be attributed largely to the implementation of effective vaccines and other medical interventions that have helped to cut down children's exposure to infections.

Young Adulthood through Old Age

Young Adults Aged 15–24

Young people between the ages of 15 and 24 are particularly prone to accidental or violent death. This is especially so for men, whose rates of accidental or violent death have been approximately three to five times greater than those of women since the 1930s. This differential has not changed by much over time. As Table 7.5 shows, the leading cause of death among 15- to 24-year-olds in 1931 was TB, which killed more women than men earlier in the century. By mid-century, motor vehicle accidents had surpassed TB as the leading cause of death among men in this aged group. Overall, the dramatic improvement in young adult mortality can be attributed in large part to the dramatic decline of TB.

An encouraging trend is the reduction in motor vehicle fatalities among young adults, especially since the early 1970s. Among the factors involved in this trend are laws making the use of seat belts mandatory, stiffer penalties for impaired driving, better and safer vehicle construction, and, perhaps, a greater awareness overall of road safety fostered through public health campaigns. Unfortunately, motor vehicle accidents, along with violence and suicide, continue to claim a disproportionate number of young lives. Meanwhile, cancer and cardiovascular disease remain rare among young adults, and death rates associated with these causes have been declining.

Adults Aged 25–44

In 1931, the overall death rate for men between the ages of 25 and 44 was 410 per 100 000; the rate for women was 440 per 100 000. By the end of the century, these rates had dropped to 126 and 68 for men and women, respectively (see Table 7.6). The higher overall rate for women in 1931 was the result of a combination of conditions, including higher rates of TB, cancer, cardiovascular disease, and nephritis, and complications associated with childbirth. But as conditions improved for women midway through the century, death rates for men surpassed those for women in every major cause category except cancer. At the same time, some of the most lethal diseases of earlier periods—TB, appendicitis, ulcers of the stomach and duodenum, and intestinal obstruction—began to recede to the point where they no longer constituted major risks.

For both men and women in this age category, death from cardiovascular disease rose until the early 1970s and has been declining ever since, following a pattern that has been observed in other industrialized countries. Most scholars agree that reductions in cigarette smoking, the introduction of new treatments to control hypertension, increased consciousness of the importance of diet in health maintenance, and the control of cholesterol levels through

TABLE 7.6   Death rates (per 100 000 population) for Canadian men and women by broad age category, cause of death, and period, 1931–2000

Age and cause of death	Males						Females					
	1931	1951	1971	1981	1991	2000	1931	1951	1971	1981	1991	2000
Age 1–4												
Diarrhea/enteritis	92	41	1	0	0	0	70	9	1	0	0	0
Accidents/violence	81	48	41	28	13	7	50	61	28	19	7	4
Influenza/bronchitis/pneumonia	59	98	8	2	0	0	160	40	10	2	0	0
Tuberculosis	51	31	0	0	0	0	45	14	0	0	0	0
Diphtheria	36	11	0	0	0	0	34	1	0	0	0	0
Whooping cough	21	16	0	0	0	0	32	3	0	0	0	0
Total	**679**	**399**	**91**	**59**	**39**	**23**	**612**	**205**	**78**	**46**	**28**	**18**
Age 5–14												
Accidents/violence	46	45	34	24	11	7	15	16	17	12	5	4
Tuberculosis	23	6	0	0	0	0	28	8	0	0	0	0
Appendicitis	17	2	2	0	0	0	16	2	2	0	0	0
Influenza/bronchitis/pneumonia	14	5	0	0	0	0	16	5	0	0	0	0
Diphtheria	11	1	1	0	0	0	12	1	0	1	0	0
Total	**185**	**89**	**53**	**37**	**23.2**	**16**	**162**	**59**	**35**	**24**	**17**	**12**
Age 15–24												
Tuberculosis	71	18	0	0	0	0	118	24	0	0	0	0
Motor vehicle accidents (MVAs)	22	37	73	66	38	22	5	10	23	18	12	9
Other accidents/violence	67	41	40	35	19	14	9	5	9	8	4	4
Influenza/bronchitis/pneumonia	19	5	2	1	0	0	13	4	2	1	0	0
Cardiovascular	14	8	4	3	3	2	16	7	3	2	2	2
Cancers	7	10	9	6	6	6	5	6	6	4	2	4
Suicide	6	6	18	28	29	21	4	2	4	5	4	5
Total	**284**	**161**	**158**	**150**	**110**	**78**	**269**	**92**	**57**	**46**	**37**	**34**

(continued)

TABLE 7.6   (continued)

Age and cause of death	Males						Females					
	1931	1951	1971	1981	1991	2000	1931	1951	1971	1981	1991	2000
Age 25–44												
Tuberculosis	86	28	1	0	0	0	110	26	1	0	0	0
Motor vehicle accidents (MVAs)	27	41	39	39	19	21	5	6	12	10	7	4
Other accidents/violence	54	120	59	24	11	19	7	20	10	7	5	5
Cardiovascular	43	59	46	32	20	16	48	34	18	12	8	7
Influenza/bronchitis/pneumonia	31	6	4	1	2	1	26	5	3	1	1	1
Cancers	25	25	29	23	21	19	53	45	37	28	29	26
Suicide	19	12	24	26	28	25	7	4	9	9	8	6
Total	**410**	**252**	**218**	**174**	**153**	**126**	**440**	**183**	**118**	**87**	**76**	**68**
Age 45–64												
Cardiovascular	352	687	597	454	272	171	319	376	199	160	98	62
Cancer	202	243	286	309	305	227	267	266	238	250	240	207
Tuberculosis	90	48	6	2	1	0	61	21	3	1	0	0
Influenza/bronchitis/pneumonia	89	35	34	17	17	15	71	25	14	8	10	12
Nephritis/nephrotis	86	30	5	5	4	4	89	27	4	4	4	2
Motor vehicle accidents (MVAs)	39	44	35	32	14	10	12	10	14	11	7	5
Other accidents/violence	58	49	52	37	24	23	13	10	17	13	8	8
Suicide	37	25	32	29	25	22	8	9	14	12	7	8
Total	**1 249**	**1 336**	**1 208**	**1 044**	**804**	**591**	**1 118**	**868**	**599**	**552**	**449**	**364**

TABLE 7.6   (continued)

Age and cause of death	Males						Females					
	1931	1951	1971	1981	1991	2000	1931	1951	1971	1981	1991	2000
Age 65–74												
Cardiovascular	1754	2488	2271	1827	1243	1228	1532	1862	1201	986	599	586
Cancer	763	783	1034	1073	1127	907	698	618	566	610	659	732
Influenza/bronchitis/pneumonia	332	170	193	100	110	153	366	127	60	42	50	93
Nephritis/nephrotis/renal failure	329	105	15	25	28	34	338	97	12	16	19	20
Accidents/violence (–MVAs)	155	141	111	105	33	34	82	56	58	42	25	20
Tuberculosis	107	72	14	5	2	2	85	35	6	2	1	1
Total	**4352**	**4309**	**4174**	**3703**	**3135**	**2603**	**3835**	**3207**	**2215**	**1901**	**1679**	**1505**
Age 75+												
Cardiovascular	5247	7456	7025	5740	4237	3454	5302	7005	5662	4514	3466	2884
Cancer	1186	1446	1880	2074	2247	1279	1016	1137	1088	1084	1190	2044
Influenza/bronchitis/pneumonia	1147	890	836	593	663	863	1136	808	453	326	433	507
Senility	1021	234	40	23	8	6	1205	273	45	27	4	40
Nephritis/nephrotis/renal failure	945	335	50	124	156	170	824	357	38	79	101	114
Accidents/violence (–MVAs)	316	331	259	216	102	104	458	376	217	172	254	268
Hernia/intestinal obstruction	128	74	55	47	37	33	85	57	48	41	40	41
Diabetes	93	101	206	160	197	37	132	140	207	170	180	40
Diarrhea/enteritis	81	74	13	9	0	0	97	31	9	10	2	1
Suicide	35	31	27	32	18	14	5	6	4	12	7	5
Total	**11881**	**12169**	**11446**	**10410**	**9531**	**8567**	**11635**	**11059**	**8329**	**7190**	**6863**	**6617**

Notes: Death rates have been rounded to whole numbers. MVAs = motor vehicle accidents.

Source: Trovato (1994): 22–64; data for 1991 and 2000 from World Health Organization, www3.who.int/whosis/menu.cfm?path=whosis,mort&language=english (accessed 10 April 2006).

medication, as well as better management of lifestyles, all helped reduce vascular disease mortality (Levy, 1981; Martikainen et al., 2005; Rothenberg and Koplan, 1990; Thom, 1989). Declines in cancer mortality have been less impressive, though major improvements in treatment are likely to be reflected in changing rates (Collins and Barker, 2007; Rothenberg and Koplan, 1990). Cancer is the number-one cause of death for women in this age category.

Suicide, despite declining rates since around the mid-1980s, remains a leading cause of premature death for people aged 25–44, especially men. Declines in the suicide rate have not prevented it from replacing motor vehicle accidents as the principal cause of death among 24- to 44-year-old men. The prevalence of suicide among men is not unique to Canada, but is common in other high-income countries as well (Ahlburg and Schapiro, 1984; Pampel, 1996, 1998; Stack, 2000a, 2000b). Fred Pampel has observed that suicide rates for young adult males are highest in societies characterized by a high degree of individualism versus collectivism. Suicide rates are lower in societies where the social system protects those in need (the unemployed, the disadvantaged, etc.). He notes that the situation is worst in individualistically oriented social contexts where young men experience high rates of unemployment and belong to a large birth cohort (which reduces chances for the individual in gaining access to jobs under difficult economic conditions).

Adults Aged 45–64

In 1931, the overall death rate for men aged 45–54 was 1 249 per 100 000, while that for women was 1 118 per 100 000 (see Table 7.6). These rates have plummeted over the course of the century, to 591 and 364, respectively,

as of 2000. Mortality in this age group is now caused mainly by chronic and degenerative diseases, especially cardiovascular ailments and cancers. This pattern of disease contrasts sharply with the trends that characterized the earlier part of the twentieth century, when the major killers were influenza, bronchitis, and pneumonia (and, to a lesser degree, complications such as nephritis and nephrosis). By the late twentieth century, these and other causes (tuberculosis, syphilis, hernias, and stomach ulcers) had declined to insignificance from a population perspective.

Adults Aged 65–74

Large-scale improvements in mortality among older adults between the ages of 65 and 74 have been gained over the twentieth century. In 1931, men and women had death rates of 4 352 and 3 835 per 100 000, respectively. By the midway mark of the century, these rates had declined to 4 309 and 3 207, respectively, and further decreases over subsequent decades brought these rates to 2 603 and 1 505 as of the start of the twenty-first century (see Table 7.6). In the early 1900s, a mix of infectious and chronic diseases (in order, cardiovascular disease, cancer, influenza/bronchitis/pneumonia, nephritis, accidents, and tuberculosis) claimed many lives of seniors in this age category. Today, cardiovascular disease and cancer pose the greatest threats to people in this age category.

Cardiovascular mortality rates have been declining for both sexes since the mid-1900s, but fell faster for women from the 1950s until the 1980s. Thereafter, the decline has been faster for males. At the same time, cancer death rates in this age group have always been higher for men, even though male rates have levelled off and begun to decline in recent decades, while female cancer rates have been rising slightly since the 1970s.

Adults Aged 75 and Older

Mortality rates for Canadians aged 75 and older have been declining since early in the twentieth century. Between 1931 and the early 1980s, the overall death rate for women in this age group fell by 37 per cent, from 11 635 per 100 000 to 7190. Over the same period, the male mortality rate dropped from 11 881 to 10 410 per 100 000, for a 14 per cent decline. These trends repeat the pattern, evident in other age groups, of more precipitous declines in the death rate for women. It is worth noting, however, that between 1991 and 2000, the male death rate dropped by 10 per cent, while female mortality declined by just 3.5 per cent, indicating somewhat larger mortality improvements by men recently.

As with adults aged 65–74, cardiovascular disease and cancer are the leading causes of death in this age group. Nonetheless, it is interesting to note the declines in cardiovascular mortality for both men and women. In 1931, the cardiovascular mortality rates for men and women aged 75 and over were 5 247 and 5 302, respectively. These rates peaked in the early 1950s and have been following a downward trend ever since, to 5 749 and 4 514, respectively, in the early 1980s and 3 454 and 2 884 by 2000. The same declines have not been matched by cancer rates for this age group.

Mortality from influenza, bronchitis, pneumonia, senility, and nephritis (including renal failure), which were leading killers earlier in the century, have declined significantly over time for adults 75 years of age and over. Likewise, hernia and intestinal obstructions, diarrhea, and enteritis are now minor causes of death. However, diabetes has risen in importance. Suicide for elderly Canadian men and women has followed two trends: a decline between the early 1930s and the early part of the 1970s, and a rise thereafter until the mid-1980s, from which point the trend has been downward. Accidental and violent deaths have declined over time.

Inequalities in Health and Mortality

The Sex Differential in Mortality

The female advantage in mortality and life expectancy is one of the most entrenched differentials in human populations (Luy, 2003; Madigan, 1957; Stolnitz, 1955; Vallin, 1983). At the international level, only a few exceptions to this have been noted (Das Gupta and Shuzhuo, 2000; D'Souza and Chen, 1980; El-Badry, 1969; Mishra, Roy, and Retherford, 2004; Nadarajah, 1983).

Preston (1976) found that the sex differential in mortality tended to favour men until the period of large-scale modernization in the late nineteenth century, when the balance swung in favour of women and then began to widen over most of the twentieth century. Indeed, historical evidence for Western Europe confirms that during the late 1800s, at a time when life expectancy was much below what it is today, women's life expectancy exceeded men's by about 2 or 3 years (Acsádi and Nemeskéri, 1970; Preston, 1976). This female advantage could have been greater had it not been for high rates of maternal mortality (Henry, 1989). With gradual improvements in socioeconomic conditions and public health during the nineteenth and twentieth centuries, the rate of pregnancy-related deaths decreased, helping women to gain considerable numbers of years of life expectancy. George Stolnitz (1955) established that the sex differential in mortality started to widen after about the 1920s, and that by the 1940s, women outlived men by about 4 years on average. By the 1950s, the sex gap in the industrialized countries had grown to approximately 5 or 6 years, reaching 7 or 8 years by the 1970s (Lopez, 1983; Vallin, 1983).

The general trend in men's and women's mortality is illustrated in Figures 7.12a and 7.12b, which focus on the experience of Canada and Austria. In both countries, the difference between men's and women's longevity ranged between 3 and 4 years early in the twentieth century. The sharp drop and recovery of the differential during the early 1920s in Canada may reflect problems with

the estimated life expectancy figures, or possibly some event that produced a temporary narrowing of the sex gap in life expectancy at birth. One possible explanation is the influenza pandemic of 1918–19. During the pandemic, female mortality in the young adult ages exceeded male mortality in the United States, and women lost a portion of their mortality advantage over men for a temporary period (Noymer and Garenne, 2000; Smith, 1993: 83). Since the US, like Canada, saw a sharp drop in women's mortality advantage in the early 1920s, it is reasonable to speculate that the pandemic had similar effects on mortality differences in both countries, and that this may explain the temporary drop in the sex differential in men's and women's life expectancy in Canada during the early 1920s.

By the middle of the twentieth century, the Canadian gender gap in life expectancy had risen to about 4.5 years, and to just over 5 years in Austria. Around the same time,

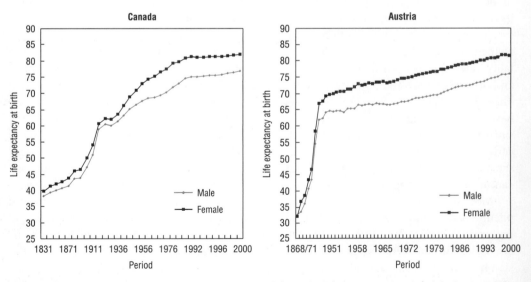

FIGURE 7.12a   Historical trend in male and female life expectancy at birth, Canada and Austria

Sources: Adapted from Bélanger (2003: 17); Nagnur (1986a); Péron and Strohmenger (1985): 115; Statistik Austria (2005:79).

the differential stood at almost 6 years in the United States and ranged between 2 and 7 years across the other industrialized countries (Lopez, 1983; Peron and Strohmenger, 1985: 121; Smith, 1993: 83). The difference reached nearly 7 years in both Canada and Austria during the early part of the 1970s. By the year 2000, gender gaps in life expectancy for the two countries were virtually identical to those recorded in the mid-1950s, around 5.5 years. This pattern of gender difference in average longevity is not unique to Canada and Austria: it has been observed across a large number of industrialized countries also. A significant exception is Japan, where the difference, in favour of women, has continued to grow (Pampel, 2002; Trovato and Heyen, 2006; Trovato and Lalu, 1996; Waldron, 1993).

In spite of the recent narrowing of the mortality differential many experts believe the gap will never close completely. This raises two important questions: why should

we expect an indefinite mortality advantage for women, and why did the differential narrow at all after increasing in favour of women over much of the twentieth century? Biological and genetic differences between the sexes help us to answer the first question; the rest of the puzzle may be explained in terms of differences in acquired risks due to behavioural differences.

Males' greater vulnerability to death begins very early in life—from the moment of conception. Sebastian Kramer (2000: 1609), after a careful review of the literature, arrived at the conclusion that males are, on most relevant measures, inherently more vulnerable owing to "the biological fragility of the male fetus." In other words, maleness seems to have some intrinsic risks that are genetic/biological in origin (Madigan, 1957; Perls and Fretts, 2002; Verbrugge, 1976, 1989; Waldron, 1976). Studies conducted on primates and humans reinforce the possibility of a hormonal basis for the higher

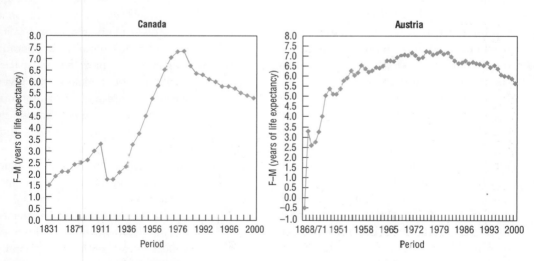

FIGURE 7.12b   Historical trend in the female–male difference in life expectancy at birth, Canada and Austria

Source: Adapted from Bélanger (2003 17); Nagnur (1986a); Péron and Strohmenger (1985): 115; Statistik Austria (2005: 79).

mortality of males. Among other things, it is believed that low *immunocompetence*—an organism's all around ability to avoid the harmful effects of parasites—in male mammals is due to the effect of testosterone, which is an immunosuppressant (Owen, 2002). The resulting differences in immunocompetence may underlie male-biased mortality from parasitic infections as well as from some other conditions. Exactly how testosterone is linked to immunosuppression is not yet fully known, but one theory is that testosterone alters the way in which males allocate resources among competing physiological needs. Males may be unable to mount an effective immune response because they face a trade-off between allocating resources to fending off disease and allocating resources to other metabolic activities (Owen, 2002). Women's stronger immune system gives them an advantage in longevity over males (Pido-Lopez, Imami, and Aspinall, 2001).

Men have higher death rates than women do from vascular diseases, especially coronary heart disease. As this is a leading cause of death, this sex differential would account for a significant portion of the overall male disadvantage in mortality risk (Rogers, Hummer, and Nam, 2000). In both men and women, the mortality rate from coronary heart disease increases exponentially with age, starting at about age 35, but the rise in the age-related rate for women lags behind that for men by 5 to 10 years (Smith, 1993: 89). It is worth noting that this lagged pattern, which contributes significantly to the gender gap in overall mortality, is generally not evident in the case of cancer, where the rise in death rates for men and women begins more or less at the same time at around the age of 35.

The female relative advantage in vascular disease has been ascribed to the protective effects prior to menopause of the female hormone estrogen, which plays a role in the modulation of cholesterol (Smith, 1993). The incidence of cardiovascular disease in women rises sharply after the menopausal transition, when female hormones, most notably estrogen, decline. It has also been observed that with menopause the levels of HDL cholesterol drop while LDL cholesterol increases, creating a situation that is conducive to an increased risk of vascular disease. Hormone replacement therapy appears to lower women's risk of this disease, suggesting that estrogen plays an important protective role in women (Mendelsohn and Karas, 2005).

A theory advanced by Thomas Kirkwood (2010b) regarding females' longevity advantage relies on evolutionary biological principles. Females' advantage may result because they are less disposable than men in an evolutionary sense. This notion makes biological sense according to Kirkwood because in humans, as in most animal species, the state of the female body is very important for the success of reproduction. Therefore, nature may protect the female body more than the male body. If the female animal's body is too much weakened by the accumulated damage that comes from the organisms' repair and maintenance processes throughout life, there is a real threat to her chances of making healthy offspring. The man's reproductive role, on the other hand, is less directly dependent on his continued good health.

In addition to these possible biological differences, the sex differential in health and longevity is largely mainly attributable to differences in modifiable risk factors associated with lifestyle and behaviour (Case and Paxson 2005; DesMeules et al., 2004; Kramer, 2000; Rogers et al., 2010; Veevers and Gee, 1986; Verbrugge, 1976; Waldron, 1976, 2000). Roughly 75 per cent of the mortality discrepancy between men and women during adulthood can be accounted for by differences between the sexes in death from lung cancer, cirrhosis of the liver, suicide, homicide, motor vehicle accidents, heart disease, and stroke—all of which have strong behavioural components (such as stress, safety, diet, and substance abuse). In the United States, Ingrid Waldron (1986) calculated that male mortality from coronary heart disease exceeded female mortality by a ratio of 2 to 1; for lung cancer the ratio was 6 to 1. Male mortality from emphysema

was five times greater than women's mortality, and men were three times as likely as women to die from motor vehicle accidents and suicides. As Table 7.7 shows, the calculated cause-specific death rate ratios for Canada and the United States tend to be above 1.0 (signifying higher male mortality).

In both Canada and the United States, the ratio of male-to-female death rate from suicide and homicide and motor vehicle accidents is most pronounced among 15- to 24-year-olds, and then for those aged 25 to 34. Expert opinion is unified in support of the proposition that, in general, the greater tendency for men to die from such causes arises largely from sociocultural conditioning, which induces greater risk-taking and aggressiveness in men (Kramer, 2000; Veevers and Gee, 1986; Verbrugge, 1976; Waldron, 1976, 2000). One of the factors underlying the propensity for young men to die from violence and accidents is a

TABLE 7.7   **Male and female crude death rates for selected causes of death and corresponding male-to-female ratios of death rates, Canada and the United States, 2000**

||||||||||||||||||| ||||||||||||||||||||||||||||||||||||||||||||||||||||||||||||||||||||||||||||||||||||||||||||||||||||||||

| Cause of death | Canada | | | United States | | |
	Male	Female	Male/Female	Male	Female	Male/Female
Infectious/parasitic	11.3	8.9	1.30	23.0	19.0	1.21
Malignant neoplasms	218.8	188.6	1.16	207.2	186.2	1.11
Lung cancer	63.3	41.7	1.52	65.5	45.4	1.44
Acute myocardial infarction	74.2	55.6	1.33	72.7	64.6	1.13
Other ischemic heart disease	79.0	67.1	1.18	116.1	113.0	1.03
Bronchitis/emphysema/asthma	35.8	27.1	1.32	43.3	42.8	1.01
Liver disease and cirrhosis	10.1	5.0	2.02	13.8	7.4	1.86
Motor vehicle fatalities	11.0	5.2	2.12	20.6	9.5	2.17
Suicide	18.4	5.2	3.54	17.1	4.0	4.28
Homicide	2.2	0.8	2.75	9.2	2.7	3.41

Source: Author's computations based on data from the World Health Organization (2006).

phenomenon that Harold Hannerz (2001: 189) has termed the "manhood trials"— dangerous rites of passage, common in most societies in various forms among boys passing into adulthood, that carry "an added mortality risk."

Returning to the question of why the longevity gap between men and women has been narrowing recently, we can look for the answer in behavioural changes between the sexes and how these changes have affected the survival probabilities of men and women. The recent literature in this area has focused on the changing role of women in industrialized societies and how it is linked to the narrowing sex difference in mortality. Other studies have examined changing patterns of smoking in men and women and their long-term effects on male and female death rates.

Constance Nathanson (1995) has hypothesized that in countries with relatively high levels of gender equality there are high levels of smoking prevalence among women, which would result in slower gains in life expectancy for women at age 40. Nathanson's cross-national analysis revealed that increased female labour-force participation is inversely associated with change in female life expectancy at age 40, and that in countries where female smoking prevalence in 1970 was relatively high, women's life expectancy gains between 1970 and 1988 were slower than in those countries characterized by low smoking prevalence. Japan, for example, with very low female smoking rates, showed the largest increases in female life expectancy between 1970 and 1988; by contrast, Denmark, with the highest smoking prevalence, had the slowest gain in female life expectancy during this period. Nathanson's results suggest that change in some aspects of the behaviour of women (in this case, increased rates of smoking) may

have adversely affected their longevity gains over recent decades.

Pampel (2002, 2003) took a different perspective on women's changing attitudes towards smoking, attributing it instead to a diffusion phenomenon. Women who increasingly over the latter part of the twentieth century took up smoking were essentially following the pattern of smoking established earlier in the century by men, forming a trend whose effects would be felt decades later, in the form of diminishing longevity gains (Lopez, Caselli, and Valkonen, 1995). Women's smoking began to rise significantly in the 1960s, at a time when men were abandoning the habit in response to intensive public health campaigns warning of the health dangers of tobacco. Owing to the differential timing of smoking initiation and cessation in men and women, the trends in lung cancer mortality (and other smoking-related diseases) for men and women have diverged. While lung cancer mortality in men peaked and levelled off in the early 1980s and has shown a downward trend recently, the corresponding rates for women rose rapidly, and only recently has there been a levelling of this trend. This differential pattern of change has contributed significantly to the recent narrowing of the sex gap in mortality and life expectancy.

As Figure 7.13 shows, the most important contributors to the narrowing of the sex difference in life expectancy in Canada have been faster declines for men in rates of death from heart disease, lung cancer, and other cancers, all of which are strongly connected to cigarette smoking. As well, men's death rates with respect accidents and violence (excluding suicide) have been falling faster in recent years, and this is another important contributor to the declining sex difference in life expectancy.

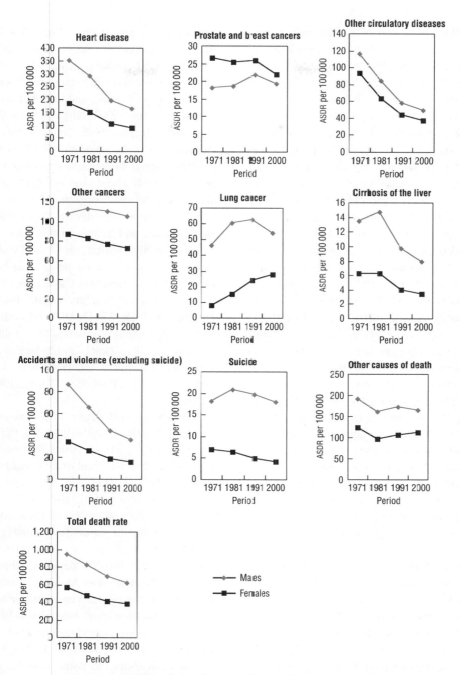

FIGURE 7.13   Age standardized death rates (ASDRS) (per 100 000 population) in Canada by sex, cause of death, and total death rate, 1971–2000

Note: The standard population is the European standard million (World Health Organization, 1998).

Source: Trovato and Lalu (2007): 112–13. Reprinted by permission of the publisher. "From Divergence to Convergence: The Sex Differential in Life Expectancy in Canada, 1971–2000" by Frank Trovato and Nirannanilathu Lalu. *Canadian Review of Sociology and Anthropology* 44, 1. Copyright © 2008, John Wiley and Sons.

Dana Glei and Shiro Horiuchi (2007) have identified another significant cause of the narrowing sex differential in life expectancy. For populations in the most advanced stage of epidemiological transition, life table survival probabilities have become increasingly rectangular over time. The degree of rectangularization has been noticeably greater for females, which means that an increasing proportion of female deaths are concentrated in the older ages. For men, the degree of rectangularization is less, and therefore deaths are more dispersed across age categories. This also implies that men have greater room for further improvements in survival probabilities as compared to women. Thus, as Glei and Horiuchi point out, this varying distribution of deaths in male and female life tables is responsible for some of the decline in sex differences in life expectancy at birth because under this circumstance the same rate of mortality decline would produce a smaller life expectancy gain for women than for men. This in turn translates into larger life expectancy gains for men than for women, serving to reduce the female–male difference in life expectancy.

The Aboriginal Disadvantage in Health and Survival

Aboriginal minorities in Canada and other parts of the world have a long history of socioeconomic disadvantage, social isolation, and relatively poor health (Hayward and Heron, 1999; Kunitz, 1990, 2000; Leonard and Crawford, 2002; Pool, 1991, 1994; Ross and Taylor, 2002; Sandefur, Rindfuss, and Cohen, 1996; Taylor, Bampton, and Lopez, 2005). Many of Canada's Aboriginal people experience socioeconomic and epidemiological conditions that can only be described as deplorable (Anderssen, 1998; Pfeiff, 2003). In many communities, especially those that are more remote, housing is generally substandard, and basic services such as fresh water, proper sewage disposal, and essential health care are unavailable (Royal Commission on Aboriginal Peoples, 1995; Young, 1994). In combination, poverty and isolation have fostered pernicious social pathologies that have been exacerbated over time by high rates of alcoholism and substance abuse (Whitehead and Hayes, 1998). The devastating effects of alcohol abuse and its role in the high incidence of family violence, crime, and violent deaths among Aboriginal people has been extensively documented in Canada and other parts of the world (Bachman, 1992; Broudy and May, 1983; De Wit, De Wit, and Embree, 2000; Gray, 1990; Hayward and Heron, 1999; Hisnanick, 1994; Hogg, 1992; Jarvis and Boldt, 1982; Kunitz, 1983, 1990, 1994; Levy and Kunitz, 1971; Pool, 1991; Young, 1988a, 1988b).

Although crude death rates have been declining (Health Canada, 1996: 17), the life expectancy of Canada's Aboriginal people is significantly lower than other Canadians, and this is also true for aboriginals in Australia, New Zealand, and the United States. Table 7.8 shows that in these countries the average length of life for Aboriginal people falls well below the respective national populations. The deficit is astonishingly large for Australian Aborigines, whose lives are on average 20 years shorter than those of non-Aboriginal Australians. In the other three nations, the disadvantage in life expectancy ranges between 6 and 7 years.

Canada's Aboriginal populations are currently undergoing the epidemiological transition, though they are lagging substantially with respect to the larger Canadian population. This is especially true for the aboriginals

TABLE 7.8 Life expectancy at birth by sex and corresponding national populations for Registered Indians and Inuit-inhabited areas in Canada, Indigenous People in Australia, Maori population in New Zealand, and American Indian and Alaska Native population of the United States (selected years)

Sex and population	Canada, 1996–2000	Australia, 1997–9	New Zealand, 1995–7	United States, 1996–8
Aboriginals				
Male	68.3	55.6	67.2	67.0
Female	74.5	56.3	71.6	74.0
Larger society				
Male	75	75	73	73
Female	81	81	79	79
Aboriginals–larger society				
Males	−6.7	−19.4	−5.8	−6.0
Females	−6.5	−14.7	−7.4	−5.0
Inuit-inhabited areas of Canada, 2001				
Male	64.4			
Female	69.8			
Difference from larger society				
Males	−10.6			
Females	−11.2			

Sources: Verma, Michalowski, and Gauvin (2004): 197–235; Population Reference Bureau, (1997, 1998); Wilkins et al. (2008): 12.

of the North, who are both socially and geographically isolated. Movement through the epidemiological transitions has brought on a new challenge for the aboriginal population: in addition to the existing problems of poverty and high levels of social pathologies, there is a rising epidemic of chronic and degenerative diseases. As a function of long-term adaptations to Western ways of living, Canadian Aboriginal people have all but lost their traditional ways of life, which once centred on hunting, fishing, and agriculture. They have become a predominantly sedentary population, and partly because of this change they now experience an increased prevalence of chronic and degenerative diseases. The four leading causes of death among Canada's First Nations are injuries and poisonings, followed by circulatory disease, cancer, and respiratory ailments (Health Canada, 2003: 26–7). Rates of heart disease and diabetes among Canada's Native people are increasing faster than in the non-Aboriginal Canadian population (Health Canada, 2003; Narayan, 1997; Ng, 1996; Young, 1997).

Table 7.9 compares health status indicators for Canadian Aboriginal people.

TABLE 7.9   Comparative mortality indicators for Canadian Aboriginal people in relation to other Canadians (Registered Indians; urban Aboriginal people)

(A) Registered Indians (RI) in relation to other Canadians (around 1999)

	RI	Canada	Ratio: RI/Other Canadians
Infant mortality rate (per 1 000 live births)	8.0	5.5	**1.45**
Stillbirth rate (1985–8)	10.6	5.1	**20.8**
Perinatal death rate	14.5	7.9	**1.83**
Cause of death in infancy (%)			
Congenital anomalies	25	28	**0.89**
Conditions originating in the perinatal period	27	45	**0.60**
SIDS	11	9	**1.22**
All other and unknown	37	18	**2.06**
Birth weight			
Low (<2 500 grams)	6.0	5.6	**1.07**
High (≥ 4 000 grams)	22.0	12.2	**1.80**

(B) Urban Aboriginal people (1991–2001)

	Death rate ratio: Aboriginal/Non-Aboriginal	
Cause of death	**Male**	**Female**
All causes	1.56	1.94
Infectious diseases	2.04	5.76
HIV/AIDS	2.03	10.65
Other infectious	2.04	4.84
Cancer	1.09	1.21
Trachea/bronchus/lung	1.42	1.33
Breast cancers	—	0.91
Other cancers	0.95	1.29
Endocrine diseases	1.42	2.61
Circulatory system	1.50	1.93
Ischemic heart disease	1.52	1.73
Other circulatory diseases	1.47	2.15
Respiratory diseases	1.72	1.91
Digestive system diseases	3.00	4.82
External causes	2.80	3.37
Suicide	1.57	2.46
Motor vehicle	3.51	4.13
Other external	3.76	—
Other external (incl. suicide)	—	3.65
Other external (excl. suicide)	—	3.16

TABLE 7.9   (continued)

All other causes	1.47	2.63
Smoking-related diseases	1.46	1.36
Alcohol-related diseases	4.55	11.44
Drug-related diseases	3.71	6.43
Amenable to medical intervention (<75 yrs)	1.80	1.99

Note: — means not applicable.

Sources: Health Canada (2003): various pages; for perinatal and stillbirth rates, Canadian Institute for Child Health (1994):143; Tjepkema et al. (2010): 12; World Health Organization (2006b).

Panel (A) shows comparative statistics on early life mortality and morbidity for the Registered Indians and for the rest of Canada's population. It highlights two areas of particular concern: the greater incidence of sudden infant death syndrome (SIDS) and infant deaths from "other or unknown" causes in the Registered Indian population. While it is impossible to say precisely what is included in the category of "other or unknown" causes, it is reasonable to assume that it includes cases that reflect poor pre- and postnatal care for mothers. There is a higher incidence of high birth weight babies in the Registered Indians population (Luo et al., 2004). Panel (B) looks at cause-specific death rate ratios (i.e., the ratio of Aboriginal death rates to non-Aboriginal death rates). With the exception of two causes (other cancers in men, and breast cancer in women) the ratios exceed a value of 1, which means higher mortality risk for Aboriginal people. Overall, Aboriginal males have a 56 per cent greater risk of death as compared to other Canadian men. For Aboriginal females the excess risk is 94 per cent. Alcohol and drug related deaths as well as accidents and injuries represent the leading causes of premature death in Aboriginal men. For Aboriginal

women, alcohol related deaths and HIV/AIDS emerge as the two most important determinants of premature death, though clearly accidents and injuries are also prominent causes.

Socioeconomic Disparities in Health and Mortality

Disparities in health and mortality by socioeconomic status have been observed for a long time in the industrialized countries. One of the key findings in this literature being the existence of an inverse socioeconomic gradient in mortality risk: as socioeconomic status increases, mortality declines, and as socioeconomic status decreases, mortality rates increase (Antonovsky, 1967; Feinstein, 1993; Hummer, Rogers, and Eberstein, 1998; Kitagawa and Hauser, 1973; Marmot, 1995, 2005b; Marmot et al., 2008; Wilkinson, 1996, 2005; Wilkinson and Marmot, 2003; Wilkinson and Pickett, 2009).

Observations in Canada are consistent with this generalization. In an early study, Russell Wilkins (1980), using the occupations of men aged 25–64 as the index of SES, investigated disparities in life expectancy at birth across districts of Montreal. He computed mortality ratios of five occupational classes (class 1 being the highest ranked and class 5 the lowest), and, using the overall average death rate across all classes as the standard, found clear evidence of an inverse gradient: the highest occupational class had the lowest relative mortality, and the lowest class showed the highest relative mortality.

More recent analyses confirm earlier findings (Wilkins, Berthelot, and Ng, 2002; Tjepkema et al., 2010: 13). Notwithstanding some narrowing of the gaps in cause-specific mortality between the richest and poorest income quintiles, the overall mortality disadvantage for men and women in the lowest class remains substantial: 41 and 30 per cent, respectively (Tjepkema et al., 2010).

As for the causal mechanisms that link socioeconomic status to health status, the importance of income is well understood: more money usually affords individuals and their families greater access to health care and insurance, as well as a host of other health-conferring benefits (Canadian Institute for Health Information, 2002: 32).

In his extensive review of the literature, Richard Wilkinson (2005: 25) identified three key social risk factors underlying the differences in health in a population, all tied to socioeconomic inequality:

1. low social status;
2. poor social affiliations; and
3. poor quality of early childhood experiences.

Poor socioeconomic conditions predispose a person to a life of physical, mental, and economic difficulties. Research has shown that infants and children who grow up in poor and disorganized socioeconomic contexts are more likely to be abused and neglected. The effects of abuse on the neural development of a child may be permanent and not easily erased by therapy or other medical interventions (Teicher, 2003). Further, as the child grows to become an adult, he or she passes these effects on to the next generation of children, thereby perpetuating a cycle of poverty and hardship.

Joseph Feinstein (1993) developed a useful framework for understanding how socioeconomic disadvantage relates to poor health. Feinstein's typology (see Table 7.10) emphasizes four sets of factors (represented by the four cells) that affect the ways that health inequalities are produced and maintained by socioeconomic status.

There is also a psychosocial dimension to the socioeconomic gradient in health and mortality. The root causes of disparities in health emanate from the effects of social exclusion and isolation and the stressful life experienced by disadvantaged people, which usually results from lack of education, poor job prospects, unemployment, and low income. A sense of fatalism and powerlessness often accompanies these conditions, leading to smoking and alcohol as means of easing stress. To this configuration of poor material conditions, add the poor nutrition and diet that are typical of impoverished socioeconomic status, and it is not difficult to see how, over the long term, a majority of socioeconomically disadvantaged individuals develop health issues. Their compromised immune systems reduce their resistance to communicable and non-communicable illness, which, combined with their susceptibility to

TABLE 7.10	Typology of socioeconomic discrepancies by type of explanation and source of health inequality		

||||||||||||||||||||||||||||||||||||||||||||||||||||||||||||||||||||||||||||||||||||||||||||||||||||||||||||||||||||||||||||||||||||||||||

		Source of inequality in health	
		Lifespan (average length of life)	**Access to and use of** health care services
Type of explanation	**Materialistic causes** (having to do with access to material resources)	• housing • overcrowding • sanitation • transit mode • occupational hazards • environmental hazards	• ability to purchase health care • ability to purchase pharmaceuticals • regular access to and ability to consult a family physician
	Behavioural/ psychosocial causes (having to do with cultural predispositions to health behaviour)	• diet • smoking • amount of exercise • choice of leisure activities • risk-taking behaviour • alcohol and substance abuse	• access to comprehensive medical information • understanding of how to "play the system" • ability to follow medical instructions • ability to self-diagnose • awareness of disease recurrence

Source: Adapted from Feinstein (1993): 279–322.

accidental and violent death, greatly increases their mortality risk (Berkman and Breslow, 1983; Cassel, 1976; Cobb, 1976; House, Landis, and Umberson, 1988; Marmot, Kogevinas, and Elston, 1987; Syme and Berkman, 1976; Wilkinson, 2005; Wilkinson and Marmot, 2003; Wilkinson and Pickett, 2009).

Canadian Mortality in Comparative Perspective

Table 7.11 compares Canada with five other wealthy nations—the United States, Japan, Sweden, the United Kingdom, and France—across several indicators of population health. These include life expectancy at birth and health-adjusted life expectancy (the average number of years a person can expect to live free of major disability). Canada's health profile compares favourably with these other countries, especially the United States, whose expenditure on health ranks highest but lowest in infant mortality, life expectancy, and healthy life expectancy. Japan and Sweden come out on top on these key indicators. The United States and United Kingdom stand out for their high rates of adolescent birth rates. As can be expected, the six countries share a preponderance of deaths due to non-communicable diseases.

TABLE 7.11　**Population health indicators for Canada and five other high-income countries around 2011**

Health Indicator	Canada	US	Japan	Sweden	UK	France
Crude death rate per 1 000 population	7	8	10	9	9	9
Infant mortality rate per 1 000 live births	5	6	2	2	4	3
Life expectancy at birth (both sexes)	81	79	83	82	81	82
Healthy life expectancy at birth (both sexes)	73	70	76	74	72	73
Healthy life expectancy as % of life expectancy	90.1	88.6	91.6	90.2	88.9	89.0
Adolescent fertility rate per 1 000 women 15–19	12	30	6	6	30	6
% deaths non-communicable diseases	89	87	80	90	88	87.0
Expenditure on health as % of GDP	11.7	17.9	9.3	9.4	9.3	11.6

Sources: Population Reference Bureau (2012); UNdata (2010); World Bank (2013)

Clearly, the data in Table 7.11 shows that higher spending on health care does not necessarily translate into best overall performance in terms of population health, as evidenced by the United States (Kunitz, 2007; Kunitz and Pesis-Katz, 2005; Torrey and Haub, 2004).

Future Prospects

Based on the trends examined, there remains little doubt that Canada is in the advanced stages of the epidemiological transition (Bah and Rajulton, 1991; Lussier, Bourbeau, and Choinière, 2008). So what is the most likely course of Canada's mortality over the twenty-first century? One encouraging trend, noted earlier, is the declining rate of cardiovascular mortality among adults and the elderly since the 1960s. A key to the decline of heart disease (which is the most important component of cardiovascular mortality) has been the reduction in cigarette smoking, the move towards healthier diets, and greater participation in

physical exercise—all of which contribute to a reduction in hypertensive complications. There are still gains to be made in the fight against heart disease. Less optimistic are the trends for cancer. As the average age of the population rises, the incidence of cancer is bound to increase over the foreseeable future (Roterman, 2006). Prospects for hope rest with continuing research, which is bound to produce favourable results (Collins and Barker, 2007; Wigle et al., 1986), and with strategies for prevention, namely the eradication of risk factors including tobacco, alcoholism, high-fat diets, and inactivity (Muir and Sasco, 1990; Rothenberg and Koplan, 1990).

Compared with those of a few decades ago, current rates of death from suicide, homicide, and motor vehicle accidents are lower and show promise of further declines. Of some concern is the large number of Canadians that perish on an annual basis as a result of respiratory conditions and, among infants, the large proportion of deaths due to congenital anomalies and other complications of the perinatal period, largely associated with low birth weight and prematurity. Although Canada's infant mortality rate is one of the lowest in the world, the lower rates of Japan and Sweden demonstrate that further progress in this area is possible.

As for reducing health and mortality disparities within Canada itself, further success will likely depend on greater public health efforts aimed at reducing inequalities along socioeconomic lines. Wide gaps in mortality remain for causes of death that are presumed to be largely amenable to greater public health interventions—for example, HIV, lung cancer, skin cancer, chronic obstructive pulmonary disease, cirrhosis of the liver, and motor vehicle accidents (James et al., 2007). Therefore greater public health efforts are required to reduce the socioeconomic gaps in Canadian health and mortality.

Conclusion

A population's overall health status is a function of a complex set of interrelated factors—environmental, institutional, socioeconomic, and genetic, among others. The epidemiological transition theory states that societies pass through several stages of development with respect to the major causes of premature death, from an early stage in which pestilence and famine predominate, to an intermediary stage of receding pandemics, to a final stage of human-caused and degenerative diseases. Recent scholars have proposed extensions to this typological explanation, including a fourth stage characterized as the age of delayed degenerative diseases. During this stage, there is a tendency for the most advanced countries to experience notable improvements in medical therapies that help to postpone not only the onset of major disabilities, such as cardiovascular disease and cancers, but also death for those afflicted with those diseases. An important point raised in the recent literature concerns the key role of lifestyle and health habits in understanding why there is so much chronic disease and premature death in today's most advanced countries. In recent years, parts of the developing world have suffered major setbacks in the fight against disease and premature death; one of the most dramatic of these setbacks is associated with the HIV/AIDS epidemic; another is the fall in life expectancy in Russia and some of the other former Soviet bloc countries. At the same time, the burden of disease due to noncommunicable diseases such as cancer and circulatory conditions is bound to worsen with time as these societies pass through the different stages of the epidemiological transition.

Notes for Further Study

It is important to recognize that the age-specific death rate and the crude death rate (CDR) are related. The crude death rate is the weighted average of a set of age-specific death rates, where the weights are the proportions of the total population at each age. Stated differently, the crude death rate is the cumulative product of a set of age-specific death rates and an age distribution for a given population. This is shown below. The symbol D means deaths, P population, x implies an age category, and M_x stands for age-specific death rate per person.

$$CDR = \frac{D}{P} \times 1000 \qquad (1)$$

$$= \frac{\sum D_x}{P} \times 1000 \qquad (2)$$

$$= \frac{\sum M_x P_x}{P} \times 1000 \qquad (3)$$

$$= 1000 \times \sum \frac{P_x}{P} \times M_x \qquad (4)$$

$$= 1000 \times \sum w_x M_x \qquad (5)$$

The numerator of the crude death rate is the sum (indicated by the Greek letter sigma, Σ) of age-specific deaths divided by the total population (equation 2), which can also be derived by taking the sum of the products of age-specific death rates multiplied by the age-specific populations, as in equation 3. Dividing this sum by the total population produces the crude death rate. The last two expressions say the same thing using different notation (P_x/P is the proportion of population in a given age category). If each age-specific proportion is multiplied by its corresponding death rate, the sum of these products would yield the crude death rate (i.e., equation 4). Equation 5 is the same as equation 4 but expressed as the sum of products—i.e., the sum of age-specific population weights ($w_x = P_x/P$) multiplied by age-specific death rates.

Health-Adjusted Life Expectancy (HALE)

A key component of the average length of life is the proportion of life that one can expect to live free of major disability. An empirical measure that takes this into account is the *health-adjusted life expectancy* (HALE). By specifying the portion of overall life expectancy spent in good health, this measure is a valuable indicator of population health. HALE takes into account the average number of years the population spends in good health free of major disability, given its overall life expectancy at birth. Table 7.12 shows life expectancy at birth for men and women, and the associated HALE values for the World Health Organization (WHO) health regions and for the world as a whole (World Health Organization, 2007).

The regional figures mask wide variations in both life expectancy and HALE across specific countries. The highest life expectancy is in Japan, where the average man lives 77 years and the average woman 86. Japan also has the highest HALE scores (72 for men, 78 for women); thus, Japanese men and women spend just over 90 per cent of their relatively long lives in good health. By contrast, the most disadvantaged country in the world is Sierra Leone, where male life expectancy is just 37 years and female life expectancy just 40. HALE values for Sierra Leone are 27 years for men and 30 years for women. So, a Sierra Leonean man can hope to live about 73 per cent of his relatively short life free of major disability, while a woman can expect her disability-free life to be 75 per cent of her life. In other words, in Sierra Leone, about one-quarter of the average citizen's life—short as it is—would be spent in a state of ill health. Many countries in sub-Saharan Africa share life expectancies below 50 years, with correspondingly low HALE values (World Health Organization, 2007: 22–30).

TABLE 7.12 Life expectancy at birth and health-adjusted life expectancy in years, by WHO region

Life expectancy at birth (e_0) or health-adjusted life expectancy at birth (HALE)	WHO region						
	African region	Region of the Americas	South-east Asia region	European region	Eastern Mediterranean region	Western Pacific region	Global
e_0 males	48	72	62	69	62	71	64
e_0 females	50	77	65	77	64	75	68
e_0 female – e_0 male	2	5	3	8	2	4	4
HALE male	40	63	54	62	53	63	56
HALE female	42	67	55	68	54	66	59
HALE (male) – HALE (female)	–2	–4	–1	–6	–1	–3	–3
% of life in good health, given e_0 (males)	83.3	87.5	87.1	89.7	84.5	88.7	87.5
% of life in good health, given e_0 (females)	84.0	87.0	84.6	88.3	84.4	88.0	86.8

Source: From *World Health Statistics 2007*, World Health Organization, p. 30, Table Health status: mortality. © 2007 World Health Organization.

Standardization of Death Rates

Age composition has a strong effect on mortality. If a relatively young population is compared to a relatively old population, the young population might actually show a lower crude death rate. To circumvent this problem, it is advisable, when comparing mortality across two or more populations, to apply statistical standardization to remove differences in age compositions of the populations being compared. There are two methods of standardization used in demographic analysis: *direct standardization* and *indirect standardization*.

Direct Standardization
In this type of standardization, an appropriate "standard population" is selected and then used to derive age-standardized death rates for the populations being compared. Essentially, the age-specific death rates of the study populations are applied to the standard population to obtain the number of expected deaths that would occur in the standard population if it had the age-specific death rates of a study population.

Standardization allows us to examine populations in a *relative* sense, even though in absolute terms the standardized rates have no real meaning (they are fictitious figures). Standardization merely allows the researcher to make relative types of comparisons. A standardized death rate, for instance, is a fictitious rate obtained through a statistical procedure under a restrictive assumption: that the study population experiences the same age distribution as the standard population.

Table 7.13 illustrates the application of direct standardization to Canada and Mexico for the year 2000. For the purpose of this example, the overall population of Canada in 2000 is used as the standard.

The age structures of Canada and Mexico are very different: Canada's is considerably older. In 2000, the crude death rate for Mexicans was lower than for Canadians.

This seems counter-intuitive, given Canada's more advanced social structure. By all relevant indicators, Canada should have lower mortality than Mexico.

In Table 7.13, columns 2 and 3 list the age-specific death rates (per person) for Canada and Mexico in 2000. Column 4 shows the age-specific population of Canada for 2000, and columns 5 and 6 include the expected

TABLE 7.13   Direct standardization of death rates for Canada and Mexico, 2000

Age	Canada age-specific death rates per person	Mexico age-specific death rates per person	Canada population (standard)	Products	
(1)	(2)	(3)	(4)	$(5) = (2) \times (4)$	$(6) = (3) \times (4)$
0	0.005164	0.017216	336 189	1 736	5 788
1–4	0.000207	0.000768	1 446 080	300	1 111
5–14	0.000142	0.000324	4 097 595	583	1 328
15–24	0.000569	0.000859	4 162 089	2 367	3 575
25–34	0.000650	0.001433	4 404 726	2 865	6 312
35–44	0.001238	0.002533	5 306 541	6 569	13 441
45–54	0.002908	0.005058	4 363 765	12 689	22 072
55–64	0.007655	0.011563	2 814 615	21 545	32 545
65–74	0.020199	0.025273	2 143 223	43 290	54 166
75+	0.073494	0.082019	1 716 011	126 117	140 746
Total			**30 790 834**	**218 061**	**281 083**
CDR per 1 000	7.082	4.423			
SDRs per 1 000	7.082	9.129			

Note: Figures in columns (5) and (6) are rounded to whole numbers. The age compositions for the two countries are shown below:

Age group	Canada %	Mexico %
<15	20.23	35.50
15–64	67.75	60.22
65+	12.02	4.28
Total population	30 790 834	98 872 000

Source: Author's computations based on data from the World Health Organization (2006a).

deaths by age, obtained by multiplying the appropriate age-specific death rates in the study population by the corresponding standard population in each age. The steps required to compute the standardized death rates are outlined below, using Mexico as the example:

1. Multiply each age-specific death rate for Mexico by the corresponding standard population in column 4; the results are shown in column 5.
2. Sum all values in column 6.
3. Divide the total from step 2 by the total standard population.

And so, the directly standardized death rate (DSDR) for Mexico is

$$DSDR = \frac{\text{sum of expected deaths}}{\text{total standard population}} \times 1000$$

$$DSDR = \frac{281083}{30\,790\,834} \times 1000 = 9.129$$

In formal terms, this can be written as

$$DSDR = \frac{\sum m_x P_x}{P}$$

where x is the age for a given group, m_x is the age-specific death rate of the population being studied, P_x is the age-specific population of the standard, and P is the total standard population.

The other computations for Mexico are executed in the same way.

Once we have calculated the directly standardized death rate, we can compare it with the crude death rate. The DSDR for Canada is 7.082 per 1000, which is exactly the same as the CDR. This is because we have used Canada's population as the standard. We find that the DSDR of 9.129 for Mexico is substantially higher than its corresponding CDR of 4.423, and therefore higher than the CDR for Canada. This is to be expected. Mexico is a developing country and Canada is highly advanced. On intuitive grounds alone we would expect Canada to have a lower mortality level than Mexico. However, the key to understanding standardized death rates is to keep in mind that the procedure eliminates statistically differences in age compositions across the populations being compared, and that comparative analysis based on the standardized death rates will typically give different results than analysis based on differences in CDRs alone.

The standardization procedure can be easily applied to cause-specific death rates as well by following the same procedures as described above. The input data will be age-specific death rates by cause of death.

Indirect Standardization

Indirect standardization is applied under different circumstances. The problem presented below illustrates when and how indirect standardization is used.

Table 7.14 includes information on age-specific death rates for Canada in 2000 and only the population distribution for Mexico in 2000, along with only the total number of deaths for Mexico. We assume for the sake of this example that we do not have any information on age-specific death rates for Mexico.

This is the sort of situation in which indirect standardization is typically used. While direct standardization depends on having the age-specific death rates of a study population, the indirect method is used when this information is not available. Instead, the indirect method applies the

TABLE 7.14 Age-specific death rates in 2000 for Canada, and the population distribution of Mexico in 2000 (indirect standardization procedure)

Age	Canada death rates	Mexico population	Products
(1)	(2)	(3)	(4) = (2) × (3)
0	0.005164	2 239 848	11 566
1–4	0.000207	9 067 087	1 881
5–14	0.000142	22 157 543	3 153
15–24	0.000569	20 243 131	11 512
25–34	0.000650	16 255 637	10 573
35–44	0.001238	11 625 327	14 391
45–54	0.002908	7 735 602	22 494
55–64	0.007655	4 872 474	37 297
65–74	0.020199	2 981 350	60 219
75+	0.073494	1 754 609	128 954
Total		**98 932 608**	**302 040**
Observed total deaths, Mexico		437 555	
CDR per 1 000, Canada	7.082		
ISDR per 1 000, Mexico		10.259	

Source: Author's computations based on data from World Health Organization (2006a).

age-specific death rates of a standard population to the age distribution of the study population to derive the number of deaths that could be expected in the study population if it experienced the age-specific death rates of the standard. The formula for the indirectly standardized death rate is

$$\text{ISDR}_j = \frac{O}{E} \times \text{CDR}_s$$

where ISDR_j is the indirectly standardized death rate for study population j, E is the number of expected deaths in the study population, O is the number of observed deaths in the study population, and CDR_s is the crude death rate of the standard population.

In the worked example in Table 7.14, we see that Mexico's ISDR is 10.259 per 1 000. This is consistent with our earlier finding based on direct standardization: Mexico has higher standardized mortality rate than Canada, even though the two standardized rates for Mexico are not identical.

Exercises

1. Table 7.15 shows age–sex-specific populations and deaths by cause for Canada in 1971 and 1998. The corresponding crude death rates (per 100 000) are also listed. With the use of a suitable spreadsheet, use these data to compute the directly standardized male cause-specific death rates per person in 1998. Use the male Canadian population in 1971 as the standard.

   Repeat these procedures for females. Use the female population in 1971 as the standard.

   Interpret your results. Do the directly standardized death rates for 1998 differ substantially from the crude death rates in 1998?

2. The questions below are to be worked out from data contained in the Canadian life tables for 1901 (Tables 7 16 and 7.17) and 2009–11 (see Table 7.1, page 272). The male and female life tables for 1901 are examples of "abridged" life tables, whereas the 2009–11 tables are single-year life tables. In the abridged tables, age is grouped into five-year categories starting from age 5. Note that infancy (age 0) and ages 1–4 are grouped differently because of the unique mortality pattern in these ages: n infancy, the death rate is relatively high, while from ages 1–4 the probability of death drops significantly. In other words, the beginning of these age intervals has considerably higher chances of death than the end points. In the age ranges between 5 and 85, it can be safely assumed that deaths are distributed more or less evenly. However, in extreme old age the even distribution assumption does not hold.

   After examining the 1901 and 2009–11 life tables, answer the following questions. All of the questions rely on the information conta ned in the survivorship (i.e., l_x) columns of these life tables. You will compute a series of probabilities. The first question is worked out to illustrate the computations.

   a) What is the probability of a newborn boy surviving to age 5 in 1901 and in 2009–11?

   Answer

   The probability of an infant boy surviving to age 5 in 1901 is obtained by dividing the l_x value for age 5 by the l_x value for age 0:

   $$\frac{78772}{100000} = 0.78772$$

   (continued)

TABLE 7.15   Populations, deaths, and death rates by cause for Canada, 1971 and 1998

1971	Population	Heart disease	Other circulatory	Lung cancer	Other cancers	Suicide	Other external	Other causes	Total deaths
Males									
0	186 400	5	6	0	17	0	204	3 575	3 807
1–4	769 100	4	3	0	76	0	329	314	726
5–14	2 345 500	12	9	0	184	14	765	270	1 254
15–24	1 981 100	40	30	1	181	358	2 357	295	3 262
25–34	1 400 200	132	54	11	190	300	1 209	291	2 187
35–44	1 298 100	910	171	124	452	344	1 031	713	3 745
45–54	1 119 200	3 247	478	563	1 124	335	986	1 502	8 235
55–64	829 300	6 687	1 236	1 322	2 363	256	779	2 625	15 268
65–74	481 700	8 747	2 554	1 535	3 267	122	551	3 866	20 642
75+	275 400	12 821	5 991	891	4 043	67	675	6 237	30 725
Total	10 686 000	32 605	10 532	4 447	11 897	1 796	8 886	19 688	89 851
CDR per 100 000		305.12	98.56	41.62	111.33	16.81	83.16	184.24	840.83
Females									
0	177 200	6	6	0	13	0	130	2 604	2 759
1–4	730 800	2	4	0	66	0	198	288	558
5–14	2 241 600	10	6	0	130	4	374	243	767
15–24	1 929 400	24	28	2	111	91	596	238	1 090
25–34	1 390 600	52	68	6	209	125	328	270	1 058
35–44	1 267 600	217	184	43	730	150	323	516	2 163
45–54	1 143 800	731	373	149	1 796	159	346	898	4 452
55–64	842 000	2 102	779	230	2 563	97	317	1 527	7 615
65–74	548 800	4 833	1 887	215	2 882	50	305	2 272	12 444
75+	366 100	12 768	7 210	164	3 570	19	745	5 049	29 525
Total	10 637 900	20 745	10 545	809	12 070	695	3 662	13 905	62 431
CDR per 100 000		195.01	99.13	7.60	113.46	6.53	34.42	130.71	586.87

TABLE 7.15   (continued)

1998

Males

Age	Population							Total
0	175 258	14	6	1	8	0	29	1 001
1–4	786 841	8	2	0	20	0	84	217
5–14	2 093 593	10	6	0	49	30	159	363
15–24	2 091 297	29	13	0	108	457	853	1 740
25–34	2 302 083	90	30	16	254	568	867	2 325
35–44	2 609 915	576	142	127	649	713	1 007	4 308
45–54	2 028 899	1 779	293	732	1 727	513	677	7 332
55–64	1 305 844	3 558	672	1 938	3 562	296	495	13 098
65–74	987 407	7 779	2 000	3 743	6 938	201	531	27 658
75+	600 064	16 893	6 042	3 459	9 624	147	1 258	54 964
Total	**14 981 201**	**30 736**	**9 206**	**10 016**	**22 939**	**2 925**	**5 960**	**113 006**
CDR per 100 000	**205.16**	**205.16**	**61.45**	**66.86**	**153.12**	**19.52**	**39.78**	**754.32**

Females

Age	Population							Total
0	167 160	13	8	0	13	0	15	809
1–4	746 253	7	1	0	24	0	52	171
5–14	1 988 231	7	4	0	51	16	98	266
15–24	1 993 166	16	13	2	60	105	266	620
25–34	2 250 342	32	28	9	212	133	256	919
35–44	2 596 641	165	110	186	946	182	328	2 478
45–54	2 037 567	490	239	635	2 103	159	267	4 791
55–64	1 343 982	1 169	460	1 190	3 275	70	216	8 083
65–74	1 138 227	3 987	1 515	2 105	5 480	59	329	17 951
75+	1 004 021	21 897	9 286	2 122	10 359	50	1 776	68 996
Total	**15 265 590**	**27 783**	**11 664**	**6 249**	**22 523**	**774**	**3 603**	**105 084**
CDR per 100 000	**182.00**	**182.00**	**76.41**	**40.94**	**147.54**	**5.07**	**23.60**	**688.37**

Source: Populations, deaths, and death rates by cause for Canada, 1971 and 1998, World Health Organization www3.who.int/whosis/mort/table1.cfm?path=whosis,mort,mort_table1&language=english. Accessed 2008. Copyright © World Health Organization.

This tells us that in 1901, the probability of survival to age 5 for a newborn baby boy was almost 79 per cent. How does this compare to 2009–11? In 2009–11, the probability of a boy infant surviving to age 5 is:

$$\frac{99\,398}{100\,000} = 0.99398$$

The chance of survival to age 5 for a newborn boy in 2009–11 is over 99 per cent, which is a significant improvement over the survival probability in 1901. These computations can be executed for an infant girl surviving to age 5 over the same two periods.

b) What is the probability of a boy aged 5 in 1901 surviving to age 65? Calculate this probability for a girl. Calculate these probabilities for 2009–11. Interpret the results.

c) What is the probability of a man aged 65 in 1901 surviving to age 80? What is the probability in 2009–11? Answer the same question for a woman.

d) What is the probability of a 15-year-old male in 1901 surviving to his twenty-fifth birthday? What is this probability for a 15-year-old female? Calculate the same probabilities for 2009–11. Interpret your results.

e) For these two periods, is the probability of a 10-year-old boy surviving to age 85 greater or smaller than the probability of a 65-year-old male surviving to age 85? Calculate these probabilities and interpret your results.

3. Discuss the health and epidemiological transitions of high-income nations and how these are similar to or different from the situation in developing countries.

4. Discuss competing theories of senescence and aging in countries in the fourth stage of epidemiological transition. Based on these theories, what are the long-term implications for societies' future burden of disease?

5. Notwithstanding universal health care in Canada, there are significant discrepancies in health and mortality across different sectors of the population. Discuss the factors responsible for these persisting differentials and how existing health disparities can be minimized or eliminated over the course of the twenty-first century. Would further increases in health care spending be effective in raising the overall health status of Canadians?

TABLE 7.16   Abridged life table for Canadian males, 1901

Age (x)	Of 100 000 born alive: Proportion of persons alive at beginning of age interval dying during interval (q_x)	Of 100 000 born alive: Number living at beginning of age interval (l_x)	Of 100 000 born alive: Number dying during age interval (d_x)	Stationary population (years lived): In the age interval (person-years lived) (L_x)	Stationary population (years lived): In this and all subsequent age intervals (T_x)	Average number of years of life remaining at beginning of age interval (e_x^0)
0	0.14398	100 000	14 398	90 353	4 714 155	47.14
1–4	0.07979	85 602	6 030	324 455	4 623 808	54.02
5–9	0.02246	78 772	1 769	388 730	4 299 353	54.58
10–14	0.01492	77 003	1 149	382 225	3 910 623	50.79
15–19	0.02190	75 854	1 661	375 389	3 528 398	46.52
20–24	0.03004	74 193	2 229	365 563	3 153 009	42.50
25–29	0.03473	71 964	2 499	353 630	2 787 446	38.73
30–34	0.03739	69 465	2 597	340 867	2 433 816	35.04
35–39	0.04107	66 868	2 746	327 570	2 092 949	31.30
40–44	0.04856	64 122	3 114	313 032	1 765 379	27.53
45–49	0.06227	61 008	2 799	295 887	1 452 347	23.81
50–54	0.08471	57 209	4 846	274 420	1 156 460	20.21
55–59	0.11892	52 363	6 227	246 853	882 040	16.84
60–64	0.16857	46 136	7 777	211 854	635 187	13.77
65–69	0.23752	38 359	9 111	169 437	423 333	11.04
70–74	0.32877	29 248	9 616	122 148	253 896	8.68
75–79	0.44219	19 632	8 681	75 755	131 748	6.71
80–84	0.57029	10 951	6 265	37 916	55 993	5.11
85–89	0.70465	4 686	3 302	14 065	18 077	3.86
90–94	0.82225	1 384	1 138	3 478	4 012	2.90
95–99	0.91057	246	224	501	534	2.17
100+	1.00000	22	22	33	33	1.50

Note: The function p_x is not shown because it is easily derivable from the q_x column by taking $1 - q_x$ for each age category.

Source: Adapted from Bourbeau, Légaré, and Émond (1997).

TABLE 7.17   Abridged life table for Canadian females, 1901

| Age (x) | Proportion of persons alive at beginning of age interval dying during interval (q_x) | Of 100 000 born alive: | | Stationary population (years lived): | | Average number of years of life remaining at beginning of age interval (e_x^0) |
		Number living at beginning of age interval (l_x)	Number dying during age interval (d_x)	In the age interval (person-years lived) (L_x)	In this and all subsequent age intervals (T_x)	
0	0.12389	100 000	12 389	91 947	5 010 903	50.11
1–4	0.07690	87 611	6 737	332 791	4 918 960	56.15
5–9	0.02177	80 874	1 761	399 285	4 586 169	56.71
10–14	0.01546	79 113	1 223	392 608	4 186 884	52.92
15–19	0.02175	77 890	1 694	385 443	3 794 276	48.71
20–24	0.02865	76 196	2 183	375 676	3 408 833	44.74
25–29	0.03309	74 013	2 449	364 004	3 033 157	40.98
30–34	0.03553	71 564	2 543	351 483	2 669 153	37.30
35–39	0.03770	69 021	2 602	338 635	2 317 670	33.58
40–44	0.04163	66 419	2 765	325 283	1 979 035	29.80
45–49	0.04955	63 654	3 154	310 602	1 653 752	25.98
50–54	0.06431	60 500	3 891	293 153	1 343 150	22.20
55–59	0.08974	56 609	5 080	270 919	1 049 997	18.55
60–64	0.13099	51 529	6 750	241 523	779 078	15.12
65–69	0.19451	44 779	8 710	202 906	537 555	12.00
70–74	0.28695	36 069	10 350	154 937	334 649	9.28
75–79	0.41160	25 719	10 586	101 794	179 712	6.99
80–84	0.56261	15 133	8 514	53 089	77 918	5.15
85–89	0.71718	6 619	4 747	19 645	24 829	3.75
90–94	0.83921	1 872	1 571	4 550	5 184	2.77
95–99	0.91694	301	276	593	635	2.11
100+	1.00000	25	25	42	42	1.66

Note: The function p_x is not shown because it is easily derivable from the q_x column by taking $1 - q_x$ for each age category.

Source: Adapted from Bourbeau, Légaré, and Émond (1997).

Additional Reading

Carey, James R. 2002. *Longevity: The Biology and Demography of Life Span*. Princeton and Oxford: Princeton University Press.

Crimmins, Eileen M., Samuel H. Preston, and Barney Cohen, eds. 2011. *Explaining Divergent Levels of Longevity in High-Income Countries*. Panel on Understanding Divergent Trends in Longevity in High-Income Countries. Committee on Population Division of Behavioural and Social Sciences and Education, National Research Council of the National Academies. Washington: The National Academies Press.

Doyle, Shane. 2013. *Before HIV: Sexuality, Fertility and Mortality in East Africa, 1900–1980*. Oxford: Oxford University Press.

Easterlin, Richard A. 2004. *The Reluctant Economist: Perspectives on Economics, Economic History, and Demography*. Cambridge: Cambridge University Press.

Finch, Caleb E. 2007. *The Biology of Human Longevity: Inflammation, Nutrition, and Aging in the Evolution of Lifespans*. Amsterdam: Academic Press.

Mukherjee, Siddhartha. 2010. *The Emperor of All Maladies: A Biography of Cancer*. New York: Scribner.

Pepin, Jacques. 2011. *The Origins of AIDS*. Cambridge: Cambridge University Press.

Quammen, David. 2012. *Spillover: Animal Infections and the Next Human Pandemic*. New York: W.W. Norton.

Wells, Spencer. 2011. *Pandora's Seed: Why the Hunter-Gatherer Holds the Key to Our Survival*. New York: Random House.

Wunch, Guillaume, Michel Mouchart, and Josianne Duchene, eds. 2002. *The Life Table: Modelling Survival and Death*. Dordrecht: Kluwer Academic.

Notes

1. For further insights on the history of plague and its impact on society, see Herlihy (1997); Scott and Duncan (2001).
2. Technically, entropy in the context of the life table is the percentage improvement in the expectation of life at age x, if a 1 per cent improvement in mortality takes place at age x and above (Keyfitz, 1977).
3. Fries (1980) prepared his estimate of average maximum human life using a linear model assuming that life expectancy at birth and life expectancy at age 65 would at some point in the future converge. That point of convergence should occur, according to Fries' calculations, around the year 2050.

PART FOUR

Demographic Processes II: Internal and International Migration

8 Internal Migration

Introduction

Migration is the third key component of population change, after fertility and mortality. Most of us will relocate at some point in our lives. Some will move to a different country from the one where we were born or raised; this is international migration, the subject of Chapter 9. Many more will relocate within Canada, however. Some will move from one end of the country to the other; others will move to a different place within their home region; some will move more than once—perhaps several times. A recent publication by Statistics Canada points to the ubiquity of migration in our lives. Between 2009–10 and 2010–11, over half a million (516 300) Canadians picked up and moved (Bohnert, 2013b: 1). Many headed for the Prairies or British Columbia. Young adults generally opt for large metropolitan areas, while seniors generally tend to gravitate towards smaller towns or rural areas (Newbold, 2011; Statistics Canada, 2002e). What all these types of internal migration have in common is the fact that they are motivated by the movers' desire for improvement—whether in their economic situation or in their overall sense of well-being.

Basic Concepts

Defining Terms

Migration

What counts as migration? Does a move from one neighbourhood to another within the same community qualify? Is a visit to another country a migration? What about the daily movement from home to workplace and back? While all these examples involve *geographic mobility*, none of them would count as an instance of migration. In demography, *migration* is usually understood to have three main features: the crossing of administrative boundaries, long-distance travel, and a permanent or semi-permanent change in residence (Yaukey, Anderton, and Hickes, 2007). As we shall see, however, not every migration meets the long-distance criterion. The duration dimension may also be problematic, since it is not always possible to determine individuals' intentions (Goldscheider, 1971; Morrison, Bryan, and Swanson, 2004; Newell, 1988; Ritchey, 1976; Shaw, 1975). In practice, therefore, most studies of migration use an operational definition based on change in place of usual residence from one administrative area to another.

Scale of Analysis

The first step in any investigation of migration is to classify the study population into two groups: those who have changed address during a specified interval and those who have not. A subset of the "movers" will be *migrants*: people who not only changed address but who moved to a different administrative jurisdiction (community, town, city, or province). Another subset will consist of people who changed their address but stayed within the same administrative area or jurisdiction. People in this category are called *non-migrants*; examples include individuals who move house within the same community and students who move away from their usual community but only for a limited period of time, to attend college or university. "Transients," who may move from one jurisdiction to another but have no fixed address and whose movements therefore cannot be easily traced, are also treated as non-migrants. These sorts of temporary and transient moves are generally not considered to fall within the definition of migration (Hinde, 1998: 191). Researchers studying the people involved treat transients as unique subpopulations in the sociological sense.

As Figure 8.1 shows, geographic mobility is analyzed at a variety of geopolitical scales, from local to international. Demographers use parallel terms to refer to migration into and out of a locality within a country or between countries. In the case of *international migration*, the term *immigrant* refers to a citizen or permanent resident of a country who moves into another country. The parallel term in cases of internal migration is *in-migrant*, denoting a person who migrates into one administrative area from another area within the same country. The corresponding terms referring to outward movement are *emigrant* and *out-migrant*. The former pertains to people who leave one country and relocate to a different one; the latter refers to those who leave one administrative area for another within the same country.

The Uniqueness of Migration

Migration, as we noted at the outset, is one of three key components of population change. It differs from the other two—fertility and mortality—in a number of ways, some fairly obvious, others less so. For instance, birth and death are once-in-a-lifetime events, whereas an individual can—and many individuals do—experience migration many times. Migration is not a biological process, and so it is not subject to biological restrictions, as fertility is: anyone can migrate, whatever their age or gender. Yet migration, unlike fertility and mortality, is not common to all societies: it is theoretically possible for a society to have no experience of migration. Finally, whereas virtually all countries require that births and deaths be reported to governmental statistical bureaus, this is not the case with migration. As we shall see in the next section, this makes collecting data on migration uniquely challenging.

Sources of Migration Statistics

Many countries (including Denmark, Finland, Sweden, Japan, the Netherlands, Bahrain, Kuwait, and Singapore) require that changes of residence be reported, and China demands that officials approve every such move in advance; but many others have no such regulations (Bryan, 2004b: 32; Shryock and Siegel, 1976: 353). In practical terms, this means that migration data

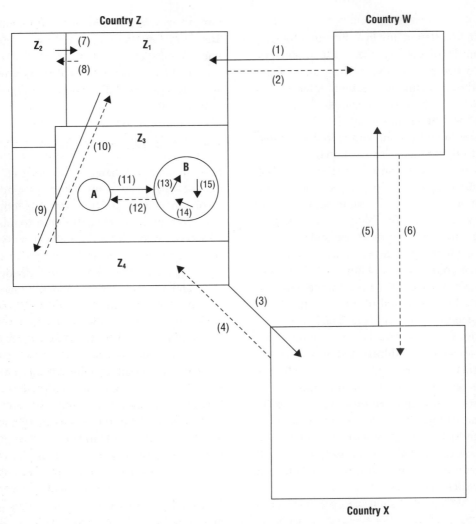

FIGURE 8.1   Conceptualizing types of geographic mobility

 (1)   immigration to country Z (emigration from country W)
 (2)   immigration to country W (emigration from country Z)
 (3)   immigration to country X (emigration from country Z)
 (4)   immigration to country Z (emigration from country X)
 (5)   immigration to country W (emigration from country X)
 (6)   immigration to country X (emigration from country W)
 (7)   in-migration to area Z1 (out-migration from area Z2)
 (8)   in-migration to area Z2 (out-migration from area Z1)
 (9)   in-migration to area Z4 (out-migration from area Z1)
(10)   in-migration to area Z1 (out-migration from area Z4)
(11)   in-migration to city B in area Z3 (out-migration from city A)
(12)   in-migration to city A in area Z3 (out-migration from city B)
(13), (14), (15) local mobility within city B

tend to be less complete than data on births, deaths, and nuptiality. For this reason, migration studies often depend on estimates produced using indirect methods.

The ideal migration data set would include, at a minimum, the following:

- data on the origins and destinations of migrants
- data disaggregated by age, sex, and other characteristics (marital status, occupation, income, race/ethnicity);
- data available in one-year age groups;
- data available annually for a large number of time periods;
- data produced in a timely manner; and
- data consistent with the relevant population base for calculating migration rates.

Ideally, these data would be available for all the major geographic units in a country, from provinces or states down through the smaller units such as counties and subcounty divisions. Unfortunately, it is not always possible to obtain such a detailed data set, and therefore many analyses of migration must be based on less extensive information. Where do we obtain migration data? There are a number of potential sources, including population registers, sample surveys, and administrative files (income tax returns, family allowance records, and so on). The most comprehensive data source, however, is the census.

Typically, the census will ask respondents to state their address at two points in time: on census day and at some earlier date (usually five years before). (A *one-year mobility question* is often included as well.) By juxtaposing respondents' addresses at the time of the census and at some earlier date, the census can tell us a good deal about respondents' movements. Table 8.1 shows the various types of geographic mobility in Canada over several census periods from 1956 to 2011. The overall consistency of these figures is remarkable. Just over half of Canadians aged five years and older do not change their place of residence in each census interval. Of those who do move, approximately half stay within the same community. This means that within any census interval, roughly one-quarter of all Canadians aged five years and older qualify as migrants, and most of them relocate within the same province (i.e., *intraprovincially*).

As important as this information is, census-based data collection is unsatisfactory for at least three reasons. First, the census question cannot detect multiple moves within the specified period. In fact, it is possible to move many times in the census period and still not be counted as having moved at all, if one happens to have returned to the original residence by the time of the next census. For this reason, census data generally underestimate the true extent of migration during a five-year period. A second problem is sampling error. For instance, with the introduction of a voluntary survey in 2011 (the National Household Survey) in place of the long-form Canadian census, the response rate to the migration questions was determined by Statistics Canada to have been only 26.1 per cent. As a result, the reliability of the estimated migration levels for relatively small subpopulations (e.g., ethnic and racial groups) and smaller geographic subunits (e.g., towns, municipalities, villages) is questionable. A third weakness of relying on censuses for migration data is that they cannot tell us anything about emigration (i.e., movement *from* Canada to another country; see Chapter 9).

TABLE 8.1   Population five years and over by mobility status and census period, Canada, 1956–61 to 2006–11 (percentages and total population aged five and over at the time of the census)

Mobility status	1956–61	1966–71	1976–81	1986–91	1991–6	1996–2001	2001–6	2006–2011
Non-migrants								
Non-movers	54.6	52.6	52.4	53.2	56.7	58.1	59.1	61.4
Local (residential) movers	25.4	23.5	24.9	23.2	23	22.4	22	20.9
Migrants								
Within same province	13.5	14.0	15.1	15.9	13.4	12.8	12.1	11.1
Different province	3.4	4.3	5.1	3.9	3.4	3.2	2.9	2.8
From abroad	3.1	4.2	2.5	3.7	3.5	3.5	3.9	3.9
Not stated[1]	0.2	1.4						
Total population aged 5+	15 302 621	19 717 210	22 280 095	24 927 870	26 604 135	27 932 590	29 544 485	30 978 630

[1] Until 1981, "not stated" responses were identified as such; since then, imputation methods have been used to allocate the "not stated" cases to the various categories of mobility.

Source: Adapted from McVey and Kalbach (1995): 123, Table 5.2; Statistics Canada (2004a, 2004b, 2007f, 2011d).

The clear advantage of census data is that they cover the entire country and make it possible to cross-classify movers by a host of individual characteristics. So, for example, analysts can classify interprovincial movers during a census interval with respect to age, sex, marital status, and education. Many other demographic characteristics can be included in a multivariate analysis (using multiple regression, for example) to ascertain the relative importance of background characteristics in explaining geographic mobility (see Long, 1988; Stone, 1978).

Migration data can also be obtained from administrative records, such as annual income tax returns. Ross Finnie (1999a), for example, used the Longitudinal Administrative Database (LAD) developed by Statistics Canada, which links individuals' income tax files over time, to categorize individuals as stayers, one-time movers, returnees, or multiple movers. He was also able to address some important questions about migration in Canada and its effects on individuals' earnings. He found, for instance, that interprovincial migration usually brings some improvement in income, though an average migrant's income may not be at par with that of the receiving population. Finnie (1999a) also noted that the size of the increase in income for interprovincial migrants depends on a number of factors, including age, gender, and the province of destination, since some provinces are more bountiful than others in terms of job opportunities and wage scales. The amount of time spent in the destination province is also important (presumably income rises with duration of residence in a new province).

The Longitudinal Administrative Database (LAD) is a 10 per cent representative sample of Canadian tax filers, followed over time and matched into family units on an annual basis. It provides individual- and family-level information on incomes, taxes, and basic demographic characteristics, including province of residence. Because the rate of tax filing in Canada is very high, the LAD's coverage of the adult population is considered to be very good (Finnie, 1999b: 231–2).

Basic Measures of Migration

In most studies of migration, the objective is, as Paul Shaw (1975: 8) put it, "to describe migration in terms of distributions by age, sex, education, occupation, etc." in order to "examine variations in the degree of intensity with which sending or receiving populations lose or gain migrants [in relation to] their varying socioeconomic contexts." To do this, analysts need to be able to compare migration rates. The problem is that the data needed to compute those rates—namely, the actual numbers of in- and of outmigrants for a given area—are frequently not available. This difficulty is generally resolved by using the demographic components equation to estimate net migration without direct knowledge of in- and outmigration frequencies (Hinde, 1998; Plane and Rogerson, 1994; see pages 354–5 for an illustration).

Migration Rates

Like marriage, divorce, or childbirth, a change of residence may be seen as a transition between two different states: a non-mover in the population of origin becomes a migrant in the population of destination. This means that changes of residence in the population are the numerators when computing rates of migration. A general migration rate can be calculated as follows:

$$\text{migration rate} = \frac{\begin{array}{c}\text{number of persons}\\\text{moving in a given}\\\text{period}\end{array}}{\begin{array}{c}\text{population}\\\text{at risk of moving}\\\text{in the period}\end{array}} \times 1\,000$$

This equation treats migration no differently from any other demographic rate. But in fact, as we noted earlier, migration is different, because—unlike fertility or mortality—it is not irreversible. Rather, migration operates in two directions: for any given area, some people will move in and others will move out. This makes it necessary to calculate two rates for any given area: a rate of in-migration and a rate of out-migration. Let us look first at out-migration:

$$\begin{array}{c}\text{out-migration}\\\text{rate for area } i\end{array} = \frac{\begin{array}{c}\text{number of out-}\\\text{migrants from}\\\text{area } i \text{ in a given period}\end{array}}{\begin{array}{c}\text{population of area}\\i \text{ at the beginning}\\\text{of the period}\end{array}} \times 1\,000$$

This formula calculates the out-migration rate for area i as the number of persons that leave area i during a given period, divided by the population of area i at the beginning of the period. In fact, since census data are usually based on the mid-interval population, the denominator is usually the census population. For example, if in a given year there are a certain number of out-migrants from area i (O_i) and the population at mid-year for this same area is given (P_i), then we can compute a central out-migration rate for area i:

$$\text{out-migration rate for area } i = \frac{O_i}{P_i} \times 1\,000$$

where O_i is the number of out-migrants from area i in the period, and P_i is the mid-year population at risk of leaving area i.

By convention, the rates are expressed as per 1 000 population.

Although it might seem that the in-migration rate could be calculated in parallel fashion, a complication arises when we try to identify the "population at risk." In theory, the population at risk should be everyone who is *not* living in area i at the beginning of the period—in other words, the population of all regions in the system being studied other than area i (Hinde, 1998: 193; Plane and Rogerson, 1994: 97). This information is often difficult to determine. Instead, in practice, the in-migration rate is calculated using the same denominator used for the out-migration rate. So, if the number of in-migrants to area i in a given period is defined as I_i, then:

$$\text{in-migration rate for area } i = \frac{I_i}{P_i} \times 1\,000$$

The use of the same denominator in the in- and out-migration rate is problematic.

On the one hand, out-migration rates make sense because the total resident population in an area at least bears some resemblance to the number of people who could move out. But this is not the case when it comes to the in-migration rate, since the resident population by definition cannot move into the area it already resides in, and its size has no direct bearing on the number of people who could move there.

On the other hand, using the same denominator for both the in- and out-migration rates does have an important advantage, in that it allows us to compute two additional rates commonly used in the literature: the *gross migration rate* (GMR) and the *net migration rate* (NMR):

$$\text{GMR}_i = \frac{I_i + O_i}{P_i} \times 1000$$

$$\text{NMR}_i = \frac{I_i - O_i}{P_i} \times 1000$$

The *gross migration rate* is a sum of two migratory flows for a given area: in-migration plus out-migration. In other words, it is the sum of the in-migration to area *i* plus the out-migration from area *i*, divided by the mid-interval population of area *i*. The usefulness of this measure is that it provides an indication of the extent of migration turnover in a given locality during a specified period. Usually, areas that attract a large number of migrants also experience substantial out-migration: in addition to those leaving the area for the first time, there are many migrants returning to their places of origin, creating a large volume of *counterstream migration*. In such cases, the gross migration rate would be substantial.

The *net migration rate* is simply the difference between the numbers of in- and

It is often assumed that areas with high in-migration rates will have low rates of out-migration. In fact, such regions typically have higher-than-average rates of out-migration as well. For example, Alberta has consistently been the most popular destination province for internal migrants since 1996, averaging between 25 000 and 30 000 in-migrants per year. However, Alberta also loses large numbers of residents to other provinces. Between 1 July 2006 and 30 June 2007, for instance, a total of 131 441 persons moved to Alberta—by far the largest in-flow recorded by any province. During the same time, however, 80 272 individuals left Alberta to go to other provinces; this was the second-largest outflow (Ontario, with 107 590 out-migrants, had the largest). The net result of this exchange was a gain of 51 169 residents for Alberta. All the other provinces except British Columbia (+10 646) experienced net losses. It is interesting to note that during the third quarter of 2007, Alberta continued to receive the largest number of interprovincial migrants (29 690), but at the same time experienced the largest outflow of all the provinces (32 690); this was the first time Alberta had experienced negative net migration since 1994 (Statistics Canada Demography Division, 2007b, 2007c).

out-migrants for a given area during a given period, divided by the population of the area. It is a useful indicator of the regional gains and losses produced by the interplay between in-migration and out-migration, and gives a good sense of the relative impact of migration on the extent of a region's overall population change. A positive net migration rate means that the population is gaining people through migratory exchanges; a negative rate means that the population is losing people. Underdeveloped regions tend to experience net losses, while more prosperous areas enjoy net gains. In this sense, the net migration rate is a good reflection of geographical disparities in socioeconomic opportunities.

Table 8.2 looks at the net balance of interprovincial migration in Canada from 1951–60 to 2006–11. Historically, there has been a directional bias in favour of Ontario, British Columbia, and Alberta. This pattern of geographic mobility can be thought of in terms of *"core–periphery" relations*: economic deprivation causes the underdeveloped peripheral regions to export people, while the economically developed core must import people in order to meet its economic objectives. Core–periphery systems reflect unequal regional development processes and the relative abundance or lack of the natural and human capital resources that stimulate economic growth. Since 1945 in Canada, the Atlantic region—especially Newfoundland and Labrador—has been a net loser in terms of net migration, while Ontario, British Columbia, and Alberta (with some periodic exceptions) have been net gainers (Bélanger, 2002; Dumas, 1990; George, 1970; Stone, 1969). However, as economic conditions fluctuate, the balance of migration can change from positive to negative (or vice versa), sometimes from one year to the next. During the early to mid-1990s, for instance, Ontario's

economy suffered a downturn, while Alberta enjoyed sustained economic growth; not surprisingly, Alberta gained a substantial number of people from elsewhere in Canada, while Ontario experienced a net loss of internal migrants. Although British Columbia experienced a net loss between 1996 and 2001, over the longer term (1991–2001) it actually gained roughly 135 000 new residents from other parts of Canada. Alberta's migratory dominance is also clearly evident in the most recent periods of observation.

Looking at the period 2006–11, only three provinces showed positive net migratory gains, with Alberta leading the way (67 482), followed by BC (51 792) and Saskatchewan (11 401). For Saskatchewan, this represents the first positive quinquennial migratory period since the early 1950s, a change connected to the increased demand worldwide of the province's leading natural resource: potash.

A significant limitation of the net migration measure becomes apparent when it is analyzed on its own, because it tells us nothing directly about the magnitudes of the two component parts that give rise to it. For example, a net migration rate of 10 for a given area could reflect any number of combinations of in- and out-migration (20–10, or 150–140, or 1180–1170, etc.). Moreover, there is no such thing as a "net migrant" in the real world—just people who are arriving at places or leaving them (Plane and Rogerson, 1994: 98).

Table 8.3, based on 2011 National Household Survey data, focuses on interprovincial migration between 2006 and 2011. This table allows for a more complete analysis of interprovincial migration as it contains migration inflows and outflows between all pairs of provinces, as well as the net migration for each province (the Canada totals across

TABLE 8.2   Interprovincial migratory balance (net migration) in Canada over five decades, 1951–60 to 2006–11

Province/territory	Period					
	1951–60	1961–70	1971–80	1981–90	1991–2001	2001–6	2006–11
Newfoundland/Labr.	–9 816	–34 537	–20 840	–30 626	–55 784	–15 114	–1 130
Prince Edward Island	–7 938	–5 732	2 927	378	2 162	–407	–1 826
Nova Scotia	–28 851	–43 521	4 165	3 331	–11 056	–7 225	–6 100
New Brunswick	–25 360	–45 277	6 441	–5 915	–12 178	–8 382	–3 364
Quebec	–72 877	–142 594	–234 163	–122 143	–130 642	–21 375	–39 987
Ontario	148 036	236 081	–96 391	184 649	26 516	–29 617	–59 067
Manitoba	–40 587	–64 161	–68 977	–37 968	–51 833	–24 892	–18 243
Saskatchewan	–87 938	–123 492	–50 603	–67 475	–60 009	–35 080	11 401
Alberta	32 858	30 022	244 991	–61 203	165 249	128 962	67 482
British Columbia	93 075	192 713	216 486	144 345	135 834	15 286	51 792
Yukon and NWT[1]	–600	519	4 036	–7 373	–8 279	–2 156	–958
Total movements	**2 962 004**	**3 660 061**	**3 849 741**	**3 168 426**	**3 257 874**	**1 398 181**	**1 400 464**

[1] Data for Nunavut (established as a separate territory in 1992) are included with Yukon and Northwest Territories.

Sources: Bélanger (2002): 58, (2003): 73; Bonnert (2013b): 1; Dumas (1990): 106; Statistics Canada Demography Division (2007b): 17–21, Table 2-4.

TABLE 8.3   Interprovincial migration in Canada, 2006–11 (population five years and over as of 2011)

Province/territory 2011	Province/territory 2006													
	Canada	NL	PE	NS	NB	QC	ON	MA	SK	AB	BC	YT	NWT	NU
Canada	855 665	23 570	8 645	54 355	36 375	84 345	225 015	48 020	43 075	189 425	130 100	3 645	6 840	2 270
NL	28 755	0	425	4 165	1 570	455	11 000	670	295	7 930	1 485	70	425	260
PE	9 165	320	0	1 855	1 235	380	2 770	115	185	1 625	580	60	35	0
NS	50 965	3 045	1 685	0	7 380	2 505	18 810	1 190	905	9 610	5 165	120	350	200
NB	36 135	1 335	1 085	7 170	0	5 545	10 535	790	355	6 650	2 270	115	220	75
QC	63 095	910	340	2 785	4 985	0	36 915	1 715	1 080	6 610	7 410	45	195	125
ON	177 600	5 180	2 230	18 235	9 790	47 555	0	12 825	4 940	36 215	38 460	425	1 070	670
MB	36 855	420	150	1 365	850	1 300	11 165	0	5 170	10 315	5 490	195	275	155
SK	58 995	450	75	1 175	490	1 555	9 475	5 875	0	29 775	9 325	260	485	50
AB	215 850	9 770	1 890	12 225	7 820	15 250	72 355	14 360	21 460	0	57 375	920	2 105	310
BC	166 455	1 395	625	4 590	1 925	9 080	49 250	10 075	8 240	78 325	0	1 350	1 315	275
YT	4 240	50	20	240	40	230	715	95	125	940	1 555	0	185	40
NT	5 195	420	85	335	185	280	1 290	165	230	1 255	770	75	0	100
NU	2 355	285	30	215	105	195	730	145	85	170	220	10	175	0
Net migration	0	5 185	−520	−3 390	−240	−21 250	−47 415	−11 165	15 920	26 425	36 355	595	−1 645	85

Note: Excludes National Household Survey data for one or more incompletely enumerated Indian reserves or Indian settlements. Global non-response rate (GNR) = 26.1%. For the 2011 National Household Survey (NHS) estimates, the global non-response rate (GNR) is used as an indicator of data quality. This indicator combines complete non-response (household) and partial non-response (question) into a single rate. The value of the GNR is presented to users. A smaller GNR indicates a lower risk of non-response bias and as a result, lower risk of inaccuracy. The threshold used for estimates' suppression is a GNR of 50% or more.

Source: Statistics Canada (2011d). Statistics Canada, 2011 *National Household Survey*, accessed September 17, 2013. Reproduced and distributed on an "as is" basis with permission of Statistics Canada.

the table represent out-migration counts from each province; the Canada column is the in-migration to each province).

As already noted, patterns of interprovincial migration can change abruptly. For instance, commenting on the situation for the interval between 2001 and 2002, Alain Bélanger (2003: 72) noticed that for the first time in 25 years, more Ontarians moved to Quebec than vice versa. This pattern was repeated between 1 July 2006 and 30 June 2007, when nearly 21 000 people moved from Ontario to Quebec while just under 17 000 left Quebec for Ontario (Statistics Canada Demography Division, 2007b). It is likely that during this period, many of those moving to Quebec were francophones returning to their home province, perhaps as a result of retirement from the labour force (Statistics Canada, 2007g: 16–17). In the most recent interval, 2006–11, the pattern of exchange between Ontario and Quebec reverted to the traditional form, with Ontario gaining at the expense of Quebec. As can be seen in Table 8.3, between 2006 and 2011, 47 555 Quebecers moved to Ontario. At the same time, 36 915 persons left Ontario to move to Quebec. Subtracting these two figures obtains a positive net migration of 10 640 in favour of Ontario.

Stream-specific Migration Rates
In many cases, analysts are interested in the exchange of migratory flows or streams between two places. The intensity of migration between origin place i and destination place j (MR_{ij}) can be computed as:

$$MR_{ij} = \frac{M_{ij}}{P_i} \times 1000$$

where M_{ij} is the number of people moving from place i to place j, and P_i is some measure of the population at risk of moving away from place i

The intensity of migration in the opposite direction—from place j to place i—would then be:

$$MR_{ji} = \frac{M_{ji}}{P_j} \times 1000$$

where M_{ji} is the number of people moving from place j to place i, and P_j is some measure of the population at risk of moving away from place j.

Ideally, in these formulas the population at risk would be the population at the start of the interval; however most often, in practice we have only the mid-interval population as the denominator.

Analysis of Migration Frequencies

Where absolute numbers—or "frequencies"—are available, they show exactly how many people are moving into or out of a given area during a given interval; they give us a concrete sense of the volume of migration, and of its possible impact on both sending and receiving populations.

Migration Efficiency
Internal migration essentially redistributes a nation's population through flows and counterflows between its various geographical subunits. An important measure of migration that reflects this principle is *migration efficiency* (also referred to as *migration effectiveness*). Closely connected to the gross and net migration concepts discussed earlier, migration efficiency is measured as the ratio of net migration to total migration (in plus out), denoted below as MER (migration efficiency ratio):

$$\text{MER}_i = \frac{I_i - O_i}{I_i + O_i} \times 100$$

This formula says that the efficiency of migration to area i is the *net migration for that area* (the sum of total inflow to area i from all other areas minus total outflow for area i) divided by the *gross migration for this same area* (the sum of total inflows to area i from all other areas plus the sum of total outflow from area i). As J. Stillwell and colleagues (2000: 19) explain, migration efficiency

> measures the degree of imbalance, or asymmetry, between a pair, a set, or system of migration flows and counterflows. Symmetrical flows suggest that migration operates primarily as an exchange process which serves to maintain the settlement system in dynamic equilibrium. Significant population exchanges take place because individual areas that perform specific roles within the settlement system (such as cities) attract migrants at certain life course stages, or with particular motivations, from other areas. But these flows are often balanced, to a greater or lesser degree, by other migrants drawn in the reverse direction by a different set of needs, motives, opportunities, or aspirations. In this situation, migration therefore acts as a mechanism for rejuvenation and renewal of population structures, and restores imbalances brought about by other demographic processes such as aging and mortality, but may bring about little if any net redistribution of population.

By convention, migration effectiveness ratios are expressed as percentages, so in the case of an area-specific ratio the MER will range between –100 and +100. High negative or positive values would indicate that net migration is an efficient mechanism for population redistribution, generating a large net effect for the given volume of movement. Conversely, values closer to zero indicate that inter-area flows are more balanced and migration serves to maintain a dynamic equilibrium in terms of population distribution across geographic areas.

If 100 people migrate to a given area i and 100 individuals leave it, the efficiency of migration to area i is zero, since:

$$\frac{100 - 100}{100 + 100} = \frac{0}{200} = 0$$

In this case, where equal numbers of migrants were received and sent out by area i there is equilibrium. However, if 100 people move into area i and only 10 leave, the efficiency ratio increases substantially:

$$\frac{100 - 10}{100 + 10} \times 100 = \frac{90}{110} \times 100 = 81.82$$

In this case, for every 100 people received and sent out, area i receives a net inflow of 82 individuals. This indicates a very high degree of efficiency. If we were to turn this example around, so that area i sends 100 out-migrants to other places and receives only 10 in-migrants, the efficiency ratio would be –81.82 (i.e., $[10 - 100]/[10 + 100] \times 100 = -81.82$), meaning that for every 100 migrants it gains or loses, area i sends a net outflow of 82 persons to other places; here, too, the degree of efficiency is very high, but this time it operates in the opposite direction, redistributing migrants to other regions. Migration effectiveness can be measured at different levels—for a specific area (as above), between two or more regions, for pairs of origin and destination areas, or for an entire system such as a country.

In some applications, analysts may be interested in studying the effectiveness of individual *migration streams* (M_{ji}) and *counterstreams* (M_{ij}) between pairs of origin and destination areas (i.e., *stream-specific effectiveness ratios*). The migration effectiveness ratio (MER$_{ij}$) for any two pairs of origin and destination areas *i* and *j* can be expressed as follows:

$$MER_{ij} = \frac{M_j - M_{ij}}{M_j + M_{ij}} \times 100$$

where M_{ji} is the migration from *j* to *i* (the stream), and M_{ij} is the migration in the opposite direction (the counterstream).

An MER$_{ij}$ value of zero would imply equilibrium in the migratory exchanges between the two places *i* and *j*. A positive value would indicate that for every 100 movements between *i* and *j*, area *i* would be the net gainer (meaning that area *i* is the more attractive area), and therefore this particular migratory stream is efficient in redistributing population from *j* to *i*. A negative MER$_{ij}$ value would suggest the opposite: that area *j* is a net gainer in relation to area *i* (or that area *j* is the more attractive place), and that this stream is efficient in redistributing population from area *i* to area *j*.

If all the area-specific, or stream-specific, efficiency ratios are summed for a given geographical system (e.g., summing province-specific MERs to derive an overall migration efficiency value for Canada), we can obtain an overall *migration efficiency index* (MEI) for the system as a whole. To do so, we sum the *absolute* values of the net migration balances for all the geographical sub-units in the system, and then divide this sum by the sum of all the gross inflows and outflows for all the subunits in the system:

$$MEI = \frac{\sum_i \left| M_{ji} - M_{ij} \right|}{\sum_i (M_{ji} + M_{ij})} \times 100$$

Whereas the two efficiency measures outlined previously had a broad range (between –100 and +100), this overall migration efficiency index has a more limited range, with values between 0 and 100. High positive values in this case would indicate that inter-area migration is an efficient factor for population redistribution, generating a substantial net effect in relation to the total volume of movement in the system as a whole. This index can be compared over time periods in order to gauge the extent of migration efficiency in a particular geographical system. For instance, Stillwell and colleagues (2000, 2001) discovered that the migration efficiency declined in magnitude in both Australia and the United Kingdom between 1976–81 and 1991–6. Changes in the migration efficiency index may reflect demographic changes (e.g., differential population aging across regions), shifts in economic opportunities across regions, or innovations (e.g., new communication and transportation technologies) that serve to either increase or decrease net shifts in population across geographic areas. For example, a declining rate of population growth may have the effect of reducing inter-area migration. On the other hand, trends towards population aging and early retirement may serve to increase movement towards locations attractive to seniors. Structural changes in the economy can produce asymmetries in inter-area migration, as some regions enjoy economic booms while others suffer downturns.

A system-wide migration efficiency measure summarizes the extent to which migration is transforming the pattern of human habitation, while reflecting "the human response to spatial variations in opportunities and constraints" and the degree of "equilibrium or disequilibrium in the flows between geographical areas that constitute the migration system" (Stillwell et al., 2000: 19). The calculation of migration efficiency for different levels of analysis is best illustrated with actual data. The Notes for Further Study and Exercises at the end of this chapter include further

information as well as worked-out examples at the levels of individual provinces, pairs of provinces, and the Canadian system as a whole.

Estimating Migration Using Residual Methods

We have already noted that the data necessary to compute actual rates of migration are not always available. In such circumstances we must rely on estimates produced using indirect or "residual" methods. There are several ways of doing this. One approach is

MIGRATION UP AND DOWN THE URBAN HIERARCHY

Migratory movements within a country can be viewed from the perspective of inflows and outflows across the *rural–urban hierarchy* encompassing places of varying population sizes: rural, small urban, middle-sized urban, large urban, and dominant metropolitan areas. Which urban size category attracts the most internal migrants in Canada? Which place category loses the most through net migration? Is movement up and down the rural–urban hierarchy age-selective? These questions have been addressed by Bruce Newbold (2011) in an analysis of migratory patterns across rural–urban size categories in Canada between 1996 and 2001. Newbold's analytical approach involves the calculation of migration effectiveness (i.e., efficiency) for the various place size categories.

His study reveals the presence of a large volume of intermetropolitan migration net movement out of Canada's largest metropolitan areas of Montreal, Toronto, and Vancouver. At the same time, there is continued movement up the urban hierarchy into other large urban centres via a largely stepwise pattern of migration. Migration across the urban–rural hierarchy is found to be age-selective, with the largest flows into Canada's large urban areas observed for 20- to 29-year-olds. Young adults share a definite tendency to leave rural areas in particular, and small urban centres. Older Canadians are more inclined to move down the rural–urban hierarchy and into smaller urban places, and at the same time more likely to leave large urban areas. Among those above age 65, there is a tendency to gravitate to medium and small urban places.

to use the *demographic components equation*, based on the numbers of births and deaths during the period in question, along with the total population sizes at the beginning and the end of the period. With such data net migration can be worked out by rearranging the components equation as follows:

$$\text{net migration} = (P_1 - P_0) - (B - D)$$

where B and D represent the number of births and deaths during the interval, and P_0 and P_1 are the population totals at the start and the end of the period, respectively.

To illustrate, we'll apply this formula to the population of Nunavut for the period 1992–6 (data in Bélanger, 2003: 104). Nunavut's net migration for this period is calculated to be –1300:

$$\text{NM}_{\text{Nunavut, 1992–6}} = (25\,300 - 22\,500)$$
$$- (3\,600 - 500) = -1300$$

This procedure can be extended to subgroups in the population (e.g., employed, unemployed, single, married, etc.) and for specific combinations of age and sex categories (e.g., males aged 20–24; females aged 20–24), assuming that the necessary information is available. In such cases, we need to know the populations at the beginning and end of a specific period for a given age–sex group, and how many people in that group have died during the interval in question, taking into account the fact that everyone will be n years older at the second point in time. (Note that except in the youngest age groups, births do not figure into the calculation.) Unfortunately, it is not always possible to know the exact number of deaths within an age cohort over n years

during a given time interval. This problem is particularly acute in the case of smaller administrative units, such as counties or municipalities, for which the required data are typically unavailable. In such cases, analysts usually rely on a residual method called the *survival rate method*. This is an advanced topic in formal demographic analysis. Explanation and examples are found in Morrison, Bryan, and Swanson (2004) and in Siegel and Swanson (2004).

Explanations of Migration

Why does population movement take place? Why are some locations within a geographical system more attractive to migrants than others? What is the relationship between socioeconomic modernization and geographical mobility? How do individual and societal factors influence migration? A number of explanatory frameworks and models have been proposed to address these and other migration-related questions.

The "Laws" of Migration

In the late 1800s, E.G. Ravenstein (1885, 1889) outlined a number of propositions that he called "laws of migration." Here is a summary of those "laws":

1. *Migration and distance*. (A) Most migrants travel short distances, and the volume of migration from one area to another decreases as the distance between them increases. (B) People who travel long distances tend to gravitate towards the largest urban centres, where the economic opportunities are greatest.

2. ***Migration by stages***. Urban expansion tends to have a gradual effect on migration. People living close to the city move there to take up newly created jobs, then migrants from more remote areas of the country move in to take up jobs in the places that have been vacated.

3. ***Stream and counterstream***. For every stream of migration in one direction, there is a corresponding counterstream of migration.

4. ***Urban–rural differences in propensity to migrate***. Migration is more likely among rural than urban populations.

5. ***Predominance of women among short-distance migrants***. Women tend to outnumber men in short-distance migration, and men outnumber women in long-distance migration.

6. ***Technology and migration***. Technological development, to the extent that it reflects economic growth and related developments (e.g., improvements in transportation), tends to stimulate migration.

7. ***Dominance of economic motives***. Economic considerations are the most important determinants of migration.

Propositions 1, 3, and 7 have received wide support in the literature, especially the last one, the economic motive as principal cause of geographic mobility (see, for example, Brown and Neuberger, 1977; Cadwallader, 1992; Cebula, 1979; Frey, 2003; Lansing and Mueller, 1973; Lewis, 1982; Ritchey, 1976; Shaw, 1975; Shin and Ram, 2008; Smith, Tayman, and Swanson, 2001; Stone, 1974; Tobler, 1995). Summarizing a large number of studies, G.J. Lewis (1982: 118) concluded that "taking a job" and "looking for work" were the most frequent responses when migrants were asked about their motivations.

The Mobility Transition

Another important contribution to our understanding of migration is the theoretical framework developed by Wilbur Zelinsky (1971, 1979), who looked at geographic mobility as both a consequence and a cause of broader societal changes. Starting from the proposition that socioeconomic modernization over the last two centuries has produced a *mobility transition* paralleling the demographic transition of the Western world, Zelinsky identified seven types of geographic mobility (see Figure 8.2) and charted their evolution through five numbered "phases" representing different degrees of socioeconomic complexity. Phase I represents the most primitive, pre-transitional type of society, while phase V represents the most advanced, in which economic activity is largely post-industrial (i.e., a technologically advanced service- and information-based economy).

In the first phase, the *pre-modern traditional* society, people live in small communities and rely on the land for sustenance. There is little genuine residential migration in this type of society and only limited movement (for purposes such as agriculture, social visits, commerce, warfare, or religious observance). The next phase, the *early transitional*, is characterized by massive rural-to-urban relocation (sparked in Western Europe by the Industrial Revolution) and internal migration to "colonization frontiers." In addition, as the population expands rapidly, this phase may be marked by massive emigration to foreign lands. In the *late transitional* phase, rural-to-urban migration levels off and the population movement becomes increasingly urban-to-urban, though there may also be increasing

A. International

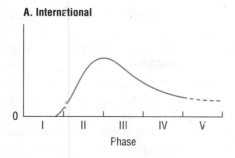

Phase

B. Frontierward (domestically)

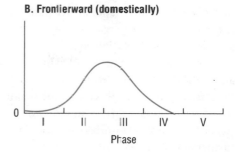

Phase

C. Rural–urban

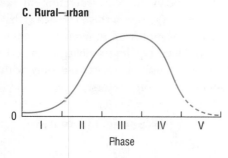

Phase

D. Urban–urban and intraurban

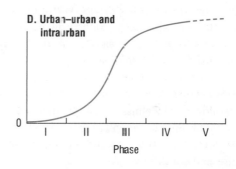

Phase

E. Circulation

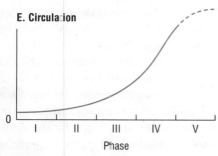

Phase

F. Potential migration absorbed by circulation

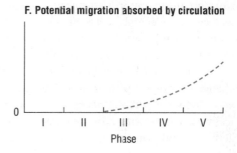

Phase

G. Potential circulation absorbed by communication systems

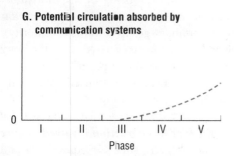

Phase

FIGURE 8.2   Changing levels of various forms of mobility through time: A schematic representation

Source: Zelinsky (1971). Zelinsky, Wilbur, 'The Hypothesis of the Mobility Transition', in *Geographical Review* 61(2) published by the American Geographical Society of New York, 1971. Reproduced with permission of the American Geographical Society in the format Republish in a book via Copyright Clearance Center.

movement of international migrants in response to labour demand. The direction and volume of these international migrations depend on economic circumstances and conditions in the receiving nations. In the *advanced society* (phase IV), the majority of the population lives in urban areas. Accordingly, rural-to-urban migration is further reduced, and city-to-city mobility becomes the most important type of movement. In this phase, a country in need of workers may attract significant numbers of unskilled and semi-skilled immigrants from underdeveloped areas of the world. However, in the more advanced stages of development, Zelinsky assumes that international migration will decline gradually as levels of socioeconomic development rise and states begin to impose strict controls on immigration. Advanced societies will experience high levels of "circulation mobility"—any form of territorial movement that involves at least one night away from home but does not entail a permanent change of residence (Bell, 2001: 5; Prothero and Chapman, 1984); this pattern is typically associated with economic and leisure activity. Finally, in the *super advanced society*, sophisticated communication technologies, such as the Internet, that allow people to work from home eliminate the need for much day-to-day circulation mobility, including the journey to and from work.

Typological Models of Migration

So many factors—individual and societal, personal and psychological, economic and structural—play a role in migration that it may not be possible to formulate an overarching theory. For this reason, some scholars have proposed typologies of migration. Typologies are conceptual schemata that describe a phenomenon—in this case, migration—in relation to selected factors deemed relevant towards an understanding of it. The advantage of the typological approach is that it offers a way to impose conceptual order on sets of factors presumed to be involved in generating migration. A disadvantage of this approach is that it may oversimplify an inherently complex process, since typologies do not deal directly with causal structure, but only with associations among factors.

Conservative versus Innovating Migration

William Petersen (1958) developed a complex typology based on the various forces that may trigger migration and the two fundamentally different states of mind that may be associated with two types of movement: *innovating* (motivated by the desire to improve one's socioeconomic status) and *conservative* (motivated by the desire to escape a situation that poses a significant threat to the well-being of the individual, such as a war or systematic persecution by a dominant group towards a minority). Specifically, Petersen arrived at his typology by juxtaposing the type of migration—whether innovating or conservative—with three factors:

1. *the type of interaction involved:* nature and humans, state (or equivalent) and humans, humans and their norms, collective behaviour;
2. *the migratory force assumed:* ecological push, migration policy, higher aspirations, social momentum; and

relationship between interregional wage differentials and migration rates.

The Distance–Gravity Model

Ravenstein (1885, 1889) suggested that most migrants move only a short distance, and that long-distance moves are relatively infrequent. Many of the migration models developed since his time explicitly incorporate the idea that distance is a deterrent to migration (Bogue, 1969; Cadwallader, 1992; Flowerdew and Amrhein, 1989; Goldscheider, 1971; Lee, 1966; Ritchey, 1976; Shaw, 1975; Yano et al., 2003). One important model in this tradition also incorporates the notion that different places within some defined geographical system (e.g., cities within a country) exert differential gravitational pull in the sense of attracting potential migrants. (The idea of distance–gravity developed by Zipf [1946] was inspired by Sir Isaac Newton's proposition that the gravitational force between two objects is directly proportional to their masses and inversely proportional to the square of the distance between them.) In accordance with this formulation, George Zipf (1946) proposed that the gross migration (M_{12}) between two places (e.g., cities) whose populations are P_1 and P_2, and the distance between them D, would be given by the equation:

$$M_{12} = \frac{P_1 P_2}{D}$$

which says that the volume of migration between any two places is a function of the differential force of attraction between each locality, divided by the distance separating the two places. Empirically, the relationship between distance and the probability of migration between places is not linear, but negatively exponential: there is a great deal of migration close to the point of origin, but

as distance increases from the origin the volume of migration drops abruptly to low levels. The version of the distance–gravity model frequently applied in empirical studies takes this into account:

$$M_{12} = K \frac{P_1 P_2}{D^a}$$

where M_{12} is the gross migration between any two places (i.e., the sum of in- and out-migration), and K and a are constants.

The latter term measures the exponential deterrent effect of distance on migration, while the former is an overall average value of the number of migrants. If the size of a is large, this implies that distance has a strong deterrent effect on migration: the majority of people will migrate to places that are relatively close to the point of origin, and relatively few will travel to distant locations. If a is small (or statistically insignificant) then distance is of minor importance, and the key determinant of migratory moves between places would be the relative population sizes of destinations (i.e., their relative "pull," or "gravity," in attracting migrants).

The *distance–gravity model* is intuitively appealing, as it corresponds to the basic notion of "least effort": the idea that when people are required to migrate—for example, to look for work—they would generally prefer to travel as short a distance as possible.

Why is distance so critical? As a general principle, the psychological and financial costs of migration vary in direct proportion to the distance between the places of origin and destination: the longer the distance, the greater the financial, psychological, and social costs of migration are likely to be. Viewed in this way, it is not difficult to see why distance can be a deterrent to migration. In most circumstances, the psychological costs of relocation (e.g., separation from family and friends) will be greater for long-distance migrants than for those who travel only a short distance from their community of origin. In the same way, immigrants to a new country will usually face greater social and psychological adjustments than people moving within the boundaries of their home country.

The Intervening Opportunities Model

For Samuel Stoufer (1940, 1960), by contrast, the most important factor explaining migration between places was not distance but opportunity. He proposed that the number of people moving a given distance is directly proportional to the number of opportunities at that distance and inversely proportional to the number of opportunities that intervene between places—in other words, the number of opportunities a migrant would encounter (and might decide to take up) on the way from one place to the other. In essence, Stoufer argued that for any pair of geographic places, the number of migrants from one place to the other will be determined by how many opportunities exist between the two areas. A frequent operationalization of the term in the empirical literature has been the number of jobs between places or the number of housing vacancies (see Plane and Rogerson, 1994: 206–11; Shaw, 1975: 49). However, Stoufer also pointed out that in any given destination area there would be other migrants competing for the same opportunities. Expressed mathematically, Stoufer's intervening opportunities equation is as follows:

$$M_{ij} = a \frac{\left(P_i P_j\right)^{b1}}{(O_{ij})^{b2}(C_{ij})^{b3}}$$

where M_{ij} is the number of migrants between places i and j, P_i and P_j are the population sizes of the two places, O_{ij} is the number of intervening opportunities between places i and j, and C_{ij} is the number of competing migrants seeking opportunities in place j, the destination.

The terms a, b_1, b_2, and b_3 are unknown parameters to be estimated empirically. Verbally, the model can be stated as follows: migration between i and j equals a direct function of (opportunities at place j) plus the inverse function of (opportunities intervening between places i and j) plus the inverse function of (the number of other migrants competing for opportunities at place j) (Shaw, 1975: 4). Stoufer's formulation has the advantage of recognizing that migrants, as rational actors, generally seek "opportunities" (i.e., work), and that this is a prime motivation for relocation.

Evidence from Canada seems generally consistent with the basic postulates of both the Zipf and the Stoufer models. For example, we saw in Table 8.1 that the majority of Canadians do not relocate at all between census periods, and that of those who do move, the majority remain within the same municipality; only a small proportion of people travel long distances (i.e., interprovincially). This suggests that distance is in fact a deterrent to migration, consistent with the distance–gravity model. Also supporting that model is the fact that the provinces with the largest populations tend to attract the largest volumes of both internal and international migrants (Shaw, 1985: 6).

A further test of the distance–gravity model might consider interurban migration patterns. Again, the evidence here is consistent with the basic postulates of the model. Canada's largest census metropolitan areas (CMAs) are Toronto, Vancouver, Montreal, Ottawa–Gatineau, Calgary, and Edmonton. These centres attract the largest shares of internal and international migrants (Shaw, 1985); thus at face value there appears to be a direct correlation between population size and the volume of in-migration to a CMA. It also appears to be the case that smaller urban centres generally lose more people than they gain through migratory exchanges.

Under the postulates of the distance–gravity model, it would not be surprising to find that the migratory flows between urban centres often take a step-like form, with migrants from smaller centres generally gravitating towards larger urban localities that are relatively close to the sending areas. For instance, the number of migrants moving from St John's to Halifax would be expected to exceed the number of migrants moving from St John's to Quebec City. And the volume of migration between Edmonton and Calgary would likely be much larger than the volume moving between Calgary and Thunder Bay, Ontario.

Extending this principle, we would expect to see fewer people migrating from St John's to Edmonton, or Calgary, or Vancouver, than to Toronto, since Toronto (1) is the largest urban centre in Canada, (2) is closer geographically to St John's, and (3) offers many more "opportunities" than St John's does. In fact, historically there have been large migratory flows from Newfoundland and Labrador, and the Atlantic region generally, to Toronto and other parts of Ontario. Nevertheless, sizeable migratory streams have developed between St John's and Calgary, Edmonton, and Vancouver, in spite of the long distance involved. The intervening opportunities model would say that the relative frequency of long-distance migration in this case is largely a function of fewer intervening opportunities in eastern and central Canada. In fact, Alberta has received many migrants from Newfoundland—people attracted by the large number of jobs available in Alberta as compared to the intervening provinces.

The Neoclassical Macroeconomic Model

In 1966, Ira Lowry formulated a model that incorporates indirectly some of the ideas inherent in the distance–gravity and intervening opportunity models. He wanted to test the proposition that the labour market works to allocate people more or less where they belong in terms of (a) their skills and training, and (b) the various regions' demand for specialized labour (Plane and Rogerson, 1994). The underlying premise is that differential economic opportunity structures across geographical areas are the key determinants of interregional migration patterns, and that structural conditions in the areas of origin and destination can either promote or discourage migration. Lowry (1966: 12) specified the following equation:

$$M_{ij} = k \left[\frac{U_i}{U_j} \cdot \frac{W_j}{W_i} \cdot \frac{L_i L_j}{D_{ij}} \right]$$

where M_{ij} is the number of migrants from place i to place j; k is an overall average migration rate; L_i and L_j are the number of persons in the non-agricultural labour force at i and j, respectively; U_i and U_j are unemployment as a percentage of the civilian non-agricultural labour force at i and j, respectively; W_i and W_j are the hourly manufacturing wages, in dollars, at i and j, respectively; D_{ij} is the airline distance from i to j, in miles.

Under the log transformation, Lowry's model become linear, easily estimated with multiple regression:

$$\log M_{ij} = \log k + \log U_i - \log U_j$$
$$- \log W_i + \log W_j + \log L_i$$
$$+ \log L_j - \log D_{ij}$$

The economic rationale of this model is consistent with the principle that more migrants will move from low-wage to high-wage areas than vice versa, and that unemployed people in areas with a surplus of labour should seek out opportunities where labour is in short supply. Similarly, regions with high wages will tend to retain more people than places with relatively low wages (Barsotti, 1985; Ferguson et al., 2007; Partridge, Olfert, and Alasia, 2007).

What factors besides size, distance, and socioeconomic opportunities influence migratory flows? Shaw (1985) studied this question with reference to Canadian *inter-metropolitan migration*. Among the additional factors that he identified were aspects of the labour market and the business cycle—i.e., industrial wage rate, unemployment, rate of residential building construction—as well as conditions such as weather, climate, and crime levels. Shaw (1985) suggests also that the role of economic factors as determinants of internal migration is diminishing in the post-industrial age.

In rich countries, concerns about social amenities and security become almost as important as labour market mechanisms in explaining differential migration patterns across regions. This might be particularly true of highly educated and highly skilled workers, who enjoy an exceptionally broad range of options and locational alternatives (Florida, 2002, 2005). On the whole, Shaw's analysis (see Table 8.5) suggests several generalizations:

1. Distance has declined as a deterrent to migration in Canada (though it is still important), probably because of reductions in the cost of transportation and telecommunications. "Declining transport costs are relevant to reduced 'fixed costs' of relocation whereas declining telecommunications costs are relevant to reduced 'psychic costs' of moving away from, say, friends and relatives" (Shaw, 1985: 21).

2. Areas with high proportions of highly educated people are more likely to send out migrants than are places with lower proportions of highly educated people. This is likely a reflection of the fact that people with more education have greater access to information regarding the prospects for economic gain through migration.

3. By itself, a higher incidence of violent crime in a particular CMA is not likely to deter migrants from going there; this suggests that other factors override crime as a consideration.

4. With some exceptions, places that normally experience harsh winter conditions do not attract as many migrants as CMAs that are situated in more moderate locations (e.g., Vancouver or Victoria).

TABLE 8.5   Determinants of Canadian intermetropolitan migration

Variable	Empirical measure
Labour market component	
Earnings opportunities	Industrial wage composite
Employment opportunities	Industrial composite employment growth
Unemployment	Unemployment rate
The business cycle	Residential building construction
Government transfers	
Unemployment Insurance	UIC benefits; availability
Government fiscal policy	Federal transfers to provinces
Natural resource revenues	Resource revenues
Additional economic factors	
Home ownership	Ownership, 25–34-year-olds
Housing costs	Cost of new housing units
Dual income-earning households	Female labour-force participation
Immigration	Immigration of foreign born
Information and psychic costs	
Distance	Distance between places
Language	Commonality of
Social and amenities considerations	
Crime	Crimes of violence
Climate severity	Total snowfall
Selectivity considerations	
Education	Proportion of highly educated

Source: Davis (1995): 73. Reprinted with permission of the Publisher from *Demographic Projection Techniques for Regions and Smaller Areas: A Primer* by H. Craig Davis © University of British Columbia Press 1995. All rights reserved by the publisher.

5. A CMA that attracts many immigrants from abroad is also likely to attract many internal migrants, probably because it offers greater social and economic opportunities than other areas.

The "Rational Actor" Model of Migration

All of the models outlined so far take a macro-level perspective, emphasizing spatial dynamics and macro-structural factors that influence the volume of migration. Implicitly, these models assume that migration is governed by microeconomic rationality, in which individuals make their rational choices based on available options (Burch, 1979; Da Vanzo, 1981; De Jong, 1999; Taylor, 2003; Walmsley and Lewis, 1993). Push and pull factors associated with the places of origin and destination are taken into account and are generally represented as economic costs and benefits, calculated according to the individual's own values. An influential model that explicitly incorporates this premise is Everett Lee's (1966), which will be discussed in the following section.

The foundations of the "rational actor" explanation of migration decision making can be traced to a seminal work by Larry Sjaastadt (1962), who proposed that the decision to move is based on assessment of the long-term benefits of relocation in relation to the long-term costs (psychological and material). What values and goals are most important in motivating rational actors to migrate? What is it that migrants seek? In Table 8.6, Gordon De Jong (1999: 283) offers a systematic list of goals in migration decision making. Essentially, people who move are searching for a better life: they are looking to improve their incomes, their standards of living, their access to opportunities for themselves and their children, and their lives overall.

Lee's Theory of Migration

Lee (1966) focused on the role played by structural factors in either "pushing" or "pulling" the individual to migrate. For instance, a high unemployment rate in the home community would be considered a "push" factor, compelling the individual to seek employment elsewhere. The presence of family and friends in the local area, on the other hand, would constitute a "pull," deterring out-migration. Push and pull factors, as perceived by the individual prospective migrant, also operate with respect to the area of intended destination. For instance,

Another "rational actor" approach to migration decision making is *place utility theory*, which focuses on migrants' perceptions of the advantages anticipated at the new location, usually in the context of local residential mobility (Bach and Smith, 1977; Deane, 1990; Landale and Guest, 1985; Lee, Oropesa, and Kanan, 1994; Speare, 1972; Wolpert, 1965a, 1965b). Individual actors are considered to have enough information to form a realistic picture of the chances of success in achieving their objectives. Actual behaviour (i.e., the decision to move) is contingent on the "worked out" probabilities with respect to the perceived gains and losses attached to each option (migration versus non-migration), plus considerations related to satisfaction with the current residence and neighbourhood. It is possible to incorporate into this type of decision-making model both the influence of significant others (e.g., spouse, colleague, parents) and the experience of cognitive dissonance—the tendency to hold to a decision even in the face of information that would argue against a move (see Burch, 1979: 284).

TABLE 8.6   Values and goals in migration decision-making: Some concepts from empirical research

Values	Goals
Income/wealth	Attaining desired income, affiliation, stable income, high standard of living, and employment stability
Comfort	Living in a pleasant, healthful and socially and morally acceptable community and home environment
Stimulation	Gaining entertainment and educational opportunities and variety in interpersonal relations
Affiliation	Living near family and friends, being with a spouse, and having family and friend support available
Easier lifestyle	Attaining a less strenuous and more peaceful life
Environmental quality	Having clean air and water, scenic landscapes, and low noise and pollution
Health	Preserving or improving one's physical or mental well-being
Functional independence	Attaining or maintaining self-reliance
Political and economic freedom	Having choices in economic and political behaviours

Source: De Jong (1999): 283, Table 13.2. From De Jong, Gordon F. 1999. 'Choice Processes in Migration Behavior', in K. Pandit and S. Davis Withers, eds, *Migration and Restructuring in the United States: A Geographic Perspective.* © Rowman and Littlefield. Reprinted with permission.

a pull factor would be any feature of the destination community that would offer the migrant an important relative gain or advantage, such as a greater number of jobs in the migrant's occupational class, and therefore a greater likelihood of finding employment. A push factor in the intended destination might be a geographical location associated with harsh winter conditions.

Lee considered four sets of factors:

1. factors associated with the area of origin;
2. factors associated with the area of destination;
3. intervening obstacles; and
4. personal factors.

The prospective migrant's decision about whether or not to migrate is thus based on an assessment of the pluses and minuses in both the place of origin and the potential destination. In addition to factors related with area of origin and area of destination, personal factors can also play a role in promoting or discouraging migration. Age, for instance, can be an important consideration: a plus for a young adult, but a minus for someone older. Figure 8.3 is a schematic representation of Lee's decision-making theory.

When the positives outweigh the negatives, the decision shifts heavily in favour of migration. Nevertheless, the individual must still be able to overcome what Lee (1966) calls "intervening obstacles." These intervening obstacles can take many forms, including the financial cost of moving, the emotional cost of geographic separation from family and friends, and the

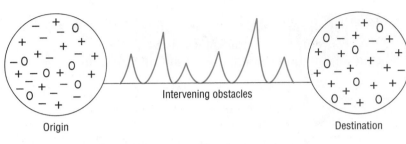

Factors at origin and destination   + attracting   O neutral   − repulsing

FIGURE 8.3   Lee's rational actor model of migration

Source: Lee (1966): 50 (Chart 1). Springer and the Population Association of America, *Demography* Vol. 3 Issue 1, 1966, "Theory of Migration" by Everett Lee, Chart 1. With kind permission from Springer Science Business and Media.

psychological insecurities associated with starting a new life in a new environment. For international migrants, one obvious obstacle would be the legal hurdles that must be cleared before gaining permission to enter a new country. Even if the pluses of migration outweigh the minuses, the intervening obstacles may still prevent the individual from moving.

Todaro's Model of Rural–Urban Migration in Developing Countries

One of the fundamental questions regarding migration in the developing countries is why large cities attract rural migrants even when the socioeconomic prospects they offer are not necessarily any better than the prospects in the rural countryside—for example, when unemployment rates in the city are high. According to Michael Todaro (1969), what matters is the perception of a significant wage differential between rural and urban areas (see also Harris and Todaro, 1970). Non-economic factors are also important, including:

- *social factors* (the desire to break away from traditional constraints or social organizations);

- *physical factors* (climate and natural disasters like floods and droughts);
- *demographic factors* (rural population growth);
- *cultural factors* (the security of urban "extended family" relationships; the allure of "bright city lights"); and
- *communication factors* (improved transportation, urban education systems, and the "modernizing" impact of media such as radio, television, and film).

As important as these non-economic factors may be, rural–urban migration in rapidly urbanizing countries largely reflects urban–rural differences in *expected*—not *actual*—earnings. According to Todaro, migrants consider the various labour market opportunities available to them in the rural and urban sectors and choose the one that maximizes their expected gains from migration to the city. (*Expected gains* can be measured by the difference in *real incomes* between rural and urban sectors and the *probability* of a new migrant obtaining an urban job.) In essence, Todaro assumes that members of the labour force, both actual and potential, compare their *expected incomes* for a given *time horizon* in the urban sector (i.e., the difference between the gains and the costs of migration) with the prevailing *average rural incomes*, and will migrate to the city if the former exceeds the latter. In other words, people from the countryside migrate to the cities because they expect that the economic opportunities there will far exceed the opportunities in the rural sector. This helps to explain the high rates of rural–urban migration in some developing countries even though the job prospects in the city may in fact be poor (Madhavan and Landau, 2011). The Todaro model may be suitably applied to less developed peripheral settings within advanced countries, such as the Canadian North (see Petrov, 2007).

Social Demographic Aspects of Migration

Selectivity of Migrants

Migration is a selective process because migrants generally do not represent a random sample of the population. Rather, they differ in their background characteristics from both the populations they leave behind and the populations they enter (Bedard and Michalowski, 1997; Geronimus, Bound and Ro, 2014; Ram and Shin, 2007). Two important observations by Lewis (1982: 97) based on his survey of the literature are:

1. Migration stimulated by economic growth and technological improvements attracts the better educated. Conversely, areas tending towards economic stagnation lose their better educated and more skilled persons first.
2. In modern technological societies, major migration streams between

metropolitan centres tend to show very little selectivity.

This last observation is especially interesting. As the overall level of migration in industrialized nations has tended to increase with increasing industrialization over the twentieth century and the expansion of commercial activity, simultaneously the selectivity in the occupational and educational characteristics of migrants has been declining or weakening (Long, 1973; Shaw, 1985; Williamson, 1965).

This is not to say that selectivity has become totally irrelevant for industrialized countries. In Canada, Kao-Lee Liaw and Mingzhu Qi (2004) analyzed 1996 census data to study Canadian-born persons aged 60 and older who, at the time of the census, resided in a province other than that of their birth. Among the strong selective forces they identified was mother tongue: specifically, the exchange of lifetime migrants between the province of Quebec (which is predominantly French-speaking) and the rest of Canada (predominantly English-speaking) had the effect of making Quebec more French—that is, Quebec gained more French-speaking people than it lost. According to Liaw and Qi (2004), instead of leading to a melting pot, the lifetime migration somewhat aggravated the spatial polarization between the two language groups. Bruce Newbold (1996) reached a similar conclusion based on his analysis of 1986 census data.

Bali Ram and Edward Shin (2007) examined the educational selectivity of migration streams across the Canadian provinces between the 1981 and 2001 censuses. They found an education gradient associated with out-migration from all regions of Canada, with the highly educated being more geographically mobile than the less educated. Interestingly, this pattern was most pronounced among the regions with persistently poor economic conditions and therefore net migratory losses over the years, namely the Atlantic region, Manitoba/Saskatchewan, and Quebec. By contrast, the three high-income provinces of Ontario, Alberta, and British Columbia not only experienced lower overall net losses, but were also less likely to lose their better-educated residents, even during bad economic times. Feng Hou and Rod Beaujot (1995) reached a similar conclusion in their investigation of interprovincial migration between Ontario and the Atlantic provinces between 1981 and 1991. The sociological implications of this educational selectivity are far-reaching, since the migration of highly educated and highly skilled persons to a few well-off provinces at the expense of the less well-off provinces will exacerbate longstanding regional socioeconomic inequalities.

Age Pattern of Migration

Age is one of a few variables that strongly affect migration probabilities; the others are education, occupation, sex, marital status, and income (Johnson et al., 2005; Ravenstein, 1885, 1889; Rogers, 1984; Shaw, 1975; Thomas, 1938). The importance of age as a determinant of migration is that it is strongly correlated with stage in the lifecycle (Greenwood, 1985). For example, entry into the work force is typically linked to the end of formal schooling, generally between the late teens and mid-twenties. Graduation usually implies the start of a search for work, often in a location other than one's community of origin. Retirement is another example of the interconnectedness of age,

lifecycle stage, and migration probabilities. For most people in the industrialized world, the official retirement age is set at 60 or 65. Upon retirement, many people migrate to locations that are geographically attractive to seniors, with a warm climate, many amenities, and so on.

So consistent is the correlation of age with migration probabilities that it has taken on the status of a general "law" in the demographic literature (Greenwood, 1985; Rees et al., 2000; Tobler, 1995). Andrei Rogers and Luis Castro (1986) have summarized this relationship mathematically (see also Bernard, Bell, and Charles-Edwards, 2014; Rogers, Castro, and Lea, 2005). There are three main segments assumed in the *age pattern of migration*:

1. *the pre-labour-force years* (childhood);
2. *the labour-force stage* (adulthood); and
3. *the post-labour-force phase* (retirement and beyond).

The mathematical specification of this model includes a term for the overall average level of migration, which is assumed to be constant across all age categories (see Figure 8.4).

In childhood, the chance of migration is relatively low and strictly tied to the family. Young adulthood typically brings a number of events: the start of university or college; entry into the labour force; marriage or co-residence with a partner; and so on. Because of all these lifecycle changes, the probability of moving is highest in young adulthood, between the ages of 18 and 24. After young adulthood, the likelihood of migration diminishes, dropping precipitously past the late thirties. By the early forties, most people are relatively settled in the mundane routines of work, family, and

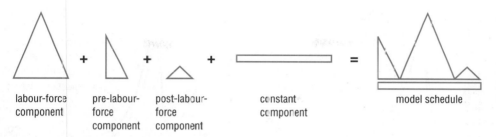

labour-force   pre-labour-   post-labour-   constant   model schedule
component   force   force   component
               component   component

FIGURE 8.4   The age pattern of migration and its components

Source: Rogers and Castro (1986): 157–208. Rogers, Andrei and Luis J. Castro, 'Migration' in Andrei Rogers and Frans J. Willkens eds, *Migration and Settlement: A Multiregional Comparative Study* 19:4. Ohio State University 1987. Reprinted with permission.

household maintenance, and the likelihood of migration is accordingly low.

A rise in the likelihood of migration in the post-retirement ages, especially after about age 75, has been identified as a characteristic feature of advanced societies (Warnes, 1992). Some of the literature concerning that rise in this area describes it as part of a general tendency among retirees to favour "sunny" regions such as Florida and California in the United States, and British Columbia in Canada (Bergob, 1992; Biggar, 1979; Chevan and Fisher, 1979; Gober, 1993; Krout, 1983; Martin et al., 1987; Northcott, 1988; Rogers, 1992a, 1992b; Serow, 1987; Sullivan, 1985; Sullivan and Stevens, 1982; Warnes, 1992). However, in Australia, Britain, and Canada, as Figure 8.5 shows, the more pronounced rise in migration probabilities at more advanced ages suggests the influence of factors associated with late life conditions.

The post-retirement period is, in fact, not a unitary phase. Merril Silverstein (1995) has identified several sub-stages in those years. With retirement many people embark on a "journey to rest," which typically means travelling to some place with a more comfortable climate than the place of origin. Eventually, the aging migrants begin to experience debilitating health problems. As they become increasingly frail, they seek either to return to their community of origin or to relocate close to children or other relatives who may offer help and support. The final move, to a hospital or nursing home, occurs when aging parents become so incapacitated that their children can no longer care for them.

Gender, the Family, and Migration

Ravenstein's (1885) early proposition that women were less likely than men to migrate over long distances and more likely to migrate short distances may no longer hold in the industrialized countries, where women are active in the labour force. As a result, gender can be expected to play a less significant role in migration today than it did in the past. One way to assess the relevance of gender in migration is by looking at indicators of long- and short-distance moves. An indirect indicator for long-distance travel is interprovincial migration. The 1991 Canadian census counted 413 060 male and 406 600 female interprovincial migrants during the five-year interval between 1986 and 1991. This is not a large differential (McVey and Kalbach, 1995: 137). Data from the 2011 Canadian Household Survey suggests a larger discrepancy today: as Tables 8.7 and 8.8 show, out of 855 665 interprovincial migrants in the period

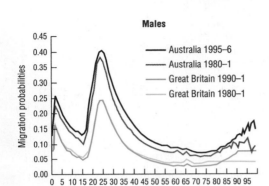

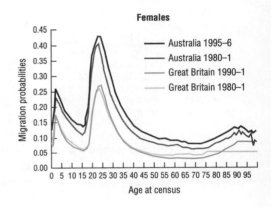

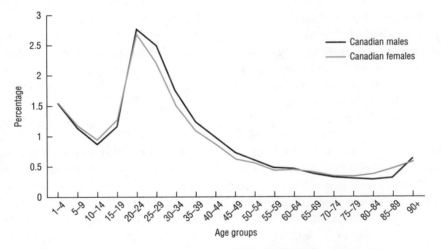

FIGURE 8.5 Age pattern of migration: Australia, Britain, and Canada

Sources: Rees, Bell, Duke-Williams, and Blake (2000): Figure 1, migration probability profiles for Australia and Britain, various years; Ram, Shin, and Pouliot (1994): 14 (figure: interprovincial migration rates for population aged 1 year and over by age group and sex, Canada, 1990–1).

2006–11, there were 11 175 more males than females. However, this represents a sex ratio (m/f) of just 2 per cent more males in relation to females (such ratios might vary more by age).

Some areas of the country send or receive more males than females, but the sex ratio of in- or out-migration across the provinces and territories do not deviate very much from a value of 1 (i.e., equal numbers of males and females). Only Prince Edward

Island and Northwest Territories appear to have a noticeable imbalance in the sex ratio of in-migration, with 111 males to 100 females in both cases (see panel [A] of Table 8.8). Some provinces tend to lose more females than males through out-migration (Prince Edward Island, New Brunswick, and Ontario).

If we look at specific migratory flows between pairs of provinces, panel (B) of Table 8.8 presents a somewhat different

WHERE DOES ALL THE TALENT FLOW?

Francoise Delisle and Richard Shearmur (2010) looked at the intraprovincial and interprovincial migration of graduates and non-graduates in Canada between 1996 and 2001. They applied a gravity model augmented by a series of structural variables to measure local characteristics as well as provincial-level characteristics in order to better separate the different patterns of geographical mobility between graduates and non-graduates aged 20 to 34. The analysis covered 375 spatial units in Canada. The criterion applied for defining migration was *moves of 50 kilometres or more*. This allowed the authors to exclude local moves (i.e., within same community). The analysis was done at two levels: at the Canada-wide scale (interregional migration); and at the intraregional level (intraregional migration).

The majority of graduates (93.5 per cent) and non-graduates (85.7 per cent) did not move 50 kilometres or more beyond their communities. So, only a relatively small proportion of young adults actually moved farther than 50 kilometres. As might be expected, the intensity of migration dropped off quite rapidly with distance.

At the Canada-wide scale (i.e., interregional migration), young non-graduates and graduates appear to behave in similar ways. Flows are weaker the farther the distance from their communities; and the origin and destination size effects are similar (i.e. larger places, whether origin or destination, exert greater influence on migrants than do smaller places). Flows are generally from low-wage to high-wage regions and localities. The only substantial difference between the two groups is that young graduates are more attracted to locations where there are already higher proportions of graduates. This can be interpreted as signifying the presence of opportunities in the knowledge-based economy, and so the attraction of graduates to such areas is to be expected.

The within region analysis produced very different results. At this scale, young non-graduates are substantially more sensitive to distance than graduates; that is, they are less likely to move longer distances. Graduates are more likely to move across places of similar population size. Non-graduates are more sensitive to agglomeration effects, meaning that larger places attract more non-graduates, and they tend to be moving from smaller to larger localities as compared to graduates. An unexpected finding was that non-graduates appear to be moving away from higher-wage localities in favour of places within a region where average wages are lower but stable. Graduates on the other hand seem to be indifferent to mean-wage levels. Finally, unlike the result in the Canada-wide analysis, this time higher concentrations of graduates at a destination area are similarly attractive to graduates and to non-graduates.

(continued)

According to Delisle and Shearmur (2010), the results for the long-distance interregional migration flows are consistent with established migration theory (i.e., distance–gravity) and theories of regional equilibrium (i.e., neoclassical economics). The intraregional findings are less intuitive. At the intraregional level, the dynamics of migration are responding to different types of conditions. One example of such variance in conditions pertains to the high-wage, resource-based localities and their ability to generate further wage increases for young workers. Delisle and Shearmur (2010) found that these resource-based localities are no longer generating economic opportunities, therefore many young adults, especially non-graduates, are leaving these localities in search of more stable, albeit less paying, work elsewhere. So, the availability of opportunities, not the average wage across areas within regions, seems to be more important as a factor of within regional migration.

The study of Delisle and Shearmur reaffirms the relevance of the distance–gravity model of migration and also the importance of the scale of analysis when studying migratory flows. The interregional part of their study provided results consistent with established theory. The findings from the within-region analysis required explanations beyond the established theories of migration, which would have been missed had these authors not looked at the lower scale of analysis within regions.

picture. In some streams, there are notably more males, while others are overrepresented by females. Those streams with the highest sex ratios (more males) all tend to reflect longer distances travelled, as the moves involve the crossing of more provinces between those of origin and destination. This might suggest support for the hypothesis that males are more migratory over long distances. But the same could be said of the female-dominant interprovincial streams because here, too, there is evidence of long-distance travel (e.g., Saskatchewan to Prince Edward Island). Overall, the evidence seems supportive of the hypothesis that males outnumber females in terms of long-distance migration by a small margin. The stream-specific flows, however, can be dominated by either sex. Analysis of intrametropolitan migration (short distance moves within a metropolitan area) suggests that here, too, males are generally more migratory than females. This casts some doubt on Ravenstein's proposition that women tend to be more mobile than men over short distances (see Figure 8.6).

Census data cannot tell us what percentage of the Canadians who relocate do so as part of a family, but the proportion is probably substantial. In single-earner families, the decision to move can be relatively straightforward, based on a rational assessment of the costs and benefits (monetary and psychic) of migrating as opposed to staying put. Things are not so simple for dual-earner couples, however. Jacob Mincer (1978) has suggested that in most such cases the wife is a "tied" or "trailing" migrant.

TABLE 8.7 Interprovincial migration in Canada, 2006–11 by sex (population five years and over; 2011 National Household Survey data)

Province/territory, 2011	Canada	NL	PE	NS	NB	QC	ON	MA	SK	AB	BC	YT	NT	NU
							Province/territory, 2006							
Males														
Canada	432 420	11 340	4 545	27 155	18 810	42 055	115 510	24 025	20 820	96 470	65 230	1 695	3 600	1 170
NL	14 625	0	185	2 070	750	185	5 580	315	140	4 210	805	0	230	140
PE	4 365	140	0	830	670	180	1 320	60	55	805	260	0	0	0
NS	25 390	1 590	830	0	3 765	1 195	9 060	660	435	5 010	2 510	45	175	115
NB	18 540	600	540	3 585	0	2 860	5 385	445	190	3 590	1 195	50	85	30
QC	31 480	455	175	1 305	2 450	0	18 200	750	550	3 645	3 740	20	125	70
ON	87 255	2 425	1 060	8 590	5 010	22 985	0	6 295	2 435	18 325	19 010	205	605	305
MA	18 570	175	85	695	460	660	5 555	0	2 435	5 435	2 775	90	135	80
SK	30 110	230	40	615	290	775	5 155	2 965	0	15 020	4 650	130	215	25
AB	112 310	4 725	1 135	6 670	4 320	8 320	38 995	7 110	10 230	0	29 035	450	1 155	165
BC	83 895	635	425	2 400	930	4 550	24 985	5 230	4 130	39 185	0	620	655	145
YT	1 995	30	0	130	15	90	290	35	45	475	750	0	110	20
NT	2 685	195	50	155	85	160	645	100	130	685	390	40	0	60
NU	1 200	145	15	110	60	100	345	75	45	90	110	0	90	0

(continued)

TABLE 8.7 (continued)

Province/territory, 2006

Province/territory, 2011	Canada	NL	PE	NS	NB	QC	ON	MB	SK	AB	BC	YT	NT	NU
Females														
Canada	423 245	12 225	4 100	27 195	17 570	42 285	109 505	23 995	22 255	92 950	64 875	1 955	3 240	1 105
NL	14 130	0	245	2 090	820	265	5 425	350	155	3 715	675	65	200	125
PE	4 800	180	0	1 025	560	200	1 445	60	130	820	320	35	1	1
NS	25 575	1 450	855	0	3 615	1 315	9 750	530	475	4 595	2 650	75	175	85
NB	17 595	735	545	3 585	0	2 680	5 150	345	165	3 065	1 080	65	135	45
QC	31 615	450	165	1 475	2 535	0	18 710	965	525	2 965	3 670	20	75	55
ON	90 345	2 755	1 170	9 650	4 775	24 570	0	6 535	2 500	17 895	19 455	220	465	365
MB	18 290	240	65	665	390	640	5 615	0	2 735	4 885	2 715	110	145	75
SK	28 885	225	40	560	205	785	4 320	2 910	0	14 755	4 670	125	265	25
AB	103 545	5 050	755	5 555	3 505	6 930	33 360	7 250	11 230	0	28 345	470	950	150
BC	82 560	755	205	2 190	995	4 530	24 265	4 850	4 115	39 140	0	730	660	130
YT	2 245	15	20	110	25	145	425	65	85	465	800	0	75	20
NT	2 510	225	35	180	100	125	650	70	105	570	375	35	0	40
NU	1 160	140	10	105	45	95	385	70	35	75	110	1	80	0

Note: NHS response rate was 26.1%.

Source: Statistics Canada (2011d). From Statistics Canada, 2011 National Household Survey. Reproduced and distributed on an "as is" basis with permission of Statistics Canada.

TABLE 8.8   Sex ratio of in- and out-migration by province and territory (A) and ten highest and lowest sex ratios of interprovincial migration streams (B); Canada 2006–11; National Household Survey data

|||||||||||||||||||||||||||||||||||||||||||||||||||||||||||||||||||||||||||||||||||||||||||||||||||||||||||||

(A)	Sex ratio (m/f) of out-migration from province/territory	Sex ratio (m/f) of in-migration to province/territory
Canada	1.02	1.02
Newfoundland/Labrador	1.04	0.93
Prince Edward Island	0.91	1.11
New Brunswick	0.99	1.00
Nova Scotia	1.05	1.07
Quebec	1.00	0.99
Ontario	0.97	1.05
Manitoba	1.02	1.00
Saskatchewan	1.04	0.94
Alberta	1.08	1.04
British Columbia	1.02	1.01
Yukon	0.89	0.87
Northwest Territories	1.07	1.11
Nunavut	1.03	1.06

(B) Ten Highest and ten lowest sex ratios of interprovincial migration streams

Stream	Highest sex ratios (m/f)	Stream	Lowest sex ratios (m/f)
PE to BC	2.07	SK to PE	0.42
PE to AB	1.50	QC to NL	0.73
NB to SK	1.41	NL to MB	0.73
MB to NB	1.29	PE to NL	0.76
NB to AB	1.23	NL to PE	0.78
AB to QC	1.23	MB to QC	0.78
NS to AB	1.20	NS to PE	0.81
QC to AB	1.20	NL to NB	0.82
ON to SK	1.19	NS to QC	0.88
NB to MB	1.18	NS to ON	0.89

Note: NHS response rate was 26.1%.

Source: Author's computations with data from Statistic Canada (2011d).

In other words, wives move because it is expected that husbands stand to gain more from relocating than wives stand to lose. Even in cases where the woman has a well-paying job, it is usually expected that the man's economic gains will compensate for her economic losses.

On the other hand, in cases where the potential gains from migration would be greater for the wife, the husband may

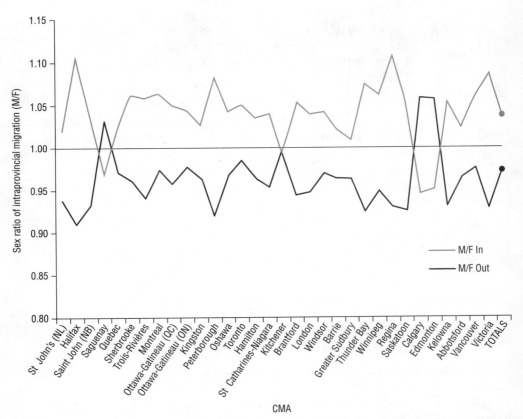

FIGURE 8.6 **Sex ratio of in- and out- migration within census metropolitan areas, 2006–10**

Dots represent overall M/F ratios for in- and out-migration

Source: Author's compilation based on data from Statistics Canada (2013m).

well be the trailing migrant. According to Mincer, however, in many such cases the wife becomes a "reluctant stayer," forgoing migration and its potential rewards in order to keep the family together. In short, traditional gender roles may still constrain married women's ability to influence family migration decisions (Cooke, 2008).

Although modern industrial society is thought to be generally egalitarian in promoting economic opportunities for men and women, much of the evidence uncovered in the context of family migration

research indicates that women are more likely than men to subordinate their careers to those of their partners. In fact, the empirical evidence indicates that the economic gains of migration tend to be substantially lower for wives than for husbands (Bonney, McCleery, and Forster, 1999; Boyle, Halfcree, and Smith, 1999; Cooke and Bailey, 1999; Green, Hardill, and Munn, 1999; Halfcree and Boyle, 1999; Lim, 1993; Shihadeh, 1991; Ten, 2010).

Migration decisions are further complicated for couples who have children or aging parents to consider. Adrian Bailey, Megan Blake, and Thomas Cooke (2004), for instance, describe how "linked lives" may either enable or constrain family migration. As we have seen, some migrants return to their former communities in order to care for parents in need of assistance (Silverstein, 1995). In some cases, three generations may live together in the same household (Knodel et al., 2000), although research based on the United States indicates that the incidence of co-residence of adult children and their elderly parents has actually declined over the course of the twentieth century (Grundy, 2000; Kobrin, 1976; Ruggles, 2007).

Migration and "Social Disorganization"

The "social disorganization" school of sociology (Durkheim, 1897 [1951]; Merton, 1964; Shaw and McKay, 1942; Wirth, 1938) has sometimes associated high rates of migration with rapid social and economic change. A central proposition in this literature is that geographic areas characterized by high rates of population mobility experience weakening of normative controls against deviant behaviours and "social pathologies." It has also been found that rates of divorce show a strong correlation with measures of migration in both the United States and Canada (Canon and Gingles, 1956; Fenelon, 1971; Glenn and Supancic, 1984; Makabe, 1980; Pang and Hanson, 1968; Trovato 1986a; Wilkinson et al., 1983), perhaps in part because of the strains that migration can introduce to a relationship. The correlation between migration and crime may be a reflection of the fact that migration is highly selective of young adult

males (Hartnagel and Lee, 1990; Hirschi, 1969; Kennedy and Forde, 1990; Kennedy and Veitch, 1997; Steffensmeir, Streifel, and Shihadeh, 1992). Other factors may also be involved, however. For instance, an economic boom might attract an influx of migrants to an area while at the same time contributing to a rise in social disorganization and a weakening of established traditions, and resulting in increased rates of crime, family dissolution, and suicide (Trovato, 1986b, 1992). On the other hand, high crime rates in a particular place might also lead to an increase in out-migration (Liska, Logan, and Bellair, 1998; Massey, Gross, and Shibuya, 1994).

Internal Migration Patterns and Differentials in Canada

The Regional Basis of Internal Migration in Canada

As we've noted already, to the extent that migrants self-select in terms of demographic and socioeconomic characteristics, high-volume migration can have significant social and economic impacts on both sending and receiving areas. Potentially, geographical mobility can help to reduce the overall level of income inequality within the larger system insofar as it allows individuals and their families to get ahead economically (Wilson, 2003). Given the selective nature of migration, however, interregional migration may actually help sustain inequalities at the regional level because underdeveloped regions will tend to lose their most skilled and productive people to more prosperous parts of the country.

Canada's history and geography have given rise to notable regional differences in economic wealth and resources. These regional differences reflect the regions' differential endowments of natural resources, proximity to natural and constructed transportation routes, political influence, and success in promoting capital investments (Bourne et al., 2011; Delisle and Shearmur, 2010; Simmons, 1982; Sitwell and Seifried, 1984). Historically, industrial activity has been concentrated in Ontario and Quebec, the industrial core of the nation, leaving other regions to rely mainly on natural resources—and, in the case of the Prairie provinces, also agriculture—as the main bases of economic growth and development. One consequence of uneven economic development has been the formation of asymmetric patterns of migration across the regions (Anderson, 1966; Barnes et al., 2000; George, 1970; Ledent, 1988; Sitwell and Seifried, 1984; Wallace, 2002; Warkentin, 1999).

In general, migrants in Canada, as elsewhere, seek to move to locations that offer good economic prospects. Areas that fail to generate sufficient employment opportunities will tend to lose many of their most skilled workers to areas that offer greater socioeconomic opportunities. Over time, this pattern of migration serves to shift the geographic concentration of specialized skills and labour in accordance with supply and demand principles (Bourne and Rose, 2001). In other words, as was explained earlier, internal migration acts as an efficiency mechanism by which workers with specialized skills are attracted to the regions where those skills are in demand and consequently will pay higher wages to workers. In this sense, internal migration plays an important redistribution function that helps to enhance the efficiency of the national economic system. But at the same time, those provinces that cannot provide sufficient economic incentives to skilled workers will progressively fall behind in their economic growth and development.

Reinforcing this idea, Liaw and Qi's (2004) analysis of lifetime interprovincial migration in Canada indicates there are substantial net transfers of migrants from the traditonal "have-not" provinces (Newfoundland and Labrador, Nova Scotia, New Brunswick, Prince Edward Island, Manitoba, Saskatchewan) to the "have" provinces (Alberta, Ontario, British Columbia, Quebec), and that migrants moving to these wealthier provinces generally achieve long-term income improvements (though generally not large enough to compensate for the disadvantages of being born in a "have-not" province). In other words, being born in a disadvantaged region is a factor in terms of the bundle of human capital (measured, for example, in education and occupational qualifications) one is able to acquire.

Ram and Shin (2007) identify another important mechanism that reinforces regional inequalities through differential patterns of internal migration in Canada. They have found that migrants are positively selected even when migration is stimulated by economic stagnation. The unemployment rate, they argue, does not necessarily influence the out-migration of less educated and less skilled persons, even though these people are typically among those with the highest rates of unemployment. Rather, it appears that unemployment actually serves as a push factor that encourages people to move if they are well educated and skilled (131). What this means in practical terms is that those regions of the country that tend towards economic stagnation will also lose much of their younger, better educated, and more skilled population first, which on the whole produces an unfavourable effect, not only in terms of demographic composition (i.e., helping to increase population aging) but also in the sense of reduced economic productivity.

It is important to note that inter-provincial migration in Canada is not unidirectional—in other words, predominantly from less developed to more developed regions. In fact, provinces that have traditionally lost out through net migration also tend to experience a significant amount of return migration. Recall Ravenstein's proposition that for every dominant stream of migration in a given direction there is typically a less dominant flow in the opposite direction. This tendency is evident in the Canadian context. For instance, historically Ontario has been the recipient of migrants from all other provinces in Canada; but for each province that sends migrants to Ontario, there is a counterflow in the opposite direction, albeit usually smaller in volume. The same point can be made with regard to Alberta and British Columbia, who over recent decades have been leading destination provinces (George, 1970; Grant and Vanderkamp, 1984; Hiller, 2009; McInnis, 1971; Rosenbaum, 1988; Stone, 1969, 1974, 1978; Vanderkamp, 1971).

So does return migration in any way help to compensate "have-not" provinces economically? John Vanderkamp (1968), in an early study, showed that the most common reasons for return migration were difficulties either in finding work or in holding onto a job in the new location. He concluded that return migration in Canada accounted for a substantial proportion of total migration, particularly during periods of economic recession. This return movement, which is positively related to unemployment, tends to be directed predominantly to regions that experience net out-migration (i.e., less prosperous regions). To the extent that this tendency prevails on a wide scale, it may be taken as indirect evidence in support of the proposition that for many, return migration represents some kind of "failure," be it in finding employment or in adjusting to life in the new province. These migrants may experience a strong longing for a more familiar social environment; others may have difficulty adjusting to a new way of life or unfamiliar workplace demands. Young single people are perhaps especially prone to these types of problems (Grant and Vanderkamp, 1985; Rosenbaum, 1988). Thus, the effects of return migration to relatively underdeveloped areas of the country may not have significant impacts on the economic development of such regions.

It should also be noted that not all cases of return migration reflect negative experiences. Young people who return to their home regions after attending university or college elsewhere are also counted as return migrants, as are older people who return to their home provinces after retiring from the labour force. These migrant categories may in fact help stimulate economic improvements in the economically disadvantaged areas. Thus, the net effect of return migration on economic growth in such regions may be negligible, as these two types of tendencies effectively cancel each other out. It thus appears that a crucial factor for a region's economic development is the extent to which the highly educated and skilled components of the labour force leave for other regions.

PUBLIC POLICY AND INTERREGIONAL MIGRATION

How important is interregional migration in explaining regional differences in economic development? Clearly, migration is important because the more prosperous regions will always be more attractive to prospective migrants. In this context, one may ask whether public policy can somehow affect interregional migratory flows. Kathleen Day and Stanley Winer (2012) have explored this question in a comprehensive analysis of interregional migration in Canada over four decades, covering data from the late 1960s to the mid-1990s. One of the central hypotheses these authors evaluated is grounded on the early work of Thomas Courcherne (1970), who proposed the transfer dependence hypothesis—that fiscally induced migration actually reduces economic efficiency in a region. That is, government support of various kinds (unemployment, welfare, etc.) of people who live in more disadvantaged regions serves to slow down economic development and regional convergence by reducing migration out of the less prosperous provinces. That is, if the unemployed and those out of the labour force with low skills can rely on government assistance, these people would have little incentive to migrate out of their region to search of work elsewhere. Courcherne had argued that this type of policy is counterproductive because it fails to stimulate labour migration among those lacking in job opportunities.

After an extensive assessment of the literature in this area and their own multivariate analysis of the evidence, Day and Winer (2012) reached the conclusion that there really is no support for the hypothesis that regional subsidization built into the employment insurance system plays an important role in maintaining regional disparities by inducing too many people to stay in relatively poorer parts of the country. Rather, the analysis lends strong support for the neoclassical economics perspective that the key determinants of internal migration across the Canadian regions are inherently economic in nature: People move in search of better wages and go to places where their skills are in demand. So, the crucial factor in interregional migration is the variations in economic growth and opportunities across the regions and the regions' ability to attract labour.

Geographic Mobility of Immigrants

Interurban Mobility

Excluding the contribution of natural increase, massive immigration from the early twentieth century to the present is the factor most responsible for the growth of North America's largest cities. The early immigrants from Europe crowded into cities, where they could most readily get jobs while establishing and maintaining their ethnic associations and ethnic-based economies (Bartel, 1989; Kritz and Nogle,

1994; Thompson, 1983; Ward, 1971; Yancey, Ericsen, and Juliani, 1976). These ethnic communities effectively sheltered newcomers from the disruptive effects of immigrating and adapting to a new society (Breton, 1964; Clark, 1972: 97).

The process of ethnic community development must be understood in the context of immigration and urbanization history. For example, the largest Italian communities in this country are concentrated in the metropolitan areas of Ontario and Quebec (namely Toronto and Montreal) because Italian immigration early in the twentieth century was largely determined by the economic exigencies of these prosperous regions—specifically, the rising demand for labour in the construction and manufacturing sectors in a context of post-war economic boom. Immigrants from Italy, as well as other parts of Europe, found jobs in construction and helped power the massive growth of Toronto as a global city. These initial settlers blazed the trail for immigrants who subsequently came to Toronto and contributed to the growth of both the city and its ethnic communities. This process has been repeated in every one of Canada's major cities, even though the principal nationalities involved may differ, depending on the region of the country. In the Prairies, for example, many of the initial settlers in Calgary, Edmonton, and Winnipeg were from Eastern Europe, especially Ukraine, Germany, and Poland. Consequently, their presence in this part of Canada is still highly noticeable.

Immigrants today continue to gravitate to Canada's largest metropolitan centres, which have become home to a large proportion of the country's total foreign-born population. In contrast, the Canadian-born population is more widely dispersed across a broad range of settlement size categories, and it is much better represented in small urban settlements. This differential pattern of concentration across urban settlements of varying size may be reinforced, in part, by interurban mobility flows among immigrants. For instance, Frank Trovato (1988) noted that the percentage of established immigrants in the largest cities is lower than the percentage of recently arrived immigrants. This difference could be attributed to differences in the out-migration rates of more established immigrants. More recent immigrants, if they do engage in interurban mobility, are more inclined to exchange one large city for another large city, or perhaps leave smaller cities for larger ones. In fact, Trovato's (1988) analysis indicates that the most dominant migration stream of foreign-born Canadians is between large urban centres, and that there is considerably less movement away from large cities towards smaller ones.

Feng Hou's (2004, 2007) studies of the Canadian "gateway cities" of Toronto, Montreal, and Vancouver reveals that during the 1970s and 1980s, the redistribution or relocation of foreign-born citizens after immigration tended to occur on just a small scale. This fact, combined with continued immigration from abroad and some internal relocation to these cities from elsewhere in Canada, produced an increasing concentration of immigrants in the three cities. In all, roughly 44 per cent of the immigrants who arrived in Canada between 1970 and the early 1980s were located in regions outside Toronto, Montreal, and Vancouver; just ten years later, this proportion had fallen to 39 per cent, suggesting a small amount of internal redistribution had taken place in favour of the gateway cities.

The propensity of foreign-born people to leave the place of initial settlement is closely linked to the size of the city and the region in which the city is situated. Metropolitan centres in prosperous regions of the country offer widespread social and economic opportunities, making out-migration less of a priority. Additionally, ethnic communities in large cities have a dampening effect on out-migration probabilities because they are made up of strong social networks joining relatives and friends of the same nationality. These communities typically support well-developed enclave economies in which many of their members are gainfully employed, which also helps to discourage out-migration (Darroch and Marston, 1988; Kobrin and Speare, 1983; Trovato, 1988).

The recent analysis by Lei Xu (2011) for the periods 1991–6 and 1996–2001 is consistent with the earlier literature: The spatial and temporal patterns of immigrants in Canada conformed to both the neoclassical economic and ethnic enclave theories. In other words, in making their decisions on departure and destination choices, the immigrants were responsive to income and employment incentives, as well as the retaining and attracting powers of ethnic communities among large metropolitan centres.

Xu (2011) also discovered an interesting temporal pattern—while the intermetropolitan migration of immigrants accentuated the over representation of the immigrants in Toronto and Vancouver in the 1991–6 period, the rise of the "secondary" metropolitan areas (e.g., Ottawa, Calgary, Edmonton, Winnipeg, Hamilton) led to increased spatial dispersal of the immigrants in the 1996–2001 period.

All things considered, it appears that once immigrants settle in metropolises like Toronto, Montreal, Vancouver, and Ottawa there is a relatively low likelihood of relocation out of these centres. Immigrants to Canada generally replicate the settlement preference of earlier generations of immigrants, taking up residence in the country's largest cities and, once established, show little inclination to leave. While certainly many immigrants do move from their initial destinations to other parts of Canada, the majority tend to move to the gateway cities: Toronto, Montreal, or Vancouver; or else to some of the secondary metropolitan areas.

The situation of refugees to Canada differs only slightly. While many are settled initially in non-gateway cities and small communities, they demonstrate an even stronger tendency to resettle in Toronto and Vancouver, although many do remain and integrate fully in their initial settlements (Hou, 2004; Krahn, Derwing, and Abu-Laban, 2005).

Geographic Mobility of Aboriginal Peoples

Indigenous minorities in New World countries—Canada, the United States, Australia, and New Zealand—differ significantly from mainstream populations, both socioeconomically and demographically. The dire conditions in which many indigenous people live led E.A. Young (1995) to describe the Aboriginal populations in these societies as representing a "Third World in the First." It is generally agreed that Aboriginal peoples' relative deprivation is a legacy of colonialism. Not surprisingly, they lag considerably on all major indicators of socioeconomic wellbeing.

Indigenous populations share some distinctive patterns of geographic mobility. John Taylor and Martin Bell (2004) explain that as a consequence of colonization, indigenous groups have experienced significant territorial displacement and have been pushed to reserves or to isolated geographic areas away from the majority population. However, since the end of World War II, the settlement and geographic mobility patterns of Aboriginal peoples have changed: they are no longer confined to remote reserve communities but dispersed across a wide variety of settings, both urban and rural. Taylor and Bell cite five other features common to indigenous populations of New World countries since the second half of the twentieth century:

1. **High levels of geographic mobility** compared with the majority population, particularly in rates of short-term circulatory movements between reserve communities and the city. This reflects unique features of Aboriginal populations, namely their participation in seasonal work; their extensive kin networks, which link individuals to both the city and the reserve; the problems they have experienced in finding adequate housing in the city; and their difficulty adjusting to the urban setting.
2. **High regional variability in geographic mobility**, reflecting the range of Aboriginal responses to regional variations in socioeconomic conditions.
3. **Sustained presence in non-metropolitan residential areas**, including reserves both close to and far removed from large urban centres.
4. **Rising post-war migration from the rural areas** (i.e., reserves) to the city, intensifying in the 1970s. Migration to urban centres has abated since the 1980s.
5. **Significant return migration** to places of Aboriginal cultural significance, such as reserves. (Taylor and Bell, 2004: 2)

The geographic mobility patterns of Aboriginal peoples in Canada have been documented extensively (see, for example, Frideres, Kalbach, and Kalbach, 2004; Maxim, Keane, and White, 2002; Norris, 1990, 1996; Norris et al., 2004). Detailed analyses of census data by Mary Norris and Stewart Clatworthy (2002) and Clatworthy and Norris (2006, 2014) point to a higher overall level of geographical mobility—local and migratory combined—among Aboriginal Canadians than among the general population. For example, between 1996 and 2001, 20.1 per cent of Aboriginal people aged five and older had been involved in migration; the figure for the general population was 16.5 per cent. During this same interval, roughly 30 per cent of Aboriginal people had changed residence locally, compared to about 22 per cent for the general population. The 2006 census gave further indication of the difference in mobility rates between Aboriginal people and other Canadians. Eight of ten First Nations people (81 per cent) lived at the same address in 2006 as they did one year before the census, compared with 86 per cent of the non-Aboriginal population. The Aboriginal population was slightly more likely than others to have either moved within the same community (11 per cent versus 8 per cent) or to have relocated to their current address from another community (8 per cent versus 5 per cent).

Table 8.9 looks at the mobility status of Registered Indians, non-status Indians, Métis, and Inuit during the 1991–6 and 1996–2001 census periods. Registered Indians and non-status Indians are

TABLE 8.9   **Mobility status of Aboriginal identity population, 1991–96 and 1996–2001, by subgroup (population aged 5+)**

IIIIIIIIIIIIIIIIIIIIIIIIIIIIIIIIIIIIIIIIIIIIIIIIIIIIIIIIIIIIIIIIIIIIIIIIIIIIIIIIIIIIIIIIIIIIIIIIIIIIIIIIIIIIIIIIIIIIIIIIIIIIIIII

	Registered Indians	Non-status Indians	Métis	Inuit
1991–96				
Local movers	40.0	26.0	23.0	14.0
Migrants	20.6	48.0	46.3	54.0
Subtotal	60.6	74.0	69.3	68.0
Non-movers	39.7	26.0	30.7	32.0
Total	100.0	100.0	100.0	100.0
1996–2001				
Local movers	29.5	32.4	31.5	36.2
Migrants	19.3	23.7	24.4	16.0
Subtotal	48.8	56.1	55.9	52.24
Non-movers	51.3	43.9	44.1	47.8
Total	100.0	100.0	100.0	100.0

Source: Adapted from Norris and Clatworthy (2003): 59, 69.

members of First Nations bands that have negotiated land treaties with the Crown. Many of these treaties established reserve lands where members of these groups have historically lived. Non-status Indians are those who are not officially registered under Canada's Indian Act; many of them are of mixed Native and non-Native parentage, and relatively few of them live on reserves. The Métis are also of mixed Aboriginal and non-Aboriginal (typically French-Canadian) ancestry, and trace their roots to the historical Red River community in western Canada. The Inuit are indigenous to northern Quebec, the Northwest Territories, Nunavut, and Labrador (Norris and Clatworthy, 2002).

The tendency for Aboriginal people to be involved in some form of geographic mobility may reflect a number of underlying factors. It may indicate that Canada's Aboriginal people find it difficult to settle down because of problems they face due to their minority status. On the other hand, it may indicate a growing tendency for Aboriginal people to integrate into urban communities while maintaining strong attachments to their indigenous cultures. Over time, more and more Aboriginal people have set up residence in urban areas, and today fewer First Nations people live on reserve than off reserve (40 per cent versus 60 per cent, as of 2006). The off-reserve population is most likely to live in urban areas of varying population size, including large metropolitan centres (Statistics Canada, 2008b). A unique feature of Aboriginal people's pattern of geographical movement is their tendency to move back and forth between the city and the reserve, often described as *circular mobility* (Norris et al., 2004; Taylor and Bell, 2004). As

Table 8.10 shows, circular mobility is most pronounced among Registered Indians.

Analyses by Clatworthy and Norris (2006, 2014) show that reserve lands are the only geographic areas to see consistent net migration gains among Aboriginal people over sequential census periods since 1971, although over recent years the gains have been diminishing. All other residential localities—rural areas, small urban areas, and large metropolitan centres—witnessed net migration losses. Reserves have experienced a net inflow of migrants, mostly at the expense of urban metropolitan and non-metropolitan areas. The greatest net losers have been rural areas and urban non-metropolitan places. Large urban centres, even though they receive a substantial number of migrants (mainly from rural areas and non-metropolitan places), still experience some net migratory deficits in certain periods (Clatworthy and Norris, 2006: 215,

TABLE 8.10 Distribution of Aboriginal migrant flows by origin, destination, and Aboriginal identity group, 1991–96 and 1996–2001 (population aged 5+)

Migration stream	Registered Indians	Non-status Indians	Métis	Inuit	Total
1991–96					
Urban to reserve	19.6	2.3	1.4	0.3	23.6
Reserve to urban	6.9	1.2	0.4	0.6	9.1
Subtotal	26.5	3.5	1.8	0.9	32.7
Rural to reserve	4.8	0.7	0.5	0.8	6.8
Reserve to rural	1.4	0.4	0.2	2.1	4.1
Subtotal	6.2	1.1	0.7	2.9	10.9
Reserve to reserve	3.1	0.2	0.0	0.0	3.3
All other streams	64.2	95.2	97.5	96.2	46.9
Total migrants aged 5+	87 340	20 130	37 460	4 760	149 690
	100.0	100.0	100.0	100.0	100.0
1996–2001					
Urban to reserve	18.2	2.3	1.2	1.8	23.0
Reserve to urban	10.7	1.5	1.2	2.7	16.1
Subtotal	28.9	3.8	2.4	4.5	39.1
Rural to reserve	5.7	0.7	0.4	2.0	9.0
Reserve to rural	1.7	0.2	0.5	1.4	3.8
Subtotal	7.4	0.9	0.9	3.4	12.8
Reserve to reserve	3.5	0.3	0.2	1.8	5.0
All other streams	60.2	95.0	96.4	90.4	43.1
Total migrants aged 5+	93 150	22 300	53 815	5 520	171 420
	100.0	100.0	100.0	100.0	100.0

Sources: Adapted from Clatworthy and Norris (2006): 214; Norris and Clatworthy (2003: 55, 69).

2014; Norris et al., 2004: 142–3). These data make it clear that the focal points of recent Aboriginal migration have been urban areas and reserves, and that large inflows to urban locations have been overshadowed by much larger outflows of urban population.

Figure 8.7 tracks the net migratory patterns for the largest of the four Aboriginal subgroups—Registered Indians—and reveals a picture consistent with what has been presented so far. Rural communities are the greatest net losers, and reserve communities the major net gainers. Metropolitan centres have witnessed an irregular pattern of ups and downs in net migration, but during the 2001–6 census period, the net balance has been clearly positive. Again, from these

trends, it is evident that the reserves have enjoyed growth as a result of the redistribution of the Registered Indian population.

The observed pattern of net gains and losses across different residential areas since 1966 shown in Figure 8.7 contradicts much of the early literature on Aboriginal mobility, which pointed to massive out-flows of Aboriginal people from reserves and rural areas to the cities (see, for example, Dosman, 1972; Hawthorne, 1966; Royal Commission on Aboriginal Peoples, 1995: 89). Some of this literature went as far as predicting an eventual extinction of many reserves. Certainly, as many scholars have noted, there was significant out-movement from reserves to cities between the 1950s and the

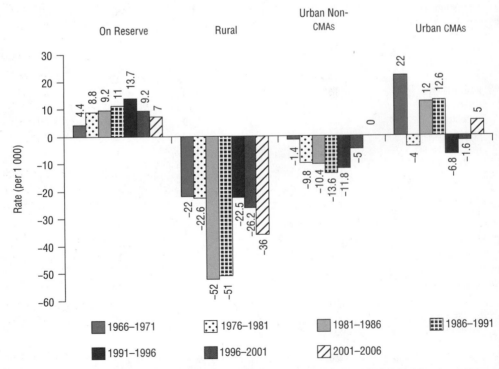

FIGURE 8.7 Average annual rate of Registered Indian net migration by location and five-year period, Canada, 1966–2006

Source: Clatworthy and Norris (2014). Clatworthy, Stewart and Mary Jane Norris, 'Aboriginal Mobility and Migration in Canada: Trends, Patterns, and Implications, 1971 to 2006.' In Frank Trovato and Anatole Romaniuk (eds.), *Aboriginal Populations—Social, Demographic and Epidemiological Perspective* ©2014 University of Alberta Press. Reprinted with permission.

early 1970s (Frideres and Gadacz, 2008: 163). How can we account for the marked change in Aboriginal migration trends?

One hypothesis for the reported rise in cityward migration in the two decades after World War II is that small levels of reserve-to-city migration were exaggerated by the fact that many Aboriginal people in the cities were, for the first time, declaring their Native ancestry on the census. Some researchers mistakenly interpreted this rise in urban Aboriginal numbers as having been generated by migration from reserves (Norris et al. 2004). In reality, as Norris and associates (2004) argue, there was—as there continues to be—a great deal of return migration from the city to the reserve. Further, they argue that from the 1950s through the 1970s, the most significant migration streams were from rural non-reserve places to reserves, and from rural non-reserve areas to urban areas. Thus, far from there having been a unidirectional flow from reserves to cities, both reserves and urban areas were involved as net migration gainers during the post-war years (Norris et al., 2004; Clatworthy and Norris, 2006). In fact, then, Aboriginal migration to the reserve is not a new trend but one that has been going on since the 1950s.

Factors in Aboriginal Geographic Mobility

In examining the factors behind Aboriginal geographic mobility it is important to remember that although this is a marginalized population, Aboriginal people are not completely isolated from mainstream Canadian people and institutions. They face many of the same life situations that other Canadians do, and many of the factors that stimulate mobility in the general population—such as opportunities for employment and education—are of equally great importance to Aboriginal people. That said, there are important differences between the experiences of Aboriginal Canadians and those of the majority population, and these

bear particularly on Aboriginal circular mobility and return to reserve communities.

Many Aboriginal people return to their home reserves after struggling to find jobs or adapt generally to life in the city. Many also have difficulty finding affordable housing, which serves as a major push factor out of the city. Those Aboriginal people who do take up residence in cities tend to be disproportionately concentrated in the poorest and most run-down neighbourhoods, where crime and other social problems abound. The social context of the reserve community, where conditions are far more welcoming, affords these individuals a reprieve from the chronic problems and stress of city life. In fact, data from the Aboriginal Peoples' Survey, reviewed by Norris and associates (2004), indicates that 'family reasons" are the most frequently cited motives for moving back to the reserve, which reinforces the idea that social networks play a key role in the circular movements of Aboriginal people.

Some of the net migration gains by reserve areas may be attributed to legislative changes associated with Bill C-31, which provided a mechanism for restoring official Indian status lost through marriage. Prior to 1985, when the bill was introduced, Registered Indian women who married non-Native or non-status Indian men lost their own status, as did their children. Bill C-31 may have prompted reinstated Registered Indians living in the city to seek residence on reserves, where they could enjoy certain legal benefits not available to those living off-reserve (such as free housing and education).

Finally, many reserves are located close to a major city, which allows Aboriginal people to move conveniently from reserve to city on a regular basis. Many Aboriginal people live on reserve for part of the year and then move to the city to gain seasonal

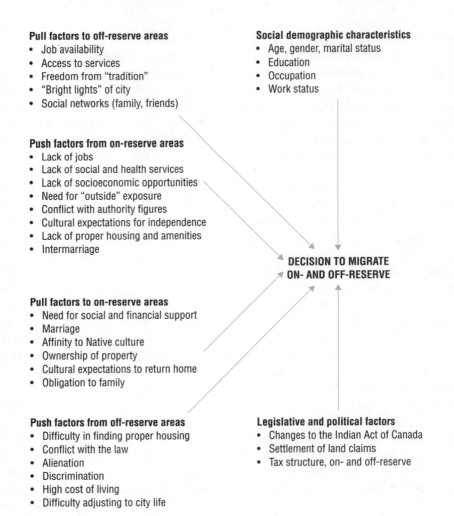

Pull factors to off-reserve areas
- Job availability
- Access to services
- Freedom from "tradition"
- "Bright lights" of city
- Social networks (family, friends)

Social demographic characteristics
- Age, gender, marital status
- Education
- Occupation
- Work status

Push factors from on-reserve areas
- Lack of jobs
- Lack of social and health services
- Lack of socioeconomic opportunities
- Need for "outside" exposure
- Conflict with authority figures
- Cultural expectations for independence
- Lack of proper housing and amenities
- Intermarriage

DECISION TO MIGRATE ON- AND OFF-RESERVE

Pull factors to on-reserve areas
- Need for social and financial support
- Marriage
- Affinity to Native culture
- Ownership of property
- Cultural expectations to return home
- Obligation to family

Push factors from off-reserve areas
- Difficulty in finding proper housing
- Conflict with the law
- Alienation
- Discrimination
- High cost of living
- Difficulty adjusting to city life

Legislative and political factors
- Changes to the Indian Act of Canada
- Settlement of land claims
- Tax structure, on- and off-reserve

FIGURE 8.8 Determinants of on- and off-reserve migration among Aboriginal people in Canada

employment, returning to the reserve once the work is no longer available. This phenomenon contributes to the high degree of circular migration characteristic of the Aboriginal population (Norris et al., 2004; Trovato, Romaniuc, and Addai, 1994).

In summary, the city and the reserve present a series of "pulls" and "pushes" that affect decisions about where to live.

Difficulties of integration and adjustment may push many Aboriginal people from the city, while the more congenial social context of the reserve may be a strong pull factor. Then again, many Aboriginal people have friends and relatives in the city, representing a strong pull factor. Reserves that show a greater degree of socioeconomic development offer pull factors in the form of opportunities for work and social resources. On the other hand, a disproportionately high sex ratio (i.e., a greater number of men than women) can be a push factor. Emma LaRocque (1994) has identified physical and sexual abuse among Aboriginal women within their reserve communities as a powerful factor that pushes them to leave the reserve for the city. Figure 8.8 presents an assemblage of conceivable push and pull factors for Aboriginal migration. It lists individual characteristics such as age, sex, marital status, employment status, and education, as well as larger structural factors, such as the proximity of a reserve to a city (Gerber, 1984).

Conclusion

Internal migration—as distinct from local or residential mobility—is an important subject of demographic analysis. This chapter has explained various measures of migration and introduced several typologies and models of geographic mobility. The last section of the chapter focused on sociological aspects of migration, including the selectivity of migrants, patterns of mobility among immigrant communities, the relevance of gender to family migration, and the association of migration with social disorganization. In Canada, broadly speaking, interregional migration patterns have changed little since the mid-twentieth century. Regions with prosperous economies have tended to attract a large share of internal migrants from the poorer regions, deepening long-standing regional inequalities in socioeconomic development. Interregional migration pattern are subject to fluctuations in response to changing economic conditions across the provinces. Finally, differentials in geographic mobility, nationality, ethnicity, and language reflect a host of factors, some economic and others non-economic, that can either enhance or reduce internal migration probabilities.

Notes for Further Study

Migration Efficiency

Table 8.11 contains worked-out examples of how migration efficiency is calculated at (a) the level of the province, (b) the migration stream, and (c) the systemic level. The information is confined to Alberta, Ontario, and British Columbia over the one-year interval 1 July 2006–30 June 2007. For illustrative purposes we may view these three provinces as comprising a single migration system. The elements in all three sub-tables are interprovincial migration flows; therefore, all diagonal cells are blank.

In Table 8.11a, the elements in the cells can be read as follows. Over the study period under consideration, 31 189 persons left Alberta to go to British Columbia, and 14 474 Albertans went to Ontario. Alberta received 29 213 people from British Columbia and another 45 144 from Ontario. British Columbia welcomed 19 128 migrants from Ontario, while 14 099 British Columbians moved east to Ontario. Also shown in this sub-table, for each province, are the following:

- in-migration
- out-migration
- net migration
- gross migration
- the efficiency of migration

TABLE 8.11A   Interprovincial migration matrix: Alberta, British Columbia, and Ontario; 1 July 2006 to 30 June 2007

Origin (out)	Destination (in)		
	Alberta	British Columbia	Ontario
Alberta		31 189	14 474
British Columbia	29 213		14 099
Ontario	45 114	19 128	
Migration measures for each province			
In-migration	74 327	50 317	28 573
Out-migration	45 663	43 312	64 242
Net migration	28 664	7 005	−35 669
Gross migration	119 990	93 629	92 815
Migration efficiency ratio*	**23.89**	**7.48**	**−38.43**

$$\textit{Migration efficiency index for the system} = \frac{\left|28\,664\right| + \left|7\,005\right| + \left|-35\,669\right|}{119\,990 + 93\,629 + 92\,815} \times 100$$

$$= \frac{71\,338}{306\,434} \times 100$$

$$= 23.28$$

* Refer to the text for the migration efficiency formulas and their description.

TABLE 8.11B   Net migration between pairs of provinces (stream analysis)

Origin (out)	Destination (in)		
	Alberta	British Columbia	Ontario
Alberta	0	1 976*	−30 640**
British Columbia		0	−5 029***
Ontario			0

* Net gain for BC in its exchange with Alberta.
** Net loss for Ontario in its exchange with Alberta.
*** Net loss for Ontario in its exchange with BC.

TABLE 8.11C   Gross migration between pairs of provinces (stream analysis)

Origin (out)	Destination (in)		
	Alberta	**British Columbia**	**Ontario**
Alberta	0	60 402*	59 588**
British Columbia		0	33 227***
Ontario			0

* Total migratory exchange between Alberta and BC.
** Total migratory exchange between Alberta and Ontario.
*** Total migratory exchange between BC and Ontario.

TABLE 8.11D   Calculation of stream-specific migration efficiency ratios based on pairs of provinces and overall index of migration efficiency for the system

Origin (out)	Destination (in)		
	Alberta	**British Columbia**	**Ontario**
		(1)	(2)
Alberta	0	$\dfrac{1\,976}{60\,402} \times 100 = 3.27$	$\dfrac{-30\,640}{59\,588} \times 100 = -51.42$
British Columbia		0	(3) $\dfrac{-5\,029}{33\,227} \times 100 = -15.14$
Ontario			0

$$\text{Migration efficiency index for the system} = \frac{|1\,976| + |-30\,640| + |-5\,029|}{60\,402 + 59\,588 + 33\,227} \times 100$$

$$= \frac{35\,669}{153\,217} \times 100$$

$$= 23.28$$

Notes: The interpretation of cells (1) to (3): (1) for every 100 migrants BC receives from and sends to Alberta, BC gains net 3.27 migrants from Alberta; (2) for every 100 migrants Ontario receives from and sends to Alberta, Ontario loses net 51.42 migrants to Alberta; (3) for every 100 migrants Ontario receives from and sends to BC, Ontario loses net 15.14 migrants to BC.

Data source: Statistics Canada Demography Division (2007b): 41, table 5. From Statistics Canada, *Annual Demographic Estimates. Canada, Provinces, and Territories, 2007*. Reproduced and distributed on an "as is" basis with permission of Statistics Canada.

The overall index of migration efficiency for the system is shown at the bottom of this sub-table.

Table 8.11b derives from the information in Table 8.11a; it is a migration stream analysis, showing the net migratory exchanges between pairs of provinces. Table 8.11c lists the gross migration frequencies between each pair of provinces. Table 8.11d lays out the calculations for the computation of migration efficiency measures for each of the individual migration streams based on the figures in Tables 8.11b and 8.11c.

The computed efficiency ratios in Table 8.11a indicate that in a comparative sense there is greater migration efficiency to Ontario and Alberta than to British Columbia. The efficiency of migration to Alberta is 23.9, and to Ontario it is −38.4; it is 7.5 in the case of British Columbia. Thus, for every 100 migrants Alberta receives and sends out, it gains net almost 24 people, redistributed there from the other two provinces. This also indicates a notable level of asymmetry in terms of migratory exchanges involving Alberta and the other provinces, with Alberta as a net beneficiary. By comparison, for every 100 people Ontario receives and sends out, it experiences a net loss of about 38 persons.

This indicates that Ontario is an important agent in redistributing migrants elsewhere in the system. The case of British Columbia is one of almost dynamic equilibrium: for every 100 people it receives and sends out, it gains net only 7 migrants from elsewhere. (Note that these results would differ considerably if all the Canadian provinces were included in the analysis.)

The overall efficiency of migration index encompassing the three provinces as a system is calculated by dividing the *absolute value* of all three provinces' net migration by the total gross migration across these same provinces, and then multiplying this quotient by 100. The efficiency of migration for this system is 23.3 per cent, meaning that for every 100 migrants received and sent out within this system, 23 persons are redistributed. This indicates a fair degree of asymmetry in the migratory flows between the provinces that constitute this system.

Table 8.11d shows the computation of migration efficiency ratios for individual migration streams (shown within the cells), and the overall migration efficiency index for the system as a whole. Note that the value of the index is identical to the value obtained in Table 8.11a, as it should be.

Exercises

Refer to Table 8.7 on page 375 in this chapter. Using the data for males only, execute the following calculations and answer the corresponding questions.

1. Identify the five most dominant interprovincial migration streams (i.e., the largest migration flows in absolute numbers). For each of these five streams determine the net exchanges between the provinces of origin and destination. Discuss how different theoretical models of migration might lead to different interpretations of the observed net migration losses and gains.

2. Calculate the in-, out-, net, and gross migration figures for each of the provinces. Are there any patterns that emerge from these data? Is there any discernible relationship between in and out-migration across the provinces? Which provinces and regions gain and lose through net migration? Why do some provinces experience relatively high gross migration levels and yet end up losing through net migration?

3. Table 8.12 includes interprovincial migration streams for 25- to 34-year-old men and women in Canada, based on the 1996 census. What can you conclude on the basis of the overall pattern of interprovincial migration in Canada for men and women aged 25–34? Explain.

TABLE 8.12   Interprovincial migration 1991–6, Canadian males and females aged 25–34 in 1996

Province/ territory in 1996	\multicolumn{12}{c}{Province/territory in 1991}
	NL	PE	NS	NB	QC	ON	MB	SK	AB	BC	YT	NU
Males 25–34												
NL	0	45	490	205	80	1 165	60	30	170	95	0	60
PE	125	0	245	160	45	160	20	10	65	55	0	10
NS	760	315	0	1 025	515	2 470	190	115	610	740	0	55
NB	355	140	1 245	0	780	1 635	110	50	300	255	10	30
QC	135	55	590	970	0	7 470	380	205	815	1 130	0	40
ON	2 465	305	3 185	1 860	8 705	0	2 140	1 005	4 070	4 055	70	155
MB	145	0	220	175	350	2 070	0	905	1 380	900	25	25
SK	10	30	150	75	200	1 030	1 065	0	3 035	1 135	40	120
AB	1 115	105	1 205	780	1 090	6 375	2 425	4 335	0	6 025	115	425
BC	1 100	90	1 935	835	3 435	15 535	2 835	2 130	11 600	0	365	240
YT	65	0	25	10	35	125	85	60	195	245	0	25
NU	160	10	110	45	70	325	75	110	435	125	15	0
Females 25–34												
NL	0	35	570	195	95	1 555	55	20	170	110	0	45
PE	85	0	315	185	45	335	10	0	120	25	0	0
NS	885	385	0	970	580	2 785	200	100	620	560	10	25
NB	435	140	1 230	0	920	1 765	100	35	320	165	0	20
QC	130	70	480	800	0	7 460	330	140	705	845	20	50
ON	2 330	340	3 315	1 680	10 030	0	2 225	985	4 320	3 990	45	130
MB	85	30	330	100	325	1 935	0	1 025	1 325	795	15	55
SK	10	30	110	70	180	1 005	1 010	0	3 020	985	45	95
AB	850	135	1 090	590	1 060	5 925	2 285	4 240	0	5 715	155	425
BC	825	110	1 635	475	3 015	14 115	2 750	2 025	11 730	0	410	265
YT	50	0	40	25	30	170	50	60	190	260	0	30
NU	140	20	115	40	60	295	95	115	430	135	25	0

Source: Adapted from Statistics Canada (1999). Adapted from Statistics Canada, Five-Year Mobility Data, 1996 Census (1999).

4. Table 8.13 shows the number of internal migrants across a selected number of census metropolitan areas (CMAs) over the period 2007–11. From these figures it is possible to compute the difference between any pair of CMAs.

   Select a reference CMA (e.g., Edmonton) and compute the in-, out-, and net migration between this CMA and each of the other CMAs listed below (excluding the reference CMA you have chosen). Then graph these in-, out-, and net migration figures.

   - Victoria
   - Vancouver
   - Calgary
   - Edmonton
   - Saskatoon
   - Winnipeg
   - Thunder Bay
   - London
   - Greater Sudbury
   - Toronto
   - Ottawa–Gatineau
   - Montreal
   - Quebec City
   - Halifax
   - Saint John (New Brunswick)
   - St John's (Newfoundland and Labrador)

   Repeat the same computations, but this time use a different CMA as the reference CMA. Then graph these in-, out-, and net migration figures.

   What geographical patterns of migration can you discern from these computations? What theories/models of internal migration might be useful in the interpretation of your results? Explain.

5. Execute the following computations and then interpret your results:

   (a) all the possible pair-wise migration efficiency ratios (MERs) for the following CMAs: Toronto, Montreal, Vancouver, Ottawa–Gatineau, Edmonton, and Calgary

   (b) the migration efficiency index (MEI) for the system made up of these six CMAs

TABLE 8.13   Intermetropolitan migration, 2007–11 (selected CMAs)

CMA in 2011 (destination)	CMA in 2007 (origin)															
	Calgary	Edmonton	Greater Sudbury	Halifax	London	Montreal	Ottawa–Gatineau ON	Ottawa–Gatineau QC	Quebec	Saint John	Saskatoon	St John's	Thunder Bay	Vancouver	Victoria	Winnipeg
Calgary	0	17 806	223	2 510	1 298	3 433	3 420	350	410	524	3 554	1 325	541	15 203	4 746	3 644
Edmonton	21 186	0	182	1 813	961	2 072	3 228	302	360	597	2 971	1 474	393	11 767	3 792	2 564
Greater Sudbury	314	327	0	133	632	238	1 852	162	26	14	108	64	204	287	84	98
Halifax	3 107	2 159	77	0	473	1 411	3 836	342	277	821	211	1 628	85	1 716	1 452	538
London	2 252	1 489	460	587	0	803	2 304	129	61	45	210	211	280	1 703	560	432
Montreal	8 651	4 676	277	1 331	1 010	0	10 511	9 507	18 398	237	814	249	82	6 665	869	931
Ottawa–Gatineau ON	3 378	3 038	760	3 017	1 672	5 999	0	12 677	615	205	384	626	510	4 085	1 808	1 111
Ottawa–Gatineau QC	284	311	89	194	89	7 394	12 617	0	2 888	13	27	53	20	344	156	150
Quebec	645	540	20	329	46	17 462	1 087	2 959	0	31	40	34	19	564	250	172
Saint John	725	807	13	1 300	90	200	382	30	16	0	31	179	14	352	120	75
Saskatoon	3 345	2 959	29	210	170	360	576	61	34	30	0	32	56	1 653	636	1 009
St John's	1 323	1 393	43	1 471	206	253	818	65	18	135	47	0	34	474	220	167
Thunder Bay	794	606	341	125	318	88	640	26	18	17	112	40	0	439	163	744
Toronto	19 485	14 943	2 580	4 874	12 410	12 961	19 061	988	702	638	4 109	1 866	1 264	21 485	2 977	4 210
Vancouver	13 889	9 946	161	1 698	1 375	5 550	4 306	324	388	778	1 747	486	323	0	13 251	3 252
Victoria	2 781	2 185	32	1 222	308	648	1 772	126	159	65	305	166	88	12 578	0	593
Winnipeg	5 907	4 218	79	653	529	1 135	2 122	278	99	79	1 010	144	674	5 742	1 272	0

Source: Statistics Canada (2013n). Statistics Canada, CANSIM Table 111-0030, In-out- and net-migration estimates by geographic regions of origin and destination, 2003. Reproduced and distributed on an an "as is" basis with permission of Statistics Canada.

Additional Reading

Day, Kathleen M., and Stanley L. Winer. 2012. *Interregional Migration and Public Policy in Canada*. Montreal and Kingston: McGill-Queen's University Press.

Frey, William H., and Alden Speare, Jr. 1988. *Regional and Metropolitan Growth and Decline in the United States*. New York: Russell Sage Foundation.

Hiller, Harry H. 2009. *Second Promised Land: Migration to Alberta and the Transformation of Canadian Society*. Montreal and Kingston: McGill-Queen's University Press.

Kono, Shigemi, and Mitsuru Shio. 1965. *Inter-Prefectural Migration in Japan, 1956 and 1961: Migration Stream Analysis*. Bombay: Asia Publishing House.

Miller, Tom. 2012. *China's Urban Billion: The Story behind the Biggest Migration in Human History*. New York: Zed Books.

Price, Marie, and Lisa Benton-Short. 2008. *Migrants to the Metropolis: The Rise of Immigrant Gateway Cities*. Syracuse, NY: Syracuse University Press.

Rogers, Andrei. 1995. *Multiregional Demography: Principles, Methods and Extensions*. New York: Wiley.

Shaw, Paul R. 1985. *Intermetropolitan Migration in Canada: Changing Determinants over Three Decades*. Toronto: NC Press.

Stillwell, John, and Maarten van Ham, eds. 2010. *Ethnicity and Migration*. Dordrecht: Springer.

Teixeira, Carlos, Wei Li, and Audrey Kobayashi, eds. 2012. *Immigrant Geographies of North American Cities*. Toronto: Oxford University Press.

9 International Migration

Introduction

In 2013, more than 230 million people around the world were living in a country other than the one in which they were born. Just over 135 million of these migrants were in the more developed countries, and about 96 million in less developed areas of the world. International migrants represented just over 3 per cent of the world's population, but almost 11 per cent of the population of the more developed countries, taken together (United Nations Department of Economic and Social Affairs Population Division, 2013d). A host of intersecting social, economic, political, and demographic dimensions continues to produce and sustain large-scale migrations today. The number of countries involved in migration, either as sources or as receivers, continues to grow, and societies that once exported many of their nationals to other countries now receive significant numbers of immigrants themselves. Meanwhile, in countries with longer immigration histories, the foreign-born populations are growing, and their societies are being transformed as a result (Parsons and Smeeding, 2006).

The intensification of migration (including refugee movements) beginning in the latter half of the twentieth century can be partly attributed to political upheavals, including the collapse of the Soviet Empire in the late 1980s and the civil unrest that has occurred in parts of Africa, Asia, and Eastern Europe (Castles and Miller, 2009). *Economic globalization* has played a part as well by freeing up the movement both of work and of workers, which has spurred international migration—sometimes permanent, sometimes temporary—to and from all parts of the globe. Moreover, clandestine migration remains an ongoing concern for the receiving societies, especially the United States and countries in southern and Western Europe.

This chapter begins with an overview of international migration. An introduction to basic concepts and measures is followed by a brief outline of human migratory patterns from prehistory to the post-industrial age and a review of prominent theories of international migration. Also included is a survey of Canadian immigration history and associated social demographic features—in particular, the changing nature of immigration and its impact on the social demographic composition of the country. The chapter concludes with a look at the philosophical questions around international migration that the world's liberal democracies now face.

The Complex Nature of International Migration

Migration usually represents a response to "push" and "pull" factors in the countries of origin and destination, respectively. In both cases, there will be demographic, economic, political, and social consequences associated with migration (see Figure 9.1). As with internal migration, the decision to emigrate is usually made on the basis of rational cost–benefit principles: people will move if there is something important to be gained (Lee, 1966). One of the most striking examples of voluntary migration in modern times was the movement from Europe to the New World, which saw in the course of a century (*c.*1850–1950) some 60 million people leave their homelands in search of socioeconomic opportunities in North America (Petersen, 1975: 279).

But history is also full of migrations that have been involuntary—forced or coerced (Crépeau et al., 2006). International movement resulting from persecution and conflict is known as *asylum migration*; those involved in asylum migration are *refugees*, defined by the United Nations as persons who have been forced to flee their country because of a real threat of persecution or death for reasons of race, religion, nationality, or political opinion. It is estimated that as of 2013, the number of refugees around the world was close to 10.4 million. When persons in refugee-like situations and internally displaced persons are also taken into account, the total number of people of concern to the UN agency responsible for the welfare of refugees (the United Nations High Commissioner for Refugees, or UNHCR) was over 35 million at the beginning of 2012 (United Nations High Commissioner for Refugees, 2013). A separate agency, the United Nations Relief and Works Agency for Palestine Refugees in the Near East, was formed in 1949 to provide education, health care, and social services to the refugees—now numbering nearly 5 million—in Jordan, Lebanon, the West Bank, the Gaza Strip, and in war-torn Syria, where over 2 million people have been uprooted (United Nations High Commission for Refugees, 2013).

Any major sociopolitical outbreak in a given part of the world will generally produce refugees and internally displaced people. Currently, the largest number of

FIGURE 9.1 **Macro-level determinants and consequences of international migration**

refugees and internally displaced persons is found in Asia (about 50 per cent), followed by Africa (about 28 per cent).

In addition to those people recognized as refugees are unknown numbers of undocumented migrants. It is virtually impossible for a receiving country to know precisely how many of these people may be living within its borders. For instance, estimates of "illegal aliens" in the United States in the late 1990s alone have ranged from roughly 5 million (Borjas, 1999: 41) to over 6 million, most of which are thought to have been from Mexico (Bean, Edmonston, and Passel, 1990; Garip, 2012; Massey and Espana, 1987; Massey et al., 1987; Massey and Singer, 1995; Massey and Pren, 2012). The annual numbers of illegal migrants in the United States have fluctuated wildly over the years, largely due to changing economic circumstances in Mexico and the United States as well as shifts in US immigration policy (Massey and Pren, 2012).

Temporary migration is another important phenomenon today (Castles and Miller, 2009; Edmonston and Michalowski, 2004: 458). Temporary migrants maintain a particular place of residence but spend varying amounts of time working or studying in another country. In Western Europe, laws allow citizens free movement among the countries that form the European Union, enabling many temporary migrants to cross borders on a daily, weekly, or seasonal basis. Segments of the Canada–US border are also crossed daily by people who live on one side and work on the other; this is the case for many auto workers in the neighbouring cities of Windsor and Detroit, for example. Similarly, many Mexicans find seasonal work in the US agricultural sector. In some cases, temporary migrants may be permitted to settle permanently in the host country if, for example, political circumstances in their country of origin mean that returning there would put them at risk of persecution or death (Castles and Miller, 2009).

Basic Concepts

Of the components of population change, international migration is the one that is most directly affected by legal restrictions and government planning. According to the United Nations, *international migrants* are people who change their country of abode (i.e., the country in which they spend most of their sleeping hours over the course of a year) (Edmonston and Michalowski, 2004: 456). Countries impose strict border controls and make a strict differentiation between permanent and temporary migrants. Applicants may be refused admission on many grounds, including lack of desired occupational skills, a history of criminal offences, or adherence to an ideology that the state considers subversive.

Classification of International Migrants

International migration can be broken down into various categories. Some moves are voluntary; others are forced or compelled by war or persecution. Instances of migration may also be classified according to whether they are peaceful or non-peaceful, civilian or military, and work-related (or study-related) as opposed to optional, for purposes such as tourism (Edmonston and Michalowski, 2004: 456). The following box contains a detailed classification of international migrants.

LEGAL CATEGORIES OF INTERNATIONAL MIGRANTS

R.E. Bilsborrow and colleagues (1997: 36–9) offer a useful classification of international migrants. From the point of view of a receiving country, the people seeking entry fall into two general groups: citizens returning home and foreigners (the latter consisting of various sub-categories, including regular immigrants, asylum migrants, and undocumented migrants).

A   Citizens

1. *Returning migrants* are persons who have been abroad as migrants in a country other than their own and who return to their own country to settle in it. Among persons entering their own country, returning migrants should be distinguished on the basis of the time that they have spent abroad and the time that they intend to spend in their country of citizenship. A year is a reasonable cut-off point in both cases, so that returning migrants are citizens who have been abroad for at least a year and who intend to remain in their own country for more than a year.

B   Foreigners

2. *Returning ethnics* are persons who are admitted by a country other than their own because of their historical, ethnic, or other ties with that country, and who are immediately granted the right of permanent abode in that country or who, having the right to citizenship in that country, become citizens within a short period after admission.

3. *Migrants with the right to free movement* are persons who have the right to enter, stay, and work within the territory of a state other than their own by virtue of an agreement or treaty concluded between their state of citizenship and the state in which they reside.

4. *Foreigners admitted for special purposes:*

   (a) *Foreign students* are persons admitted by a country other than their own for the specific purpose of following a particular program of study. In some countries, foreign students are allowed to work under certain conditions.

   (b) *Foreign trainees* are persons admitted by a country other than their own to acquire particular skills through on-the-job training. Foreign trainees are therefore allowed to work only in the specific institution providing the training and are allowed to stay for a limited period.

   (c) *Foreign retirees* are persons beyond retirement age who are allowed to stay in the territory of a state other than their own provided that they do not become a charge to that state. They are generally allowed to be accompanied by their spouses.

5. *Settlers* are persons who are granted the right to stay indefinitely in the

territory of a country other than their own and to enjoy the same social and economic rights as the citizens of that country. Settlers are usually accorded the opportunity to become naturalized citizens of the receiving state once minimum requirements have been met. (The terms *permanent migrants* or *immigrants* are often used to refer to settlers.)

6   *Migrant workers* are persons admitted by a country other than their own for the explicit purpose of exercising an economic activity:

(a) *Seasonal migrant workers* are persons employed in a state other than their own for only part of a year because the work they perform depends on seasonal conditions.

(b) *Project-tied migrant workers* are workers admitted to the state of employment for a defined period of work solely on a specific project carried out in that state by the migrant workers' employer. The employer is responsible for providing the inputs needed to complete the project, including labour. The employer of an agent who may have acted as an intermediary must ensure that project-tied migrant workers leave the country of employment once the work is completed.

(c) *Contract migrant workers* are persons working in a country other than their own under contractual arrangements that set limits on the period of employment and on the specific job held by the migrant. Once admitted, contract migrant workers are not allowed to change jobs and are expected to leave the country of employment upon completion of their contract, irrespective of whether the work they do continues or not. Although contract renewals are sometimes possible, departure from the country of employment may be mandatory before the contract can be renewed.

(d) *Temporary migrant workers* are persons admitted by a country other than their own to work for a limited period in a particular occupation or a specific job. Temporary migrant workers may change employers and have their work permits renewed without having to leave the country of employment.

(e) *Established migrant workers* are migrant workers who, after staying some years in the country of employment, have been granted the permission to reside indefinitely and work without major limitations in that country. Established migrant workers need not leave the country of employment when unemployed and are usually granted the right of being joined by their immediate family members, provided certain conditions regarding employment and housing are met.

(f) *Highly skilled migrant workers* are migrant workers who, because of their skill, are subject to preferential treatment regarding admission to a country other than their

(continued)

own and are therefore subject to fewer restrictions regarding length of stay, change of employment, and family reunification.

7. **Economic migration** covers persons who move internationally in connection with the exercise of an economic activity that is either not remunerated from within the country of destination or demands a certain investment from the migrant concerned:

   (a) **Business travellers** are foreigners admitted temporarily for the purpose of exercising an economic activity remunerated from outside the country of destination.

   (b) **Immigrating investors** are foreigners granted the right to long-term residence on the condition that they invest a minimum amount in the country of destination or start a business employing a minimum number of persons in the country of destination.

8. **Asylum migration** covers the whole spectrum of international movements caused by persecution and conflict. Specific types of migrants that are part of asylum migration are listed below:

   (a) **Refugees** are persons who, owing to a well-founded fear of being persecuted for reasons of race, religion, nationality, membership of a particular social group, or political opinion, are outside of their country of nationality and are unable or, owing to such fear, are unwilling to avail themselves of the protection of that country. Persons recognized as refugees under this definition are sometimes called *Convention refugees* and are usually granted an open-ended permission to stay in the country of asylum. When they are admitted by another country for resettlement, they are called *resettled refugees*.

   (b) **Persons admitted for humanitarian reasons** are persons who, being outside of their country of nationality, are in refugee-like situations because they cannot avail themselves of the protection of the state in which they find themselves. Sometimes such persons are characterized as *refugees type B* because they do not fully meet

The Canadian Immigration System

The Canadian immigration program offers a specific example of how international migration is codified and controlled by a receiving country. It also illustrates the legal complexities involved in immigration. There are two main ways for foreigners to legally enter Canada for periods longer than those allowed under short-term tourist and business-travel arrangements: (1) with *permanent residence* status granted through the criteria stipulated in the 1951 Convention. They usually receive treatment equal to that of Convention refugees.

(c) *Asylum seekers* are persons who file an application for asylum in a country other than their own. They remain in the status of asylum seeker until their application is considered and adjudicated.

(d) *Persons granted temporary protected status* are persons who are outside their country of nationality and cannot return to that country without putting their lives in danger. The temporary protected status granted to them by the country in which they find themselves allows them to stay for a limited though often open-ended period (as long as return to their country is considered detrimental to their security).

(e) *Persons granted stay of deportation* are persons who have been found not to qualify for refugee status or to be in an irregular situation and who are under deportation orders but who have been granted a temporary reprieve from being deported because their lives would be in danger if they returned immediately to their country of nationality.

9. *Irregular migrants* are persons in a state other than their own who have not fully satisfied the conditions and requirements set by that state to enter, stay, or exercise an economic activity in that state's territory.

10. *Migrants for family reunification* are persons admitted by a country other than their own for the purpose of accompanying or joining close relatives migrating to that country or already living in that country. Because most migrants for family reunification are relatives of other migrants, they should be considered as a distinct sub-category of that to which the primo-migrant belongs.

Source: Bilsborrow et al. (1997). Copyright © 1997 International Labour Organization.

the permanent immigration program, and (2) on a *temporary residence* basis as students, refugee claimants, or temporary workers. It is possible, under certain conditions, for temporary residents to gain permanent status as *landed immigrants*. Permanent resident status may be granted to several classes, of migrants, including independents (which comprises several categories), refugees, and family (see Table 9.1).

Each entry class has its own requirements. For example, family-class applicants must be sponsored by someone who is either

TABLE 9.1   Permanent residents in Canada by immigration category, 2012

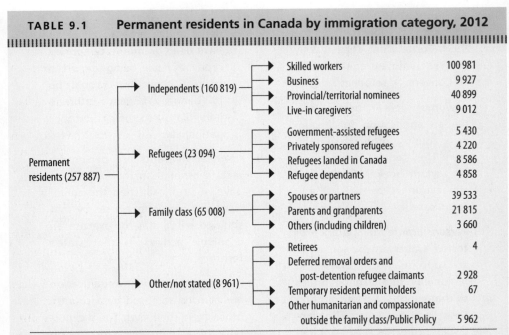

Permanent residents (257 887)		
Independents (160 819)	Skilled workers	100 981
	Business	9 927
	Provincial/territorial nominees	40 899
	Live-in caregivers	9 012
Refugees (23 094)	Government-assisted refugees	5 430
	Privately sponsored refugees	4 220
	Refugees landed in Canada	8 586
	Refugee dependants	4 858
Family class (65 008)	Spouses or partners	39 533
	Parents and grandparents	21 815
	Others (including children)	3 660
Other/not stated (8 961)	Retirees	4
	Deferred removal orders and post-detention refugee claimants	2 928
	Temporary resident permit holders	67
	Other humanitarian and compassionate outside the family class/Public Policy	5 962

Source: Adapted from Citizenship and Immigration Canada (2013). *Permanent residents in Canada by immigration category, 2012*. Citizenship and Immigration Canada (2013), Facts and figures 2012 - Immigration overview: Permanent and temporary residents. www.cic.gc.ca/english/resources/statistics/facts2012/permanent/02.asp

a Canadian citizen or a permanent resident. Skilled workers must meet certain educational, occupational, and work experience criteria and pass a minimum language proficiency test, among other selection factors (i.e., age, adaptability to Canada, and whether one has arranged employment in Canada). Business-class applicants are required either to make a minimum investment in a Canadian business or to establish, purchase, or invest in a designated business that will create employment for others. To qualify for immigration under the Federal Skilled Trades Program, one must have a trade that is in high demand in Canada. Selected refugees who qualify under the criteria of the UN Convention are always admitted, and those who do not qualify as Convention refugees may still be admitted on humanitarian grounds as judged by the appropriate government authorities. Under

the general heading of "refugee" are three sub-categories: (1) *government-assisted refugees*, selected abroad; (2) *privately sponsored refugees*, also selected abroad; and (3) *asylum seekers*, who first arrive in the country and then claim refugee status. Among the third group, only those whose claims are subsequently found to be valid in the eyes of officials (i.e., the members of a refugee board) are allowed to remain in the country.

Data Sources and Basic Measures

Data on internal migration, as we have seen, can be obtained from a variety of sources, including administrative records and the census. The situation with international migration is more complicated: though virtually all countries collect information on in-bound migration, most do not systematically monitor out-bound migration. Countries may co-operate bilaterally by trading information about the number of nationals they exchange as a result of cross-border moves. Canada and the United States, for example, share information on the numbers of the other country's nationals crossing their respective borders. This type of co-operation allows such countries to produce annual estimates of emigration.

Barry Edmonston and Margaret Michalowsky (2004: 458) identify five classes of international migration data:

1. statistics collected at the points where people move across international borders (i.e., at border crossings, seaports, and airports)—these data are gathered mostly from border-control operations and lists of passengers on sea or air transport manifests;
2. statistics regarding passports and applications for passports, visas, work permits, and other documents for international migration;
3. statistics obtained through population registers recording movement into and out of a country as well as births, deaths, and internal movements (most countries do not have population registers);
4. statistics obtained from censuses or periodic national population surveys through inquiries regarding previous residence, place of birth, nationality, or citizenship; and
5. statistics collected through various special or periodic inquiries (e.g., surveys, registration of aliens, and enumeration of citizens overseas).

Unfortunately, the most accessible data source, the census, does not distinguish between the different categories of immigrants. Nor do censuses usually identify the legal status of immigrants (e.g., illegal or undocumented, as opposed to legal permanent residents, refugees or asylum seekers, and temporary immigrants). Numbers of illegal migrants are usually estimated using indirect methods based on a combination of data sources (e.g., administrative, census, and even survey data). For example, administrative records provide data on individuals who may have entered a country legally but stayed longer than the regulations permit. It is also possible to obtain information based on decedents who are later determined to have been in the country illegally. Border-crossing data can be used to identify visitors who have not left within the allotted time. Censuses and current population surveys can be used to estimate the size of the illegally resident population by subtracting the legally resident "foreign-born" population, adjusted for census undercount, from the total foreign-born population (Yaukey, Anderton, and Hickes, 2007). The margin of error associated with indirect methods such as these can be quite substantial, however.

Estimating International Migration

In the absence of actual statistics, countries can produce estimates of net international migration using a variety of following demographic methods.

Vital Statistics Method

One such approach to estimating net migration is called the *vital statistics method*. Let us recall the growth equation, $P_{t1} - P_{t0} =$

It is possible to apply the vital statistics method to specific age–sex combinations. If we know (a) the size of a given age–sex cohort at the beginning and the end of the interval, and (b) the number of deaths that occurred in the cohort, then we can obtain an estimate of net migration for this cohort. This approach to estimating net migration generalizes to any additional factors (e.g., net migration for age–sex–regional categories).

$(B_{t0,t1} - D_{t0,t1}) + (IN_{t0,t1} - OUT_{t0,t1})$. This equation can be rearranged to obtain an estimate of net international migration between two time points ($NM_{t0,t1}$):

$$NM_{t0,t1} = (IN_{t0,t1} - OUT_{t0,t1}) = (P_{t0} - P_{t1}) - (B_{t0,t1} - D_{t0,t1})$$

Thus, net international migration equals the difference between two population counts from two censuses, minus the difference between the number of births and deaths that occurred in the interval.

This type of indirect estimation is far from satisfactory. Besides the potential for error in the components parts of the equation (i.e., births, deaths, and population), which could affect the derived net migration estimate, net migration measured in this way is a residual figure that cannot differentiate between the two migration streams—those entering the country and those leaving it. All it can tell us is the net balance of migration. Thus, we have no way of knowing whether a net balance of zero means equal numbers of immigrants and emigrants or no migration at all. Nevertheless, residual measures are frequently used in some contexts because direct information on immigration—and especially emigration—is lacking. This problem is most in evidence at the sub-national level.

Residual Method of Estimating Emigration

Most countries collect immigration data from their periodic censuses and annual administrative records of new arrivals. (In Canada, the agency responsible for collecting this information is Citizenship and Immigration Canada.) The more difficult aspect of measuring net international migration is the emigration component, for which direct information is often difficult to obtain. As most countries do not routinely collect information on emigration, for an accurate account we would need to know how many people leave the country, when they leave, and where they go. Knowledge of whether emigrants are native- or foreign-born would also be useful.

The *residual method of estimating emigration* uses population data from two successive censuses, plus the numbers of births, deaths, and persons entering the country in the interval between the two censuses. To illustrate, let us recall the components of growth equation cited previously. Population growth between two points in time is a function of the interplay of births and deaths during the interval, plus the difference between immigration and emigration. In practice, of course, the numbers of emigrants are usually not known. Therefore, we need to derive an indirect estimate of emigration ($E_{t0,t1}$), as follows:

$$E_{t0, t1} = [P_{t1} - P_{t0}] - [B_{t0, t1} - D_{t0, t1} + I_{t0, t1}]$$

where $E_{t0, t1}$ is the estimated number of emigrants between two time points, t_0 and t_1;

P is the census population at two time points, t_0 and t_1;

B is the number of births between t_0 and t_1;

D is the number of deaths between t_0 and t_1;

I is the number of immigrants between t_0 and t_1;

t_0 is the start of the interval; and

t_1 is the end of the interval.

The census populations at the beginning and end of the interval are included in this equation. But since the census is seldom a wholly accurate count of the population, the estimate produced by this formula is usually adjusted for census undercoverage.

Other Methods

In practical applications, estimating emigration (and net international migration) is much more complicated. Statistics Canada's estimates of emigration have three components: (1) emigration of Canadian citizens and alien permanent residents, (2) return of emigrants, and (3) net emigration of Canadian residents temporarily abroad. The first two components are estimated using a model based on administrative data, extracted by the Canada Customs and Revenue Agency from the federal Canada Child Tax Benefit program. Information is provided only on families that are entitled to the benefit (based on income and the presence of children under the age of 18). Statistics Canada also uses data collected by the US Immigration and Naturalization Service on Canadian residents admitted to the United States for permanent residence. The third component, Canadians temporarily abroad, is estimated using a technique called the reverse record check (Edmonston and Michalowski, 2004: 482).

Statistics Canada, in its estimate of emigration, takes into account the following flows:

- the emigration of permanent citizens and landed immigrants;
- the return migration of permanent citizens and landed immigrants;
- the number of new immigrants coming into the country in a given interval;
- the number of non-permanent residents that leave the country; and
- the number of non-permanent residents that return to Canada.

Non-permanent residents are foreigners in Canada for a limited stay and who are expected to leave after their stay expires. This category includes people claiming refugee status and others on student or work visas; non-permanent residents may eventually become landed immigrants.[1] The data used to produce estimates of the number of non-permanent residents are obtained from Citizenship and Immigration Canada. Statistics Canada also distinguishes between permanent and temporary migration. (Permanent leaves may be taken by citizens, landed immigrants, and temporary residents who exit the country permanently.)

Once all these data have been assembled, a total emigration component is calculated to reflect the net flows of permanent, returning, and temporary emigrants, all of this representing a net loss of population through emigration. The formula developed by Statistics Canada Demography Division (2003: 85) is

$$E_{(t,t+i)} = PE_{(t,t+i)} - RE_{(t,t+i)} + \Delta TE_{(t,t+i)}$$

where $E_{(t,t+i)}$ is the number of total emigrants over the period $(t,t+i)$;

t is the start of the interval and $t+i$ is the end point of the interval;

$PE_{(t,t+i)}$ is the number of permanent emigrants over the period $(t,t+i)$;

$RE_{(t,t+i)}$ is the number of returning emigrants over the period $(t,t+i)$; and

$\Delta TE_{(t,t+i)}$ is the change in the number of temporary emigrants over the period $(t,t+i)$.

Once immigration is measured from official statistics and emigration has been estimated in this way, net migration is computed by taking the difference between these two components.

Table 9.2 breaks down Canada's population growth from 1991–2 to 2004–5 into its individual components, including natural increase and the various aspects of immigration and emigration, as well as net international migration. Note that the net migration column (column 12) is derived as follows: net migration = (number of immigrants − number of emigrants − number of net temporary emigrants + number of return emigrants + number of net non-permanent residents).

Migration in History: An Overview

Migration has been a ubiquitous feature of the human experience ever since our earliest ancestors began moving out of Africa and into Asia and Europe, eventually spreading to Oceania and, most recently, the Americas (Balter, 2001; Cavalli-Sforza and Cavalli-Sforza, 1995; Diamond, 1999; Livi-Bacci, 2012; Manning, 2005). Many of these movements have been forced by humans' desire to expand beyond their territory; by wars, conquest, and persecution; and by the strong tendency among peoples of diverse civilizations to establish contacts with others through trade and exploration (Fairchild, 1925; Hoerder, 2002; Harzig and Hoerder, 2009; McNeill, 1984). In the more recent history of international migration, labour and settlement movements have figured prominently as well.

Figure 9.2 shows Jared Diamond's (1999: 37) interpretation of the prehistoric migratory experience of *Homo*. It is generally agreed that *Homo erectus* had moved out of Africa by about 1 million years ago, first to the Middle East and parts of Southeast Asia, and by 500 000 BCE (possibly much earlier) to the European continent. Modern humans— *Homo sapiens sapiens*—first appeared in Africa about 200 000 years ago; and out of Africa there occurred migrations to Eurasia and other regions. By about 45 000–35 000 years before the present, *Homo sapiens* had displaced the *Neanderthals* in Europe. Humans are thought to have reached Australia and New Guinea by 40 000–30 000 years ago, and probably arrived in North America around 12 000 BCE, crossing from northern Asia to the region that is now Alaska either by boat or on foot across the narrow land bridge that at that time connected the two continents. Migrations southward to the temperate areas of North America were followed by further southward movements to the tropical regions of North and South America, the Caribbean, and finally the temperate regions of South America and its highlands. These dates and

TABLE 9.2   Components of population growth in Canada, 1991–92 to 2012–13

Period	Population[1]	Non-permanent residents	Births	Deaths	Natural increase	Immigrants	Emigrants[2]	Returning emigrants	Net temporary emigrants	Net non-permanent residents[3]	Net migration	Residual deviation[4]	Total growth[5]
(1)	(2)	(3)	(4)	(5)	(6)	(7)	(8)	(9)	(10)	(11)	(12)	(13)	(14)
1991/1992	28 037 420	395 077	403 107	196 967	206 140	244 281	45 633	15 899	19 741	−42 919	151 887	24 183	382 210
1992/1993	28 371 264	352 158	392 181	201 808	190 373	266 890	43 993	15 279	19 744	−71 185	147 247	24 120	361 740
1993/1994	28 684 764	280 973	386 159	206 464	179 695	235 360	49 456	16 358	19 746	−22 196	160 320	24 116	364 131
1994/1995	29 000 663	258 777	381 998	209 389	172 609	220 738	52 069	18 388	19 745	−14 152	153 160	24 121	349 890
1995/1996	29 302 311	244 625	372 453	209 766	162 687	217 478	48 396	19 035	19 745	−826	167 546	22 326	352 559
1996/1997	29 610 218	243 799	357 313	217 221	140 092	224 857	52 815	18 956	25 564	182	165 616	9 978	315 686
1997/1998	29 905 948	243 981	345 123	217 688	127 435	194 459	51 816	18 671	25 563	−3 983	131 768	9 978	269 181
1998/1999	30 155 173	239 990	330 295	217 632	120 663	173 194	48 008	17 491	25 567	18 317	135 427	9 977	266 067
1999/2000	30 401 286	258 315	336 912	217 229	119 683	205 710	48 089	17 680	25 564	25 032	174 769	10 008	304 460
2000/2001	30 685 730	283 347	327 107	219 114	107 993	252 527	47 766	17 910	25 563	39 592	236 700	9 827	354 520
2001/2002	31 019 020	322 939	328 155	220 494	107 661	256 405	48 984	25 734	27 655	33 478	238 978	8 817	355 456
2002/2003	31 353 656	356 657	330 523	223 905	106 618	199 170	52 171	29 333	27 655	36 733	185 410	8 816	300 844
2003/2004	31 639 670	393 390	337 762	228 829	108 933	239 083	55 951	30 501	27 654	10 302	196 281	8 840	314 054
2004/2005	31 940 676	403 692	339 270	229 906	109 364	244 578	54 016	31 796	27 649	9 101	203 810	8 814	321 988
2005/2006	32 245 209	412 793	346 082	225 489	120 593	254 374	57 851	34 855	27 652	15 852	219 578	12 030	352 201
2006/2007	32 576 074	428 645	360 916	233 825	127 091	238 125	61 940	39 474	18 406	27 397	224 650	34 318	386 059
2007/2008	32 927 517	456 042	373 695	236 525	137 170	249 622	60 980	33 431	18 408	51 422	255 087	34 412	426 669
2008/2009	33 317 662	507 464	379 290	237 708	141 582	245 289	55 056	31 850	18 414	71 863	275 532	34 316	451 430
2009/2010	33 726 915	579 327	379 373	237 138	142 235	270 581	52 335	34 415	18 408	34 531	268 784	34 316	445 335

(continued)

TABLE 9.2 (continued)

Period	Population[1]	Non-permanent residents	Births	Deaths	Natural increase	Immi-grants	Emi-grants[2]	Returning emigrants	Net temporary emigrants	Net non-permanent residents[3]	Net migration	Residual deviation[4]	Total growth[5]
(1)	(2)	(3)	(4)	(5)	(6)	(7)	(8)	(9)	(10)	(11)	(12)	(13)	(14)
2010/2011	34 126 547	613 858	376 951	244 968	131 983	259 106	56 766	36 643	18 411	14 380	234 952	29 429	396 364
2011/2012	34 483 975	684 214	378 762	244 645	134 117	260 115	56 909	36 645	18 412	55 976	277 415	0	411 532
2012/2013	34 880 491	733 555	383 822	253 241	130 581	262 947	57 110	36 645	18 412	49 341	273 411	0	403 992

Notes: The estimate of non-permanent residents represents the number of non-permanent residents residing in Canada on the first day of the month beginning the quarter (the figures pertain to the third quarter of each year). The following groups are referred to as non-permanent residents: (1) persons with a usual place of residence in Canada who are claiming refugee status and the family members living with them; (2) persons with a usual place of residence in Canada who hold study permits and the family members living with them; and (3) persons with a usual place of residence in Canada who hold work permits and the family members living with them.

[1] Population at the beginning of the period.

[2] Emigration figures are estimated by Statistics Canada.

[3] "Net non-permanent residents" is estimated separately by Statistics Canada, and then it is added into the net migration estimate (i.e., net migration = immigrants − emigrants − net temporary emigrants + returning emigrants + net non-permanent residents).

[4] The "residual" column is an adjustment by Statistics Canada (the error of closure) used to reconcile the population estimates at the end of each period with the population at the beginning of the interval, once growth due to net migration and natural increase have been taken into account. Values for beyond 2001 not yet available, as they can only be derived once the next round of postcensal population estimates has been undertaken based on the population data from the 2006 census.

[5] The "total growth" column is the sum of columns (6) and (12) plus column (13).

Source: Adapted from Statistics Canada (2006b): 23, Table 1.2; and Statistics Canada (2013b, c, o).

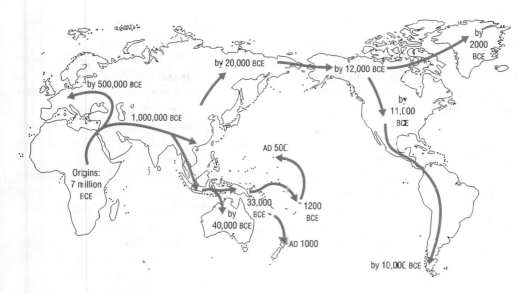

FIGURE 9.2   The spread of humans around the world

Source: Diamond (1999): 37. "The Spread of Humans around the World," from *Guns, Germs, and Steel: The Fates of Human Societies*, by Jared Diamond, copyright © 1997 by Jared Diamond. Used by permission of W.W. Norton & Company, Inc.

evidence about our early origins are approximations and subject to revision as new data are uncovered (see Hammer, 2013; Henn, Cavalli-Sforza, and Feldman, 2012; Skorecki and Behara, 2013; Stringer, 2012).

Among the forces that provoked primitive migrations, major ecological pushes due to drastic climate change and the quest for food must have been of central importance. People moved nomadically out of necessity, whether following game or seeking more favourable environmental conditions. With the development of agriculture and the domestication of animals, beginning around 8000 BCE, humans started forming settled communities, some of which would eventually develop into cities. The rise of cities marked the beginning of what we call civilization. At that point in history, as competition for territory and resources increased, the reasons for migration expanded to include forcible relocation by invading armies. Ongoing exploration

and colonization led to new migrations, and trade and commerce helped to spread knowledge and skills across civilizations (Hoerder, 2002; McNeill, 1984: 4).

Historians generally place the beginning of the "modern era" around the year 1500 (Barzun, 2001: xxi). Immigration history since that time can be subdivided into four distinct phases (Massey, 1999):

1. the mercantile period;
2. the industrial period;
3. a period of limited migration between the two world wars; and
4. the post-industrial period (since the 1960s).

Migration during the Mercantile Period

The main impetus for transnational movements during the mercantile period (1500–1800) was European colonization of the

New World: the Americas, parts of Africa, Asia, and Oceania. As these areas were settled, their new economies required abundant labour. According to Douglas Massey (1999), emigrants from Europe during this period generally fell into three categories: a relatively large number of agrarian settlers; a smaller number of administrators and artisans; and an even smaller number of entrepreneurs who established plantations to produce raw materials (sugar and rubber, for example) for Europe's growing mercantile economies. The rise of plantations meant that an outside source of cheap labour had to be found to sustain colonial economies. It was in response to this need that the slave trade and system of indentured labour developed. Over the course of three centuries between 1500 and 1800, as many as 12–13 million Africans were forcibly taken to the Americas (Hoerder, 2002; Holdren, 2013: 2961; Livi-Bacci, 2012: 16–17).

Migration during the Industrial Period

The industrial period (1800–1914) was an especially important part of modern migration history. During the nineteenth century, New World nations—particularly Canada, the United States, Australia, New Zealand, Argentina, and South Africa—were eager for European migrants to help populate their lands and develop their economies. The migratory flow that took place during this period is not likely ever to be matched for magnitude, intensity, or impact on sending and receiving areas. According to William Petersen (1975: 279), some 60 million Europeans settled in the Americas between 1800 and 1950, and perhaps another 7 million relocated to Australia and New Zealand. The key sending countries were Britain,

Italy, Norway, Portugal, Spain, and Sweden. Between 1850 and 1914, emigration accounted for a cumulative loss of more than one-tenth of Europe's population (Easterlin, 1961a).

The European migration to the New World was propelled by interrelated demographic, economic, and social forces, both within Europe and between Europe and the New World. Among the forces identified by Richard Easterlin (1961a) were increased population pressures in Europe and relatively low wages there compared with what could be earned in the emerging nations of the New World. The economic prosperity of the New World, most notably of the United States, was a strong "pull" factor enticing many immigrants from various parts of Europe. The Industrial Revolution, which destabilized Europe's rural economies, also played a major role: while some of those who were left out of work during the shift to manufacturing managed to find jobs in the factories, many others decided to seek opportunities overseas (Hatton and Williamson, 1994, 1998; Livi-Bacci, 2012; B. Thomas, 1954; D. Thomas, 1941). Once these settlers became established in their adoptive countries, they encouraged other family members to join them. For prospective migrants, this type of social networking helped to reduce the financial and psychological costs of migration and settlement in a new land. By the late 1800s, however, demographic and economic pressures within Europe were diminishing in strength as stimulants of emigration. Emigration became less desirable as wages and living conditions in Europe began to catch up with those in the New World. As a result, the European attraction to the New World waned, and emigration rates fell sharply even before the outbreak of World War I. It is interesting to note that emigration

EUROPEAN MASS EMIGRATION TO THE NEW WORLD, 1840–1932

Citing only the major senders from Europe during 1840–1932, Massimo Livi-Bacci (2012: 53) provides the following statistics on European emigration to the New World: There were a total of 18 million departures during this time from Great Britain and Ireland, 11.1 million from Italy, 6.5 million from Spain and Portugal, 5.2 million from Austria-Hungary, 4.9 million from Germany, 2.9 million from Poland and Russia, and 2.1 million from Sweden and Norway. What were the major destinations? The United States tops the list with 34.2 million arrivals; Argentina and Uruguay received 7.1 million migrants; Canada 5.2 million; Brazil 4.4 million; Australia and New Zealand 3.5 million; and Cuba 0.9 million. Notwithstanding these large migratory volumes to the New World, there was also substantial return migration to Europe.

contributed somewhat to this convergence of wages and living standards between Europe and the New World by effectively transferring socioeconomic inequalities from Europe to the New World. Once in the new country, newcomers would take their place at the bottom of the receiving country's income and occupational hierarchy and gradually work their way up.

Migration during the Interwar Period

Together, the two world wars (1914–18 and 1939–45) and the Great Depression of the 1930s severely limited international migration during the first half of the twentieth century. Major receiving countries like the United States and Canada, believing that nationals should have priority access to whatever work was available, set legal restrictions on immigration. Some governments, including those of the US and France, even encouraged foreign residents to return to their own countries (Taft, 1936).

In Canada, the number of newcomers in 1931 was just 27 530, down from 135 982 in 1926, and by the start of World War II, in 1939, the annual total was a mere 9 329—the lowest in Canadian history (see Figure 9.3).

Although voluntary migration was limited during this period, the two world wars uprooted and displaced massive numbers of people from their homelands, in Europe and elsewhere. For instance, in Asia Minor, the Russian Empire, and the Balkans, the deportation of entire peoples after World War I amounted to a kind of ethnic cleansing. The Ottoman-led expulsion of Armenians from Turkey, in what is known as the Armenian Holocaust, is but one instance that occurred during this time. This kind of forced displacement, representing a systematic attempt to exterminate an entire ethic community, has unfortunately been seen, both previously and since, in many other times and in many different contexts (see Charny, 1999). In the 1930s, the Japanese invasion of Manchuria forced many Chinese to flee. In the 1940s, following the Fascist victory in the Spanish Civil War, large numbers of Spaniards were forced to leave the country. And during Stalin's regime in the Soviet Union, there were large-scale deportations of different categories of peoples, like the close to 2 million kulaks (land owners, viewed as the enemies of the workers), who were moved to labour camps in Siberia (Polian, 2004). In the context of World War II, an estimated 7 million people threatened by the Nazi regime fled their homes, many of

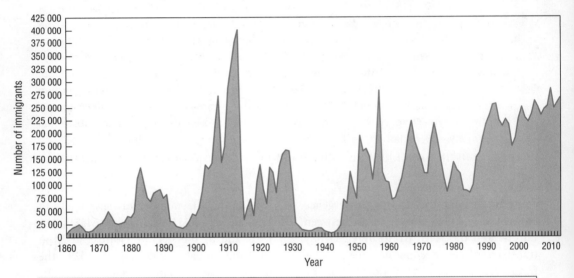

Where immigrants came from (top 10)											
1913		**1957**		**1974**		**1991**		**2001**		**2011**	
Origin	**%**	**Origin**	**%**	**Origin**	**%**	**Origin**	**%**	**Origin**	**%**	**Origin**	**%**
UK	37.4	UK	38.6	UK	17.6	Hong Kong	9.7	China	16.1	Philippines	14.1
USA	34.5	Hungary	11.2	US	12.1	Poland	6.8	India	11.1	China	11.5
Russian	4.6	Germany	10.0	Portugal	7.4	China	6.0	Pakistan	6.1	India	10.0
Ukrainian	4.3	Italy	9.8	India	5.8	India	5.6	Philippines	5.2	US	3.5
Italian	4.1	Netherlands	4.2	Hong Kong	5.8	Philippines	5.3	Rep. Korea	3.8	Iran	2.7
Chinese	1.8	US	3.9	Jamaica	5.1	Lebanon	5.2	US	2.4	UK	2.6
Hebrew Russian	1.5	Denmark	2.7	Philippines	4.3	Vietnam	3.9	Iran	2.3	Haiti	2.5
German	1.2	France	2.0	Ireland	2.3	UK	3.3	Romania	2.2	Pakistan	2.4
Bulgarian	1.1	Austria	2.0	Haiti	2.2	El Salvador	3.0	Sri Lanka	2.2	France	2.3
Polish Russian	1.1	Greece	1.9	Trinidad & Tobago	2.2	Sri Lanka	3.0	UK	2.1	United Arab Emirates	2.1
Total	**404 432**	**Total**	**282 164**	**Total**	**218 465**	**Total**	**228 557**	**Total**	**250 346**	**Total**	**248 748**

Where immigrants settled (region)											
Region	**%**	**Region**	**%**	**Region**	**%**	**Region**	**%**	**Region**	**%**	**Region**	**%**
BC	14.8	BC	13.3	BC	15.7	BC	13.8	BC	15.3	BC	20.8
Prairies	35.3	Prairies	13.1	Prairies	10.9	Prairies	10.9	Prairies	9.2	Prairies	14.0
Ontario	31.1	Ontario	52.1	Ontario	55.0	Ontario	51.4	Ontario	59.3	Ontario	40.0
Quebec	14.9	Quebec	19.5	Quebec	15.3	Quebec	22.4	Quebec	15.0	Quebec	22.5
Atlantic	3.7	Atlantic	1.8	Atlantic	2.8	Atlantic	1.3	Atlantic	1.2	Atlantic	2.7

FIGURE 9.3   Immigration to Canada, 1867–2012

Source: Citizenship and Immigration Canada (2002, 2005, 2006, 2012); *Globe and Mail* (1992, 2003).

them Jews, the population that, at the hands of the Third Reich, suffered the worst genocide in history (Charny, 1999; Kraft, 2005).

Migration in the Post-industrial Period

Migration history since World War II may be divided into two periods. First, from 1945 to roughly 1970, the countries of the Western world needed migrant labour to help rebuild their economies. During this period, many people from peripheral areas of the Mediterranean region (Italy, Spain, Portugal, Greece, Turkey) migrated to the industrialized north, particularly to countries such as West Germany, Belgium, France, Austria, Switzerland, the Netherlands, England, and Wales, which had recently established "guest worker" systems. These countries also saw a large influx of workers from their former colonies due to the process of *decolonization*, which culminated by the early 1970s as these countries gained independence. During this time, there was also a heavy amount of permanent settlement migration to Canada, the United States, and Australia (Castles and Miller, 2009).

The second period may be said to have begun in 1973, when a severe oil shortage sparked a major economic recession that subsequently led to a fundamental restructuring of the world economy. Steven Castles and Mark Miller identify a number of ways in which this development significantly altered migratory movements, including:

- changes in global investment patterns, with increased capital exports from developed countries and the establishment of manufacturing industries in some previously underdeveloped areas;

- the micro-electronic revolution, which reduced the need for manual workers in manufacturing;
- the erosion of traditional skilled manual occupations in highly developed countries;
- the expansion of the service sector, with increased demand for both high-skilled and low-skilled workers;
- the growth of informal sectors in the economies of developed countries;
- the "casualization" of employment, with increasing part-time work and less secure employment conditions; and
- increased differentiation of labour forces on the basis of gender, age, and ethnicity, through mechanisms that have pushed many women, young people, and members of ethnic minorities into casual or informal-sector work while forcing workers with outmoded skills into early retirement.

To adapt to this configuration of globalizing forces, corporations throughout the industrialized world have tried to restructure and to find ways to reduce costs—notably by exporting manufacturing operations to the developing countries, where growing populations with minimal economic prospects are eager to be given factory work, even at very low wages. In some developing regions, this has had important transformative effects, leading to rapid industrialization and economic development; the development of the Organization of Petroleum Exporting Countries in the Gulf Region is an early example. In other developing regions, such as Africa, the pace of economic growth has been less impressive.

In Western Europe, the dawn of globalization in the post-industrial period had a devastating effect on the migrant workers of the 1950s and 1960s, who for the most part had limited education and few skills beyond those required for their work, mainly in manufacturing and construction. Rates of unemployment among these immigrants increased significantly, and many older workers became permanently jobless (Therborn, 1987). To cope with demographic aging and a labour force that was shrinking during the 1970s, 1980s, and 1990s, many of these Western European countries adopted a second generation of policies designed to entice workers from abroad to settle on a temporary basis.

Overall, immigration has intensified dramatically since the early 1970s, thanks largely to *economic globalization*, with all regions of the globe (and a far broader range of both sending and receiving areas) participating in one way or another. The increasing global demand for labour and the relative ease of modern transportation make it possible for people in many parts of the world beyond Europe to emigrate. The majority of immigrants to major receiving countries—including Canada, the United States, Germany, France, Belgium, Switzerland, Sweden, and the United Kingdom—now come from the developing world: Africa, Asia, Latin America, and the former Soviet Bloc countries of Eastern Europe. At the same time, nations that traditionally exported immigrants—countries like Italy, Spain, Greece, and Portugal—are now receiving many immigrants themselves (Coleman, 2002; Livi-Bacci, 2012; Therborn, 1987). Oil-rich countries like Saudi Arabia and Kuwait have been importing labour, much of it from developing countries, to work in their growing oil-based economies. And since the 1980s, there has been much more active migration to, from, and within the newly industrializing centres of Asia—South Korea, Taiwan, Hong Kong, Singapore, Malaysia, and Thailand. Figure 9.4 shows the major migratory flows since the 1970s. All of this movement of labour has been facilitated by the creation of regional trade pacts among blocks of countries, examples being the North American Free Trade Agreement (NAFTA) between Canada, the United States, and Mexico; and the expansion of the European Union within Europe.

The major features of international migration since the late twentieth century can be summarized as follows (Castles and Miller, 2009):

1. Migration has become a global process as opposed to a localized regional phenomenon.
2. The volume and pace of international migration have reached unprecedented levels.
3. Migration has become increasingly differentiated, as migrants to receiving countries are ethnically and racially heterogeneous.
4. Immigration no longer is male-dominated, as women are increasingly participating in transnational movements (owing in part to the growing demand for female labour in certain economic sectors and to family reunification policies implemented by some major receiving countries).
5. Immigration has become highly politicized, especially in the major receiving countries, where the public hold perceptions that immigration threatens national security and challenges host nations' sense of nationhood. Some European countries have taken controversial measures to curb immigration, partly in response to such fears.

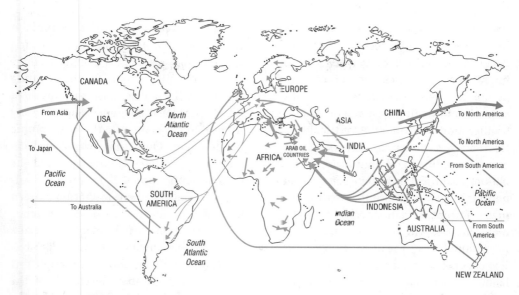

FIGURE 9.4 **Globa migratory movements from 1973**

Note: Arrow dimensions give only a rough indication of the size of the movement.

Source: Castles and Miller (2003): 6, Figure 10. From Stephen Castles and Mark J. Miller, *The Age of Migration: International Population Movements in the Modern World*, published in 2003 by Palgrave Macmillan. Reproduced by permission of Guilford Press and Palgrave Macmillan.

Theories of International Migration

Systems Perspective

Mary Kritz, Lin Lean Lim, and Hania Zlotnik (1992) point out that the world today is characterized by a number of *migration systems*: ongoing patterns of migratory exchange in which some countries and regions function as core immigration magnets and others as peripheral sending areas. In the North American migration system, for instance, the United States and (to a lesser extent) Canada are the core receiving countries, while Mexico, parts of Central and South America, and a number of countries in Asia and Europe are the primary sending areas, with relatively minor counterstreams from the two core countries to these other parts

of the world. This particular system has existed for some time and is likely to continue indefinitely.

Massey and associates (1998) identify four principal systems, in addition to the North American one, centring on Europe, the Gulf states, the Asia–Pacific region, and South America. Each system has its own unique dynamics, but there are some common features as well. How did these systems develop? What are the root causes of international migration today? Though no single theory explains everything, different theories focusing on different dimensions can provide valuable insight into the complex nature of international migration, its determinants, and its consequences.

Kritz, Lim, and Zlotnik (1992: 3) note that each migration system is situated within particular contexts (social, political, demographic, economic). These contexts, conditioned largely by previous migrations and policies in the core and peripheral countries, dictate the extent of migratory flows in a system. For example, immigration laws may be restricted and then relaxed under conditions of economic downturns and upturns in the core nation. Historical links between core and periphery, such as those that exist among many European nations and their former colonies, will have some bearing on migration flows. The demographic context becomes particularly important when labour shortages in the core nations spark a demand for workers from countries in the periphery, especially those with labour surpluses.

Economic and Sociological Perspectives

In their review of migration theories, Massey and colleagues (1993) begin with *neoclassical economics*, according to which migration decisions are driven primarily by differences in economic opportunities between sending (peripheral) and receiving (core) countries. The idea that workers in peripheral countries are motivated by the desire for employment in countries that offer higher wages implies that international migration will continue if wage differentials persist and diminish if they decrease. Theorists in the neoclassical economics tradition (e.g., Harris and Todaro, 1970; Sjaastad, 1962; Todaro, 1969) believe that the possibility exists for migration between the established sending and receiving countries to cease at some point in the future, since the intensification of migration over time will

result in lower wages in the destination country while at the same time reducing the supply of labour in the sending country. Meanwhile, wages in the sending country will gradually rise as a result of remittances (that is, money sent home by those who have emigrated) and economic development. Over time, wage levels in the two countries will converge, and the need for emigration will diminish accordingly. In general, then, migration as seen from this perspective is the consequence of uneven economic development across countries and therefore uneven distribution of capital and labour. Although this explanation is usually developed at the macro level, it can also be used at the micro level to explain how individuals, perceiving differences between countries or regions, understand the potential gains and losses associated with moving or not moving.

Essentially, the neoclassical economics theory is the one used earlier in this chapter to explain the course of the great European migration to the New World. But it has some limitations. First, given the wide income disparities that exist between regions, it suggests that migration rates around the world ought to be much higher than they are; but as we have already noted, only about 3 per cent of the world's people are migrants. Second, it does not take into account non-economic factors such as state policies that prevent the free movement of labour across borders. In fact, it says nothing at all about the role of the state. And although it implies that governments in sending and/or receiving countries can control immigration by influencing labour markets, it does not specify how this might be done (Massey et al., 1998). Nor does it recognize the role played by earlier emigrants who persuade other family members and friends to join them and facilitate their migration by providing information and assistance.

A variant on this theory (Stark, 1997) shifts the emphasis from the macro level of core–periphery differences to the micro level of the family seeking to diversify its sources of income and minimize its exposure to risk—a particular concern in developing countries, where insurance to safeguard against calamities such as crop failure or unemployment is either non-existent or too costly for the majority of people. One way of reducing risk is to have some family members working in the local economy and others working in foreign labour markets. A family using this strategy might be able to ride out a period of economic difficulty at home with the help of remittances from abroad. At the same time, financial support from abroad might enable a family to improve its situation without having to borrow money from a bank; this strategy might be especially useful in countries where capital markets are weak, access to banking may be difficult, and a family may not have adequate collateral to secure a loan.

In emphasizing "push" factors such as the need to reduce risk and the desire for institutional features such as insurance and bank loans, the "new economics" perspective suggests that migration could well continue even if wage differentials between sending and receiving countries were eliminated. It also suggests that immigrant remittances could tend to accentuate socioeconomic inequalities in the local community, as receiving families would use the income to raise their standard of living and invest in livestock, equipment, schooling, and so on.

One consequence of this process might be to generate feelings of relative deprivation among other households in the community. This in turn would generate further waves of emigration, as other families seek to close the wealth gap between themselves and the families of previous migrants (Zlotnik, 2006).

A related perspective focuses on the social networks that link migrants to family and friends back home. *Network theory* defines networks as interpersonal ties based on commonality of background, relations, and obligations (Boyd, 1989). As the numbers of international migrants increase, so do the numbers of social networks in operation, creating strong synergetic forces that promote additional migration. In this process, known as *cumulative causation*, each act of migration from the local community alters the social context within which subsequent migration decisions are made, typically in ways that make additional movement more likely (Massey and Espana, 1987).

By contrast, *dual labour market theory* focuses on the "pull" side of the equation, specifically capitalist societies' chronic need for foreign labour (Piore, 1979). It is the chronic need for foreign labour in wealthy nations that stimulates immigration.

One of the key reasons for this need is the demography of advanced capitalist societies. As the average age of these populations continues to rise, certain sectors of their workforce will shrink over time. This is especially true of the entry level, where wages are typically below average. In the past, industrial economies could rely on teenagers and women to fill those low-paying jobs, because work for these social categories was typically transient. In recent decades, however, the pool of entry-level workers has shrunk considerably as a result of two factors: first, the long-term decline in fertility and the extension of formal schooling, both of which have reduced the number of young adults entering the labour force; and, second, the urbanization of society, which has virtually eliminated rural areas as a source of entry-level labour. The imbalance between demand and supply at this level increases the long-term demand for foreign workers in industrial societies.

Other structural features of advanced economies also help generate an ongoing need for immigrants. Highly skilled workers in such countries, most of whom are native born, expect pay superiority, job security, and status recognition over the less educated and less skilled sectors of the workforce, who despite of their lower status perform jobs that few find desirable, and in this sense represent an essential component of the labour force. This inherent feature of capitalist economies poses a dilemma for employers. On the one hand, they need to attract workers to take on the low-status jobs; on the other they cannot pay high wages to achieve this goal without upsetting the socially defined relationship between status and remuneration. That is, an increase in wages at the bottom would necessitate raising wages at all other ranks of the occupational hierarchy, which would be excessively costly to employers. Reliance on foreign labour solves the dilemma because immigrants are generally willing to accept low-paying jobs that have little prestige and security. This solution is responsible for the development and maintenance of a *segmented labour force* in advanced economies, whereby one sector of the workforce, mainly native born, enjoys pay and status superiority over

workers occupying low-end jobs often filled by immigrants. Therefore, immigration policies in these countries would be highly attuned to serving the interests of employers and big business.

Finally, *world systems theory* explains international migration as a consequence of the expansion of the capitalist economy into the "peripheral" (i.e., developing) regions of the world. World systems theorists maintain that this process has been underway and gaining in intensity since the sixteenth century (Braudel, 1979; Wallerstein, 1974). Driven to increase profits and wealth, capitalist firms enter ("penetrate") poor countries on the periphery of the world economy in search of raw materials, labour, and new consumer markets.

With the spread of capitalism from its centres in Western Europe, North America, Oceania, and Japan, an increasing proportion of the world's population is being incorporated into the global market economy. And as those people in peripheral regions leave rural agricultural areas for the cities in search of work in the new economy (thus contributing to over-urbanization and urban poverty), others are drawn abroad. In the process, an uprooted proletariat is created that then becomes a part of the international movement of labour to the core capitalist economies. And as we have already seen in connection with migration systems, cultural and historical linkages between core and peripheral regions also facilitate migration, so that many developing nations and one-time colonies of Western countries have linkages that promote or ease migration to the former imperial powers.

In short, the world systems theory sees the core countries' domination (*hegemony*) of peripheral and semi-peripheral

WHEN DID GLOBALIZATION START?

While the term *globalization* has been popular since about the mid-1980s, the interconnectedness of the world's markets has been prevalent for so much longer. Scholars such as Kevin O'Rourke and Jeffrey Williamson (2002) argue that it was the sudden decrease in transportation costs in the nineteenth century that really allowed the convergence of Europe and Asian markets. Others believe the impetus for globalization was even earlier, pointing to Christopher Columbus' discovery of the Americas in 1492 as the driving force. While O'Rouke and Williamson claim that fifteenth-century discoveries of trade routes to America and Asia had little effect on world markets, economic historians suggest that the newly found silver mines of the Americas had a huge impact on the economies of Europe. Silver was generally the basis for currencies at that time, and the influence of the resulting "price revolution" on European and Asian markets should not be underestimated.

Going back even earlier into history, Andre Gunder Frank argues that the growth of trade and market integration between the Sumer and Indus civilizations of the third millennium BCE can be seen as the start of globalization. Others point to the trade links between China and Europe that first grew during the Hellenistic Age. Economist Adam Smith points more simply to primitive hunter-gatherers trading with the next village. Global historians such as Anthony Hopkins (2002) and Christopher Bayly (2004) also highlight the importance of the pre-modern exchange of ideas and knowledge as part of globalization's larger sphere.

It is clear that globalization is not simply a process that started in the last few decades. It has a history that may be almost as old as humans, starting with Smith's hunter-gatherers and developing into the interconnected societies of today. Whether you think globalization is a "good thing" or not, it appears to be an essential element of our economic history.

Source: Adapted from *The Economist* (2013b).

regions as a multidimensional phenomenon involving past as well as present political, economic, and cultural influences. Seen in this context, international migration has little to do with wage rates or employment differentials between countries. Rather, it is a product of the expansion of markets within a global political and economic hierarchy. One weakness of the world systems explanation is its vast scope. In this sweeping perspective, migration is only a small (though important) part of the picture, and some of the finer points highlighted by other theories are inevitably missed. Finally, the world systems theory does not differentiate between the varieties of international migration. Thus, it does not address the fact that transnational migration today can take a number of forms besides the one associated with capitalist penetration of peripheral regions.

Other Factors
The State

Each of the theories reviewed here has something of value to say about the determinants of international migration. None of them, however, directly or systematically addresses the role that the state plays in migration. If it were not for modern states' regulation of migration (through their immigration policies), the numbers of international migrants around the world would be significantly larger than they are. We noted earlier that, despite the inequalities that exist around the globe, just over 3 per cent of the world's people took part in international migration in 2013. According to Aristide Zolberg (1981), the reason this percentage is so low is that the world is organized into mutually exclusive and legally sovereign states. As sociopolitical entities, states try to maximize the well-being of their citizens both by forging trade and immigration agreements with one another and by controlling the flow of outsiders across their borders and determining who will and will not be allowed to gain citizenship. In fact, every modern state has laws and regulations stipulating the conditions under which foreigners will be allowed entry.

Transnationalism

Transnationalism is the name given to the relatively new tendency among immigrants to retain multiple national identities. Together, the reality of globalization, the ease of travel, and the speed of communication technologies, combined with the desire of many immigrants to maintain social, cultural, and even economic ties to their countries of origin, have fostered a strong sense of belonging to two (or more) worlds simultaneously. One of the terms used to refer to this phenomenon is *diaspora*.

In English, the term *diaspora* originally referred specifically to the dispersion of the Jewish people, beginning about the sixth century BCE. More recently it has been applied to the Africans who were forcibly transported to the New World as slaves, and to the Armenians who were driven from their homes in the Ottoman Empire during and immediately after World War I (Cohen, 1997: ix; Sheffer, 2003). The displacement of Palestinians following the creation of Israel in 1948 may be viewed as a further example of diaspora.

Common to all diasporic communities is the experience of displacement, forcible or voluntary, from an "old country" that retains some claim on the loyalty and emotions of those displaced, as well as "a sense of co-ethnicity with others of a similar background" (Cohen, 1997: xi).

In the contemporary literature, *diaspora* generally refers to ethnic minorities that maintain strong sentimental and material links with their countries of origin while gradually adopting a new identification with the host society. The persistence of an emotional attachment to the homeland is not new, of course. What is different today is the ease with which emigrants are able to maintain their connections not only with their home countries but with their fellow emigrants living in other host countries. Immigrants seeking economic advancement and social recognition are typically active in a variety of spheres—cultural, social, economic, political—and may pursue those interests in both their original and adopted countries. In this way, dense networks are created across political borders by people who live a kind of dual life, moving easily between cultures and in some cases even maintaining homes in two countries.

This concept of *transnationalism* defies the usual notion of immigration as a matter of leaving one's own country to settle permanently in a new society. It also raises the question whether transnational migrants can be described as citizens at all in the usual sense of the term—as persons who participate in one particular society and identify with one particular state. Closely related to the contemporary concept of *diaspora* is the notion of *transnational communities*, whose members live between nations and may not feel much allegiance to any one nation as such. If the trend towards transnationalism and multiple citizenship continues, the sense of attachment to any one country may become increasingly instrumental rather than emotional. Ultimately, it may become necessary to rethink what it means to be a citizen in a globalizing world (Braziel and Mannur, 2003; Levitt, DeWind, and Vertovec, 2003; Satzewich and Wong, 2006.)

Immigrant Integration in Host Societies

Another important aspect of migration not addressed in the theories reviewed so far is the reception that immigrants receive in their new countries and the process by which they become integrated, both as individuals and as groups. Some receiving societies have opted for full integration, allowing newcomers equal access to all the benefits enjoyed by the native-born population and

making it relatively easy to gain full citizenship. Others are not so accommodating (see Carmel, Cerami, and Papadopoulos, 2012). Different citizenship rules reflect different national ideologies and may have little or nothing to do with the origins or characteristics of migrants themselves.

There are two basic principles that citizenship ideologies—hence, models of immigrant integration—may follow: the "law of the blood" (*jus sanguinis*) and the "law of the land" (*jus soli*). According to the first of these ideologies, what matters is ethnicity—common descent or blood ties. According to the second, what matters is the territory in which one is born (Castles and Miller, 2009; Koser, 2007).

In practice, most modern states combine these two principles, although one or the other tends to be dominant. An exception is Israel, where *jus sanguinis* is the only principle of citizenship. This means that in awarding Israeli citizenship, preference is given to Jews over members of all other ethnic or religious groups. Israel's Law of Return, in conjunction with its citizenship law, grants automatic citizenship to Jewish immigrants to the country. Through these laws, Israel gives priority to Jews over the many Palestinians who fled or were driven from the country during wars in 1948 and 1967. In addition, Israel's marriage law treats Israeli citizens of Palestinian origin (i.e., Israeli Arabs) as second-class citizens. Israeli Arabs who marry Palestinian residents of the West Bank or Gaza must abandon Israel to live with their families, since the law does not permit the reunification of families split between Israel and the occupied territories. This makes it very difficult for Palestinians in the occupied territories to join their families in Israel, but promotes the movement from Israel of

ANTI-IMMIGRANT SENTIMENTS IN WESTERN SOCIETIES

Do Western populations view immigration as a positive force in their societies? Or do they view immigration as a potential threat to national identity and social stability? Public concern is often grounded on the perception that new-wave immigrants (i.e., post 1970s) are different from earlier waves because they are from cultures that seem incompatible with the Western way of life. Sociological evidence shows that there is indeed a great deal of anti-immigrant sentiment across Western countries, even though their degree of hostility towards foreigners is far from uniform. Research by Moshe Semyonov and colleagues (2006) and by Rima Wilkes and associates (2007) indicates that hostility is strongest where the size of an immigrant out-group is relatively large, presumably because these large groups may be perceived as being more threatening. However, hostility seems to be less pronounced where economic conditions are prosperous. This suggests the presence of a strong interaction effect between the state of the economy of a host country and the relative size of the immigrant population. Greater degree of hostility towards immigrants is more likely where both conditions are present: large size of the out-group and deteriorating economic conditions. Another important research finding is that highest levels of anti-immigrant sentiment and distrust are found in host countries where extreme right-wing political parties enjoy a great deal of support, a situation often exploited by such parties for their own political ends (Schuck, 2007). Finally, hostility towards immigrants (especially Muslim immigrants) usually increases after a terrorist event that has been perpetrated by an extremist Islamist group (Legewie, 2013).

Notwithstanding these research findings, it may be that in general immigrant group will be greeted with some degree of hostility and apprehension by the receiving population. In varying degrees, this seems to be a common historical experience by all immigrant groups, irrespective of their national origins.

Israeli Arabs who wish to join their families in the occupied territories (Mariner, 2003).

An interesting case is that of Germany, which has recently changed its citizenship laws to include *jus soli* as a basis for obtaining citizenship. Prior to 2000, the country's citizenship laws were based on the *jus sanguinis* principle of descent. As a result, before the new law was passed, the children and grandchildren of post-war migrant workers (many of whom were from Turkey) were excluded from citizenship, even though most of them had been born and raised in Germany. The *jus sanguinis* principle also meant that when East and West Germany were reunified after the fall of the Berlin Wall, ethnic Germans who had lived outside the country for generations (mostly in Eastern Europe and the former Soviet Union) were automatically granted German citizenship. By contrast, in countries such as Canada, the United States, Australia, and the United Kingdom—all of which follow the *jus soli* principle—a child born to a legal immigrant is automatically entitled to full citizenship. With its new law, Germany joins these and many other countries in granting citizenship based on the *jus soli* principle.

Most countries allow migrants who have been legally resident for a certain number of years to become "naturalized" citizens. The principle behind this practice is known as *jus domicile*. In Canada and Australia, the residence requirement is three years; elsewhere (e.g., in Austria and Germany) it may be as long as eight or ten years. Some countries (like Canada) permit dual nationality, but others (Austria, for instance) demand that migrants give up their original nationality as a condition for acquiring citizenship.

The extent to which immigrants are expected to assimilate to their new society varies. In some countries, newcomers are expected to give up their original cultures and adopt the host culture as their own. In others, immigrants are legally permitted to pursue and maintain their own languages and cultures. These two very different situations correspond to two opposite models of immigrant integration: *assimilation* and *multiculturalism*. In *assimilationist* contexts, immigrants are expected to give up their distinctive linguistic, cultural, and social characteristics in order to blend in with the majority host population. A variation on this theme is the *republican model*, which sees the nation based on a constitution and a system of laws defining citizenship, and which is therefore willing to accept newcomers as long as they abide fully by the political rules and are prepared to adopt the culture of the receiving nation (Castles and Miller, 2009; Koser, 2007: 23). The *multicultural model* differs from the republican model in that it does not demand

assimilation from immigrants; instead, it accepts and promotes existing cultural differences among subgroups in the population, primarily because this type of orientation is believed to enhance integration.

Historically, Canada, the United States, and Australia have relied on immigration as part of their nation-building strategy, and have generally encouraged permanent settlement, at least among immigrants from "desirable" countries of origin. Therefore, the official policies of these countries have shifted over time away from assimilation and towards multiculturalism. By contrast, countries that do not seek immigrants and whose laws make it difficult or impossible for immigrants to attain citizenship status have tended to foster the development of marginalized ethnic enclaves as opposed to fully integrated ethnic communities, which may actually impede the integration of immigrants to the larger society (Castles and Miller, 2009).

Canadian Immigration History

Immigration and Nation-building

Immigration has featured prominently in Canada's development as a nation. In its first century alone (1867–1967), it admitted an estimated 8 million immigrants (Hawkins, 1988). Table 9.3 outlines the connections between immigration and the major stages in Canada's economic and sociopolitical development. Conditions in the nineteenth century were particularly favourable to immigration, as the spread of industrialization created a rapidly growing demand for labour, and the new nation formed in 1867 sought to populate the vast territories to the west of Upper Canada. But interest in western settlement was limited: in 1891, the population living west of Ontario amounted to roughly 350 000—just 7.2 per cent of the

TABLE 9.3   **Immigration and Canadian nation-building: Sociopolitical, demographic, and economic contexts, pre-1850–present**

Features	Pre-1850 period	1850–1950	1950–70	1970–present
Sociopolitical	English–French dualism; French and British seen as "founding" ("charter") groups, Aboriginal people treated as subordinate. British and French define Canada as a Nation.	English–French dualism (the "two solitudes"); Canada established as a nation (Confederation).	Canada as a democratic welfare state. Multiculturalism and bilingualism become official policies. Widening regional economic inequalities. British–French dualism; threat of Quebec separation.	English–French dualism continues, but with increasing recognition of Aboriginal people, the injustice done to them in the past, and the need to settle outstanding land claims and establish some form of self-government.
Social demographic	Ethnic composition mainly British and French.	British and French backgrounds still dominate, followed by other European origins (German, Italian, etc.).	British and French still dominate, but ethnic composition becomes increasingly diverse; Canada is increasingly seen as a land of immigrants and their descendants. In the 1960s 16 per cent of the total population was foreign-born.	Increasing ethnic diversity. "Visible minority" becomes an official social category. Sustained low fertility in the post–baby boom years and increasing aging of the population.
Economic	Staples-based economy (e.g., fur trade) gives way to industrialization.	With industrialization, central Canada becomes the economic centre. Increasing demand for labour attracts large-scale immigration from Europe. Settlement of the West (mass migration of Europeans).	Post-war economic recovery; rapid economic growth, periodic recessions starting in the early 1970s.	Annual immigration targets raised. Policy changes emphasize humanitarian principles (family reunification and refugees) and qualifications such as education and skills are central features of policy. Growing concerns of increased concentration of immigrants in the largest cities; post-9/11 security issues.

TABLE 9.3   (continued)

Features	Pre-1850 period	1850–1950	1950–70	1970–present
Immigration	Immigrants come from Britain, the US, northwestern Europe.	British immigrants continue to dominate until after World War II. Active exclusion of some categories of immigrants. Significant wave of immigrants from southern Europe in the 1950s.	Immigration from southern Europe slows in the late 1960s as "New Wave" immigration (non-European origins) begins. Non-discriminatory point system introduced in 1967. New policy emphasizes economic/demographic sustainability and humanitarian principles.	Most immigrants now come from Asia, Latin America, Africa, and the Caribbean. Refugees come from all regions of the world, including Eastern Europe (breakup of Soviet Empire).

country's population. It was not until the turn of the century, when the Laurier government began offering free land for homesteading, that prospective settlers flocked to the Prairies and British Columbia. According to Marvin McInnis (2000a: 533), this was one of the most important episodes in Canadian history, helping to transform Canada into a fully continental economy. As part of this movement, in 1913 alone, Canada welcomed more than 400 000 immigrants—an annual total that remains unmatched to this day (see Figure 9.3 on page 428).

It is interesting to note that the periods with the highest volumes of immigration to Canada have not necessarily been the periods with the highest net migration figures. Between 1901 and 1921, for instance, immigration reached unprecedented levels, but emigration was also very high. Thus, net migration, while substantial, was actually lower than it has been in more recent years, when emigration rates have been much lower (McVey and Kalbach, 1995: 100). The volume of emigration declined from over 65 000 in 1970–1 to just under 36 000 by 2004–5 (Verma, 2006; Statistics Canada, 2006b: 23).

Immigration and Sociocultural Diversity

In 2011, almost 21 per cent of Canada's population was foreign-born (i.e., nearly 6.8 million). This is the highest proportion among the G-8 countries (Statistics Canada 2013p: 1) The United States has the world's largest immigrant population in absolute terms, at 45.8 million; it holds over 20 per cent of the world's total immigrant stock (see Table 9.4). Although Canada as a nation has been built on immigration and the significant contributions of the Aboriginal peoples, its social demographic fabric continues to be shaped by new waves of immigration. Until not very long ago, one could speak of Canada as being a country of two charter groups, the English and the French, and the First Nations. This is still the case today, but this picture fails to capture the growing sociocultural diversity

TABLE 9.4   **The 20 countries or areas with the most international migrants in 2013**

Rank	Country	Migrant stock	International migrants as a percentage of country's population	International migrants as a percentage of world's migrants	Cumulative percentage
1.	United States	45 785 090	14.3	19.8	19.8
2.	Russia	11 048 064	7.7	4.8	24.6
3.	Germany	9 845 244	11.9	4.3	28.9
4.	Saudi Arabia	9 060 433	31.4	3.9	32.8
5.	United Arab Emirates	7 826 981	83.7	3.4	36.2
6.	United Kingdom	7 824 131	12.4	3.4	39.6
7.	France	7 439 086	11.6	3.2	42.8
8.	Canada	7 284 069	20.7	3.1	45.9
9.	Australia	6 468 640	27.7	2.8	48.7
10.	Spain	6 466 605	13.8	2.8	51.5

Source: United Nations Department of Economic and Social Affairs Population Division (2013e).

of the population that has resulted to a large extent from immigration over the years and the consequent intermixture of ethnicities arising from intermarriage.

Change in the National Origins of Immigrants

The shift in the major source countries of immigrants in recent decades has changed the composition of the foreign-born population. One of the most important developments in this regard has been the growth of *visible minorities* in Canada, as the range of sending areas has continued to become more varied. In 1991, Hong Kong contributed almost 10 per cent of all immigrants to Canada. The only "traditional" sending country in the top ten was the United Kingdom, which ranked eighth that year, just ahead of El Salvador and Sri Lanka. By the turn of the new millennium, the majority of immigrants came from Asia, Africa, and Latin America. The top four source countries in 2012 were China, India, Pakistan, and the Philippines.

In 1913, more than 70 per cent of the immigrants admitted to Canada came from the United Kingdom and the United States; the rest came mainly from Russia, Ukraine, Italy, China, Germany, Bulgaria, and Poland (see Figure 9.3). Europe would continue to account for the great majority of immigrants through to the 1960s.

The return of peace following the end of World War II brought an increase in immigration to Canada. In the context of a booming economy, over 430 000 immigrants were admitted between 1946 and 1950, exceeding the numbers in the preceding 15 years. Legislative amendments to the Immigration Act provided for the admission of people who had been displaced during the war, and the toll taken on Europe's economy by

DISCRIMINATORY IMMIGRATION POLICY IN EARLY CANADIAN HISTORY

During the first two decades of the twentieth century, Canada passed a number of immigration Acts that were clearly discriminatory. They were meant to bar entry to nationalities or races that the government at the time considered undesirable. Two examples illustrate the racist elements inherent in Canadian immigration law during this time.

The first case concerns immigrants from China. After the Canadian Pacific Railroad was completed in 1885, the many Chinese workers that had been recruited to help build the railway were no longer wanted in Canada. The Chinese Immigration Act of 1885, which imposed a $50 fee on any Chinese person entering Canada, was part of an effort to restrict further immigration of settlers from China, including spouses and children of those already in the country. When the new fee failed to stem Chinese immigration, it was raised, in 1900, to $100, and just three years later to $500. (By comparison, today's Right of Landing fee is only $490.) Because some Chinese immigration continued in spite of these prohibitive entry fees, the Canadian government in 1923 passed the Chinese Exclusion Act, which banned Chinese immigration altogether; it was not repealed until 1947, when, in the aftermath of World War II, the Canadian government felt it could no longer abide by such a discriminatory policy directed against a specific nationality.

The second case that illustrates the government's orientation to 'undesirables' involved immigrants from India. The *Komagata Maru* was a Japanese steamliner that in 1914 arrived in Vancouver from Hong Kong via Shanghai and a number of other ports along the way. Among the passengers were 342 Sikhs, 24 Muslims, and 12 Hindus, all subjects of the British Empire. After two months of deliberation, during which the ship's passengers suffered deteriorating conditions in limbo offshore, Canadian authorities barred the immigrants from landing, and the ship was turned back. This shameful incident is viewed by many historians of a prime example of Canada's early-twentieth-century 'White Canada' policy.

In 1967, Canada's new Immigration Act struck down all references to 'preferred nationalities, ethnicities or races', heralding a new era of immigration policy driven mainly by Canada's desire to expand demographically while espousing humanitarian principles.

the heavy costs of waging war meant that people from different parts of Europe were seeking to emigrate; Canada was an attractive destination.

During the 1950s, European immigrants continued to come to Canada in large numbers, including many from southern Europe. The peak year for immigration was

1957, when Canada received over 282 000 immigrants. More than 31 000 Hungarians were admitted, mostly on humanitarian grounds, after the uprising of 1956. Italians, Germans, Dutch, and Portuguese continued to arrive in large numbers until the early 1970s.

By the late 1980s, Western Europe and the United States together accounted for only about one-third of Canada's immigrants; another third came from Asia, and the remaining third from the rest of the world, especially South America, the Caribbean, Central America, and Eastern Europe. At the root of this shift was the new Immigration Act adopted in 1967, which introduced a new point system for assessing applicants. Potential immigrants were to be judged and assigned a score on the basis of their education and skills, rather than on characteristics such as ethnicity or national background, which had been used as immigration criteria in the past. The official policy of multiculturalism, introduced just four years later, in 1971, was designed to promote equality among Canada's three founding cultures (Aboriginal, French, and English) and the growing number of groups of other ethnic backgrounds. Further revisions to the Immigration Act, in 1990, reflected the growing sense that immigration numbers had to increase if Canada was to avoid significant labour shortages in the future. Currently, annual immigration targets are in the range of 250 000—a significant increase over the target of 100 000 set in 1967, when Canada's population was just over 20 million.

Ethnocultural Origins

Table 9.5 shows the distribution of Canadians' ethnic origins as determined by the National Household Survey (NHS) in 2011. The NHS allowed for single as well as multiple responses to the question on ethnic ancestry, "What were the ethnic or cultural origins of this person's ancestors?" More than 200 ethnic origins were reported in the NHS. Thirteen of these ethnicities, alone or in combination with other ethnicities, comprised 1 million or more people.

In 2011, nearly 58 per cent of the Canadian population listed themselves as having a single ethnicity, while 42 per cent stated multiple ethnic origins. This large percentage of multiple ethnicities is understandable given Canada's long history of immigration and the consequent intermixing of diverse sociocultural groups.

About 31 per cent of those stating a single ethnicity listed "Canadian" as being their ethnic origin (5.8 million out of 19 million cases). The second most frequent single response was an Asian origin ethnicity (21 per cent out of a total of 19 million). British (13.3 per cent) and French (6.2 per cent) together comprised 19.4 per cent of all single responses. First Nations, Inuit, and Métis accounted for 3.3 per cent of all single ethnic origins, and 3.3 per cent of all multiple ethnicities.

Among those that reported a multiple ethnic origin, the most frequently cited ethnicity was British (34 per cent out of 26 million multiples). Thus, it appears that many Canadians are descendants of mixed ethnicities whereby at least one parent must have been of British origin. As might be expected, "all other ethnic origins" represent

IMMIGRATION AND DIVERSITY—LONG-TERM VS SHORT-TERM PERSPECTIVE

The full impact of immigration on receiving societies such as Canada and the United States is often obscured in detailed analyses that focus on the short-term problems of immigrant adjustment and the problem of accommodating to the diversity which immigrants bring to their new world. Building on this idea, Charles Hirschman (2006) suggests that a longer-term perspective on immigration and its sociological impact on host societies is essential. The longer-term perspective should include in particular the socioeconomic roles of the children of immigrants. It turns out, based on Hirschman's analysis of the American experience with immigration, that the descendants of immigrants have had a profound effect in defining the nature of American society. According to Hirschman, major waves of immigration create population diversity with new languages and cultures, but over time, while immigrants and their descendants become more integrated into the host society, the character of the society and culture is transformed.

For instance, Hirschman points out that in the early decades of the twentieth century, immigrants and their children were the majority of the workforce in many of the largest industrial cities in the United States (and this is true in Canada as well). In recent decades, the arrival of new waves of immigrants and their families

has helped to slow the demographic and economic decline of some American cities, according to Hirschman. Moreover, in the economic realm, the presence of immigrants probably creates as many jobs for native-born workers as are lost through displacement. Intermarriage between the descendants of immigrants and old-stock Americans has helped to foster a national identity based on civic participation rather than ancestry.

Immigrants and their children have made important and lasting contributions to twentieth-century North American society across a wide array of areas, from politics to popular culture. For example, during the middle decades of the twentieth century a number of prominent film directors with immigrant origins, including Frank Capra (Italy), William Wyler (Germany), Lewis Milestone (Russia), among others, produced some of the most memorable Hollywood films of the twentieth century. Among second generation immigrant directors, Hirschman points to the contributions of John Ford (*The Grapes of Wrath*) and Joseph L. Mankiewicz (*A Letter to Three Wives*). George Stevens, Robert Wise, Oliver Stone, and Steven Spielberg are cited as examples of highly influential directors of third and higher generation immigrant status.

Source: Charles Hirschman (2005), "Immigration and the American Century." *Demography* 42 (4): 595–620.

a substantial category of all multiple ethnicities (21.3 per cent).

Although not shown in Table 9.5, next to Canadian, English is the most frequently cited ethnicity either alone or in tandem with other ethnic origins (6.5 million people). This was followed by French (5.1 million), Scottish (4.7 million), Irish (4.5 million), and German (3.2 million). Among those ethnic origins

(either as single or multiple) that surpassed the 1-million mark include Italian, Chinese, First Nations, Ukrainian, East Indian, Dutch, and Polish (Statistics Canada 2013p: 13).

It should be noted that the tendency to list a single or a multiple ethnicity is largely contingent on whether one is a first-generation immigrant or of a higher generational status. For instance, over 80 per

TABLE 9.5   Distribution of ethnicities (single, multiple); Canada National Household Survey, 2011

Ethnicity	Single + multiple	Frequencies		Column %	
		Single	Multiple	Single	Multiple
First Nations (North American Indian)	1 369 115	517 550	851 565	2.72	3.28
Inuit	72 615	42 705	29 910	0.22	0.12
Métis	447 655	68 205	379 450	0.36	1.46
Canadian	10 563 805	5 834 535	4 729 270	30.65	18.19
British Isles origins	11 343 710	2 521 360	8 822 350	13.25	33.93
French origins	5 077 215	1 170 620	3 906 595	6.15	15.02
Other European origins	3 748 565	3 542 295	206 270	18.61	0.79
Latin, Central & South American origins	544 380	285 070	259 310	1.50	1.00
African origins	766 735	465 235	301 500	2.44	1.16
Asian origins	5 011 220	4 022 085	989 135	21.13	3.80
All other origins	6 092 695	566 635	5 526 060	2.98	21.25
Total ethnicities listed	**45 037 710**	**19 036 295**	**26 001 415**	**100**	**100**
Total (individuals)	Single + multiple	Single	Multiple		
	32 852 320	19 036 295	13 816 025		
%	100.0	57.9	42.1		

Source: Author's computations; data source: Statistics Canada (2013q).

cent of the first generation reported a single ethnic origin. Of these, Chinese, East
Indian, and English were the top three. The
most frequently reported origins among the
second generation (children born in Canada
of at least one immigrant parent) in 2011,
either alone or in combination with other
ethnic origins, were English, Canadian,
and Scottish. The highest proportion (49.6
per cent) of multiple ethnicities was among
the third generation. For these individuals,
the most common ethnic origins reported,
either alone or with other ethnicities, were
Canadian, English, and French (Statistics
Canada 2013p: 14).

Geographic Distribution of Immigrants

Traditionally, Ontario, Quebec, and British
Columbia have attracted the majority of
immigrants to Canada (see Figure 9.3). To
a large extent, the uneven distribution of
immigrant settlement across the regions
reflects longstanding regional discrepancies in economic development (Sitwell and
Seifried, 1984). Ontario's dominance as a
destination was firmly established by the
second decade of the twentieth century.

In every region, newcomers generally choose to settle in large urban centres.
Two reasons in particular account for this
pattern. First is the strong "pull" of established ethnic communities in the city, where
others of the same national background can
assist in the settlement process; second is
the wide availability of jobs, amenities, and
resources, both within the ethnic economy
itself and within the larger context of the
city (Fong, 2005; Fong and Shibuya, 2005;
Hou, 2004).

Table 9.6 shows the distribution of total
Canadian population, the immigrant population, and the population of recent immigrants (2006–11) by census metropolitan

area (CMA) in 2011. In 2011, there were 6.8
million immigrants in Canada. Of these, 91
per cent lived in one of the country's 33 census metropolitan areas. Together, Toronto,
Montreal, and Vancouver comprised 63.4
per cent of the total immigrant population,
and nearly 63 per cent of all recent arrivals.
In contrast, these three CMAs house just
over one third (35.2 per cent) of the total
Canadian population. This discrepancy
clearly highlights the great attraction of
these three urban areas for immigrants.

Especially strong is the pull of Toronto,
which in 2011 had the largest share of
Canada's foreign-born at 37.5 per cent (2.54
out of 6.8 million). Immigrants represented
nearly half of the population of Toronto (46
per cent). Meanwhile in Vancouver, immigrants' share of that city's population was 40
per cent (913 000 immigrants). In Montreal,
its 846 600 immigrants comprised nearly
23 per cent of the population. Beyond these
three CMAs, Calgary and Ottawa-Gatineau
had the fourth and fifth largest foreign-born
populations, respectively. As shown in Table
9.6, the propensity to settle in the largest
metropolitan areas is even greater among
recent newcomers to Canada. Over 62 per
cent of the 1.16 million arrivals between
2006 and 2011 chose to settle in Toronto
(32.8 per cent), Montreal (16.3 per cent), and
Vancouver (13.3 per cent). Far behind these
three CMAs, Ottawa–Gatineau, Calgary, and
Edmonton were the most attractive cities
for recent arrivals, the latter two having seen
an increasing share of new immigrants over
recent years.

Visible Minorities

In 2001, 13 per cent of Canada's people
identified themselves as belonging to a
visible minority (Statistics Canada, *The*

TABLE 9.6 Count, percentage distribution and relative ratio of total population, immigrant population and recent immigrants, in Canada and by census metropolitan areas, 2011 (NHS)

	Total population		Immigrants			Recent immigrants (2006 to 2011)		
	Number	Percentage	Number	Percentage	Relative ratio[1]	Number	Percentage	Relative ratio[1]
Canada	32 852 320	100.0	6 775 765	100.0	—	1 162 915	100.0	—
Toronto	5 521 235	16.8	2 537 405	37.4	2.2	381 745	32.8	2.0
Montreal	3 752 475	11.4	846 645	12.5	1.1	189 730	16.3	1.4
Vancouver	2 280 700	6.9	913 310	13.5	1.9	155 125	13.3	1.9
Ottawa–Gatineau	1 215 735	3.7	235 335	3.5	0.9	40 420	3.5	0.9
Ottawa–Gatineau (QC part)	310 830	0.9	30 910	0.5	0.5	7 760	0.7	0.7
Ottawa–Gatineau (ON part)	904 910	2.8	204 450	3.0	1.1	32 660	2.8	1.0
Calgary	1 199 125	3.7	313 880	4.6	1.3	70 700	6.1	1.7
Edmonton	1 139 580	3.5	232 195	3.4	1.0	49 930	4.3	1.2
Quebec	746 685	2.3	32 880	0.5	0.2	10 665	0.9	0.4
Winnipeg	714 635	2.2	147 295	2.2	1.0	45 270	3.9	1.8
Hamilton	708 175	2.2	166 755	2.5	1.1	18 775	1.6	0.7
Kitchener–Cambridge–Waterloo	469 935	1.4	108 720	1.6	1.1	15 245	1.3	0.9
London	467 260	1.4	87 655	1.3	0.9	11 905	1.0	0.7
Halifax	384 540	1.2	31 260	0.5	0.4	8 305	0.7	0.6
St Catharines–Niagara	383 965	1.2	64 385	1.0	0.8	5 650	0.5	0.4
Oshawa	351 690	1.1	56 175	0.8	0.8	4 080	0.4	0.3
Victoria	336 180	1.0	60 075	0.9	0.9	6 440	0.6	0.5
Windsor	315 460	1.0	70 290	1.0	1.1	9 225	0.8	0.8
Saskatoon	256 435	0.8	27 355	0.4	0.5	11 465	1.0	1.3
Regina	207 215	0.6	21 735	0.3	0.5	8 150	0.7	1.1
Sherbrooke	196 675	0.6	12 115	0.2	0.3	4 045	0.3	0.6
St John's	193 825	0.6	5 875	0.1	0.1	1 615	0.1	0.2
Barrie	184 330	0.6	22 350	0.3	0.6	2 135	0.2	0.3

TABLE 9.6   (continued)

	Total population			Immigrants			Recent immigrants (2006 to 2011)		
	Number	Percentage		Number	Percentage	Relative ratio[1]	Number	Percentage	Relative ratio[1]
Kelowna	176 435	0.5		24 450	0.4	0.7	3 150	0.3	0.5
Abbotsford	166 680	0.5		39 035	0.6	1.1	5 935	0.5	1.0
Greater Sudbury	158 260	0.5		9 775	0.1	0.3	665	0.1	0.1
Saguenay	154 235	0.5		1 705	0.0	0.1	535	0.0	0.1
Kingston	153 900	0.5		18 085	0.3	0.6	1 740	0.1	0.3
Trois-Rivières	146 930	0.4		4 045	0.1	0.1	1 570	0.1	0.3
Guelph	139 670	0.4		27 515	0.4	1.0	3 025	0.3	0.6
Moncton	135 520	0.1		5 995	0.1	0.2	2 250	0.2	0.5
Brantford	133 250	0.4		15 080	0.2	0.5	985	0.1	0.2
Saint John	125 010	0.4		5 365	0.1	0.2	1 290	0.1	0.3
Thunder Bay	119 140	0.4		10 895	0.2	0.4	850	0.1	0.2
Peterborough	116 175	0.4		9 495	0.1	0.4	535	0.0	0.1

Note: — means not applicable.

[1] The ratios show whether the share of immigrants or recent immigrants in a given location is higher than the share of the total population in the same location. For example, if 5 per cent of recent immigrants live in a place and the same share (5 per cent) of the total population lives there, then the ratio will be 1.0.

Source: Statistics Canada (2013p): 12. From Statistics Canada, *National Household Survey, 2011, Immigration and Ethnocultural Diversity in Canada, 2013.* Reproduced on an "as is" basis with permission of Statistics Canada

Daily, 2005b). By 2011, this group's representation had grown to nearly 6.3 million, 19.1 per cent of the total Canadian population (Statistics Canada, 2013p: 14). *Visible minorities* is an official designation based on either self-designation in the census or cross-classification of birthplace, ancestry, language, and religion. Most members of a visible minority in Canada today are first-generation immigrants, but their Canadian-born descendants may also qualify for the "visible minority" designation.

The Employment Equity Act defines *visible minorities* as persons, other than Aboriginal people, who are non-Caucasian in race or non-white in colour. The ten groups in this category are Chinese, South Asian, Black, Filipino, Latin American, Southeast Asian, Arab, West Asian, Japanese, and Korean (Statistics Canada, *The Daily*, 2005b). The visible minority population today is growing much faster than the overall population (see Table 9.7).

Projections indicate that by 2031 roughly three in ten Canadians could be a member of a visible minority, accounting perhaps between 11.4 and 14.4 million people, depending on the projection scenario. South Asians and Chinese would be expected to be the largest visible minority groups in 2031 (Statistics Canada, 2010). Almost all of visible minorities would live in metropolitan areas, especially in Vancouver, Montreal, and—above all—Toronto.

It is sometimes suggested that immigrants in general, and visible minority immigrants in particular, experience some occupational discrimination that results in a loss of income (Samuel, 1987). This

is a difficult proposition to test directly. Still, the literature on inequality leaves little doubt that economic integration is a serious problem for recent immigrants in general. Ever since John Porter's (1965) analysis revealed the extent of Canada's social stratification on the bases of race and ethnicity, sociologists using a variety of measures have found that immigrants generally and certain minorities in particular do not fare as well as the larger Canadian society. For instance, the average earnings of immigrants have fallen in recent decades and immigrants during their first year in Canada are significantly more likely than those born in Canada to fall below the low-income cut-off (McMahon, 2013; Picot, Hou, and Coloumbe, 2007).

That recent arrivals are worse off than longer established immigrants may be attributed, at least in part, to the time of their arrival, since employment opportunities vary from year to year, depending on the state of the economy. But such findings are not easily explained by one or two factors alone (see, for example, Aydemir and Borjas, 2006). Some research suggests that many visible minority immigrants work within in their ethnic enclaves, where jobs are generally not as well-paying as jobs in the larger economy. And in such contexts, the immigrants are not in a position to learn English or French because their daily interactions are mainly with others of their own ethnic community (Li and Dong, 2007) This suggests that part of the immigrant disadvantage in earnings may be explained by the very features that make the presence of an ethnic enclave attractive to new immigrants.

TABLE 9.7   Visible minorities in selected census metropolitan areas of Canada, 1981–2011

Canada	Population	Visible minority population	% Visible minority	Top three visible minority groups in 2011
1981	24 083 495	1 131 825	4.7	
1991	26 994 040	2 525 480	9.4	
2001	29 639 030	3 983 845	13.4	
2011	32 852 325	6 264 755	19.1	S. Asian, Chinese, Black
Montreal				
1981	2 798 040	146 365	5.2	
1991	3 172 005	349 415	11.0	
2001	3 380 640	458 330	13.6	
2011	3 752 475	762 325	20.3	Black, Arab, L. American
Toronto				
1981	2 975 495	404 790	13.6	
1991	3 868 875	997 500	25.8	
2001	4 647 955	1 712 530	36.8	
2011	5 521 235	2 596 420	47.0	S. Asian, Chinese, Black
Vancouver				
1981	1 250 610	173 300	13.9	
1991	1 584 195	379 480	24.0	
2001	1 967 480	725 655	36.9	
2011	2 280 695	1 030 335	45.2	Chinese, S. Asian, Filipino
2011				
Ottawa–Gatineau	1 215 735	234 015	19.2	Black, Arab, Chinese
Calgary	1 199 125	337 420	28.1	S. Asian, Chinese, Filipino
Edmonton	1 139 585	254 990	22.4	S. Asian, Chinese, Filipino
Winnipeg	714 635	140 770	19.7	Filipino, S. Asian, Black
Hamilton	708 175	101 600	14.3	S. Asian, Black, Chinese

Sources: Statistic Canada (2003d): 44, 45; (2013p): 17.

Aboriginal Population

A.J. Jaffe (1992) has correctly stated that the Aboriginal populations of North America are the "first immigrants from Asia," the ones that first settled the American continent some 12 000 years ago. The Aboriginal population of Canada consists of four identifiable subgroups: the Inuit, the Métis, and the North American Indians (also known as First Nations) subdivided into Registered and Non-Registered Indians. The Registered Indians account for about 75 per cent

TABLE 9.8 North American Indian, Métis, and Inuit populations of Canada (1871–2006) by ancestry and identity.

Year	North American Indian Ancestry	Identity	Métis Ancestry	Identity	Inuit Ancestry	Identity
1871	23 035		2			
1881	108 547					
1891						
1901	93 460		34 481			
1911	105 611					
1921	110 814				3 269	
1931	122 911				5 979	
1941	118 316		35 416		7 205	
1951	165 607					
1961	208 286				11 835	
1971	295 215				17 550	
1981	313 655		76 520		23 200	
1986		286 230		59 745		27 290
1991		443 285		128 700		35 495
1996		535 075		210 055		41 085
2001		608 850		292 310		45 070
2006		698 025		389 785		50 485
2011		851 560		451 795		59 445

Sources: Goldmann and Delic (2014); and Statistics Canada (2013r): 7.

of all First Nations peoples. Table 9.8 shows the historical pattern of population growth for the North American Indians, Métis, and Inuit as reflected in two census indicators: ancestry and identity. Geographically, the Inuit are concentrated primarily in Nunavut, the Northwest Territories, Northern Quebec, and Labrador. The Métis and Indians live in the urban and periurban areas, with a notable proportion of Indians residing in rural remote reserves. The Non-Registered Indians and the Métis tend to be the most urbanized groups. Most Métis live in the Prairies, Ontario, and Quebec, while the Registered and Non-Registered Indians are mostly in Ontario, British Columbia, and the Prairie provinces.

Owing to their higher birth rates and a significant amount of *ethnic mobility*, the Aboriginal identity population has been growing faster than the national average. In 2001, the *aboriginal identity* population numbered 976 305 (3.3 per cent of Canada's overall population). In 2011, there were over 1.4 million people with an Aboriginal identity, accounting for 4.3 per cent of the Canadian population. A distinguishing feature of the Aboriginal population is its youth, their median age being 28 years as compared to 41 for all Canada in 2011. The Inuit are the youngest of the Aboriginal groups, with a median age of only 23 (Statistics Canada, 2013r).

International Migration: The Future

Aging Western societies are being transformed by the immigrants they depend on to sustain their labour forces. Ultimately, these societies may have to renounce the idea of the nation as a singular homogeneous cultural entity and revise their self-concept to embrace ethnic diversity.

Imagined Futures

Can theories of international migration help immigrant-receiving nations respond to this challenge? Of the theories outlined earlier in this chapter, none in itself can adequately cover the diversity of issues pertaining to the formulation of immigration policy. For example, the economic and dual labour market theories focus exclusively on economic considerations; they have nothing to say about issues of national self-determination or national identity. Nor do the theories address directly how future worker power needs will evolve in the most advanced economies and how immigration will help solve this problem given that immigrants may be increasingly needed but not necessarily wanted as citizens (Piché, 2013).

Alan Simmons (1999, 2010: 59–61) has proposed that immigrant-receiving countries (liberal democracies) can adopt what he calls an *imagined futures* approach to designing immigration policy. Under the imagined futures approach, a country would set immigration policy in light of its economic goals and its ideas about its cultural identity (see

Figure 9.5). A nation would also consider its sociopolitical and economic position in the international context and then develop appropriate policies regarding not only trade and commerce with other nations but also immigration in general and immigration targets specifically. This would require that national leaders have a clear image of their country's future, specifically whether or not that future includes immigrants as fully integrated citizens. According to Simmons, once an imagined future has been formulated, immigration policies consistent with this vision can be designed.

To some extent, this approach resembles Canada's perspective on immigration since the 1967 reforms. The nation's view of itself is clearly multicultural, and its immigration policy has helped bring about this reality. At the same time, Canada is a leading economic player in the world economy, and its immigration targets are set with an eye to ensuring that its economic needs are satisfied over the long term. By contrast, countries like Japan and those of Western Europe have taken a different approach. These countries, historically, have not been countries of immigration, seeing themselves as distinct and rather homogeneous nations. But in the light of continued immigration they could perhaps benefit from an *imagined futures* perspective.

Immigration and Population Aging

Immigration has been proposed as a possible solution to combat the effects of demographic aging and below-replacement fertility levels in advanced societies. The United Nations report *Replacement Migration* (United Nations Department of Economic and Social Affairs Population Division, 2000) suggested that immigration could be used by countries as a strategy to avoid population decline in

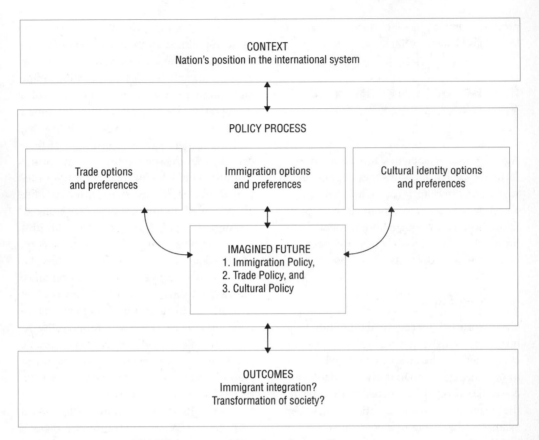

FIGURE 9.5   Imagined futures and immigration policy

Source: Simmons, Alan B. 1999. "Immigration Policy: Imagined Futures", in Shiva S. Halli and Leo Dridger, eds, *Immigrant Canada: Demographic, Economic, and Cultural Challenges*. Toronto: University of Toronto Press.: 35, Fig. 2.1. Reprinted with permission of the publisher.

the near future. We can think of *replacement migration* as the number of immigrants needed for a country to maintain its current size of the labour force population (aged 15–64) over an indefinite period of time.

A related question is whether immigration can be adjusted to stave off the effects of demographic aging. Research on this question demonstrates that it could, but that the number of immigrants needed to offset declines in the working-age population are significantly larger than those needed to offset total population decline. The UN concluded that the levels of migration needed to

offset population aging (i.e., to maintain the current balance of dependants to workers in the population) would be extremely large, and in all cases entail vastly more immigration than occurred in the past. Scholars such as David Coleman (2002) and Geoffrey McNicoll (2000) have estimated that immigration can only prevent population aging at unprecedented, unsustainable, and increasing levels that would generate rapid population growth and eventually displace the original population from its majority position. It seems doubtful, therefore, that increased immigration in Japan and the rich countries of Western Europe can be viewed as a viable remedy to demographic aging.

Open Borders?

A number of scholars (see, for example, Carens, 1987, 1999; Hayter, 2000; Legrain, 2006; Moses, 2006) have argued that migration is a fundamental human right, and that immigration controls should therefore be abolished. The issue of "open borders," they argue, strikes at the heart of what is morally just in a world that is increasingly divided along socioeconomic lines. Is it a violation of a fundamental human right—the freedom to choose where to live—for a privileged nation to deny someone from a less privileged country the opportunity to immigrate? Is there any moral objection to the adoption of an "open borders" policy?

Having examined three theories of moral justice (Rawlsian, Nozichean, and utilitarian), Joseph Carens (1987) found that even though they differed on some critical issues, they all concurred that states have an obligation to respect all human beings as free and equal moral persons, and that part of that commitment should entail "open borders." To prohibit people from entering a territory because they do not hold citizenship there is no part of any state's legitimate mandate (Carens, 1987: 255).

On the other hand, proponents of the communitarian perspective (Isbister, 2000; Meilaender, 1999; Walzer, 1992) have suggested that unrestricted immigration would restrict a nation's right to self-determination and its citizens' right to economic well-being, while threatening not only the national cultures of receiving societies but possibly even liberal democratic values and liberties. To these arguments, proponents of open borders would respond that the real purpose of immigration controls is to protect the privileges that the affluent societies of Europe and North America enjoy over the less fortunate societies of Africa and Asia—in short, that border controls have less to do with restricting people than with controlling economic resources. Advocates of open borders would acknowledge that such a policy would require that the society relinquish some control over its cultural and demographic compositions; however, they contend, open borders would in no way prevent such a state from functioning. These theorists would therefore insist that moral justice requires open borders. Critics of the open borders idea (Isbister, 2000; Meilaender, 1999; Walzer, 1992) would agree that liberal states have a moral obligation to aid poor countries in need, but only so long as the "costs" to the providers of assistance are not too high. These critics do not advocate abolition of immigration to Western liberal democracies, but they do insist that states have a moral obligation to place the interests of their own citizens first.

Whether open borders would be a practical option for liberal states remains a question for further debate (see Coleman, 2002; Golini, 2003; Keely, 2001; Romellón, 2001). Carens (1987) himself has acknowledged that on practical grounds and issues of national sovereignty and security, liberal democracies are not likely to accept free migration to all as a policy option. This view would seem applicable today and into the foreseeable future. Liberal democracies are bound to stay the course with their immigration policies, emphasizing a balance between national self-interest and the promotion of humanitarian principles (i.e., regarding asylum seekers, refugees, and family reunification). In any event, under existing conditions, immigrant-receiving liberal democracies cannot avoid the kinds of challenges associated with the integration of an increasing number of newcomers and the resultant ethnic diversity.

Conclusion

To a great extent the history of humanity is a history of migration. From our early ancestors to the rise of *Homo sapiens sapiens* people have been involved in migratory movements, each governed by its own set of dynamic forces—e.g., environmental pushes arising from climate change, natural disasters forcing people to flee their territory; the quest to explore new lands or to conquer and colonize others; the need of some societies to build their economies through the labour of migrants from less privileged regions to the disruptive effects of civil conflict, and war. Today, virtually every corner of the globe is being affected by migration, either as a predominantly receiving country or as a predominantly sending country, while some of the countries that at one time sent out its people to other parts of the globe have recently turned into major receiving areas for international migrants. Such is the world today. The sociological consequences of earlier migratory movements and encounters of different civilizations continue to be felt today, as reflected, for example, by ongoing racial tensions characteristic of societies such as the United States, Canada, Australia, and South Africa among others. As explained in this chapter, international migration today is complex and multifaceted. Many liberal democracies today rely increasingly on immigration as a means to supplements their growing demographic deficit resulting from decades of below replacement fertility. In many such cases, immigrants are often allowed to establish their own ethnic communities and to even gain citizenship. However, at the other extreme are countries where immigrants are wanted only as temporary workers and not as potential citizens. Clearly, the sociological conditions in these extreme types of settings pose radically different implications for both immigrants and their host societies. As the world becomes increasingly interconnected economically, immigration will continue to represent a major transformative force of both sending and receiving societies.

Notes for Further Study

If appropriate data are available, it is possible to compute rates and various ratios of international migration.

International Migration Ratios and Rates

Ratios

A set of migration measures may be based solely on frequencies. Edmonston and Michalowski (2004: 484) present six migration ratios, expressing relations among immigration, emigration, and net migration:

$$\frac{\text{emigration}}{\text{immigration}} = \frac{E}{I} \tag{1}$$

$$\frac{\text{net immigration}}{\text{immigration}} = \frac{I-E}{I} (\text{where } I > E) \tag{2}$$

$$\frac{\text{net emigration}}{\text{immigration}} = \frac{E-I}{I} (\text{where } E > I) \tag{3}$$

$$\frac{\text{immigration}}{\text{gross immigration}} = \frac{I}{I+E} \tag{4}$$

$$\frac{\text{emigration}}{\text{gross migration}} = \frac{E}{I + E} \qquad (5)$$

$$\frac{\text{net migration}}{\text{gross migration}} = \frac{I - E}{I + E} \qquad (6)$$

Which of these ratios is most appropriate depends on the purpose of the analysis and the migration characteristics of the area or country under study.

Rates

Migration rates have a general form that can apply to either internal or external types of movement. We will look at five migration rates, all crude rates. Below, we assume that the denominator for the rates is the mid-year population of a country, typically the census population; and the symbols I and E represent the volume of immigration and emigration, respectively, during a given interval:

$$\text{crude immigration rate} = \frac{I}{P} \times 1\,000 \qquad (7)$$

$$\text{crude emigration rate} = \frac{E}{P} \times 1\,000 \qquad (8)$$

$$\text{crude net migration rate} = \frac{I - E}{P} \times 1\,000 \qquad (9)$$

$$\text{crude gross migration rate} = \frac{I - E}{P} \times 1\,000 \qquad (10)$$

Table 9.9 shows cross-national examples of each of these migration rates around 1995. Note the variations across the countries. Israel and Ecuador, for instance, have relatively high net migration rates (especially Israel), while the other countries are far behind in this measure. The reason for this is readily seen: the other countries have relatively high emigration rates, which are substantially lower their net migration rates. Notice as well the gross migration rates, which combine immigration and emigration into one measure. This rate may be viewed as an overall indication of population turnover in a country. On this account, Ecuador surpasses Israel, though this is clearly a function of Ecuador's much higher rate of emigration: while a lot of people move into Ecuador, a significant number also leave the country. By contrast, most of Israel's high gross migration rate can be accounted for by its high immigration rate combined with its low emigration.

TABLE 9.9   Various rates of migration for selected countries, c.1995

Country and year (1995 unless noted otherwise)	(1) Immigration[1]	(2) Emigration[1]	(3) Population[2] (in thousands)	(4) Immigration rate (1)/(3) × 1000	(5) Emigration rate (2)/(3) × 1000	(6) Net migration rate [(1) − (2)]/(3) × 1000	(7) Gross migration rate [(1)+ (2)]/(3) × 1000
South Africa	5 064	8 725	41 244	0.1	0.2	−0.1	0.3
Zimbabwe	2 901	3 282	11 526	0.3	0.3	<0.05	0.5
Canada	300 313	165 725	29 615	10.1	5.6	+4.5	15.7
USA[3]	878 288	263 232	262 765	3.3	1.0	+2.3	4.3
Ecuador	471 961	348 845	11 221	42.1	31.1	+11.0	73.1
Venezuela	62 482	77 388	19 787	3.2	3.9	−0.8	7.1
Indonesia	218 952	57 096	194 755	1.1	0.3	+0.8	1.4
Israel (1990)	197 533	14 191	4 660	42.4	3.0	+39.3	45.4
Japan	87 822	72 377	125 197	0.7	0.6	+0.1	1.3
South Korea	101 612	403 522	45 093	2.3	8.9	−6.7	11.2
Belgium	62 950	36 044	10 137	6.2	3.6	+2.7	9.8
Germany	1 096 048	698 113	81 661	13.4	8.5	+4.9	22.0
Italy (1994)	99 105	65 548	57 204	1.7	1.1	+0.6	2.9
Poland (1994)	6 907	25 904	38 544	0.2	0.7	−0.5	0.9
Russian Fedn (1994)	1 146 735	337 121	147 968	7.7	2.3	+5.5	10.0
Sweden	45 887	33 984	8 831	5.2	3.8	+1.3	9.0
Switzerland	90 957	69 357	7 041	12.9	9.9	+3.1	22.8
UK	245 452	191 570	58 606	4.2	3.3	+0.9	7.5
Australia	253 940	149 360	18 049	14.1	8.3	+5.8	22.3

[1] Long-term immigrants: non-residents, or persons who have not continuously lived in the country for more than one year, arriving for a length of stay of more than one year. Long-term emigrants: residents, or persons who have resided continuously in the country for more than one year, who are departing to take up residence abroad for more than one year.

[2] Estimated mid-period population.

[3] US Census Bureau estimate: immigration includes refugees and illegal entrants as well as legal permanent residents; emigration includes departures of legal foreign-born and native residents.

Source: Adapted from Edmonston and Michalowski (2004): 487.

Exercises

1. The period since the 1960s has been described by some as the "age of migration." Others have referred to "worlds in motion." In the same context, it has been written that in comparison to earlier modern history, there has been "an acceleration of migration"; and that "migration is "highly differentiated" and increasingly "politicized." Write an essay on how global migration patterns have changed in the post-World War II years. What is the possible future of immigration for liberal democracies?
2. Receiving societies can be located along a continuum of "exclusiveness–inclusiveness" with respect to their reception of and treatment of immigrants. Discuss this idea in relation to different countries in the world that receive a substantial number of immigrants. What are the immigration policy challenges for societies at different locations on the continuum?
3. Write a critical essay on the role that ethnic communities play in the integration of immigrants into North American society.

Additional Reading

Betts, Alexander, ed. 2011. *Global Migration Governance*. Oxford: Oxford University Press.

Czaika, Mathias, and Carlos Vargas-Silva, eds. 2012. *Migration and Economic Growth*. Elgar Research Collection. The International Library of Studies on Migration. Cheltenham, UK: Elgar.

Hatton, Timothy J., and Jeffrey G. Williamson. 2005. *Global Migration and the World Economy: Two Centuries of Policy and Performance*. Cambridge, MA: MIT Press.

Hoerder, Dirk. 2002. *Cultures in Contact; World Migrations in the Second Millennium*. Durham, NC: Duke University Press.

Koslowsky, Ray, ed. 2011. *Global Mobility Regimes*. New York: Palgrave Macmillan.

Livi-Bacci, Massimo. 2012. *A Short History of Migration*. Cambridge: Polity Press.

Ness, Emmanuel, general ed. 2013. *The Encyclopedia of Global Human Migration*, 5 vols. Chichester: Wiley-Blackwell.

Portes, Alejandro, and Josh DeWind, eds. 2007. *Rethinking Migration: New Theoretical and Empirical Perspectives*. New York: Berghahn Books.

Simmons, Alan B. 2010. *Immigration and Canada: Global and Transnational Perspectives*. Toronto: Canadian Scholars Press.

Wells, Spencer. 2010. *The Journey of Man: A Genetic Odyssey*. Princeton: Princeton University Press.

Note

1. In addition to the categories listed, non-permanent residents include people in Canada who hold a Minister's permit and non-Canadian-born dependants of (a) people claiming refugee status or (b) people holding student authorization, employment authorization, or a Minister's permit. Children born in Canada to parents of non-permanent resident status are considered Canadian by birth and have all rights and privileges associated with citizenship (Statistics Canada Demography Division, 2003: 31, 65).

PART FIVE

Population Change and Societal Interrelationships

Urbanization

Introduction

The world is becoming increasingly urbanized. Four decades ago, Kingsley Davis (1970: 4) observed that before 1850 no society could be described as predominantly urbanized, and that by 1900 only Great Britain could be seen as being more urban than rural. By 1800, London, then the largest city on earth, had a population of almost 1 million; Paris had over 500 000 inhabitants and Vienna about 200 000. By 1950, the populations of London and Paris were ranked third and fourth largest in the world, respectively, by the United Nations. In 2011, neither London nor Paris was among the top ten largest cities in the world. Among the 20 largest cities today only 5 are in industrialized countries: Tokyo, New York, Los Angeles, Moscow, and Osaka-Kobe; the rest are in the developing countries (United Nations Department of Economic and Social Affairs Population Division, 2012b). This sweeping historical account gives us a sense of the dramatic changes in global urbanization over a relatively recent segment of the broad spectrum of human history.

The urbanization process—as measured by the proportion of the population living areas defined as urban—varies considerably across the regions; it has slowed considerably in the industrialized countries, as many are approaching a saturation point in their levels of urban growth. However, since the mid-twentieth century, urbanization has occurred rapidly in the developing countries, where migration to the cities is widespread, motivated by the combination of rapid population growth and extreme poverty and hardship in the countryside. As these countries industrialize, there is great unevenness in the extent and pace of economic development, and of urbanization. In many parts of the developing world, large primate cities are growing faster than other urban settlements, and the rural areas have fallen behind in development as a result of inattention by governments focused on promoting the urban sector of their economies. Given this uneven development, large urban centres are often viewed by rural dwellers as attractive places, where they can establish a better life for themselves and their families. In many respects, this situation in the world's poorer countries is reminiscent of the experience nearly 200 years ago of countries in the West as they underwent the upheavals associated with a rapidly changing economy brought on by the Industrial Revolution and rapid urbanization.

Basic Concepts and Measures

Urbanization is a complex process of change affecting both the population and the geography of a country or region. It is characterized particularly by three developments:

1. a progressive concentration of people and economic activity in cities and towns, which alters the general scale of population settlement;

2. a shift in the national economy, in which the non-agricultural mode of production, situated predominantly in areas of the country designated as "urban," becomes dominant; and

3. an increasing diffusion of technological innovation spreading from larger to smaller urban centres and eventually to rural areas, so that in the advanced stages of urbanization the urban and the rural become similar in the extent and intensity of technological adoption as well as in certain sociopsychological aspects, including lifestyles, values, and attitudes

The homogenizing sociopsychological effect of urban living on the population is what defines *urbanism*, a term referring to the style of life found in urban areas. The sociological implications of urbanism have preoccupied scholars for well over a century; notable contributions to the study of urbanism have come from such eminent sociologists as Ferdinand Tönnies (1883 [1995]), Max Weber (1905 [1958]), George Simmel (1903 [1969]), Ernest Burgess (1925), and Robert Park (1916, 1929 [1959]). In sociopsychological terms, as well as in demographic and economic terms, urbanization is a transforming process. In the initial stages of urbanization, there are sharp sociological differences between the urban and the rural populations. Early theorists tended to characterize life in the city as impersonal and isolating, detached from the traditional forms of living characteristics of the rural folk community. Simmel, for example, viewed urban life as psychologically overwhelming—so much so that

it drove city-dwellers to detach themselves from others and compartmentalize their lives in order to make them more manageable (Sennett, 1969: 8–9).

As countries in the West have become predominantly urban, sociologists have developed new conceptions of urbanism. One view sees the city as a culturally heterogeneous place whose benefits outweigh the characteristically urban disadvantages of crime, deviancy, and poverty. Jane Jacobs (1967), for instance, championed cities—especially neighbourhoods—as places that provide close affiliation for their citizens and, in this way, a natural form of protection against crime. Moreover, in the anonymous environment of the city it is possible for people of like orientations to form associations for the purposes of promoting activities of common interest; this is what makes cities places of innovation and cultural creativity (Fischer, 1975, 1976). Still, the darker aspects of city life cannot be ignored, and it is fair to say that urbanization is a process that produces both negative and positive results in a country: on the one hand, it creates problems associated with socioeconomic inequalities, such as poor housing and urban crime, and promotes congestion, encroachment on agricultural land, and environmental degradation; on the other hand, it engenders, for many people, a better standard of living, material and social progress, and greater cultural diversity.

Having progressed through a century or more of sustained industrialization, most Western countries and Japan have reached what appears to be a peak level of urbanization, and the pace of additional urban growth is occurring at a slower and slower rate. Currently, the proportion of the population living in urban areas of Europe, North America, and Latin America exceeds

75 per cent (Jones, 2003: 952), and few substantial differences in lifestyle, values, and attitudes remain between the urban and the rural sectors. Indeed, we can question the degree to which urban and rural populations really differ at all with respect to these sociological dimensions in an age in which television, radio, the Internet, computers, wireless communication networks, and interconnected systems of transportation are commonplace (Small and Witherick, 1986: 225). The same cannot be said of the developing countries, where large segments of the population are rural and without ready access to advanced communication technologies. Nevertheless, as urbanization intensifies through the urban hierarchy and diffuses to the rural areas of these countries, a blurring of urban–rural lifestyle differences, similar to what has occurred in the industrialized countries of the West, seems inevitable.

What Is "Urban"?

The term *urban* is used frequently in the popular media and in everyday conversation, though its precise meaning is elusive. This is the case even in demography. For instance, what exactly constitutes an *urban area*? Variations in the definition of "urban" across countries make this seemingly simple question difficult to answer, and make international comparisons of urbanization challenging to carry out.

In the United States and in Mexico, a place must have a population of at least 2500 to qualify as urban. These definitions of urban, though they are not consistent, are straightforward compared with how the term is defined in other countries. In India, for example, an urban area is any place with 5000 or more inhabitants, a density of no fewer than 1000 persons per square mile

(or 390 per square kilometre), and at least three-quarters of the adult male population employed in pursuits other than agriculture. In China, an urban population is designated according to its role in the country's economy or political administration: any area in which the dominant economic activity is agriculture is considered rural, while administrative centres and places that are predominantly industrial are considered urban (Brockerhoff, 2000: 6). Despite attempts by the United Nations to standardize the use of "urban," wide variations exist in how the term is applied in different countries (McKibben and Faust, 2004: 105–23; United Nations Department of Economic and Social Affairs Population Division, 2002).

In Canada, until recently, Statistics Canada defined the urban population as comprising all incorporated places with a population of at least 1000 and a density of at least 400 persons per square kilometre; and all remaining areas were classified as rural (Statistics Canada, 2003e: 104). Beginning with the 2011 census, this definition has been modified to better reflect the existence of a rural/urban continuum. The term *population centre* replaces the term *urban area*. A population centre is defined as a population of at least 1000 and a density of 400 or more people per square kilometre. All areas outside population centres will continue to be defined as rural area. Population centres are divided into three groups based on the size of their population: (a) small population centres, with a population of between 1000 and 29999; (b) medium population centres, with a population of between 30000 and 99999; (c) large urban population centres, consisting of a population of 100000 and over. This new approach to defining urban allows for a more dynamic understanding of the rural–urban continuum (Statistics Canada, 2011e).

This recent change by Statistics Canada recognizes that in today's context the diffusion of lifestyles, values, and attitudes from urban to rural areas through urbanization has erased many of the once widely accepted differences that distinguished cities from smaller communities (see Table 10.1). For this reason, the rural–urban dichotomy, once commonly used to describe the social, demographic, economic, and spatial dimensions of urban and rural areas, is too simplistic for modern contexts and should probably be abandoned. Significant changes in communication technologies, transportation, and economic activity have brought about new forms of urbanization that are best studied using a multidimensional rather than a unidimensional conceptualization of settlement systems (Hugo, Champion, and Lattes, 2003). Consider some of the ways in which urban and rural functions are increasingly intermixed. To cite just one example, advances in transportation and communication technologies have enabled many people to commute daily from homes in rural areas to jobs in the nearby city.

Many parts of the world today are experiencing changes to settlement patterns that cannot be observed through the traditional measure of urbanization, the "per cent urban." For example, in Europe, the traditional monocentric form of the urban region is disappearing. It is being replaced by a variety of polycentric urban configurations, ranging in scale from individual metropolitan areas in which centres subsidiary to the main core can be identified along the lines of the city's edge, to

TABLE 10.1   Some widely accepted differences between urban and rural populations

Dimension	Urban	Rural
Economy	dominated by secondary and tertiary activities	predominantly primary industry and activities supporting it
Occupational structure	manufacturing, construction, administration, and service activities	agriculture and other primary industry occupations
Education levels and availability	higher than national averages	lower than national averages
Accessibility to services	high	low
Accessibility to information	high	low
Demography	low fertility and mortality	high fertility and mortality
Politics	greater representation of liberal and radical elements	conservative, resistance to change
Ethnicity	varied	more homogeneous
Migration levels	high and generally net in-migration	low and generally net out-migration

Source: Hugo, Champion, and Lattes (2003): 279, Table 1. Copyright © 2004 John Wiley and Sons."Toward a New Conceptualization of Settlements for Demography" by Graeme Hugo, Anthony Champion, Alfredo Lattes, in *Population and Development Review* vol. 29, issue 2. Copyright © 2003 The Population Council Inc.

much wider urban fields that incorporate several polynuclear metropolitan regions to form even larger urban systems, or *megalopolises*. Similar changes are taking place in the developing countries. For instance, the Philippines and Thailand are witnessing the growth of extended metropolitan regions characterized by a mixture of urban and rural features and linked by urban development along major transport routes. New spatial forms such as these challenge the usual conception of what constitutes a city (Hugo, Champion, and Lattes, 2003).

Basic Measures of Urbanization

In this section, we look at some of the more widely used measures of urbanization. None of the simple measures reviewed here can tell us anything about the causes and consequences of urbanization, or even why levels of urbanization change; these measures are but a starting point to a more substantive analysis of the phenomenon of urbanization.

Urban population change is usually described in terms of three commonly adopted measures:

1. the urban proportion and its change over time;
2. the distribution of population in accordance with size of settlement and change in these distributions; and
3. the urban growth rate and its change over time.

While considering the usefulness and applicability of these measures, it is important to keep in mind the preceding discussion of the limits to unidimensional measures of urbanization and the conceptual problems of defining "urban."

Urban Proportion

Urban proportion refers to the percentage of a country's population that resides in areas that are designated as "urban." That is,

$$\% \text{ urban} = \left[\frac{\text{urban population}}{\text{urban population} + \text{rural population}} \right] \times 100$$

The data required to compute this measure is easy to obtain for countries that take periodic censuses of their populations. Usually, tabulations are compiled showing the distribution of population according to the type of residence, rural or urban. For example, the UN's *2000 Demographic Yearbook* (United Nations Department of Economic and Social Affairs Population Division, 2002) gives Ireland's total population for 1996 as 3 626 087, of which 2 107 991 lived in urban areas, and 1 518 096 resided in rural localities. Therefore, the urban proportion for Ireland in 1996 was

$$\frac{2\,107\,991}{3\,626\,087} \times 100 = 58.13\%$$

A recent UN report on world urbanization shows that in 2011, the population of the world was just over 52 per cent urbanized. In that year, there were 3.63 billion people living in urban places and 3.34 billion living in rural areas. In the same year, the population of the more developed regions (as defined by the United Nations) was estimated to be 1.24 billion, and that of the less developed regions 5.73 billion. As Table 10.2 shows, the urban proportion was 77.7 per cent for the more developed countries, and 46.5 per cent for the less developed countries (United Nations Department of Economic and Social Affairs Population Division, 2012b: 4).

TABLE 10.2   Urban and rural population by major world area, 2011

Region	Population (in billions)			Percentage		
	Urban	Rural	Total	Urban	Rural	Total
World	3.63	3.34	6.97	52.1	47.9	100
More developed countries	0.96	0.28	1.24	77.7	22.9	100
Less developed countries	2.67	3.07	5.73	46.5	53.5	100

Source: Adapted from United Nations Economic and Social Affairs Population Division (2012b): 4.

A drawback of this measure is the wide variation, noted earlier in the chapter, in how "urban" is defined internationally. This can make it difficult to compare rates of different nations. However, the index can be used unambiguously to measure the extent to which a country's population resides in urban areas, and it can be applied without complication to measure levels of urbanization within countries—across provinces, states, and so on.

Percentage Change in Urban Proportion

In many applications, we are interested in looking at the extent of change over time in the percentage of the population that lives in urban areas. The *percentage change in urban proportion* measures (in percentage terms) the magnitude of increase or decrease, between any two points in time, of the population living in urban areas. The formula for this index of urbanization is as follows:

% change in urban population =

$$\left[\frac{\% \text{ urban population}, t_1 - \% \text{ urban population}, t_0}{\% \text{ urban population}, t_0} \right] \times 100$$

We'll continue with the example of Ireland. In 1978, Ireland was 52.00 per cent urbanized (Population Reference Bureau, 1978). As we saw earlier, by 1996, the percentage had grown to 58.13. Thus, the percentage change in the urban proportion over this period was

$$\frac{58.13 - 52.00}{52.00} \times 100 = 11.79\%$$

We can also apply this measure on a global scale. In 1950, the world's urban and rural proportions were 29.1 and 70.9 per cent, respectively. By the year 2000, the proportions were 47.1 per cent urban and 52.9 per cent rural (United Nations Department of Economic and Social Affairs Population Division, 2004b: 5). The percentage change in the urban proportion was therefore

$$\frac{47.1 - 29.1}{29.1} \times 100 = 61.86\%$$

and the corresponding change in the rural proportion was

$$\frac{52.9 - 70.9}{70.9} \times 100 = -25.39\%$$

Rate of Growth of Urban Population

In many cases, we wish to examine the rate of growth in the actual number of people that live in urban areas over some specified interval, rather than looking at change in the urban proportion. To do this, we would take the difference between *actual* population counts for the urban population. There are three different growth rates that can be considered: the *arithmetic*, the *exponential*, and the *geometric*. If the time interval is relatively short, the arithmetic average is adequate. However, if the interval is long—say five years or longer—then either the exponential or the geometric would be more appropriate (see the discussion of population growth models in Chapter 3).

The *arithmetic rate of growth* of urban population between two points in time, t_0 and t_1, can be computed as follows:

$$\frac{\left[\frac{\text{urban population, } t_1 - \text{urban population, } t_0}{\text{urban population, } t_0} \right]}{n}$$

where n is the number of years in the interval between t_0 and t_1.

This formula gives the arithmetic average annual rate of change (either positive or negative) of the urban population over an interval between t_0 and t_1 but the rate can also be expressed as a percentage by multiplying the quotient by 100.

As an illustration, let's consider the case of Canada over the 30-year interval 1871–1901. The census of 1871 counted 722 343 Canadians living in urban areas. In 1901, the number of Canadians living in urban areas was 2 014 222 (Basavarajappa and Ram, 1983: A67–74). The arithmetic average rate of growth of the urban population during this interval was

$$\frac{\left[\frac{2\,014\,222 - 722\,343}{722\,343} \right]}{30} = 0.05962 \,/\, \text{year}$$

Expressed in percentage terms, this translates into an average annual growth rate of 5.96 per cent over the 30-year interval.

If the change of the urban population is assumed to follow an *exponential* progression over time, the formula can be reworked using natural logarithms of the populations divided by the number of years in the interval. The exponential average growth rate of urban population between t_0 and t_1 is as follows:

$$\frac{\ln P_1 - \ln P_0}{n}$$

where ln stands for "natural logarithm."

Using the information from the example above, this works out to

$$\frac{\ln 2\,014\,222 - \ln 722\,343}{30} = 0.0342$$

This tells us that the annual average exponential growth rate of the urban population between the two time points is 3.42 per cent.

If growth between periods is thought to follow a *geometrical* progression, then the formula changes as follows:

$$\left[\frac{P_1}{P_0} \right]^{1/n} - 1$$

Using the same population data as before, this formula yields an average annual growth rate of urban population of 3.48 per cent per year. That is,

$$\left[\frac{2\,014\,222}{722\,343} \right]^{-1/30} - 1 = 0.0348, \text{ or } 3.48\% \,/\, \text{year}$$

As we can see, the exponential and geometric rates are quite similar.

Distribution of Urban Population by Size of Settlement

In spatial terms, urbanization implies (among other things) a rise in the extent to which the population of a nation or region is concentrated in towns and cities (Davis, 1973: 47). In order to measure this aspect of urbanization, we need to incorporate categories of urban settlement defined by population size. The first step would be to create size categories of settlements (e.g., small, medium, large), and then classify the population according to these categories. This approach requires us to define what we mean by "small urban," "medium urban," "large urban," and so on. The way these categories are defined would depend on the country and also the historical period being analyzed. In a country with a population of, say, 200 million, "small" settlements might be localities with populations of less than 5 000. In a country with a much smaller population, this designation might apply to places with populations of less than 1 000.

By classifying the urban population according to settlement size, it is possible to see how uniformly the population is distributed across settlements of different sizes. In some regions, for instance, the urban population may be heavily concentrated in the largest urban centres of a country, with a relatively small proportion of the people living in smaller settlements. In other cases, the distribution may be more even. An analyst could use this measure to study the extent to which the overall urban population of a particular country is concentrated in, say, cities of one million population or greater, or cities with less than 500 000 people, and so forth. As a general formula, we may write the following:

% urban population living in settlements of size k at time t

$$= \frac{N_{k,t}}{\sum N_{k,t}} \times 100$$

where $N_{k,t}$ is the number of people residing in urban places of size k at time t, and $\sum N_{k,t}$ is the total number of people across all k categories of urban population size (i.e., the total urban population of the country) at time t.

Table 10.3 shows that just over half of the world's urban population resides in places with fewer than 500 000 inhabitants. Between 1975 and 2011, however, the proportion of the urban population living in places of this size declined, from 53.30 to 50.9 per cent. In 2011, about 21 per cent of the world's urban population lived in settlements of between 1 million and 5 million residents. In proportionate terms, this settlement size increased slightly from 22 per cent in 1975. Urban places of 10 million or more inhabitants (known as *megacities*) have seen their share of the world's urban population increase over this interval from 4.3 per cent to nearly 10 per cent, the largest gain over this period across all five urban size classes. And although the population in settlements of between 5 million and 10 million grew in absolute terms (from 131 million to 283 million) over the interval, the share of population for this

TABLE 10.3   World population distribution by area of residence (urban, rural) and size class of urban settlement, 1975 and 2011

IIIIIIIIIIIIIIIIIIIIIIIIIIIIIIIIIIIIIIIIIIIIIIIIIIIIIIIIIIIIIIIIIIIIIIIIIIIIIIIIIIIIIIIIIIIIIIIIIIIIIIIIIIIIII

Area and urban size class	Population (in millions)		Percentage (based on total urban population)	
	1975	2011	1975	2011
Total world population	4 068	3 970		
Urban population	1 516	3 630	100	100
10 million or more	65	359	4.3	9.9
5 million to 10 million	131	283	8.6	7.8
1 million to 5 million	333	776	22.0	21.4
500 000 to 1 million	179	365	11.8	10.1
Fewer than 500 000	808	1 849	53.3	50.9
Rural population	2 552	3 334		

Source: Adapted from United Nations Economic and Social Affairs Population Division (2006b): 11; (2012b): 5.

urban size category declined in proportionate terms from 8.6 to 7.8 per cent.

Change in the Number of Settlements of a Given Population Size

The data in Table 10.3 show how the global population changed, over a 36-year interval, for five categories of urban settlement classed according to population size. Another way to chart these changes would be to look at the increase and decrease in the number of settlements of each size. So, for example, we could look at the change in the number of cities exceeding a population of 100 000 across several time periods. The percentage change in the number of settlements of size k between t_0 and t_1 can be computed as follows:

$$\left[\frac{\text{number of settlements of size } k, t_1 - \text{number of settlements of size } k, t_0}{\text{number of settlements of size } k, t_0} \right] \times 100$$

As we discussed earlier, we can obtain an arithmetic average annual rate of change for this measure by dividing the percentage by n, the number of years in the interval between t_0 and t_1. For example, Davis (1973) determined that between 1950 and 1960, the number of cities worldwide with 125 000 or more inhabitants grew from 757 to 1 071. Thus, for urban settlements of this size, the absolute change was 314. The corresponding percentage change in the number of settlements of this size over the ten-year interval was

$$\frac{1 071 - 757}{757} \times 100 = 41.48\%$$

The annual arithmetic average rate of growth for cities over 125 000 between 1950 and 1960 was thus

$$\frac{41.48}{10} = 4.15\% \, / \, \text{year}$$

On a global level, in 1975 the world contained 21 "urban agglomerations" with

5 million or more inhabitants. By 2003, that number had risen to 46, for an absolute change of 25 and a corresponding percentage growth of 119 per cent (United Nations Department of Economic and Social Affairs Population Division, 2004b: 14). The average arithmetic annual percentage change in the number of cities with populations of 5 million or more over the 28-year interval was therefore 4.25 per cent per year. Most of this increase may be attributed to growth in the world's less developed regions, which were home to 33 of the 46 urban agglomerations of this size in 2003.

Components of Urbanization

As a demographic process, urbanization is driven by changes in fertility and mortality (natural increase) and in internal and external migration (net migration). In general, the greater the rate of growth of the national population, the faster the rate of urbanization (Davis, 1955). But urbanization is also a spatial phenomenon, and an administrative one. *Annexation* is the process in which a city artificially expands its geographical boundaries and also its population size by appropriating adjacent land or territory that typically contains sparsely or densely populated smaller settlements. *Incorporation* of new places is a legal/administrative process that formalizes the establishment of settlements as towns or cities. Incorporation essentially increases the number of towns and cities in a country.

The relative contribution of natural increase and net migration to urban growth has varied over history. Prior to the Industrial Revolution, from the thirteenth century through the seventeenth century, European cities grew mostly through migration rather than through natural increase. These cities were generally characterized by high mortality rates that would typically exceed birth rates by a significant margin, thus accounting for negative rates of natural increase. The high mortality was due to underdeveloped socioeconomic conditions and widespread infectious diseases, including the notorious pandemic known as the Black Death, which wiped out about a quarter of Western Europe's population during its most devastating period, between 1348 and 1350 (Langer, 1973). The population levels of cities subject to such adverse demographic conditions could be maintained by migration from the countryside (Davis, 1973: 102–3; de Vries, 1984: 199–200; United Nations Department of Economics and Social Affairs Population Division, 1973: 196).

Cities in Europe did not reach self-maintenance (in terms of population growth through natural increase) until the eighteenth and nineteenth centuries. Paris and London achieved self-maintenance by the close of the eighteenth century, while a number of German and Swedish cities gained this status during the first half of the nineteenth century (United Nations Department of Economics and Social Affairs Population Division, 1973: 196). Between 1841 and 1911, towns and cities in England and Wales grew more by natural increase than by net in-migration. In urban areas as a whole, net migration was responsible for only one-sixth of the overall population growth in England and Wales. The city of London grew from 2.3 million to 7.3 million during this time, with natural increase accounting for 3.8 million of this growth and net migration 1.3 million (or roughly 33 per cent) (Hinde, 2003: 251).

In general, we can say that over the nineteenth and twentieth centuries, natural increase replaced migration as the main factor in urban growth. This is particularly true of the industrialized countries, where urbanization has peaked and the rural populations are relatively small. Today, mortality and fertility rates in the urban and rural populations of industrialized countries are no longer very different (both being generally low), and it is fair to conclude that future urban population growth will occur mainly through natural increase. In major immigrant-receiving nations like Canada and the United States, urban growth through natural increase will be supplemented by significant international migration.

Natural increase is responsible for a large portion of urban population growth in most contemporary developing countries, accounting for over half of urban population growth in some cases. It is also true that the contributions to urban growth of natural increase and net migration are not uniform across regions in the developing world (Beier, 1976; Gugler, 1988; McGee and Griffith, 1998; National Research Council, 2003; Preston, 1979).

However, it seems reasonable to suggest that, in general, high rates of urban growth are at least as much a function of natural increase as of rural-to-urban migration. The National Research Council (2003) has confirmed that in an overall sense, about 60 per cent of urban growth in the developing countries can be attributed to the effect of natural increase, and the balance left to migration and reclassification.

Urbanization History

Early Cities

Urbanization as a historical process cannot be understood in isolation from the development of early cities in the ancient world. The very concept of human civilization is inextricably tied to the development of cities (De Coulanges, 1956; Faris, 1963: 341; Hall, 1998; Mumford, 1961; Scott, 1988; Weber, 1905 [1958]). Civilization in its etymology means urbanization, cities being the points of political and cultural progress through history, and the places where modern economies developed (Keyfitz, 1996b: 269).

The oldest village known is thought to have been a place just outside of present-day Jericho, in Palestine as early as circa 9000 BCE, which later evolved into a small farming village. Along with Jericho, Catal Huyuk, located in Anatolia in present Turkey, is considered as the oldest known pre-urban settlement, its origins dating back to about 6500 BCE. The first urban centres—cities with organized bureaucracies, differentiated economic activities, and socially stratified power structures—first emerged about 5 500 years ago (or about 3500 BCE). It appears that such early cities arose in more than one place in the *Old World*: in Mesopotamia (mainly present-day Iraq) and certain regions of Turkey, Egypt, China, and India. There is evidence of early cities in the *New World*, dating back about 3 700 years ago in Peru, and in Mesoamerica about 1 300 years ago (Douglas, 2013; Tellier, 2009).

The emergence of pre-urban settlements, and later the early cities, coincided partly with peoples' quest for seeking protection in large numbers and for co-operative mutual benefit. Early settlements were often places where different peoples would come together to trade in goods, such as pottery and metals, as well as for religious observance. Beginning about 8 000 years ago, people would discover how to domesticate animals and plants, thereby allowing for the formation of settled communities and the production of abundant food to sustain such settlements. This period of human history is known as the *Neolithic* (or *Agricultural*) *Revolution* (Cipolla, 1962; Gist and Favia, 1974). This was a turning point in human history, as it represented the beginnings of modern civilization, encompassing art, organized religion, architecture, writing, cities, and even humanity's darker features, such as war, social inequality, and exclusion (Balter, 2005: 3).

The fertile agricultural lands in parts of the Ancient World, such as the valleys of the Tigris and Euphrates rivers of Mesopotamia (the "Fertile Crescent"), the Yellow River in China, and the Nile in Egypt, served as ideal settings, not only for agriculture but also for the beginnings of urban life. By 4500 BCE, the surplus food produced in these alluvial regions would sustain a number of prospering cities, including Uruk, Ur, Susa, Sialk, Mashkan-shapir, Babylon, Nippur, Kish, and Tepe Yahya (Kenoyer, 2005; Lamberg-Karlovsky and Lamberg-Karlovsky, 1971 [1973]; McDowell, 2005; Stone and Zimanky, 2005). By 2500 BCE, cities had also emerged in the Indus valley of present-day Pakistan (e.g., Harappa) and in the middle reaches of the Yellow River in China (Gates, 2011; Sjoberg, 1965 [1973]). In the New World, the ancient peoples of Mesoamerica, the Mayas, Zapotecs, Mixtecs, and Aztecs, and in South America, the Incas, had developed urban communities on a major scale long before the arrival of Europeans (Gist and Favia, 1974; Sjoberg, 1965 [1973]; Tellier, 2009). In their day, many of these early urban centres would form interconnections with other settlements or cities through trade, co-operation, or competition for resources and even warfare. These varied types of interconnections

through history represent an essential feature of early urbanization and civilization (Turchin et al., 2013).

In his "The Urban Revolution," V Gordon Childe (1950) listed ten other elemental features of early cities:

1. concentration of a relatively large number of people in a restricted area;
2. developed social stratification;
3. non-agricultural occupations in addition to farming: craft specialists, priests, traders, administrators, etc.;
4. the production of an economic surplus and its appropriation by a central authority, such as a king or a deity;
5. writing, to record economic activity and the myths, and other ideological issues that served to justify the discrepancies between the privileged and lower classes;
6. exact and predictive sciences, to forecast the weather for agricultural production;
7. monumental public architecture, which could include such structures as temples, palaces, fortifications, and tombs;
8. figural art;
9. foreign trade; and
10 residence-based group membership, in which people of all professions and classes could share in a sense of community.

These elemental features of early cities encompass demographic, geographical, social, economic, and ideological dimensions of urban development.

Many of the early cities eventually disappeared as a result of warfare, epidemic diseases, and other catastrophic developments; a number of them were rediscovered and resettled, only to disappear under conditions of war, invasion, disease, natural

CATAL HUYUK AND OTHER SETTLEMENTS OF THE NEOLITHIC

In 1958, excavations in southern Anatolia (Turkey), led by the British archaeologist James Mellaart, revealed the remains of an 8000-year old settlement, Catal Huyuk (i.e., "pitchfork-shaped mound" in Turkish), which dates to about 6500 BCE. With a population of about 10 000, Catal Huyuk is thought to be the largest and best-preserved site of the Neolithic Age, the age in which agriculture developed. Among the many findings uncovered in this prototypical Neolithic village is evidence that the people of Catal Huyuk were among the world's first farmers and artisans, and that they buried their dead under the plastered floors of their houses. In fact, skeletal evidence has led archaeologists to surmise that the people of Catal Huyuk must have had elaborate burial rituals that likely reflected deep expressions of emotional ties to their departed (Balter, 1998, 2005).

disaster, neglect, and mass abandonment. Cities such as Babylon, Ur, Uruk, Nippur, Kish, and Mashkan-shapir all became extinct (Johnson, 1954 [1973]; Proskouriakoff, 1955 [1973]; Stone and Zimansky, 2005). Others, though, including Jericho, Rome, Athens, and Istanbul, have managed to survive through periods of decline and ascendancy. What distinguished this latter group of cities was their ability to reconstruct, adapt and innovate, and ultimately flourish as centres of commerce, trade, culture, knowledge, religion, and political influence (Hall, 1998; Sjoberg, 1965 [1973]: 24–5; Taylor, 2012; Tellier, 2009).

With the progression of history, there emerged different city forms—from the feudal towns of the Middle Ages to the pre-industrial city, and later, the urban-industrial city after the Industrial Revolution (Sjoberg, 1960; Weber, 1905[1958]). These changes in the form of cities reflect the changing nature of economic and social reproduction at each stage of their development. For instance, the feudal European city was typically small, not larger than a town, with unpaved streets and small houses surrounding the landlord's imposing estate, and usually a monastery. The medieval era in Europe brought early signs of the rise of pre-industrial European cities, where political power became consolidated in impressive complexes of technological, cultural, religious, and governmental structures. Later, as Europe entered the Industrial Age in the eighteenth and nineteenth centuries, financial and commercial organizations took over as the dominant urban forms alongside these other institutions (Hall, 1998; Mumford, 1961; Sjoberg, 1960). In today's context, urban form is even more complex, as reflected in suburban sprawl, multiple nuclei cities, mega cities, and *global cities* (Taylor, 2012).

Industrialization and the Second Urban Revolution

Urbanization progressed gradually over most of human history but has accelerated significantly during the last two centuries, driven largely by industrialization. The Industrial Revolution began in the mid-1800s in England and Wales, before spreading to other areas of northern, western, and southern Europe and eventually to the countries of the New World: Canada, the United States, Latin America, Australia, New Zealand, and also Japan. This part of urbanization history has been described as the *second urban revolution*, distinct from the *first urban revolution* that is characterized by the emergence of early cities of the Neolithic Age (Tellier, 2009; Soja, 2000). Why does industrialization lead to rising levels of urbanization? To answer this question, one needs to examine in detail the contribution of technology and in particular the development of efficient communication and transport systems that allowed for economic activity to diffuse geographically, and for people to move beyond the reaches of their immediate environments. One elemental corollary of the second urban revolution is rural-to-urban migration.

During the early stages of the population explosion in Europe, from the mid-nineteenth century to the early twentieth century, the majority of the population lived on farms in rural communities. Sustained high rates of natural increase during this part of European history sparked unprecedented levels of population growth in the then largely rural sector. The effect of population growth on rural communities soon became evident to the people: for every time two or more children came of age within a family, the land had to be divided in order for the young to establish themselves. As a result, parcels of farmland became smaller and smaller, and people in the countryside began to look towards

the towns and cities, where jobs in factories were becoming abundantly available (Davis, 1963; Friedlander, 1969; Kennedy, 1973). It was this shift to an economy based on urban industrial manufacturing that sparked the rural exodus in Europe during the nineteenth and twentieth centuries. We can argue that the spread of urbanization in the modern demographic history of the Western world can be attributed largely to the destabilizing effects of the Industrial Revolution on the agrarian system of economic production. And as was discussed earlier, only later, once the majority of a country's population has become concentrated in its cities and towns, does natural increase take over as the leading factor in urban population growth.

Global Urbanization since 1950

According to the 2011 UN revision of *World Urbanization Prospects*, the percentage of the world's urban population rose from 29.4 in 1950 to 52.1 in 2011 (United Nations Department of Economic and Social Affairs Population Division, 2012b). This accounts for a change in the absolute number of people living in urban areas from 0.75 billion in 1950 to 3.63 billion in 2011. In 2011, the world's urban and rural percentages had practically converged, with the urban proportion reaching 52.1 per cent. Figure 10.1 shows the historical and projected trends in urban and rural populations for the world and major development regions.

The annual rate of urbanization worldwide has been declining, from 1.89 per cent in 1950–70, to 1.55 per cent between 1970 and 2011. This slowdown in the overall rate of urban growth has to do with the declining pace of urbanization in the more developed

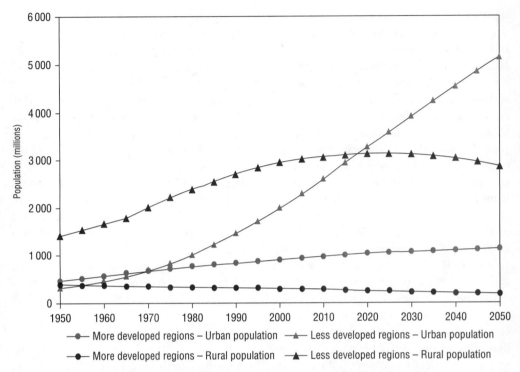

FIGURE 10.1   Urban and rural populations of the world, overall and by development region, 1950–2050

Source: United Nations Department of Economic and Social Affairs Population Division (2012b): 3. From World Urbanization Prospects: The 2011 Revision, United Nations Department of Economic and Social Affairs Population Division. © 2012 United Nations. Reprinted by permission of the United Nations.

countries, where urbanization is reaching a limit, and the contribution of the developing countries, where rates of urbanization, though greater than in the more developed countries, are expected to follow a declining trend over time. By 2030, the urban share of the world's population is projected to reach 60 per cent, and will likely grow to almost 70 per cent by the year 2050. In spite of the anticipated slowdown in the rate of urbanization, these projections, together with past trends, point to the inescapable conclusion that our planet is becoming increasingly urbanized, and that most of the world's population will soon be living in urban areas (see Figure 10.2).

Urban Systems

Within countries or regions, urbanized human settlements tend to naturally arrange themselves in what geographers call *urban systems*. These are networks consisting of cities, towns, and smaller urban settlements connected by roads, communication systems, and social and economic activity. The constituent parts of an urban system are interdependent: no one town or city in the system is wholly self-sufficient, and each one relies in varying degrees on the goods and services produced by other centres within the system. Urban systems are also characterized by a high level of social interaction

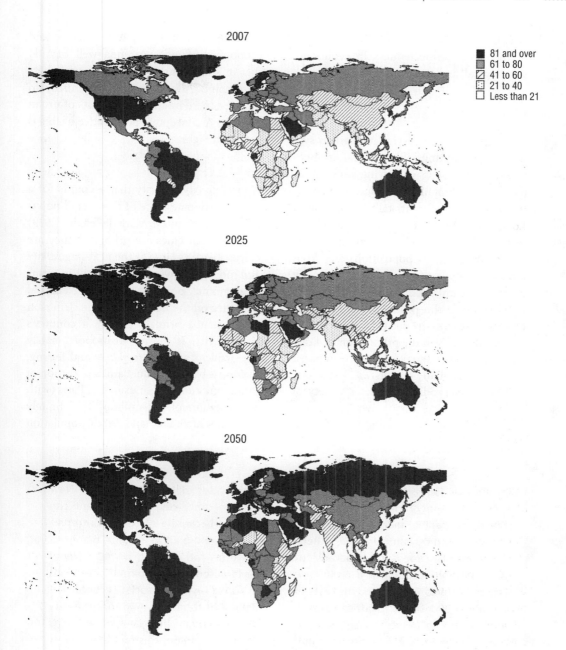

FIGURE 10.2 Distribution of the world urban population by major area, 1950, 2011, 2050

Source: United Nations Department of Economic and Social Affairs Population Division (2012b): 10.

among the constituent centres as a result of their interconnectedness in economic, sociological, and geographic terms.

Urban Hierarchy

Geographers typically view the urban system as constituting a hierarchical arrangement of settlements of varying sizes within a defined geographic space, such as a country or a province (Christaller, 1933 [1966]; Losch, 1940 [1954]). In strictly demographic terms, urban places tend to arrange themselves according to population size, from largest to smallest (or *vice versa*). Strongly correlated with population size (in direct proportion) is the primacy and centrality of urban centres in social and economic terms, especially in the production and distribution of goods and services. Compared to smaller urban centres, a large city will typically produce a greater variety of goods and services for its own population and for those of its surrounding areas and

hinterlands. Thus, its sphere of social and economic influence extends well beyond that of smaller urban places. Geographers have coined the term *urban hierarchy* to describe these interrelated aspects of urban systems. A conceptual perspective of this is shown in Figure 10.3.

Primate Cities

A *primate city* is a city that accounts for a disproportionate share of the overall population of a country. Mark Jefferson (1939) specified that cities are primate if they are at least twice as large as the next largest city and more than twice as significant in terms of economic, political, social, and cultural influence on the nation or region. Jefferson added that a primate city, as a country's leading city, is always disproportionately expressive of national capacity and feeling, making it both a product and a reflection of its nation's culture. For example, Paris (with a population of 2.2 million) is definitely the focus of France and has a population

In the late 1930s, Jefferson (1939: 227) coined the term *primate city* to describe the demographic and economic bases that favoured certain cities over others. A city may become primate because of its favourable location in a productive region. Jefferson pointed to the cases of Chicago (field crops), Seattle (forests), and Pittsburgh (minerals) as American examples of cities whose rise to prominence had been fuelled by favourable natural factors. It is also possible that a city may become dominant because of its advantageous situation on lines of communication or transportation, as in the cases of New Orleans and New York. In other cases, a dominant city emerges because a successful entrepreneur has chosen it as a site of manufacturing (as with Detroit, home to Henry Ford's automobile empire). These kinds of forces—natural, social, economic— often act together. And once a city becomes larger than any other in its country or region, this fact alone gives it an impetus to grow even more. It draws people from surrounding cities and gains character by virtue of being the best market for exceptional products and ideas.

1. Independent local centres, no hierarchy

2. A single strong centre

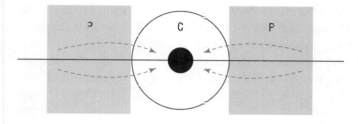

3. A single national centre, strong peripheral subcentres

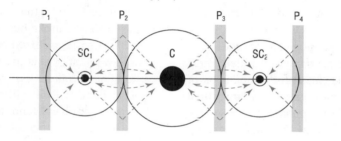

4. A functionally interdependent system of cities

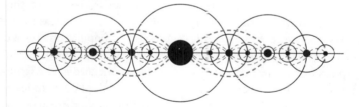

FIGURE 10.3 A sequence of stages in spatial organization

Note: C = Dominant centre; P = Periphery; SC1 and SC2 = Secondary centres; P_1 to P_4 = Peripheral regions between centres. The arrows can be thought of as indicating the direction of migratory attraction of a centre and therefore its political and economic geospatial dominance. In (3), the peripheral areas exert pressures on the centres for economic and political integration. In (4), a complex interdependent urban system evolves, with some centres being dominant and others less dominant in economic and political influence.

Source: CITIES, POVERTY AND DEVELOPMENT: URBANIZATION IN THE THIRD WORLD 2E by Alan Gilbert & Joseph Gugler (1992) Figure 2.1 from p. 39.

more than double that of the country's second largest city (Marseilles, population 800 000). The United Kingdom's primate city, London, has a population nearly seven times as great as that of the second largest city, Birmingham (6.9 million versus 1 million). Similarly, Mexico City (population 9.8 million in the city; 16.6 million in the metropolitan area) outshines Guadalajara (1.7 million), and a huge divide exists between Bangkok (population 5.9 million) and Thailand's second largest city, Nakhon Ratchasima (278 000) (United Nations Department of Economic and Social Affairs Population Division, 2002).

Based solely on the demographic criterion for primacy (i.e., having a disproportionately large population) not every country has a primate city. India's most populous city, Delhi, with its population of 22.7 million, is not significantly larger than Mumbai (formerly Bombay), which is home to nearly 20 million; Kolkata (formerly Calcutta) is the country's third-largest city with 14.4 million inhabitants, and Chennai (formerly Madras) is fourth, with 8.5 million. China, Canada, Australia, Brazil, and the United States are other examples of countries without primate cities; in none of these countries is there a vast difference between the top city and the second and third-ranked cities.

Besides having large populations and embodying their national cultures, primate cities are major centres of economic and social activity; they dominate the country—and, in some cases, the areas beyond their national boundaries. Size and influence are strong pull factors that attract additional residents, causing the primate city to grow at a much greater rate than the smaller cities in the country. A primate city is often also a capital city and thus a centre of political power. In this respect, it is important to note that primacy is not simply a matter of population size (Small and Witherick, 1986: 170). If one applies the size and rank criteria alone to define primacy, then some of the largest metropolitan areas of the world—including, for example, New York, Karachi, and Mumbai (Bombay)—are not primate. However, if one considers primacy in its broader sense, as embodying a nation's culture and dominant influence in social, political, cultural, and economic matters, then these cities are clearly primate cities.

Rank-Size Rule of Cities

Running counter to the principle of primacy is a view of urban hierarchy known as the *rank-size rule of cities*. Empirical studies have shown that in a set of statistical observations (such as incomes, population sizes, housing prices) there will be a few very large values or objects, and that as the value decreases, the number of items or cases increases in a fairly regular way. In 1949, George Zipf devised the theory of rank-size rule as an expression of this fundamental principle.[1] His goal was to explain that with respect to population size, a country's cities follow a general rule based on a relationship between the size of the largest city and the relative rank of cities of lesser size. In general, the number of small towns in a country exceeds the number of medium-sized towns, which outnumber the large towns.

Based on the rank-size rule, Zipf (1949) devised a general theory of how settlements develop within a region. Settlement patterns, he argued, are determined by the opposing forces of *diversification* and *unification*. Diversification tends to promote the establishment of small communities scattered over territory in locations best situated for gathering raw materials for economic production. Under these conditions, communities are widely spread and largely autonomous. Unification operates in an opposite manner. As economic activity becomes more diversified and complex, it becomes more efficient for production and consumption to take place in one big city. Unification tendencies minimize the costs and difficulties associated with transporting manufactured goods. Optimum population distribution is thought to occur when both forces, diversification and unification, are operating in a geographical system, so that the ratio of large to medium and small settlements remains consistent as the overall population grows.

Figure 10.4 is early evidence that the urban hierarchy of some countries fits Zipf's model fairly well. However, there are in some cases notable deviations from the expected distribution (Clarke, 1970). Indeed, most geographers now expect deviations to

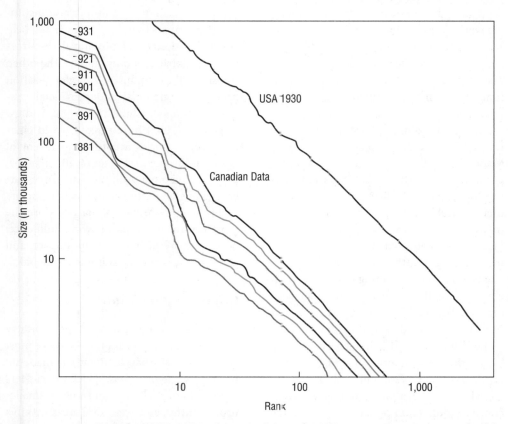

FIGURE 10.4   Canada 1881–1931: Communities of 1000 or more persons, ranked in the decreasing order of population size

Note: The Canadian urban system has conformed fairly consistently to the rank-size rule. As urbanization brought increased populations to cities at every level in the urban hierarchy, the rank-size graph has shifted to the right.

Source: Zipf (1949): 417

occur in any empirical application of the Zipf equation, and as a result it is now commonly viewed as a probability model rather than a "law" (Brackman et al., 1999; Reed, 1988). (Please refer to the Notes for Further Study section of this chapter for more on this point.)

Global Cities

An important category of cities today is the *global city*. Global cities have large populations, though they are not necessarily among the world's largest cities, nor are they necessarily primate in their own countries, as defined strictly in terms of population size. They are distinguished by their specialized functions, which give them a wide sphere of influence in the global arena (Hall, 1996; Sassen, 2000, 2001a, 2001b; Taylor, 2012). London, Amsterdam, Genoa, Lisbon, and Venice have all been global cities at some point in history. These were important centres that gained this distinction by virtue of their centrality with respect to trade, commerce, and political influence worldwide. Paris, Rome, and Vienna became global cities in the eighteenth century, just as others, like Genoa, were becoming much less influential. Over the course of the nineteenth century, Berlin, Chicago, Manchester, and New York emerged as leading global cities, while Venice receded in importance.

In the contemporary world, with the acceleration of economic globalization, global cities are associated less with the concentration of imperial power and the orchestration of trade than with key features of today's global economy, such as transnational corporate organizations, international banking and finance, international non-governmental agencies, and supranational governance. The global cities of today may be thought of as command centres for the world's flow of scientific, technological, and cultural information, the production of new knowledge, the dissemination of global culture, and the control of finance and investing. Cities like New York, Miami, Los Angeles, London, Brussels, Paris, Tokyo, Hong Kong, Singapore, and Johannesburg are highly interconnected along these critical dimensions, and in this sense they provide an interface linking the global to the local. In other words, they feature the economic, cultural, and institutional structures that, on the one hand, help channel national and provincial resources into the global economy, and on the other, transmit the impulses of globalization back to the national and provincial centres. Christopher Chase-Dunn and Andrew Jorgensen (2003) have ranked world cities in three categories according to extent of global influence (see Figure 10.5): alpha, beta, and gamma Although all three categories of global cities are important and are highly interconnected, alpha cities are the most central in terms of world influence; beta cities are of intermediate impact, and gamma cities are of least influence globally.

Urban Agglomerations

As we have discussed, not every country has a primate city or a global city. In most countries, the urban landscape is made up of *urban agglomerations*, which are clusters of interconnected cities and towns, smaller urban centres, and even rural areas within a specified region. From a sociological standpoint, agglomerations in North America are useful units of study, since they tend to be highly integrated socially and economically, with commuter populations travelling daily between the home community and the

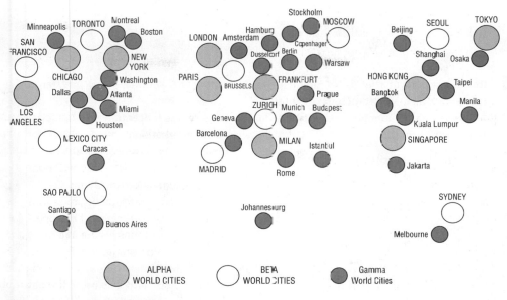

FIGURE 10 5   Globalization and world cities

Source: Chase-Dunn and Jorgenson (2003): 142. Republished with permission from Cengage Learning, from *Encyclopedia of Population* by Paul Demeny and Geoffrey McNicoll, eds. 'Systems of Cities' by Christopher Chase-Dunn and Andrew Jorgenson, 2003. Permission conveyed through Copyright Clearance Center, Inc

urban core. However, the urban agglomeration is essentially a statistical construct: they are intended to impose a relative degree of homogeneity on a given geographic area with respect to demographic, economic, social, historical, or cultural characteristics (Plane, 2004: 86).

Census Metropolitan Areas

The concept of agglomeration is associated with an important urban designation: the *metropolitan area*. The nomenclature and criteria used to define a metropolitan area vary from country to country. For instance, in Canada these areas are called census metropolitan areas, or CMAs. In the United States, they are called metropolitan statistical areas (MSAs). It is important to note that as with urban agglomerations, the metropolitan area is a statistical construct created by national bureaus of statistics for ease of collecting and comparing data.

In Canada, the metropolitan area is a statistical construct that includes both *census metropolitan areas* (CMAs) and *census agglomerations* (CAs). Both of these units, as defined by Statistics Canada, are formed by one or more adjacent municipalities centred on a *population centre*, known as the *core*. The "core" may be thought of as the largest city, and which gives its name to the census agglomeration or census metropolitan area. For example, the Montreal CMA encompasses nearly 100 municipalities, including Laval, Longueuil, La Prairie, and Mirabel; the city of Montreal, on the island of Montreal, is the central municipality for which the CMA is named. A census agglomeration must have a core population of at least 10 000. A census metropolitan area must have a total population of at least 100 000, of which 50 000 or more live in the core. For a municipality to be considered part of an adjacent CMA or CA, it must have

SEVEN KEY FEATURES OF GLOBAL CITIES

In their review of the global city, Paul Knox and Sallie Marston (2004: 404) list a number of key functional characteristics of world cities:

1. They are the sites of most of the leading global markets for commodities, commodity futures, investment capital, foreign exchange, equities, and bonds.
2. They are home to clusters of specialized advanced business services, especially those that are international in scope and that are attached to finance, accounting, advertising, property development, and law.
3. They house concentrations of corporate headquarters—not just of transnational corporations but also of major national firms and large foreign firms.
4. They house concentrations of national and international headquarters of trade and professional associations.
5. They are sites of leading non-governmental organizations (NGOs) and intergovernmental organizations (IGOs) that are international in scope.
6. They are headquarters for the most powerful and internationally influential media, news and information services, and culture industries (including art and design, fashion, film, and television).
7. They attract, because of their importance and visibility, many terrorist acts.

a high degree of integration with the core, as measured by commuting flows derived from census place of work data. A census agglomeration can lose its designation if its core population falls below 10 000, but a census metropolitan area retains its status even if its total population or core population falls below the minimum requirements.

CMAs and CAs can contain within their boundaries cities and towns of varying population size (i.e., *population centres*) as well as rural places. Small *population centres* with a population count of less than 10 000 that are not contiguous with the core or *secondary core* (i. e., a population centre within a CMA that has at least 10,000 persons and was the core of a CA that has been merged with an adjacent CMA) are called *fringe*. All territory within a CMA or CA that is not classified as a core or fringe is classified as *rural area*.

Megacities

Megacities are urban agglomerations of 10 million persons or more. In 2011, the proportion of people around the world living in its 23 megacities was about 10 per cent of the world's population. The number of megacities is projected to increase to 37 in 2025, at which point they are anticipated to account for 13.6 per cent of the global population (United Nations Department of Economics and Social Affairs Population Division, 2012b: 6). In 1950, there were just

TABLE 10.4 Population of urban agglomerations with 10 million inhabitants or more in 2011 and their average annual rates of change; selected periods, 1950-2011, and projected to 2025

Rank in 2011	Urban agglomeration	Population (millions)				Average annual rate of change (%)[c]		
		1970	1990	2011	2025	1970–90	1990–2011	2011–25
19	Lagos, Nigeria	1.4	4.8	11.2	18.9	6.08	4.08	3.71
9	Dhaka, Bangladesh	1.4	6.6	15.4	22.9	7.86	4.02	2.84
22	Shenzhen, China	0.0	0.9	10.6	15.5	18.44	11.89	2.71
11	Karachi, Pakistan	3.1	7.1	13.9	20.2	4.15	3.16	2.68
2	Delhi, India	3.5	9.7	22.7	32.9	5.07	4.03	2.67
8	Beijing, China	4.4	6.8	15.6	22.6	2.14	3.96	2.66
21	Guangzhou, Guangdong, China	1.5	3.1	10.8	15.5	3.45	6.01	2.54
5	Shanghai, China	6.0	7.8	20.2	28.4	1.30	4.52	2.43
15	Manila, Philippines	3.5	8.0	11.9	16.3	4.07	1.89	2.26
7	Mumbai (Bombay), India	5.8	12.4	19.7	26.6	3.80	2.20	2.12
18	Istanbul, Turkey	2.8	6.6	11.3	14.9	4.30	2.58	2.00
20	Al-Qahirah (Cairo), Egypt	5.6	9.1	11.2	14.7	2.42	1.00	1.98
10	Kolkata (Calcutta), India	6.9	10.9	14.4	18.7	2.26	1.33	1.87
3	Ciudad de México (Mexico City), Mexico	8.8	15.3	20.4	24.6	2.79	1.38	1.32
13	Los Angeles–Long Beach–Santa Ana, USA[b]	8.4	10.9	13.4	15.7	1.31	0.99	1.13
6	São Paulo, Brazil	7.6	14.8	19.9	23.2	3.31	1.42	1.08
4	New York–Newark, USA[a]	16.2	16.1	20.4	23.6	−0.03	1.12	1.05
12	Buenos Aires, Argentina	8.1	10.5	13.5	15.5	1.30	1.20	0.98
23	Paris, France	8.2	9.3	10.6	12.2	0.64	0.62	0.97
14	Rio de Janeiro, Brazil	6.6	9.6	12.0	13.6	1.84	1.05	0.93
16	Moskva (Moscow), Russian Federation	7.1	9.0	11.6	12.6	1.17	1.22	0.56
17	Osaka–Kobe, Japan	9.4	11.0	11.5	12.0	0.80	0.19	0.33
1	Tokyo, Japan	23.3	32.5	37.2	38.7	1.67	0.64	0.27

Notes: Urban agglomerations are ordered according to their population size in 2011.
[a] Refers to the New York–Newark urbanized area.
[b] Refers to the Los Angeles–Long Beach–Santa Ana urbanized area.
[c] Rates calculated by the exponential growth formula.

Source: United Nations Department of Economic and Social Affairs Population Division (2012b): 8. From World Urbanization Prospects: The 2011 Revision, United Nations Department of Economic and Social Affairs Population Division. © 2012 United Nations. Reprinted by permission of the United Nations.

two megacities in the world—New York (12.3 million) and Tokyo (11.3 million). Today, Tokyo is the largest megacity, with over 37.2 million people. Table 10.4 lists the world's megacities and their changing growth trends from 1970 and projected to 2025.

MEGACITIES—SOME ARE LARGER THAN COUNTRIES!

If it were a country, what city would be the thirty-fourth largest on earth? Tokyo! Based on censuses, the UN Population Division estimates that Tokyo would be larger than 209 of the world's countries. The "Tokyo" referred to here is the Kanto Major Metropolitan Area (MMA), as defined by the Japan Statistics Bureau. Tokyo's population in 2012 was 37 million, just behind Poland and just ahead of Algeria, Uganda, and Canada.

Currently, 30 per cent of Japan's population resides in the MMA, but it wasn't always that way. In the aftermath of World War II, just 14 per cent of the country's population lived in the MMA. From 1950 to 1970, Tokyo grew at a speedy 3.6 per cent every year. Today, however, growth is much more modest at 0.7 per cent per year. What is remarkable about the Tokyo metro area is its comparatively compact size at roughly 120 kilometres (70 miles) across. Compare that to the Washington, DC,

metro area, which is about 250 kilometres (150 miles) at its widest point and a population of nearly 6 million.

Expansion of Tokyo geographically is limited by the ocean on one side and mountains to the west. As a result, its population density is about 2.5 times that of Bangladesh.

Mention should also be made of Tokyo's competitor for the top spot—Delhi. India's capital is expanding rapidly in all directions, and its annual growth rate is 3.1 per cent. In 1950, Delhi was not even ranked in the UN's list of the 30 largest metro areas; the city first appeared ranked 30 in 1965 when its population was around 3 million. By 2012, it had grown to 23 million and is projected to reach 33 million by 2025, just 12 years away. Delhi can be expected to pass Tokyo not long after 2030.

Source: Adapted with permission from the Population Reference Bureau from Carl Haub "Cities Larger Than Many Countries", 2013.

Some urban systems extend beyond metropolitan urban agglomerations to form a *megalopolis*. Jean Gottman (1961) coined this term based on his observations of the almost continuous and densely populated urban and suburban area stretching from Boston to Washington, DC, in the United States. In a more general sense, the concept refers to the growing together and integration of large urban agglomerations into a higher order of urban structure or complex. Megalopolitan areas are discernible in highly urbanized countries. Examples include the Axial Belt

of Britain; the Pacific coastlands of Honshu, Japan; the Rhone valley of France, between Lyon and Marseilles; the region of California between Los Angeles and San Diego; and the Pearl River Delta in China (Knox and Marston, 2004; Small and Witherick, 1986).

Figure 10.6 shows the megalopolitan system of North America, which extends through parts of eastern and western Canada and the United States. In Canada, the St Lawrence River and Great Lakes urban system encompasses some of the country's oldest and largest urban centres.

THE URBANIZATION TRAP

As a general rule, moving to work in cities is synonymous with economic growth, and the more people do the first, the more countries get of the second. But general rules are made to be broken. As the chart below shows, in many African countries an increase in the size of the urban population has not necessarily been associated with growth. Excluding the extreme case of Liberia (which had a civil war during the period in question), several of Africa's largest countries, notably Nigeria, saw a big increase in what seem like relatively unproductive slums, and those countries that are following the Asian example (Kenya, Ghana, and Ethiopia) are doing so modestly and tentatively.

Urbanization and income

Change between 1985 and 2010

East Asia and Pacific

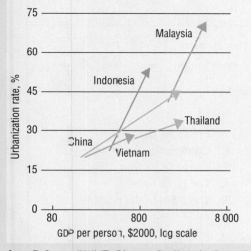

Sub-Saharan Africa

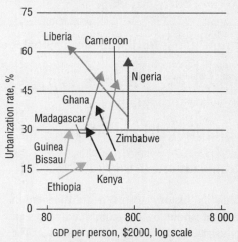

Source: *The Economist* (2012). "The Urbanization Trap: Moving from Farms to Cities Doe Not Always Translate to Gains in Income." *The Economist*, www.economist.com/blogs/graphic detail/2012/10/daily-chart (downloaded 2 October 2012). © The Economist Newspaper Limited, London (2 October 2012).

It begins in the easternmost Atlantic region with Halifax and St John's, extends down through the many cities, towns, and villages along the shores of the St Lawrence River between Quebec City and Montreal, and reaches across the densely populated cities and surrounding urban areas of Ontario, including Kingston, Ottawa, Toronto, Hamilton, London, St Catharines–Niagara, and Windsor, among other localities. About 45 per cent of Canada's population lives in this megalopolitan system.

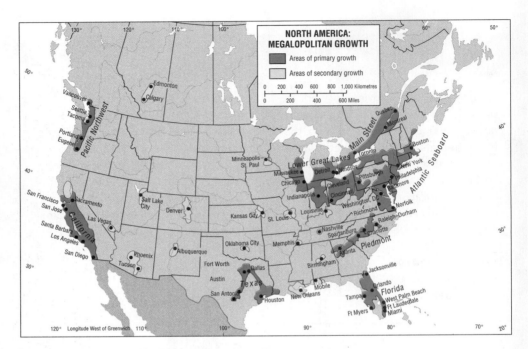

FIGURE 10.6   North American megalopolitan growth

Source: de Blij, H.J., and Alexander B. Murphy. 2003. Human Geography: Culture, Society, and Space, 7th edn. New York: John Wiley: p. 356. Copyright © 2002. Reprinted with permission of John Wiley & Sons, Inc.

Canadian Urbanization

Urbanization History

Canada's history traces a transformation brought about by the combined forces of industrialization and urbanization. The country has passed through several economic regimes, from the mercantilist era prior to 1800 to the current post-industrial age, characterized by rapid economic globalization. As part of its transformation, the country has witnessed major interrelated demographic, technological, and social changes (see Table 10.5). Broadly speaking, Canada's urbanization history can be divided into five stages:

1. Pre-Confederation
2. Confederation to 1900
3. The early 1900s to 1931
4. The 1930s to 1951
5. The 1950s to the present

1. Pre-Confederation

In the early stages of Canada's development, population growth was largely a rural phenomenon, as most people lived and worked on farms. In the early period of colonization, during the seventeenth century, the process of settlement formation was in its incipient phase. The priority for early settlers was to establish safe settlements near natural transportation routes (rivers, lakes,

TABLE 10.5 Canada's population by urban and rural residence and various measures of change, 1871–2011

Period	Population			% change from previous period:	%		% change from previous period		% change in urban and rural proportions (change from previous period)	
	Total	Urban	Rural	total Population	Urban	Rural	Urban	Rural	Urban	Rural
1871	3 689 257	723 094	2 966 163		19.6	80.4				
1881	4 324 810	1 111 476	3 213 334	17.2	25.7	74.3	53.7	8.3	31.1	−7.6
1891	4 833 239	1 536 970	3 296 269	11.8	31.8	68.2	38.3	2.6	23.7	−8.2
1901	5 371 315	1 874 589	3 496 726	11.1	34.9	65.1	22.0	6.1	9.7	−4.5
1911	7 206 643	3 012 377	4 194 266	34.2	41.8	58.2	60.7	19.9	19.8	−10.6
1921	8 787 949	4 165 488	4 622 461	21.9	47.4	52.6	38.3	10.2	13.4	−9.6
1931	10 376 786	5 447 813	4 928 973	18.1	52.5	47.5	30.8	6.6	10.8	−9.7
1941	11 506 655	6 409 207	5 097 448	10.9	55.7	44.3	17.6	3.4	6.1	−6.7
1951	14 009 429	8 811 931	5 197 498	21.8	62.9	37.1	37.5	2.0	12.9	−16.3
1956	16 080 791	10 709 807	5 370 984	14.8	66.6	33.4	21.5	3.3	5.9	−10.0
1961	18 238 247	12 803 249	5 434 998	13.4	70.2	29.8	19.5	1.2	5.4	−10.8
1966	20 014 880	14 690 922	5 323 958	9.7	73.4	26.6	14.7	−2.0	4.6	−10.7
1971	21 568 310	16 521 325	5 046 985	7.8	76.0	23.4	12.5	−3.2	4.4	−12.0
1976	22 992 605	17 566 350	5 426 255	6.6	76.4	23.6	6.3	7.5	−0.3	0.9
1981	24 343 000	18 549 366	5 793 634	5.9	76.2	23.8	5.6	6.8	−0.3	0.8
1986	25 309 000	19 412 003	5 896 997	4.0	76.7	73.3	4.7	1.8	0.7	2.1
1991	27 297 000	21 073 204	6 223 716	7.9	77.2	22.8	8.6	5.5	0.7	−2.1
1996	28 847 000	22 644 895	6 202 105	5.7	78.5	21.5	7.5	−0.3	1.7	−5.7
2001	30 007 094	23 915 654	6 091 440	4.0	79.7	20.3	5.6	−1.8	1.5	−5.6
2006	31 612 897	25 290 318	6 322 579	5.4	80.0	20.0	5.8	3.8	0.4	−1.5
2011	33 476 688	27 147 774	6 329 414	5.9	81.1	18.9	1.4	5.5	1.4	−5.5

Notes: Definitions of "urban" and "rural" have changed over the censuses as follows: from 1871 to 1941, "urban population" means population living in incorporated villages, towns, and cities regardless of size; all remaining population is "rural." In 1951, the definition of "urban" was changed to all persons living in cities, towns, and villages of 1 000+, whether incorporated or not, plus the urban fringes of census metropolitan areas; "rural" included the remaining population. In 1956, "urban population" was defined as the population living in cities, towns, and villages of 1 000+, whether incorporated or not, plus the urban fringe of census metropolitan areas, plus the urban fringe of major urban areas (cities with a population of 25 000–50 000); "rural" included the remaining population. For 1961 and 1971, "urban" was defined as (1) population of incorporated cities, towns, and villages with a population of 1 000 and over, plus (2) unincorporated places of 1 000 and over having a population density of at least 1 000 per square mile, plus (3) built-up fringes of (1) and (2) having a minimum population of 1 000 and a density of at least 1 000 per square mile. For 1976 and beyond, "urban population" is population living in an area having a population concentration of 1 000 or more and a population density of at least 400 per square kilometre; "rural" is the remaining population (Leacy, 1983: A54–93).

The urban and rural populations for 2006 were estimated based on the assumption that the urban population represents 80 per cent of the total population of Canada in 2006.

Sources: Leacy (1983); Statistics Canada (2002f, 2005a, 2007h, 2013s); Haines and Steckel (2000): 702–3; Table A.4; McVey and Kalbach (1995): 149.

oceans) that would facilitate trade with Europe. In the period from about 1760 to 1849, known as the pre-industrial stage or staples economy stage (Innis, 1930),[2] urbanization proceeded gradually. By the first quarter of the nineteenth century, Quebec (then Lower Canada) had two cities of over 20 000 (Montreal and Quebec City) that comprised more than 5 per cent of the entire colonial population of British North America; this made Canada one of the most urbanized regions of the world at that time.

Urbanization gained momentum in the latter half of the nineteenth century (from roughly 1849 to 1896) as the nation reoriented itself towards an industrial-based economy. With the construction of the Canadian Pacific Railway, completed in 1885, the interior hinterland of the country (Manitoba and the rest of the Prairies, and the westernmost province of British Columbia) attracted increasing numbers of settlers, many from western, northern, and eastern Europe. Although this settlement of the West involved a great deal of movement to farms and homesteads in rural areas, increases in agricultural production combined with a gradual shift towards a service economy did, in time, stimulate significant urban growth, as more and more people relocated to the towns and cities. Taken together, the early urban settlements of Upper and Lower Canada (i.e., Quebec and Ontario) and the easternmost areas of the country, plus the emerging settlements in the interior, accounted for an urbanization level of roughly 16 per cent by 1861 (McVey and Kalbach, 1995: 146–7; Stone, 1969: 29).

2. Confederation to 1900

By 1867, the year of Confederation, the number of urban settlements in the country had grown steadily, so that in 1871, the proportion of the population living in urban locations (at that time mostly in Ontario, Quebec, and the Maritimes) had risen to nearly 20 per cent (see Table 10.6 and Figure 10.7). The scale and speed of urbanization during this part of Canada's history was quite dramatic.[3] Indeed, the decade after Confederation can be seen as marking the nation's "take-off" towards higher levels of urbanization (Stone, 1969). The large-scale shift towards a concentration of the population in medium- and large-sized cities, away from the rural areas and smaller towns, had truly begun, and by 1901, out of a population of approximately 5.4 million, roughly 35 per cent of Canadians were urban dwellers.

Census figures for 1891 give an indication of how Canada's population was distributed among cities of various size. In that year, Canada's census recorded a total of 4.8 million inhabitants, of whom nearly 30 per cent were living in urban settlements (Leacy, 1983: A67–74; Stone, 1969: 39). Out of an overall urban population of about 1.5 million living in incorporated centres of at least 1000 persons, about 30 per cent of Canadians were located in places with a population of between 1000 and 4999. An almost equal proportion were settled in incorporated places of over 100 000 (27.6 per cent) and places of between 5000 and 29 999 (27.1 per cent); another 16 per cent resided in localities of between 30 000 and 99 999 population (Leacy, 1983: A67–74).

3. The Early 1900s to 1931

Although urbanization was well underway by the start of the twentieth century, the majority of Canadians still lived a life centred on the land, the homestead, the village, and the parish. Life was in many respects regulated by the seasons: the spring and summer months were typically spent cutting

TABLE 10.6   Canadian society and urban evolution

Period	Pre-1900	1900–45	1945–75	1975–2000+
Regime	Mercantile	"Great Transforma-tion"; early industrial capitalism, early industrial society	Post-war economic boom; advanced capitalism	Post-industrial shift; globalization
Prevailing technology	Sail, horse and cart, water, early steam power	Steel, rail, early automobiles, tele-phone, telegraph	Auto, aviation, television	Expressways, telecommunications
Urban system	Small number of port cities acting as entrepôts; hierarchy of service centres develops as agriculture expands	Industrial core (Windsor to Quebec City) and resources-based periphery; incipient decline in eastern provinces	Metropolitan dominance; rapid increase in pro-portion of urban population	Toronto gains primacy; shift to the West; Quebec's system becomes more autonomous, some centres decline
Urban economy	Staples-based	Early corporate capitalism; Fordism	Advanced corporate capitalism; late Fordism	Deindustrialization; shift to service economy
Urban demographics	Immigration (primarily European) is major input to population growth	Urbanization growth slowed by World War I, Great Depression, and World War II	Baby boom; high rates of post-war immigration	Baby bust; population growth becomes a function of immigration (mainly from non-traditional sending areas)
Political agenda	From colonies to Confederation	Nationalism: trans-portation, protective tariffs, regional support	Keynesian policies; federal transfers; regional economic development	Federalism under siege; NAFTA; multi-culturalism; retrench-ment of welfare agenda
Canadian distinction	Colonialism	Staples base	Welfare state	Multiculturalism

Sources: Adapted from Bunting and Filion (2000): 54; Bourne (2000): 32.

down trees to clear new land for planting, tilling the soil and preparing it for seeding, and, later on in the season, harvesting crops. Much of the rhythm of daily activity was directed to the production of basic neces-sities to last through the long and harsh winter months (Fingard, 1974). But these conditions were changing, and over the early decades of the new century, Canada, in the throes of rapid urbanization, began its inexorable move from being a folk society to becoming an urban industrial nation.

It was not until the early 1920s that the share of Canada's population living in

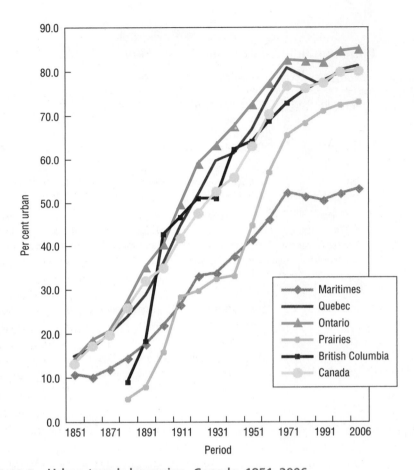

FIGURE 10.7   Urban trends by region, Canada, 1851–2006

Notes: For Canada total prior to 1951, Newfoundland is excluded. Nunavut came into existence in 1998 (formerly part of the Northwest Territories). From 1851 to 1911 the urban population figures refer to incorporated cities, towns, and villages of 1000 and over only. From 1921 to 1951, the percentages are estimates of the percentages that would have been reported in the respective censuses had the 1961 census definition and procedures been used. For the regions, per cent urban in 2006 was extrapolated based on the historical series. For changes in the definition of "urban" since 1871, refer to the note under Table 10.5 (page 477).

Sources: Haines and Steckel (2000): 702–3, Table A.4; Kubat and Thornton (1974): Table P1; Leacy (1983); McVey and Kalbach (1995): 149; Statistics Canada (2002f, 2005a, 2005b); Stone (1969): 29; United Nations Department of Economic and Social Affairs Population Division (2007).

urban localities reached 48 per cent (Stone, 1969). At that time, there were just six cities in Canada with populations in excess of 100 000. But it was during this period that the process of urbanization picked up momentum. By 1931, over 45 per cent of Canadians had their homes in cities of 100 000 and over, and a declining proportion (about 16 per cent) of the people were situated in the smaller settlements of between 1000 and 4 999 population (Leacy, 1983: A67–74). The census of 1921

For an interesting account of life during Quebec's frontier society in the early 1900s, see Louis Hémon's novel *Maria Chapdelaine* (1914). The ongoing struggle to tame the harsh farmland is the backdrop to this classic of world literature, which is set in Quebec's Lac Saint-Jean region. When the heroine of the novel rebuffs a wealthy American suitor to marry a French-Canadian farmer, she effectively chooses to continue the same difficult life she and her family have always known. Her devotion to traditional values, writes Paul Socken (1997), "symbolizes Quebec's determined struggle to secure a foothold for rural, Catholic, French society away from the onslaught of modern, urban, English-dominated life."

system had been established (McInnis, 2000a). We can make this claim based on three criteria:

1. the timing at which the current census metropolitan areas reached 25 000 people;
2. the degree of growth of centres of 25 000 people; and
3. the evolution of places with populations of 2 500 or more. (McInnis, 2000a)

By 1901, ten of the current census metropolitan areas of Canada had passed the 25 000 mark in population. One-fifth of the nation's population resided in those ten centres, the five largest of which were Montreal (368 000), Toronto (240 000), Quebec City (104 000), Ottawa–Hull (58 000), and Halifax (51 000). Edmonton and Calgary were among the cities that had not yet surpassed 25 000 inhabitants, whereas Winnipeg had already reached a population of 48 000 people. In 1901, Vancouver was still comparatively small, with just 33 000 people. (By comparison, in 1901 the United States had 160 cities with populations over 25 000, together accounting for 26 per cent of its national population.) By 1931, all but one (Sudbury) of the CMAs listed in Table 10.7 (page 486) had passed the 25 000 mark in population, and the portion of the Canadian population living in these centres had reached just over 39 per cent.

In terms of the second criterion, by 1931 Canada had added 14 cities of 25 000 or more, bringing the overall percentage of the population living in CMAs to just over 42 per cent. As for the third and broadest of the three criteria of urbanization, population in places of 2 500 or more, the proportion of the Canadian population that

recorded a total population of about 8.8 million, representing an increase of 22 per cent over the previous decade and a dramatic rise of 63 per cent from the population enumerated in 1901 (5.4 million). Between 1901 and 1911, the urban share of the total population had risen to about 42 per cent; by the early 1920s, it reached about 47 per cent. Significant during this part of the nation's history was the massive immigration from the European continent, particularly Eastern Europe. A large share of the immigrants settled in rural areas, but many others ended up in the growing cities (McVey and Kalbach, 1995).

By the start of the Great War of 1914–17, Canada's shift to an industrial-based economy had been firmly imprinted, and by the start of the Great Depression of 1929–39, the composition of today's Canadian urban

could be considered "urban" had, by the third decade of the twentieth century, risen to almost 50 per cent (McInnis, 2000a: 558–64). Stone's analysis (1969: 39), based on the percentage of the population classified as urban, confirms that, indeed, 1931 was the turning point at which Canada's population attained a 50 per cent level of urbanization.

4. The 1930s to 1951

During the 1930s and 1940s, urbanization proceeded at a slower pace than in earlier decades. The depression of the 1930s brought high levels of unemployment and a crisis in the agricultural economy (owing in part to draught and dust-bowl conditions on the Prairies and in the plains of the US), which slowed internal migration from the countryside to the city considerably. Leroy Stone (1969: 21) points out that the period from the start of the Great Depression up to the Second World War was marked by an enormous dampening of the factors promoting urbanization. Immigration and population growth decelerated markedly, as did the demand for the products of non-primary activities; the rate of investments in new technologies also dropped.

Faced with the harsh realities of the day, many city-dwellers returned to the countryside, seeking refuge with family and relatives in the rural areas. As a result, city growth slowed. According to Marvin McInnis (2000a: 566), the Atlantic region, which had been an area of heavy emigration in the 1920s, ceased to lose people. Cities in Quebec barely retained their natural increase, and Toronto, Hamilton, and London—the major urban centres of Ontario—probably did not retain their natural increase. Winnipeg's population kept constant, and Vancouver grew by barely 10 per cent. Rural-to-urban migration had essentially stopped, and interregional migration dropped to a low level. Many Prairie residents, driven off their farms during the severe draught, had nowhere promising to go. Only British Columbia grew substantially, with gains derived from both natural increase and net international migration.

During World War II, Canada entered a recovery phase of unprecedented industrialization. New industries developed to meet the wartime demand for such items as synthetic rubber, roller bearings, diesel engines, antibiotics, high-octane gasoline, aircraft, ships, and other industrial products. The steel industry boomed. This new wave of industrialization caused heavy declines in the agricultural working force in the 1940s, and these changes, combined with a period of unprecedented prosperity following the war, were tied to a marked upsurge in urbanization. By 1951, the national level of urbanization had surpassed the 60 per cent mark (Stone, 1969: 22).

5. The 1950s to the Present

Aided by the high fertility of the baby boom years (1946–66) and augmented by large waves of immigrants from all over the world, Canada in the 1950s and 1960s underwent another period of intense urbanization. By 1961, almost three-quarters of the population was classified as urban. The prosperous postwar urban economy played a major role in this trend, as the rural sector underwent significant depopulation through large outflows of migrants headed for the country's metropolitan centres. By the early 1960s, nearly 8 million people, out of a national population of just over 18 million, lived in 18 urban places with populations of 100 000 or more, and by 1971, the number of CMAs in Canada had grown to 23.

The 1960s brought a significant development in Canada's urbanization: the "flight to suburbia." Canada's inner cities underwent decline as the growth of industry in the urban fringes, combined with the development of efficient systems of roadways and transportation routes linking the core and surrounding areas, enabled people to commute between the suburbs and other sections of the metropolitan system on a daily basis. People could live in the suburbs, where real estate properties were more affordable, and commute fairly easily to work either in the city or in other surrounding urban localities.

In the 1970s and 1980s, Canada went through two successive economic recessions. The first one, sparked by the oil crisis of 1973, hit the economies of central Canada (Ontario and Quebec) particularly hard. Meanwhile, the discovery of abundant oil reserves in Alberta promoted staggering economic growth in this part of the country. The economic boom in Alberta during the 1970s drew internal migrants from virtually every part of Canada, and while urban centres in the east were experiencing a slowdown in population growth, cities such as Calgary and Edmonton grew rapidly, aided by the significant endowments of a resource-based economy. Further west, Vancouver was also benefitting from rapid population growth.

In the early 1980s, when the census recorded a 76 per cent level of urbanization, Canada was hit with another economic downturn. Immigration to Canada slowed considerably and fertility rates, which had

been dropping since the early 1960s, continued to fall. Unlike the 1970s economic downturn, which favoured western Canada, the recession of the 1980s hurt the economies of the western provinces (particularly Alberta's), forcing many people to the urban areas of central Canada to look for work opportunities. Most immigrants coming to Canada likewise headed to metropolitan areas like Toronto, Ottawa–Hull, and Hamilton in the east, and to Vancouver in the west. Population growth in Calgary and Edmonton therefore slowed considerably. In Quebec, Montreal continued to experience net migratory losses that began in the aftermath of the separatist Parti Québécois's win in the 1976 provincial election (Shaw, 1985); Montreal would not see net migration gains until the early years of the new millennium (Statistics Canada, *The Daily*, 2004: 11). By 1981, Toronto had replaced Montreal as the leading metropolis in the country, with Vancouver forming the third-largest population across Canadian metropolises.

By 2001, approximately 80 per cent of Canada's population was urban. Of the total population of just over 30 million, about one-third lived in just three urban centres: Toronto, Montreal, and Vancouver. The 2006 census saw the number of CMAs increase to 33, up from 27 in 2001. The six additions were Kelowna, British Columbia; Barrie, Brantford, Guelph, and Peterborough, in Ontario; and Moncton, New Brunswick.

In 2011, these 33 CMAs comprised 69.1 per cent of Canada's total population, an increase from 64.3 per cent in 2001. Moreover, the share of Canada's population living in Toronto, Montreal, and Vancouver rose to 35 per cent. The growing demographic weight of these three centres means that to a large extent Canada's demographic trends are being shaped by what takes place in these metropolitan centres.

Among the other CMAs, Calgary and Edmonton have seen significant growth over recent censuses, much of it attributable to migratory gains due to Alberta's strong economy. By 2011, both cities had surpassed the 1.2 million mark, making them the two fastest growing metropolises in the country over 2006–11, at 12.6 and 12.1 per cent, respectively (see Tables 10.7 and 10.8). Also in the Prairies, the recent economic boom in Saskatchewan has led to notable population increases in its two CMAs, Saskatoon and Regina (11.4 per cent and 8 per cent, respectively) over this same interval. On the west coast, Vancouver continues to experience major growth. By 2011, this metropolitan area consisted of over 2.3 million people. Also in British Columbia, Kelowna and Abbotsford CMAs have seen steady growth recently. In the east, beside Toronto and Montreal, Ottawa ranks among the fastest growing CMAs in recent years, having grown from 1.13 million in 2006 to 1.24 million in 2011.

Over the second half of the twentieth century a number of CMAs passed through periods of population decline and recovery. For example, London, Windsor, and Sudbury lost population between 1971 and 1981, but have seen steady gains thereafter; between 1991 and 2011, Sudbury, Saint John, and Thunder Bay lost population. Sudbury has also lost population between 2001 and 2011. Between 2006 and 2011, Windsor showed a negative change in population growth. For the most part, such changes in population growth reflect periodic shifts in the global demand for goods and materials connected to the main economic activities of these cities and the effect of this on population mobility.

Canada's Metropolitan System

Throughout most of its history, Canada has not had a single, dominant primate metropolis (McInnis, 2000a). However, there is little doubt that, overall, Montreal and Toronto have shared dominance in terms of population growth and economic centrality to Canada. As early as 1871, Montreal, with 153 516 residents, and York (Toronto), with 115 974, had populations well above the third-ranked Canadian City (Quebec). By the turn of the century, Montreal's population had risen to just over 371 000, while Toronto's was notably smaller, at 272 663 (Dominion Bureau of Statistics, 1953: 6-25, 6-54). Between 1901 and 1931, Toronto grew more rapidly than Montreal, yet its population at the end of this period was still just 80 per cent of Montreal's. It was not until the mid-twentieth century that Montreal and Toronto (with 1.1 million people and 1.4 million people, respectively) had roughly equal populations. By the time of the 1981 census, Toronto had gained supremacy, reaching close to 3 million as compared to Montreal's population of 2.8 million (McInnis, 2000a: 560, 597). The 2001 census counted Toronto's population as being almost 4.7 million, and that of Montreal just over 3.4 million. In 2011, the census showed a population of 5.58 million for Toronto and 3.82 million for Montreal.

It is clear that the population gap between Canada's two largest CMAs has stretched quite substantially over the last quarter of the twentieth century, and it is even greater today (see Table 10.7). In 2001, the population of Toronto CMA exceeded that of Montreal's by approximately 1.2 million people; by 2006 the difference had grown to 1.5 million; and in 2011 the gap had widened by 1.76 million in favour of Toronto. There are several factors to consider in

FIGURE 10.8   The Canadian Urban System—census metropolitan areas and census agglomerations

Note: Blue dots refer to census agglomerations.

Source: Bourne, Larry S. 2000. 'Urban Canada in Transition to the Twenty-First Century: Trends, Issues, and Visions', in Trudi Bunting and Pierre Filion, eds, *Canadian Cities in Transition: The Twenty-First Century* 2/e. Don Mills, ON: Oxford University Press.: p. 27.

regards to this development, an important one being Toronto's stronger attraction to international migrants. As well, Toronto's amalgamation of municipalities surrounding its metropolitan region may also be a contributing factor. Finally, Montreal has tended to experience periods of net migratory losses, especially after the rise of the separatist party Parti Québécois in 1976.

Following Toronto and Montreal in Canada's metropolitan system is the CMA of Vancouver, with a population of 2.31 million in 2011. The combined CMA of the National Capital Region, comprising Ottawa and Gatineau, and the CMAs of Calgary and Edmonton round off the top six

metropolitan areas. As of 2011, the remaining CMAs had populations well below these five, the smallest being the recently added CMA of Peterborough, with a population of 118 975. In total, the combined populations of Toronto, Montreal, and Vancouver CMAs in 2011 comprised over 11.7 million people (nearly 30 per cent of the total population of Canada); if we add the combined populations of Ottawa, Calgary, and Edmonton this would account for over 15 million people, or a cumulative total of just over 40 per cent of Canada's population.

A number of interrelated factors account for the noted patterns of metropolitan development in Canada. The location

TABLE 10.7   Populations of the metropolitan areas of Canada in 2011, traced back to 1901

CMA	1901	1931	1951	1961	1971	1981	1991	2001	2011
Toronto	240 000	828 000	1 117 000	1 824 000	2 628 043	2 999 000	3 893 045	4 682 897	5 583 064
Montreal	368 000	1 040 000	1 395 000	2 110 000	2 743 208	2 828 000	3 127 240	3 426 350	3 824 221
Vancouver	33 000	333 000	531 000	790 000	1 082 352	1 268 000	1 602 500	1 986 965	2 313 328
Ottawa–Gatineau	98 000	188 000	282 000	430 000	602 510	718 000	920 855	1 063 664	1 236 324
Edmonton		84 000	173 000	337 568	495 702	657 000	839 920	937 845	1 214 839
Calgary		84 000	139 000	279 062	403 319	593 000	754 030	951 395	1 159 869
Winnipeg	48 000	289 000	354 000	475 989	540 262	585 000	652 355	671 274	730 018
Quebec City	104 000	188 000	275 000	357 568	480 502	576 000	645 550	682 757	765 706
Hamilton	68 000	175 000	260 000	395 189	498 523	542 000	599 760	662 401	721 053
St Catharines–Niagara	35 000	100 000	162 000	150 226	303 429	304 000	364 550	377 009	392 184
London	43 000	78 000	122 000	181 283	286 011	284 000	381 525	432 451	474 786
Kitchener		53 000	63 000	154 864	226 846	288 000	356 420	414 284	477 160
Halifax	51 000	79 000	134 000	183 946	222 637	278 000	320 500	359 183	390 328
Victoria		61 000	104 000	154 152	195 800	233 000	287 900	311 902	344 615
Windsor		115 000	158 000	193 365	258 643	246 000	262 075	307 877	319 246
Oshawa		34 000	52 000	80 918	112 093	154 000	240 105	296 298	356 177
Saskatoon		44 000	55 000	95 526	126 449	154 000	210 025	225 927	260 600
Regina		57 000	71 000	112 141	140 734	164 000	191 695	192 800	210 556
St John's			68 000	90 838	131 814	155 000	171 855	172 918	196 966
Greater Sudbury		25 000	71 000	110 694	155 424	150 000	157 610	155 601	160 770
Chicoutimi–Jonquière (Saguenay)*		31 000	56 000	105 009	133 703	135 000	154 030	154 938	157 790
Sherbrooke		37 386	62 166	70 253	84 570	115 983	139 195	153 811	201 890
Abbotsford–Mission								147 370	170 191

TABLE 10.7 (continued)

CMA	1901	1931	1951	1961	1971	1981	1991	2001	2011
Kingston**				53 526	59 047	109 000	136 401	146 838	159 561
Trois-Rivières		50 000	68 000	83 659	97 930	111 000	136 300	137 507	151 773
Saint John		50 000	78 000	95 563	106 744	114 000	124 980	122 678	127 761
Thunder Bay		46 000	66 000	110 920	112 093	121 000	124 430	121 986	121 596
Barrie***									187 013
Brantford***									135 501
Guelph***									141 097
Kelowna***									179 839
Moncton***									138 644
Peterborough***									118 975
Total population of Canada	5 371 000	10 377 000	14 009 000	18 238 247	21 568 310	24 343 185	27 296 860	30 007 094	33 476 688
Total CMAs population	1 088 000	4 069 386	5 916 166	9 026 259	12 228 388	13 825 599	17 394 851	19 296 926	23 123 441
CMAs as % of total population	20.3	39.2	42.2	49.5	56.7	56.8	63.7	64.3	69.1
Toronto, Montreal, Vancouver share of total population	11.9	21.2	21.7	25.9	29.9	29.1	31.6	33.6	35.0

Notes: To be included in 1901, 1931, and 1951, the population must have been at least 25 000.
*Since 2002, Chicoutimi–Jonquière CMA has been renamed Saguenay CMA.
**Figures for Kingston in 1961 and 1971 pertain to the central city (urban core) of Kingston.
*** Barrie, Brantford, Guelph, Kelowna, Moncton, and Peterborough became CMAs in 2006.

Sources: Adapted from Dominion Bureau of Statistics (1953, 1962); McInnis (2000a): 597–8; McVey and Kalbach (1995): 71, 163; Statistics Canada (1973, 1982, 1992, 2005c, 2013t); Stone (1969): 175.

TABLE 10.8   Population of Canada's census metropolitan areas in 2006 and 2011, showing percentage change over this period

CMA	Province	Population 2006	Population 2011	Percent change
Toronto	ON	5 113 146	5 583 064	9.2
Montreal	QC	3 635 571	3 824 221	5.2
Vancouver	BC	2 116 581	2 313 328	9.3
Ottawa–Gatineau	ON/QC	1 130 761	1 236 324	9.3
Calgary	AB	1 079 310	1 214 839	12.6
Edmonton	AB	1 034 945	1 159 869	12.1
Quebec City	QC	715 515	765 706	7.0
Winnipeg	MB	694 668	730 018	5.1
Hamilton	ON	692 911	721 053	4.1
London	ON	457 720	474 786	3.7
Kitchener	ON	451 235	477 160	5.7
St Catharines–Niagara	ON	390 317	392 184	0.5
Halifax	NS	372 858	390 328	4.7
Oshawa	ON	330 594	356 177	7.7
Victoria	BC	330 088	344 615	4.4
Windsor	ON	323 342	319 246	−1.3
Saskatoon	SK	233 923	260 600	11.4
Regina	SK	194 971	210 556	8.0
Sherbrooke	QC	186 952	201 890	8.0
St John's	NL	181 113	196 966	8.8
Barrie	ON	177 061	187 013	5.6
Kelowna	BC	162 276	179 839	10.8
Abbotsford	BC	159 020	170 191	7.0
Greater Sudbury	ON	158 258	160 770	1.6
Kingston	ON	152 358	159 561	4.7
Saguenay	QC	151 643	157 790	4.1
Trois-Rivières	QC	141 529	151 773	7.2
Guelph	ON	127 009	141 097	11.1
Moncton	NB	126 424	138 644	9.7
Brantford	ON	124 607	135 501	8.7
Thunder Bay	ON	122 907	121 596	−1.1
Saint John	NB	122 389	127 761	4.4
Peterborough	ON	116 570	118 975	2.1

Sources: Adapted from Statistics Canada (2007a): 22; (2013t).

of the nation's initial settlements and economic specialization in certain kinds of industries in different parts of the country figure prominently. Most important, according to McInnis (2000a), is the fact that the Canadian urban system has historically divided economic functions in a way that has precluded the emergence of a single dominant metropolis. Canada's major cities have essentially been ports.

In the nineteenth century, Toronto was an inland port, on the same lake and river system as Montreal, which was the leading commercial centre of Canada. In the latter half of the nineteenth century, Montreal reinforced its position as the country's leading Atlantic port even though it was more than a thousand kilometres from the ocean. Quebec City, prior to the middle of the nineteenth century, had been the principal Atlantic port, but Montreal took over that role after the river channel was dredged to allow ocean ships to reach it. Had Montreal been the leading port from the outset and not had to share economic functions with Quebec City, it might have established a position of dominance earlier. Toronto, meanwhile, became the leading urban centre and eventually the metropolitan focus of industrial Canada. Vancouver, initially, was less a port city than a commercial centre for BC's logging industry; however, with the opening of the Panama Canal in 1914, Vancouver's position as a port city was greatly enhanced, and it remained the only major city on Canada's Pacific coast (McInnis, 2000a: 560–1).

Recent Developments

Data released from the 2006 census confirm that while most of Canada's population is concentrated in the central municipalities comprising the census metropolitan areas, the peripheral municipalities—*exurbia*—surrounding the CMAs have been experiencing faster growth. This pattern of urban development, which has been going on since the mid-twentieth century, is a product of urban sprawl, which occurs when sustained population growth in a municipality sparks rapid development of the lands surrounding the municipality, which become suburban communities. Statistics Canada (2007a: 22) reports that between 2001 and 2006, the growth rate of peripheral municipalities within the 33 CMAs—11.1 per cent—was double the national average. During the same period, the central municipalities of the CMAs grew more slowly, at the rate of over 4.2 per cent (see Table 10.9).

This trend seems to have persisted into the most recent census period. Between 2006 and 2011, urban centres other than the core city of the largest six metropolitan areas in Canada grew the fastest; the core cities

| TABLE 10.9 | Population growth of central municipalities and peripheral municipalities for the 33 census metropolitan areas, 2001 to 2006 |

Region	2001	2006	Growth (%)
Central municipalities	12 230 443	12 739 103	4.2
Peripheral municipalities	7 891 108	8 769 472	11.1
Total of census metropolitan areas	20 121 461	21 508 575	6.9

Source: Adapted from Statistics Canada (2007a): 31. From Statistics Canada, Portrait of the Canadian Population in 2006, 2006 Census © 2007. Reproduced and distributed on an "as is" basis with permission of Statistics Canada

themselves experienced relatively modest increases in population (see Table 10.10). For example, within the Toronto CMA, the core city of Toronto grew by 8 per cent over this interval, but other urban centres (of varying sizes) within the Toronto CMA grew by nearly 39 per cent. In Montreal and Calgary, the rural areas within these metropolitan areas experience greater growth rates than their respective core cities. All this of course, must be kept in proper perspective because as we have seen with the new changes to the definition of urban introduced by Statistics Canada, the category "rest urban" in Table 10.10 encompasses an amalgam of centres varying in population size from

TABLE 10.10   Population change in Canada's largest CMAs between 2006 and 2011; core, urban, and rural portions

CMA	Population 2011	Population 2006	Per cent change
Toronto CMA	5 583 064	5 113 149	9.2
Toronto core	5 132 794	4 753 120	8.0
Rest urban	311 261	224 334	38.7
Rural	139 009	135 695	2.4
Montreal CMA	3 824 221	3 635 571	5.2
Montreal core	3 407 963	3 316 615	2.8
Rest urban	310 200	221 327	40.2
Rural	106 058	97 629	8.6
Vancouver CMA	2 313 328	2 116 581	9.3
Vancouver core	2 135 201	1 953 252	9.3
Rest urban	125 546	112 380	11.7
Rural	52 581	50 949	3.2
Ottawa–Gatineau CMA	1 236 324	1 130 761	9.3
Ottawa–Gatineau core	933 596	860 928	8.4
Rest urban	159 838	136 884	16.8
Rural	142 890	132 949	7.5
Calgary CMA	1 214 839	1 079 310	12.6
Calgary core	1 095 404	988 079	10.9
Rest urban	81 186	58 213	39.5
Rural	38 249	33 018	15.8
Edmonton CMA	1 159 869	1 034 945	12.1
Edmonton core	960 015	862 544	11.3
Rest urban	104 134	80 042	30.1
Rural	95 720	92 359	3.6

Sources: Adapted from Statistics Canada (2013u, 2013v).

small (1000–29000) to large (100000 and over). Nonetheless, these data point to the same conclusion: the core cities of Canada's CMAs are growing but not as fast as the other urban areas within their metropolitan geographic confines. A large proportion of these other urban localities appear to be new growth areas surrounding the large central cities.

Between 2001 and 2006, heading the list of Canada's fastest-growing *exurbia* was Okotoks, Alberta, population 17145, which experienced an astonishing growth rate of 46.7 per cent between 2001 and 2006. Three other places in Alberta—Wood Buffalo, Grande Prairie, and Red Deer, all three within the influence of Calgary and Edmonton CMAs—enjoyed growth rates of between 24 and 22 per cent. Near Montreal CMA, St-Jean-sur-Richelieu, with a population of almost 88000 in 2006, grew by almost 10 per cent. The rapid growth of such small towns and rural areas on the outskirts of metropolitan centres is a testament to the importance of modern communications systems and efficient roadways that facilitate commuting between the larger municipalities of a CMA system and its remoter places. It is clear, too, that the growth of these smaller centres is contingent on their proximity to urban centres where jobs are abundant. Most of the mid-sized urban centres whose population declined between 2001 and 2006 are located in regions where the economy depends partly or completely on the exploitation of natural resources, most notably forests. Many, for instance, are in remote areas of British Columbia, which have been hurt in recent years by the Canada–US softwood lumber dispute, although clearly this is not the sole cause of decline.

Similar patterns of growth and decline was also observed by the 2006 census among Canada's rural areas. Two types of rural places are distinguishable: those that are close to urban centres and those that are more remote. In rural areas that are close to urban centres, more than 30 per cent of the labour force commutes to work in the urban centre. The growth rate of these places between 2001 and 2006 was 4.7 per cent, which was just below the national growth rate of 5.4 per cent. Key to this growth in rural areas is the existence of highway access to and from the nearby urban centre (Statistics Canada, 2007a: 36). By contrast, the 25 small towns and rural communities that experienced the fastest population declines between 2001 and 2006—Crowsnest Pass in Alberta, Marystown in Newfoundland and Labrador, Flin Flon in Manitoba, to name just a few—were all located far from large urban centres.

The Effects of Urbanization on Rural and Small-Town Canada

In a nation that is becoming increasingly urbanized, Canada's small towns and rural villages face an uncertain future. Some of these places thrive, others decline, and still others undergo slumps and recovery in cycles. The reasons for this are linked mainly to the changing nature of the rural economy. Unlike past times, when rural areas relied almost exclusively on the products of independent family farms and rural communities were essentially isolated from urban centres, conditions today dictate a very high degree of spatial interdependence when it comes to social and economic activity. Rural-based processing and manufacturing has become almost fully amalgamated into the larger urban economy (Beckstead et al., 2003; Coffey, 1994; Wallace, 2002).

There are those who argue that the fondly held image of rural Canada as a blend of farmland, mining towns, mill towns, and railroad towns is more a product of nostalgia than a realistic portrayal of life outside of Canada's largest cities. The remnants of resource-based industries are still found in rural areas and small towns, but the way they are organized is not the same as it once was. Large corporations have replaced small agricultural producers. Small woodlots, sawmills, and bush camps of the forestry sector have been overtaken by vast timber reserves, and there is long-haul trucking of timber to large, centralized pulp or sawmills. Multinational corporations buy and sell materials. Small fishing boats are less commonly found in the picturesque harbours of Canada's east and west coasts, and sea products are caught, cleaned, and frozen at sea on large vessels, or else farmed in pens according to a business model typically controlled and administered by large conglomerate corporations (Reimer, 2005: 79–80).

These widespread changes have dramatically altered many rural settlements and small towns, in some cases quite negatively. For instance, as many of the traditional rural jobs are taken over by highly efficient new technologies, young men and women must look for employment in the city. Depopulation and economic stagnation are the too-often inevitable outcomes of all such changes. Regions that have been hit especially hard include parts of Newfoundland and Labrador, Cape Breton Island, northern New Brunswick, the Gaspé region of Quebec, and rural Saskatchewan (Beshiri and Bollman, 2001; Bollman, 2000; Catto, 2003; Dale, 1988; Hodge and Qadeer, 1983; Reimer, 2005).

On the other hand, some parts of rural Canada have not fared as badly. Parts of the North, central British Columbia, southwestern Quebec, and rural regions surrounding larger cities in the Atlantic provinces have experienced population growth over the last 20 years. Recognizing the diversity of rural and small-town Canada, Liz Hawkins and Ray Bollman (1994: 78–80) have suggested a seven-category typology of settlements:

1. **Primary settlements**—census divisions containing the largest cities in Canada; these areas have growing populations and high levels of net migration.
2. **Urban frontier**—rural areas strongly integrated into the economic activities of urban regions, with characteristics similar to primary settlements, though less pronounced.
3. **Rural nirvana regions**—areas that have positive population growth, especially as a result of the in-migration of young workers; these rural areas do relatively well economically and socially, and are typically situated near large urban centres.
4. **Agro–rural**—small, dispersed, agriculture-based settlements in the Prairies, southern Quebec, the Annapolis Valley region of Nova Scotia, and parts of British Columbia.
5. **Rural enclave**—rural areas, mainly in the Atlantic provinces and the Gaspé region of Quebec, that have low rates of economic activity and high rates of unemployment; they are highly dependent on government social transfer payments.
6. **Resource areas**—areas rich in forests and in mineral and petroleum resources, located in northern regions of

WHICH OF CANADA'S LARGEST CMAs IS MOST RURAL?

It may seem contradictory, but CMAs do contain rural areas. The 2011 census data shows that among the largest CMAS with populations over 1 million—i.e., Toronto, Montreal, Vancouver, Ottawa–Gatineau, Calgary, and Edmonton—the most rural is Ottawa–Gatineau, with almost 12 per cent of its CMA population living in areas designated as rural. Edmonton CMA, however, has the largest percentage of its population that lives in places designated as "small urban" (9 per cent), even though its percentage rural of 8.3 per cent is not very far from the level of Ottawa–Gatineau's.

TABLE 10.11   Proportion of CMA population that is rural or small urban; Canada's largest CMAs, 2011

CMA	Area within the CMA	Population, 2011	%
Toronto	small urban	154 809	3.0
	rural	139 009	2.5
Montreal	small urban	122 767	3.2
	rural	106 058	2.8
Vancouver	small urban	43 178	1.9
	rural	52 581	2.3
Ottawa–Gatineau	small urban	53 078	4.7
	rural	132 890	11.6
Calgary	small urban	33 622	3.2
	rural	33 249	3.1
Edmonton	small urban	104 134	9.1
	rural	95 720	8.3

Note: The population size classes within CMAs, as defined by Statistics Canada, are as follows: (a) small population centres, with a population of between 1 000 and 29 999; (b) medium population centres, with a population of between 30 000 and 99 999; (c) large urban population centres, consisting of a population of 100 000 and over.

Sources: Compiled with data from Statistics Canada (2013u).

the western provinces and territories, northern Ontario, and Labrador; these areas have a high proportion of young people and low percentage of elderly.

7. *The Native North*—areas of the sub-arctic and arctic regions of Canada that have growing populations, relatively low education, and low economic activity.

Two elements seem particularly important in the success of rural places and small towns: proximity to urban centres, and availability of natural amenities and resources, such as raw materials, natural attractions for tourism, and natural transport routes like rivers and lakes (Biggs and Bollman, 1994; Bollman and Biggs, 1992; Bryant and Joseph, 2001; Hamilton, 2002, 2004; Holubitsky, 2005; Reimer, 2005). Rural communities that lie relatively close to large urban centres benefit from a wider range of goods and services for their residents, and from a regular influx of city-dwellers and tourists in search of recreational properties and nature parks outside the city.

Urban Change in the Future

In general, countries pass through three stages of urbanization: an initial stage, followed by a stage of acceleration, and then a stage of maturity (see Figure 10.9). What lies beyond this third stage is a question of considerable interest, especially for the advanced countries, where the level of urbanization has reached or is fast approaching a plateau. These societies may be moving into a fourth but uncertain stage of urban development.

Between the 1960s and the 1990s, three unexpected urbanization trends took place in the high-income countries. First, following widespread urbanization in the post-war years, these societies underwent a period of *counterurbanization*, characterized by the growth of small centres at the expense of the large urban areas. Second, by the late 1970s and early 1980s, the counterurbanization trend had slowed and seemingly reached an end. It was then followed by a

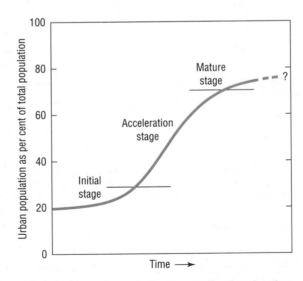

FIGURE 10.9   **The urbanization curve and stages of urbanization**

Source: A MODERN DICTIONARY OF GEOGRAPHY 3E by John Small & Michael Witherick (1995) Figure "The urbanization curve and stages of urbanization" from p. 235. Reprinted by permission of Oxford University Press, USA.

third development, a return to the traditional pattern of urbanization, referred to in the literature as *reurbanization* (Champion, 2001; Fielding, 1989 [1996]; Frey, 1987, 1989, 1990; 1993; Frey and Speare, 1992; Geyer and Kontuly, 1993, 1996; Glaeser and Shapiro, 2003; Morrison and Wheeler, 1976; Vining and Kontuly 1978 [1996]).

The counterurbanization phenomenon was first observed in the United States, where it lasted for about a decade beginning in the early 1970s. It was later recognized in Western Europe, Japan, Australia and New Zealand, parts of Eastern Europe, and some of the more developed industrializing countries, like South Korea (see Fielding, 1989 [1996]; Vining and Kontuly, 1978 [1996]. The rise of counterurbanization as the dominant force shaping American settlement systems was seen by many as a turning point. Brian Berry (1976 [1996]) characterized it as a movement from a state of more concentration to a state of less concentration. He showed that American metropolitan regions grew slower than the nation as a whole and lost, through net migration, about 1.8 million people to non-metropolitan areas between March 1970 and March 1974. This development stood in sharp contrast to what had occurred during all proceeding decades dating as far back as the early nineteenth century. What was more, it was the largest metropolitan areas in the country—those exceeding populations of 3 million, including New York, Boston, Los Angeles, Chicago, Philadelphia, San Francisco, and Washington—that accounted in greatest measure for the decline in metropolitan growth. In contrast, rapid growth had taken place in smaller metropolitan areas, particularly those situated in the state of Florida; in the South and the West; in exurban counties

beyond metropolitan areas, with large commuter populations; and in counties not tied to metropolitan labour markets (Beale, 1975, 1977 [1996]; Frey, 1990; Gordon, 1979 [1996]; Morrison and Wheeler, 1976; Lichter, 1985 [1996]; Vining and Strauss, 1977 [1996]; Wardwell, 1977; Zelinsky, 1978).

Outside of the United States, D.R. Vining and T.M. Kontuly (1978 [1996]) studied the time trend of net migration across settlements of varying size in a number of European and non-European countries, covering the period between 1950 and the mid-1970s. They noted rising levels of net migration to the cities during the 1950s and 1960s, followed by a general pattern of declining net migration in the 1970s. This development could not be explained by changes to the boundaries of metropolitan areas. One country where this trend was pronounced was Japan. Historically, Japan had seen a general flow of population from the peripheral areas of the country into the core region of Hanshu, stretching back from the port cities of Tokyo, Osaka, and Nagoya, and the Tokkaido megalopolis (the Kanto, Tokai, and Kinki regions). The growth of these centres was particularly strong in the 1960s: in certain years of that decade, these regions gained over half a million people through net migration. But this general and sustained movement of population towards the Pacific coast of central Honshu came to an end in the 1970s. In 1971, for instance, the region's net migration gain was around 430 000 persons; in 1976, the net gain was just 9 000. Statistics for Italy, Norway, Denmark, New Zealand, Belgium, France, West Germany, East Germany, and the Netherlands confirmed the counterurbanization trend. These countries all showed either a reversal in the direction of net population flow from periphery to core or a drastic reduction in the level of this net flow.

What caused the population turnaround? The literature highlights a number of possible explanations, ranging from a desire to "get back to nature" and a renewed appreciation of rural life to the far-reaching effects of regional economic restructuring (Frey, 1990). Counterurbanization may have represented a response to the increasingly hectic way of life associated with city living. P.A. Morrison and J.P. Wheeler (1976) found evidence of this mindset among the American people, and argued that with the rise of affluence and better means for commuting daily from a rural home to a job in the city, many Americans were able to realize this preference by moving to smaller urban settlements and rural areas. Innovations in communication and transportation technology have made access to the city and its amenities possible without necessarily living in the city (Long, 1981).

Regional economic restructuring is another compelling explanation for counterurbanization. The economic dislocations that occurred during the 1970s, sparked in part by the oil crisis, led to deindustrialization and the development of a new geography of production based predominantly on advanced service delivery, high-tech research, and recreation and leisure-time activities. Those metropolitan areas that failed to adapt to the post-industrial circumstances experienced population decline. At the same time, better roads and highways helped to increase the geographic range of rural towns, linking them together and making possible a new territorial division of labour in the non-metropolitan areas. These efficiencies of communication and transportation effectively reduced the constraints of distance.

By the early 1980s, the counterurbanization trend had slowed considerably. The pattern that was so prevalent during the 1970s began to reverse, and metropolitan areas again experienced significant population growth, mostly through net migration. Following a decade of shifting population trends in favour of peripheral regions within countries of the more developed Western world, the early 1980s marked the recovery of core regions (Champion, 1988 [1996]). This new tendency was apparent in parts of Western Europe and especially in the United States, where the annual average rate of growth for central cities was 0.64 per cent, up from 0.09 per cent in the 1970s (Cochrane and Vining, 1988 [1996]; Vining and Pallone, 1982). American metropolitan areas with 1 million or more people in the 1980s had grown by 12 per cent over the previous decade, with much of this growth occurring in the southern and the western states, and in certain larger centres of the north, notably New York and Boston (Frey and Speare, 1992).

Compared with the extensive urban growth that occurred in the United States, the phenomena of counterurbanization and reurbanization were relatively minor developments in Canada (Keddie and Joseph, 1991). Even so, the 1980s saw a significant return of population gains to Ontario, most notably the census metropolitan area of Toronto, which grew by almost 1 million people between 1981 and 1991 (a 30 per cent growth rate); this was twice the city's growth rate during the 1970s (Champion, 2001: 156). Though it was the outer urban areas that contributed most of these gains to Toronto CMA, Larry Bourne and A.E. Olvet (1995) have noted that there was an inner-city recovery during this time. The urban centre of Toronto, which experienced a

16 per cent decline in population during the 1970s, saw a gain of 6 per cent in the 1980s. Other Canadian investigators have documented similar inner-city growth rates (see Champion, 2001; Ley, 1992; Ram, Norris, and Skof, 1989).

The counterurbanization phenomenon and subsequent reurbanization may suggest that urban systems in the advanced countries simply went through a temporary deviation in the general pattern of urbanization established over the past century and are now back on track. Yet it is far from certain what the future holds. The industrialized world may currently be passing through a transitional period, moving perhaps towards some new development, with no clear outcome in sight (Champion, 2001).

Today, most advanced societies are undergoing a mixture of urbanization trends. Many regions are experiencing suburbanization or reurbanization, and others are experiencing both processes simultaneously. Some urban centres are losing population to the smaller settlements while others are gaining. In assessing this situation, Anthony Champion (2001: 158) has remarked that "if there is one certainty to be drawn from this review of urban population trends, it is that nothing is the same as it was in those apparently straightforward days when 'urbanization' meant greater population concentration in any geographical framework used." Contemporary suburbanization processes appear to be very different from those that shaped the "dormitory-style" bedroom communities of the past. Suburbs are increasingly becoming "urbanized" in the sense that they are home to occupational and resource facilities traditionally associated with the inner city. This suggests that the advanced economies have

moved recently into a situation "beyond urbanization" (Champion, 2001: 159).

Canada, like all other major industrialized nations, is now at an uncertain juncture in its urbanization process. There cannot be much more rural-to-urban migration, as the proportion of rural inhabitants has essentially bottomed out. On the other hand, suburban expansion is bound to continue. It would seem inconceivable that the suburbs would falter in continuing to attract urban dwellers, given that they now offer many of the functional properties and amenities that were once the purview of the urban core, including places to shop and work, leisure facilities, and arts centres (Smith, 2000). In all likelihood, Canada will also continue to see an increasing concentration of its population in the largest metropolitan areas, with some peripheral growth among the surrounding zones of the larger urban centres due to urban sprawl. The ability of the large urban centres to attract migrants will, of course, fluctuate in response to economic periods of boom and bust in different regions of the country (Bourne and Rose, 2001; Coffey, 2000; Keil and Kipfer, 2003; Wallace, 2002). As the metropolitan areas increase in size, their infrastructures will require constant maintenance and upgrading (Henderson, 2003; Ley, 2000; Zolnik, 2004). City planners will face enormous challenges from a list of growing concerns that includes, among other items,

- increased congestion;
- the need to provide housing for the poor;
- the need to revitalize older neighbourhoods;
- the possibility of escalating crime rates; and

- rising health concerns associated with pollution and the spread of communicable diseases (Gillis, 2005; Kazemipur and Halli, 2000; Peressini, 2005).

Global Outlook

On a global scale, the most striking feature of urbanization over the past 50 years and, projected, over the first half of the twenty-first century is the pronounced difference in the pace and magnitude of growth in the world's more and less developed areas. The United Nations 2011 *Revision of World Urbanization Prospects* (United Nations Department of Economic and Social Affairs Population Division, 2012b), in its forecast for world population growth to 2050, has made the following observations and predictions:

1. The world urban population is expected to increase from 3.6 billion in 2011 to 6.3 billion in 2050.
2. By mid-century, the world urban population will likely be the same size as the world's total population in 2002.
3. Virtually all of the world's population growth will be absorbed by the less developed regions, whose urban population is projected to increase from 2.7 billion in 2011 to 5.1 billion in 2050.
4. The urban population of the more developed regions is projected to increase modestly, to 1.13 billion in 2050.
5. Globally, the level of urbanization is expected to rise from 52 per cent in 2011 to 67 per cent in 2050. More developed regions are expected to see their level of urbanization rise from 78 per cent to 86 per cent over the same period. In the less developed regions, the proportion

urban will likely increase from 46 per cent in 2011 to 64 per cent in 2050.
6. There are marked differences in the size of the urban population and the proportion of urban dwellers among the major areas of the world. By 2050, Asia and Africa will each have more urban dwellers than any other major area, with Asia alone accounting for over half of the urban population of the world.

These trends imply a variety of social, economic, and environmental implications and challenges. Approximately 2 per cent of the earth's total land area is occupied by urbanized places (Redman and Jones, 2004); however, as urbanization continues, the densely populated core urban areas encroach inexorably on the low-density city fringes and the countryside surrounding cities. Urban population growth in most countries is now outstripping overall population growth. As urbanized areas expand into the hinterlands, where the land is primarily agricultural or "natural" (i.e., forests, wetlands, grasslands), urbanization will impose significant challenges on ecosystems, hydrological systems, and local climates. These challenges may, in turn, affect human health. Compounding these potentially adverse environmental scenarios is people's increasing reliance on automobiles for transportation, which add pollutants to the environment while necessitating the construction or expansion of roads and highways (Redman and Jones, 2004).

To maintain order and essential services in the growing urban centres of the developing world, exceptional resources and planning will be required. Urbanization unfolds fairly smoothly in the developed countries, but the same cannot be expected in the developing world, where expanding cities lack the means to provide essential services like housing, education, health care, police protection, and affordable transportation (Jones, 2002). Health care is particularly important, since the higher population density of cities helps the spread of lethal communicable diseases (Aguirre, Pearl, and Patz, 2004; Dyson, 2003; Nsiah-Gyabaah, 2004; Redman and Jones, 2004). Yet many of the world's poorest countries have other issues of great concern to contend with, including collapsing economies, civil war, and anarchy (Linden, 1996). The large-scale flow of rural migrants into the cities adds an almost unmanageable level of complexity to these problems, as many among the growing numbers of poor rural migrants are forced to set up makeshift urban shanty-towns in the face of extreme poverty and severe housing shortages.

An emerging challenge facing many urban centres throughout the world—in developing and more developed countries alike—is the growing risk of environmental hazards, from such possible occurrences as cyclones to droughts, earthquakes, floods, and landslides to volcanic eruptions. The urban areas that seem especially vulnerable, according to the UN, are coastal cities, some of which house very large populations. For example the five most populated cities in 2011 are situated in areas with exposure to at least one of these hazards: Tokyo, Delhi, Mexico City, New York–Newark, and Shanghai. Tokyo is located in a region with high risk of floods and cyclones; Delhi is potentially affected by high risk of floods and medium risk of droughts; Mexico City has a high risk of floods, medium risk of landslides, and low risk of droughts; the region of New York–Newark is at high risk of floods and medium risk of cyclones; and Shanghai is at high risk of floods (United Nations

Department of Economic and Social Affairs Population Division, 2012b: 18).

Given these emerging challenges cities of the world must also grow in terms of degree of innovation in order to sustain their ever growing populations. Not only does the pace of life increase with city size, but so also must the rate at which new major adaptations and innovations need to be introduced (Bettencourt et al., 2007).

Conclusion

The world is becoming increasingly urbanized, and over the course of the twenty-first century most people on the planet will be living in areas designated as urban places. In this chapter, we have looked at the fundamental concepts of urbanization as a demographic, geographical, economic, and sociological process, all of which are inseparable dimensions of this complex global phenomenon.

Notes for Further Study

Zipf's Rank-Size Rule and Zipf's "Law"

The literature distinguishes between Zipf's "law" and Zipf's rule. Zipf's "law" is, in essence, a special case of Zipf's rank-size rule.

Zipf's rule states that if all settlements of a country or region are ranked, from largest to smallest, according to their population size, the population (P_n) of the nth settlement in the list will be $1/n$th that of the largest settlement (P). So, the population of a given city (P_r) is determined by $P(1/r)$, where r is the rank of the given city in relation to the largest city. For example, if the largest city in a country contained 1 million citizens, the second city would contain half (1/2) as many as the first, or 500 000 people; the third would contain one-third (1/3) the population of the largest, or 333 333; the fourth would hold a quarter (1/4), or 250 000; and so forth. When graphed, this equation produces an inverted *J*-shaped curve between rank (*x*-axis) and population size (*y*-axis). However, if rank and population size are transformed to logarithms, the graph becomes a straight line.

Fundamentally, Zipf's "law" can be explained as follows. Consider a set of data values, ordered as $x(1) \geq x(2) \geq \ldots \geq x(n)$, in the reverse of the conventional arrangement (i.e., with the largest value ranked first). We may think of r as the rank and $x(r)$ as the absolute size of the rth data value in the ordered set. Zipf noticed that the relationship $rx(r)$ was a constant, and that this seemed to hold for various kinds of objects, including cities by population, books by number of pages, and biological genera by number of species (Reed, 1998: 674). From this equation, it is possible to derive the rank-size distribution: $rx(r)$ = a constant. Under Zipf's "law," the parameter $q = 1$. So, the rank-size "law" is actually a special case of the rank-size distribution. If in empirical study the value of the parameter q differs from unity, then we have a "rank-size function," or "rank-size distribution" as opposed to Zipf's "law."

In empirical applications, it is customary to use the log-linear version of Zipf's "law":

$$\log (\text{population size}) = \log (\text{constant}) - q\,[\log (\text{rank})]$$

If q is 1, then the plot of log (population size) against log (rank) will be a strong inverse relationship (as depicted in Figure 10.4, page 469). If q is less than 1, the slope of the curve would be flatter, with a more even distribution of city sizes than predicted by Zipf's "law." If q is greater than 1, then large cities are larger than predicted under Zipf's "law," and there will be a wider dispersion of city sizes.

It is interesting to note that Gabaix (1999: 740) computed for the metropolitan areas of the United States in 1991 a value of $q = 1.005$. For the Netherlands, Brackman et al. (1999) reported values of $q = 0.55$ for 1600, $q = 1.03$ for 1900, and $q = 0.72$ for 1990. This suggests that the value of q is not always constant over time, meaning that in some cases urban growth is not proportional. Sometimes, the urban population becomes more concentrated in the larger cities (which increases the value of q), whereas during other periods the urban population becomes more evenly distributed across the various cities (which decreases q). (Gossman and Odynak [1983] provide additional insights into the applicability of Zipf's "law" to Canadian data.)

Exercises

1. Visit the United Nations' Population Division website, www.un.org/en/development/desa/
    population/ and look for the latest revision of *World Urbanization Prospects*. The UN usually
    posts with each new revision the relevant urbanization data (typically a Microsoft Excel
    file). Download the appropriate data to conduct an analysis of a highly developed country,
    a developing country, and a least developed country of your choice with respect to the
    following measures over the period 1950–2000:

    a) total population
    b) rural population
    c) urban population
    d) per cent urban
    e) per cent rural
    f) urban annual growth rate
    g) rural annual growth rate
    h) total annual growth rate
    i) annual rate of change of percentage urban
    j) annual rate of change of percentage rural

    Graph each of these measures for the three countries.

    -   What differences and patterns do you observe in these figures?
    -   Which of the three countries is the most urbanized?
    -   What is the projected level of urbanization to the year 2050 for these countries?
    -   Discuss possible demographic, economic, and sociological implications of urbanization
        across the three countries over the first half of the twenty-first century.

2. Describe the urbanization process from prehistory to the present. What is the future of
    urbanization for the developed and the developing countries?
3. Why do some cities get very large and others do not? What are the factors responsible for
    this differential growth?
4. What are some of the most pressing challenges that cities in the developing world face
    today and over the course of the twenty-first century? Can you propose some solutions?
5. What are some of the most pressing policy issues facing Canadian cities today?
6. Write an essay on the social and demographic conditions facing rural Canada today. How
    are rural localities to cope with increasing urbanization on the one hand and the tendency
    for rural youth to flock to the cities on the other?

Additional Reading

Angel, Shlomo. 2012. *Planet of Cities*. Cambridge, MA: Lincoln Institute of Land Policy.

Beall, Jo, Basudeb Guha-Khasnobis, and Ravi Kanbur. 2010. *Urbanization and Development: Multidisciplinary Perspectives*. Oxford: Oxford University Press.

Derudder, Ben, Michael Hoyler, Peter J. Taylor, and Frank Witlox, eds. 2011. *International Handbook of Globalization and World Cities*. Cheltenham, UK: Edward Elgar.

Douglas, Ian. 2013. *Cities: An Environmental History*. London: I.B. Tauris & Co.

Gates, Charles. 2011. *Ancient Cities: The Archaeology of Urban Life in the Ancient Near East and Egypt, Greece, and Rome*. London: Routledge.

Hohenberg, Paul M., and Lynn Hollen Lees. 1985. *The Making of Urban Europe: 1000–1950*. Cambridge, MA: Harvard University Press.

Soja, W. Edward. 2000. *Postmetropolis: Critical Studies of Cities and Regions*. Oxford: Blackwell.

Taylor, Peter. 2013. *Extraordinary Cities: Millennia of Moral Syndromes, World-Systems and City/State Relations*. Cheltenham, UK: Edward Elgar.

Tellier, Luc-Normand. 2009. *Urban World History: An Economic and Geographical Perspective*. Quebec: Presses de L'Université du Québéc.

Wu, Fulong, Fangzhu Zhang, and Chris Wesbster, eds. 2014. *Rural Migrants in Urban China: Enclaves and Transient Urbanism*. London: Routledge.

Notes

1. Clarke (1970: 51) points out that even though the rank-size rule is attributed to Zipf, often others preceded Zipf in developing this "rule," most notably Felix Auerbach (1913) in Germany, and Lotka (1925) in the United States.

2. See Watkins (1963) and Bertram (1963) for extensions of the ideas of Innis (1930).

3. For a useful overview of the historical evolution of the Canadian settlement system, see Dahms (1990).

11 Population and Resources

Introduction

The idea that human population growth must be controlled in the interest of societal well-being has been a subject of attention and controversy for centuries, and the debate is no less heated now than it was in the past. This chapter examines opposing views on the importance of population to environmental and societal well-being. The chief spokesmen for the opposing viewpoints are Thomas Malthus and Karl Marx (with Frederick Engels). The chapter will also look at some of the predecessors of Malthus and Marx, as well as a number of the authors who have followed in their footsteps—the neo-Malthusians and the neo-Marxists. Other perspectives on the possible impact of population growth on ecological sustainability are discussed in the context of contemporary research and theorizing in this area.

POPULATION: THE ONGOING DEBATE

A Sampling of Views from the Mid-1700s to the Twenty-First Century

> "The Almighty will bless, protect, and maintain a people that obey His Command to multiply and populate the Earth."

(Johan Peter Sussmilch, 1741, from *The Divine Order in the Transformation of the Human Race as Demonstrated through Birth, Death, and the Multiplication of the Same*)

> " . . . by then men will know that, if they have a duty toward those who are not yet born, that duty is not to give them existence but to give them happiness . . . "

(Marie Jean Antoine-Nicolas de Caritat, marquis de Condorcet, 1794, "The Tenth Stage," *Sketch for a Historical Picture of the Progress of the Human Mind*)

> "The power of population is indefinitely greater than the Power in the Earth to produce subsistence in men."

(continued)

(Thomas Malthus, 1798, from *An Essay on the Principle of Population; or a View of Its Past and Present Effects on Human Happiness, with an Inquiry into our Prospects respecting the Future Removal or Mitigation of the Evils which it Occasions*)

"Is it necessary for me to give any more details of the vile and infamous doctrine [Malthus's population theory], this repulsive blasphemy against man and nature, or to follow up its consequences any further? Here, brought before us at last, is the immorality of the economists in its highest form."

(Frederick Engels, 1844, from *Outlines of a Critique of Political Economy*)

"Malthus, that master in plagiarism (the whole of his population theory is a shameless plagiarism . . . quite commonplace and known to every schoolboy)."

(Karl Marx, 1867, from *Das Kapital*)

"In terms of the practical problems that we must face in the next few generations . . . it is clear that we will greatly increase human misery if we do not, during the immediate future, assume that the world available to terrestrial human population is finite. 'Space' is no escape."

(Garret Hardin, 1968, from "The Tragedy of the Commons," *Science* 162, 3859 [13 December 1968]: 1243–8)

"One hears that 'we' have more people than 'we' have 'need' of, though 'we' inevitably goes undefined. What amazing arrogance and self-centredness!"

(Julian Simon, 1990, from *Population Matters*)

"Scarcities of renewable resources are already contributing to violent conflicts in many parts of the developing world. These conflicts may foreshadow a surge of similar violence in coming decades, particularly in poor countries where shortages of water, forests and, especially, fertile land, coupled with rapidly expanding populations, already cause great hardship."

(Thomas F. Homer-Dixon, J.H. Boutwell, and G.W. Rathjens, 1993, from "Environmental Change and Violent Conflict," *Scientific American* 268, 2 [February]: 38–45)

"We are not running out of energy or natural resources. There will be more and more food per head of the world's population. Fewer and fewer people are starving. . . . Mankind's lot has actually improved in terms of practically every measurable indicator."

(Bjorn Lomborg, 2001, from *The Skeptical Environmentalist*)

"Environmental problems have contributed to numerous collapses of civilizations in the past. Now, for the first time, a global collapse appears likely. Overpopulation, overconsumption by the rich and poor choices of technologies are major drivers; dramatic cultural change provides the main hope of averting calamity."

(Paul R. Ehrlich and Anne H. Ehrlich, 2013, from "Can a Collapse of Global Civilization be Avoided?" *Proceedings of the Royal Society* 280: 1–9).

Population Thought through History

Views on population had been expressed as early as the classical periods of ancient Greece, Rome, and China. Later in this chapter, we shall examine the ideas of Thomas Malthus (1766–1834) concerning his *principle of population* as detailed in his famous *Essay* published in 1798 and later revised through six subsequent editions. Before doing so, it will be important to consider a brief overview of pre-Malthusian thought on population. Charles Stangeland (1904: 14), in his authoritative study of population thought, claims that "as a matter of historical fact, [population] has occupied the attention of thoughtful men in nearly all ages." To this, he adds the early Greek philosophers Plato (c.424–348 BCE) and Aristotle (384–322 BCE), who had proposed remedies of various kinds to avert the human misery associated with overpopulation.

Stangeland (1904: 16–17) identified seven pre-Malthusian perspectives on population. Some are pronatalist, while others advocate restraint in matters of procreation and sexuality. The importance of marriage as a vehicle to promote population growth is prominent in these early writings. Another recurring theme is the quandary that states would face under conditions of excess population on the one hand and deficits on the other, and the appropriate means to intervene under these radically different conditions. Finally, some of the early thoughts on population are highly embedded in moral religious arguments and the tension these moral arguments posed for state and individual, whose interests are not always in harmony.

1. *The primitive attitude, usually expressed in religious veneration of the procreative powers.* Many ancient pagan rituals began as ways to encourage humans to procreate (examples include phallic cults and bacchanalia festivals in the ancient world). Perhaps these rituals represented a way for early societies to stimulate population growth in the light of recurrent epidemics of disease and war that decimated their numbers.

2. *The Greek view, which saw procreation as a civic duty, hence something to be regulated according to the needs of the city state.* In Ancient Greece, both public sentiment and written law punished celibacy. Frequent wars and epidemics had to be countered by population growth, which was best achieved through early marriage and procreation. In this context, Plato expressed the view that all personal ends had to be subordinated to the common good, and therefore marriage, as a means to propagate the race, was a personal duty to the state. On the other hand, Plato maintained that if a city state grew beyond a certain limit, which he estimated to be a population of 5 040, it would be morally acceptable for couples to resort to infanticide and abortion.

3. *The Roman policy of promoting continuous population growth, with a view to the indefinite expansion of the Roman state.* As with the ancient Greeks, the Romans viewed marriage primarily as a vehicle for rearing offspring and therefore a duty owed to the state. Heavy taxes were imposed on bachelors, while laws like the *lex Papia Poppaea* were passed to promote marriage and fecundity. In accordance with Roman law, widows and divorced women had to remarry within one or two years. Childless couples were accorded a low status in Roman society, while those with children enjoyed important privileges (such as the succession of property to their offspring). In addition to marriage and procreation, the Romans saw the conquest of new lands as an important mechanism for avoiding underpopulation within their territories.

4. *The Medieval Christian conception of sexual relations, which emphasized the moral superiority of celibacy.* Unlike the Ancient Greeks and Romans, who favoured early and widespread marriage and procreation, the Medieval Christian writers advocated celibacy and the ascetic life, which they considered more consistent with Christian morality. In fact, this view may have developed as a reaction to the immoral conditions that prevailed in the early Roman Empire. Thus, Christian scholars such as Saint Paul (d. 64/67CE), Saint Augustine (354–430), and, later, Saint Thomas Aquinas (1225–74) abhorred marriage and preferred chastity as a path bringing them closer to Christ. But though they considered celibacy the superior lifestyle, they acknowledged that marriage played a salutary role in society.

5. *The attitude of the humanists, who echoed the Greeks in emphasizing the need to regulate population.* During the Renaissance, a number of humanist scholars endorsed the view that population should be controlled. Among those was Sir Thomas More (1478–1535), who, in his work *Utopia*, presented a model of the ideal city-state and suggested that cities be composed of small groups of people, not to exceed 6 000. Families, he recommended, should have no fewer than 10 members and no more than 16.

6. *The individualistic and anti-ascetic attitude of the Reformation (1517–1648).* In reaction to the asceticism of the Medieval Christian scholars, the Reformation period, which began with Martin Luther's (1483–1546) criticism of Church doctrine in 1517, promoted the

view that virtuosity and marriage are not incompatible. Luther himself advocated that young men should marry not later than the age of 20, and women no later than 18.

7. **The mercantilist attitude, favouring population growth as a way of maintaining national economic and political power.** The mercantilist writers believed that the wealth of the nation was more important than the good of the individual. The greater the population, they reasoned, the greater the state's productivity and, hence, prosperity. They believed that population could be increased by imposing taxes on celibates, by excluding unmarried men from public office, and by rewarding those who married with tax exemptions. An early and well-known proponent of mercantilist thought was Niccolò Machiavelli (1469–1527), who championed the idea that population growth, in conjunction with agriculture, industry, and trade, would guarantee tangible socioeconomic benefits to a city-state. He warned, however, that population could at some point increase beyond the capacity of the city-state's limited territory, and that war, want, and disease would be the likely results of this situation.

Thomas Malthus (1766–1834): The Principle of Population

Thomas Robert Malthus was born in 1766 in Surrey, England, the sixth of eight siblings. After four years at Cambridge University (1784–8), he took holy orders in the Church of England, and from 1793 served as a curate in Surrey. Five years later, in 1798, his *Essay on the Principle of Population as It Affects the Future Improvement of Society, with Remarks on the Speculations of Mr. Godwin, M. Condorcet, and other Writers* was published anonymously. The subtitle Malthus attached to subsequent six editions—*A view of its past and present effects on human happiness, with an inquiry into our prospects respecting the future removal or mitigation of the evils which it occasions*—gives a good indication of the tone of the work. As indicated by the title of his *Essay*, Malthus's arguments were especially directed at countering the views of utopian philosophers and specifically those of the Marquis de Condorcet (1743–94) and William Godwin (1756–1836).

Condorcet, in his *History of Human Progress from Its Outset to Its Imminent Culmination in Human Perfection* (1794), believed that humans were inherently good but that social institutions were problematic and needed to be brought in line with the inherent goodness of humans (these thoughts would later influence the thinking of Karl Marx, whose ideas are discussed in the second part of this chapter). Condorcet also believed it to be an immutable principle of human society that population would never exceed the means of subsistence. If population growth should ever threaten to outpace the growth of the means of subsistence, the problem could be solved by society through the application of reason and technological innovation. William Godwin (1756–1836), best known for his *Enquiry Concerning the Principle of Political Justice* (1793), denounced society's established institutions as "obstacles to human development" (Petersen, 2003: 468). And later, in his *Of Population* (1820), he too posed the argument that the growth of population could not possibly outgrow humanity's ability to provide sufficient food and resources for the population—the sort of utopian thinking that Malthus set out to refute in his *Essay*.

In his 1798 *Essay*, Malthus dismissed as overly optimistic Godwin's and Condorcet's opinions that humankind and society were perfectible and that subsistence would always outpace population growth. He then proposed his principle of population:

> I think I may fairly make two postulata. First, that food is necessary to the existence of man. Secondly, that the passion between the sexes is necessary, and will remain nearly in its present state. . . . Assuming then, my postulates as granted, I say, that the power of population is indefinitely greater than the power in the earth to produce subsistence for man. Population, when unchecked, increases in a geometrical ratio. Subsistence increases only in an arithmetical ratio. A slight acquaintance with numbers will show the immensity of the first power in comparison of the second. (Malthus, 1798 [1960], 9/12; vol. 1 in Wrigley and Souden, 1986: 8)

In the sixth and final edition of the *Essay*, Malthus reaffirmed three key propositions:

1. Population is necessarily limited by the means of subsistence.
2. Population invariably increases where the means of subsistence increase, unless prevented by some very powerful and obvious checks.
3. These checks, and the checks which repress the superior power of population, and keep its effects on a level with the means of subsistence, are all resolvable into moral restraint, vice, and misery (Malthus, 1826, 22/4, vol. 1 in Wrigley and Souden, 1986: 20–1).

In short, Malthus argued that population growth will tend to surpass the means available to sustain humanity, and that unchecked population increases geometrically (1, 2, 4, 8, 16, 32, etc.), while food and other items necessary to sustain human existence increase only arithmetically (1, 2, 3, 4, 5, 6, 7, etc.) (see Figure 11.1).

Malthus argued that in the long run the difference in growth rates between population and food would produce its own remedies in the forms of what he called "misery" (including famine, war, disease, and pestilence) and "vice" (including all the ways that humans had then discovered to avoid unwanted conceptions and children, notably abortion and infanticide). Malthus described the "miseries" as *positive checks* on population growth because they all contributed to increasing the death rate, thereby helping to lower population to the point where the resources available would once again be sufficient to sustain it. The "vices" he described as *preventive checks*, as they all served to lower the birth rate. It is clear that Malthus disapproved strongly of these behaviours, which he considered illicit and immoral. His preferred remedy to reduce fertility was the voluntary adoption of licit preventive checks more consistent with a moral and Christian way of life—specifically sexual abstinence outside of marriage and the postponement, or even avoidance, of marriage itself. He also referred to these as *moral restraint* because they represented

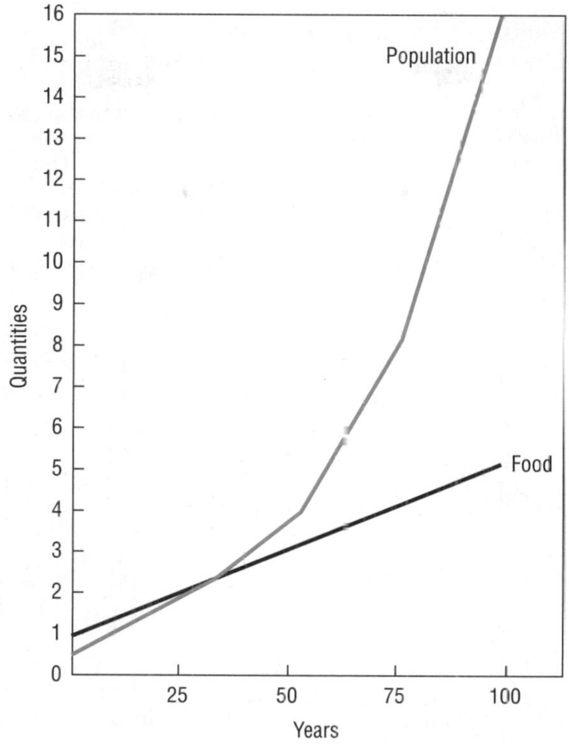

FIGURE 11.1   The two rates of increase as Malthus saw them

Source: Adapted from Overbeek (1974) 43. From *History of Population Theories by Johanne Overbeek*, 1974, Rotterdam University Press. Reprinted with permission.

the application of morally sound actions towards a desirable societal goal. Table 11.1 clarifies these distinctions. Moreover, he reasoned, by postponing marriage until the people concerned were capable of supporting a family, individuals and society would both benefit. And by working longer before establishing a family, people would be able to save more of their income, thus helping to reduce poverty and raise the overall level of well-being. In this sense, Malthus's theorizing has helped to raise awareness that effective population control in rapidly growing societies—where the balance between population and resources may be precarious ultimately rests on the private decisions of individuals.

As already indicated, Malthus elaborated on these ideas through several revisions of his *Essay*. The basic Malthusian principles—that population growth will always tend to outpace growth in the means of subsistence and must be held in check one way or the other—remained central, but he later outlined a more complex, and surprisingly modern, framework in which population change in any particular society depends on a variety of factors specific to that society. These factors—the level of technology; the level of available natural resources; the rates of usurpation of productive surplus by centres of political power; the competitiveness of markets; and, implicitly, the normative standards of living that influence

TABLE 11.1   **Malthusian checks on population**

IIIIIIIIIIIIIIIIIIIIIIIIIIIIIIIIIIIIIIIIIIIIIIIIIIIIIIIIIIIIIIIIIIIIIIIIIIIIIIIIIIIIIIIIIIIIIIIIIIIIIIIIIIIIIIIIIIIIIIIIIIIIIIII

Positive checks – conditions that increase the death rate (*misery*)	*Preventive checks* – behaviours that act on the birth rate	
	Illicit (*vice*)	**Licit (*moral restraint*)**
• unwholesome occupations • severe labour • exposure to the seasons • bad and insufficient food and clothing arising from poverty • bad nursing of children • excesses of all kinds • famine • pestilence • disease • war • infanticide	• all forms of contraception and "unnatural acts that prevent the consequences of irregular connections" • abortion	• permanent celibacy or late marriage • "strictly moral conduct toward sex"

Source: Adapted from Flew (1970).

how much each member consumes and, hence, what is available for consumption by others (Turner, 1995: 12)—are outlined in Figure 11.2.

Modern Criticism of Malthus

Modern critics have faulted Malthus for not anticipating how the worst consequences of overpopulation might be mitigated. For example, some say that he failed to take full account of human resilience in the face of difficult predicaments. Throughout history, humans have been remarkably good at problem-solving. Julian Simon (1995, 1996) has suggested that progress in science, technology, and socioeconomic well-being has moved in tandem with population growth. Similarly, Robert Fogel and Dora Costa (1997) have argued that the exponential rise of population in modern times has been accompanied by exponential advances in scientific understanding and technological innovation (see Figure 11.3). In fact, Ester Boserup (1965, 1981) proposed a thesis that in a sense reverses the Malthusian causal order: whereas Malthus argued that an increase in the food supply would translate into increased birth rates and lower mortality, hence population growth, Boserup argued that, historically, increasing population density was itself the driving force behind agricultural and technological innovations that increased the food supply, promoted economic growth, and raised standards of living. Population growth and density, according to Boserup, provided the impetus for the specialization of economic activities, such that people would produce and trade in the market the wide variety of goods and services needed by an expanding population. This, in turn, served to stimulate economic growth and well-being.

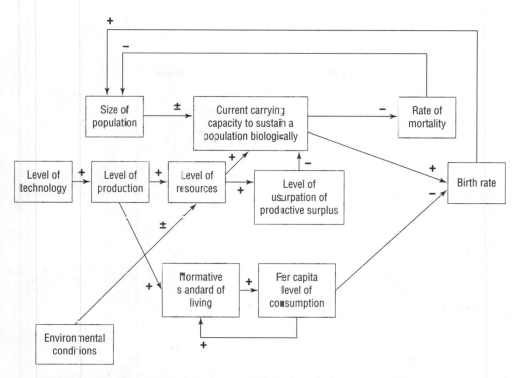

F GURE 11.2   Malthus's model of population dynamics

Note: The + and - signs signify positive and negative effects, respectively, among variables; In some cases the relationship between variables can be either positive or negative.

Source: Jonathan H. Turner. 1995. *Macrodynamics: Toward a Theory on the Organization of Human Populations*. Copyright © 1995 by Jonathan H. Turner. Reprinted by permission of Rutgers University Press.

Malthus suggested that population and the means of subsistence must be in balance. But what constitutes optimum population size is difficult to specify. It depends not only on the resources available but on the culture's standards regarding the appropriate level of subsistence for individuals. Social standards vary from society to society and from one historical period to another. The more developed the society, the higher its expectations. As material aspirations rise, so do levels of consumption. Increased consumer demand for material goods means greater economic activity, but increases in economic activity also heighten the risk of environmental damage, increased pollution, and resource depletion (Cohen, 1995, 2003; Ehrlich and Ehrlich, 1990). Consider that even the most useful technological innovations often have undesirable by-products or side effects. For example, the automobile has transformed society by allowing people to move about faster and more efficiently than ever before; yet over the years since its invention, automobile emissions have contributed significantly to environmental pollution. It is true that technologies have been developed to counteract harmful side effects; thus, it has become

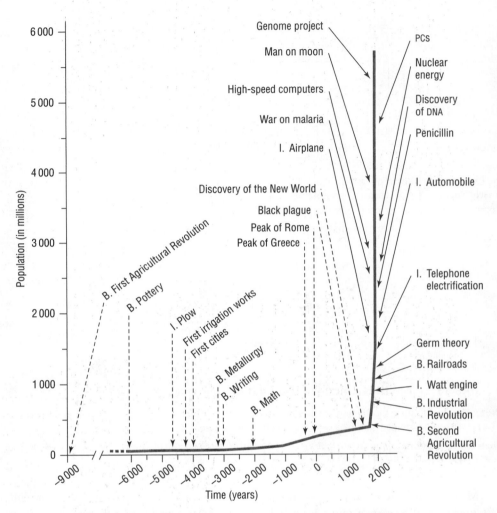

FIGURE 11.3 **The growth of the world population and some major events in the history of technology**

Notes: I = invention; B = beginning. There is usually a lag between the invention of a process or a machine and its general application to production. "B" is intended to identify the beginning, or earliest stage, of this diffusion process.

Source: Fogel and Costa (1997), 50. Springer, *Demography* vol. 34, issue 1, 1997, pp. 49-66, "A Theory of Technophysio Evolution, with Some Implications for Forecasting Population, Health Care Costs, and Pension Costs" by Robert W. Fogel and Dora L. Costa. With kind permission from Springer Science and Business Media.

standard practice among car manufacturers to install catalytic converters to reduce carbon emissions. This technology is just one example of the measures that wealthy, highly industrialized countries have relied on to limit automobile-related pollution.

Poorer countries, however, may not be able to afford such costly techno-fixes. In other words, sustainability and optimum population size are so closely interrelated that it is virtually impossible to say at what point exactly a certain population has reached the limits to its growth. However, various attempts have been presented recently to measure the human impact on the environment and resources (see box, page 515).

Because Malthus viewed birth control as being a vicious practice that ran counter to God's beneficent design for humanity, he is often regarded as more of a moralist than a scientist. Yet, it may be unfair to accuse him of excessive moralism. Malthus was not an anti-populationist. His main concern was that society ought to strive to attain a sustainable balance between population and resources as to engender an optimal state of well-being for all. And his recommendation that people delay marriage and save their money before starting a family seems, by today's standards, like perfectly sound advice consistent with the modern idea of family planning.

Although Malthus addressed the role of migration in population change, he could not have anticipated the large-scale emigration by European society in the nineteenth century to relieve population pressure. Between 1850 and 1950, some 50 million people left Europe for the New World (Kennedy, 1993: 6; Petersen, 1975: 279). This massive exodus served as a "safety valve" during the stage of the Western demographic transition when Western Europe faced a prolonged period of rapid population growth. Having said that, it is highly unlikely that emigration on such a scale would ever be possible for the less developed countries today.

Finally, if economic growth is equated with overall well-being and prosperity in the human population, then Malthus's dire predictions were once again off the mark. Since the Industrial Revolution, global production of goods and services has expanded to a degree that few if any, in his time could have imagined. The International Monetary Fund (2000) has estimated that between 1750 and the early 1900s population growth exceeded world gross domestic product (GDP); yet from the early 1900s onward, real GDP has outstripped world population growth by a significant degree. The world's economic productivity is sustaining a larger population than ever seen in the history of humanity, and overall, standards of living around the world have been improving over time, though clearly significant regional disparities persist and remain a source of ongoing concern for the global community (Goklany, 2007; United Nations Department of Economic and Social Affairs Population Division, 2001: 8–9).

The Importance of Malthus to Population Studies

Malthus explained clearly and forcefully how rapid population growth could be detrimental to humanity. Through his insistence on the application of moral restraint, he also emphasized the responsibility of the individual. His work has sparked much research on the question of population and its relationship to social and economic development and questions pertaining to environmental sustainability.

Recently, scholars have questioned the value of Malthusian theory in the light of (a) the contemporary demographic outlook for an increasing number of countries facing demographic maturity and low or even declining annual rates of natural increase, and (b) the significant improvements achieved in food production (e.g., the green revolution), health, and standards of living since his time. So, should Malthus be retired? Clearly, moral objections to birth control and family planning have no place in the twenty-first century, but many of the issues Malthus raised are not irrelevant in a world characterized by unequal population growth across regions, ecological and environmental instability, and widening socioeconomic inequalities across and within nations. We shall return to some of these issues later.

We must remind ourselves that in spite of advancements in overall standards of living, a significant portion of the global population—perhaps a billion of the earth's inhabitants—still live in abject poverty under precarious circumstances, besieged by war, famine, disease, and other calamities (Barro and Sala-i-Martin, 2004; Goklany, 2007; Livi-Bacci and De Santis, 1998). The battle to extirpate poverty and human suffering is far from over. In the poorest countries of the world—particularly those of Tropical Africa and Central Asia—poverty is a cause of rapid population growth, and rapid population growth compounds these societies' ability to reduce poverty. A vicious cycle prevails, producing a "poverty trap" from which these countries cannot seem to escape (Brown, 2011; Sachs, 2007, 2008).

We may credit Malthus with laying the foundations of modern demography (Winch, 2003: 619). For Roland Pressat (1985: 133), Malthus was "unquestionably one of the most influential figures in the development of population studies as well as an economist of the first rank." Along with the demographic transition theory, Malthusian theory represents the starting point of any serious analysis of population dynamics (Petersen, 1975: 144; Singer, 1971; Zimmerman, 1989). The classical sociological theorists—Auguste Comte (1798–1857), Herbert Spencer (1820–1903), and Émile Durkheim (1858–1917)—found

many of their insights on the sociological significance of population size and density in Malthus. Clearly, there were others, some of whom have been mentioned already (see Chapter 2), whose contributions to the development of population studies cannot be denied—William Petty, John Graunt, Gregory King, Edmund Halley, and Johan Peter Sussmilch are but just a few. What distinguishes Malthus, however, is that he went so far as to develop a system of thought on population and its interactions with biology, social structure, and resources, thus laying the foundation of a longstanding debate on population matters, which no serious scholar can overlook.

Karl Marx (1818–83)

Karl Marx was born in Trier, Germany, and received his doctorate in philosophy in 1841. As a young man, he worked as a journalist and edited a newspaper that was suppressed by the authorities because of its overly liberal content. Throughout his life, Marx combined scholarly research and writing with political activism. He moved to Paris in 1842 to continue his editorial work, but was expelled from the city in 1845 at the request of the Prussian government. He then sought refuge first in Brussels and eventually in London, where he settled with his family in 1849 and lived until his death in 1883.

In the mid-1840s, Marx found a close friend and collaborator in Frederick (Friedrich) Engels (1820–95). Together, Marx and Engels published a booklet that was to become one of the most frequently cited works in the history of social thought: the *Communist Manifesto* (1847). Among the goals it set out were the following:

THE LOGISTIC EQUATION, THE CONCEPT OF "CARRYING CAPACITY"

Another example of the Malthusian influence on the study of population is the development of the *logistic equation*. The logistic equation is a way of calculating the growth rate of a population by taking into account its current size. Mathematically, the logistic equation takes the form, $dN(t)/dt = rN(t)(1-N(t)/K)$, where $N(t)$ is the population, t is time, r is the growth rate, and K represents the maximum sustainable population size. For a constant K and r, the solution is an S-shaped function saturating to a constant population size as N approaches K.

This logistic equation was formulated in 1838 by Pierre François Verhulst (1804–49) in reaction to Malthus's description of population growth as indefinitely exponential. Exponential growth cannot actually proceed indefinitely, and so Verhulst sought a more realistic description of population growth over time, one that would take into account how populations adjust as they grow larger under the combined pressures of crowding and resource depletion (Leschaeghe, 2003).

In 1920, without prior knowledge of Verhulst's early work, Raymond Pearl (1879–1940) and Lowell Reed (1886–1966) produced the same mathematical model. Like Verhulst, Pearl and Reed saw the logistic equation as an expression of a natural, self-regulating process whereby human populations undergo three successive stages of growth: first slow, then rapid, and finally slow again

as the populations' numbers approach some upper limit (i.e., K). Pearl (1927) suggested that as a population approached the limits of the resources available to sustain it, certain controls would kick in to reduce the rate of growth. This kind of reaction to population growth may be thought of as a *density-dependent effect*. For example, in animal populations in the wild, a prolonged period of high growth and increased density usually leads to a period of increased death rates, which then reduces the population to levels consistent with the food supply. Lotka (1925) and Volterra (1926) independently expressed this idea in mathematical form to describe the rise-and-fall sequences of two species in the wild characterized by a *predator–prey relationship*.

This type of mechanism was precisely what concerned Malthus, with the exception that humans, unlike animals, have the ability to regulate population growth through *preventive checks*, and thus avoid the *positive checks* (Cohen, 1995; Lutz and Qiang, 2002; Sibly and Hone, 2002). Thus, in the logistic equation, exponential rate of growth and the absolute size of a population change in inverse proportion over time: as population size increases, the rate of exponential growth declines. And it is this pattern that gives the logistic curve its characteristic elongated S-shape.

These thoughts about the logistic equation bear close resemblance to the more recent concept of *carrying*

(continued)

capacity—the sustainability of the earth's ecosystem given the food, habitat, water, and other ecosystem necessities required to support the human population. Underlying the concept is a fundamental question: What is the number of persons that the earth can support without significant negative impacts to both humans and the planet? Arriving at an answer is not straightforward. For one thing, unlike animal species, whose relationship to the ecosystem entails mainly their interactions for food and habitable space, humans bring many more complex variables to the equation. For instance, along with our tendency to take resources from the earth, we also try to replace what we have removed (for instance, by planting seedlings to replenish forests). And as self-reflexive agents, humans are capable of considering how our behaviours may be damaging the environment and take steps to modify our behaviour to avert potential disaster in the long run. Whether we are succeeding remains an important question subject to further study (see, for example, Meadows, Randers, and Meadows, 2005; Randers, 2012).

- abolition of property in lands (i.e., an end to private landownership);
- abolition of all rights of inheritance;
- introduction of a progressive (graduated) income tax;
- nationalization of the means of transportation and commerce;
- compulsory labour for all; and
- free education, and an end to child labour. (Bogardus, 1960: 252)

Marx's magnum opus, however, was *Das Kapital*, an analysis of the evolution of capitalism. The first volume was published in 1867; the remaining two volumes, still incomplete at his death, were edited by Engels and published in 1885 and 1895. Marx argued that under advanced capitalism, wealth becomes increasingly concentrated in fewer and fewer hands. In order to survive, those without the capital assets needed to produce wealth themselves—the "proletariat"—are forced to sell their labour power, and to do so in a marketplace in which competition for jobs is ensured by the constant presence of what Marx called the "industrial reserve army" of the unemployed. This competition allows employers to keep wages below what they would be if workers were paid the full value of their labour. It is in this way—by appropriating to themselves the "surplus value of labour"— that capitalists exploit the working class. Yet this exploitation cannot continue forever, according to Marx: for as capitalism advances, so too will the workers' "class consciousness." Awareness of their common suffering and exploitation will lead to class action through powerful labour organizations, and the proletariat will eventually win the class struggle, overthrowing the capitalists and seizing control of the means of production.

Marxist thought offers no systematic theory of population (Bogue, 1969, 16–17; Linder, 1997). The closest Marx comes to considering population dynamics is in his discussion of the "reserve army" of labour—but this is a feature of advanced capitalism, not of human populations in general. Whereas Malthus proposed a general principle of population, a universal natural law applicable in all places and times, Marx insisted that the population of any society is determined by the prevailing social and economic conditions. Each specific societal stage (or *mode of production*) creates its own law of population. As Marx put it (1867 [1967]: 631–2):

> The laboring population . . . produces, along with the accumulation of capital produced by it, the means by which [it] itself is made relatively superfluous, is turned into a relative surplus-population; and it does this to an always increasing extent. This is a law of population peculiar to the capitalist mode of production; and in fact every special historic mode of production has its own special laws of population, historically valid within its limits alone. An abstract law of population exists for plants and animals only, and only in so far as man has not interfered with them.

In other words, for Marx the "reserve army" of unemployed labour is not the inevitable product of biological urges—what Malthus called "the passions between the sexes." Rather, it is generated primarily by capital itself as the capitalist class invests in new machinery, which displaces workers from their jobs and adds them to the "reserve army." The ongoing process of capital investment serves to maintain a reserve army of labour large enough to keep workers' wages low and employers' profits high.

Believing that society's greatest problem was not population but the capitalist system, Marx did not propose any alternative to Malthus's theory. Engels, like Marx, believed that the Malthusian principle of population was terribly mistaken, arguing that there was no proof that productivity of land increases in arithmetical progression, as Malthus believed. Moreover, he added, even if population grows geometrically, as Malthus claimed, science is just as limitless and grows at least as rapidly as population. For Engels, science and technology could easily solve any problems that might result from population growth (Engels, 1844 [1971]).

Nevertheless, Marx's theory of capitalism clearly included demographic dimensions, for in his view the size and strength of the industrial reserve army depended not only on the displacement of workers from the industrial production process by new technology but also on rural-to-urban migration of workers from the countryside and high fertility rates among the labouring class and the poor. These demographic realities, Marx suggested, helped to perpetuate the surplus of workers in the capitalist system despite the high mortality rates characteristic of the working class. Figure 11.4 is a rendition of these ideas connecting demography and capitalism.

Modern Perspectives on Marx's View of Population

Marx's analysis of socioeconomic inequality is an outstanding contribution to our understanding of society. With respect to demography, however, his views have been largely set aside. Even China—a communist

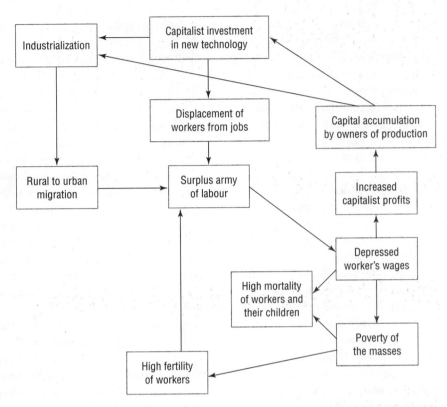

FIGURE 11.4 Marx's implicit model of population dynamics in the capitalist system of production

Source: Author's rendition.

state—recognized decades ago that slowing population growth, in the long term, is essential to societal well-being. With few exceptions, developing countries around the world have come to recognize the importance of controlling population growth and have abandoned the Marxist perspective, at the same time adopting organized family planning.

Just as Malthus has been criticized for rejecting contraception on moral grounds, Marx has been criticized for failing to recognize that uncontrolled population growth can be detrimental

to human well-being. In their classic study, *Population Growth and Economic Development in Low-Income Countries*, Ansley Coale and Edgar Hoover (1958) identified three ways in which rapid population growth has hampered economic development in India and Mexico. First, the larger a population becomes, the more resources it needs for health care, education, and other important services; this will make it difficult for a government with limited resources to meet its service obligations. Second, the more rapidly a population grows, the more resources it will need in order to achieve a given standard of living. Third, a rapidly growing population will typically have a sizable economic burden of dependent children and youths (as a result of persistently high birth rates) and a relatively small working-age population to carry it. A society with a relatively large working-age population will generally enjoy higher per capita income "as a direct result of having a higher fraction of its population eligible on account of age for productive work" (Coale and Hoover, 1958: 24). It is no coincidence that the fastest-growing populations in the world tend to have relatively low rates of economic growth and high rates of social and political instability. Population may not be the only cause of such problems, but it seems clear that rapid population growth can exacerbate whatever other structural difficulties a society may face.

As for Marx's prediction that the capitalist system would be overthrown, in reality capitalism has withstood repeated crises historically, only to rebound as a viable system, notwithstanding its inherent contradictions and continuing problems. But historically, to a significant extent, instead of increasing misery and discontent, on the whole, the working classes—and society in general—have experienced significant improvements in their lives as a result of the scientific and technological advances brought on and promoted by capitalism (Hayek, 1998: 296). Among the other societal benefits associated with industrialization and capitalism, Julian Simon (1995) notes the dramatic decline in infant mortality, longer life expectancy, good health and nutrition, better education, more money, more leisure time, and greater individual freedom and happiness (see also Goklany, 2007; Leisinger, Schmitt, and Pandya-Lorch, 2002: 4–5).

Finally, some analysts have attributed the socioeconomic difficulties experienced by the less advantaged regions of the world to their historical experience of colonialism and peripheral capitalism (e.g., Frank, 1969, 1991; Myrdal, 1957). Yet, the argument has been posed that what these societies really need may be more, not less, capitalism, in order to provide meaningful productive work, a better standard of living, and greater individual freedom (Bhagwati, 2000). The collapse of the Soviet system strongly suggests that communism is not a viable solution for poor countries (Rusmich and Sachs, 2003). Of course, capitalism alone, in the absence of major developments in other spheres of a society, will not solve the problems of poor countries. Above all, together with capitalism, there must be democratic governance and political stability. In addition, human rights and individual freedoms must be promoted and protected to allow people the confidence to explore profitable enterprises that help to stimulate economic growth and overall well-being.

The Importance of Marxist Thought to Population Studies

As we have seen, there is actually very little demographic theory in Marx. Perhaps his most important contribution to the field has been his insistence that socioeconomic inequality is inherent in the nature of capitalism itself. Even in the most advanced societies, overall income may rise without diminishing the relative gap between the wealthy and the poor (Fischer, 2003; Galbraith, 2002; Piketty, 2014; Sarin, 2003). Marx's penetrating analysis helps to bring into focus the fact that the rise of wealth and socioeconomic well-being around the world has not occurred equitably. This is significant because as the developing countries proceed through their socioeconomic and demographic transitions—some faster than others—many may enjoy an increase in their overall national wealth, yet this rise in national wealth will not necessarily translate into a more equitable distribution of income within society. It is possible for within-country income inequality to increase even as between-country inequality diminishes (see Firebaugh, 2003).

Malthus and Marx Contrasted

Table 11.2 juxtaposes Malthus and Marx on several issues related to population: their views of humanity; their basic theses regarding the role of population in societal problems; the contemporary schools of thought based on their theories; and their impact on population policy. From the works of these two scholars, Malthus appears to have been somewhat pessimistic about the future of humanity, while Marx perhaps was more optimistic. Unlike Malthus, Marx felt the capitalist system could be changed for the better through a revolution of the proletariat; Malthus was less sanguine about humanity's ability to overcome what he saw as biological tendencies that drive humankind to live at the brink of subsistence. Nevertheless, undoubtedly both thinkers have offered important insights on the human condition. In terms of impact on population policy, however, Malthus has been more influential; few if any countries today outwardly accept Marxism as a guiding doctrine towards the solution of population problems—certainly not China with its one-child policy.

In recent decades, virtually all developing countries have embraced one key element of the neo-Malthusian remedy as a means of tackling rapid population growth, most notably through a combination of family planning, reproductive health campaigns, and increased education for boys and girls—interventions that have been quite effective in reducing fertility rates on the one hand, and lowering death rates on the other.

Contemporary Perspectives

Contemporary perspectives on population can be classified under three headings: neo-Malthusianism, neo-Marxism, and revisionism. Scholars within the first of these schools are often referred to as *pessimists* (Bloom, Canning, and Sevilla, 2003) because they embrace the Malthusian *principle of population* and its potentially negative ramifications for society. The other two perspectives are more optimistic (i.e., *optimists*) in their outlook about the human condition, even though the scholars in these camps are not necessarily commonly united under Marxism or revisionism as such and can be from varied disciplinary backgrounds.

Neo-Malthusianism

Paul Ehrlich (1995: 3), a prominent population ecologist, exemplifies the neo-Malthusian position:

> I predict that the most important demographic development in the next 50 years will be the worldwide recognition that there is an intimate connection between the size of the human population and the state

TABLE 11.2   A summary of Malthusian and Marxist perspectives

Dimension	Malthusian	Marxist
View of humanity	Pessimistic: humans will always live at the edge of subsistence because—contrary to utopian visions of their perfectibility—the majority will not exercise the self-restraint necessary to control "the passion between the sexes."	Optimistic: the capitalist system is unjust, but it will eventually be overthrown through a revolution of the proletariat.
View of population	Population grows geometrically, while the food supply grows arithmetically; therefore, a rapid increase in population promotes poverty. Population and resources (i.e., food supply) must be in balance.	Population, as a problem, is secondary to the poverty and inequality on which the capitalist system depends. Capitalism produces an oversupply of workers, and this helps capitalists keep wages in check. This relationship reinforces the capitalist system of production and exploitation of the working classes: the larger the number of workers, the larger the supply of labour, which in turn has the effect of keeping workers' wages lower than they should be.
Evidence	That rapid population growth is detrimental to economic growth is a proposition that has been supported by Coale and Hoover (1958) and by more recent evidence showing that countries that grow rapidly tend to have relatively young populations and also significant social and economic problems and political instability. At the same time, population growth contributes to rapid urbanization, increased pollution, and deforestation.	In many contexts (i.e., in poor developing countries), poverty has been shown to be associated with high fertility, which in turn accounts for explosive rates of population growth. Marxists essentially turn Malthus upside down by arguing that it is poverty that causes high birth rates and therefore high rates of population growth, not the other way round.
Intervention	Responsibility for solving the "population problem" lies with the individual. The licit "preventive checks" of moral restraint (i.e., celibacy and late marriage) are preferable to "positive checks" associated with misery (famine, pestilence, disease, war) and vice (abortion, infanticide, contraception—i.e., illicit "preventive checks").	Capitalism must be overthrown through a revolution of the proletariat. If population grows exponentially, "necessity" provokes among humans a search for solutions through the application of science and technology.
Criticism	• Too pessimistic about humans' ability both to practise self-restraint and find innovative solutions to address the subsistence problem. • Objected, on moral grounds, to the use of contraceptive devices.	• Underestimated the problems associated with overpopulation. • Failed to foresee that even communist societies (e.g., China) would reject the Marxist view and adopt a plan to curb population growth consistent with Malthusian principles.

(continued)

TABLE 11.2   (continued)

IIIIIIIIIIIIIIIIIIIIIIIIIIIIIIIIIIIIIIIIIIIIIIIIIIIIIIIIIIIIIIIIIIIIIIIIIIIIIIIIIIIIIIIIIIIIIIIIIIIIIIIIIIIIIIIIIIIIII

Dimension	Malthusian	Marxist
	• Failed to foresee that advances in agriculture, etc. could extend the bounds of subsistence or that migration could relieve population pressures. • Did not foresee the population decline in contemporary industrialized nations, where the problem is not that population is pressing on resources, but that the economy presses on a slowly growing (even declining) population (i.e., a Malthusian inversion situation).	• Perhaps underestimated the positive aspects of capitalism, such as its tendency to promote innovation and create the jobs necessary to raise standards of living of poor countries.
Contemporary Schools	• *Neo-Malthusians* believe that population is a key factor in social, economic, and environmental matters; most demographers implicitly or explicitly agree. • They advocate population control through family planning and believe that to avert global ecological breakdown, immediate action must be is taken to curb population growth and consumption. Among their recommended interventions are (a) family planning; (b) development aid and debt relief to poor countries. • Some neo-Malthusians see globalization as a positive force to the extent that it helps developing countries attain higher standards of living. Others—especially environmentalists—oppose globalization because it promotes excessive economic growth through the exploitation of resources (oil, forests, fresh water, etc.). • Environmentalists argue that population growth is a multiplier: more people means a greater demand for goods; increasing demand increases resource depletion, pollution, global warming, etc.	• *Neo-Marxists* (including dependency/world systems theorists and antiglobalists) blame the capitalist system for economic and political inequalities around the world. • They believe overpopulation is not a cause of human suffering but a consequence of poverty; eliminating world regional inequality—a legacy of colonialism and unequal political and economic relations between the superpowers and the rest of the world—will take care of the population problem. • Today's multinationals control an increasing share of global wealth, while populations in developing countries represent both a source of cheap labour and an expanding consumer market. • Neo-Marxists are generally wary of globalization because it increases inequality and helps rich countries exploit poor countries.
Impact on population policy	Significant: neo-Malthusian ideas underlie family planning and reproductive health programs across the developing world.	Minimal: although Marxist doctrine was reflected in some aspects of population policy under the communist regimes of the former Soviet Bloc (i.e., antagonistic to contraception but liberal with respect to abortion), today most countries, including China, have abandoned Marxism and actively promote family planning to curb population growth.

of Earth's life support systems. This will be accompanied by a realization that current levels of overpopulation greatly increase the vulnerability of humanity to catastrophe, and that it is in the common interest of both rich and poor to work together to solve the human predicament. That should lead to a determined effort to: (1) gradually and humanely reduce human population size (especially in the rich countries which have disproportionate per-capita impacts); (2) limit wasteful consumption among the rich to make room for needed growth among the poor; (3) transition to much more efficient, environmentally benign technologies and cultural practices. Whether this can be accomplished in time to avoid an enormous increase in death rates from wide-spread loss of agricultural productivity and/or deterioration of the epidemiological environment is inherently unpredictable at the moment. (Reprinted by permission of the author).

Two decades earlier, Donella Meadows and colleagues (1972) carried out a massive computer simulation designed to project future environmental and resource sustainability. They concluded that if the then-current trends "in world population, industrialization, pollution, food production, and resource depletion" were to continue, the "limits to growth" on earth would be reached within a century: "The most probable result," in their view would be "a rather sudden and uncontrollable decline in both population and industrial capacity." Ultimately, continuing human population growth, excessive consumption, and incessant economic

production would together usher in ecological breakdown. Implicit in the neo-Malthusian view is the belief that the world would be a better place if it contained fewer people. In contrast to Malthus himself, however, neo-Malthusians promote contraception and family planning as crucial elements in the control of population growth.

Consistent with these ideas, Ehrlich and associates (1977) have proposed the so-called IPAT equation: I = PAT, which says that the impact (I) on the environment is a product of population size (P), multiplied by the level of affluence of the society (A) and its technology (T). Its utility has been called into question—some authors consider it unconvincing (Demeny, 1998; Preston, 1998) because in fact rich countries are less polluting than some developing countries (rich countries can afford to clean up the environment and have laws in place to reduce pollution). But the formula does help in presenting a visualization of neo-Malthusian thinking: Population, in interaction with affluence (wealthy countries consume more) and technology (more technology means more need for energy resources), determines the degree of impact (i.e., degradation) on the environment.

Figure 11.5 is a more elaborate conceptual rendition of the basic neo-Malthusian view of the links between population growth, resources, and environment. Overpopulation in this is seen as exerting pressure on resources and environment through complex series of interrelationships with other variables in the system, including increased consumption and demand for natural and non-renewable resources. Note also that there are various feedback loops in the system, such as the indirect effect of environmental degradation on the death rate and then on population itself. When neo-Malthusians attribute environmental and resource problems to population, therefore, what they are really referring to are the sorts of complex mechanisms depicted in Figure 11.5.

Has the situation reached a critical point? What is the causal connection from population size and growth rates to social and ecological conditions? From the point of view of the industrialized countries, it may be that the real problem is not population directly but rather overconsumption and its subsequent effects on resource depletion and

environmental stresses (Schumacher, 1974). Eric Woolmington (1985) has even thought of an inverted Malthusian scenario—a *Malthusian inversion*—suggesting that in countries where population growth rates continue to decline (i.e., the rich world), it is the economy that presses on the population rather than the other way around, as was suggested by Malthus, because ever-increasing rates of consumption and production are required by a slow growth population in order to maintain economic growth.

More recent works in the neo-Malthusian tradition have probed further

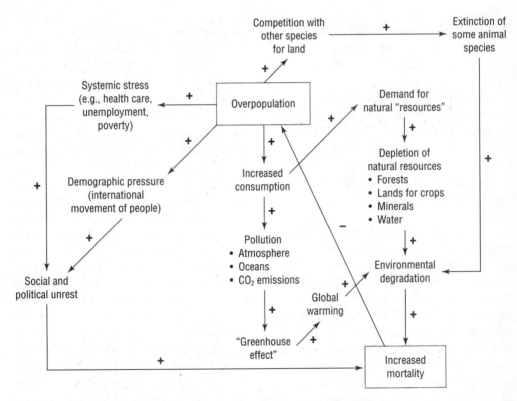

FIGURE 11.5   A neo-Malthusian model of the relationship between population and ecological stability

Note: A plus sign implies an increasing effect; a negative sign implies a decreasing effect.

Source: Author's rendition.

into the relationship of population growth and sustainability. In *Countdown*, Alan Weisman (2013) asks whether a sustainable balance between nature and the human population can ever be achieved. His main message is that no matter what environmental, ecological, or social predicament we face, it should be easier to solve with fewer people. A sustainable future, therefore, is achievable if we slow population growth and reduce the number of people on the planet. In *10 Billion*, Stephen Emmott (2013) gives a pessimistic outlook on our collective future. He points out that human activity is responsible for global environmental stresses, including global warming and climate change, water shortages, and other serious ecological problems; and producing new technologies many not be the answer to solving our global problems because technology itself is a contributing factor. Thus, neo-Malthusians continue in many ways to address the questions that were raised years ago by Ehrlich in *The Population Bomb* and by the 1972 study of Meadows and colleagues, *The Limits to Growth*. From the perspective of these scholars, another half-century of "business as usual" in regard to consumption patterns and economic production cannot possibly lead to a desirable future for humanity (see also Randers, 2012; Rockström and Klum, 2013; Smil, 2008, 2012; Tyrell, 2013). So, we must either find ingenious ways of reducing environmental and socioeconomic problems that accompany a growing global population, or nature will ultimately find its own solution by unleashing the Malthusian positive checks.

Neo-Marxism

To some extent, neo-Marxist scholars can be described as *optimists* because besides challenging the Malthusian principle, they believe that a different more equitable world is possible once the capitalist system of economic production and its iniquitous underpinnings are overthrown, the world can create a new more equitable social system. Neo-Marxists believe the real problem facing the world is not over-population; rather, it is widening socioeconomic inequalities between countries (and also within countries). Capitalism breeds inequality in access to resources and income, and in the global arena some countries are destined to remain relatively deprived and dependent on the wealthy more privileged countries. Thus, for neo-Marxists, social inequality is the foundation of all of the major ills that plague humanity—from poverty to crime, to war and sociopolitical instability. These are the major problems to be tackled.

Thus, whereas neo-Malthusian scholars see the world's growing human population as central to environmental problems, neo-Marxist writers maintain that to fixate on overpopulation as the root cause of human suffering is to obscure the reality that the world is divided into wealthy and relatively poor regions, and that this divide is widening. Neo-Marxists argue that the population predicament of poor developing nations, for instance, is largely a function of their relative economic deprivation and continued dependency on the industrialized nations. They view the source of the problem as economic inequality, not overpopulation. Neo-Marxists would look at the global economy so grounded in capitalism as inherently problematic that it is bound to ultimately collapse under the weight of its own contradictions. There are entrenched and persisting imbalances in economic and political power across nations, with some nations enjoying inordinate influence in the global arena and others almost none. The globalization of capital—seen by many writers as offering the developing nations the opportunity to emulate the "success story" of the West—is seen by neo-Marxists as exacerbating rather than diminishing socioeconomic disparities within and across societies (Wimberly, 1990).

As we saw in Chapter 3, it was the neo-Marxist scholar Andre Gunder Frank (1991) who coined the phrase "underdevelopment of development" to refer to the chronic dependence of the developing regions in a world where the great economic powers exercise overwhelming influence and control. Development—or, more precisely, underdevelopment—serves the interests of powerful nations (see also Wallerstein, 1974, 1980). The aid that poor nations receive comes at the cost of persistent dependence on the aid providers. Imbalances in the distribution of wealth, resources, and political influence have exacerbated socioeconomic inequality, poverty, and other social problems. Again, from this perspective, therefore, overpopulation is not the prime cause of human suffering, as the neo-Malthusians contend, but the result of a complex chain of causation arising from power imbalances in international political and economic relations (Myrdal, 1957).

The challenge, as the neo-Marxists see it, is to distribute the benefits of progress equitably among the peoples of the world. The consumerism of wealthy regions and their overwhelming economic and political influence over the less advantaged nations is one of the impediments to this goal.

Cornucopianism

Another group of scholars that fall under the heading of "optimists" have no particular allegiance or affinity to Marxist theory as such. We may refer to these analysts at *cornucopians* because they believe in the power of market (i.e., the invisible hand) to solve our human predicaments. They disagree with the neo-Malthusians that population growth necessarily impedes economic development (Aligica, 2007; Goklany, 2007; Lam, 2013; Lomborg, 2001; Simon, 1995; 1996). This accords with the argument, outlined earlier in this chapter, that throughout human history, population growth has been associated with progress, innovation, specialization of economic activity, rising incomes, and improved standards of living. Cornucopians point, for instance, to the fact that even though between 1960 and 2000 the world's population doubled and continues to grow, per capita incomes worldwide have not fallen but have actually increased significantly and poverty levels have been declining. They find that the prices of raw materials have been declining, while overall standards of living are improving. They argue that many of society's undesirable features, which neo-Malthusians often blame on population growth, are actually related not to population as such, but to inefficient government policies and institutions. Regarding poverty, *The Economist* (2013c) explains that the threshold for dire poverty in developing countries today is typically set at $1.25 a day of consumption (rather than income)—a figure is arrived at by averaging the poverty lines in the 15 poorest countries (not because $1.26 spells comfort).

Using this yardstick by which poverty reduction in poor countries is measured, it has been reported that since 1990, the poverty rate has halved worldwide, from 43 per cent in 1990 to 21 per cent in 2010. Almost all of the fall in the poverty rate should be attributed to economic growth, according to *The Economist*. Moreover, "Fast-growing economies in the developing world have done most of the work. Between 1981 and 2001 China lifted 680 million people out of poverty. Since 2000, the acceleration of growth in developing countries has cut the numbers in extreme poverty outside China by 280 million" (*The Economist*, 2013c).

This is promising news for the world. But unfortunately, there remain about a billion poor people to be helped out of poverty. Many of these people are in the less prosperous parts of India and in the most fragile states of sub-Saharan Africa (e.g., Congo and Somalia). Still, one can take some solace in knowing that "shifting people above the threshold that marks dire poverty has begun to look achievable within a generation" (*The Economist*, 2013d).

Revisionism

Revisionists (many of whom are neoclassical economists) subscribe neither to neo-Marxism nor to neo-Malthusianism. One particular area of interest to these analysts is the link between rapid population growth and economic development.

A report by the United States National Research Council (1986) marked a turning point in the economic demography literature. Between the mid-1960s and the early 1990s, economic demographers tended to emphasize the deleterious effects of rapid population growth on a country's ability to generate sufficient economic growth. The standard explanation for this effect is the Coale and Hoover (1958) model, in which rapid population growth causes the age structure to widen in the youthful age groups, thus posing a serious youth dependency problem for governments attempting to raise average incomes. The National

Research Council report did indicate that on balance slower population growth would indeed be beneficial to economic development for most developing countries. However, it questioned the often assumed idea that reducing population growth rates is the key to taking a poor country out of poverty. It asserted that the relationship between population growth and poverty for developing countries holds up only to a limited degree. For instance, if the population of Bangladesh were halved, its status as a poor nation would not change appreciably; it would move from the second poorest nation to thirteenth poorest in the world. This suggests that other factors in addition to population growth must be considered in any cross-national analysis of poverty levels.[1]

According to David Bloom, David Canning, and Jaypee Sevilla (2003), countries with rapidly growing populations do typically show slower rates of economic growth in general, but this negative correlation tends to disappear or even change direction (i.e., the correlation becomes positive) once other relevant factors are brought into the equation—for example, country size, openness to trade, quality of civic and political institutions, and overall level of education.

As was noted in Chapter 4, a country's GDP can take a turn for the better if a period of sustained fertility increases is followed by a rapid fertility decline. This scenario can represent a "window of opportunity" for developing countries because it would create an optimal shift in the age structure, whereby more young adult workers are present to fill a country's labour demands. Revisionist scholars acknowledge this important demographic phenomenon, but consistent with Bloom and colleagues (2003), also point out the crucial role of social and political institutions in a country's ability to take full advantage of this one-time "demographic bonus." If economic success is to follow, a government must provide adequate education and training for its labour force and find ways to create jobs for an expanding, youthful working-age population (Ahlburg, 1998; Birdsall, Kelley, and Sinding, 2001; Cincotta and Engelman, 1997; Clarke, 1996; Evans, 1998; Preston, 1998).

On the question of the environment and resources, the United States National Research Council (1986) report suggested that the relationship between population growth and the depletion of non-renewable resources is statistically weak and often exaggerated. It found income growth and excessive consumption to be more important factors. A world with a rapidly growing population but slow income growth might deplete its resources more slowly than one with a stationary population but rapidly increasing income. It was also argued in the report that while population is directly related to the growth of large cities in the developing world, its role in urban problems is likely secondary; ineffective or misguided government policies tend to play a more important role.

Population, Environment, Resources: Complex Interrelationships and Challenges

Notwithstanding the differing perspectives on the question concerning population, environment, and resources, it seems axiomatic that in a real-world sense population cannot be dismissed as a factor in matters of global socioeconomic and ecological sustainability; in one way or another population is a component of a large equation explaining global challenges in their various forms and dimensions. Here, we examine a number of socioeconomic, environmental, and resource concerns—all interrelated with population—facing our collective future as we move forward into the twenty-first century.

Socioeconomic Challenges

Jobs

The population of the world has surpassed 7 billion. Medium-range projections prepared by the UN indicate that by the year 2050 the global population could soar to 9.6 billion. If we consider the ages between 15 and 65 as a rough indication of the potential workforce, it is clear that the number in this age range worldwide has been growing. However, this growth of potential workforce is uneven across the regions; in some of the industrialized countries, the labour-force population is already in a state of constriction while in most developing countries, it is growing, in many cases quite rapidly. The rich countries will likely have to rely increasingly on immigration to meet their labour demands. On the other hand, these countries are in a better position to build human capital to make their labour forces more efficient; they have the resources to do this, even in the face of possible population decline (Elgin and Tumen, 2012). For the poorer countries, the challenge is how to create sufficient job creation, as population growth may outstrip growth in job creation (Brown, Gardner, and Halweil, 1999: 53; International Labor Organization, 2008). This type of problem is especially acute in in the poorest regions of the globe.

Rapid Urbanization

The world has become increasingly urbanized over the past half-century. The trend towards greater levels of urbanization is expected to continue (United Nations Department of Economic and Social Affairs Population Division, 2012b). Although urbanization brings with it positive socioeconomic change, among the most obvious potentially negative consequences, particularly in the developing countries are rampant urban poverty, rising crime rates, air pollution, and the rapid spread of communicable diseases because of overcrowding and, in many cases, underdeveloped sanitary systems. The more developed countries are not immune to these types of problems, but would be in a better position to deal with them due to having access to advanced resources and means.

Infectious Disease Epidemics

The specific causes of any communicable disease epidemic—whether of HIV/AIDS, SARS, or avian flu (to name just a few)—are complex and multivariable. It is clear, however, that factors such as high population density, crowding, deforestation, global travel, and forced migratory movements may all play contributing roles by amplifying the potential spread of infectious diseases. This is something that can potentially affect all corners of the globe.

Food Insecurity

Some regions of the globe are experiencing serious food shortages. According to Danielle Nierenberg's (2013) analysis, estimates of the number of chronically hungry people worldwide are in the range of 815

million, which is a modest decline from the 956 million estimated in 1970. Most of those are in India and Asia, although the most acute hunger crises are localized in sub-Saharan Africa. More than 239 million people in sub-Saharan Africa are considered undernourished, but overall Asia has a largest number of undernourished people, with an estimated 578 million in 2010. In Latin America and the Caribbean, hunger has receded since the 1990s, but there are still 53 million undernourished people. Meanwhile, food prices internationally have continued to rise, by as much as 70 per cent since 2007. This situation appears to be even more severe in many of the developing countries, where poverty rates are still quite high. Tragically, a lot of food goes to waste—as much as 30 per cent of yearly harvests is wasted because of poor or inadequate storage and processing facilities (Nierenberg, 2013).

Resource Scarcity and State Conflict

In some parts of the planet, as resources like fresh water and arable land become increasingly scarce, interstate violence becomes more likely (Homer-Dixon, 1999; Homer-Dixon, Boutwell, and Rathjens, 1993). The most common types of these conflicts, according to Thomas Homer-Dixon (1999: 5), are ethnic clashes and civil strife. In these circumstances, population pressure may be an exogenous factor leading countries to resort to violence as a way of either obtaining or protecting the scarce resources (e.g., fresh water and arable land). Poor countries seem particularly vulnerable to this kind of conflict because they lack both the material and the human capital resources to buffer themselves against the effects of such environmental scarcities. In some of these countries affected by the HIV/AIDS epidemic, ongoing conflict exacerbates the spread of this deadly disease (Mills et al., 2006). In others, climate change may precipitate depletions of water and agricultural land, and these could induce existing tensions between states (Burke et al., 2009; Hsiang, Meng, and Cane, 2011). Although these interactions seem plausible, it would seem highly likely that conflict between countries is highly dependent on many additional social, economic, and political factors.

Environmental/Ecological Stresses

Over the past 60 years the earth's climate has been undergoing a warming trend. There is growing (some say indisputable) evidence that human activity—primarily increased carbon emissions from industrial production— has contributed significantly to this phenomenon (Mann, 2014; Pebley, 1998; Stern, 2007). The UN's Intergovernmental Panel on Climate Change (2013) has concluded in its report of 2013 that it is extremely likely that humans are responsible for climate change over the past half-century. Indeed, key indicators in the climate change models analyzed by the Panel point in the same direction: temperatures across the world's regions and oceans have been rising, carbon emission increasing, and sea ice levels in the Arctic and Antarctic falling. The Panel looked at various scenarios to project possible levels of future warming. Based on that analysis, it concluded that global surface temperature change for the end of the twenty-first century is likely to exceed 1.5°C relative to 1850 to 1900 in all but the lowest scenario considered, and likely to exceed 2°C for the two high scenarios. All this suggests that the earth may be approaching a crossing point between

a tolerable level of warming (i.e., 2°C) and that which is dangerous to human well-being (i.e., above 2°C). Meanwhile, carbon dioxide emissions appear to be increasing worldwide, which can only exacerbate matters from the point of view global warming and climate change (Singer, 2013).

Research by Johan Rockström and colleagues (2009) of the Stockholm Resilience Centre shows that the earth is reaching a point where critical planetary boundaries are being stressed. These authors have identified nine such critical boundaries (see Figure 11.6). The evidence strongly suggests that the human imprint on the planet's environment is now so vast that the current geological period should be labelled the "Anthropocene"—the Age of Man, they claim. Figure 11.6 encompasses critical ecological sustainability dimensions, from climate change, to ocean acidification, to pollution, ozone depletion of the stratosphere, biodiversity, and land and freshwater reserves. According to these scholars, human pressure has reached a scale where the possibility of abrupt or irreversible global change, challenging our own well-being, can no longer be excluded. We are the first generation with the knowledge of how our activities influence the earth as a system, and thus the first generation with the power and the responsibility to change our relationship with the planet. Effective global stewardship can be built around the "planetary boundaries" concept, which aims to create a scientifically defined safe operating space within which humanity can continue to evolve and develop (Stockholm Resilience Centre, 2013: 11).

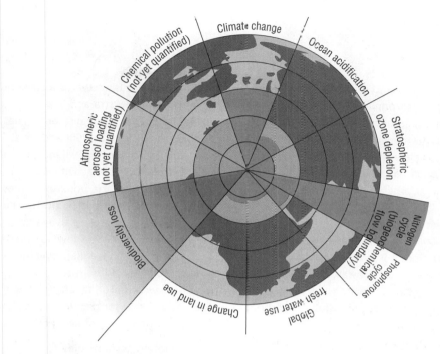

FIGURE 11.5   Planetary Boundaries

Note: The dark blue wedges represent an estimate of the current position of each boundary. The inner light grey shading represents the proposed safe operating space. Three boundaries have already been exceeded: rate of biodiversity loss; climate change; human interference with the nitrogen cycle.

Source: Rockström, Johan, Will Steffen, Kevin Noone, A. Persson, et al. (2009): 472. "A Safe Operating Space for Humanity." *Nature* 461: 472–475. Reprinted by permission from Macmillan Publishers Ltd.

Towards a Synthesis

However deeply their economic and political ideologies may differ, Marxists and free-market cornucopians share a basic optimism with regard to the future. Most environmentalists, by contrast, share the Malthusian view. The cornucopians, many of whom are economists, believe that population growth can fuel economic growth, hence well-being, and that problems such as vanishing resources and environmental degradation can be solved through technical and scientific innovation. Environmentalists are not so confident.

Nathan Keyfitz (1993) has asked why economics and the natural sciences (biology, ecology, etc.) generally differ so radically in the ways they conceptualize issues pertaining to population, environment, and resources. He suggests that more progress would be made in formulating an appropriate population policy if the two camps could agree on the nature of the problems involved and their urgency. But biologists/ecologists and economists perceive the world in very different ways. As Keyfitz explains it, part of the problem is that economists tend to see humans as the central fact of life on earth, whereas ecologists and biologists see

THE ECOLOGICAL FOOTPRINT

The overall impact of human activities on the environment can be estimated by calculating the so-called *ecological footprint* developed by Mathis Wackernagel and William Rees (1996). The exercise is designed to answer the question: *How much of the regenerative capacity of the biosphere is occupied by human activities?* The result is an account like the GDP or a bank statement, but rather than money, it adds up how much land and water is necessary to provide the resources we consume and to absorb the waste we generate (Global Footprint Network, 2013).

The World Wildlife Fund and the Global Footprint Network's *Living Planet Report 2012* shows that humanity's ecological footprint has increased to the point where the earth is unable to replace resources at the rate at which humans are consuming them; our footprint now exceeds the world's ability to regenerate by about 30 per cent. This means that the world is currently moving dangerously towards a state of "overshoot" (Hoekstra and Wiedmann, 2014). Demand on natural resources has doubled since the mid-1960s and we are currently using the equivalent of 1.5 planets to support our activities.

In Figure 11.7, the horizontal lines across the two graphs indicate the level of *ecological reserve* available to the average person. As shown in these graphs, this level has fallen over time, as the ecological footprints across the regions have risen. The *Living Planet Report 2012* calls for people to adopt a more sustainable way of living by:

- promoting technologies that lighten our footprint, especially those that can reduce climate-threatening carbon dioxide emissions;
- safeguarding ecosystems, especially fisheries and forests; and
- stemming biodiversity loss by protecting vital natural habitats in the earth's ecosystem.

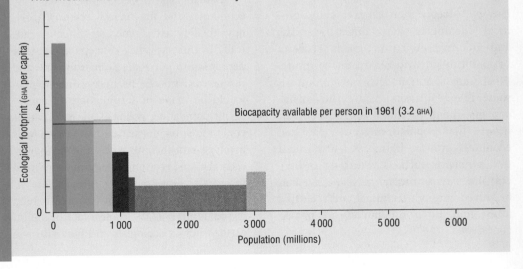

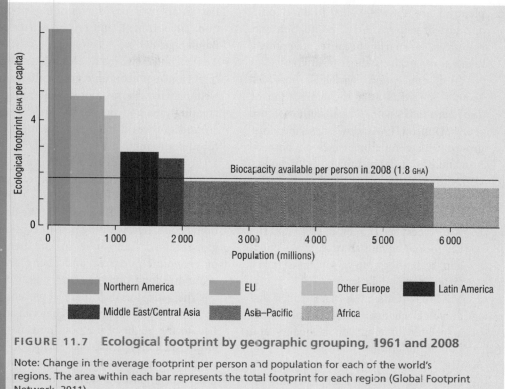

FIGURE 11.7 **Ecological footprint by geographic grouping, 1961 and 2008**

Note: Change in the average footprint per person and population for each of the world's regions. The area within each bar represents the total footprint for each region (Global Footprint Network, 2011).

Source: World Wildlife Fund and Global Footprint Network (2012): 9, Figure 5. Copyright © 2000 WWF (panda.org). (WWF/ZSL/GFN). Some rights reserved.

humans as just one species among many in the web of life. Economics has a time scale of years or decades at most, whereas biology and ecology are accustomed to thinking about evolutionary processes operating over millennia. Economics is concerned with inputs and outputs within a particular human economy; biology and ecology are concerned with the biosphere that sustains all life. Economics deals with two parts of a truncated commodity cycle—production and consumption; biology and ecology look at the much longer cycle of production,

consumption, and waste, and how all these affect the ecosystem.

As it turns out, the data these two disciplines have generated on the effects of population on the environment are far from conclusive. Keyfitz recognizes that statistical correlations cannot provide definitive answers to such complex questions. Biologists and ecologists see no need for a general law to prove the harm that would be done if the earth's human population were to continue growing. On the other hand, the data compiled by economists, though plentiful, are not well suited to developing any sort of general law of population and resources, primarily because economists take a comparatively short-term view.

Is a conceptual synthesis possible? Twenty-one years after the publication of *The Limits to Growth*, the lead author of that report, Donella H. Meadows, described four groups with competing views on population and ecological sustainability. Meadows (1993) identified each of these groups with a colour:

1. The "blues" see economic growth as the key to solving human problems. Capital and technology, they say, must grow faster than population.
2. The "reds" follow the Marxist idea that a radical change in the social system is needed to eradicate inequality and human suffering in the world.
3. The "greens" are environmentalists, concerned above all with sustaining the planetary ecosystem for all the earth's species. They believe that the global economy is too big and growing too fast, promoting over-consumption, and that long-term survival depends on reducing consumption and production as well as human population growth.
4. The "whites" emphasize self-reliance and put the local community ahead of the larger social system. They object to elite experts telling the people what they must do to deal with problems. Whites focus their efforts on making their local communities self-sufficient.

As different as these schools of thought appear, Meadows (1993) urged that they be reconciled, since each is correct in some respects and has something valuable to contribute to our greater understanding of the complex issues surrounding population, environment, and resources (see also Bandarage, 1997).

The blues, for instance, emphasize the importance of economic growth to human welfare. Growth promotes well-being by creating jobs and raising incomes. People around the world need to have meaningful and productive work in order to live a good life and provide for their families, and as long as economic progress continues, the population can enjoy a rising standard of living. The people of the developing countries, with the help of economic globalization, can share in the benefits of economic progress and rising socio-economic conditions.

The reds, for their part, represent the collective social conscience. They call attention to the plight of the poor and marginalized, and they insist that socioeconomic inequalities must be eliminated. Once this task is accomplished, the pace of population growth in the poor countries will slow and stabilize in line with the world average.

The greens focus on the environment and its fragility in the face of economic growth and globalization. But economic progress and environmental sustainability need not be opposing goals (Demeny, 1998). The world community should be able to achieve both objectives: increasing economic growth and ecological sustainability alike.

Finally, the whites emphasize the value of smallness and reliance on local community to find co-operative solutions to human challenges (e.g., Schumacher, 1974). If human communities can become more self-sufficient, the need for widespread economic production will be reduced, and, with it, the overuse of natural resources.

CANADA'S CARBON FOOTPRINT

Canada ranks among the most advanced industrialized countries of the world. As with other highly industrialized countries it too contributes to the growing problem of carbon emissions. Between 1990 and 2009, Canada's emission of CO_2 increased by over 20 per cent.

How does Canada compare in this regard to other OECD countries? Don Kerr (2014) has addressed this question. His report shows that relative to most other OECD countries, Canada has a higher level of carbon emissions.

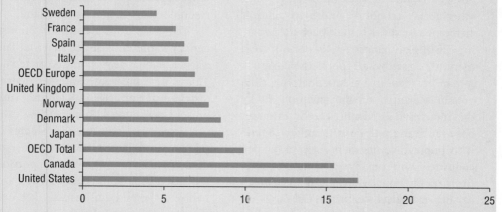

Source: Don Kerr. 2014. "Population growth, energy use, and environmental impact: Comparing the *Canadian and Swedish records* on CO_2 emissions." *Canadian Studies in Population* 41 (1 -2): 120 -143. Figure 1, page 122.

How can one explain Canada's relatively high carbon footprint?

According to Kerr, the reality is that Canada is a resource-rich country with major reserves of fossil fuels. This means that the incentive for moving away from fossil fuels is not strong as compared to countries with fewer reserves (e.g., Sweden). Much of its production of fossil fuels is generated for export, which represents a substantial source of revenues. Canada imposes relatively lower energy consumption taxes and prices on consumers and on industry for such things as gasoline, for example. Finally, Canada has strong resource-based economy that relies heavily on the use of fossil fuels for production and extraction purposes (e.g., mining of aluminum, copper, gypsum, nickel, potash fertilizers, and for production of wood pulp, etc.).

Conclusion

This chapter has looked at the Malthusian and Marxist perspectives on population and resources and their contemporary variants. Notwithstanding the divergence of opinions across the various schools of thought, rapid population growth can, and often does, have very serious consequences for society, resources, and the environment, even though its role is often indirect through other social, economic, and even political factors, or serves as a multiplier exacerbating existing problems. Yet, as we have seen, there are cases where population plays a minor or even inconsequential role. The pressures exerted on the environment by the industrialized countries, for instance, have much more to do with affluence than with population numbers. Less developed countries with rapidly growing but relatively poor populations have had much smaller ecological footprints. On the other hand, we might reasonably expect wealthy nations to more than poor ones to mitigate the damage they do to the environment. Transitional societies undergoing rapid industrialization—such as China and India, both population billionaires—will play an increasingly significant role in terms of pollution and resource depletion in the future, unless of course they find ways to avoid excessive damage to the environment during their rapid industrialization. The challenge for these societies is to promote economic growth while also accepting the costs of limiting environmental damage. In summary, population does play a role in ecological and resource problems, but its effects are synergetic or indirect, produced in interaction with other factors such as a society's level of affluence and consumption patterns, rapid economic growth, and the willingness and ability of governments to promote appropriate solutions to solve problems.

Notes for Further Study

Malthusian theory implies that unless population growth is checked, at some point density will increase to such an extent as to cause depletion of the food supply and other resources like water and arable land.

The simplest measure of population density is the ratio of people to all land in a given habitat (e.g., country or territory). This simple measure expresses density in terms of persons per unit of area (usually persons per square kilometre).

There are two main problems with the people-to-land ratio, however. First, it does not take into account the portions of any given geographic territory that are not habitable—mountains, rivers, lakes, oceans, deserts, and so forth (Foley et al., 2011). Second, as Ehrlich, Ehrlich, and Holdren (1977: 717) have pointed out, population density itself does not take into account the fact that it takes more than physical space to support a population. A shortage of fresh water or fertile soils, or a climate unsuitable for agriculture, for instance, "may make it difficult to supply even a sparse population in a given area with the necessities of existence. Large parts of Africa, North and South America, and Australia are or could quickly become overpopulated in this respect despite their low densities because over large areas they lack sufficient dependable water, good soils, or a moderate climate."

From the Malthusian point of view, the real concern is the number of people in a given area in relation to the means of subsistence in that area. The people-to-land ratio should therefore be refined to

$$\frac{\text{Population of geographic area } i}{\text{means of subsistence in geographic area } i}$$

A ratio greater than 1 would indicate "overpopulation"—the greater the ratio, the greater the degree of overpopulation. A ratio below 1 would denote overabundance of land or subsistence in relation to the number of people in that habitat.

In societies that rely mainly on agriculture, "means of subsistence" would include, at a minimum, the amount of land suitable for agricultural production, or the amount of the land area that is occupied by fresh water and other resources essential for the production of food. In an industrial economy, agricultural land remains essential, but other types of resources are also important: for instance, the raw materials and energy sources needed for technological development and economic productivity; education and health services for the labour force; capital investment; and so forth.

An important problem in such measures of population density is how to identify the "essential resources" for a given population in a given geographic area, and then to clearly specify measureable indicators of "essential resources." Various refinements to the measure of population density are presented by Plane and Rogerson (1994) and also by Shryock and Siegel (1972: 71).

Exercises

1. Write a brief essay on the applicability of Malthusian theory to today's population and resource situation in regard to the more developed and less developed countries. What new issues do we face today that Malthus could not have foreseen? Suggest interventions to help solve identified concerns.

2. Examine the Marxist theory of population and write a brief essay on its present and possible future applicability towards explaining the population and resources problems faced by the contemporary least developed nations (i.e., the poorest nations in the world). Is a Marxist analysis of the situation of any value from the point of view of population policy in these poor countries?

3. What are the major resource and environmental challenges facing the world in the twenty-first century? How does population figure in your assessment of this question?

Additional Reading

Cafaro, Philip, and Eileen Crist, ed. 2012. *Life on the Brink: Environmentalists Confront Overpopulation*. Athens, GA: University of Georgia Press.

Charbit, Yves. 2009. *Economic, Social and Demographic Thought in the XIXth Century: The Population Debate from Malthus to Marx*. Dordrecht: Springer.

Heilbroner, Robert L. 1999. *The Worldly Philosophers: The Lives, Times and Ideas of the Great Economic Thinkers*, 7th edn. Ney York: Simon and Schuster.

Hollander, Samuel. 1997. *The Economics of Thomas Robert Malthus*. Toronto: University of Toronto Press.

Lutz, Wolfgang, William P. Butz, and K. C. Samir, eds. 2014. *World Population and Human Capital in the Twenty-First Century*. Oxford: Oxford University Press.

Petersen, William. 1979. *Malthus*. Harvard, MA: Harvard University Press.

Randers, Jørgen. 2012. *2050: A Global Forecast for the Next Forty Years: A Report to the Club of Rome Commemorating the 40th Anniversary of the Limits to Growth*. White River Junction, VT: Chelsea Green Publishing.

Rockström, Johan, and Mattias Klum. 2013. *The Human Quest: Prospering Within Planetary Boundaries*. Stockholm: Langenskiolds.

Tyrell, Toby. 2013. *On Gaia: A Critical Investigation of the Relationship Between Life and Earth*. Princeton: Princeton University Press.

Wrigley, E.A., and David Souden. 1986. *The Works of Thomas Robert Malthus* (8 vols.) London: William Pickering.

Note

1. Additional reviews based on the National Research Council report are found in the World Bank's *World Development Report for 1992* (World Bank, 1992).

Demographic Change and Policy Concerns

Introduction

Momentous change on a global scale often results from complex socioeconomic processes unfolding over long stretches of time. Unfortunately, in many cases, our understanding of causal dynamics responsible for change can only be retrospective. The global financial crisis of 2008 exemplifies this type of conundrum. The global community seemed unprepared for the massive downturn catapulted by years of mismanagement within the financial system. Could the financial crisis have been averted? What policies would have been necessary to avert this crisis? These are the types of questions policy analysts ask when assessing long-term consequences of current trends within their disciplinary domains. The task of population analysts is to evaluate long-term social, economic, and environmental consequences of demographic trends in order to inform government officials on possible policy options to affect desirable change for the benefit of their societies.

Proper assessment of population dynamics and their wider sociological consequences is crucially important for planning purposes. Demography lies at the core of all major sociological change, and plays a role in many of the existing social, economic, and environmental challenges confronting the global community. For example, population growth along with accelerated industrial and urban expansion over the twentieth century is a contributing factor for rising levels of carbon emissions and thereby climate change (Barnosky et al., 2011; Mann, 2014; Smil, 2008). Clearly, the role population plays with such problems is complex and is seldom a direct causal factor; nonetheless, it seems undeniable that more people in conjunction with growing affluence exacerbate resource and environmental dilemmas at both national and global scales.

As indicated by Dirk Helbing (2013), the world today consists of complex networks of interdependent systems that are vulnerable to failure at all scales. An adverse change in one system will have adverse cascading effects on other systems. Population is an inseparable component of these systems. A global economic crisis, for instance, will catapult crises in global systems of production and trade, as well as other systems including agriculture and health care; increased unemployment worldwide would provoke more organized criminal activity and there would be more clandestine movements of people across international borders.

Clearly, given the interconnected nature of systems central to our well-being as a global community, countries cannot view themselves as independent disconnected entities invulnerable to developments elsewhere on the planet. For instance, emergent lethal viruses can spread rapidly across international borders as a function of both our access to advanced systems of transport and travel, and the variable efficacy of national health systems in coping with communicable disease epidemics.

With specific reference to global population, the world has seen major fertility declines over recent decades and rates of natural increase have been falling for some time. However, population growth is far from over. In 1950, world population stood at 2.5 billion. By 1990, it had doubled to 5 billion, and according to United Nations projections, it will have tripled by 2020. Notwithstanding declining growth rates since the early 1970s, the population will continue increase over the twenty-first century, will likely reach 9.6 billion in 2050, and possibly exceed 10 billion by 2100 (United Nations Department of Social and Economic Affairs Population Division, 2013a: 2).

In fact, there is considerable *momentum* for further growth that is inherent in the current age structure of the world's population. Most of this momentum is due to the relative youthfulness of the age compositions of the developing countries, and, in particular, the least developed countries. As a whole, the percentage of population under 25 years of age in the less developed countries represents nearly 50 per cent of their total population (United Nations Department of Economic and Social Affairs Population Division, 2013a: 7). This means that over the course of the remaining portion of the twenty-first century, the world will see millions of reproducing young couples, which will account for considerable growth. Among the possible consequences of this demographic situation, the countries affected—and more broadly, the world—may see a rise in sociopolitical instability if this large youthful component of the population in poor countries is deprived of meaningful employment and a decent standard of living.

High rates of population growth and deteriorating standards of living cannot be seen as challenges restricted solely to the developing countries. Rapid population growth coupled with rising poverty, unemployment, and sociopolitical conflict in poor countries are key reasons behind the rising waves of illegal and asylum-seeking migrations to some of the wealthy nations, which, at the same time, must rely increasingly on labour migration to help combat their growing demographic deficit and supplement a dwindling native born workforce. Yet, as was indicated in Chapter 9, for some receiving countries in the West and also Japan, immigration has come to be viewed as both a problem and a solution: immigrants are increasingly needed, though not necessarily wanted as citizens (Castles and Miller, 2009; Marfleet, 2006). How receiving countries cope with this conundrum represents a very challenging problem. How can the world's developed countries cope with their shortfall in fertility and consequent demographic maturity over the long term? Is increased immigration the most viable solution?

And what can poor countries do to cope with their demographic and socioeconomic problems? How can they help themselves out of the poverty trap? Are reduced rates of population growth the answer? In this chapter, we will address these questions through a discussion of population policy and its relationship to broader sociological and socioeconomic trends. We will begin by examining population policy as a concept, before making an overview of current demographic policy concerns among developed and developing countries, and concluding with a discussion of population policy issues from the point of view of Canadian society.

Population Policy

Population policy may be defined as an objective plan formulated by government to reduce, increase, or stabilize population growth rates over some specified period of time. Population policies are usually

---

Sociologists often speak of inequality in "life chances" between social categories. By this, it is meant that there is inequality in not only how long people live but also variation in the quality of life. The following table summarizes a few macro-level indicators of the disparate life chances between the ten poorest countries in Africa and the ten richest countries in the world, looked at two points in time: mid-1990s and early 2000s. As can be easily seen from these data, the two sets of countries differ noticeably along the various indicators.

Two worlds, different life chances; ten poorest countries in Africa and the ten richest countries in the world, mid-1990s and early 2000s

1. GNP per capita	1996	2003	Absolute Change
Average, ten poorest countries in Africa	$227	$174	−$53
Average, ten richest countries in the world	$13 020	$32 623	+$19 603
2. Life expectancy at birth (years)	**1992**	**2003**	**Absolute Change**
Average, ten poorest countries in Africa	46.8	44.3	−2.5
Average, ten richest countries in the world	76.1	78.8	+2.7
3. Risk of maternal death		**2000**	
Average, ten poorest countries in Africa		1 in 10	
Average, ten richest countries in the world		1 in 9 040	
4. Infant mortality rate per 1 000 live births	**1995**	**2005**	**Absolute Change**
Average, ten poorest countries in Africa	122.5	84.5	−38
Average, ten richest countries in the world	6.47	4.1	−2.37

Note: The ten poorest countries in Africa are Ethiopia, Burundi, Congo (DRC), Sierra Leone, Malawi, Niger, Mozambique, Rwanda, Uganda, and Central Africa Republic. The ten richest countries are represented by Norway, Switzerland, USA, Japan, Denmark, Sweden, UK, Finland, Austria, and the Netherlands.

Sources: Adapted from data in Turshen (2010): 245–64. Also, some information taken from the Population Reference Bureau World Population Data Sheets for the years indicated.

motivated by a government's perceived need to avert foreseen problems of a social, economic, or environmental nature thought to be linked to prevailing and projected demographic conditions. A policy aimed at affecting the demography of a nation is therefore also viewed as a vehicle for engendering desirable long-term socioeconomic outcomes, and is best understood as part of a broader set of societal concerns by governments.

Strictly speaking in regard to demography itself, the aim of population policies is to effect *quantitative change* through one or more of the three major demographic variables—fertility, mortality, and migration—in order to reduce or increase the rate of population growth. Less often, governments may implement policies directed at changing the composition of their population, thus effecting *qualitative demographic change*. For example, a country's immigration policy may be modified to encourage immigration from certain areas of the world with the goal of changing the county's racial or ethnic composition.

Policies with a direct bearing on fertility, mortality, or migration are called *direct population policies*. There is a long history of such policies in the developing countries. Family planning programs are a good example. Aimed at affecting birth rates, family planning programs are designed to bring about fertility decline by giving women access to effective contraceptives and education about fertility so that they may gain greater control over their reproductive lives, particularly in terms of the number and spacing of children they have.

Indirect policies are programs designed to influence non-demographic variables that have an indirect impact on the key demographic variables. Indirect policies include programs aimed at improving population health, such as immunization programs and anti-malaria campaigns in poor countries. These types of programs, if successful, can reduce rates of infant, childhood, and maternal mortality. Over the long term, these same programs may cause, indirectly, a decline in parents' demand for children, because as child survival probabilities improve, parents will desire fewer offspring. Policies aimed at improving the status of women could be expected to have a similar indirect effect on fertility rates: as women's status improves, women gain greater autonomy over their personal lives, which we would expect to translate into delayed marriage and later timing of childbearing (National Research Council and Institute of Medicine, 2005).

Figure 12.1 summarizes the stages of population policy creation. Typically, population policy is formulated on the basis of past and current trends in fertility, mortality, and migration; rate of natural increase and age structure; and the anticipated future trajectory of these variables. Population projections over some specified period (usually 25 or 50 years) are formed by taking the central demographic variables of fertility, mortality, and migration and applying different assumptions about whether, when, how, and to what extent current trends might change over the projection period. Projections are usually executed under "high," "medium," "low," and "no change" scenarios to account for varying degrees of change in the variables. These scenarios provide an indication of the extent of population growth that could be expected as well as what changes in age structure may result

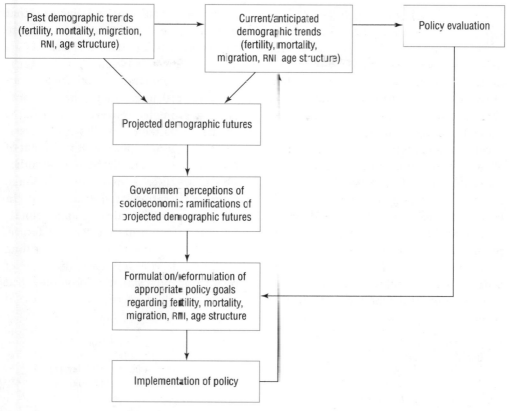

FIGURE 12.1   Demographic policy process

from the interplay of natural increase and net migration.

Governments tend to take very seriously the projection exercise and the possible socioeconomic ramifications of the projected demographic futures. Attention then turns to what policy or policies may be implemented to alter the projected increase/decrease in population and effects on age structure. For example, in populations where fertility has been below replacement for many years, population projections could forecast eventual deficits in the working-age population. Officials might wish to respond to such a prognosis by introducing policies to increase birth rates. The opposite scenario could prevail in poor developing countries, where persisting high birth rates might lead to predictions of continued population growth and a superabundance of workers. In such circumstances, officials would likely recommend policies aimed at fertility reduction. Once a policy has been devised and implemented, governments need to monitor the demographic trends over time in order to gauge the effectiveness of the policy, which may need to be adjusted or replaced if it fails to produce the desired demographic changes.

Population Policy–Societal Interrelationships

As already suggested, the process of formulating and implementing population policy always takes place within a broader societal context. No policy is ever implemented without first having some idea of the socioeconomic and environmental implications of current and projected population trends (Birg, 1995). In this sense, population policy is but one part of a broader societal configuration involving—beside demographic considerations—social structure, economy, polity, and culture.

Figure 12.2 is intended to map out, broadly, the complex interrelationship between population policy and the key government and societal factors that shape it. The diagram assumes a close connection (though not necessarily a perfect correlation) between type of government (i.e., democratic or otherwise) and other societal forces that either promote or fail to promote the overall well-being of citizens. This sketch implies that societal well-being is an important determinant of a country's demographic regime—in other words, whether it is post-transitional, transitional, or delayed transitional. In turn, the prevailing demographic conditions and those projected into the future, as understood and perceived by a ruling government, will influence the type of population policy that is promoted and implemented. Governments in liberal

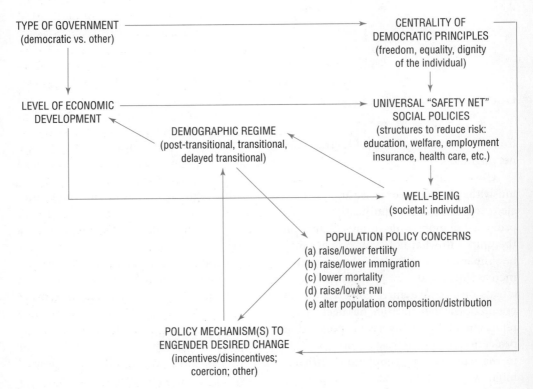

FIGURE 12.2   **Population policy in societal context**

democracies by their very nature must promote policies that are consistent with the basic principles of democracy: freedom, equality, and dignity of the individual. These principles are not always upheld by non-democratic governments, which, as a result, may be much more assertive in the kinds of policies they introduce into their societies. For example, officials in non-democratic regimes would see the principle of individual freedom as secondary to what the state perceives as most important.

Depending on how they perceive the demographic and socioeconomic conditions of their country, government officials—democratically elected or not—will devise population policies according to four different aims:

1. to raise the rate of natural increase;
2. to reduce the rate of natural increase;
3. to maintain the current rate of natural increase; and
4. to achieve population growth through immigration.

In liberal democracies, impediments to population policy include the lack of a political basis for long-term planning (since elected politicians typically hold office for just a few years), the emphasis on individual freedom and welfare as paramount to broader societal objectives, and the difficulty of addressing environmental concerns in any policy aimed at promoting population growth rather than decline in the future. Apart from these obstacles, there is a tendency for government officials in democratic societies to see their constituencies only in terms of organized groups, and so the government's role becomes one of arbitrating

competing claims. The interests of organized groups in democratic societies may relate less to the population as a whole than to specific concerns, such as family, feminism, the environment, health, multiculturalism, refugees, and so forth. Furthermore, demographic policy matters seldom receive widespread attention from the public in democratic societies (McNicoll, 1995).

Non-democratic regimes have significantly greater leeway in the realm of population policy. For example, China's family planning program, with its one-child policy as its centrepiece, was introduced in 1979 amid a belief among governing officials that it was necessary for the good of the nation to curb population growth rates. Chinese officials wanted to actualize a predictable trajectory of population growth with the goal of eventually stabilizing population at about 1.2 billion by the end of the twentieth century (Bongaarts and Greenhalgh, 1985; Greenhalgh, 1986). To do this, they devised a set of regulations governing family size. With some exceptions, all Chinese couples in urban areas and all government employees must opt for a one-child limit or else they will face a variety of penalties administered by family planning committees at the provincial and local levels. Couples who wish to have more than one child may be allowed to pay a large fine (known as a "social maintenance fee") over many years; the funds generated by these fines are used by the government to cover costs of education and other basic services for "extra" children (Greenhalgh, 1986; Winckler, 2002).

China's one-child policy is not applied universally across the country. Instead, the Chinese government has divided the country into three regions, each with its own fertility targets and, accordingly, its own degree of flexibility in how the policy is applied. In the first region, only 20 to 50 per cent of childbearing women are permitted to have a second child. Among the provinces in this group are Hubei and those lying along a narrow coastal strip running from Heilongjiang to Zhejiang, where about a third of China's population lives. A second region, which comprises roughly 55 per cent of China's population, includes the central and southern provinces. Here, parents are allowed a second child if the first is a girl or if the parents are experiencing significant hardship because they have only one child. The local cadres are left the task of judging what constitutes "significant hardship." Under these conditions, 50 to 70 per cent of the women in this region would be allowed to have a second child. The third group of provinces, which includes Guizhou, Hainan, Nei Menggu, Ningxia, Qinghai, Tibet, Xinjiang, and Yunnan, contains the greatest proportion of ethnic minorities. Here, the rules are more permissive: at least 70 per cent of women are allowed to have a second child, and in Xinjiang, approximately 40 per cent of women are allowed a third (Attané, 2002: 104).

In strictly demographic terms, China's one-child policy has been highly successful. In 1975, China's rate of natural increase was one of the highest in the world (1.7 per cent); by 1985, after several years of the one-child policy, it had declined to 1.1 per cent and to just 0.6 per cent in 2006, well below the world rate of 1.2 per cent (Population Reference Bureau, 1975, 1985, 2006). From a human rights perspective, however, the one-child policy has some distinct problems (see Aird, 1990; Berelson and Lieberson, 1979; Lim, 2006; McLarty, 2006; Potts,

2006; Smith, 2006). Most notably, it has created a certain disdain for female infants, and as a result, there has been an increase in the level of sex-selective abortions in the country and more reported cases of neglect, abandonment, and even infanticide of newborn girls (Bongaarts, 2013). As a consequence of almost three decades of imbalanced sex ratios, young Chinese men today are having difficulty finding young marriageable brides. The rapid decrease in fertility rates in conjunction with improved mortality conditions has led to an increased proportion of elderly people in the population. With the lack of adequate pension coverage, more and more young Chinese couples will be solely responsible for the care of one child and four parents, a situation that has been called the 4:2:1 problem (Hesketh, Lu, and Xing, 2006). All this has led analysts Weng Feng, Yong Cai, and Baochang Gu (2012: 126–7) to declare:

History will remember China's one-child policy as the most extreme example of state intervention in human reproduction in the modern era. History will also likely view this policy as a very costly blunder, born of the legacy of a political system that planned population numbers in the same way that it planned the production of goods. It showcases the impact of a policy making process that, in the absence of public deliberations, transparency, debate, and accountability, can do permanent harm to the members of a society. The one-child policy will be added to the other deadly errors in recent Chinese history, including the famine in 1959–61 caused largely by the industrialization

BABY BOOM A PERK THAT ONLY ELITE CAN AFFORD

The rich and famous are paying exorbitant fines to bypass China's controversial one-child policy

China's controversial one-child policy, which has led to forced abortions and sterilizations, is facing a new assault from an unexpected group: the rich and famous.

The *nouveaux riches*, an increasingly powerful class in China, are paying big money to be exempted from the one-child limit, and this could jeopardize efforts to control the growth of the world's most populous nation, a Chinese official warned.

Some wealthy families and show-business celebrities are paying $20,000 or more in official penalties for evading the one-child limit, and they see it as a small price to pay for the privilege, Chinese media have reported.

The latest revelations will fuel the outrage of the ordinary masses, already bitterly resentful of the perks and privileges of the wealthy. The widening gap between the rich and poor has sparked fears among government officials who worry that the gap will destabilize Chinese society and trigger class conflict.

The one-child policy was introduced in 1979 to restrain China's fast-rising population, which has reached 1.3 billion today. Most urban couples are limited to one child and most rural couples are limited to two children.

The policy, enforced with ruthless zeal in some parts of the country, has managed to moderate the growth of China's population over the past two decades. But now there is a growing risk of a "population rebound," according to the latest warning.

Zhang Weiqing, the top Chinese family-planning official, said the widening gap between rich and poor is threatening the one-child policy, since wealthy families often "disdain" the policy and simply "pay to have as many children as they like," the state-run Xinhua news agency reported yesterday.

The gulf between China's rich and poor grows wider every year. In 2005, the most recent data available, the top 10 per cent of urban dwellers were earning 9.2 times more than the bottom 10 per cent. The gap had increased from the previous year, when the richest were earning 8.9 times more than the poorest.

At the same time, the average urban resident is earning 3.2 times more than the average farmer, an "alarming" gap in comparison to other countries, another Chinese official said in February.

While this widening income gap is dangerous enough, some of the most extreme anger is aimed at business tycoons and wealthy showbiz personalities who seem to consider themselves above the law.

(continued)

"We found out that most celebrities and rich people have two children, and 10 per cent have three," Yu Xuejun, a senior official of China's population and family planning commission, said in an interview with a Beijing newspaper in March.

"This phenomenon must be stopped," he said.

The government vowed that any celebrities or tycoons who violate the one-child policy will be prohibited from receiving awards or honours in the future. The idea is to hit the celebrities in their public image, rather than just their pocketbook. "They will have to pay a dear price," Mr. Yu declared.

But it's unclear whether the penalties are working. One affluent Beijing woman said she and her husband had happily paid $13,000 for the right to have a second child. "This sum of money is nothing to our family," she said to a reporter from China Youth Daily.

Some wealthy families have reportedly paid more than $100,000 for the right to have a second child.

Earlier this year, an opinion survey of almost 8,000 people on a Chinese website found that the vast majority were outraged that wealthy families could violate the one-child policy.

One professor at a Beijing university commented that the exemption is the same as allowing a wealthy person to drive through the red lights at traffic intersections.

Other commentators have criticized celebrities such as basketball star Yao Ming and Hollywood actress Zhang Ziyi, both of whom have casually remarked in interviews that they might decide to have several children.

Population rebound

China's vigorous economic growth has produced an increasingly powerful wealthy class that doesn't mind paying fines for an exemption to the country's one-child policy.

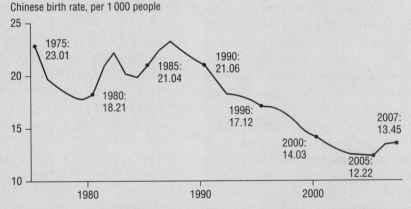

Chinese birth rate, per 1 000 people

1975: 23.01
1980: 18.21
1985: 21.04
1990: 21.06
1996: 17.12
2000: 14.03
2005: 12.22
2007: 13.45

Source: Carrie Cockburn/The Globe and Mail; World Development Indicators; CIA World Fact Book.
Note: 2006 and 2007 are estimates.

and collectivization campaign of the later 1950s, and the Cultural Revolution of the late 1960s and early 1970s. While these grave mistakes both cost tens of millions of lives, the harms done were relatively short-lived and were corrected quickly afterward. The one-child policy, in contrast, will surpass them in impact by its role in creating a society with a seriously undermined family and kin structure, and a whole generation of future elderly and their children whose well-being will be seriously jeopardized. (Reprinted by permission of John Wiley and Sons).

In recent years, the one-child policy has been relaxed somewhat. The most recent revision, introduced in late 2013, allows families to have a second child if either parent is an only child (Ouyang, 2013). Notwithstanding this change, there is little doubt that the policy is fundamentally coercive, still affecting about two-thirds of the Chinese population (Cai, 2012). This change does nothing by way of recognizing or respecting a couple's freedom to choose the number of children they want; this element of state control over the individual remains steadfast in the policy. Clearly, the Chinese population policy would be inconceivable in a democratic society, not only because of its punitive dimensions but because it violates fundamental principles of democracy.

We can compare policies aimed at curbing population growth in China with similar efforts in India, the world's largest democracy. With its 1.5 per cent rate of natural increase in 2013—still above the world level of 1.2 per cent (Population Reference Bureau, 2013)—India maintains one of the highest rates of natural increase among transitional societies. Since gaining independence in 1947, India's population has trebled in size, and projections indicate that India's 2013 population of 1.28 billion will likely reach 1.44 billion in 2025 and 1.65 billion by 2050 (Dyson, Cassen, and Visaria, 2004; Jones and Leete, 2002; Population Reference Bureau, 2013). Table 12.1 has a breakdown of

TABLE 12.1   Demographic indicators in 2013 and population projections to 2025 and 2050 for China and India

	China	India
Population (billions)	1.36	1.28
Rate of natural increase (%)	0.5	1.5
CBR per 1 000 population	12	22
CDR per 1 000 population	7	7
Total fertility rate per woman	1.5	2.4
Infant mortality rate per 1 000 live births	13	44
% population < 15	13.0	30.0
% population 15–65	73.0	64.0
% population 65+	9.0	6.0
Population projection, 2025 (billions)	1.41	1.44
Population projection, 2050 (billions)	1.31	1.65

Source: Population Reference Bureau (2013), *World Population Data Sheet*. Reprinted with permission.

India's and China's varying demographic profiles as of 2013.

In its implementation of population policies, India has been less successful than might have been expected. One of the reasons stems from low popular acceptance of family planning programs. In the early days of the program, Indian government officials tried to promote the rhythm method and the widespread use of condoms. It soon became clear that this approach was not working. In desperation, the government began a campaign of wide-scale sterilization. Mass vasectomy "camps" were established in the early 1970s, and in some parts of the nation large incentives were offered to men who agreed to the procedure. The campaign resulted in more than 2 million sterilizations in 1972 and over 3 million in 1973. A year later, however, the program was abandoned owing to a combination of problems, including funding cuts, a large incidence of health complications related to the procedure, and rising doubts among officials about the effectiveness of this policy intervention. The government also attempted to reformulate the abortion law to make the procedure more accessible to women, but with limited success.

In 1976, a new sterilization campaign was initiated. New laws made sterilization mandatory for couples with three or more children. Though these laws were never actually accepted by the Indian president, many local administrators adopted the policy of compulsory sterilization and attempted to achieve the "targets" set by government officials by relying on police and bully squads to round up men for the operation (Potts and Selman, 1978: 318). Ultimately, the excesses of this campaign helped to bring down the government of Indira Ghandi and set back the progress of family planning.

In spite of the many problems that India has faced in applying its family planning policies over the years, there is undeniable evidence that these policies have had some effect in lowering fertility: "In short," Tim Dyson, Robert Cassen, and Leela Visaria (2004: 348) write, "the program has facilitated the country's fertility decline." Undoubtedly, China's relative success in meeting demographic goals through family planning policy can be attributed to the Chinese government's much greater freedom to impose tough policies under little risk of popular rebellion.

Figure 12.2 (page 544) suggested that a country's demographic regime—whether post-transitional, transitional, or delayed transitional—is closely linked to the level of societal well-being: the greater the level of well-being, the greater the likelihood that birth and death rates will be under control, keeping population growth rates at desirably low levels. The historical experience of Western societies fits this proposition. The West's fertility transition occurred as standards of living improved. Better socioeconomic conditions brought lower rates of infant and childhood mortality, which meant couples, confident that their children would reach adulthood, could plan to have fewer children. Mortality improvements have helped promote the small-family ideal, keeping fertility levels low in Western societies. By contrast, fertility rates and rates of natural increase are typically high in settings characterized by high levels of poverty, where having a large family is seen as a way to minimize risk and uncertainty. In countries frequently afflicted by famines, droughts, and other natural calamities, children are long-term investments that help reduce risk for families and ensure security for parents in old age (Cain, 1982, 1983, 1985, 1987; Caldwell, 1982; Dercon, 2005).

POPULATION POLICY IN ROMANIA

A famous piece of population policy was put into effect in Romania by the country's totalitarian leader Nicolae Ceausescu. In 1957, Ceausescu's communist government issued a decree making abortion available, on request, to Romanian women. Given that birth control was then generally unavailable, abortion became the principal means of fertility control in Romania. In 1965, for example, 80 per cent of all conceptions ended in abortion (Berelson, 1979; Frejka, 1983; Pop-Eleches, 2006).

As the birth rate fell to low levels, Ceausescu and his officials began to worry that population declines, were they not to reverse, would jeopardize the country's economic progress. Thus, in 1966, the government changed its policy, restricting abortion, making it available only under certain restrictive conditions, such as risk to the life of the mother, risk of deformity to the fetus, and rape. With the sudden withdrawal of abortion on demand, the birth rate jumped, in 1967, to an unprecedented rate of 27.4 per 1000 population. Fertility rates would eventually level off and, by the late 1970s, return to "normal" levels. However, the boost in fertility brought about by the draconian policy restricting abortion actually created an unanticipated baby boom of a magnitude similar to the one experienced in the United States after World War II (Berelson, 1979). The long-term sociological effects of the abortion decree are still being felt today in Romania. For instance, an ongoing matter for the society is the care of an estimated 170000 orphaned children as they progress through life, the remnants of the aggressive policy to boost the national birth rate through abortion restrictions (Nelson, Fox, and Zeanah, 2013).

Social Policy and Its Connection to Population Policy

As we noted earlier, in general, the idea behind population policy is to intervene in demographic matters to ultimately enhance the well-being of the population. Closely related to population policy is social policy. *Social policy* refers to the legal structures created and maintained by a government to ensure minimum standards of well-being for the population (also known as *public policy*). It typically operates through one of two principles: (1) the mitigation of risk for individuals and their families under conditions of loss (examples include employment insurance, health insurance, and welfare), and (2) the maintenance of equity standards in access to socioeconomic opportunities and human rights (such as rights and freedoms of the individual, universal education, old-age security, safety standards on the road and in the workplace, etc.).

Social policy has an indirect bearing on the demography of a society because it aims to reduce insecurity and hardship among the people while enhancing their overall socioeconomic well-being; in these conditions, there is a greater likelihood that fertility rates may be controlled.

Democratic societies are often called "welfare democracies" because they are based on the principle of the *social contract*—the idea that the people agree to be governed by elected individuals who, in turn, are expected to act in the best interests of the electorate and society at large. It is understood that citizens are to help pay for the services and benefits received from government (universal health care, education, public pensions, and so on); as a result, workers pay a portion of their wages or salary to the government, which in turn uses the revenues for the wider benefit of the society. Those with greater income are expected to contribute more so as to maintain equity. Democratic governments may also generate revenue by collecting corporate taxes and by taking interest from government investments. All of these funds are used to help maintain societal well-being through the provision of "safety nets" (social security systems) designed to protect the citizen who, by virtue of misfortune or circumstance, suffers a setback in life (e.g., disability, illness, unemployment).

Not all governments can or are willing to exercise the degree of political will required to implement the extensive social security systems found in most Western democracies. In the extreme, this is often true of despotic regimes whose main interests lie in preserving power and achieving (through corruption) financial gain. In other cases, where the political will is present, the cost of building up an extensive

"safety net" is prohibitive. This situation characterizes many poor developing countries today.

To use statistical terms, the correlation between type of government and level of socioeconomic development is certainly not perfect. However, as measured in Human Development Index (HDI) scores, it is true that liberal democratic regimes provide greater social and economic stability than do authoritarian regimes (United Nations Development Programme, 2002). Democratic countries are generally more successful at promoting economic growth while maintaining individual freedoms. The greater a government's ability to generate wealth, the greater its ability to implement and maintain safety net structures for the benefit of its citizens. It is partly because of their success in achieving wealth that many welfare democracies enjoy a level of well-being and prosperity that is unmatched by poor developing countries.

China may prove to be an example of a non-democratically governed society that experiences significant economic growth. However, it remains, in important respects, a problematic exception to the principle that democratic countries have healthier social systems. Economic development in the country is occurring very unevenly. Certainly, as a by-product of the country's "economic miracle," wages have risen, and the middle class is getting larger. But while millions of Chinese people have become richer, hundred of millions of others have not, and inequality is actually increasing. Moreover, more than half of the Chinese population still toils in agriculture, many of them living in abject poverty. With the country undergoing a transition to a market economy, the program of lifetime employment once guaranteed to

ON HUMAN RIGHTS

On 10 December 1948, the General Assembly of the United Nations adopted and proclaimed the *Universal Declaration of Human Rights*. Its key principle is that all human beings are born with equal and inalienable rights and fundamental freedoms. Among its articles are the following three, dealing with freedom of movement, family and marriage, and the right for adequate standards of living.

Article 13

(1) Everyone has the right to freedom of movement and residence within the borders of each State.

(2) Everyone has the right to leave any country, including his own, and to return to his country.

Article 14

(1) Everyone has the right to seek and to enjoy in other countries asylum from persecution.

Article 16

(1) Men and women of full age, without any limitation due to race, nationality, or religion, have the right to marry and to found a family. They are entitled to equal rights as to marriage, during marriage and its dissolution.

(2) Marriage shall be entered into only with the free and full consent of the intending spouses.

(3) The family is the natural and fundamental group unit of society and is entitled to protection by society and the State.

Article 25

(1) Everyone has the right to a standard of living adequate for the health and well-being of himself and of his family, including food, clothing, housing, and medical care and necessary social services, and the right to security in the event of unemployment, sickness, disability, widowhood, old age, or other lack of livelihood in circumstances beyond his control.

(2) Motherhood and childhood are entitled to special care and assistance. All children, whether born in or out of wedlock, shall enjoy the same social protection (United Nations, 1998).

all Chinese citizens is now eroding fast. Millions of workers have lost their jobs in the wake of economic restructuring. All the while, human rights in China exist only on paper; there has been no significant liberalization of political freedoms in China to speak of, according to Human Rights Watch (2013: 300–13).

Demographic Concerns: A Global Perspective

The Demographic Divide

There exists a vast demographic divide between the developed and developing countries. On one side are the impoverished countries (once called "The Third World," currently numbering 49 countries, according to the UN) with relatively high birth and death rates and low life expectancies; on the other are the mostly wealthy countries characterized by low birth rates and high life expectancies, very low annual rates of population growth, if not decline, and demographic aging. Somewhere in between these two extremes are the emerging economies (i.e., transitional societies). Of growing concern are the growing disparities between the poorest countries and the rest in terms of standards of living, health conditions, and socioeconomic well-being (Sutcliffe, 2001; Therborn, 2006). The tripartite conception of countries masks wide variations within each of set of countries. In any case, the notion of a developed and a developing world is somewhat incomplete in describing the broad contours of the world's demography. For example, in some developed regions (such as Eastern Europe), population decline is already underway, while in others (the United States, for instance), population continues to grow with no sign of imminent decline. At the same time, some more advanced countries of the developing world (such as South Korea) have been experiencing below-replacement birth rates for quite some time and are facing the prospect of population decline in the near future.

Mary Kent and Carl Haub (2005: 9) are among those who have asked what explains the widening demographic divide between the poorest countries and the rest of the world. Among the world's most underdeveloped nations, some factors we can point to are widespread poverty, populations that are predominantly rural, high rates of illiteracy, limited family planning efforts by governments, and very weak or absent "safety nets" for the people. Given these prevailing conditions, relatively high fertility and rapid population growth are bound to persist in the poorest countries. At the other end of the spectrum, argue Kent and Haub (2005), the persistence of sub-replacement fertility in wealthy countries may be attributed to a combination of sociological and economic factors, including the disjuncture between material expectations and rising economic uncertainty among young couples, the inhibiting effects of this condition on marriage and childbearing, the difficulty for young people of securing permanent employment, and the problem of securing independent housing as a result of the rising cost of living. Clearly, the conditions giving rise to high or low fertility are quite different. It follows, therefore, that population policy orientations for these two sets of societies would be vastly different.

As a way to help poor countries improve their standards of living and their levels of social and economic development, the United Nations in 2000 initiated a multi-year program that would provide tangible benchmarks for measuring progress in eight areas, each having various numbers of targets and indicators. The UN's *Millennium Development Goals* (MDGs), designed to be achieved by 2015, are as follows:

1. Eradicate extreme hunger and poverty by halving the number of people living

on less than $1 a day and halving the number of people suffering from malnutrition.

2. Make primary education universal by ensuring that all children are able to complete primary schooling.

3. Eliminate gender disparities in primary and secondary schooling, preferably by 2005 and no later than 2015.

4. Reduce child mortality by cutting the under-five death rate by two-thirds.

5. Improve maternal health by reducing the maternal mortality rate by three-quarters.

6. Halt and reverse the spread of HIV/AIDS, malaria, and other deadly diseases.

7. Reduce by half the number of people living without access to safe drinking water and sanitation.

8. Develop a global partnership for development by reforming aid and trade programs, with special treatment for the poorest countries. (Cheru and Bradford, 2005; Sachs and McArthur, 2005; United Nations Development Programme, 2005: 39)

As noted by UN Secretary-General Ban Ki-moon in *The Millennium Development Goals Report 2013*, substantial progress has been made in meeting many of the targets—including halving the number of people living in extreme poverty and the proportion of people without sustainable access to improved sources of drinking water. Remarkable gains have been made in the fight against malaria and tuberculosis (United Nations, 2013a). There have been visible improvements in critical health areas, especially the reduction of under-five mortality and maternal mortality, as well as improved access to antiretroviral therapy for those afflicted with HIV. And primary

education levels have increased substantially among boys and girls.

The *Report* also points to critical areas in need of greater effort. Notwithstanding progress in reducing hunger in poor countries, much more effort is needed in this area. As well, there is growing need to improve maternal health because too many women die in childbirth. More than 2 billion people lack basic sanitation facilities. Major gaps remain in basic knowledge about HIV and its prevention in the regions hardest hit by the epidemic; access to antiretroviral therapy must therefore expand significantly. Too many children are still denied primary education. Environmental sustainability is under severe threat.

Wide gaps remain among regions in degree of success towards meeting the MDGs targets, especially in the area of population health. For instance, mortality to children under age five has improved in the Americas, Europe, and western Pacific regions, much in line with expectations, but insufficient progress has been made in Africa, Eastern Mediterranean, and Southeast Asia. There has been insufficient improvement in extent of coverage of measles immunization, contraceptive prevalence, access to skilled birth attendance, and basic sanitation facilities (Moran and Stevenson, 2014: 528; World Health Organization, 2014).

The United Nations in collaboration with governments, civil society and other partners, has proposed a post-2015 development plan: *The Millennium Sustainability Goals* (MSGs).[1] These new goals are grounded on a transformative agenda aimed at ending extreme poverty in the world, improve health and education, as well as tackle more novel problems, including more transparent governance; the building of peace and solidarity among nations; the transition to low-carbon energy by 2050; the protection of critically endangered biodiversity; the improvement of farm yields with reduced environmental costs; and the reshaping of cities to be much more energy-efficient and resilient to rising temperatures and sea levels (*The Economist*, 2013e). The transformative principles underlying the MSGs are as follows:

1. *Leave No One Behind:* Ensure that no person, regardless of ethnicity, gender, geography, disability, race or other status, is denied universal rights and basic economic opportunities.
2. *Put Sustainable Development at the Core:* The universal challenge for all every country is integrate social, economic, and environmental dimensions of sustainability in order to halt the alarming pace of climate change and environmental degradation.
3. *Transform Economies for Jobs and Inclusive Growth:* Governments must aim to attain sustainable patterns of consumption and production to help end extreme poverty and improve livelihoods.
4. *Build Peace and Effective, Open, and Accountable Public Institutions:* A universal agenda for all countries to recognize peace and good governance as core elements of well-being; to exercise openness and transparency in order to promote the rule of law, property rights, freedom of speech and the media, open political choice, access to justice, and accountable government and public institutions.
5. *Forge a New Global Partnership:* A new spirit of solidarity among nations, co-operation and mutual accountability based on a common understanding

of our shared humanity, underpinning mutual respect and mutual benefit in a shrinking world (United Nations, 2013b).

From Bucharest to Cairo and Beyond: Shifts in Global Population Policy Orientations

There have been a number of shifts in global population policy orientations over the past six decades. In the 1960s and 1970s, the leading demographic issue from a global perspective was rapid population growth and high fertility rates. The world's population had grown to 3 billion, and rates of natural increase had risen to their highest levels in history at over 2 per cent per annum. Neo-Malthusians sounded the alarm over the devastating long-term effects of rapid population growth on the environment, resources, and socioeconomic stability.

Shortly after the publication of *The Population Bomb* (Ehrlich, 1968) and *The Limits to Growth* (Meadows et al., 1972), the demographic community gathered in 1974 at the World Population Conference in Bucharest, Romania. As expected, issues and debates surrounding world population growth dominated the agenda. Representatives of the developed countries argued in favour of vigorous family planning programs as a means to curb the developing world's explosive rates of population growth. Representatives of the developing world countered that family planning could not possibly work in the context of poor underdeveloped nations; instead, they argued, these developing countries would benefit most from increased economic development and assistance from the wealthy countries. The belief was that economic development would enable poor countries to get out of the poverty trap. Mortality rates would fall as a consequence, to be followed, eventually, by falling fertility rates, all leading to lower rates of population growth. Among professional demographers, Kingsley Davis (1967) and Judith Blake (1969) were two of the fiercest critics of organized family planning programs. They criticized the multi-billion-dollar-a-year establishment for promoting a naive approach to population control, since family planning, they argued, would do nothing to alter the motivation of couples to want large families.

At subsequent conventions, in Mexico City in 1984 and in Cairo in 1994, opposition to family planning programs was considerably milder. A number of studies based on empirical evidence from the 1970s and 1980s left little doubt about the effectiveness of family planning programs in those countries in which they had been adopted (see Berelson, 1969; Berelson et al., 1990; Mauldin and Berelson, 1978; Mauldin and Ross, 1991; Potts and Selman, 1978: 215; Rathor, 2004; Ross and Mauldin, 1996; Tsui, 2001). At the 1984 conference, most representatives of the developing countries expressed strong acceptance of family planning programs in recognition of the successes achieved by those countries that had adopted such programs during earlier decades.

By the early 1990s, rates of population growth in the world had dropped considerably from the high levels of the 1960s and early 1970s. With the exception of sub-Saharan Africa and parts of Asia, most developing countries had progressed to advanced stages of the fertility transition, and by the 1990s, many African countries were beginning to see some fertility declines as well. Consequently, the focus of the 1994 International Conference on Population and Development had shifted to issues of reproductive health and women's autonomy as new policy concerns (May, 2012; Rao and Sexton, 2010).

What was especially significant about the issue of reproductive health was that it was viewed primarily as a human rights issue and only secondarily as a demographic concern (Chasteland, 2006; Kantner and Kantner, 2006; Locoh and Vandermeersch, 2006; McNicoll, 2001). Many experts attending the Cairo conference believed that women should have access not just to family planning measures but to pre- and postnatal care and to health education, all to help reduce the risk of infections and illness among mothers and their children. Reproductive health, as it was embraced by the United Nations Fund for Population Activities (UNFPA) at the Cairo conference, encompassed family planning, maternal and infant health, sexual health, and the prevention of AIDS (Haberland and Measham, 2002; Sai, 2002). Fertility programs since Cairo have increasingly been designed with the view that family planning and reproductive health are both integral aspects of population health policy that, along with the goal of controlling the spread of HIV/AIDS, should be pursued in developing countries (Kantner and Kantner, 2006; Locoh and Vandeermeersch, 2006).

As indicated by these changes in population policy orientations, unlike the situation of the past, today there is less overt consideration of the benefits of population stabilization or decline—i.e., the neo-Malthusian perspective. Yet, our growing preoccupation with global warming and its sociological and ecological ramifications dictates an urgent need to reconsider the population factor in searching for solutions to looming environmental and resource crises facing the planet (see for example, *Philosophical Transactions of the Royal Society B*, 2009; *Proceedings of the Royal Society*, 2012). But, as noted by Diana Coole (2013), the problematization of population numbers is widely disavowed today, even regarded with suspicion among many academics. According to Coole, five overlapping tendencies serve to foreclose public debate on the population question:

1. ***Population-shaming:*** The shaming of those who espouse the Malthusian view that population is growing too fast globally, based on the idea that there is actually no demographic growth problem today, and limiting population would be akin to limiting categories of people that are considered redundant or undesirable—e.g., the global South.

2. ***Population-skepticism:*** Two variants: (1) the position that the global demographic transition is coming to an end with fertility falling across all regions, and therefore there is no need for population control measures; (2) the view that population growth notwithstanding, free markets and technological advancements will help society solve sustainability problems, and therefore there is no need to control population growth.

3. ***Population-declinism:*** The perspective that in the advanced societies there is now a problem of slow growth accompanied by population aging, and this means decline and loss of influence in the world; the remedy is renewed growth through the application of pronatalist policies and increased immigration.

4. ***Population-decomposing:*** This position disavows the very framework of aggregate population concerns; population issues (e.g., fertility and reproduction) are fundamentally matters of personal choice; therefore, policy should be aimed at improving such things as reproductive rights and maternal and child health rather than focused on aggregate population issues.

5. ***Population-fatalism:*** Continued global population growth over the twenty-first century is assumed as given and cannot be averted; we must therefore identify the socioeconomic and environmental impacts of growth and determine ways to abate these impacts; an explicit population policy aimed at affecting population growth is not needed; environmental impacts of population growth can be mitigated by technological solutions.

These discourses are mutually supporting in their silencing effects. Coole (2013: 212) adds that, in particular, population-shaming and population-skepticism are especially powerful; the first renders the population question morally treacherous; the second is overly congenial to hegemonic pro-growth ideologies. However, in agreement with Coole, none of the five arguments provides "good enough reason for suppressing discussion about population numbers and the merits of fewer people, especially as renewed public concerns emerge over resource insecurity, biodiversity, climate change and high-density urban living" (Coole, 2013: 212–13).

UNMET NEED FOR FAMILY PLANNING

The number of developing countries with family planning programs has grown from only 2 in 1960 to 115 by 1996 (Cleland et al., 2006, 2012). Significant progress has been achieved by the programs, but there remains a huge unmet need for further reproductive health services, especially in the poorest countries (Ahmed et al., 2012; Ezeh, Bongaarts, and Mbaru, 2012; Peterson, Darmstadt, and Bongaarts, 2013; Potts, 2014). Table 12.2, from Herbert Peterson and colleagues (2013: 1697), looks at one aspect of the problem—the unmet need for contraception—among women in the developing countries. As noted in the table, the estimated extent of unmet need for contraceptives in 2012 varies depending on the measure used. For example, the lowest estimate in this table (column 4) indicates that 10 per cent of all women in the childbearing ages (153 million) who do not want a pregnancy have no access to any contraceptives; if only married women are considered, the unmet need is in the range of between 12.6 and 24.5 per cent.

TABLE 12.2 Estimates of unmet need for contraception among women in the developing countries according to two different studies

Women in developing countries with unmet need for contraception in 2012	Not wanting pregnancy, but:	Alkema et al. (2013) study (millions; %)	Darroch and Singh (2013) study (millions; %)
All women	No modern method (%)		222 (15.0%)
All women	No method (%)		153 (10.0%)
Married women	No modern method (%)	196 (18.5%)	191 (18.3%)
Married women	No method (%)	134 (12.6%)	130 (12.6%)
All women wanting to avoid pregnancy	No modern method (%)		222 (26.0%)
All women wanting to avoid pregnancy	No method (%)		153 (18.0%)
Married women wanting to avoid pregnancy	No modern method (%)	196 (24.6%)	191 (24.4%)
Married women wanting to avoid pregnancy	No method (%)	134 (16.8%)	130 (16.8%)

Source: Peterson, Herbert B., Gary L. Darmstadt, and John Bongaarts (2013), "Meeting the Unmet Need for Family Planning: Now Is the Time." *Lancet* 381 18 May): 1696–9. Copyright 2013 with permission from Elsevier.

Current Population Policy Concerns through the Eyes of Government Officials

The United Nations routinely surveys national governments to gauge their perceptions of population change in their countries (United Nations Department of Economic and Social Affairs Population Division, 2013f). Officials in each country are asked to comment on broad variety of population issues, including explicitly demographic ones—population size and growth, population age structure, spatial distribution, fertility, mortality, and migration. As one might expect, the policy concerns differ significantly between developing and developed countries.

Table 12.3 shows that on a global level, violence against women, non-communicable diseases (chronic/degenerative), and HIV/AIDS are considered to be the three most significant population issues of concern to officials. In the more developed countries, the leading three issues are overweight and obesity, non-communicable diseases, and violence against women, followed by population aging and irregular migration. Officials in the less developed countries share a longer list of population challenges, from violence against women; to high rates of non-communicable diseases, HIV/AIDS, tuberculosis, and malaria; to high rates of fertility. Among the least developed countries, HIV/AIDS and high levels of child mortality are tied as the leading areas of concern, followed by violence against women and low life expectancy. The high rate of population growth and uneven spatial distribution of the population are also ranked highly as additional items of concerns among officials in the least developed countries.

The next section summarizes selected policy concern outlined in the United Nations' *World Population Prospects, 2012 Revision* (United Nations Department of Economic and Social Affairs Population Division, 2013a), specifically with regard to the following variables: population age structure, fertility and family planning, health and mortality, spatial distribution and internal mobility, and international migration.

Population Age Structure

Recent estimates based on a variety of new indicators of population aging developed by Wolfgang Lutz, Warren Sanderson, and Sergi Scherbov (2008) suggest that by any of these measures, demographic aging worldwide is increasing rapidly; it is likely to peak sometime between 2020 and 2030 before slowing down. Older persons are the fastest growing population group. Globally, during 2005–10, the annual growth rate for the population aged 60 years or over (2.6 per cent) was more than twice that recorded for the total population (1.2 per cent). The number of persons aged 60 and older is projected to increase from 784 million in 2011 to more than 2 billion in 2050. During this same period, the number of "oldest old" (80 years or over) is projected to grow from 109 million to 402 million. Most developed countries and some developing countries with low fertility already face significant population aging. However, in absolute numbers, the majority of old people live in developing countries. In 2010, 65 per cent of the world's population aged 60 years or over lived in developing countries, and by 2050 this proportion is projected to increase to 79 per cent (United Nations Department of Economic and Social Affairs Population Division, 2013a: 18).

TABLE 12.3   Population issues of concern to governments in 2011 (issues that were a major concern or unacceptable to at least 50 per cent of governments in 2011, by level of development)

World		More Developed Regions		Less Developed Regions		Least Developed Countries	
Issue	Percentage	Issue	Percentage	Issue	Percentage	Issue	Percentage
Violence against women	92	Overweight and obesity	96	Violence against women	92	HIV/AIDS	100
Non-communicable diseases	86	Non-communicable diseases	94	Non-communicable diseases	83	Child mortality	100
HIV/AIDS	80	Violence against women	94	HIV/AIDS	87	Violence against women	98
Overweight and obesity	75	Population ageing	88	Tuberculosis	78	Life expectancy at birth	98
Irregular migration	75	Irregular migration	77	Child mortality	77	Tuberculosis	96
Adolescent fertility	65	Low fertility	65	Maternal mortality	76	Maternal mortality	96
Child mortality	64	Size of working-age population	64	Irregular migration	73	High fertility	92
Under-nutrition in children	64	Low rate of population growth	53	Adolescent fertility	73	Malaria	88
Maternal mortality	62			Overweight and obesity	67	Adolescent fertility	82
Size of working-age population	61			Pattern of spatial distribution	64	High rate of population growth	80
Life expectancy at birth	56			Life expectancy at birth	63	Irregular migration	78
Pattern of spatial distribution	55			Size of working-age population	61	Size of working-age population	76
Population ageing	54			Malaria	53	Pattern of spatial distribution	75
				High fertility	52	Non-communicable diseases	63

Source: United Nations Department of Economic and Social Affairs Population Division (2013F): 5. From *World Population Policies 2011*, United Nations Department of Economic and Social Affairs Population Division. © 2013 United Nations. Reprinted by permission of the United Nations.

Change in the age structure occurs at the bottom, at the top, and in the middle of the age pyramid. With regards to aging at the middle, an issue of critical importance is the size of the working-age population. Given their demographic history, the developed countries are concerned about impending labour-force shortages. In contrast, the developing countries are worried about having working-age populations that are too large, a situation that threatens to cause high unemployment rates. While developed countries are trying to find ways to reduce the consequences of aging in the middle and at the top by increasing the legal retirement age, eliminating early retirement incentives, and encouraging more women to enter the labour force, the developing countries have fewer available measures for minimizing the projected influx of young adults in the labour force; the key challenge will be to generate jobs for an expanding youthful labour force (Birdsall, Kelley, and Sinding, 2001).

Fertility and Family Planning
As we have seen in earlier chapters, fertility worldwide has been declining for well over three decades. Total fertility has declined from 4.4 children per woman in 1970–75 to 2.5 in 2005–10. The developed countries as a group averaged at 1.6 children per woman in 2005–10. Fertility has continued to fall in the vast majority of developing countries, and 32 of these countries had already reached below replacement level fertility in 2005–10. Yet, in 2005–10, total fertility remained high at 4 children per woman or greater in 47 developing countries, including 26 countries where total fertility was 5 children per woman or greater (United Nations Department of Economic and Social Affairs Population Division, 2013a: 25).

Due to the relatively slower progress of the fertility transition in most of Africa, a significant policy development has been the increase in the number of African government officials that reported to have policies to reduce fertility. In 1976, 25 per cent of governments in Africa had policies aimed at lowering fertility. This percentage increased to 68 per cent in 1996, and further to 72 per cent in 2011 (United Nations Department of Economic and Social Affairs Population Division, 2013f: 29).

For Europe, the percentage of governments that had policies to raise fertility has increased steadily from 24 per cent in 1976 to 70 per cent in 2011. The situation in Asia is mixed, where a considerable proportion of governments, 36 per cent in 2011, continued to have policies to lower fertility, while the percentage that had policies to raise fertility increased from 5 per cent in 1976 to 30 per cent in 2011.

Governments in many developed countries have used measures such as baby bonuses; family allowances; maternal, paternal, and parental leave; subsidized childcare; tax incentives; subsidized housing; flexible work schedules; and campaigns to promote the sharing of parenting and household work between spouses. Overall, the evidence offers mixed conclusions about the effects of pro-natalist policies in Western countries; on balance, the best that can be said is that the impact of these policies on period fertility rates is positive but not very strong (Calot, 2006; Corman, 2002; De Santis, 2006; Douglass, 2005; Gauthier, 2005, 2007; Gauthier and Hatzius, 1997; Kohler, Billari, and Ortega, 2006). Meanwhile, the countries of Eastern Europe continue to experience very low fertility, irrespective of any pro-natalist policy, due to a combination of sociopolitical uncertainty, and declining per capita income and living standards.

If pro-natalist policies are not the key to raising fertility, what is? Hans-Peter Kohler and colleagues (2006) suggest it is crucial for countries that wish to raise their birth rates to continue to focus on policies designed to make childbearing more compatible with labour-force participation of women. At the same time, they must also devise strategies aimed at reducing the socioeconomic uncertainty for young adults in a context of persistently high unemployment levels. Others have expressed the view that the key to raising fertility levels in high-income nations depends on effecting a change of outlook regarding the gendered division of labour in the home. Berna Miller Torr and Susan Short (2004), for instance, argue that too many women are burdened by what they refer to as "the second shift"—the tendency for women to work outside the home and to then handle the care of children as well as routine domestic chores without much assistance and support from their male partners. In other words, there is an unfinished gender-role revolution. Women have made significant advances towards gaining "institutional" equality (i.e., in opportunities for education and work), but have had less success in gaining equality in the home (Epsing-Andersen, 2009; McDonald, 2000; Ray, Gornick, and Schmitt, 2008).

Meanwhile, in many of the poorest countries there remains an unfinished family planning agenda: There is still a huge *unmet need for family planning* services. This situation is most severe in sub-Saharan Africa. In order to increase access to family planning in resource-poor areas, Ndola Prata (2009) proposes four critical steps for governments to take:

1. increase knowledge about the safety of family planning methods;
2. ensure contraception is genuinely affordable to the poorest families;

3. ensure that there is an adequate supply of contraceptives by making family planning a permanent line item in government budgets for health care; and
4. take immediate action to remove barriers hindering access to family planning.

John Bongaarts (1994) had also proposed that governments of poor countries should introduce measures to reduce the large number of unwanted births (especially to teen mothers).

Health and Mortality

As with the demographic transition, individual countries are at different stages of the epidemiological transition. In Africa, for example, we have seen that life expectancy at birth is the lowest in the world, estimated to be 55.6 years in 2005–10 (United Nations Department of Economic and Social Affairs Population Division, 2013a: 15). The majority of deaths annually in this region are due to communicable diseases (infectious/parasitic), and maternal, perinatal, and nutritional conditions. This indicates that this region is still in the early stages of the epidemiological transition. Progress in reducing mortality in this region has been hampered significantly by the HIV epidemic in conjunction with a host of other factors, including armed conflict, economic stagnation, and resurgent infectious diseases such as tuberculosis and malaria. Although conditions are expected to improve in Africa during this century, the UN projections to 2045–50 show this region as holding a life expectancy below other areas of the world. In contrast, in developed countries, excluding some of the former Soviet Bloc countries in Eastern Europe and some transitional economies in southeastern Europe, life expectancy at birth is around 80 years and well over 80 per cent of deaths are now due to non-communicable diseases, as would be expected for countries in the advanced stages of epidemiological transition. Although proportionately fewer, non-communicable diseases also account for the majority of deaths in Asia, Latin America and the Caribbean. Most countries in these regions are approaching the final stage of the epidemiological transition.

Under current epidemiological conditions, the developing countries—some more than others—are seeing both persistence of high rates of infectious diseases, coupled with a growing burden of non-communicable diseases such as cancer and cardiovascular complications. Public health interventions must therefore target at all sectors of the age structure, from infancy and childhood, to adulthood and old age:

- reduce further the rates of infant and child mortality;
- reduce undernutrition levels in children;
- reduce rates of maternal mortality by providing greater levels of assistance to expectant mothers (the major causes of mortality being hemorrhage, sepsis, unsafe abortion, hypertensive disorders, and obstructed labour);
- reduce harmful, yet modifiable risk factors in the population, especially the use of tobacco and alcohol, and obesity, which are strongly linked to major chronic degenerative diseases;
- increase efforts to further reduce infections from tuberculosis, malaria, and HIV/AIDS, which in combination claim millions of lives annually; and
- improve measures to help reduce the rate of new infections of HIV, including routine screening of the blood

supply; education and communication campaigns on the prevention and treatment of HIV/AIDS; better access to anti-retroviral treatment; legal measures to protect against HIV/AIDS-related discrimination; improved effort to more widely distribute condoms; and reduction of mother-to-child transmission of HIV. (Ezzati and Riboli, 2013; Lozano et al., 2012; United Nations Department of Economic and Social Affairs Population Division, 2013a, 2013f).

Spatial Distribution and Internal Migration

The UN survey of government officials uncovered a number of principal concerns related to urbanization and population spatial distribution, the greatest urgency expressed by officials from the developing countries (64 per cent versus 27 per cent, developed countries):

- the high rate of rural to urban migration;
- the high rate of inflow of large numbers of migrants to the megacities, which strains the capacities of local city governments to provide basic services (e.g., health care, clean water, sanitation, public transportation); and
- the large percentage of population that lives in environmentally fragile areas and that could potentially be displaced internally (United Nations Department of Economic and Social Affairs Population Division, 2013).

Added to these concerns is the growing number of people living in slums in the large cities, as well as the environmental implications of rapid population growth (May, 2012; National Research Council,

2003; United Nations Human Settlement Programme, UN-Habitat, 2013).

International Migration

The complex nature of contemporary international migration has been treated at length in Chapter 9. It suffices to say that the topic remains an extremely sensitive yet important policy domain. The extent of migratory movements across the globe keeps increasing; and while the majority of migrants seek a better life in the more developed countries, lately, many developing countries have been experiencing significant increases in international migration due to labour-induced movements and refugee crises (United Nations Department of Economic and Social Affairs Population Division, 2013g).

It is known that migration entails positive and negative consequences for sending and receiving countries. A key policy concern for sending countries includes, among others, controlling the extent to which they experience "brain drain" (i.e., the loss of highly educated and skilled people to other countries). On the other hand, poor sending countries benefit from the income immigrants remit to their families back home, which helps boost economic development significantly (Ngoma and Ismail, 2013).

Unsurprisingly, the immigration policies of receiving countries are very selective, favouring the admission of people who meet specific labour needs or who have skills considered to be in short supply. Notwithstanding this fact, the rich countries compete among themselves to attract the best talent from the developing world (i.e., "brain gain"). At the same time, these countries must be vigilant in policing their borders against clandestine entry of illegals. These issues intersect with national demographic concerns, particularly over population aging and growing labour-force needs. As their reliance on immigrant labour grows, they must face the challenge of integrating a growing and diverse migrant population into their social fabric. For some countries more than others, this is a complicated and difficult matter. In Western European countries, there has been increasing levels of xenophobia towards immigrants over recent years (see, for example, Semyonov, Rijman, and Gorodzeisky, 2006; Wilkes, Guppy, and Farris, 2007).

The UN survey of government officials from more developed and less developed countries tend to confirm divergent concerns and needs with respect to immigration. Those representing more developed countries are more inclined to say that their countries want more immigrants, though at the same time they are likely to declare immigration levels as being too high. There seems to be strong desire on the part of these officials to wish for more skilled workers, however. They are also more open to policies favouring family unification and the integration of non-nationals to their societies, but the issue of irregular (i.e., clandestine) migration remains a dominant concern. For officials from the developing countries, a critical point of major concern is emigration of their nationals and the loss of skilled workers to the more developed prosperous countries of the world (United Nations Department of Economic and Social Affairs Population Division, 2013f).

Canadian Population Policy Concerns

Canada's Population: From Frontier Society to the Twenty-First Century

In 1867, the year of Confederation, Canada's population numbered just under 3.5 million people. The population was predominantly rural and most people lived in farming communities. As of April 2014 the population stood at 35.4 million, the vast majority concentrated in towns and cities. By the year 2036, the population could reach nearly 44 million, and possibly rise to just under 53 million by 2061 (Statistics Canada Demography Division, 2010). As the fertility rate is assumed to remain below replacement levels, future growth will depends heavily on immigration levels. And given the sharp declines in fertility over the past five decades, population aging will accelerate between 2010 and 2031, a period during which all baby boomers will reach age 65. Beyond this point, the expectation is that aging would continue at a slower pace.

A characteristic feature of the Canadian population is its ethnocultural diversity. Each census in Canada's history is reflective of this fact. For instance, the census of 1901 testifies to the dominance of English and French ethnic origins along with the growth of immigrant groups from Western and Eastern Europe (Darroch, 2014; Kralt, 1990). Eleven decades later, the census of 2011 reveals a Canadian population that is getting increasingly more heterogeneous ethnoculturally and unevenly distributed geographically, with a disproportionately large share of the population concentrated in the largest metropolitan areas—i.e., Toronto, Montreal, Vancouver, Ottawa–Gatineau, Calgary, Edmonton, and Winnipeg.

What differs today from the immigration of past is the origins of immigrants. In the past, the vast majority were from European origins; today, most newcomers are from countries outside Europe. It is not surprising, therefore, that population projections show that by 2031, about one in three Canadians is expected to be a member of a visible minority (in Toronto and Vancouver they would account for 60 per cent of the population—thus, a majority); about a third of Canada's population will have a mother tongue that is neither English nor French; and about 55 per cent of persons living in CMAs in 2031 will be either immigrants or the Canadian-born children of immigrants—these proportions are expected to reach 78 per cent in Toronto, and 70 per cent in Vancouver (Statistics Canada Demography Division, 2010).

Social Policy in Canada: Shifting Orientations

Canada, like other Western nations, has over its history developed social policies in reaction to economic and demographic changes (Aysan and Beaujot, 2009). As indicated in Table 12.4, early in the twentieth century, the main concern was safeguarding the family and children. As the country changed from a predominantly agricultural to an urban industrial economy, its demography also changed, and public policy focused on the implementation of pensions for an expanding workforce. In the 1950s and 1960s, the attention shifted to the expanding family of the baby boom period and the creation of a universal health care system to complete other

TABLE 12.4   Demographic and social policy orientation: Canada, 1840 onward

	1840–90	1891–1940	1941–74	1975–
Population	Fast growth; high fertility and immigration; mortality declining	Continued growth; slow immigration in 1930s; continuing fall of early life mortality and to women in reproductive ages; low fertility in 1930s	Continued growth; post-war immigration; early life mortality falls to historic low levels; death rates falling faster in adults and those over age 60; post-war baby boom (1946–66) and subsequent baby bust	Continued growth; post-1960s new wave immigration; most survival improvements concentrated in the older ages; below-replacement fertility
Age structure	Young	Young	1970s: transition to an aging population	Aging population structure; aging of baby boom generations
Economy	Population mainly rural; urbanization intensifying; economy mainly agricultural	1931, population crosses 50% urbanization; economy becomes mainly industrial, and resource-based	Population mostly urban; growth of metropolitan areas, driven by post-war prosperity and immigration; early 1970s the post-industrial economy	Urban, post-industrial economy; globalization; prominence of Toronto, Montreal, and Vancouver CMAs
Social Policy Orientation	The protection of family institution; compulsory education; public health	1941: Workman's Compensation Act; 1916: Mothers' Allowance; 1927: Old Age Pension for destitute over age 70; 1930: Unemployment Relief Camps; 1935: Dominion Housing Act; 1940: Federal Unemployment Insurance Act; government begins collecting taxes	The welfare state; 1956: Unemployment Assistance Act; 1963: Canada Pension Plan, Canada Assistance Plan (unemployment assistance), Medicare, Guaranteed Income Supplement; 1964: National Housing Act amended; 1968: Immigration Act amended; Divorce Act; 1971: Unemployment Insurance Act expanded; Family Allowance expanded; 1978: Child Tax Credit (but Family Allowance reduced)	1970s: Improvement in the social safety net: Old-Age Security, Guaranteed Income Supplement, Unemployment Insurance, Family Allowance; 1980s onward: erosion of the safety net, contain rising costs, reduce Old-Age Security benefits at middle income and above, eliminate family allowances, reduce range of workers covered by the benefits available under unemployment insurance, Canada Health Act

Source: Compiled by author based on Moscovitch (2013).

aspects of the Canadian "safety net." In those historical contexts, seniors represented a relatively small segment of the population. But as the baby boom came to an end, increasingly the attention has shifted towards meeting the safety-net needs of a growing senior population, perhaps at some expense of the younger generations, and especially among those in the family-building stages of the lifecycle (Beaujot, Ravanera, and McQuillan, 2007: 12).

Population Policy Challenges over the Twenty-First Century

We can identify three broad policy approaches that demographically mature societies have considered at various times:

1. policies that encourage childbearing among younger couples;
2. policies that increase immigration of working-age people; and
3. public policies aimed at improving the negative effects of the demographic trends.

The last category includes measures such as raising the age of retirement, encouraging more women to enter the workforce, guaranteeing flexible work hours for parents of young children, ensuring the availability of childcare, and extending parental leave (Gauthier, 2007; Grant et al., 2004).

In Canada, most of the attention in the social policy and population literature has been directed towards the second of these three policy orientations: immigration. With the exception of Quebec, where a baby bonus was introduced in 1988 to help boost fertility (and then abandoned in 1992, when it was deemed unsuccessful) (Milligan, 2002), Canada has had no pro-natalist policies. There are several possible reasons for

this. First, as we've seen earlier, it is difficult for governments of liberal democracies to affect private behaviour, most especially reproduction (Demeny, 2003). As well, population change is a slow process, and the results of a policy implemented now could take many years to bear fruit. Policies aimed at increasing fertility in order to ensure a viable future labour force would take at least one generation before society would see any real change in the number of new labour-force entrants. From a political standpoint, these kinds of policies are not appealing. As a result, public policy has usually focused on programs designed to generate more immediate change in society: by altering immigration policy to either increase or decrease the number of newcomers admitted, by introducing incentives for businesses to hire more entry-level workers, by increasing labour-force participation rates, and by modifying the laws regarding legal age of retirement from the labour force, and other similar strategies (Grant et al., 2004).

Policies that Can Affect Fertility

Persistent low fertility in Canada and other Western societies (and also Japan) is primarily the result of delays in family formation among young people. This makes union formation (or marriage) one of the most important proximate determinants of fertility, along with contraceptive use, abortion, and breastfeeding. Any pro-natalist policy, if it is to be effective, must operate through these proximate determinants. For obvious practical and ethical reasons, democratic governments cannot possibly reduce access to contraception and abortion as a way to boost birth rates. Thus, if fertility in Canada is to increase above its current rate of 1.6 children per woman, it will be necessary to introduce policies that in the least would help young couples attain a more balanced work and family life. Canada can implement "family-friendly" social policies that, first, remove workplace and career impediments to child-drearing and, second, promote union formation among young adults (Beaujot, Ravanera, and Burch, 2005; Grant et al., 2004).

The review by Jonathan Grant and colleagues (2004) reinforces the view that fertility rates in liberal democracies respond positively when governments implement social policies that benefit families. For instance, Hyatt and Milne (1991) found that 1 per cent increase in real value of unemployment insurance maternity benefits could produce an increase in the total fertility rate of between 0.09 and 0.26 per cent. This is not a large effect, but it is noteworthy, and it can be achieved by paying more into social programs that economically benefit couples who have children. This is of crucial importance because even a small increase in the total fertility rate could help to slow down the pace of demographic aging while boosting natural growth of the population (Beaujot, 1990; Beaujot, Ravanera, and Burch, 2005; Goldstein, Sobotka, and Jasilionene, 2009). Perhaps some of Canada's existing social programs could be modified with these goals in mind. The tax system could be modified to substantially increase tax breaks for couples with young children; family allowance benefits could be made universal for all low- and middle-income families with young children; young parents could be provided with more generous parental leaves from work; and quality daycare could be made available with government subsidies to working parents. It is likely that many young adults today are postponing union formation and childbearing because of economic insecurity. Alleviating this type of insecurity among young adults should be made a priority. Social and economic policies and programs such as these would provide a more economically secure foundation for both young families just starting out and those who already have children. As pointed out by Anne Gauthier (2007), social policies of this nature would be costly. On the other hand, the costs may be viewed as an investment in the future of the country. Even if the period TFR could be raised by 0.3 of a child to a constant birth rate of 1.8, this would have significant long-term benefits to Canadian society. At this level of fertility, immigration targets could be reduced from present levels.

The Immigration Option

Immigration forms an essential policy anchor for Canada's future. There will never be a shortage of immigrants hoping to establish residence in this country. Therefore, presumably, Canada can manage long-term demographic change by periodically altering its immigration policy. Immigration targets can be raised to grant entry to more workers as needed.

Yet this solution is not problem-free. Some critics have taken exception to the idea that immigration can solve Canada's demographic and economic challenges (see, for example, Francis, 2002; Green and Green, 1999; Paquet, 2010; Romaniuk, 2012). Among the problems associated with immigration is the uneven geographic distribution of immigrant settlement and their socioeconomic integration. As we have already noted, most immigrants choose to settle in Ontario, Quebec, and BC, and specifically in the largest census metropolitan areas. This uneven settlement pattern accentuates existing disparities in regional economic development and amplifies problems of population density and congestion in the largest cities. Another concern with increased immigration are the social and economic costs of integrating newcomers into Canadian society, many of whom are from national origins whose cultures differ significantly from the culture of North America (Koopmans, 2013).

On demographic considerations alone, it is doubtful that increased immigration could substantially raise the prevailing low levels of fertility in Canada. It is true that, generally speaking, immigrants have higher fertility than Canadian-born citizens, but the difference is small (Bélanger, 2006). With respect to population aging, immigration levels could be adjusted annually to affect population size and growth rate, but the number of immigrants needed would be very large, and they would have to be predominantly young if this measure were to appreciably slow demographic aging in Canada (George and Loh, 2007; Seward, 1986). Further, Frank Denton, Christine Feaver, and Byron Spencer (2002) have indicated that even if immigration numbers were increased from their current levels of about 200 000–250 000 annually to 450 000 per year, the impact on the age distribution of Canada's population would be quite minor. For immigration to have an appreciable impact on the age composition, the annual number of newcomers to Canada would have to exceed half a million. Given these large numbers, increased immigration much beyond the current targets as a means of solving the country's demographic deficit may be difficult and not likely to receive widespread acceptance by the public.

Canada's Aging Population: Societal Implications in the Twenty-First Century

Some of the major policy challenges to be faced by Canada over the course of the twenty-first century will be associated with the increasing aging of the population. According to population projections from Statistics Canada (2010), the proportion of seniors aged 65 years or over would represent between 23 and 25 per cent of the population by 2036, compared to 14 per cent in 2009 (the base period for the projections). This would mean that by 2036, the number of seniors would be more than double the number observed in 2009 and would vary between 9.9 and 10.9 million persons. It is anticipated that there would be more people aged 65 years or over than the number of children. Moreover, it is envisioned that the proportion that represents the working-age population among the total population would decrease progressively up to the year 2036 to reach about 60 per cent and would then remain fairly stable (in 2009, the proportion was 69 per cent). The population aged 80 years or over would likely reach 3.3 million in 2036 (2.6 times than in 2009); and the median age of the population could be as high as 45 years (Statistics Canada, 2010).

The unfolding of these demographic trends over the twenty-first century will have far reaching societal implications. According to Roderic Beaujot (2012), the demographic conditions of the past were relatively easy to adjust to from a societal perspective. However, adjusting to the future may not be so straightforward. For example, if we think of the 1970s, the beginning of the ongoing low fertility regime in Canada, this change meant greater freedom for adults as they would have fewer child dependents. Reduced fertility meant more women could participate in the paid labour force. Later, through the 1980s and 1990s, the large baby boom generation was moving through the age structure, contributing to large increases in the size of the labour force. Accommodation to this development was also relatively easy, as it meant for Canada a younger, larger, and better educated labour force.

But as we move into the 2000s and beyond, the baby boomers are approaching the later phases of their working years, the ages of less labour productivity. The over-60 population is enjoying unprecedented survival gains (Denton and Spencer, 2011; Foot and Venne, 2011; Wister, 2005), largely due to declines in mortality from cardiovascular disease and to a lesser extent cancer. At the same time, the proportion of frail elderly is increasing.

Thus, what we are now facing is the aging of the Canadian labour force. The share of the population aged 15–64 has already started to decline for the first time—along with a shrinking supply of young entry-level workers. The first of the boomers turned 65 in 2011, and before long those over 65 will, for the first time, outnumber those under 15—the next generation of workers about to enter the labour force (Friesen, 2013; Statistics Canada, 2007a).

In the mid-1970s, there were many more young adults to enter the labour force. As we move farther into the twenty-first century, the long-term expectation is that there will be relatively fewer entry-level workers as compared to older workers. Consequently, the Canadian labour force will grow more slowly. The fact that there will be fewer workers paying income tax in the near future will have important implications because it is those workers who will have to support the growing population of retirees. The expected shortage of workers will lead to a greater need for immigrants in the prime working ages.

As explained by Beaujot (2012), younger generations of Canadians have been told to invest in their education as a way to get ahead in life. By staying longer in school, they delay entering the labour force in the hopes of securing themselves

a better future (Marshall, 2011). But their socioeconomic aspirations may be seriously thwarted, as population aging may actually imply a compromised opportunity structure if the general tendency among the older generations of workers is to stay in the workplace longer. Indeed, there are signs that young Canadians are already encountering problems of findings adequate employment.

Diane Galarneau, René Morissette, and Jeannine Usalcas (2013) note that youth employment has tended to be significantly lower than older Canadians. In 1976, the maximum full-time employment rate among those aged 34 and under was reached at age 25. In 2012, the maximum rate was reached at the age of 31. In 2012, the unemployment rate of 15–24-year-olds was 14.36 per cent, a rate twice the national average of 7.2 per cent. Canada is not alone in this type of situation; a blighted opportunity structure for young people is a common feature across many demographically mature countries— and for different sets of reasons, also in many developing countries (*The Economist*, 2013f, 2013g). Beside these issues of concern facing younger generations of Canadians, it is also more likely many of them will also experience the so-called *sandwich effect*— caught in a situation of simultaneously raising a young family while also having to take care of elderly parents (Williams, 2005).

Below, we outline some specific public policy implications of Canada's aging population, drawing largely from the evaluation of Beaujot (2012), with respect to three public policy pillars:

1. Canada/Quebec Pension Plan and intergenerational transfers;
2. health care; and
3. the labour force and age at retirement.

When Canada's social programs were being established or enhanced in the 1960s (refer to Table 12.4, page 566), it was easy to plan for increased benefits for the elderly, who were an important pocket of poverty at that time. With a growing population, growing economy, a small proportion of elderly, and larger cohorts following behind, it was not impossible to have income levels for the elderly that were comparable to the income they had while in the labour force. Canada's social programs were set up when there was a small proportion elderly in the population and a breadwinner model of families prevailed. Now our policies need to adapt to a situation where there are increased proportions of elderly, fewer people at ages 15–64, and the vast majority are in two-earner rather than breadwinner families.

In the late 1960s, the Canada/Quebec Pension Plan (C/QPP) was gathering contributions from all workers, while only paying out to those who had made contributions after the plan had started in 1967. The plan quickly developed a surplus, and it was very tempting to use the plan to deal with poverty for elderly persons who had made minimal contributions. In effect, the plan was changed so that contributors could get the full benefit if they had made full contributions (at the rate of 3.6 per cent) for at least 10 years. The C/QPP was a very good investment for people who retired in the late 1970s, with a contribution rate of 3.6 per cent and full benefits after 10 years of contributions. In contrast, today's young people do not see it as such a good investment. To get the same full benefits, they have to contribute for 40 years (ages 18–65 minus 15 per cent grace period), at the rate of 9.9 per cent (see also Denton and Spencer, 2011).

Until those who were 18 in 2003, when the contribution rate was raised to a sustainable level (9.9 per cent), there will have been transfers from younger to older generations through the C/QPP. That is, while the benefits have remained the same, the program has different meaning and value relative to contributions, across cohorts. Inter-generational transfers have benefitted today's seniors more than will be the case for tomorrow's seniors. The relative size of cohorts also plays a role, as does the extent of overall population and economic growth, since transfers are easier in times of growth and when larger cohorts follow smaller ones. That is no longer the case.

Compared to pensions, health is very much funded on a pay-as-you-go basis, and except for the lucky few with "civil service–type benefits in retirement," there is a lack of options for saving during younger years in a private plan that provides benefits at older ages. Since health care is largely funded at the societal level, there should have been savings while the baby boom was at prime labour-force ages. Instead, governments have lowered taxes and increased deficits.

With the oncoming decline in the proportion of the population aged 15–64, and with better health at older ages, we are seeing delays in retirement. This is likely to gather momentum as the age of eligibility for Old-Age Security is pushed back. However, as discussed by Beaujot (2012), there are other issues to bring into the picture. An important inequality to consider when pushing back the age of retirement is the health status by socioeconomic status. With a three- or four-year difference in life expectancy over income categories, eligibility at age 67 rather than 65 makes a much larger difference for the poorer segments of the population, especially those in poor health. There are other ways to reduce the costs of Old-Age Security that would not be to the disadvantage of the poorer segments. One possibility is to lower the income at which clawbacks apply.

Pushing back the age of retirement is a potential solution for people who have insufficient savings, but this also affects other parts of the population especially the young. Young people have been looking forward to the retirement of the baby boom in order to have a better opportunity structure. They have maximized their education and delayed their labour-force entry, just to find that the baby boom is still plugging up the system. The boomer generations seem to want to keep on working rather than retire and leave space in the labour force for younger generations (see also Foot and Stoffman, 2000; Foot and Venne, 2011).

Other Areas of Policy Concern

Other areas of policy concerns as Canada progresses through the twenty-first century include the following:

- the increasing congestion of Canada's largest cities and urban sprawl;
- the decline of small towns exacerbated by the out-migration of youth;
- the concentration of newcomers in the largest cities and the need to develop smaller centres as possible attraction areas to help reduce uneven regional economic development;
- rising levels of economic inequality;
- urban planning for an aging population (changes in transportation, housing, services);
- widening regional inequalities in economic development exacerbated differential attraction of labour; and
- the need to eliminate inequalities in health and mortality by socioeconomic status, and in particular improve the health of Aboriginal peoples.

Conclusion

In some respects, governments are constrained in their ability to implement policies designed to alter demographic behaviours such as childbearing, which most citizens consider a private matter. In liberal democracies, the basic principles of freedom, equality, and dignity of the individual must be upheld; government policies cannot violate these tenets. Governments of liberal democracies, then, face considerable obstacles in any attempt to promote directly pro-natalist policies. And even if such policies were truly effective, the financial costs would be large. As a result, many liberal democracies look to a combination of public policies directed at easing the dual responsibilities of work and family life for young adults, which hold promise as indirect mechanisms to boost period total fertility rates. Non-democratic governments have much greater leeway in the type of policies they can implement.

Canada's population policy concerns and challenges overlap with those of other demographically mature countries of the West and Japan, which are likewise facing low fertility and increased population aging and therefore labour-force shortages. Policy mechanisms for addressing the birth deficit would likely include programs aimed at helping young couples—and especially women, who take on a disproportionate share of the burden known as the "double shift"—achieve a better balance between work and family life, all of which might serve to stimulate aggregate fertility increases. Exclusive reliance on immigration as a demographic policy option is not a problem-free solution. Immigration levels, even if they were to be increased substantially from their current targets, would bring only minor change to the age distribution of Canada's population; and immigration policy cannot be exercised in isolation of broader sociological concerns.

Exercises

1. *Population policy cannot be viewed independently of other aspects of the social system.* Evaluate this statement. How are population policy and social policy interrelated?
2. Discuss the claim that the most successful population policies have been implemented in non-democratic societies. How would one define "successful" in this case? Give examples of some success stories and also of some failed policies. Should governments have any role at all in affecting demographic behaviour?
3. What would be the justification for wanting to raise fertility in liberal democracies when most of the world's population is faced with serious population pressures? Would it not be more sensible for low-fertility societies to increase their immigration targets as a means to avert long-term population decline? Isn't immigration a relatively "easy" solution to demographic aging for low-fertility societies? Critically evaluate these questions.

Additional Reading

Betts, Alexander, ed. 2011. *Global Migration Governance*. Oxford: Oxford University Press.

Conway, Gordon. 2012. *One Billion Hungry: Can We Feed the World?* Ithaca, NY: Comstock.

Goldstone, Jack, Eric Kaufmann, and Monica Duffy Toft. 2012. *Political Demography: How Population Changes Are Reshaping International Security and National Politics*. Oxford: Oxford University Press.

Greenhalgh, Susan. 2010. *Cultivating Global Citizens: Population in the Rise of China*. Cambridge, MA: Harvard University Press.

Hoff, Derek S. 2012. *The State and the Stork: The Population Debate and Policy Making in US History*. Chicago: The University of Chicago Press.

Last, Jonathan V. 2013. *What to Expect When No One's Expecting: America's Coming Demographic Disaster*. New York: Encounter Books.

McNicoll, Geoffrey, John Bongaarts, and Ethel P. Churchill, eds. 2012. *Population and Public Policy: Essays in Honor of Paul Demeny*. Supplement to vol. 38, Population and Development Review. New York: The Population Council.

May, John. 2012. *World Population Policies: Their Origin, Evolution, and Impact*. Dordrecht: Springer.

Philosophical Transactions of the Royal Society B. 2009. *The World in 2050: The Impact of Population Growth on Tomorrow's World*. Theme Issue edited by Roger V. Short and Malcolm Potts. Vol. 364, 1532 (27 October).

Rao, Mohan, and Sarah Sexton, eds. 2010. *Markets and Malthus: Population, Gender, and Health in Neo-Liberal Times*. Los Angeles: Sage.

Takayama, Noriyuki, and Martin Werding, eds. 2011. *Fertility and Public Policy: How to Reverse the Trend of Declining Birth Rates*. Cambridge, MA: MIT Press.

Note

1. The Millennium Sustainability Goals consist of 12 "Universal Goals": 1. End poverty; 2. Empower girls and women and achieve gender equality; 3. Provide quality education and lifelong learning; 4. Ensure healthy lives; 5. Ensure food security and good nutrition; 6. Achieve universal access to water and sanitation; 7. Create sustainable energy; 8. Create jobs, sustainable livelihoods, and equitable growth; 9. Manage natural resource assets sustainably; 10. Ensure good governance and effective institutions; 11. Ensure stable and peaceful societies; 12. Create a global enabling environment and catalyze long-term finance (United Nations, 2013b).

abridged life table A life table based on grouped age categories with the exception of infancy and the very last (oldest) age group, which is typically an open-ended category.

age The interval of time, expressed in completed years, between the date of birth and the present. Age is a fundamental characteristic of population structure. One may distinguish between biological aging (the aging of the organism—i.e., maturation) from chronological aging (i.e., the accumulation of calendar time), even though in actual fact both types of processes are inseparable.

age of delayed degenerative diseases The fourth stage of the epidemiologic transition.

age pattern of migration The graphical representation of the varying probabilities of geographic mobility across age categories.

age–sex pyramid The graphic representation (e.g., a histogram or vertical bar chart) portraying the relative number of males and females in the population in accordance with age category. Because of the interplay of fertility and mortality, and to a lesser extent migration, such a chart often assumes the shape of a pyramid (or triangle). In fact, however, the shape of the age distribution of a population can take on a variety of forms that can deviate substantially from a pyramid.

age-specific fertility rate Fertility rate based on the number of children born to women in a given age category.

asylum migration Forced movement due to the presence of conditions in a country that threaten the lives of individuals (e.g., civil war; ethnic conflict, etc.).

average human lifespan The average lifespan of a population as measured by life expectancy at birth.

baby boom A significant surge in the number of births taking place in a population over a protracted period (e.g., the post-war baby boom in Europe, North America, Australia, and New Zealand between 1946 and 1966, with its peak around 1960). The sharp decline in births after a baby boom is often referred to in the literature as a *baby bust*.

birth cohort A group of individuals born during a specified period of time, usually a given calendar year or interval (e.g., five-year period).

carrying capacity The maximum population sustainable by a given territory under specific conditions, such as a given level of land use and consumption of natural resources.

cause-specific death rate A measure of the extent of mortality due to a given cause in relation to the population at risk of dying from that cause.

census A periodic accounting of the population taken by countries usually every five or ten years.

census agglomerations (CA) Clusters of interconnected cities and towns, smaller urban centres, and even rural areas within a specified region.

census metropolitan area (CMA) A statistical construct describing a large agglomeration of urban centres that show a high level of economic integration with a central city, from which the metropolitan area derives its name (e.g., Toronto metropolitan area). Different countries have different statistical criteria to define a metropolitan area. In Canada, a census metropolitan area must have a population size of at least 100 000, and the majority of the population in the agglomeration must be involved in non-agricultural economic activity.

cohabitation (consensual union) A type of conjugal union involving two persons of the opposite sex or (since 2001) of the same sex living together, possibly with children. This kind of union, often referred to as either a *consensual union* or *common-law marriage*, is not formalized though legal or religious marriage rites.

cohort fertility The reproductive experience of a particular birth cohort of women or of women belonging to a specific marriage cohort, as observed at the end of the cohort's childbearing years (i.e., cohort completed fertility). This type of fertility is often contrasted with *period fertility*, which measures the reproductive experience at one point in time as produced by different cohorts at different stages in their childbearing years passing though the given point of observation together (this yields the *period total fertility rate*).

cohort (or generational) life table A type of life table that is specific to a given generation.

compression of morbidity and mortality The theory that we can postpone the onset of major disability in life to older and older ages without postponing the average timing of death. This essentially means that we can live healthier lives until very close to the point at which we die. It also means that the average age at death (life expectancy) is fixed.

counterurbanization A phenomenon, observed during the 1970s in the United States and some other industrialized countries, in which rural areas and smaller urban settlements grew faster than large urban centres, largely as a function of net migration stimulated by economic restructuring, and partly because of a general preference among some people to reside away from the city. This development was facilitated by the existence of effective systems of roadways linking city and countryside.

demographic balancing equation (demographic components equation) An expression of the change in population as a function of change in births, deaths, and migration. This equation is often referred to as the *components equation* because it expresses population change as a function of two components: natural increase and net migration.

demographic dividend The combination of demographic and economic conditions that can propel a developing country out of poverty by virtue of having a large youthful labour force and along with structural conditions favourable to economic growth; however, this window of opportunity to capture this benefit is limited in time.

demographic transition theory A theory of demographic change based on the idea that all populations pass through stages, beginning with high birth and death rates, followed by a stage where birth and death rates fall but fertility rates remain high, to an eventual stage in which both death and birth rates are low and therefore natural increase is also low.

dependency ratio A ratio intended to indicate the balance of the population in the ages needing support to those in the labour-force ages who are economically productive. There are various such measures, including the total dependency ratio, the youth dependency ratio, and the old-age dependency ratio.

direct standardization A statistical method applied to control for confounding effect of characteristics differences, such as age composition, on differences in demographic rates, such as mortality. The method calls for the application of age-specific rates of a study population to the age distribution of a standard population.

distance-gravity model A mathematical description of the tendency for migration to decline with distance from a given origin and to be influenced by differential population sizes of places in a geographical system.

doubling time The number of years a population would take to double its current size if the current rate of growth remained constant.

early neonatal mortality (and death rate) Mortality to infants occurring between birth and the first week of life.

ecological footprint A measure of the overall impact of human activities on the environment. The ecological footprint gives a quantitative account of how much land and water is necessary to provide the resources we consume and to absorb the waste we produce.

exogenous mortality Mortality due to external conditions such as accidents, violence, and suicide.

expansion of survival The view that survival probabilities in the life table when plotted over time points increasingly shift to the right on the age axis. This implies that average age at death is not fixed.

exponential model Essentially the same as the geometric model, except that it considers compounding to occur instantaneously (i.e., continuously). The exponential and geometric converge to the same model if the time interval is made sufficiently small.

family planning In a general sense, this is the exercise of conscious effort by couples or individuals to control the number and spacing of births. At the societal level, *family planning* refers to organized efforts by governments to provide the necessary means and services for couples to achieve the family size they desire and at the same time for the population to reduce its fertility rate.

fecundity The physiological capability of a woman, a man, or a couple to produce a live birth.

fertility Along with mortality and migration, one of the fundamental processes responsible for change and renewal of a population.

fetal deaths Fetal deaths occurring during the gestation period (i.e., stillbirths).

first urban revolution The term signifies the advent of the first cities in Old World between roughly 5000 and 2500 years ago. This is distinguished from the *second urban revolution*, which came about after the discovery of the Americas, and in particular following the Industrial Revolution.

gains to marriage The perspective of Gary Becker that men and women have different interests in marriage, and that therefore the partners are in essence in a trading type of relationship. In the traditional context, men provided economic security and women traded domestic services, including childbearing and childrearing. Today, families dissolve because these trading principles no longer work as well as in the past.

generation In the sociological sense, a group of individuals, not necessarily part of the same birth cohort, but who experience in common some important sociohistorical event (e.g., living through a war or a major economic depression) that shapes for these people a collective identity that differentiates them from the rest of the population. In demography, generation means the average difference in age between mothers and daughters—i.e., the mean length of a generation.

geometric model A mathematical model that considers compounding at set intervals (e.g., annually on 31 December).

global city A city distinguished by its interconnected specialized functions that gives it a wide sphere of influence in the global economy.

gross reproduction rate (GRR) The average number of daughters born to a hypothetical cohort of mothers that experience the prevailing age-specific fertility rates of the population.

health transition A theoretical perspective that describes the improvements in life expectancy and overall health of populations over the historical spectrum, going beyond the scope covered by epidemiological transition theory.

hybristic (stage) A stage that is describes the role of lifestyle and behavioural factors as important aspects of the epidemiological profile of societies in the fourth stage of epidemiologic transition.

indirect standardization A statistical method applied to control for confounding effect of characteristics differences (such as age composition) on differences in demographic rates (such as mortality). The method calls for the application of a standard set of age-specific rates to the age distribution of a study population.

intergenerational contract The idea that all societies have an implicit understanding that all persons go through life stages in which they move from a state of dependency from childhood to youth, to a stage of producer during the working years, and ultimately again to a state of dependency in old age; therefore, societies have a moral obligation to provide support to those unable to be economically productive by virtue of being too young or past labour-force age.

intermediate variables In fertility analysis, *intermediate variables* are those that are assumed to affect fertility directly and are intermediate to the influence of societal factors. For example, an increase in a society's average income may affect the birth rate only through one or more of the intermediate variables, which include the timing and extent of marriage of women, the extent to which contraception is used, the extent to which abortion is practised, and the duration of breastfeeding. The term has been replaced recently by an alternative term, the *proximate determinants of fertility*.

intervening opportunities model A migration model that predicts the volume of migration between places as a function of the number of opportunities (jobs) between places available to potential migrants.

intrinsic rate of natural increase (intrinsic rate of growth) A population that has been subjected to constant age-specific schedules of mortality and fertility over many years and is closed to migration will eventually converge to a stable population. The difference between the stable birth and death rates (i.e., intrinsic birth and intrinsic death rates) in this population is the intrinsic rate of natural increase (or intrinsic growth rate).

late neonatal mortality (and death rate) Mortality to infants occurring between the first week of life and the first month of life.

life expectancy A measure derived from the life table that indicates the average number of years one can expect to live given a current age.

lifespan The length of life of an individual.

linear model (arithmetic model) A mathematical equation based on the assumption that population growth follows a linear trend with no compounding.

logistic model A mathematical model of population growth characterized by an S-shaped curve, denoting slow population growth initially, followed by a period of rapid growth, and then finally, once the population approaches a maximum level, decreasing rates of growth.

maximum average human lifespan The maximum average age at death of a population (i.e., life expectancy at birth).

maximum observed lifespan The maximum lifespan of an individual that has been proven to have lived the longest among all humans.

maximum potential lifespan The theoretically possible maximum lifespan for a species. This is not possible to know; all we can know is the observed maximum lifespan.

mean length of a generation The average age at which mothers give birth to their daughters.

median age The age that is greater than the age of one half of the population and lower than the other half. The median age of population is usually preferred to the mean age of population, or arithmetic average age, because it is not affected by extreme values.

megacities Urban places of 10 million or more inhabitants.

megalopolis A large, almost contiguous, and densely populated urban system that extends beyond metropolitan urban agglomerations. In a more general sense, the term refers to the integration of large urban agglomerations into an even higher order of urban structure and complexity. An example of megalopolis is the Eastern Seaboard and St Lawrence–Great Lakes urban system that straddles eastern United States and eastern Canada.

migrants People who cross significant administrative political boundaries and whose moves are not local (i.e., within the same community of residence).

migration The movement of individuals or groups of people involving a permanent or semi-permanent change of residence. Along with fertility and mortality, one of the fundamental processes responsible for change and renewal of a population.

Millennium Development Goals (MDGs) A series of objectives ratified by the United Nations in agreement with the countries of the world aimed at reducing poverty and improving health and socioeconomic conditions in the poorest countries of the world by the year 2015.

mobility transition A theoretical framework that describes the historical pattern of geographic mobility, from primitive society to the super-advanced society.

mortality The process whereby deaths occur in a population. Along with fertility and migration, one of the fundamental processes responsible for population change.

natural fertility Fertility that prevails in underdeveloped societies (e.g., pre-industrial) characterized by the absence of conscious planning of births by couples.

neoclassical economics (model) A model of human action that considers rational decision making as the basis for action (e.g., migration), whereby the individual evaluates the possible gains and possible losses of an intended behaviour before actually executing the behaviour.

neo-Malthusians Contemporary followers of Malthus who believe that population growth must be controlled; unlike Malthus himself, they advocate the use of birth control (including contraception and even induced abortion) to reduce population growth rates.

neo-Marxists Contemporary followers of Marx who believe that population growth is an issue of secondary concern to such problems as poverty and inequality in the world.

net reproduction rate The same as the gross reproduction rate, but *net reproduction rate* further assumes that there is some risk of mortality to women in the reproductive ages.

patriarchy The core principle of traditional family systems in which older males have authority and control over the younger members of the family.

perinatal mortality (and death rate and ratio) Late fetal deaths plus early neonatal infant deaths.

period life table (or synthetic life table) A life table that is calculated on the basis of current age-specific death rates.

polygyny A form of plural marriage in which a man is allowed to have more than one wife (as opposed to polyandry, in which one woman is allowed more than one husband).

population estimates Derived population counts for off-census years based on information from previous actual censuses.

population momentum Additional population growth resulting from the current age structure of a population. It can be positive if the population structure is young and there are disproportionate numbers of women in the childbearing ages because of past high fertility. Alternatively, the momentum can be negative if the age structure is old due to past sub-replacement fertility levels.

population policy An objective plan devised and implemented by governments to affect population change in a desired direction.

population projections An estimate of the future population based on assumptions about anticipated changes in fertility and mortality (and where appropriate also net migration).

post-neonatal mortality (and death rate) Mortality to infants between the first month of life and the twelfth month of life.

proximate determinants of fertility A quantitative version of the intermediate variables.

quantum effect (on fertility) The contribution of cohort completed fertility to the current total fertility rate.

rank-size rule of cities A mathematical expression that expresses a relationship between the size of the largest city and the relative rank of cities of lesser size: In general, the number of small towns

in a country exceeds the number of medium-sized towns, which outnumber the large towns.

record lifespan The highest observed age at death, a record held by Jeanne Calmant, who died at age 122.

rectangularization of survival The idea that as death rates fall to very low levels, the survival curve in the life table of a population becomes increasingly rectangular in shape, meaning that conditional survival probabilities improve upwards towards 100 per cent survival, though never reaching 100 per cent.

refugees An official UN designation of people that flee their countries due to a well-founded fear of persecution due to their race or nationality.

replacement fertility The fertility level that a population must achieve, given its mortality level, to replace itself in the long term. The usual replacement rate is 2.1 children per woman, but this figure would need to be adjusted upwards in contexts where female death rates are high.

second demographic transition A theoretical perspective that explains the growing diversity of family and partnership bevaviours in post-modern societies that have long passed through the demographic transition.

second urban revolution The latest and ongoing wave of world urbanization that began after the Industrial Revolution.

senescent mortality (endogenous mortality) Mortality associated with aging. This type of mortality excludes mortality related to conditions external to the functioning of the organism—e.g., accidents, violence, and suicide.

sex ratio The balance of men to women in a population or within an age category, expressed as the ratio of males to females multiplied by 100.

single years of age life tables Life tables that are based on single years of age rather than grouped age categories.

stable population A population closed to migration with unchanging age-specific death and fertility rates and age-sex structure, that increases (or decreases) at a constant rate.

stationary population A stable population that has a constant intrinsic rate of natural increase equal to zero. In the life table, the L_x column is a stationary population.

sterility The inability to conceive. In the case of *primary sterility*, a woman has never been able to conceive; *secondary sterility* occurs after a woman has given birth to at least one child.

survival ratios A measure of survival derived from the life table. It is the ratio of the number of person-years lived by a cohort at given age x, out of an initial 100 000 births.

tempo effect The effect of period conditions on the timing of an event in cohorts (e.g., births) as measured by the mean age or duration at which cohort members experience the event (e.g., childbearing).

total fertility rate The sum of age-specific fertility rates for a given period over the whole range of reproductive ages (15–49). This measure is interpreted as the number of children a woman would have during her lifetime if she were to experience the age-specific fertility rates in the given period of observation.

underlying cause of death The initial cause or condition (e.g., injury) that determines the morbid process that ultimately leads to death. This is the cause of death that is given in published official statistics, even though in actuality death certificates can contain more than one cause of death.

unmet need for family planning Women with an unmet need for family planning are those who are fecund and sexually active but are not using any method of contraception, although they report not wanting any more children or wanting to delay the next pregnancy.

urbanism A term referring to the style of life found in urban areas—i.e., the homogenizing sociopsychological effect of urban living on the population.

urbanization The process by which the population concentration intensifies in localities defined by a country as "urban." The criteria for what constitutes urban vary considerably across countries.

visible minorities An official designation based on either self-designation in the census or cross-classification of birthplace, ancestry, language, and religion. Canada's Employment Equity Act defines *visible minorities* as persons, other than Aboriginal people, who are non-Caucasian in race or non-white in colour. The ten groups in this category are Chinese, South Asian, Black, Filipino, Latin American, Southeast Asian, Arab, West Asian, Japanese, and Korean.

vital statistics system A continuous registration system of vital events, including births, deaths, marriages and divorces.

Aarssen, Lonnie W. 2005. "Why Is Fertility Lower in Wealthier Countries? The Role of Relaxed Fertility-Selection," *Population and Development Review* 31, 1: 113–26.

Acemoglu, Daron, and James A. Robinson. 2013. *Why Nations Fail: The Origins of Power, Prosperity, and Poverty*. New York: Crown Business.

Acsádi, Gy, and J. Nemeskéri. 1970. *History of Human Life Span and Mortality*. K. Balas, trans. Budapest: Akademiai Kiado.

Agadjanian, Victor, and Ndola Prata. 2002. "War, Peace, and Fertility in Angola," *Demography* 39, 2: 215–31.

Aguirre, A. Alonso, Mary C. Pearl, and Jonathan Patz. 2004. "Urban Expansion Impacts on the Health of Ecosystems, Wildlife and Humans," www.populationenvironmentresearch.org (29 November–15 December 2004).

Ahlburg, Dennis A. 1998. "Julian Simon and the Population Growth Debate," *Population and Development Review* 24, 2: 317–27.

———, Allen C. Kelley, and Karen Oppenheim Mason. 1996. "Editors' Introduction," in Dennis A. Ahlburg, Allen C. Kelley, and Karen Oppenheim Mason, eds, *The Impact of Population Growth on Well-Being in Developing Countries*. Berlin: Springer.

———, and M.O. Schapiro. 1984. "Socioeconomic Ramifications of Changing Cohort Size: An Analysis of US Postwar Suicide Rates by Age and Sex," *Demography* 21, 1: 97–108.

Ahmed, Saifuddin, Qingfeng Li, Li Liu, and Amy O. Tsui. 2012. "Maternal Deaths Averted by Contraceptive Use: An Analysis of 172 Countries," *Lancet* 380: 111–25.

Aird, John. 1990. *Slaughter of the Innocents*. Washington, DC: American Enterprise Institute.

Akers, Donald S. 1967. "On Measuring the Marriage Squeeze," *Demography* 4: 907–24.

Alchon, Suzanne Austin. 2003. *A Pest in the Land: New World Epidemics in a Global Perspective*. Albuquerque: University of New Mexico Press.

Aligica, Paul Dragos. 2007. *Prophecies of Doom and Scenarios of Progress: Herman Kahn, Julian Simon, and the Prospective Imagination*. New York: Continuum International.

Alkema, L., V. Kantorova, C. Menozzi, and A. Biddlecom. 2013. "National, Regional, and Global Rates and Trends in Contraceptive Prevalence and Unmet Need for Family Planning Between 1990 and 2015: A Systematic and Comprehensive Analysis", *Lancet* 381: 1642–52.

Allard, Michel, Victor Lebre, Jean-Marie Robine, and Jean Calment. 1998. *Jeanne Calment: From Van Gogh's Time to Ours: 122 Extraordinary Years*. New York: W.H. Freeman.

Andersen, Stacy L., Paola Sebastiani, Daniel A. Dworkis, Lori Feldman, and Thomas T. Perls. 2012. "Health Span Approximates Life Span among Many Supercentenarians: Compression of Morbidity at the Approximate Limit of Life Span," *Journal of Gerontology A: Biological and Medical Sciences* 67A, 4: 395–405.

Anderson, Barbara A. 2003. "Russia Faces Depopulation? Dynamics of Population Decline," *Population and Environment* 23, 5: 437–64.

———, and Brian D. Silver. 1989. "Patterns of Cohort Mortality in the Soviet Population," *Population and Development Review* 15, 3: 471–502.

Anderson, I.B. 1966. *Internal Migration in Canada, 1921–1961*. Economic Council of Canada, Staff Study no. 13. Ottawa: Queen's Printer.

Anderson, Margo J. 2003. "Census," in Paul Demeny and Geoffrey McNicoll, eds, *Encyclopedia of Population*, vol. 1. New York: Macmillan Reference USA/Thomson Gale.

Anderssen, E. 1998. "Canada's Squalid Secret: Life on Native Reserves," *Globe and Mail* (12 October): A1, A3.

Andorka, Rudolph. 1978. *Determinants of Fertility in Advanced Societies*. London: Methuen.

Antonovsky, Aaron. 1967. "Social Class, Life Expectancy and Overall Mortality," *The Milbank Quarterly* 45, 4: 151–93.

———, and Judith Bernstein. 1977. "Social Class and Infant Mortality," *Social Science and Medicine* 11: 453–70.

Ariès, Philippe. 1980. "Two Successive Motivations for Declining Birth Rates in the West," *Population and Development Review* 6: 645–50.

———. 1974. *Western Attitudes toward Death: From the Middle Ages to the Present*. Patricia M. Ranum, trans. Baltimore, MD: Johns Hopkins University Press.

———. 1960. "Interprétations pour une histoire des mentalités," in Hélène Berques et al., *La Prévention des naissances dans la famille: ses origines dans les temps modernes*. National Institute for Demographic Studies, monograph no. 35. Paris: Presses Universitaires de France.

Attané, Isabelle. 2013. *The Demographic Masculinization China: Hoping for a Son*. INED Population Studies, vol. 1. Dordrecht: Springer.

———. 2002. "China's Family Planning Policy: An Overview of Its Past and Future," *Studies in Family Planning* 33, 1: 103–13.

Auerbach, Felix. 1913. "Das Gesetz der Bevoelkerungskoncentration," *Petermanns Geographische Mitteilungen* 59: 74–6.

Aydemir, Abdurrahman, and George . Borjas. 2006. "A Comparative Analysis of the Labor Market Impact of International Migration: Canada, Mexico, and the United States," National Bureau of Economic Research, Working Papers www.nber.org/papers/w12327. pdf.

Aysan, Mehmet F., and Roderic Beaujot. 2009. "Welfare Regimes for Aging Populations: No Single Path for Reform," *Population and Development Review* 35, 4: 701–20.

Bach, R.L., and J. Smith. 1977. "Community Satisfaction, Expectations of Moving, and Migration," *Demography* 14: 147–67.

Bachman, Ronet. 1992. *Death and Violence on the Reservation: Homicide, Family Violence, and Suicide in American Indian Populations*. New York: Auburn House.

Bah, S.M., and Fernado Rajulton. 1991. "Has Canadian Mortality Entered the Fourth Stage of the Epidemiologic Transition?" *Canadian Studies in Population* 18, 2: 18–41.

Bailey, Adrian J., Megan K. Blake, and Thomas J. Cooke. 2004. "Migration, Care, and the Linked Lives of Dual-Earner Households," *Environment and Planning A* 36: 1617–32.

Balakrishnan, T.R., George E. Ebanks, and Carl F. Grindstaff. 1979. *Patterns of Fertility in Canada, 1971*. Cat. no. 99-759. Ottawa: Statistics Canada.

———, Karol J. Krotki, and Evelyn Lapierre-Adamczyk. 1993. *Family and Childbearing in Canada: A Demographic Analysis*. Toronto: University of Toronto Press.

———, K.V. Rao, E. Lapierre-Adamcyk, and K.J. Krotki. 1987. "A Hazard Model Analysis of the Covariates of Marriage Dissolution in Canada," *Demography* 24: 395–406.

Balter, Michael. 2005. *The Goddess and the Bull*. New York: Free Press.

———. 2001. "In Search of the First Europeans," *Science* 291, 5509 (2 March): 1722–5.

———. 1998. "Why Settle Down? The Mystery of Communities," *Science* 282 (20 November): 1442–7.

Bandarage, Asoka. 1997. *Women, Population and Global Crisis: A Political Economy Analysis*. London: Zed Books.

Banister, Judith, and Ansley J. Coale. 1994. "Five Decades of Missing Females in China," *Demography* 31: 459–79.

Barash, David P., and Judith Eve Lipton. 2001. *The Myth of Monogamy: Fertility and Infertility in Animals and People*. New York: W.H. Freeman.

Barbi, Elisabetta, John Bongaarts, and James W. Vaupel, eds. 2008. *How Long Do We Live?: Demographic Models and Reflections on Tempo Effects*. Heidelberg: Springer-Verlag.

Barbieri, Magali, and Nadine Ouellette. 2012. "The Demography of Canada and the United States from the 1980s to the 2000s: A Summary of Changes and a Statistical Assessment," *Population-E* 67, 2: 177–280.

Barker, David J.P. 2012. "Sir Richard Doll Lecture. Developmental Origins of Chronic Disease," *Public Health* 126: 185–9.

———. 2004. "The Developmental Origins of Adult Disease," *Journal of the American College of Nutrition* 23, 6: 588S–95S.

———. 1998. *Mothers, Babies and Health in Later Life*. Edinburgh: Churchill Livingstone.

———, and C. Osmond. 1986. "Infant Mortality, Childhood Nutrition, and Ischaemic Heart Disease in England and Wales," *The Lancet* (May 10): 1077–81.

Barclay, George W. 1958. *Techniques of Population Analysis*. New York: John Wiley & Sons.

Barnes, Trevor J., John H. Britton, W.J. Coffey, et al. 2000. "Canadian Geography at the Millennium," *The Canadian Geographer* 44, 1: 4–24.

Barnosky, Anthony D., Nicholas Matzke, Susumu Tomiya, Guinevere O.U. Wogan, Brian Swartz, et al. 2011. "Has the Earth's Sixth Mass Extinction Already Arrived?" *Nature* 471: 51–57.

Barro, Robert J. 1997. *Determinants of Economic Growth: A Cross-Country Empirical Study*. Cambridge, MA: MIT Press.

———, and Sala-i-Martin. 2004. *Economic Growth*, 2nd edn. Cambridge, MA: MIT Press.

Barsotti, Odo. 1985. "Cause e Effetti Della Immigrazione Regionale," in Alberto Bonaguidi, ed., *Migrazioni e Demografia Regionale in Italia*. Milano: Franco Angeli.

Bartel, A.P. 1989. "Where Do New Immigrants Live?" *Journal of Labor Economics* 7: 371–91.

Barzun, Jacques. 2001. *From Dawn to Decadence: 500 Years of Western Cultural Life 1500 to the Present*. New York: Harper Perennial.

Basavarajappa, K.G., and Bali Ram. 1983. "Population and Migration," in F.H. Leacy, ed., *Historical Statistics of Canada*. Ottawa: Statistics Canada.

Bateson, Patrick, David Barker, Timothy Clutton-Brock, Debal Deb, et al. 2004. "Developmental Plasticity and Human Health," *Nature* 430 (22 July): 419–21.

Bayly, Christopher A. 2004. *The Birth of the Modern World 1780–1914: Global Connections and Comparisons.* London: Blackwell.

Beale, Calvin L. 1977 [1996]. "The Recent Shift of United States Population to Nonmetropolitan Areas, 1970–75," in H.S. Geyer and T.M. Kontuly, eds, *Differential Urbanization: Integrating Spatial Models.* London: Edward Arnold.

———. 1975. "The Revival of Population Growth in Nonmetropolitan America," ERS 605. Washington, DC: United States Department of Agriculture.

Bean, Frank D., Barry Edmonston, and Jeffrey S. Passel. 1990. "Introduction," in Frank D. Bean, Barry Edmonston, and Jeffrey S. Passel, eds, *Undocumented Migration to the United States: IRCA and the Experience of the 1980s.* Santa Monica, CA: RAND Corporation.

Beaujot, Roderic. 2012. "Aging in Canada, 2011: The Aging of the Past Will Be Different from the Aging of the Future," *Population Change and Lifecourse Strategic Knowledge Cluster* http://sociology.uwo.ca/cluster/en/ (accessed 5 August 2013).

———. 2000. *Earning and Caring in Canadian Families.* Toronto: Broadview.

———. 1995. "Family Patterns at Mid-life (Marriage, Parenting and Working)," in Jean Dumas, ed., *Family over the Life Course: Current Demographic Analysis.* Cat. no. 91-543-E. Ottawa: Statistics Canada.

———. 1990. "The Challenge of Changing Demographics," *Policy Options/Options Politiques* (December): 19–22.

———. 1978. "Canada's Population: Growth and Dualism," *Population Bulletin* 33, 2. Washington, DC: Population Reference Bureau.

———, and Don Kerr. 2004. *Population Change in Canada*, 2nd edn. Don Mills, ON: Oxford University Press.

———, Karol J. Krotki, and P. Krishnan. 1978. "Socio-cultural Variations in the Applicability of the Economic Model of Fertility," *Population Studies* 32, 2: 319–25.

———, and Kevin McQuillan. 1982. *Growth and Dualism: The Demographic Development of Canadian Society.* Toronto: Gage.

———, Zenaida Ravanera, and Thomas K. Burch. 2005. "Toward an SDC (Social Development Canada) Family Research Framework," Issues Paper for Social Development Canada Roundtable on Families (1–2 December 2005).

———, ———, and Kevin McQuillan. 2007. "Population Change in Canada to 2017 and Beyond: The Challenges of Policy Adaptation," *Horizons* 9, 4: 3–17, special issue on *Population at 2017: The Many Dimensions of Population Aging.*

Beaver, M.W. 1975. "Population, Infant Mortality and Milk," *Population Studies* 27, 2: 243–54.

Becker, Gary S. 1991. *A Treatise on the Family*, enlarged edn. Cambridge, MA: Harvard University Press.

———. 1974. "A Theory of Marriage: Part II," *Journal of Political Economy* 82: S11–26.

———. 1973. "A Theory of Marriage: Part I," *Journal of Political Economy* 81, 4: 813–46.

———. 1960. "An Economic Analysis of Fertility," in *Demographic and Economic Change in Developed Countries.* A Conference of the Universities, National Bureau Committee for Economic Research, Special Conference Series 11. Princeton, NJ: Princeton University Press.

———, Elisabeth M. Landes, and Robert T. Michael. 1977. "An Economic Analysis of Marital Instability," *Journal of Political Economy* 85, 6: 1141–87.

———, and H.G. Lewis. 1973. "On the Interaction between the Quantity and Quality of Children," *Journal of Political Economy* 81, 2: S279–88.

———, K.M. Murphy, and R. Tamura. 1990. "Human Capital, Fertility and Economic Growth," *Journal of Political Economy* 81, 5: S12–37.

Beckstead, Desmond, Mark Brown, G. Gellatly, and C. Seaborn. 2003. *A Decade of Growth: The Emerging Geography of New Economy Industries in the 1990s.* The Canadian Economy in Transition Research Paper Series 11-622-MIE2003003. Analytical Studies Branch. Ottawa: Statistics Canada.

Bedard, Mario, and Margaret Michalowski. 1997. *Advantages of the One Year Mobility Variable for Breaking Down Interprovincial Migration by Age, Sex and Marital Status.* Cat. no. 91F0015MIE1997004. Ottawa: Statistics Canada.

Beier, George J. 1976. "Can Third World Cities Cope?" *Population Bulletin* 31, 4. Washington: Population Reference Bureau.

Bélanger, Alain. 2006. *Report on the Demographic Situation in Canada: 2003 and 2004.* Cat. no. 91-209-XIE. Ottawa: Statistics Canada.

———. 2003. *Report on the Demographic Situation in Canada: 2002.* Cat. no. 91-209-XPE. Ottawa: Statistics Canada.

———. 2002. *Report on the Demographic Situation in Canada: 2001.* Cat. no. 91-209-XPE. Ottawa: Statistics Canada.

———, and Jean Dumas. 1998. *Report on the Demographic Situation in Canada: 1997.* Cat. no. 91-209-XPE. Ottawa: Statistics Canada.

———, and S. Gilbert. 2003. "The Fertility of Immigrant Women and Their Canadian-born Daughters," in Alain Bélanger, ed., *Report on the Demographic Situation in Canada 2002: Current Demographic Analysis,* 127–51. Ottawa: Minister of Industry.

———, and Geneviève Ouellet. 2002. "A Comparative Study of Recent Trends in Canadian and American

Fertility, 1980–1999," in Alain Bélanger, *Report on the Demographic Situation in Canada in 2001*. Cat. no. 91-209-XPE. Ottawa: Statistics Canada.

Bell, Martin. 2001. "Understanding Circulation in Australia," *Journal of Population Research* 18, 1: 1–18.

Bellis, Mark A., Tom Hennell, Clare Lushey, et al. 2007. "Elvis to Eminem: Quantifying the Price of Fame through Early Mortality of European and North American Rock and Pop Stars," *Journal of Epidemiology and Community Health* 61: 896–901.

Berelson, Bernard. 1979. "Romania's 1966 Abortion Decree: The Demographic Experience of the First Decade," *Population Studies* 33, 2: 205–22.

———. 1969. "Beyond Family Planning," *Studies in Family Planning* 38 (February): 1–16.

———, Shireen J. Jejeebhoy, Allen C. Kelly, et al. 1990. "The Great Debate on Population Policy: An Instructive Entertainment," *International Family Planning Perspectives* 16, 4: 126–48.

———, and Jonathan Lieberson. 1979. "Government Efforts to Influence Fertility: The Ethical Issues," *Population and Development Review* 54, 4: 581–614.

Bergob, Michael J. 1992. "Where Have all the Old Folks Gone? Interprovincial Migration of the Elderly in Canada: 1981–1986," *Canadian Studies in Population* 19, 1: 17–25.

Berkman, Lisa F. 2005. "Tracking Social and Biological Experiences: The Social Etiology of Cardiovascular Disease," *Circulation* 111: 302–24.

———, and Lester Breslow. 1983. *Health and Ways of Living: The Alameda County Study*. New York: Oxford University Press.

———, and Leonard S. Syme. 1979. "Social Networks, Host Resistance and Mortality: A Nine-Year Follow-up Study of Alameda County Residents," *American Journal of Epidemiology* 109, 2: 186–204.

Bernard, Aude, Martin Bell, and Elin Charles-Edwards. 2014. "Improved Measures for the Cross-National Comparison of Age Profiles of Internal Migration," *Population Studies* 68, 2: 179–95.

Bernhardt, Eva. 2003. "Cohabitation," in Paul Demeney and Geoffrey McNicol, eds, *Encyclopedia of Population*. New York: Macmillan Reference USA/Thomson Gale.

Bernstein, Peter L. 1996. *Against the Gods: The Remarkable Story of Risk*. New York: John Wiley & Sons.

Berry, Brian J.L. 1976 [1996]. "The Counterurbanisation Process: Urban America since 1970," in H.S. Geyer and T.M. Kontuly, eds, *Differential Urbanization:Integrating Spatial Models*. London: Edward Arnold.

Berry, Linda G. 1977. "Age and Parity Influences on Maternal Mortality: United States, 1919–1969," *Demography* 14, 3: 297–310.

Bertram, Gordon W. 1963. "Economic Growth in Canadian Industry, 1870–1915: The Staple Model and the Take-off Hypothesis," *The Canadian Journal of Economics and Political Science* 29, 2: 159–84.

Beshiri, R., and Ray D. Bollman. 2001. "Population Structure and Change in Predominantly Rural Regions," *Rural and Small Town Canada Analysis Bulletin*. Cat. no. 21-006-0XIE, no. 2.

Betencourt, Luís M.A., José Lobo, Dirk Helbing, Christian Kuhnert, and Geoffrey B. West. 2007. "Growth, Innovation, Scaling, and the Pace of Life in Cities," *Proceedings of the National Academies of Science* 104, 17: 7301–6.

Bhagwati, Jagdish. 2002. *Free Trade Today*. Princeton, NJ: Princeton University Press.

———. 2000. *The Wind of the Hundred Days*. Cambridge, MA: MIT Press.

Bhat, Mari P.N., and Shiva S. Halli. 1999. "Demography of Brideprice and Dowry: Causes and Consequences of the Indian Marriage Squeeze," *Population Studies* 53, 2: 129–48.

Bielby, W.T., and D.D. Bielby. 1992. "I Will Follow Him: Family Ties, Gender-Role Beliefs, and Reluctance to Relocate for a Better Job," *American Journal of Sociology* 97, 5: 1241–67.

Biggar, Jeanne C. 1979. "The Sunning of America: Migration to the Sunbelt," *Population Bulletin* 34, 1. Washington: Population Reference Bureau.

Biggs, Brian, and Ray D. Bollman. 1994. "Urbanization in Canada," in Craig McKie and Keith Thompson, *Canadian Social Trends*, vol. 2, 67–72. Toronto: Thompson.

Billari, Francesco, and Hans-Peter Kohler. 2004. "Patterns of Low and Lowest-Low Fertility in Europe," *Population Studies* 58, 2: 161–76.

Bilsborrow, R.E., ed. 1998. "The State of the Art and Overview of the Chapters." in Richard E. Bilsborrow, ed., *Migration, Urbanization and Development: New Directions and Issues*. New York: United Nations Population Fund and Kluwer Academic Publishers.

Bilsborrow, R.E., G. Hugo, A.S. Oberai, and H. Zlotnik. 1997. *International Migration Statistics: Guidelines for Improving Data Collection Systems*. Geneva: International Labour Office.

Biraben, Jean Noel. 2006. "The History of the Human Population from the First Beginnings to the Present Day," in Graziella Caselli, Jacques Vallin, and Guillaume Wunsch, eds, *Demography. Analysis and Synthesis: A Treatise in Population Studies*, vol. 3, 5–17. Amsterdam: Academic Press

———. 2003a. "The Rising Numbers of Humankind," *Population and Societies* 394 (October). Also available at www.ined.fr/englishversion/ publications/pop_et_soc/index.html.

———. 2003b. "World Population Growth," in Paul Demeny and Geoffrey McNicoll, eds, *Encyclopedia of Population*. New York: Macmillan Reference USA/Thomson Gale.

———. 1979. "Essai sur l'Évolution du nombre des hommes," *Population* 34, 1: 13–25.

Birdsall, Nancy, Allen C. Kelley, and Steven Sinding, eds. 2001. *Population Matters: Demographic Change, Economic Growth, and Poverty in the Developing World*. Oxford: Oxford University Press.

———, and Steven W. Sinding. 2001. "How and Why Population Matters: New Findings, New Issues," in Nancy Birdsall, Allen C. Kelley, and Steven W. Sinding, eds, *Population Matters: Demographic Change, Economic Growth, and Poverty in the Developing World*. Oxford: Oxford University Press.

Birg, Herwig. 1995. *World Population Projections for the 21st Century: Theoretical Interpretations and Quantitative Simulations*. Frankfurt and New York: Campus Verlag and St Martin's.

Blake, Judith. 1969. "Population Policy for Americans: Is the Government Being Misled?" *Science* 164, 3879: 522–9.

———. 1968. "Are Babies Consumer Durables?" *Population Studies* 22, 1: 5–25.

Blankenhorn, David. 2007. *The Future of Marriage*. New York: Encounter Books.

Blauner, Robert. 1966. "Death and Social Structure," *Psychiatry* 29: 378–94.

Bloom, David E., and David Canning. 2001. "Cumulative Causality, Economic Growth, and the Demographic Transition," in Nancy Birdsall, Allen C. Kelley, and Steven W. Sinding, eds, *Population Matters: Demographic Change, Economic Growth, and Poverty in the Developing World*. Oxford: Oxford University Press.

———, and ———. 2000. "The Health and Wealth of Nations," *Science* 287: 1207–9.

———, ———, and Jaypee Sevilla. 2003. "The Demographic Dividend: A New Perspective on the Economic Consequences of Population Change," *Population Matters: A RAND Program Policy-Relevant Research Communication*. Santa Monica, CA: RAND Corporation.

———, and Jeffrey G. Williamson. 1998. "Demographic Transitions and Economic Miracles in Emerging Asia," *The World Bank Economic Review* 12, 3: 419–55.

Blue, Laura, and Thomas J. Espanshade. 2011. "Population Momentum across the Demographic Transition," *Population and Development Review* 37, 4:721–47.

Bobak, Martin, and Arjan Gjonca. 2001. "The Seasonality of Live Birth Is Strongly Influenced by Socio-Demographic Factors," *Human Reproduction* 16, 7: 1512–17.

Bocquet-Appel, Jean-Pierre. 2011. "When the World's Population Took off: The Springboard of the Neolithic Demographic Transition," *Science* 333 (29 July): 560–1.

———, and Ofer Bar-Yosef, eds. 2008. *The Neolithic Demographic Transition and its Consequences*. New York: Springer Science + Business Media.

Bogardus, Emory S. 1960. *The Development of Social Thought*, 4th edn. New York: Longmans, Green, and Co.

Bogue, Donald J. 1969. *Principles of Demography*. New York: John Wiley & Sons.

Bohnert, Nora. 2013a. *Mortality: Overview, 2008 and 2009*. Component of Statistics Canada Catalogue no. 91-209-X, Report on the Demographic Situation in Canada: Ottawa: Minister of Industry.

———. 2013b. *Migration: Interprovincial, 2009/2010 and 2010/2011*. Component of Statistics Canada Catalogue no. 91-209-X. Report on the Demographic Situation in Canada.

Bollman, Ray D. 2000. *Rural and Small Town Canada: An Overview*. www.statcan.ca:8096/bsolc/english/ bsolc?catno=21F0018X&CHROPG=1.

———, and Brian Biggs, eds. 1992. *Rural and Small Town Canada*. Toronto: Thompson.

Bonaguidi, Alberto, ed. 1985. *Migrazioni e Demografia Regionale in Italia*. Milano: Franco Angeli.

Bongaarts, John. 2013. "The Implementation of Preferences for Male Offspring," *Population and Development Review* 39, 2: 185–208.

———. 2009. "Human Population Growth and the Demographic Transition," *Philosophical Transactions of the Royal Society B* 364: 2985–90.

———. 2008. "Fertility Transitions in Developing Countries: Progress or Stagnation?" *Studies in Family Planning* 39, 2: 105–10.

———. 2006. "How Long Will We Live?" *Population and Development Review* 32, 4: 605–28.

———. 2004. "Population Aging and the Rising Cost of Public Pensions," *Population and Development Review* 30, 1: 1–24.

———. 2003. "Proximate Determinants of Fertility," in Paul Demeny and Geoffrey McNicoll, eds, *Encyclopedia of Population*. New York: Macmillan Reference USA/Thomson Gale.

———. 1994. "Population Policy Options in the Developing World," *Science* 263 (11 February): 771–6.

———. 1978. "A Framework for Analyzing the Proximate Determinants of Fertility," *Population and Development Review* 4, 1: 105–32.

———. 1975. "Why High Birth Rates Are So Low," *Population and Development Review* 1, 2: 289–96.

———, and Rodolfo A. Bulatao, eds. 2000. *Beyond Six Billion: Forecasting the World's Population*. Washington, DC: National Academies Press.

———, and Griffith Feeney. 1998. "On the Quantum and Tempo of Fertility," *Population and Development Review* 24, 2: 271–92.

———, and Susan Greenhalgh. 1985. "An Alternative to the One-Child Policy in China," *Population and Development Review* 11, 4: 585–618.

———, W. Parker Mauldin, and James F. Philips. 1990. "The Demographic Impact of Family Planning Programs," *Studies in Family Planning* 21, 6: 299–310.

———, François Pelletier, and Patrick Gerland. 2011. "Global Trends in AIDS Mortality," in R.G. Rogers and

E.M. Crimmins, eds, *International Handbook of Adult Mortality*, 171–83. New York, NY: Springer.

——, and Robert G. Potter. 1983. *Fertility, Biology, and Behavior: An Analysis of the Proximate Determinants.* New York: Academic Press.

——, and Steven W. Sinding. 2009. "A Response to Critics of Family Planning Programs," *International Perspectives on Sexual and Reproductive Health* 35, 1: 39–44.

——, and Tomas Sobotka. 2012. "A Demographic Explanation for the Recent Rise in European Fertility," *Population and Development Review* 38, 1: 83–120.

——, and Susan Cotts Watkins. 1996. "Social Interactions and Contemporary Fertility Transitions," *Population and Development Review* 22, 4: 639–82.

Bonney, Norman, Alison McCleery, and Emma Forster. 1999. "Migration, Marriage and the Life Course: Commitment and Residential Mobility," in Paul Boyle and Keith Halfcree, eds, *Migration and Gender in the Developed World.* London: Routledge.

Booth, Alan, David R. Johnson, Lynn White, et al. 1984. "Women, Outside Employment, and Marital Instability," *American Journal of Sociology* 90: 567–83.

Booth, Frank W., and P. Darrell Neufer. 2005. "Exercise Controls Gene Expression," *American Scientist* 93 (January–February): 28–35.

Borjas, George J. 1999. *Heaven's Door: Immigration Policy and the American Economy.* Princeton, NJ: Princeton University Press.

Boserup, Ester. 1981. *Population and Technological Change: A Study of Long-Term Trends.* Chicago: The University of Chicago Press.

——. 1965. *The Conditions of Agricultural Growth.* Chicago: Aldine.

Bourbeau, Robert, Jacques Légaré, and Valerie Émond. 1997. *New Birth Cohort Life Tables for Canada and Quebec, 1801–1991.* Current Demographic Analysis no. 3. Cat. no. 91F0015MPE. Ottawa: Statistics Canada.

Bourgeois-Pichat, Jean. 1986. "The Unprecedented Shortage of Births in Europe," *Population and Development Review* 12 (supp.): 3–25.

Bourgeois-Pichat M.J. 1952. "Essai sur la mortalité 'biologique' de l'homme," *Population* 3 (July–September): 381–94.

——. 1951 [1981]. "Measuring Infant Mortality," *Population* (Selected Papers no. 6). Paris: National Institute of Population Studies.

Bourne, Larry S. 2000. "Urban Canada in Transition to the Twenty-First Century: Trends, Issues, and Visions," in Trudi Bunting and Pierre Filion, eds, *Canadian Cities in Transition: The Twenty-First Century.* Don Mills, ON: Oxford University Press.

——, Tom Hutton, Richard G. Shearmur, and Jim Simmons, eds. 2011. *Canadian Urban Regions: Trajectories of Growth and Change.* Toronto: Oxford University Press.

——, and A.E. Olvet. 1995. *New Urban and Regional Geographies in Canada: 1986–91 and Beyond.* Major Report 33. Toronto: Centre for Urban and Community Studies.

——, and Damaris Rose. 2001. "The Changing Face of Canada: The Uneven Geographies of Population and Social Change," *The Canadian Geographer* 45, 1: 105–19.

Boyd, Monica. 1989. "Family and Personal Network in International Migration: Recent Developments and New Agendas," *International Migration Review* 23, 3: 638–70.

Boyd, Monica, and Elizabeth Grieco. 1998. "Triumphant Transitions: Socioeconomic Achievements of the Second Generation in Canada." *International Migration Review* 32, 4: 857–876.

Boyd, Monica, and Michael Vickers. 2000. "100 Years of Immigration." *Canadian Social Trends* 58: 2–12.

Boyle, Paul, Keith Halfcree, and Dareen Smith. 1999. "Family Migration and Female Participation in the Labour Market: Moving Beyond Individual-level Analyses," in Paul Boyle and Keith Halfcree, eds, *Migration and Gender in the Developed World.* London: Routledge.

Bozon, Michel. 2003. "At What Age Do Women and Men Have Their First Sexual Intercourse? World Comparisons and Recent Trends," *Population & Societies* 391 (June): 3. INED www.ined.fr/english version/pop_et_soc/index.html.

Brackman, S., H. Garretsen, C. Van Marrewijk, et al. 1999. "The Return of Zipf: Towards a Further Understanding of the Rank-Size Distribution," *Journal of Regional Science* 39: 183–213.

Braudel, Fernand. 1979. *Civilization and Capitalism, 15th–18th Centuries.* 3 vols. Siân Reynolds, trans. Vol. 1: *The Structures of Everyday Life;* vol. 2: *The Wheels of Commerce;* vol. 3: *The Perspective of the World.* New York: Harper and Row.

——. 1966. *The Mediterranean and the Mediterranean World in the Age of Philip II,* vol. 1. Berkley: University of California Press.

Braziel, Jana Evans, and Anita Mannur, eds. 2003. *Theorizing Diaspora: A Reader.* Malden, MA: Blackwell.

Breton, Raymond. 1964. "Institutional Completeness of Ethnic Communities and the Personal Relations of Immigrants," *American Journal of Sociology* 70: 193–205.

Brewster, Karin L., and Ronald R. Rindfuss. 2000. "Fertility and Women's Employment in Industrialized Nations," *Annual Review of Sociology* 26: 271–96.

Brian, Eric, and Marie Jaisson. 2007. *The Descent of Human Sex Ratio at Birth: A Dialogue between Mathematics, Biology and Sociology.* Dordrecht: Springer.

Brockerhoff, Martin P. 2000. "An Urbanizing World," *Population Bulletin* 55, 3. Washington, DC: Population Reference Bureau.

Broudy, D.W., and P.A. May. 1983. "Demographic and Epidemiologic Transitions among the Navajo Indians," *Social Biology* 30:1–16.

Brown, Alan A., and Egon Neuberger. 1977. "Comparative Analysis of Internal Migration: An Overview," in Alan A. Brown and Egon Neuberger, eds, *Internal Migration: A Comparative Perspective*. New York: Academic Press.

Brown, Lester R. 2011. *World on the Edge: How to Prevent Environmental and Economic Collapse*. New York: W.W. Norton.

———, Gary Gardner, and Brian Halweil. 1999. *Beyond Malthus: Nineteen Dimensions of the Population Challenge*. New York: W.W. Norton.

Bryan, Thomas. 2004a. "Population Estimates," in Jacob S. Siegel and David A. Swanson, eds, *The Methods and Materials of Demography*, 2nd edn, 523–60. San Diego, CA: Elsevier.

———. 2004b. "Basic Sources of Statistics," in Jacob S. Siegel and David Swanson, eds, *The Methods and Materials of Demography*, 2nd edn. San Diego, CA: Elsevier.

Bryant, Christopher R., and Alun E. Joseph. 2001. "Canada's Rural Population: Trends in Space and Implications in Place," *The Canadian Geographer* 45, 1: 132–7.

Budinski, Ron, and Frank Trovato. 2005. "The Effect of Premarital Cohabitation on Marital Stability over the Duration of Marriage," *Canadian Studies in Population* 32, 1: 69–95.

Buhaug, Halvard. 2010. "Climate Not to Blame for African Civil Wars," *Proceedings of the National Academy of Sciences of the United States of America* 107, 38:16477–82.

Bulatao, Rodolfo A. 2001. "Introduction," in Rodolfo A. Bulatao and John B. Casterline, eds, *Global Fertility Transition*, supp. to *Population and Development Review* 27. New York: Population Council.

———, and John B. Casterline, eds. 2001. *Global Fertility Transition*, supp. to *Population and Development Review* 27. New York: Population Council.

Bumpass, Larry L. 1990. "What's Happening to the Family? Interactions between Demographic and Institutional Change," *Demography* 27: 483–98.

———, James A. Sweet, and Andrew Cherlin. 1991. "The Role of Cohabitation in Declining Rates of Marriage," *Journal of Marriage and the Family* 53: 913–27.

Bunting, Trudy, and Pierre Filion, eds. 2000. *Canadian Cities in Transition: The Twenty-First Century*, 2nd edn. Don Mills, ON: Oxford University Press.

Burch, Thomas K. 2002a. "Teaching the Fundamentals of Demography: Ten Principles and Two Rationales," *Genus* LVIII, 3–4: 21–34.

———. 2002b. "Teaching the Fundamentals of Demography: A Model-based Approach to Family and Fertility," *Genus* LVIII, 3–4: 73–90.

———. 1979. "The Structure of Demographic Action," *Journal of Population* 2, 4: 279–93.

———. 1966. "The Fertility of North American Catholics: A Comparative Overview," *Demography* 3, 2: 174–87.

Bureau de la Statistique du Québec. 1997. *La Situation démographique au Québec: édition 1997*. Quebec City: Les Publications du Québec.

Burger, Oskar, Annette Baudisch, and James W. Vaupel, 2012. "Human Mortality Improvement in Evolutionary Context," *Proceedings of the National Academies of Science* 109, 44:18210–14.

Burgess, Ernest W. 1925. "The Growth of the City," in Robert E. Park, Ernest W. Burgess, and R.D. MacKenzie, *The City*. Chicago: Chicago University Press.

Burke, M.B., E. Miguel, S. Satyanath, J.A. Dykema, and D.B. Lobell. 2009. "Warming Increases the Risk of Civil War in Africa," *Proceedings of the National Academy of Sciences of the United States of America* 106, 4: 20670–4.

Bushnik, Tracey, Jocelynn L. Cook, A. Albert Yuzpe, Suzanne Tough, and John Collins. 2012. "Estimating the Prevalence of Infertility in Canada," *Human Reproduction* 27, 3: 738–46.

Butz, William P., and Michael P. Ward. 1979a. "The Emergence of Countercyclical US Fertility," *The American Economic Review* 69, 3: 318–28.

———. 1979b. "Will US Fertility Remain Low? A New Economic Interpretation," *Population and Development Review* 5, 4: 663–88.

Cadwallader, Martin. 1992. *Migration and Residential Mobility: Micro and Macro Approaches*. Madison, WI: The University of Wisconsin Press.

Cai, Yong. 2012. "China's Demographic Reality and Future," *Asian Population Studies* 8 (1): 1–13.

———. 2010. "China's Below-Replacement Fertility: Government Policy or Socioeconomic Development?" *Population and Development Review* 36, 3: 419–40.

———, and Wang Feng. 2005. "Famine, Social Disruption, and Involuntary Fetal Loss," *Demography* 42, 2: 301–22.

Cain, Mead. 1993. "Patriarchal Structure and Demographic Change," in Nora Federici, Karen Oppenheim Mason, and Solvi Sogner, eds, *Women's Position and Demographic Change*. Oxford: Clarendon.

———. 1987. "The Consequences of Reproductive Failure: Dependence Mobility and Mortality among the Elderly of Rural South Asia," *Population Studies* 40, 3: 375–88.

———. 1985. "On the Relationship between Landholding and Fertility," *Population Studies* 39: 5–15.

——. 1983. "Fertility as an Adjustment to Risk," *Population and Development Review* 9, 4: 688–702.

——. 1982. "Perspectives on Family and Fertility in Developing Countries," *Population Studies* 36, 2: 159–75.

Caldwell, John C. 2006. "On Net Intergenerational Wealth Flows: An Update," in John C. Caldwell ed., *Demographic Transition Theory*. Dordrecht: Springer.

——. 2001. "The Globalization of Fertility Behavior," in Rodolfo A. Bulatao and John B. Casterline, eds, *Global Fertility Transition*, supp. to *Population and Development Review* 27. New York: Population Council.

——. 1991. "Introductory Thoughts on Health Transition," in John C. Caldwell, et al., eds, *What We Know about Health Transition: The Cultural, Social and Behavioural Determinants of Health*, 2 vols. Proceedings of an International Workshop (May 1989). Canberra: Australian National University.

——. 1986. "Routes to Low Mortality in Poor Countries," *Population and Development Review* 12, 2: 171–220.

——. 1982. *Theory of Fertility Decline*. London: Academic Press.

——. 1976. "Toward a Restatement of the Demographic Transition Theory," *Population and Development Review* 2, 3–4: 321–66.

——, and Pat Caldwell. 1997. "What Do We Know about the Fertility Transition?" in Gavin W. Jones, et al., eds, *The Continuing Demographic Transition*. Oxford: Clarendon.

——, and ——. 1990. "High Fertility in Sub-Saharan Africa," *Scientific American* (May): 118–25.

——, ——, Bruce K. Caldwell, and Indrani Pieris. 1998. "The Construction of Adolescence in a Changing World: Implications for Sexuality, Reproduction, and Marriage," *Studies in Family Planning* 29, 2: 137–53.

——, and Thomas Schindlmayr, 2003 "Explanations of the Fertility Crisis in Modern Societies: A Search for Commonalities," *Population Studies* 57, 3: 241–63.

Calot, Gérard. 2006. "The Effect of Pronatalist Policies in Industrialized Countries," in Graziella Caselli, Jacques Vallin, and Guillaume Wunsch, eds, *Demography: Analysis and Synthesis*. Amsterdam: Elsevier.

Cambois, Emmanuelle, Jean-Marie Robine, and Mark D. Hayward. 2002. "Social Inequalities in Disability-Free Life Expectancy in the French Male Population, 1980–1991," *Demography* 38, 4: 513–24.

Campbell, Kenneth L., and James W. Wood, eds. 1994. *Human Reproductive Ecology: Interactions of Environment, Fertility, and Behavior*, vol. 709. New York: The New York Academy of Sciences.

Canada Dominion Bureau of Statistics. 1923. *Vital Statistics 1921*. First Annual Report. Ottawa: F.A. Acland, Printer to the King's Most Excellent Majesty.

Canadian Broadcasting Corporation (CBC). 2004. "Chechnya," *The Passionate Eye* (aired 15 November).

Canadian Institute for Child Health. 1994. *The Health of Canada's Children: A CICH Profile*, 2nd edn. Ottawa: CICH.

Canadian Institute for Health Information. 2002. *Health Care in Canada*. Ottawa: CIHI.

Canon, Kenneth L., and Ruby Gingles. 1956. "Social Factors Related to Divorce Rates for Urban Counties in Nebraska," *Rural Sociology* 21: 34–40.

Carens, Joseph H. 1999. "Reconsidering Open Borders," *International Migration Review* 33, 4: 1082–97.

——. 1987. "Aliens and Citizens: The Case for Open Borders," *Review of Politics* 49, 2: 251–73.

Carey, James R. 2003a. "Life Span," in Paul Demeny and Geoffrey McNicoll, eds, *Encyclopedia of Population*. New York: Macmillan Reference USA/Thomson Gale.

——. 2003b. "Life Span: A Conceptual Overview," in James R. Carey and Shripad Tuljapurkar, eds, *Life Span: Evolutionary, Ecological, and Demographic Perspectives*, supp. to *Population and Development Review* 29. New York: Population Council.

——, and Debra S. Judge. 2001. "Principles of Biodemography with Special Reference to Human Longevity," *Population: An English Selection* 13, 1: 9–40.

——, and Shripad Tuljapurkar, eds. 2003. *Life Span: Evolutionary, Ecological, and Demographic Perspectives*, supp. to *Population and Development Review* 29. New York: Population Council.

Carlson, Elwood. 2008. *The Lucky Few: Between the Greatest Generation and the Baby Boom*. New York: Springer.

Carlson, Gosta. 1966. "The Decline in Fertility: Innovation or Adjustment Process," *Population Studies* 20: 149–74.

Carmel, Emma, Alfio Cerami, and Theodoros Papadopoulos, eds. 2012. *Migration and Welfare in the New Europe: Social Protection and the Challenges of Integration*. Bristol, UK: The Policy Press.

Case, Anne, and Christina Paxson. 2005. "Sex Differences in Morbidity and Health," *Demography* 42, 2: 189–214.

Caselli, Graziella, F. Meslé, and J. Vallin. 2002. "Epidemiologic Transition Theory Exceptions," *Genus* LVIII, 1: 9–52.

——, and Jacques Vallin. 1990. "Mortality and Population Ageing," *European Journal of Population* 6, 11–25.

——, ——, and Guillaume Wunsch, eds. 2006. *Demography. Analysis and Synthesis: A Treatise in Population Studies*, 4 vols. Amsterdam: Academic Press.

Caspi, Avshalom, Bradley, R. Entner Wright, T.E. Moffitt, et al. 1998. "Early Failure in the Labor Market: Childhood and Adolescent Predictors of

Unemployment in the Transition to Adulthood," *American Sociological Review* 63, 3: 424–51.

Cassel, J. 1976. "The Contribution of the Social Environment to Host Resistance," *American Journal of Epidemiology* 104: 107–23.

Casterline, John B. 2001. "The Pace of Fertility Transition: National Patterns in the Second Half of the Twentieth Century," in Rodolfo A. Bulatao and John B. Casterline, eds, *Global Fertility Transition*, supp. to *Population and Development Review* 27. New York: Population Council.

Castles, Steven, and Mark J. Miller. 2009. *The Age of Migration: International Population Movements in the Modern World*, 4th edn. New York: Guilford.

Catalano, Ralf, J. Ahern, T. Bruckner, E. Anderson, and K. Saxton. 2009. "Gender-Specific Selection in Utero among Contemporary Human Birth Cohorts," *Paediatric Perinatal Epidemiology* 23: 273–8.

———, T. Bruckner, A.R. Marks, and B. Eskenazi. 2006. "Exogenous Shocks to the Human Sex Ratio: The Case of September 11, 2001 in New York City," *Human Reproduction* 21: 3127–31.

———, J. Goodman, C.E. Margerison-Zilko, K.B. Saxton, E. Anderson, and M. Epstein. 2012a. "Selection against Small Males in Utero: A Test of the Wells Hypothesis," *Human Reproduction* 27, 4: 1202–8.

———, K.B. Saxton, T. Bruckner, and et al. 2012b. "Hormonal Evidence Supports the Theory of Selection in Utero," *American Journal of Human Biology* 24: 526–32.

———, T. Yorifuji, and I. Kawachi. 2013. "Natural Selection in Utero: Evidence from the Great East Japan Earthquake," *American Journal of Human Biology* 25: 555–9.

———, C.E. Zilko, K.B. Saxton, and T. Bruckner. 2010. "Selection in Utero: A Biological Response to Mass Layoffs. *American Journal of Human Biology* 22: 396–400.

Catto, Susan. 2003. "A Slow Death," *Time* (Canadian edn) 13 October: 49–59.

Caughley, Graeme. 1966. "Mortality Patterns in Mammals," *Ecology* 47, 6: 906–18.

Cavalli-Sforza, L., and Francesco Cavalli-Sforza. 1995. *Great Human Diasporas: The History of Diversity and Evolution*. Sarah Thorne, trans. New York: Addison-Wesley (Helix Books).

Cebula, Richard J. 1979. *The Determinants of Human Migration*. Lexington, MA: Lexington Books.

Cesario, Sandra K. 2002. "The 'Christmas Effect' and Other Biometeorologic Influences on Childbearing and the Health of Women," *Journal of Obstetrics Gynecology and Neonatal Nursing* 31, 5: 526–35.

Chahnazarian, Anouch. 1988. "Determinants of the Sex Ratio at Birth: Review of Recent Literature," *Social Biology* 35: 214–35.

Chamie, Joseph, and Robert Mirkin. 2011. "Same-Sex Marriage: A New Social Phenomenon," *Population and Development Review* 37, 3: 529–51.

Champion, Anthony H. 2001. "Urbanization, Suburbanization, Counterurbanization and Reurbanization," in Ronald Paddison, ed., *Handbook of Urban Studies*. London: Sage.

———. 1988 [1996]. "The Reversal of the Migration Turnaround: Resumption of Traditional Trends?" in H.S. Geyer and T.M. Kontuly, eds, *Differential Urbanization: Integrating Spatial Models*. London: Edward Arnold.

Chappell, Neena L., Ellen M. Gee, L. MacDonald, and M. Stones. 2003. *Aging in Contemporary Canada*. Toronto: Prentice-Hall.

Charbonneau, Hubert. 1977. "Les regimes de fecondite naturelle en Amerique du Nord: Bilan et analyse des observations," in Henri Leridon and Jane Menken, eds, *Natural Fertility*. International Union for the Scientific Study of Population. Liege: Ordina Editions.

———. 1975. *Vie et mort de nos ancêtres*. Montreal: Les Presses de l'Université de Montréal.

———, Bertrand Desjardins, Jacques Legare, and Hubert Denis. 2000. "The Population of the St Lawrence Valley, 1608–1760," in Michael R. Haines and Richard H. Steckel, eds, *A Population History of North America*. Cambridge: Cambridge University Press.

Charles, Enid. 1948. *The Changing Size of the Family in Canada*, Census Monograph no. 1, Eighth Census of Canada, 1941. Ottawa: King's Printer.

Charny, Israel W. 1999. *The Encyclopedia of Genocide*. Santa Barbara, CA: ABC-CLIO.

Charon, Joel M. 1998. *The Meaning of Sociology*, 6th edn. Upper Saddle River, NJ: Prentice Hall.

Chase, Helne C. 1969. "Registration Completeness and International Comparisons of Infant Mortality," *Demography* 6, 4: 425–33.

Chase-Dunn, Christopher, and Andrew Jorgenson. 2003. "Systems of Cities," in Paul Demeny and Geoffrey McNicoll, eds, *Encyclopedia of Population*. New York: Macmillan Reference USA/Thomson Gale.

Chasteland, Jean-Claude. 2006. "World Population Growth and the International Community from 1950 to Present Day," in Graziella Caselli, Jacques Vallin, and Guillaume Wunsch, eds, *Demography: Analysis and Synthesis*. Amsterdam: Elsevier.

Chen, Jiajian, and Wayne J. Millar. 2000. "Are Recent Cohorts Healthier than Their Predecessors?" *Health Reports* 11, 4: 9–23.

Chen, Yu, Weifeng Liang, Shigui Yang, et al. 2013. "Human Infections with the Emerging Avian Influenza A H7N9 Virus from Wet Market Poultry: Clinical Analysis and Characterisation of Viral Genome," *Lancet* (25 April) http://dx.doi.org/10.1016/S0140-6736(13)60903-4.

Cherlin, Andrew J. 2012. "Goode's World Revolutions and Family Patterns: A Reconsideration at Fifty Years," *Population and Development Review* 38, 4: 577–608.

——. 2004. "The Deinstitutionalization of American Marriage," *Journal of Marriage and the Family* 66: 848–61.

——. 2003. "Family Demography," in Paul Demeny and Geoffrey McNicoll, eds, *Encyclopedia of Population*. New York: Macmillan Reference USA/Thomson Gale.

——. 1981. *Marriage, Divorce, and Remarriage*. Cambridge, MA: Harvard University Press.

Cheru, Fantu, and Colin Bradford, eds. 2005. *The Millennium Development Goals: Raising the Resources to Tackle World Poverty*. London and New York: Zed Books.

Chesnais, Jean-Claude. 1992. *The Demographic Transition: Stages, Patterns and Implications*. Elizabeth and Philip Kreager, trans. Oxford: Clarendon.

Cheung, Siu Lan Karen, Jean-Marie Robine, Edward J.C. Tu, et al. 2005. "Three Dimensions of the Survival Curve," *Demography* 42, 2: 243–58.

Chevan, A., and L.R. Fischer. 1979. "Retirement and Interstate Migration," *Social Forces* 57: 1365–80.

Chiang, Chin Long. 1984. *The Life Table and Its Applications*. Malabar, FL: Robert E. Krieger.

Childe, V. Gordon. 1950 "The Urban Revolution," *The Town Planning Review* 21, 1: 3–17.

Choudhry, Misbah T., and I. Paul Elhorst. 2010. "Demographic Transition and Economic Growth in China, India and Pakistan," *Economic Systems* 34: 218–36.

Christaller, Walter. 1933 [1966]. *Central Places in Southern Germany*. Carlisle Baskin, trans. Englewood Cliffs, NJ: Prentice Hall.

Christensen, Kaare, Gabriele Doblhammer, Roland Rau, and James W Vaupel. 2009. "Ageing Populations: The Challenges Ahead," *Lancet* 374, 9696: 1196–1208.

Chui, Tina W.L., and Frank Trovato. 1989. "Ethnic Variations in Fertility: Microeconomic and Minority Group Status Effects," *International Review of Modern Sociology* 19, 1: 80–92.

Cincotta, Richard P., and John Doces. 2012. "The Age-Structural Maturity Thesis: The Impact of the Youth Bulge on the Advent and Stability of Liberal Democracy," in Jack A. Goldstone, Eric P. Kaufmann, and Monica Duffy Toft, eds, *Political Demography: How Population Changes Are Reshaping International Security and National Politics*, 98–116 Boulder, CO: Paradigm Publishers.

——, and Robert Engelman. 1997. "Economics and Rapid Change: The Influence of Population Growth," Occasional Paper no. 3 (October). Washington, DC: Population Action International.

Ciocco, Antonio. 1938. "The Masculinity of Stillbirths and Abortions in Relation to the Duration of Uterogestation and to the Stated Causes of Foetal Mortality," *Human Biology* 10, 2: 235–50.

Cipolla, Carlo M. 1962. *The Economic History of World Population*. Harmondsworth, UK: Penguin.

Citizenship and Immigration Canada. 2013. *Facts and Figures 2012—Immigration Overview: Permanent and Temporary Residents*. www.cic.gc.ca/english/resources/statistics/facts2012/permanent/02.asp (accessed 28 September 2013).

——. 2012. Canada Facts and Figures 2012: Immigration Overview Permanent and Temporary Residents. Ottawa: Minister of Public Works and Government Services.

——. 2006. *Annual Report to Parliament on Immigration 2006*. Cat. no. C&I-831-10-06.

——. 2005. *Facts and Figures 2004: Immigration Overview: Permanent and Temporary Residents*. Cat. no. C&I-743-08-03E. www.cic.gc.ca/english/pub/facts2004/overview/1.html (accessed 30 September 2005).

——. 2002. *Facts and Figures 2000: Immigration Overview: Permanent and Temporary Residents*. www.cic.gc.ca/english/pub/facts2001/1imm-05.html.

Clark, S.D. 1972. "Rural Migration and Patterns of Urban Growth," in Edward B. Harvey, ed., *Perspectives on Modernization: Essays in Memory of Ian Weinberg*. Toronto: University of Toronto Press.

Clark, Warren. 2007. "Delayed Transitions of Young Adults," *Canadian Social Trends*. Statistics Canada (Catalogue No. 11-008): 13–21.

Clarke, John I. 2003. "Sex Ratio," in Paul Demeny and Geoffrey McNicoll, eds, *Encyclopedia of Population*. New York: Macmillan Reference USA/Thomson Gale.

——. 2000. *The Human Dichotomy: The Changing Numbers of Males and Females*. Amsterdam: Pergamon.

——. 1997. *Predictions: The Future of Population*. London: Phoenix.

——. 1996. "The Impact of Population Change on Environment: An Overview," in Bernardo Colombo, Paul Demeny, and Max F. Perutz, eds, *Resources and Population: Natural, Institutional, and Demographic Dimensions of Development*. Oxford: Clarendon.

——. 1970. *Population Geography*. Oxford: Pergamon.

Clatworthy, Stewart, and Mary Jane Norris. 2014. "Aboriginal Mobility and Migration in Canada: Trends, Patterns, and Implications, 1971 to 2006," in Frank Trovato and Anatole Romaniuk, eds, *Aboriginal Populations—Social, Demographic and Epidemiological Perspectives*. Edmonton: University of Alberta Press.

——, and ——. 2006. "Aboriginal Mobility and Migration; Trends, Recent Patterns, and Implications: 1971–2001," in Jerry P. White, Susan Wingert, Dan

Beavon, and Paul Maxim, eds, *Aboriginal Policy Research: Moving Forward, Making a Difference*, 4: 207–34. Toronto: Thompson.

Cleland, John. 2001. "The Effects of Improved Survival on Fertility: A Reassessment," in Rodolfo A. Bulatao and John B. Casterline, eds, *Global Fertility Transition*, supp. to *Population and Development Review* 27. New York: Population Council.

———. 1996. "Population Growth in the 21st Century: Cause for Crisis or Celebration?" *Tropical Medicine and International Health* 1, 1: 15–26.

———, Stan Bernstein, Alex Ezeh, et al. 2006. "Family Planning: The Unfinished Agenda," *Lancet* 368 (18 November): 1810–27.

———, Austin Conde-Agudelo, Herbert Peterson, John Ross, and Amy Tsui. 2012. "Contraception and Health," *Lancet* 380 (July 14): 149–56.

———, and John Hobcraft. 1985. *Reproductive Change in Developing Countries: Insights from the World Fertility Survey*. Oxford: Oxford University Press.

———, and Christopher Wilson. 1987. "Demand Theories of the Fertility Transition: An Iconoclastic View," *Population Studies* 41, 1: 5–30.

Coale, Ansley J. 1996. "Age Patterns and Time Sequence of Mortality in National Populations with the Highest Expectation of Life at Birth," *Population and Development Review* 22, 1: 127–36.

———. 1991. "Excess Female Mortality and the Balance of the Sexes in the Population: An Estimate of the Number of Missing Females," *Population and Development Review* 17: 517–23.

———. 1986. "The Decline of Fertility in Europe since the Eighteenth Century as a Chapter in Demographic History," in Ansley J. Coale and Susan Cotts Watkins, eds, *The Decline of Fertility in Europe*. Princeton, NJ: Princeton University Press.

———. 1983. "Recent Trends in Fertility in Less Developed Countries," *Science* 221: 828–32.

———. 1974. "The History of the Human Population," *The Human Population*, special issue of *Scientific American*. San Francisco: W.H. Freeman.

———. 1973. "The Demographic Transition Reconsidered," in *Proceedings of the International Population Conference*. Liege, BE: Liege International Union for the Scientific Study of Population.

———. 1972. *The Growth and Structure of Human Populations: A Mathematical Investigation*. Princeton, NJ: Princeton University Press.

———. 1969. "The Decline of Fertility in Europe from the French Revolution to World War II," in S.J. Behrman, Leslie Corsa Jr, and Ronald Freedman, eds, *Fertility and Family Planning: A World View*. Ann Arbor, MI: The University of Michigan Press.

———. 1964. "How a Population Ages or Grows Younger," in Ronald Freedman, ed., *Population: The Vital Revolution*. Garden City, NY: Doubleday (Anchor Books).

———. 1957a. "How the Age Distribution of a Human Population Is Determined," *Cold Spring Harbor Symposia on Quantitative Biology* 22: 83–9.

———. 1957b. "A New Method for Calculating Lotka's *r*— The Intrinsic Rate of Growth in a Stable Population," *Population Studies* 11, 1: 92–4.

———, and Paul Demeny. 1983. *Regional Model Life Tables and Stable Populations*, 2nd edn. New York: Academic Press.

———, and Edgar M. Hoover. 1958. *Population Growth and Economic Development in Low-Income Countries*. Princeton, NJ: Princeton University Press.

———, and Susan Cotts Watkins, eds. 1986. *The Decline of Fertility in Europe*. Princeton, NJ: Princeton University Press.

Cobb, S. 1976. "Social Support as a Moderator of Life Stress," *Psychosomatic Medicine* 38: 300–14.

Cochrane, S.G., and D.R. Vining Jr. 1988 [1996]. "Recent Trends in Migration between Core and Peripheral Region in Developed and Advanced Developing Countries," in H.S. Geyer and T.M. Kontuly, eds, *Differential Urbanization: Integrating Spatial Models*. London: Edward Arnold.

Coffey, William J. 2000. "Canadian Cities and Shifting Fortunes of Economic Development," in Trudy Bunting and Pierre Filion, eds, *Canadian Cities in Transition: The Twenty-First Century*, 2nd edn. Don Mills, ON: Oxford University Press.

———. 1994. *The Evolution of Canada's Metropolitan Economies*. Montreal: The Institute for Research on Public Policy.

Cohen, Joel E. 2003. "Human Population: The Next Half Century," *Science* 302 (14 November): 1172–5.

———. 1995. *How Many People Can the Earth Support?* New York: W.W. Norton.

Cohen, Robin. 1997. *Global Diasporas: An Introduction*. Seattle: University of Washington Press.

Cohn, Samuel Jr. 2003. "Black Death," in Paul Demeny and Geoffrey McNicoll, eds, *Encyclopedia of Population*. New York: Macmillan Reference USA/Thomson Gale.

Coleman, David. 2002. "Replacement Migration, or Why Everyone Is Going to Have to Live in Korea: A Fable for Our Times from the United Nations," *Philosophical Transactions of the Royal Society of London B* 357: 583–98.

Collins, Francis S., and Anna D. Barker. 2007. "Mapping the Cancer Genome," *Scientific American* 296, 3 (March): 50–7.

Coltrane, S. 1996. *Family Man: Fatherhood, Housework and Gender Equity*. New York: Oxford University Press.

Columbia Encyclopedia, 6th edn. 2003. New York: Columbia University Press. www.bartleby.com/65/.

Cooke, Lynn Prince, and Janeen Baxter. 2010. "'Families' in International Context: Comparing Institutional Effects across Western Societies," *Journal of Marriage and Family* 72: 516–36.

Cooke, Thomas J. 2008. "Gender Role Beliefs and Family Migration," *Population, Space and Place* 14: 163–75.

———, and Adrian Bailey. 1999. "The Effect of Family Migration, Migration History, and Self-selection on Married Women's Labour Market Achievement," in Paul Boyle and Keith Halfcree, eds, *Migration and Gender in the Developed World*. London: Routledge.

Coole, Diana. 2013. "Too Many Bodies? The Return and Disavowal of the Population Question," *Environmental Politics* 22, 2: 195–215.

Copen, Casey E., Kimberly Daniels, Jonathan Vespa, and William D. Mosher. 2012. "First Marriages in the United States: Data from the 2006–2010 National Survey of Family Growth," *National Health Statistics Reports* 49 (22 March).

Corman, Diana. 2002. "Family Policies, Work Arrangements and the Third Child in France and Sweden," in Erik Klijzing and Martine Corijn, eds, *Dynamics of Fertility and Partnership in Europe: Insights and Lessons from Comparative Research*, vol. 2. New York and Geneva: UN.

Costa, Dora L. 2000. "Understanding the Twentieth-Century Decline in Chronic Conditions among Older Men," *Demography* 37, 1: 53–72.

Côté, James, and John M. Bynner. 2008. "Changes in the Transition to Adulthood in the UK and Canada: The Role of Structure and Agency in Emerging Adulthood," *Journal of Youth Studies* 11, 3: 251–68.

Courchene, Thomas J. 1970. "Interprovincial Migration and Economic Adjustment," *Canadian Journal of Economics* 3: 550–76.

Cowgill, Donald O. 1971. "The Use of the Logistic Curve and the Transition Model in Developing Nations," in Ashish Bose, P.B. Desai, and S.P. Jain, eds, *Studies in Demography*. Chapel Hill, NC: The University of North Carolina Press.

Crenshaw, Edward M., Ansari Z. Ameen, and Matthew Christenson. 1997. "Population Dynamics and Economic Development: Age-specific Population Growth Rates and Economic Growth in Developing Countries," *American Sociological Review* 62, 6: 974–84.

Crépeau, Francois, Delphine Nakache, Machale Collyer, et al., eds. 2006. *Forced Migration and Global Processes: A View from Forced Migration Studies*. Lenham, UK: Lexington Books.

Crimmins, Eileen M., Melanie L. Johnston, Mark Hayward, and Teresa E. Seeman. 2006. "Age Differences in

Allostatic Load: An Index of Frailty," in Zeng Yi, et al., eds, *Longer Life and Healthy Aging*. Dordrecht: Springer.

Croll, Elisabeth J. 2000. *Endangered Daughters*. London: Routledge.

Cummings, David R. 2003. "The Influence of Latitude and Cloud Cover on the Seasonality of Human Births," *Social Biology* 50, 1–12: 23–41.

Cutler, David, A. Deaton, and A. Lleras-Muney. 2006. "The Determinants of Mortality," *The Journal of Economic Perspectives* 20: 97–120.

———, and Grant Miller. 2005. "The Role of Public Health Improvements in Health Advances: The Twentieth Century United States," *Demography* 42, 1: 1–22.

Da Vanzo, Julie. 1981. "Microeconomic Approaches to Studying Migration Decisions," in G.G. De Jong and R.W. Gardner, eds, *Migration Decision Making*. New York: Pergamon.

Dahms, F.A. 1990. "The Evolution of Settlement Systems: A Canadian Example, 1851–1970," in Gilbert A. Stelter, ed., *Cities and Urbanization: Canadian Historical Perspectives*. Toronto: Copp Clark Pitman.

Dale, Edmund H, ed. 1988. *The Future of Saskatchewan Small Town*. Victoria, BC: Department of Geography, University of Victoria.

Dalla Zuanna, Gianpiero. 2006. "Induced Abortion," in Graziella Caselli, Jacques Vallin, and Guillaume Wunsch, eds, *Demography: A Treatise in Population Studies*, vol. 1. Amsterdam: Elsevier and Academic Press.

Darroch, Gordon, ed. 2014. *The Dawn of Canada's Century: Hidden Histories*. Kingston and Montreal: McGill-Queen's University Press, 2013.

———, and W.G. Marston. 1988. "Patterns of Urban Ethnicity: Toward a Revised Ecological Model," in M. Iverson, ed., *Urbanism and Urbanization: Views, Aspects, and Dimensions*. Leiden: E.J. Brill.

Darroch, J.E, and S. Singh. 2013. "Trends in Contraceptive Need and Use in Developing Countries in 2003, 2008, and 2012: An Analysis of National Surveys", *Lancet* 381: 1756–62.

Das Gupta, Monica, and Lee Shuzhuo. 2000. "Gender Bias in China, South Korea and India 1920–1990: Effects of War, Poverty and Fertility," in Shahra Razavi, ed., *Gendered Poverty and Well-Being*. Oxford: Blackwell.

David, Henry P., and Joanna Skilogianis, eds. 1999. *From Abortion to Contraception: A Resource to Public Policies and Reproductive Behavior in Central and Eastern Europe from 1917 to the Present*. Westport, CT: Greenwood Press.

Davis, Craig H. 1995. *Demographic Projection Techniques for Regions and Smaller Areas: A Primer*. Vancouver: University of British Columbia Press.

Davis, Hugh, Heather Joshi, and Romana Peronacci. 2000. "Forgone Income and Motherhood: What

Do Recent British Data Tell Us?" *Population Studies* 54, 3: 293–305.

Davis, Kingsley. 1986. "Low Fertility in Evolutionary Perspective," in Kingsley Davis, Mikhail S. Bernstam, and Rita Ricardo-Campbell, eds, *Below-Replacement Fertility in Industrial Societies: Causes, Consequences, Policies*, supp. to *Population and Development Review* 12.

———. 1984. "Wives and Work: The Sex Role Revolution and Its Consequences," *Population and Development Review* 8, 3: 397–417.

———. 1973. "The Evolution of Western Industrial Cities," *Readings from Scientific American*, in Kingsley Davis, ed., *Cities: Their Origins, Growth and Human Impact*. San Francisco: W.H. Freeman.

———. 1970. "The Urbanization of the Human Population," *Scientific American*. New York: Alfred Knopf.

———. 1967. "Population Policy: Will Current Programs Succeed?" *Science* 158, 3802 (10 November): 730–9.

———. 1963. "The Theory of Change and Response in Modern Demographic History," *Population Index* 29, 4: 345–66.

———. 1956. "The Amazing Decline of Mortality in Underdeveloped Areas," *The American Economic Review* 46, 2: 305–18.

———. 1955. "The Origin and Growth of Urbanization in the World," *American Journal of Sociology* 60 (March): 429–37.

———. 1945. "The World Demographic Transition," *The Annals of the American Academy of Political and Social Science* 235: 1–11.

———, and Judith Blake. 1956. "Social Structure and Fertility: An Analytical Framework," *Economic Development and Cultural Change* 4, 4: 211–35.

———, and Pietronella van den Oever. 1982. "Demographic Foundations of New Sex Roles," *Population and Development Review* 8, 3: 495–511.

Davis, Mike. 2000. "The Origins of the Third World," *Antipode* 32, 1: 48–9.

Day, Kathleen M., and Stanley L. Winer. 2012. *Interregional Migration and Public Policy in Canada*. Montreal and Kingston: McGill-Queen's University Press.

Day, Lincoln H. 1992. *The Future of Low-Birthrate Populations*. London: Routledge.

———. 1985. "Illustrating Behavioral Principles with Examples from Demography: The Causal Analysis of Differences in Fertility," *Journal for the Theory of Social Behaviour* 15, 2: 189–201.

———. 1978. "What Will a ZPG Society Look Like?" *Population Bulletin* 33, 3. Washington: Population Reference Bureau.

———. 1968. "Natality and Ethnocentrism: Some Relationships Suggested by an Analysis of Catholic-Protestant Differentials," *Population Studies* 22: 27–50.

de Blij, H.J., and Alexander B. Murphy. 2003. *Human Geography: Culture, Society, and Space*, 7th edn. New York: John Wiley.

De Coulanges, Fustel. 1956. *The Ancient City: A Classic Study of the Religious and Civil Institutions of Ancient Greece and Rome*. Garden City, NY: Doubleday (Anchor Books).

De Jong, Gordon F. 1999. "Choice Processes in Migration Behavior," in K. Pandid and S. Davis Withers, eds, *Migration and Restructuring in the United States: A Geographic Perspective*. Lanham, MD: Rowman and Littlefield.

De Moivre, 1752. *A Treatise of Annuities on Lives*. London, 1725. de Rooij, Susanne R., Hans Wouters, Julie E. Yonker, Rebecca C. Painter, and T.J. Rosenboom. 2010. "Prenatal Undernutrition and Cognitive Function in Late Adulthood," *Proceedings of the National Academies of Science* 107, 39: 16881–6.

De Santis, Gustavo. 2006. "Pronatalist Policy in Industrialized Nations," in Graziella Caselli, Jacques Vallin, and Guillaume Wunsch, eds, *Demography: Analysis and Synthesis*. Amsterdam: Elsevier.

de Vries, Jan. 1984. *European Urbanization 1500–1800*. Cambridge, MA: Harvard University Press.

De Wit, Margaret L., David J. De Wit, and Brian G. Embree. 2000. "'Natives' and Non-Natives' Relative Risk of Children's Exposure to Marital Dissolution: The Role of Family Volatility and Implications for Future Nuptiality in Native Populations," *Canadian Studies in Population* 27, 1: 107–33.

Deane, Glenn D. 1990. "Mobility and Adjustments: Paths to the Resolution of Residential Stress," *Demography* 27, 1: 65–77.

Delisle, Francoise, and Richard Shearmur. 2010. "Where Does All the Talent Flow? Migration of Young Graduates and Nongraduates, Canada 1996–2001," *The Canadian Geographer* 54, 3: 305–23.

Demeny, Paul. 2003. "Population Policy Dilemmas in Europe at the Dawn of the Twenty-First Century," *Population and Development Review* 29, 1: 1–28.

———. 1998. "Population Size and Material Standards of Living," in Paul Demeny and Geoffrey McNicoll, eds, *The Earthscan Reader in Population and Development*. London: Earthscan.

Denton, Frank T., Christine H. Feaver, and Byron G. Spencer. 2002. "Alternative Pasts, Possible Futures: A 'What if' Study of the Effects of Fertility on the Canadian Population and Labour Force," *Canadian Public Policy* 28, 3: 443–59.

———, ———, and ———. 2000. "The Future Population of Canada and Its Age Distribution," in Frank T. Denton, Deborah Fretz, and Byron G. Spencer, eds, *Independence and Economic Security in Old Age*. Vancouver: University of British Columbia Press.

——, and Byron G. Spencer. 2011. "Age of Pension Eligibility, Gains in Life Expectancy, and Social Policy," *Canadian Public Policy* 37, 2: 183–99.

——, and ——. 1999. "How Old Is Old? Revising the Definition Based on Life Table Criteria," *Mathematical Population Studies* 7, 2: 147–59.

——, and ——. 1975. *Population and the Economy.* Lexington, MA: Saxon House/Lexington Books.

Dercon, Stefan. 2005. "Risk, Insurance, and Poverty: A Review," in Stefan Dercon, ed., *Insurance against Poverty.* Oxford: Oxford University Press.

DesMeules, Marie, Douglas Manuel, and Robert Cho. 2004. "Mortality: Life and Health Expectancy of Canadian Women" *BioMed Central (BMC) Women's Health* 4 (supp. 1): S9. www.biomedcentral.com/1472-6874/4/SI/S9.

Diamond, Jared. 1999. *Guns, Germs, and Steel: The Fates of Human Societies.* New York: W.W. Norton.

Dicken, Peter. 2011. *Global Shift: Mapping the Changing Contours of the World Economy.* Los Angeles: Sage.

Dickinson, John, and Brian Young. 2003. *A Short History of Quebec,* 3rd edn. Montreal and Kingston: McGill-Queen's University Press.

Dixon, Ruth B. 1971. "Explaining Cross-Cultural Variations in Age at Marriage and Proportions Never Marrying," *Population Studies* 25: 215–33.

Dobyns, Henry F. 1983. *Their Numbers Become Thinned: Native American Population Dynamics in Eastern North America.* Knoxville, TN: The University of Tennessee Press.

Dominion Bureau of Statistics. 1962. "Population: Incorporated Cities, Towns and Villages," *Census of Canada, 1961* 1: 1–6.

——. 1960. *Canadian Life Tables, 1950–1952, 1955–1957.* Cat. no. 84-510.

——. 1953. *Ninth Census of Canada, 1951,* vol. 1: Population: General Characteristics. Ottawa: The Queen's Printer.

——. 1947. *Life Tables for Canada and Regions, 1941 and 1931.* Cat. no. 84-515.

——. 1923. *Vital Statistics, 1921.* First Annual Report.

Donaldson, Loraine. 1991. *Fertility Transition: The Social Dynamics of Population Change.* Cambridge, MA: Basil Blackwell.

Dong, Maxia, Wayne H, Giles, Vincent J. Felitti, et al. 2004. "Insights into Causal Pathways for Ischemic Heart Disease: Adverse Childhood Experiences Study," *Circulation* 110: 1761–6.

Dorland's Pocket Medical Dictionary, 22nd edn. 1977. Philadelphia: W.B. Saunders.

Dosman, E.J. 1972. *Indians: The Urban Dilemma.* Toronto: McClelland and Stewart.

Douglas, Ian. 2013. *Cities: An Environmental History.* London: IB Tauris & Co.

Douglass, Carrie B. 2005. *Barren States: The Population "Implosion" in Europe.* Oxford: Berg.

Drolet, Marie. 2003. "Motherhood and Paycheques," *Canadian Social Trends* 68 (Spring): 19–21.

D'Souza, Stan, and Lincoln C. Chen. 1980. "Sex Differential in Mortality in Rural Bangladesh," *Population and Development Review* 6, 2: 257–70.

Dumas, Jean. 1990. *Report on the Demographic Situation in Canada: 1990.* Cat. no. 91-209E. Ottawa: Statistics Canada.

Duncan, Greg J., W. Jean Yeung, Jeanne Brooks-Gunn, et al. 1998. "The Effects of Childhood Poverty on the Life Chances of Children," *American Sociological Review* 63, 3: 406–23.

Durkheim, Émile. 1897 [1951]. *Suicide: A Study in Sociology.* New York: Free Press.

Dyson, Tim. 2012. "Causes and Consequences of Skewed Sex Ratios," *Annual Review of Sociology* 38: 443–61.

——. 2010. *Population and Development: The Demographic Transition.* London: Zed Books.

——. 2003. "HIV/AIDS and Urbanization," *Population and Development Review* 29, 3: 427–42.

——, Robert Cassen, and Leela Visaria, eds. 2004. *Twenty-First Century India: Population, Economy, Human Development, and the Environment.* Oxford: Oxford University Press.

——, and Mike Murphy. 1985. "The Onset of Fertility Transition," *Population and Development Review* 11, 3: 399–440.

Easterlin, Richard A. 2004. "How Beneficent Is the Market? A Look at the Modern History of Mortality," in Richard A. Easterlin, *The Reluctant Economist: Perspectives on Economics, Economic History, and Demography,* 101–38. Cambridge: Cambridge University Press.

——. 1999. *Growth Triumphant: The Twenty-First Century in Historical Perspective.* Ann Arbor: University of Michigan Press

——. 1987. *Birth and Fortune,* 2nd edn. Chicago: University of Chicago Press.

——. 1983. "Modernization and Fertility: A Critical Essay," in Rodolfo A. Bulato and Ronald D. Lee, eds, *Determinants of Fertility in Developing Countries,* vol. 2. New York: Academic Press

——. 1980. *Birth and Fortune: The Impact of Numbers on Personal Welfare.* New York: Basic Books.

——. 1978. "The Economics and Sociology of Fertility: A Synthesis," in C. Tilly, ed., *Historical Studies of Changing Fertility.* Princeton, NJ: Princeton University Press.

——. 1975. "An Economic Framework for Fertility Analysis," *Studies in Family Planning* 6, 3: 54–63.

——. 1969. "Towards a Socio-economic Theory of Fertility: A Survey of Recent Research on Economic Factors in American Fertility," in S.J. Berham, et al., eds, *Fertility and Family Planning: A World View*. Ann Arbor: University of Michigan Press.

——. 1961a. "The American Baby Boom in Historical Perspective," *American Economic Review* 51: 869–911.

——. 1961b. "Influences in European Overseas Immigration Before WWI," *Economic Development and Cultural Change* 9: 331–51.

Easterly, William. 2006. *The White Man's Burden: Why the West's Effort to Aid the Rest Have Done So Much Harm and So Little Good*. New York: Penguin.

——. 2002. "How Did Heavily Indebted Poor Countries Become Heavily Indebted? Reviewing Two Decades of Debt Relief," *World Development* 30, 10: 1677–96.

Eastwood, Robert, and Michael Lipton. 2011. "Demographic Transition in Sub-Saharan Africa: How Big Will the Economic Dividend Be?" *Population Studies* 65, 1:9–35.

Eaton, J.W., and A.J. Mayer. 1953. "The Social Biology of Very High Fertility among the Hutterites: The Demography of a Unique Population," *Human Biology* 25: 206–64.

Eberstadt, Nicholas. 2011. "The Global War against Baby Girls," *The New Atlantis* (Fall): 3–18.

——. 1997. "World Population Implosion?" *The Public Interest* 129: 3–20.

Ebrahim, Shah, and Liam Smeeth. 2005. "Non-communicable Disease in Low and Middle-Income Countries: A Priority or a Distraction?" *International Journal of Epidemiology* 34: 961–6.

Economist, The. 2013a. "Angry Young Indians. What a Waste: How India Is Throwing Away the World's Biggest Economic Opportunity," (11 May). www.economist.com/news/leaders/21577372-how-india-throwing-away-worlds-biggest-economic-opportunity-what-waste (accessed 2 April 2014).

——. 2013b. "When Did Globalisation Start?" (23 September). www.economist.com/blogs/freeexchange/2013/09/economic-history-1 (accessed 2 July 2014).

——. 2013c. "How Did the Global Poverty Rate Halve in 20 Years?" (2 June). www.economist.com/blogs/economist-explains/2013/06/economist-explains-0 (accessed 11 October 2013).

——. 2013d. "The World Has an Astonishing Chance to Take a Billion People out of Extreme Poverty by 2030," (1 June). www.economist.com/news/briefing/21578643-world-has-astonishing-chance-take-billion-people-out-extreme-poverty-2030-not (accessed 11 October 2013).

——. 2013e. "Free Exchange—The Next Frontier," (21 September). www.economist.com/news/finance-and-economics/21586512-guest-article-jeffrey-sachs-director-earth-institute-columbia (accessed 2 April 2014).

——. 2013f. "The Economist Explains: Why Is Youth Unemployment So High?" (8 May). www.economist.com/blogs/economist-explains/2013/05/economist-explains-why-youth-unemployment-so-high (accessed 2 July 2014).

——. 2013g. "Youth Unemployment: Generation Jobless," (27 April). www.economist.com/news/international/21576657-around-world-almost-300m-15-24-year-olds-are-not-working-what-has-caused (accessed 2 July 2014).

——. 2012. "The Urbanization Trap: Moving from Farms to Cities Does Not always Translate to Gains in Income," (2 October). www.economist.com/blogs/graphicdetail/2012/10/daily-chart (accessed 2 October 2013).

——. 2011a. "Corrosive Corruption: A Correlation between Corruption and Development," (2 December). www.economist.com/blogs/dailychart/2011/12/corruption-and-development (accessed 18 July 2013).

——. 2011b. "Add Sugar and Spice: India's Sex Ratio Is Getting Worse. The Trend Can be Reversed," (7 April). www.economist.com/node/18530101 (accessed 18 April 2014).

——. 2004. "Japan: A Shrinking Giant," (8 January): 38.

——. 2003a. "Congo's War: Waiting to be Rescued," (17 May): 40–1.

——. 2003b. "Sudan's War: Peace, the Unimaginable," (17 May): 41–2.

Edmonston, Barry. 2014. "Two Centuries of Demographic Change in Canada," *Canadian Studies in Population* 41 (1–2): 1–37.

——, and Margaret Michalowski. 2004. "International Migration," in Jacob S. Siegel and David A. Swanson, eds, *The Methods and Materials of Demography*, 2nd edn. Amsterdam: Elsevier.

Egolf, Brenda, Judith Lasker, S. Wolf, et al. 1992. "The Roseto Effect: A 50-Year Comparison of Mortality Rates," *American Journal of Public Health* 82, 8: 1089–92.

Ehrlich, Paul R. 1995. "Our Demographic Future: Predictions for the Next 50 Years," *Population Today* 23: 2–3.

——. 1968. *The Population Bomb*. New York: Ballantine Books.

——, and Ann H. Ehrlich. 1990. *The Population Explosion*. London: Hutchinson.

——, ——, and John P. Holdren. 1977. *Ecoscience: Population, Resources, Environment*. San Francisco: W.H. Freeman.

Eichler, Margrit and Anne-Marie Pedersen. 2013. "Marriage and Divorce." *The Canadian Encyclopedia*. www.thecanadianencyclopedia.com/articles/marriage-and-divorce.

El-Badry, M.A. 1969. "Higher Female than Male Mortality in Some Countries of South Asia: A Digest," *Journal of the American Statistical Association* 64: 1234–44.

Elgin, Ceyhun and Semih Tumen. 2012. "Can Sustained Economic Growth and Declining Population Coexist?" *Economic Modeling* 29: 1899–1908.

Emlen, Merritt J. 1970. "Age Specificity and Ecological Theory," *Ecology* 51, 6: 588–601.

Emmott, Stephen. 2013. *10 Billion*. London: Allen Lane.

Engelhardt, Henriette, Thomas Kogel, and Alexia Prskawetz. 2004. "Fertility and Women's Employment Reconsidered: A Macro-level Time Series Analysis for Developed Countries, 1960–2000," *Population Studies* 58, 1: 109–120.

Engels, Friedrich. 1884 [1964]. *The Origin of the Family, Private Property and the State*. New York, NY: International Publishers.

———. 1844 [1971]. "Outlines of a Critique of Political Economy," in Ronald L. Meek, ed., *Marx and Engels on the Population Bomb*. Dorothea L. Meek and Ronald L. Meek, trans. Berkeley, CA: Ramparts.

Epsing-Andersen, Gosta. 2009. *The Incomplete Revolution: Adapting to Women's New Roles*. Cambridge, UK: Polity Press.

Ermisch, John F. 2003. *An Economic Analysis of the Family*. Princeton, NJ: Princeton University Press.

———. 1981. "Economic Opportunities, Marriage Squeezes, and the Propensity to Marry: An Economic Analysis of Period Marriage Rates in England and Wales," *Population Studies* 35: 347–56.

Esteve, Albert, Ron Lesthaeghe, and Antonio López-Gay. 2012. "The Latin American Cohabitation Boom, 1970–2007," *Population and Development Review* 38, 1: 55–81.

Evans, L.T. 1998. *Feeding the Ten Billion: Plants and Population Growth*. Cambridge: Cambridge University Press.

Evans, Robert G., and G.L. Stoddart. 1990. "Producing Health, Consuming Health Care," *Social Science and Medicine* 31: 1347–63.

Ezeh, Alex C., John Bongaarts, and Blessing Mberu. 2012. "Global Population Trends and Policy Options," *Lancet* 380 (14 July): 142–8.

Ezzati, Majid, and Elio Riboli. 2013. "Behavioral and Dietary Risk Factors for Noncommunicable Diseases," *New England Journal of Medicine* 369: 954–64.

———, and ———. 2012. "Can Noncommunicable Diseases Be Prevented? Lessons from Studies of Populations and Individuals," *Science* 337 (21 September): 1482–7.

Fair, Martha M. 1994. "The Development of National Vital Statistics in Canada: Part I—From 1605 to 1945," *Health Reports* 6, 3: 356–7.

Fairchild, Henry Pratt. 1925. *Immigration*. New York: Macmillan.

Faitosa, M.F., and H. Krieger. 1992. "Demography of the Human Sex Ratio in Some Latin American Countries, 1967–1968," *Human Biology* 64, 4: 523–30.

Faris, Robert E.L. 1963. "Interrelated Problems of the Expanding Metropolis," *The Canadian Journal of Economics and Political Science* 5, 3: 341–7.

Fauci, Anthony S., and David M. Morens. 2012. "The Perpetual Challenge of Infectious Diseases," *New England Journal of Medicine* 366: 454–61.

Faust, Kimberly. 2004. "Marriage, Divorce and Family Groups," in Jacob A. Siegel and David A. Swanson, eds, *The Methods and Materials of Demography*, 2nd edn. Amsterdam: Elsevier.

Fawcett, James T. 1983. "Perceptions of the Value of Children: Satisfactions and Costs," in Rodolfo A. Bulatao and Ronald D. Lee, eds, *Determinants of Fertility in Developing Countries, vol. 1: Supply and Demand for Children*. New York: Academic Press.

Feinstein, Joseph. 1993. "The Relationship between Socio-economic Status and Health: A Review of the Literature," *The Milbank Quarterly* 71: 279–322.

Ferelon, Bill. 1971. "State Variations in United States Divorce Rates," *Journal of Marriage and the Family* 33: 321–7.

Feng, Weng, Yong Cai, and Baochang Gu. 2012. "Population, Policy, and Politics: How Will History Judge China's One-Child Policy?" in Geoffrey McNicoll, John Bongaarts, and Ethel P. Churchill, eds, *Population and Public Policy: Essays in Honor of Paul Demeny*, 115–29. Supplement to Volume 38, *Population and Development Review*. New York: The Population Council.

Ferguson, Mark, Kamar Ali, Rose M. Olfert, and Mark Partridge. 2007. "Voting with Their Feet: Jobs versus Amenities," *Growth and Change* 38, 1: 77–110.

Ferguson, Niall. 2011. *Civilization: The West and the Rest*. London: Penguin.

Fernández, Raquel. 2013. "Cultural Change as Learning: The Evolution of Female Labor Force Participation over a Century," *American Economic Review 2013* 103, 1: 472–500.

Field, Alexander J. 1984. "Microeconomics, Norms and Rationality," *Economic Development and Cultural Change* 32, 4: 279–93.

Fielding, A.J. 1989 [1996]. "Migration and Urbanization in Western Europe Since 1950," in H.S. Geyer and T.M. Kontuly, eds, *Differential Urbanization: Integrating Spatial Models*. London: Edward Arnold.

Filmer, Deon, and Lant Pritchett. 1999. "The Impact of Public Spending on Health: Does Money Matter?" *Social Science and Medicine* 49: 1309–23.

Finch, Brian Karl. 2003. "Early Origins of the Gradient: The Relationship between Socioeconomic Status and Infant Mortality in the United States," *Demography* 40, 4: 675–99.

Fingard, Judith. 1974. "The Winter's Tale: The Seasonal Contours of Pre-industrial Poverty in British North America," Canadian Historical Association, *Historical Papers*: 65–94.

Finnie, Ross. 1999a. "The Patterns of Inter-provincial Migration in Canada 1982–95: Evidence from Longitudinal Tax-based Data," *Canadian Studies in Population* 26, 2: 205–34.

———. 1999b. "Inter-provincial Migration in Canada: A Longitudinal Analysis of Movers and Stayers and the Associated Income Dynamics," *Canadian Journal of Regional Science* 22, 3: 227–62.

Firebaugh, Glenn. 2003. *The New Geography of Global Income Inequality*. Cambridge, MA: Harvard University Press.

Fischer, Claude S. 1976. *The Urban Experience*. New York: Harcourt Brace Jovanovic.

———. 1975. "Toward a Subcultural Theory of Urbanism," *American Journal of Sociology* 80: 1319–41.

Fischer, Stanley. 2003. "Globalization and its Challenges," *The American Economic Review* 93, 2: 1–30.

Fishbein, Martin. 1972. "Toward an Understanding of Family Planning Behaviors," *Journal of Applied Social Psychology* 2: 214–27.

Fisher, Ronald A. 1930. *The Genetical Theory of Natural Selection*. Oxford: Clarendon Press.

Fleischman, John. 1999. "Why Are You Alive?" *Old Farmer's Almanac*. Dublin, NH: Yankee Publishing Inc.

Flew, Antony, ed. 1970. *Malthus: An Essay on the Principle of Population*. Harmondsworth, UK: Penguin.

Florida, Richard. 2005. *The Flight of the Creative Class: The New Global Competition for Talent*. New York: Harper Business/HarperCollins.

———. 2002. *The Rise of the Creative Class: And How It's Transforming Work, Leisure, Community, and Everyday Life*. New York: Basic Books.

Flowerdew, Robin, and Carl Amrhein. 1989. "Poisson Regression Models of Canadian Census Division Migration Flows," *Papers of the Regional Science Association* 67: 89–102.

Fogel, Robert W. 2004a. *The Escape from Hunger and Premature Death, 1700–2100*. Cambridge: Cambridge University Press.

———. 2004b. "Changes in the Process of Aging during the Twentieth Century: Findings and Procedures of the Early Indicators Project," in Linda J. Waite, ed., *Aging, Health, and Public Policy: Demographic and Economic Perspectives*, supp. to *Population and Development Review* 30. New York: Population Council.

———, and Dora L. Costa. 1997. "A Theory of Techno-physio Evolution, with Some Implications for Forecasting Population, Health Care Costs, and Pension Costs," *Demography* 34, 1: 49–66.

Folbre, Nancy. 1988. "The Black Four of Hearts: Toward a New Paradigm of Household Economics," in Daisy Dwyer and Judith Bruce, eds, *A Home Divided: Women and Income in the Third World*. Stanford, CA: Stanford University Press.

———. 1983. "Of Patriarchy Born: The Political Economy of Fertility Decisions," *Feminist Studies* 9: 261–84.

Foley, Jonathan A., Navin Ramankutty, Kate A. Brauman, Emily S. Cassidy, et al. 2011. "Solutions for a Cultivated Planet," *Nature* 478: 337–42.

Fong, Eric. 2005. "Immigration and the City," in Harry H. Hiller, ed., *Urban Canada: Sociological Perspectives*. Don Mills, ON: Oxford University Press.

———, and Kumiko Shibuya. 2005. "Multiethnic Cities in North America," *Annual Review of Sociology* 31: 1–20.

Fontana, Luigi, Linda Partridge, and Valter D. Longo. 2010. "Extending Healthy Life Span—From Yeast to Humans," *Science* 328 (16 April): 321–6.

Foot, David, and Daniel Stoffman. 2000. *Boom, Bust & Echo: Profiting from the Demographic Shift in the New Millennium*. Toronto: Stoddart.

———, and ———. 1998. *Boom, Bust & Echo 2000: Profiting from the Demographic Shift in the New Millennium*. Toronto: Macfarlane, Walter & Ross.

———, and Rosemary A. Venne. 2011. "The Long Goodbye: Age, Demographics, and Flexibility in Retirement," *Canadian Studies in Population* 38 (3–4): 59–74.

Foreign Policy, 2005. "The Failed States Index," *Foreign Policy* 149 (July–August): 56–65.

Foster, Caroline. 2000. "The Limits to Low Fertility: A Biosocial Approach," *Population and Development Review* 26, 2: 209–34.

Francis, Diane. 2002. *Immigration: The Economic Case*. Toronto: Key Porter.

Frank, Andre Gunder. 1991. "The Underdevelopment of Development," *Scandinavian Journal of Development Alternatives* 10, 3: 5–72.

———. 1984. "Political Ironies in the World Economy," *Studies in Political Economy* 15 (Fall): 119–49.

———. 1969. *Capitalism and Underdevelopment in Latin America*. New York: Monthly Review Press.

Frejka, Tomas. 2004. "The Curiously High Fertility of the USA," *Population Studies* 58, 1: 77–92.

———. 1983. "Induced Abortion and Fertility: A Quarter Century of Experience in Eastern Europe," *Population and Development Review* 9, 3: 494–520.

———, and Jean-Paul Sardon. 2004. *Childbearing Trends and Prospects in Low-Fertility Countries: A Cohort Analysis*. Dordrecht: Kluwer Academic Publishers.

Frenk, Julio, Louis Bobadilla, Claudio Stern, et al. 1991. "Elements for a Theory of the Health Transition," *Health Transition Review* 1: 21–38.

Freud, Sigmund. 1930 [2005]. *Civilization and Its Discontents (Unbehagen in der Kultur)*. James Strachey, trans. New York: Norton.

Frey, W.H. 2003. "Internal Migration," in Paul Demeny and Geoffrey McNicoll, eds, *Encyclopedia of Population* vol. 2, 545–8. New York: Macmillan Reference USA/Thomson Gale.

———. 1993. "The New Urban Revival in the United States," *Urban Studies* 30, 4–5: 741–74.

———. 1990. "Metropolitan America: Beyond the Transition," *Population Bulletin* 45, 2. Washington: Population Reference Bureau.

———. 1989. "United States: Counterurbanisation and Metropolis Depopulation," in A.G. Champion, ed., *Counterurbanisation: The Changing Pace and Nature of Population Deconcentration*. London: Edward Arnold.

———. 1987. "Migration and Depopulation of the Metropolis: Regional Restructuring or Rural Renaissance?" *American Sociological Review* 52, 2: 240–57.

———, and Alden Speare. 1992. "The Revival of Metropolitan Population Growth in the United States: An Assessment of Findings from the 1990 Census," *Population and Development Review* 18, 1: 129–46.

Frideres, James S., and René Gadacz. 2008. *Aboriginal Peoples in Canada*, 8th edn. Toronto: Pearson.

———, Madeline A. Kalbach, and Warren E. Kalbach. 2004. "Government Policy and the Spatial Redistribution of Canada's Aboriginal Peoples," in John Taylor and Martin Bell, eds, *Population Mobility and Indigenous Peoples in Australasia and North America*, 94–114. London: Routledge.

Friedan, Betty, 1963. *The Feminine Mystique*. New York: WW Norton.

Friedlander, D. 1969. "Demographic Responses and Population Change," *Demography* 6, 4: 359–82.

Friedman, Debra, Michael Hechter, and Sitoshi Kanazawa. 1994. "A Theory of the Value of Children," *Demography* 31, 3: 375–401

Fries, James F. 2012. "The Theory and Practice of Active Aging," *Current Gerontology and Geriatrics Research*, vol. 2012, article ID 42063: 7 pages. doi:10.1155/2012/420637.

———. 1983. "The Compression of Morbidity," *The Milbank Quarterly/Health and Society* 61: 397–419.

———. 1980. "Aging, Natural Death and the Compression of Mortality and Morbidity," *The New England Journal of Medicine* 303, 3: 130–5.

———, Bonnie Bruce, and Eliza Chakravarty. 2011. "Compression of Morbidity 1980–2011: A Focused Review of Paradigms and Progress," *Journal of Aging Research*, vol. 2011, article ID 261702: 10 pages. doi:10.4061/2011/261702.

———, and Lawrence M. Crapo. 1981. *Vitality and Aging: Implications of the Rectangular Curve*. New York: W.H. Freeman.

Friesen, Joe. 2013. "The Baby Bust: In a First, the Newly Retired Outnumber the Newly Hired," *Globe and Mail* (18 February): A1, A4.

Frisbie, W. Parker. 2005. "Infant Mortality," in Dudley Poston and Michael Micklin, eds, *Handbook of Population*. New York: Kluwer Academic Publishers/Plenum.

Fukuda, M., K. Fukuda, T. Shimizu, and T. Møller. 1998. "Decline in Sex Ratio at Birth after Kobe Earthquake," *Human Reproduction* 13, 8: 2321–2.

Furedi, Frank. 1997. *Population and Development: A Critical Introduction*. New York: St Martin's.

Fussell, Elizabeth, and Alberto Palloni. 2004. "Persistent Marriage Regimes in Changing Times," *Journal of Marriage and the Family* 66, 5: 1201–13.

Fuwa, Makiko. 2004. "Macro-Level Gender Inequality and the Division of Household Labor in 22 Countries," *American Sociological Review* 69, 6: 751–67.

Gabaix, X. 1999. "Zipf's Law for Cities: An Explanation," *Quarterly Journal of Economics* 114: 739–67.

Galbraith, James K. 2002. "A Perfect Crime: Inequality in the Age of Globalization," *Daedalus* (Winter): 11–25.

Galarneau, Diane, René Morissette, and Jeannine Usalcas. 2013. "What Has Changed for Young People in Canada?" Cat. no. 75-006-X. Ottawa: Statistics Canada, *Insights on Canadian Society*. Minister of Industry.

Galley, Chris, and Robert Woods. 1999. "On the Distribution of Deaths during the First Year of Life," *Population* 11: 35–60.

Galloway, Patrick R. 1986. "Long-Term Fluctuations in Climate and Population in the Preindustrial Era," *Population and Development Review* 12, 1: 1–24.

Galor, Oded. 2011. *Unified Growth Theory*. Princeton: Princeton University Press.

Garip, Dilz. 2012. "Discovering Diverse Mechanisms of Migration: The Mexico-US Stream 1970–2000," *Population and Development Review* 38, 3: 393–434.

Gates, Charles. 2011. *Ancient Cities: The Archaeology of Urban Life in the Ancient Near East and Egypt, Greece, and Rome*. London: Routledge.

Gauri, Varun, and Peyvand Khaleghian. 2002. "Immunization in Developing Countries: Its Political and Organizational Determinants," *World Development* 30, 12: 2109–32.

Gauthier, Anne H. 2007. "The Impact of Family Policies on Fertility in Industrialized Countries: A Review of the Literature," *Population Research and Policy Review* 26: 323–46.

———. 2005. "Trends in Policies for Family-Friendly Societies," in Miroslav Macura, Alphonse L. MacDonald, and Werner Haug, eds, *The New Demographic Regime: Population Challenges and Policy Responses*. New York and Geneva: United Nations.

———, and Jan Hatzius. 1997. "Family Benefits and Fertility: An Econometric Analysis," *Population Studies* 51, 3: 295–306.

Gauvreau, Danielle. 1991. *Québec: une ville et sa population au temps de la Nouvelle France*. Montreal: Presses de l'Université du Québec.

Gee, Ellen M. 1994. "The Life Course of Canadian Women: An Historical and Demographic Analysis," in Frank Trovato and Carl F. Grindstaff, eds, *Perspectives on Canada's Population: An Introduction to Concepts and Issues*. Don Mills, ON: Oxford University Press.

———, and Gloria M. Gutman, eds. 2000. *The Overselling of Population Aging: Apocalyptic Demography, Intergenerational Challenges, and Social Policy*. Don Mills, ON: Oxford University Press.

Gelbard, Alene, Carl Haub, and Mary M. Kent. 1999. "World Population Beyond Six Billion," *Population Bulletin* 54, 1. Washington: Population Reference Bureau.

Gems, David, and Linda Partridge. 2013. "Genetics of Longevity in Model Organisms: Debates and Paradigm Shifts," *Annual Review of Physiology* 75:621–44.

George, Lianne. 2007. "Making Moms: Can We Feed the Need to Breed?" *Maclean's* (28 May).

George, M.V. 1970. *Internal Migration in Canada*. 1961 Census Monograph. Ottawa: Statistics Canada.

———, and Shirley Loh. 2007. "Projected Population Size and Age Structure for Canada and Province: With and without International Migration," *Canadian Studies in Population* 34, 2: 103–27.

———, ———, Ravi P. Verma, and Y. Edward Shin. 2001. *Population Projections for Canada, Provinces and Territories, 2000–2026*. Cat. no. 91-520-XPB. Ottawa: Statistics Canada.

Gerber, Linda M. 1984. "Community Characteristics and Out-Migration from Canadian Indian Reserves: Path Analysis," *Canadian Review of Sociology and Anthropology* 21, 2: 145–65.

Geronimus, Arline T., John Bound, and Annie Ro. 2014. "Residential Mobility across Local Areas in the United States and the Geographic Distribution of the Healthy Population," *Demography* 51: 777–809.

Geyer, H.S., and T. Kontuly, eds. 1996. *Differential Urbanization: Integrating Spatial Models*. London: Edward Arnold.

———, and ———. 1993. "A Theoretical Foundation for the Concept of Differential Urbanization," *International Regional Science Review* 15: 157–77.

Giddens, Anthony. 1992. *The Transformation of Intimacy: Sexuality, Love and Eroticism in Modern Societies*. Stanford, CA: Stanford University Press.

Giere, Ronald N. 1999. *Science without Laws*. Chicago: The University of Chicago Press.

Gilbert, Alan, and Joseph Gugler. 1992. *Cities, Poverty and Development: Urbanization in the Third World*, 2nd edn. Oxford: Oxford University Press.

Gillis, Ron. 2005. "Cities and Social Pathology," in Harry H. Hiller, ed., *Urban Canada: Sociological Perspectives*. Don Mills, ON: Oxford University Press.

Gist, Noel P., and Sylvia Fleis Favia. 1974. *Urban Society*, 6th edn. New York: Thomas Y. Crowell.

Gjonca, Arjan. 2001. *Communism, Health and Lifestyle: The Paradox of Mortality Transition in Albania, 1950–1990*. Westport, CT: Greenwood.

———, Christopher Wilson, and Jane Falkingham. 1997. "Paradoxes of Health Transition in Europe's Poorest Country, Albania 1950–1990," *Population and Development Review* 23, 3: 585–609.

Glaeser, Edward L., and Jesse M. Shapiro. 2003. "Urban Growth in the 1990s: Is City Living Back?" *Journal of Regional Science* 43, 1: 139–65.

Glei, Dana A., and Shiro Horiuchi. 2007. "The Narrowing Sex Differential in Life Expectancy in High-Income Populations: Effects of Differences in the Age Pattern of Mortality," *Population Studies* 61, 2: 141–59.

Glenn, Norvall D., and M. Supancic. 1984. "The Social and Demographic Correlates of Divorce and Separation in the United States: An Update and Reconsideration," *Journal of Marriage and the Family* 46: 563–79.

Global Footprint Network. 2013. www.footprintnetwork. org/en/index.php/GFN/ (accessed 4 July 2014).

———. 2011. *The National Footprint Accounts*. Global Footprint Network, San Francisco, California (accessed 20 February 2012).

Globe and Mail. 2003. "Portrait of Canadian Immigration," (25 January): A5.

———. 1992. "Canadian Immigration Trends," (20 June): A4.

Gluckman, Peter D., and Mark A. Hanson. 2004. "Living with the Past: Evolution, Development, and Patterns of Disease," *Science* 305: 1733–5.

———, ———, and Catherine Pinal. 2005. "The Developmental Origins of Adult Disease," *Maternal and Child Nutrition* 1: 130–41.

Gober, Patricia. 1993. "Americans on the Move," *Population Bulletin* 48, 3. Washington: Population Reference Bureau.

Goklany, Indur M. 2007. *Improving State of the World: Why We're Living Longer, Healthier, More Comfortable Lives on a Cleaner Planet*. Washington, DC: Cato Institute.

Goldmann, Gustave, and Senada Delic. 2014. "Counting Aboriginal Peoples in Canada," in Frank Trovato and Anatole Romaniuk, eds, *Aboriginal Populations–Social, Demographic, and Epidemiological Perspectives*. Edmonton, AB: University of Alberta Press.

———, Norbert Robitaille, and Sacha Sénecal. 2014 "Another Look at Definitions and Growth of Aboriginal Populations in Canada," in Frank Trovato and Anatole Romaniuk, eds, *Aboriginal Populations— Social, Demographic, and Epidemiological Perspectives*. Edmonton, AB: University of Alberta Press.

Goldscheider, Calvin. 1971. *Population, Modernization, and Social Structure*. Boston: Little, Brown.

———, and Peter H. Uhlenberg. 1969. "Minority Group Status and Fertility," *American Journal of Sociology* 74: 361–72.

Goldscheider, Frances K., and Linda J. Waite. 1991. *New Families, No Families? The Transformation of the American Home.* Berkeley: University of California Press.

———, and ———. 1986. "Sex Differences in the Entry into Marriage," *American Journal of Sociology* 92: 91–109.

Goldstein, Joshua R., and Thomas Cassidy. 2012. "How Slowing Senescence Translates into Longer Life Expectancy," *Population Studies* 66, 1: 29–37.

———, Tomas Sobotka, and A. Jasilioniene. 2009. "The End of Lowest-Low Fertility?" *Population and Development Review* 35, 4: 663–99.

Goldstone, Jack, Eric Kaufmann, and Monica Duffy Toft. 2012. *Political Demography: How Population Changes Are Reshaping International Security and National Politics.* Oxford: Oxford University Press.

Golini, Antonio. 2003. "Current Demographic Setting and the Future of Aging: The Experience of Some European Countries," *Genus* LIX, 1: 15–49.

———, and Raffaella Iacoucci. 2006. "Demographic Trends and Relationships between Generations," in Graziella Caselli, Jacques Vallin, and Guillaume Wunsch, eds, *Demography: Analysis and Synthesis—A Treatise in Population Studies,* 4 vols, 305–25. Amsterdam: Academic Press.

Gomez, Rafael, and Danielle Lamb. 2013 "Demographic Origins of the Great Recession: Implications for China," *China and World Economy* 21, 2: 97–118.

Gompertz, Benjamin. 1825. "On the Nature of the Function Expressive of the Law of Mortality," *Philosophical Transactions* 27: 513–82.

Goode, William J. 1963. *World Revolution and Family Patterns.* New York: Free Press.

Goodkind, Daniel. 1996. "On Substituting Sex Preferences Strategies in East Asia: Does Prenatal Sex Selection Reduce Postnatal Discrimination?" *Population and Development Review* 22, 1: 111–25.

Goody, Jack. 1996. "Comparing Family Systems in Europe and Asia," *Population and Development Review* 22, 1: 1–20.

Gordon, P. 1979 [1996]. "Deconcentration without a 'Clean Break,'" in H.S. Geyer and T.M. Kontuly, eds, *Differential Urbanization Integrating Spatial Models.* London: Edward Arnold.

Gortmaker, Steven L., and P.H. Wise. 1997. "The First Injustice: Socio-economic Disparities, Health Services Technology, and Infant Mortality," *Annual Review of Sociology* 23: 147–70.

Gossman, Charles, and David Odynak. 1983. "The Canadian Census and the Rank-Size Rule," in N. Waters,

ed., *Cartography and Physical and Human Geography: The Douglas College Papers,* BC Geographical Series, no. 40. Occasional Papers in Geography. Vancouver, BC: Tantalus Research Limited.

Gottlieb, Beatrice. 1993. *The Family in the Western World from the Black Death to the Industrial Age.* New York: Oxford University Press.

Gottman, Jean. 1961. *Megalopolis: The Urbanized Northeastern Seaboard of the United States.* New York: The Twentieth-Century Fund.

Gourbin, Catherine. 2006. "Fetal Mortality," in Graziella Caselli, Jacques Vallin, and Guillaume Wunsch, eds, *Demography: Analysis and Synthesis,* vol. 1. Amsterdam: Elsevier.

Gove, Walter R. 1973. "Sex, Marital Status and Mortality," *American Journal of Sociology* 79: 45–67.

Gowder, John. 1993. "The Canadian Syndrome of Regional Polarities: An Obituary," *Canadian Review of Sociology and Anthropology* 30, 10: 1–12.

Gracey, Michael, and Malcom King. 2009. "Indigenous Health Part 1: Determinants and Disease Patterns," *Lancet* 374: 65–75.

Grant, E. Kenneth, and John Vanderkamp. 1985. "Migrant Information and the Remigration Decision: Further Evidence," *Southern Economic Journal* 51: 1202–15.

———, and ———. 1984. "A Descriptive Analysis of the Incidence and Nature of Repeat Migration within Canada, 1968–71," *Canadian Studies in Population* 11, 1: 61–78.

Grant, Jonathan, Stijn Hoorens, Suja Sivadasan, et al. 2004. *Low Fertility and Population Ageing Causes, Consequences, and Policy Options.* Santa Monica: RAND Corporation.

Gray, Alan. 1990. *A Matter of Life and Death: Contemporary Aboriginal Mortality.* Canberra: Aboriginal Studies Press.

Green, Alan, and David Green. 1999. "The Economic Goals of Canada's Immigration Policy: Past and Present," *Canadian Public Policy* 24: 425–51.

Green, Anne, Irene Hardill, and Stephen Munn. 1999. "The Employment Consequences of Migration: Gender Differentials," in Paul Boyle and Keith Halfcree, eds, *Migration and Gender in the Developed World.* London: Routledge.

Greenhalgh, Susan. 1986. "Shifts in China's Population Policy," *Population and Development Review* 12, 3: 491–516.

Greenwood, Michael J. 1985. "Human Migration: Theory, Models and Empirical Studies," *Journal of Regional Science* 25, 4: 521–44.

Greksa, Lawrence P. 2003. "Birth Seasonality in the Old Order Amish," *Journal of Biosocial Science* 36: 299–315.

Grigoriev, Pavel, France Meslé, Vladimir M. Shkolnikov, Evgeny Andreev, A. Fihel, M. Pechholdova, and J. Vallin. 2014. "The Recent Mortality Decline in Russia: Beginning of the Cardiovascular Revolution?" *Population and Development Review* 40, 1: 107–129.

Grindstaff, Carl F. 1995. "Canada's Continued Trend of Low Fertility," *Canadian Social Trends* (Winter): 12–16.

——. 1994. "The Baby Bust Revisited: Canada's Continuing Pattern of Low Fertility," in Frank Trovato and Carl F. Grindstaff, eds, *Canada's Population: Introduction to Concepts and Issues*. Don Mills, ON: Oxford University Press.

——. 1985. "The Baby Bust Revisited: Canada's Continuing Pattern of Fertility," *Canadian Studies in Population* 12, 1: 103–10.

——. 1981. *Population and Society: A Sociological Perspective*. West Hanover, MA: Christopher Publishing House.

——. 1975. "The Baby Bust: Changes in Fertility Patterns in Canada," *Canadian Studies in Population* 2: 15–22.

——, T.R. Balakrishnan, and David J. Dewit. 1992. "Educational Attainment, Age at First Birth and Lifetime Fertility: An Analysis of Canadian Fertility Survey Data," *Canadian Review of Sociology and Anthropology* 28, 3: 324–39.

——, and Frank Trovato. 1990. "Junior Partners: Women's Contribution to Family Income in Canada," *Social Indicators Research* 22: 229–53.

Grossbard-Schechtman, Shoshana. 1995. "Marriage Market Models," in Mariano Tommasi and Kathryn Ierulli, eds, *The New Economics of Human Behavior*. Cambridge: Cambridge University Press.

Grundy, E. 2000. "Co-residence of Mid-life Children with their Elderly Parents in England and Wales: Changes between 1981 and 1991," *Population Studies* 54: 193–206.

Guengant, Jean-Pierre, and John May. 2009. *Proximate Determinants of Fertility in Sub-Saharan Africa and Their Possible Use in Fertility Projection*. United Nations Expert Group Meeting on Recent and Future Trends in Fertility (2 December). New York: UN.

Gugler, Joseph. 1988. "The Urban Transition in the Third World: Introduction," in Joseph Gugler, ed., *The Urbanization of the Third World*. Oxford: Oxford University Press.

Guillard, Achille. 1855. *Eléments de statistique humaine, ou démographie comparée*. Paris: Guillaumin et cie Libraires.

Guillot, Michel. 2003. "Life Tables," in Paul Demeny and Geoffrey McNicoll, eds, *Encyclopedia of Population*. New York: Macmillan Reference USA/ Thomson Gale.

Guilmoto, Christophe Z. 2012. "Skewed Sex Ratios at Birth and Future Marriage Squeeze in China and India, 2005–2100," *Demography* 49: 77–100.

Guimond, Eric. 1999. "Ethnic Mobility and the Demographic Growth of Canada's Aboriginal Populations from 1986 to 1996," in Alain Bélanger, *Report on the Demographic Situation in Canada: 1998 and 1999*. Cat. no. 91-209-XPE. Ottawa: Statistics Canada.

——, Norbert Robitaille, and Sacha Sénecal. 2014. "Another Look at Definitions and Growth of Aboriginal Populations in Canada," in Frank Trovato and Anatole Romaniuk, eds, *Aboriginal Populations— Social, Demographic, and Epidemiological Perspectives*. Edmonton, AB: University of Alberta Press.

Guindon, Hubert. 1988. *Quebec Society: Tradition, Modernity, and Nationhood*. Toronto: University of Toronto Press.

Gunderson, Morley. 1998. *Women and the Canadian Labour Market: Transitions Towards the Future*. Ottawa and Toronto: Statistics Canada and ITP Nelson.

Gurunath S., Z. Pandian, R.A. Anderson, and S. Bhattacharya. 2011. "Defining Infertility—A Systematic Review of Prevalence Studies," *Human Reproduction Update* 17, 5: 575–88.

Gurven, Michael, and Hillard Kaplan. 2007. "Longevity among Hunter-Gatherers: A Cross-cultural Examination," *Population and Development Review* 33, 2: 321–65.

Gusfield, Joseph R. 1967. "Tradition and Modernity: Misplaced Polarities in the Study of Social Change," *American Journal of Sociology* 72: 351–62.

Guttentag, Marcia, and Paul F. Secord. 1983. *Too Many Women? The Sex Ratio Question*. Beverly Hills, CA: Sage.

Haberland, Nicole, and Diana Measham, eds. 2002. *Responding to Cairo: Case Studies of Changing Practice in Reproductive Health and Family Planning*. New York: Population Council.

Haines, Michael R., and Richard H. Steckel. 2000. *A Population History of North America*. Cambridge: Cambridge University Press.

Hajnal, John. 1965. "European Marriage Patterns in Perspective," in D.V. Glass and D.E.C. Eversley, eds, *Population in History: Essay in Historical Demography*. London: Edward Arnold.

——. 1953. "Age at Marriage and Proportion Marrying," *Population Studies* 7, 2: 111–36.

Halfcree, Keith, and Paul Boyle. 1999. "Introduction: Gender and Migration in Developed Countries," in Paul Boyle and Keith Halfcree, eds, *Migration and Gender in the Developed World*. London: Routledge.

Hall, David R., and John Z. Zhao. 1995. "Cohabitation and Divorce in Canada: Testing the Selectivity Hypothesis," *Journal of Marriage and the Family* 57: 421–7.

Hall, Peter. 1998. *Cities in Civilization*. London: Weidenfeld & Nicolson.

———. 1996. "The Global City," *International Social Science Journal* 48: 15–23.

Halli, Shiva S. 1990. "The Fertility of Ethnic Groups," in Shiva S. Halli, Frank Trovato, and Leo Driedger, eds, *Ethnic Demography: Canadian Immigrant, Racial and Cultural Variations*. Ottawa: Carleton University Press.

Halweil, Brian. 2003. "Grain Production Drops," in *Vital Signs*, 28–9. The Worldwatch Institute. New York: W.W. Norton.

Hamilton, Graeme. 2004. "Mission Aims to SeduceStudents to Gaspé Charms," *National Post* (18 March): A5.

———. 2002. "People Don't Even Say Hello Anymore," *National Post* (21 September): A3.

Hammer, Michael F. 2013. "Evolution. Human Hybrids," *Scientific American* 308 (May): 66–71.

Hannerz, Harald. 2001. "Manhood Trials and the Law of Mortality," *Demographic Research* 4, 7 (May): 185–202. www.demographic-research.org.

Hansen, Dorthe, Henrik Møller, and Jørn Olsen. 1999. "Severe Periconceptional Life Events and the Sex Ratio in Offspring: Follow up Study Based on Five National Registers," *British Medical Association Journal* 319: 548–9.

Hardy, Melissa A., and Linda Waite. 1997. "Doing Time: Reconciling Biography with History in the Study of Social Change," in Melissa A. Hardy, ed., *Studying Aging and Social Change: Conceptual and Methodological Issues*. Thousand Oaks, CA: Sage.

Harris, J.R., and M.P. Todaro. 1970. "Migration, Unemployment, and Development: A Two-Sector Analysis," *American Economic Review* 60, 1: 126–42.

Hartnagel, Tim F., and G.W. Lee. 1990. "Urban Crime in Canada," *Canadian Journal of Criminology* 32: 591–606.

Harvey, David. 1975. "The Geography of Capitalist Accumulation: A Reconstruction of the Marxian Theory," *Antipode* 7, 2: 9–21.

Harzig, Christiane, and Dirk Hoerder. 2009. *What Is Migration History?* Cambridge: Polity Press.

Hassold, Terry, S.D. Quillen, and J.A. Yamane. 1983. "Sex Ratio in Spontaneous Abortions," *Annals of Human Genetics* 47 (January) (Part I): 39–47.

Hatton, Timothy J., and Jeffrey G. Williamson. 1998. *The Age of Mass Migration: Causes and Economic Impact*. New York: Oxford University Press.

———, and ———. 1994. "What Drove the Mass Migrations from Europe in the Late Nineteenth Century?" *Population and Development Review* 20, 3: 503–31.

Haub, Carl. 2013. "Cities Larger than Many Countries," Population Reference Bureau, demographics revealed (accessed 26 June 2013).

———. 1987. "Understanding Population Projections," *Population Bulletin* 42, 4. Washington: Population Reference Bureau.

Hawkins, Freda. 1988. *Canada and Immigration: Public Policy and Public Concern*, 2nd edn. Kingston and Montreal: McGill-Queen's University Press.

Hawkins, Liz, and Ray D. Bollman. 1994. "Revisiting Rural Canada: It's Not All the Same," *Canadian Agriculture at a Glance*, 78–80. Ottawa: Statistics Canada. Cat. no. 96-301.

Hawthorne, H B., ed. 1966. *A Survey of the Contemporary Indians of Canada: Report on the Economic, Political, Educational Needs and Policies*, 2 vols. Ottawa: Indian Affairs Branch.

Hayek, F.A. 1998. "The Extended Order and Population Growth," in Paul Demeny and Geoffrey McNicoll, eds, *The Earthscan Reader in Population and Development*. London: Earthscan.

Haynes, Michael, and Rumy Husan. 2003. *A Century of State Murder? Death and Policy in Twentieth-Century Russia*. London: Pluto.

Hayter, Teresa. 2000. *Open Borders: The Case against Immigration Controls*. London: Pluto.

Hayward, Mark D., and Bridget K. Gorman. 2004. "The Long Arm of Childhood: The Influence of Early-Life Social Conditions on Men's Mortality," *Demography* 41, 1: 87–107.

———, and Melonie Heron. 1999. "Racial Inequality in Active Life among Adult Americans," *Demography* 36, 1: 77–92.

Hazelrigg, Lawrence. 1997. "On the Importance of Age," in Melissa A. Hardy, ed., *Studying Aging and Social Change: Conceptual and Methodological Issues*. Thousand Oaks, CA: Sage.

Health Canada. 2003. *A Statistical Profile on the Health of First Nations in Canada* (various pages).

———. 1996. "Trends in First Nations Mortality 1979–1993." Cat. no. 34-79/1993E.

Heilig, Gerhard, Thomas Buttner, and Wolfgang Lutz. 1990. "Germany's Population: Turbulent Past, Uncertain Future," *Population Bulletin* 45, 4. Washington: Population Reference Bureau.

Hekimi, Siegfried, and Leonard Guarente. 2003. "Genetics and the Specificity of the Aging Process," *Science* 299 (28 February): 1351–4.

Helbing, Dirk. 2013. "Globally Networked Risks and How to Respond," *Nature* 497: 51–59.

Held, David, Anthony McGrew, David Goldblatt, et al. 1999. *Global Transformations: Politics, Economic and Culture*. Stanford, CA: Stanford University Press.

Hémon, Louis. 1914 [1965]. *Maria Chapdelaine*. Toronto: Macmillan.

Henderson, Robert. 1915. *Mortality Laws and Statistics*. New York: John Wiley.

Henderson, Vernon. 2003. "The Urbanization Process and Economic Growth: The So-What Question," *Journal of Economic Growth* 8: 47–71.

Henn, Brenna M., Luigi. L. Cavalli-Sforza, and Marcus W. Feldman. 2012. "The Great Human Expansion," *Proceedings of the National Academies of Science* 109, 44: 17758–64.

Henrich, Joseph, Robert Boyd, and Peter J. Richerson. 2011. "The Puzzle of Monogamous Marriage," *Philosophical Transactions of the Royal Society B* 367: 657–69.

Henripin, Jacques. 2003. *La métamorphose de la population canadienne*. Montreal: Les Éditions Varia.

———. 1994. "From Acceptance of Nature to Control: The Demography of the French Canadians since the Seventeenth Century," in Frank Trovato and Carl F. Grindstaff, eds, *Perspectives on Canada's Population: An Introduction to Concepts and Issues*. Don Mills, ON: Oxford University Press.

———. 1972. "Trends and Factors of Fertility in Canada," *1961 Census Monograph*. Ottawa: Statistics Canada.

———. 1954. *La population canadienne au début du XVIIIè siècle*. Paris: Institut National d'Études Démographiques.

———, and Yves Péron. 1972. "The Demographic Transition of the Province of Quebec," in D.V. Glass and Roger Revelle, eds, *Population and Social Change*. London: Edward Arnold.

Henry, Louis. 1989. "Men's and Women's Mortality in the Past," *Population* 44 (English selection no. 1): 177–201.

———. 1961. "Some Data on Natural Fertility," *Eugenics Quarterly* (now *Social Biology*) 8: 81–91.

Henshaw, Stanley K. 2003. "Abortion: Prevalence," in Paul Demeny and Geoffrey McNicoll, eds, *Encyclopedia of Population*, 529–31. New York: Macmillan Reference USA/Thompson Gale.

Herlihy, David. 1997. *The Black Death and the Transformation of the West* (edited and with an introduction by Samuel K. Cohn Jr). Cambridge, MA: Harvard University Press.

Hesketh, Therese, Li Lu, and Zhu Wei Xing. 2006. "The Effect of China's One-Child Family Policy after 25 Years," *New England Journal of Medicine* 353 (15 September): 1171–6.

———, and Zhu Wei Xing. 2006. "Abnormal Sex Ratios in Human Populations: Causes and Consequences," *Proceedings of the National Academy of Sciences* 103, 36: 13271–5.

Hess, Gregory. 2004. "Marriage and Consumption Insurance: What's Love Got to Do with It?" *Journal of Political Economy* 112, 2: 290–318.

Heuveline, Patrick, Michel Guillot, and Davidson R. Gwatkin. 2002. "The Uneven Tides of the Health Transition," *Social Science and Medicine* 55: 313–22.

———, and Jeffrey M. Timberlake. 2004. "The Role of Cohabitation in Family Formation: The United States in Comparative Perspective," *Journal of Marriage and the Family* 66: 1214–30.

Hiedemann, B., O. Suhomlinova, and A.M. O'Rand. 1998. "Economic Independence, Economic Status, and Empty Nest in Midlife Marital Disruption," *Journal of Marriage and the Family* 60: 219–31.

Hill, Allan G. 1990. "Understanding Recent Fertility Trends in the Third World," in John Landers and Vernon Reynolds, eds, *Fertility and Resources*, 146–63. Cambridge: Cambridge University Press.

Hill, Kenneth. 2004. "War, Humanitarian Crises, Population Displacement, and Fertility: A Review of Evidence." Roundtable on the Demography of Forced Migration Committee on Population. National Research Council of the National Academies. Washington: The National Academies Press.

Hiller, Harry H. 2009. *Second Promised Land: Migration to Alberta and the Transformation of Canadian Society*. Montreal and Kingston: McGill-Queen's University Press.

Himes Norman E. 1936 [1963]. *A Medical History of Contraception*. 1st Gamut Press edn. New York: Gamut Press.

Hinde, Andrew. 2003. *England's Population: A History since the Domesday Survey*. New York: Oxford University Press.

———. 1998. *Demographic Methods*. London: Edward Arnold.

Hirschi, Travis. 1969. *Causes of Delinquency*. Berkley, CA: Free Press.

Hirschman, Charles. 2005. "Immigration and the American Century," *Demography* 42, 4: 595–620.

———. 1994. "Why Fertility Changes," *Annual Review of Sociology* 20: 203–33.

Hisnanick, John J. 1994. "Comparative Analysis of Violent Deaths in American Indians and Alaska Natives," *Social Biology* 41, 1–2: 96–109.

Hobcroft, John N. 2004. "Method, Theory, and Substance in Understanding Choices about Becoming a Parent: Progress or Regress?" *Population Studies* 58, 1: 77–92. Discussion of the paper by John Caldwell and Thomas Schindlmayer in *Population Studies* 57, 3 (2003).

Hodge, Gerald, and Mohammad A. Qadeer. 1983. *Towns and Villages in Canada: The Importance of Being Unimportant*. Toronto: Butterworths.

Hoekstra, Arjen Y., and Thomas O. Wiedmann. 2014. "Humanity's Unsustainable Environmental Footprint," *Science* 344, 6188: 1114–17.

Hoerder, Dirk. 2002. Cultures *in Contact: World Migrations in the Second Millennium*. Durham: Duke University Press.

Hoffman, Lois Wladis, and Martin L. Hoffman. 1973. "The Value of Children to Parents," in James T.

Fawcett, ed. *Psychological Perspectives on Population*, 19–76. New York: Basic Books.

Hogg, Robert. 1992. "Indigenous Mortality: Placing Australian Aboriginal Mortality within a Broader Context," *Social Science and Medicine* 35, 3: 335–46.

Holdren, Nate. 2013. "Transatlantic Slave Trade," in Emmanuel Ness (general editor), *The Encyclopedia of Global Human Migration*, vol. V, 2961–6. Chichester: Wiley-Blackwell.

Hollander, Samuel. 1997. *The Economics of Thomas Robert Malthus*. Toronto: University of Toronto Press.

Holubitsky, Jeff. 2005. "Tiny Alberta Village Turns Its Fortunes around," *Edmonton Journal* (17 April): A1, A7.

Homer-Dixon, Thomas. 1999. *Environment, Scarcity, and Violence*. Princeton, NJ: Princeton University Press.

———, J.H. Boutwell, and G.W. Rathjens. 1993. "Environmental Change and Violent Conflict," *Scientific American* 268, 2 (February): 38–45.

Hoogvelt, Ankie. 2001. *Globalization and the Postcolonial World: The New Political Economy of Development*, 2nd edn. London: Palgrave.

———. 1976. *The Sociology of Developing Societies*. New York: Macmillan.

Hopkins, A.G. (ed.) 2002. *Globalization in World History*. New York: W.W. Norton

Horiuchi, Shiro 2003. "Mortality, Age Patterns," in Paul Demeny and Geoffrey McNicoll, eds, *Encyclopedia of Population*, 649–54. New York: Macmillan Reference USA/Thompson Gale.

———. 1991. "Assessing Effects of Mortality Reduction on Population Aging," *Population Bulletin of the United Nations* 31: 38–51.

———, and John R. Wilmoth. 1998. "Deceleration in the Age Pattern of Mortality at Older Ages," *Demography* 35, 4: 391–412.

Hou, Feng. 2007. "Changes in the Initial Destinations and Redistribution of Canada's Major Immigrant Groups: Reexamining the Role of Group Affinity," *International Migration Review* 41, 3: 680–605.

———. 2004. "The Initial Destinations and Re-distribution of Canada's Major Immigrant Groups: Changes over the Past Two Decades," Working Paper series, Business and Labour Market Analysis Division, Ottawa: Statistics Canada.

———, and Rod Beaujot. 1995. "A Study of Interregional Migration between Ontario and Atlantic Canada: 1981–1991," *Canadian Journal of Regional Science* 28: 147–60.

House, James S., Karl R. Landis, and Debra Umberson. 1988. "Social Relationships and Health," *Science* 2441: 540–5.

Howson, C.P., M.V. Kinney, and J.E. Lawn (eds). 2012. *Born Too Soon: The Global Action Report on Preterm Birth*. March of Dimes, PMNCH, Save the Children, World Health Organization. Geneva: World Health Organization. www.who.int/pmnch/media/news/2012/preterm_birth_report/en/index.html (accessed 9 September 2013).

Hrdy, Sarah Blaffer. 1999. *Mother Nature: A History of Mothers, Infants and Natural Selection*. New York: Pantheon.

Hsiang, Solomon, M., Kyle C. Meng, and Mark A. Cane. 2011. "Civil Conflicts Are Associated with the Global Climate," *Nature* 476: 438–41.

Hugo, Graeme. Anthony Champion, and Alfredo Lattes. 2003. "Toward a New Conceptualization of Settlements for Demography," *Population and Development Review* 29, 2: 277–97.

Human Rights Watch. 2013. *World Report 2013. Events of 2012*. New York.

Hummer, Robert, Richard G. Rogers, and Isaac W. Eberstein. 1998. "Socio-economic Differentials in Adult Mortality: A Review of Analytic Approaches," *Population and Development Review* 24, 3: 553–78.

———, ———, Charles B. Nam, and C.G. Ellison. 1999. "Religious Involvement and U.S. Adult Mortality," *Demography* 36, 2: 273–85.

Hurd, W. Burton. 1965. "Ethnic Origin and Nativity of the Canadian People," *1941 Census Monograph*. Ottawa: Queen's Printer.

Hyatt, Douglas E., and William J. Milne. 1991. "Can Public Policy Affect Fertility?" *Canadian Public Policy* 17, 1: 77–85.

Inglehart, Ronald. 1997. *Modernization and Postmoderrization: Cultural, Economic, and Political Change in 43 Societies*. Princeton, NJ: Princeton University Press.

Inkeles, Alex, and David Horton Smith. 1974. *Becoming Modern: Individual Change in Six Developing Countries*. Cambridge, MA: Harvard University Press.

Innis, Harold A. 1930. *The Fur Trade in Canada: An Introduction to Canadian Economic History*. New Haven: Yale University Press.

Institut National d'études demographiques (INED). 2013. *Database on Developed Countries*. www.ined.fr/en/pop_figures/developed_countries_database/ (accessed 1 May 2014).

Intergovernmental Panel on Climate Change. 2013. "Summary for Policymakers," in Climate Change 2013: The Physical Science Basis. Contribution of Working Group I to the Fifth Assessment Report of the Intergovernmental Panel on Climate Change. Cambridge, UK, and New York: Cambridge University Press.

International Labor Organization. 2008. *Global Employment Trends: January 2008*. Geneva: International Labor Office.

International Monetary Fund. 2000. *World Economic Outlook 2000*. Washington, DC.

Isbister, John. 2000. "A Liberal Argument for Border Controls: Reply to Carens," *International Migration Review* 34, 2: 629–35.

Islam, Mazharul M., M. Ataharul Islam, and Nitai Chakroborty. 2003. "Fertility Transition in Bangladesh: Understanding the Role of the Proximate Determinants," *Journal of Biosocial Science* 36: 351–69.

Jacobs, Jane. 1967. *Death and Life of Great American Cities*. Harmondsworth, UK: Penguin.

Jaffe, A.J. 1992. *The First Immigrants from Asia: A Population History of the North American Indians*. New York: Plenum.

James, Paul D., Russell Wilkins, Allan S. Detsky, et al. 2007. "Avoidable Mortality by Neighbourhood Income in Canada: 25 Years after the Establishment of Universal Health Insurance," *Journal of Epidemiology and Community Health* 61: 287–96.

James, William. H. 2012. "Hypotheses on the Stability and Variation of Human Sex Ratios at Birth," *Journal of Theoretical Population Biology* 310: 183–6.

———. 2004. "Further Evidence that Mammalian Sex Ratios at Birth Are Partially Controlled by Parental Hormone Levels around the Time of Conception," *Human Reproduction* 19, 6:1250–56.

———. 1996. "Evidence that Mammalian Sex Ratios at Birth Are Partially Controlled by Parental Hormone Levels at the Time of Conception," *Journal of Theoretical Biology* 180: 160–75.

———. 1987a. "The Human Sex Ratio: Part I. A Review of the Literature," *Human Biology* 59, 5: 721–52.

———. 1987b. "The Human Sex Ratio: Part II. A Hypothesis and a Program of Research," *Human Biology* 59, 5: 873–900.

Jarvis, George K., and Menno Boldt. 1982. "Death Styles among Canada's Indians," *Social Science and Medicine* 16: 1345–52.

Jefferson, Mark. 1939. "The Law of the Primate City," *The Geographical Review* 29: 226–32.

Jeffery, Roger, and Patricia Jeffery. 1997. *Population, Gender and Politics: Demographic Change in Rural North India*. Cambridge: Cambridge University Press.

Jeune, Bernard, and Axel Skytthe. 2001. "Centenarians in Denmark in the Past and the Present," *Population: An English Selection* 13, 1: 75–94.

Johansson, S. Ryan. 1991. "The Health Transition: The Cultural Inflation of Morbidity during the Decline of Mortality," *Health Transition Review* 1, 1: 39–68.

Johnson, Jothan. 1954 [1973]. "The Slow Death of a City," *Readings from Scientific American*, in Kingsley Davis, ed., *Cities: Their Origin, Growth and Human Impact*. New York: W.H. Freeman.

Johnson, Kay. 1996. "The Politics of the Revival of Infant Abandonment in China, with Special Reference to Hunan," *Population and Development Review* 22, 1: 77–98.

Johnson, Kenneth M., Paul R. Voss, Roger B. Hammer, Glenn V. Fuguitt, and Scott McNiven. 2005. "Temporal and Spatial Variations in Age-specific Net Migration in the United States," *Demography* 42, 4: 791–812.

Johnson, Nan E. 1979. "Minority-Group Status and the Fertility of Black Americans," *American Journal of Sociology* 84: 1386–1400.

———, and Suwen Lean. 1985. "Relative Income, Race and Fertility," *Population Studies* 39: 99–112.

Jones, Gavin W. 2007. "Delayed Marriage and Very Low Fertility in Pacific Asia," *Population and Development Review* 33, 3: 453–78.

———. 2003. "Urbanization," in Paul Demeny and Geoffrey McNicoll, eds, *Encyclopedia of Population*, 951–4. New York: Macmillan Reference USA/ Thompson Gale.

———. 2002. "Southeast Asia Urbanization and the Growth of Mega-urban Regions," *Journal of Population Research* 19, 2: 119–36.

———, and Richard Leete. 2002. "Asia's Family Planning Programs as Low Fertility is Attained," *Studies in Family Planning* 33, 1.

Jones, Larry E., Alice Schoonbroodt, and Michele Tertilit. 2011. "Fertility Theories: Can They Explain the Negative Fertility-Income Relationship?" in John B Shoven, ed., *Demography and the Economy*, 43–100. Chicago: University of Chicago Press.

———, and Michéle Tertilt. 2008. "An Economic History of Fertility in the U.S.: 1826–1960," in P. Rupert, ed., *Frontiers of Family Economics*, vol. 1, 165–230. Bingley, UK: Emerald Press.

Jones, Owen R., Alexander Scheuerlein, Roberto Salguero-Gomez, Carlo Giovanni Camarda, et al. 2014. "Diversity of Ageing across the Tree of Life," *Nature* 505: 169–74.

Junhong, Chu. 2001. "Prenatal Sex Determination and Sex-Selective Abortion in Rural Central China," *Population and Development Review* 27, 2: 259–82.

Kalbach, Warren, E. 1970. *The Impact of Immigration on Canada's Population*. Ottawa: The Queen's Printer.

———, and Wayne McVey Jr. 1979. *The Demographic Bases of Canadian Society*, 2nd edn. Toronto: McGraw-Hill.

———, and ———. 1971. *The Demographic Bases of Canadian Society*. Toronto: McGraw-Hill.

Kalmijn, Matthijs. 2013. "The Educational Gradient in Marriage: A Comparison of 25 European Countries," *Demography* 50: 1499–1520.

———. 2007. "Explaining Cross-national Differences in Marriage, Cohabitation, and Divorce in Europe, 1990–2000," *Population Studies* 61, 3: 243–63.

Kalter, Harold. 1991. "Five-Decade International Trends in the Relation of Perinatal Mortality and Congenital Malformations: Stillbirth and Neonatal Death Compared," *International Journal of Epidemiology* 20, 1: 173–9.

Kanazawa, Satoshi, and Mary C. Still. 1999. "Why Monogamy?" *Social Forces* 78, 1: 25–50.

Kannisto, Vaino. 1996. "The Advancing Frontier of Survival," *Odense Monographs on Population Aging*, 3. Odense, DK: Odense University Press.

———, Jens Lauritsen, A. Roger Thatcher, and James W. Vaupel. 1994. "Reductions in Mortality at Advanced Ages: Several Decades of Evidence from 27 Countries," *Population and Development Review* 20, 4: 793–810.

———, Mauri Nieminen, and Oiva Turpeinen. 1999. "Finnish Life Tables Since 1751," *Demographic Research*, vol. 1 (July). www.demographic-research.org/.

Kantner, John F. and Andrew Kantner. 2006. *The Struggle for International Consensus on Population and Development.* New York: Palgrave Macmillan.

Kappeler, Peter M. 2013. "Why Male Mammals Are Monogamous," *Science* 341 (2 August) 469–70.

Kasearu, Kairi, and Dagmar Kutsar. 2011. "Patterns behind Unmarried Cohabitation Trends in Europe," *European Societies* 11, 2: 307–25.

Katz, J., C.C.L Anne, and N. Kozuki et al. 2013. "Mortality Risk in Preterm and Small-for-Gestational-Age Infants in Low-Income and Middle-Income Countries: A Pooled Country Analysis," *Lancet* 381: 417–25.

Kazemipur, Abdolmohammad, and S.S. Halli. 2000. *The New Poverty in Canada: Ethnic Groups and Ghetto Neighbourhoods.* Toronto: Thompson.

Keddie, P.D., and A.E. Joseph. 1991. "The Turnaround of the Turnaround? Rural Population Change in Canada, 1976 to 1986," *The Canadian Geographer* 35, 4: 367–79.

Keely, Charles. 2001. "Should Borders Be Open?" International Union for the Scientific Study of Population General Conference. San Salvador de Bahia, Brazil, 24 August 2001.

Keil, Roger, and Stefan Kipfer. 2003 "The Urban Experience and Globalization," in Wallace Clement and Leah F. Vosko, eds, *Changing Canada: Political Economy as Transformation*, 335–62. Montreal and Kingston: McGill-Queen's University Press.

Kennedy, Leslie W., and David R. Forde. 1990. "Routine Activities and Crime: An Analysis of Victimization in Canada," *Criminology* 28: 137–52.

———, and David Veitch. 1997. "Why Are Crime Rates Going Down? A Case Study in Edmonton," *Canadian Journal of Criminology* 97: 51–69.

Kennedy, Paul. 1993. *Preparing for the Twenty-First Century.* Toronto: HarperCollins.

Kennedy, Robert E. Jr. 1973. *The Irish: Emigration, Marriage, and Fertility.* Berkeley: University of California Press.

Kenoyer, Jonathan Mark. 2005. "Uncovering the Keys to the Lost Indus Cities," special issue, *Scientific American* 15, 1: 25–35.

Kent, Mary M., and Carl Haub. 2005. "Global Demographic Divide," *Population Bulletin* 60, 4. Washington: Population Reference Bureau.

Kerr, Don. 2014. "Population Growth, Energy Use, and Environmental Impact: Comparing the Canadian and Swedish Records on CO_2 Emissions," *Canadian Studies in Population* 41, 1–2: 120–43.

———, Melissa Moyser, and Roderic Beaujot. 2006. "Marriage and Cohabitation: Demographic and Socioeconomic Differences in Quebec and Canada," *Canadian Studies in Population* 33, 1: 83–117.

Kettle, John. 1980. *The Big Generation.* Toronto: McClelland and Stewart.

Keyfitz, Nathan. 2003. "Euler, Leonhard," in Paul Demeny and Geoffrey McNicoll, eds, *Encyclopedia of Population*, 322–3. New York: Macmillan Reference USA/Thomson Gale.

———. 1996a. "Population," *Grolier Encyclopedia* on CD-ROM.

———. 1996b. "Internal Migration and Urbanization," in Bernardo Colombo, Paul Demeny, and Max F. Perutz, eds, *Resources and Population: Natural, Institutional, and Demographic Dimensions of Development*, 259–85. Oxford: Clarendon.

———. 1993. "Are there Ecological Limits to Population?" *Proceedings of the National Academy of Sciences of the USA*, 90 (August): 6895–9.

———. 1987. "Canada's Population in Comparative Perspective," in P. Krishnan, Frank Trovato, and Gordon Fern, eds, *Contributions to Demography: Methodological and Substantive*, vol. 1: *Essays in Honor of Dr. Karol J. Krotki*, 95–110. Edmonton: Department of Sociology, University of Alberta.

———. 1986. "The Family that Does Not Reproduce Itself," in Kingsley Davis, Mikhail S. Bernstam, and Rita Ricardo-Campbell, eds, *Below-Replacement Fertility in Industrial Societies: Causes, Consequences, Policies*, 139–55, supp. to *Population and Development Review* 12.

———. 1985. *Applied Mathematical Demography*, 2nd edn. New York: Springer.

———. 1977. *Applied Mathematical Demography.* New York: John Wiley & Sons.

———. 1975. "How Do We Know the Facts of Demography?" *Population and Development Review* 1, 2: 267–88.

——. 1968. *Introduction to the Mathematics of Population*. Reading, MA: Addison-Wesley.

King, Malcolm, Alexandra Smith, and Michael Gracey. 2009. "Indigenous Health Part 2: The Underlying Causes of the Health Gap," *Lancet* 374: 76–85.

King, Margaret, John Gartrell, and Frank Trovato. 1994. "Early Childhood Mortality: 1926–1986," in Frank Trovato and Carl F. Grindstaff, eds, *Perspectives on Canada's Population: An Introduction to Concepts and Issues,* 136–41. Don Mills, ON: Oxford University Press.

Kinsella, Kevin, and Victoria A. Vlekoff. 2001. *An Aging World: 2001*. Washington, DC: U.S. Census Bureau, Series P95/01-1. U.S. Government Printing Office.

Kirk, Dudley. 1996. "Demographic Transition Theory," *Population Studies* 50: 361–87.

——. 1960. "The Influence of Business Cycles on Marriage and Birth Rates," in *National Bureau of Economic Research, Demographic and Economic Change in Developed Countries,* 241–57. Princeton, NJ: Princeton University Press.

Kirkwood, Thomas. 2010a. "Why Can't We Live Forever?" *Scientific American* 303, 3 (September): 42–9.

——. 2010b. "Why Women Live Longer," *Scientific American* (21 October): 48.

Kitagawa, Evelyn M., and Phillip M. Hauser. 1973. *Differential Mortality in the United States: A Study in Socio-economic Epidemiology*. Cambridge, MA: Harvard University Press.

Klasen, Stephan. 2003. "Sex Selection," in Paul Demeny and Geoffrey McNicoll, eds, *Encyclopedia of Population,* 879–81. New York: Macmillan Reference USA/Thomson Gale.

Kliegman, Robert M. 1995. "Neonatal Technology, Perinatal Survival, Social Consequences, and the Perinatal Paradox," *American Journal of Public Health* 85: 909–13.

Klinger, Andras. 1985. "The Fight against Infant Mortality," in Jacques Vallin and Alan D. Lopez, eds, *Health Policy, Social Policy and Mortality Prospects,* 281–97. Paris: Ordina Editions. Proceedings of a Seminar, 28 February–4 March 1983. Paris: Institut National d'Etudes Demographiques and International Union for the Scientific Study of Population.

Knodel, John. 1977. "Age Patterns of Fertility and the Fertility Transition: Evidence from Europe and Asia," *Population Studies* 31: 219–50.

——, Jed Friedman, Truong Si Anh, and Bui The Cuong. 2000. "Intergenerational Exchanges in Vietnam: Family Size, Sex Composition, and the Location of Children," *Population Studies* 54: 89–104.

Knox, Paul L., and Sallie A. Marston. 2004. "Places and Regions in Global Context," *Human Geography,* 3rd edn. Upper Saddle River, NJ: Pearson.

Kobrin, Frances E. 1976. "The Primary Individual and the Family: Changes in Living Arrangements in the United States since 1940," *Journal of Marriage and the Family* 38: 233–8.

——, and Alden Speare. 1983. "Outmigration and Ethnic Communities," *International Migration Review* 17, 3: 425–44.

Kohler, Hans-Peter. 2000. "Social Interactions and Fluctuations in the Birth Rates," *Population Studies* 54, 2: 223–37.

——, Francesco Billari, and José Antonio Ortega. 2006. "Low Fertility in Europe: Causes, Implications, and Policy Options," in Fred R. Harris, ed., *The Baby Bust—Who Will Do the Work? Who Will Pay the Taxes?* 48–109. Lanham, England: Rowman and Littlefield.

——, ——, and ——. 2002. "The Emergence of Lowest-Low Fertility in Europe during the 1990s," *Population and Development Review* 28, 4: 641–80.

Koopmans, Ruud. 2013. "Multiculturalism and Immigration: A Contested Field in Cross-national Comparison," *Annual Review of Sociology* 39:147–69.

Kormondy, Edward J. 1969. *Concepts of Ecology*. Englewood Cliffs, NJ: Prentice-Hall.

Koser, Khalid. 2007. *International Migration: A Very Short Introduction*. Oxford: Oxford University Press.

Kosinski, Leszek A. 1970. *The Population of Europe: A Geographical Perspective*. Bristol: Longman.

——, and R. Mansel Prothero, eds. 1975. *People on the Move: Studies on Internal Migration*. London: Methuen.

Kotlikoff, Laurence J., and Scott Burns. 2012. *The Clash of Generations: Saving Ourselves, Our Kids, and Our Economy*. Cambridge, MA: The MIT Press.

Kraft, Barbara Sarina. 2005. "Refugee," *Microsoft Encarta Encyclopedia*. Microsoft.

Krahn, Harvey, Tracey M. Derwing, and Baha Abu-Laban. 2005. "The Retention of Newcomers in Second- and Third-Tier Canadian Cities," *International Migration Review* 39, 4: 872–94.

Kralt, John. 1990. "Ethnic Origins in the Canadian Census: 1871–1986," in Shiva S. Halli, Frank Trovato, and Leo Driedger, eds, *Ethnic Demography: Canadian Immigrant, Racial and Cultural Variations,* 13–30. Ottawa: Carleton University Press.

Kramer, Sebastian. 2000. "The Fragile Male," *British Medical Journal* 321: (23–30 December): 1609–12.

Kreager, Philip. 2003. "Graunt, John," in Paul Demeny and Geoffrey McNicoll, eds, *Encyclopedia of Population* 1: 472–3. New York: Macmillan Reference USA/Thomson Gale.

Krishnan, P., and David Odynak. 1987. "A Generalization of Petersen's Typology of Migration," *International Migration* 25, 4: 385–97.

Kritz, M., and J.M. Nogle. 1994. "Nativity Concentration and Internal Migration among the Foreign-Born," *Demography* 31, 3: 509–24.

———, Lin Lean Lim, and Hania Zlotnik. 1992. "Global Interactions: Migration Systems, Processes, and Policies," in Mary M. Kritz, Lin Lean Lim, and Hania Zlotnik, eds, *International Migration Systems: A Global Approach*, 1–16. Oxford: Clarendon.

Krotki, Karol J. 1997. "How the Proportion of Artificial Canadians Varied between and among Regions of Canada and Ethnic Origins between 1991 and 1996," special issue, *Canadian Journal of Regional Science* 20, 1–2: 169–80.

———, and David Odynak. 1990. "The Emergence of Multiethnicities in the Eighties," in Shiva S. Halli, Frank Trovato, and Leo Driedger, eds, *Ethnic Demography: Canadian Immigrant, Racial and Cultural Variations*, 415–37. Ottawa: Carleton University Press.

Krout, J. A. 1983. "Seasonal Migration of the Elderly," *The Gerontologist* 23: 295–9.

Kubat, Daniel, and David Thornton. 1974. *A Statistical Profile of Canadian Society*. Toronto: McGraw-Hill.

Kucera, Tomas Olga Kucerova, Oksana Opara, and E. Schaich, eds. 2000. *New Demographic Faces of Europe: The Changing Population Dynamics in Countries of Central and Eastern Europe*. Berlin: Springer.

Kuhn, Randall. 2010. "Routes to Low Mortality in Poor Countries Revisited," *Population and Development Review* 36, 4: 655–92.

Kunitz, Stephen J. 2007. *The Health of Populations; General Theories and Particular Realities*. Oxford: Oxford University Press.

———. 2000. "Globalization, States, and the Health of Indigenous Peoples," *American Journal of Public Health* 90: 1531–9.

———. 1994. *Disease and Diversity: The European Impact on the Health of Non-Europeans*. New York: Oxford University Press.

———. 1990. "Public Policy and Mortality among Indigenous Populations of Northern America and Australia," *Population and Development Review* 16, 4: 647–72.

———. 1983. *Disease Change and the Role of Medicine: The Navajo Experience*. Berkeley, CA: University of California Press.

———, with Irena Pesis-Katz. 2005. "Mortality of White Americans, African Americans, and Canadians: The Causes and Consequences for Health of Welfare State Institutions and Policies," *The Milbank Quarterly* 83, 1: 5–39.

Kuznets, Simon. 1955. "Economic Growth and Income Inequality," *American Economic Review* 45: 1–28.

Lam, David. 2013. "How the World Survived the Population Bomb: Lessons from 50 Years of Extraordinary Demographic History," *Demography* 48, 4: 1231–62.

———, and Jeffrey A. Miron. 1996. "The Effects of Temperature on Human Fertility," *Demography* 33, 3: 291–305.

———, and ———. 1991. "Seasonality of Births in Human Populations," *Social Biology* 38, 1–2: 51–78.

Lamarchand, René, 2009. *The Dynamics of Violence in Central Africa*. Philadelphia, PA: University of Pennsylvania Press.

Lamb, Vicki L., and Jacob S. Siegel. 2004. "Health Demography," in Jacob S. Siegel and David A. Swanson, eds, *The Methods and Materials of Demography*, 2nd edn, 341–70. Amsterdam: Elsevier.

Lamberg-Karlovsky, C.C., and Martha Lamberg-Karlovsky. 1971 [1973]. "Readings from *Scientific American*," in Kingsley Davis, ed., *Cities: Their Origins, Growth and Human Impact*, 28–37. San Franciso: W.H. Freeman.

Lamptey, Peter, Jami L. Johnson, and Marya Khan. 2006. "The Global Challenge of HIV and AIDS," *Population Bulletin* 67, 1. Washington: Population Reference Bureau.

Landale, Nancy, and Avery M. Guest. 1985. "Constraints, Satisfaction, and Residential Mobility: Speare's Model Reconsidered," *Demography* 22: 199–222.

Landes, David S. 1999. *The Wealth and Poverty of Nations: Why Some Are So Rich and Some So Poor*. New York: W.W. Norton.

Landry, A. 1945. *Traité de Démographie*. Paris: Payot.

———. 1934. *La Révolution démographique*. Paris: Sirey.

Langer, William L. 1973. "The Black Death," *Readings from Scientific American*, in Kingsley Davis, ed., *Cities: Their Origins, Growth and Human Impact*, 106–11. San Francisco: W.H. Freeman.

Lansing, J. B., and E. Mueller. 1973. *The Geographic Mobility of Labor*. Ann Arbor: The University of Michigan, Survey Research Centre.

Lapierre-Adamcyk, Evelynne, and Carole Charvet. 2000. "Cohabitation and Marriage: An Assessment of Research in Demography," *Canadian Studies in Population* 27, 1: 239–54.

Larochelle-Côté, Sébastien, and Jason Gilmore. 2009. "Canada's Employment Downturn," *Perspectives on Labour and Income* 10, 2: 5–12. Cat. no. 75-001-X, Statistics Canada.

LaRocque, Emma D. 1994. *Violence in Aboriginal Communities*. Ottawa: Royal Commission on Aboriginal Peoples.

Last, Jonathan V. 2013. *What to Expect When No One's Expecting: America's Coming Demographic Disaster*. New York: Encounter Books.

Lavely, William, and R. Freedman. 1990. "The Origins of the Chinese Fertility Decline," *Demography* 27, 3: 357–68.

———, Jianke Li, and Jianghong Li. 2001. "Sex Preference for Children in a Meifu Li Community in Hainan, China," *Population Studies* 55, 3: 319–30.

Le Bourdais, Celine, and Evelyn Lapierre-Adamcyk. 2004. "Changes in Conjugal Life in Canada: Is Cohabitation Progressively Replacing Marriage?" *Journal of Marriage and the Family* 66: 929–42.

———, Ghyslaine Neill, and Pierre Turcotte. 2000. "The Changing Face of Conjugal Relationships," *Canadian Social Trends* 56 (Spring): 14–17.

Leacy, F.H. 1983. *Historical Statistics of Canada*, 2nd edn. Ottawa: Minister of Supply and Services.

Ledent, Jacques. 1988. "Canada," in W. Weidlich and G. Haag, eds, *Interregional Migration: Dynamic Theory and Comparative Analysis*, 101–30. Berlin: Springer.

Lee, Barret A., R.S. Oropesa, and W. Kanan. 1994. "Neighborhood Context and Residential Mobility," *Demography* 31, 2: 249–70.

Lee, Everett S. 1966. 'A Theory of Migration," *Demography* 3, 1: 47–57.

Lee, Ronald, D. 2007. *Global Population Aging and Its Economic Consequences*. The Henry Wendt Lecture Series. Washington, DC: AEI Press.

———. 2003. "The Demographic Transition: Three Centuries of Fundamental Change," *Journal of Economic Perspectives* 17, 4: 167–90.

———, and Andrew Mason, eds, 2011. *Population Aging and the Generational Economy: A Global Perspective*, 1–31. Cheltenham, UK: Elgar.

———, and ———. 2010. "Fertility, Human Capital and Economic Growth over the Demographic Transition," *European Journal of Population* 21: 31–49.

———, and David S. Reher. 2011. "Introduction: The Landscape of Demographic Transition and its Aftermath," *Population and Development Review* 37, S1: 1–7.

Legewie, Joscha. 2013. "Terrorist Events and Attitudes toward Immigrants: A Natural Experiment," *American Journal of Sociology* 118, 5: 1199–245.

Legrain, Philippe. 2006. *Immigrants: Your Country Needs Them*. London: Little, Brown.

Leherer, Evelyn L. 2008. "Age at Marriage and Marital Instability: Revisiting the Becker–Landes–Michael Hypothesis," *Journal of Population Economics* 21: 463–84.

Leibenstein, Harvey. 1982. "Economic Decision Theory and Human Fertility Behavior: A Speculative Essay," *Population and Development Review* 7: 381–400.

Leisinger, Kalus M., Karin M. Schmitt, and Rajul Pandya-Lorch. 2002. *Six Billion and Counting: Population and Food Security in the 21st Century*. Washington, DC: International Food Policy Research Institute.

Leonard, William R., and Michael H. Crawford, eds. 2002. *Human Biology of Pastoral Populations*. Cambridge: Cambridge University Press.

Leone, Tiziana, Zoe Matthews, and Gianpiero Dalla Zuanna. 2003. "Impacts and Determinants of Sex Preference in Nepal," *International Family Planning Perspectives* 29, 2: 76–83.

Leridon, Henri. 2006. "Natural Fertility and Controlled Fertility," in Graziella Caselli, Jacques Vallin, and Guillaume Wunsch, eds, *Demography: A Treatise in Population Studies*, vol. 1, 467–77. Amsterdam: Elsevier and Academic Press.

———. 1976. "Facts and Artifacts in the Study of Intra-uterine Mortality: A Reconsideration from Pregnancy Histories," *Population Studies* 39, 2: 319–35.

Leslie, Gerald R., and Sheila K. Korman. 1989. *The Family in Social Context*, 7th edn. New York: Oxford University Press.

Lesthaeghe, Ron. 2010. "The Unfolding Story of the Second Demographic Transition," *Population and Development Review* 36, 2: 211–51.

———. 2003. "Verhulst, Pierre-Francois," in Paul Demeny and Geoffrey McNicoll, eds, *Encyclopedia of Population*, 959–60. New York: Macmillan Reference USA/Thomson Gale.

———. 1995. "The Second Demographic Transition in Western Countries: An Interpretation," in Karen Oppenheim Mason and An-Margrit Jensen, eds, *Gender and Family Change in Industrialized Countries*, 17–62. Oxford: Clarendon.

———. 1983. "A Century of Demographic and Cultural Change in Western Europe," *Population and Development Review* 9, 3: 411–36.

———, and K. Neels. 2002. "From the First to the Second Demographic Transition: An Interpretation of the Spatial Continuity of Demographic Innovation in France, Belgium and Switzerland," *European Journal of Population* 18: 325–60.

———, and Johan Surkyn. 1988. "Cultural Dynamics and Economic Theories of Fertility Change," *Population and Development Review* 14, 1: 1–45.

———, and Chris Wilson. 1986. "Modes of Production, Secularization, and the Pace of the Fertility Decline in Western Europe, 1870–1930," in Ansley J. Coale and Susan Cotts Watkins, eds, *The Decline of Fertility in Europe*, 261–92. Princeton, NJ: Princeton University Press.

Levitis, Daniel A., and Daniel E. Martinez. 2013. "Two Halves of U-shaped Mortality," *Frontiers in Genetics* 4, 31: 1–6.

Levitt, Peggy, Josh DeWind, and Steven Vertovec. 2003. "International Perspectives on Transnational Migration: An Introduction," special issue, *International Migration Review* 37, 3: 565–75.

Levy, J.E., and Stephen J. Kunitz. 1971. "Indian Reservations, Anomie and Social Pathologies," *Southwestern Journal of Anthropology* 27, 2: 97–128.

Levy, Robert I 1981. "The Decline in Cardiovascular Disease Mortality," *Annual Review of Public Health* 2: 49–70.

Lewis, G. J. 1982. *Human Migration: A Geographical Perspective.* London: Croom Helm.

Ley, David. 2000. "The Inner City," in Trudy Bunting and Pierre Filion, eds, *Canadian Cities in Transition: The Twenty-First Century*, 2nd edn, 274–302. Don Mills, ON: Oxford University Press.

———. 1992. "Gentrification in Recession: Social Change in Six Canadian Cities, 1981–86," *Urban Geography* 13, 3: 230–56.

Li, Nan, and S. Tuljapurkar. 1999. "Population Momentum for Gradual Demographic Transitions," *Population Studies* 53, 2: 255–62.

Li, Peter S., and Chunhong Dong. 2007. "Earnings of Chinese Immigrants in the Enclave and Mainstream Economy," *Canadian Review of Sociology and Anthropology* 44, 1: 65–99.

Liaw, Kao-Lee, and Mingzhu Qi. 2004. "Lifetime Interprovincial Migration in Canada: Looking Beyond Short-Run Fluctuations," *The Canadian Geographer* 48, 2: 168–90.

Lichter, Daniel T., Dianne K. McLaughlin, George Kephart, and David J. Landry. 1992. "Race and the Retreat from Marriage: A Shortage of Marriageable Men?" *American Sociological Review* 57, 6: 781–99.

Liefbroer, Aart C., and Edith Dourleijn. 2006. "Unmarried Cohabitation and Union Stability: Testing the Role of Diffusion Using Data from 16 European Countries," *Demography* 43, 2: 203–21.

Lim, Lin Lean 1993. "Effects of Women's Position on their Migration," in Nora Federici, Karen Oppenheim Mason, and Solvi Sogner, eds, *Women's Position and Demographic Change*, 225–42. Oxford: Clarendon.

Lim, Meng-Kin. 2006. "China's One-Child Policy: Pseudo Economic Rationalizations" (letter), *British Medical Journal* 333 (24 August).

Linden, Eugene 1996. "The Exploding Cities of the Developing World," *Foreign Affairs* 75, 1: 52–65.

Linder, Mark. 1997. "Was Marx a Crypto-Malthusian?" in Mark Linder, *The Dilemmas of Laissez-Faire Population Policy in Capitalist Societies: When the Invisible Hand Controls Reproduction*, 146–70. Westport, CT: Greenwood.

Lindstrom, David P., and Betemariam Berhanu. 1999. "The Impact of War Famine, and Economic Decline on Marital Fertility in Ethiopia," *Demography* 36, 2: 247–62.

Liska, Allen E., John R. Logan, and Paul E. Bellair. 1998. "Race and Violent Crime in the Suburbs," *American Sociological Review* 63, 1: 27–38.

Little, Bruce. 2000. "Female Boomers Led March into the Paid Work Force," *Globe and Mail* (14 February): A2.

Livi-Bacci, Massimo. 2012. *A Concise History of World Population*, 5th edn. Malden, MA: Wiley-Blackwell.

———. 1997. *A Concise History of World Population*, 2nd edn. Malden, MA: Blackwell.

———, and Gustavo De Santis. 1998. *Population and Poverty in Developing Countries.* Oxford: Oxford University Press.

Locoh, Thérèse. 2006. "Factors in Couple Formation," in Graziella Caselli, Jacques Vallin, and Guillaume Wunsch, eds, *Demography—Analysis and Synthesis: A Treatise in Demography*, 373–96. Amsterdam: Elsevier and Academic Press.

———, and Céline Vandermeersch. 2006. "Fertility Control in Third World Countries," in Graziella Caselli, Jacques Vallin, and Guillaume Wunsch, eds, *Demography: Analysis and Synthesis*, 95–127. Amsterdam: Elsevier.

Loh, Shirley, and M.V. George. 2003. "Estimating the Fertility Level of Registered Indians in Canada: A Challenging Endeavour," *Canadian Studies in Population* 30, 1: 117–35.

Lomborg, Bjorn. 2001. *The Skeptical Environmentalist.* Cambridge: Cambridge University Press.

Long, John. 1981. *Population Deconcentration in the United States.* Washington, DC: US Bureau of the Census.

Long, Larry H. 1988. *Migration and Residential Mobility in the United States.* New York: Russell Sage Foundation.

———. 1973. "New Estimates of Migration Expectancy in the United States." *Journal of the American Statistical Association* 68, 341: 37–43.

Lopez, Alan D. 1983. "The Sex Mortality Differential in Developed Countries," in Alan D. Lopez and Lado T. Ruzicka, eds, *Sex Differentials in Mortality: Trends, Determinants and Consequences.* Canberra: Australian National University.

———, and Lado T. Ruzicka, eds. 1983. *Sex Differentials in Mortality: Trends, Determinants, and Consequences.* Canberra: Department of Demography, Australian National University Printing Press.

Lopez, Allen, Graziella Caselli and Tapani Valkonen, eds. 1995. *Adult Mortality in Developed Countries: From Description to Explanation.* Oxford: Clarendon.

Lopez, Alvaro. 1961. *Problems in Stable Population Theory.* Princeton: Office of Population Research.

Losch, August. 1940 [1954]. *The Economics of Location.* William H. Woglam, trans. New York: Yale University Press.

Lotka, Alfred J. 1925. *The Elements of Physical Biology.* Baltimore: Williams and Wilkins.

———. 1907. "Relation between Birth Rates and Death Rates," *Science*, n.s., 26: 21–22. Reprinted in David P.

Smith and Nathan Keyfitz, *Mathematical Demography: Selected Papers*. (1977). Berlin: Springer.

Lowry, Ira S. 1966. *Migration and Metropolitan Growth: Two Analytical Models*. Los Angeles, CA: Institute of Government and Public Affairs, University of California.

Lozano, Rafael, Mohsen Naghavi, Kyle Foreman, et al. 2012. "Global and Regional Mortality from 235 Causes of Death for 20 Age Groups in 1990 and 2010: A Systematic Analysis for the Global Burden of Disease Study 2010," *Lancet* 380: 2095–128.

Lukas, D., and T.H. Clutton-Brock. 2013. "The Evolution of Social Monogamy in Mammals," *Science* (2 August) 341: 526–30.

Luo, Zhong-Cheng, William J. Kierans, Russell Wilkins, et al. 2004. "Infant Mortality among First Nations versus Non–First Nations in British Columbia: Temporal Trends in Rural Versus Urban Areas, 1981–2000," *International Journal of Epidemiology* 33, 6: 1252–9.

Lussier, Marie-Hélène, Robert Bourbeau, and Robert Choinière. 2008. "Does the Recent Evolution of Canadian Mortality Agree with the Epidemiologic Transition Theory?" *Demographic Research* 18: 531–68.

Lutz, Wolfgang. 2012. "Demographic Metabolism: A Predictive Theory of Socioeconomic Change," in Geoffrey McNicoll, John Bongaarts, and Ethel P. Churchill, eds, *Population and Public Policy: Essays in Honor of Paul Demeny*, 283–301. Supplement to vol. 38, *Population and Development Review*. New York: The Population Council.

———, ed. 1994. *The Future Population of the World: What Can We Assume Today?* London: Earthscan.

———, Sylvia Kritzinger, and Vegard Skirbekk. 2006. "The Demography of Growing European Identity," *Science* 314 (20 October): 425.

———, and Ren Qiang. 2002. "Determinants of Human Population Growth," *Philosophical Transactions of the Royal Society of London B* 357: 1197–210.

———, Warren Sanderson, and Sergei Scherbov. 2008. "The Coming Acceleration of Global Population Ageing," *Nature* 451 (7 February): 716–19.

———, William P. Butz, and K. C. Samir, eds. 2014. *World Population & Human Capital in the Twenty-First Century*. Oxford: Oxford University Press.

Luy, Marc. 2003. "Causes of Male Excess Mortality: Insights from Cloistered Populations," *Population and Development Review* 29, 4: 647–76.

Lynch, Scott M., and J. Scott Brown. 2001. "Reconsidering Mortality Compression and Deceleration: An Alternative Model of Mortality Rates," *Demography* 38, 1: 79–95.

McDaniel, Susan A., and Zachary Zimmer, eds. 2013. *Global Ageing in the Twenty-First Century: Challenges, Opportunities and Implications*. Surrey, UK: Ashgate.

———., and Lorne Tepperman. 2007. *Close Relations: An Introduction to the Sociology of Families*. Toronto: Pearson/Prentice Hall.

McDonald, Kevin. 2001. "Theoretical Pluralism and Historical Complexity in the Development and Maintenance of Socially Imposed Monogamy: A Comment on Kanazawa and Still," *Social Forces* 80, 1: 343–7.

McDonald, Peter. 2000. "Gender Equity in Theories of Fertility Transition," *Population and Development Review* 26, 3: 427–40.

McDowell, Andrea G. 2005. "Daily Life in Ancient Egypt," *Scientific American* 15, 1: 68–76.

McEvedy, Colin, and Richard Jones. 1978. *Atlas of World Population History*. Middlesex, England: Penguin.

McFalls, Joseph A. Jr. 1990. "The Risks of Reproductive Impairment in the Later Years of Childbearing," *Annual Review of Sociology* 16: 491–519.

———. 1979. "Frustrated Fertility: A Population Paradox," *Population Bulletin* 34, 2. Washington: Population Reference Bureau.

McGee, Terrence G., and C.J. Griffith. 1998. "Global Urbanization: Towards the Twenty-First Century," *Population Distribution and Migration*, pp. 49–65. New York: United Nations Department of Economic and Social Affairs Population Division.

McGehee, Mary A. 2004. "Mortality," in Jacob A. Siegel and David A. Swanson, eds, *The Methods and Materials of Demography*, 2nd edn, pp. 265–300. Amsterdam: Elsevier.

McIlroy, Anne. 2004. "Some Brains Are Old at 40," *Globe and Mail* (10 June): A17.

McInnis, Marvin. 2000a. "Canada's Population in the Twentieth Century," in Michael R. Haines and Richard H. Steckel, eds, *A Population History of North America*, pp. 529–99. Cambridge: Cambridge University Press.

———. 2000b. "The Population of Canada in the Nineteenth Century," in Michael R. Haines and Richard H. Steckel, eds, *A Population History of North America*, pp. 371–432. Cambridge: Cambridge University Press.

———. 1971. "Age, Education and Occupational Differentials in Interregional Migration: Some Evidence for Canada," *Demography* 8: 195–204.

MacKellar, Landis F. 2003. "Simon, Julian L.," in Paul Demeny and Geoffrey McNicoll, eds, *Encyclopedia of Population*, pp. 888–9. New York: Macmillan Reference USA/Thomson Gale.

Mackenbach, Johan. 2013. "Political Conditions and Life Expectancy in Europe, 1900–2008," *Social Science and Medicine* 82: 134–46.

MacKenzie, Betsy. 1987. "The Decline of Stroke Mortality," *Canadian Social Trends* (Autumn): 34–7.

McKeown, Thomas. 1976. *The Modern Rise of Population*. London: Edward Arnold.

——, R.G. Brown, and R.G. Record. 1972. "An Interpretation of the Modern Rise of Populating In Europe," *Population Studies* 26, 3: 345–542.

McKibben, Jerome K., and Kimberly A. Faust. 2004. "Population Distribution: Classification of Residence," in Jacob B. Siegel and David A. Swanson, eds, *The Methods and Materials of Demography*, 2nd edn, pp. 105–23. Amsterdam: Elsevier.

MacLachlan, Malcolm. 1997. *Culture and Health*. Chichester, England: John Wiley & Sons.

McLarty, Cameron B. 2006. "Not a Policy to Emulate" (letter), *British Medical Journal* 333 (25 August).

McMahon, Tamsin. 2013. "Why the World's Best and Brightest Struggle to Find Jobs in Canada. Why Do Skilled Immigrants Often Fare Worse Here than in the U.S. and U.K.?" *Maclean's* (24 April). www2.macleans.ca/2013/04/24/land-of-misfortune/ (accessed 1 October 2013).

McMillen, Marilyn M. 1979. "Differential Mortality by Sex in Fetal and Neonatal Deaths," *Science* 204, 6 (April): 89–91.

McNeill, William. 1984. "Human Migration in Historical Perspective," *Population and Development Review* 10, 1: 1–18.

——. 1963. *The Rise of the West*. Chicago: University of Chicago Press.

McNicoll, Geoffrey. 2012. "Reflections or Post-transition Demography," *Population and Development Review* 38(S1): 3–19.

——. 2006. "Policy Lessons of the East Asian Demographic Transition," *Population and Development Review* 32, 1: 1–25.

——. 2003a. "Population," in Paul Demeny and Geoffre McNicoll, eds, *Encyclopedia of Population*, vol. 2, pp. 730–2. New York: Macmillan Reference USA.

——. 2003b. "Petty, William," in Paul Demeny and Geoffrey McNicoll, eds, *Encyclopedia of Population*, pp. 729–30. New York: Macmillan Reference USA/ Thomson Gale.

——. 2001. "Governments and Fertility in Transitional and Post-transitional Societies," in Rudolfo A. Bulatao and John B. Casterline, eds, *Global Fertility Transition*, 129–58, supp. to *Population and Development Review* 27. New York: The Population Council.

——. 2000. "Reflections on Replacement Migration," *People and Place* 8, 4: 1–13.

——. 1998. "Malthus for the Twenty-First Century," *Population and Development Review* 24, 2: 309–16.

——. 1995. "Institutional Impediments to Population Policy in Australia," Australian National University. Working Paper in Demography no. 53.

Macunovich, Diane J. 2002. *Birth Quake: The Baby Boom and Its Aftershocks*. Chicago: University of Chicago Press.

McVey, Wayne W. Jr, and Warren E. Kalbach. 1995. *Canadian Population*. Toronto: Nelson.

Madhavan, Sangeetha, and Loren B. Landau. 2011. "Bridges to Nowhere: Hosts, Migrants, and the Chimera of Social Capital in Three African Cities," *Population and Development Review* 37, 3: 473–97.

Madigan, Francis C. 1957. "Are Sex Mortality Differentials Biologically Caused?" *The Milbank Quarterly* 35, 2: 202–23.

Maier, Heiner, Jutta Campe, Bernard Jeune, Jean-Marie Robine, and James Vaupel, eds. 2010. *Supercentenarians*. Heidelberg: Springer-Verlag.

Makabe, Tomoto. 1980. "Provincial Variations in Divorce Rates: A Canadian Case," *Journal of Marriage and the Family* 42: 171–6.

Makeham, W.M. 1867. "On the Law of Mortality," *Journal of the Institute of Actuaries* 13: 325–67.

——. 1860. "On the Law of Mortality and the Construction of Annuity Tables," *Assurance Magazine* 8: 301–10.

Malenfant, Éric Caron, and Alain Bélanger. 2006. "The Fertility of Visible Minority Women in Canada," in Alain Bélanger, ed., *Report on the Demographic Situation in Canada 2003 and 2004*, pp. 79–95. Cat. no. 91-209-XIE. Ottawa: Statistics Canada.

Mamelund, Svenn-Erik. 2004. "Can the Spanish Influenza Pandemic of 1918 Explain the Baby Boom of 1920 in Neutral Norway?" *Population E* 59, 2: 229–60.

Mann, Michael E. 2014. "Climate Change. False Hope. The Rate of Global Temperature Rise May Have Hit a Plateau, but a Climate Crisis Still Looms in the Near Future," *Scientific American* 310 (April): 78–81.

Mannheim, Karl. 1923. *Essays on the Sociology of Knowledge*. London: RKP.

Manning, Patrick. 2005. *Migration in World History*. New York: Routledge.

Manton, Kenneth G. 1991. "The Dynamics of Population Aging: Demography and Policy Analysis," *The Milbank Quarterly* 69, 2: 309–38.

——. 1982. "Changing Concepts of Mortality and Morbidity in the Elderly Population," *The Milbank Quarterly/Health and Society* 60, 2: 183–244.

——, Xi Liang Gu, and Vicky Lamb. 2006. "Long-Term Trends in Life Expectancy and Active Life Expectancy in the United States," *Population and Development Review* 32, 1: 81–105.

——, and Burton Singer. 1994. "What's the Fuss about Compression of Mortality?" *Chance* 7, 4: 21–30.

——, and James W. Vaupel. 1995. "Survival After the Age of 80 in the United States, Sweden, France, England and Japan," *New England Journal of Medicine* 333: 1232–5.

——, and Anatole I. Yashin. 2006. "Inequalities of Life: Statistical Analysis and Modeling Perspectives," in Claudine Sauvain-Dugerdil, Henri Leridon, and

Nicholas Mascie-Taylor, eds, *Human Clocks: The Bio-cultural Meanings of Age*, pp. 145–70. Bern: Peter Lang.

Marfleet, Philip. 2006. *Refugees in a Global Era*. New York: Palgrave Macmillan.

Mariner, Joanne. 2003. "Israel's New Citizenship Law: A Separation Wall through the Heart," FindLaw Legal News and Commentary. writ.news.findlaw.com/mariner/20030811.html

Marks, Eli S., William Seltzer, and Karol J. Krotki. 1974. *Population Growth Estimation: A Handbook of Vital Statistics Measurement*. New York: The Population Council.

Marmot, Michael. 2005a. *The Status Syndrome. How Social Standing Affects Our Health and Longevity*. New York: Holt and Co.

——. 2005b. "Social Determinants of Health Inequalities," *Lancet* 365 (19 March): 1099–104.

——. 1995. "Social Status and Mortality: The Whitehall Studies," in Alan Lopez, Graziella Caselli, and Tapani Valkonen, eds, *Adult Mortality in Developed Countries: From Description to Explanation*, pp. 243–60. Oxford: Clarendon.

——, Sharon Friel, Ruth Bell, et al. 2008. "Closing the Gap in a Generation: Health Equity Through Action on the Social Determinants of Health," *Lancet* 372: 1661–9.

——, and Richard G. Wilkinson, eds. 2006. *The Social Determinants of Health*. Oxford: Oxford University Press.

——, G.M. Kogevinas, and M.A. Elston. 1987. "Social/Economic Status and Disease," *Annual Review of Public Health* 8: 1111–35.

Marshall, Katherine. 2011. "Generational Change in Paid and Unpaid Work," *Canadian Social Trends*. Cat. no. 11-008-X. Ottawa: Statistics Canada.

Martel, Laurent. 2013. *Mortality: Overview 2010 and 2011*. Cat. no. 91-209-X. Report on the Demographic Situation in Canada. Ottawa: Component of Statistics Canada.

——, and Alain Bélanger. 2000. "Dependence-Free Life Expectancy in Canada," *Canadian Social Trends* 58 (Autumn): 26–9.

Martikainen, Pekka, Tuija Martelin, Elina Nihtila, K. Majamaa, and S. Koskinen. 2005. "Differences in Mortality by Marital Status in Finland from 1976 to 2000: Analyses of Changes in Martial-Status Distributions, Socio-demographic and Household Composition, and Cause of Death," *Population Studies* 59, 1: 99–116.

Martin, H.W., S.K. Hoppe, C.L. Larson, and R.L. Leon. 1987. "Texas Snowbirds: Season Migrants to the Rio Grande Valley," *Research on Aging* 9: 134–47.

Marx, Karl. 1867 [1967]. *Capital: A Critical Analysis of Capitalist Production*, vol. I, ed. Frederick Engels. New York: International Publishers.

Mascarenhas, Maya, Hoiwan Cheung, Colin D. Mathers, and Gretchen A. Stevens. 2012. "Measuring Infertility in Populations: Constructing a Standard Definition for Use with Demographic and Reproductive Health Surveys," *Population Health Metrics* 10, 17: 1–11.

Masi, Ralph. 1995. "Multicultural Health: Principles and Policies," in Ralph Masi, Lynette Mensah, and K.A. McLeod, eds, *Health and Cultures*, vol. 1: *Policies, Professional Practice and Education*, 11–23. Oakville, ON: Mosaic Press.

Mason, Andrew, and Ronald D. Lee. 2011. "Population Aging and the National Economy: Key Findings," in Ronald D. Lee and Andrew Mason, eds, *Population Aging and the Generational Economy: A Global Perspective*, 1–31. Cheltenham, UK: Elgar.

Mason, Karen Oppenheim. 1997a. "Explaining Fertility Transitions," *Demography* 34, 4: 443–54.

——. 1997b. "Gender and Demographic Change: What Do We Know?" in Gavin W. Jones, et al., eds, *The Continuing Demographic Transition*, 158–82. Oxford: Clarendon.

——. 1993. "The Impact of Women's Position on Demographic Change during the Course of Development," in Nora Federici, Karen Oppenheim Mason, and Solvi Sogner, eds, *Women's Position and Demographic Change*, 19–42. Oxford: Clarendon.

——. 1988. "A Feminist Perspective on Fertility Decline," *University of Michigan Population Studies Center Research Reports*, 88–119. Ann Arbor, Michigan.

Massey, Douglas S. 1999. "Why Does Immigration Occur? A Theoretical Synthesis," in Charles Hirschman, Philip Kasinitz, and Josh DeWind, eds, *The Handbook of International Migration: The American Experience*, 34–53. New York: Russell Sage Foundation.

——, Rafael Alarcon, Jorge Durand, and Humberto Gonzales. 1987. *Return to Aztlan: The Social Process of International Migration from Western Mexico*. Berkeley: University of California Press.

——, Jaoquin Arango, Graeme Hugo, et al. 1998. *Worlds in Motion: Understanding International Migration at the End of the Millennium*. Oxford: Oxford University Press.

——, ——, ——, et al. 1993. "Theories of International Migration: A Review and Appraisal," *Population and Development Review* 19, 3: 431–66.

——, and F.G. Espana. 1987. "The Social Process of International Migration," *Science* 237: 733–8.

——, Andrew B. Gross, and Kumiko Shibuya. 1994. "Migration, Segregation, and the Concentration of Poverty," *American Sociological Review* 59, 3: 425–45.

——, and Karen A. Pren. 2012. "Unintended Consequences of US Immigration Policy: Explaining the Post-1965 Surge from Latin America," *Population and Development Review* 38, 1: 1–29.

———, and Audrey Singer. 1995. "New Estimates of Undocumented Mexican Migration and the Probability of Apprehension," *Demography* 32, 2: 203–13.

Matras, Judah. 1965. "The Social Strategy of Family Formation: Some Variations in Time and Space," *Demography* 2: 349–62.

Mauldin, Parker W., and Bernard Berelson. 1978. "Conditions of Fertility Decline in Developing Countries," *Studies in Family Planning* (9 May): 89–147.

———, and John A. Ross. 1991. "Family Planning Programs: Efforts and Ressults, 1982–89," *Studies in Family Planning* 22, 6: 350–67.

Maxim, S. Paul, Carl Keane, and Jerry White. 2002. "Urban Residential Patterns of Aboriginal People in Canada," in David Newhouse and Evelyne Peters, eds, *No Strangers in These Parts: Urban Aboriginal Peoples*, 79–91. Ottawa: Policy Research Initiative.

May, John. 2012. *World Population Policies: Their Origin, Evolution, and Impact*. Dordrecht: Springer.

Meadows, Donella H. 1993. "Seeing the Population Issue Whole," in Laurie Ann Mazur, ed., *Beyond the Numbers: A Reader on Population, Consumption, and the Environment*, 23–32. Washington, DC: Island Press.

———, Dennis L. Meadows, J. Randers, and W.W. Behrens III. 1972. *The Limits to Growth: A Report for the Club of Rome's Project on the Predicament of Mankind*. New York: Universe Books.

———, Jorgen Randers, and Dennis Meadows. 2005. *Limits to Growth: The 30 Year Update*. London: Earthscan.

Mealey, Linda. 2000. *Sex Differences: Developmental and Evolutionary Strategies*. San Diego: Academic Press.

Meilaender, Peter C. 1999. "Liberalism and Open Borders: The Argument of Joseph Carens," *International Migration Review* 33, 4: 1062–81.

Mendelsohn, Michael E., and Richard H. Karas. 2005. "Molecular and Cellular Basis of Cardiovascular Gender Differences," *Science* 308 (10 June): 1583–7.

Menken, Jane. 1985. "Age and Fertility: How Late Can You Wait?" *Demography* 22, 4: 469–483.

———, James Trussell, and Ulla Larsen. 1986. "Age and Infertility," *Science* 233, 4771: 1389–94.

Mercer, Alex J. 1990. *Disease, Mortality and Population in Transition: Epidemiological-Demographic Change in England Since the Eighteenth Century as Part of a Global Phenomenon*. Leicester, England: Leicester University Press.

———. 1986. "Relative Trends in Mortality from Related Respiratory and Airborne Infectious Diseases," *Population Studies* 40: 129–45.

———. 1985. "Smallpox and Epidemiological-Demographic Change in Europe: The Role of Vaccination," *Population Studies* 39: 287–307.

Mertens, Walter. 1976. "Canadian Nuptiality Patterns: 1911–1961," *Canadian Studies in Population* 3: 57–71.

Merton, Robert K. 1964. "Anomie, Anomia, and Social Interaction," in M.B. Clinard, ed., *Anomie and Deviant Behavior*, 213–42. New York: Free Press.

Meslé, France, and Jacques Vallin. 2011. "Historical Trends in Mortality," in R.G. Rogers and E.M. Crimmins, eds, *International Handbook of Adult Mortality*, 9–47. Dordrecht: Springer Science-Business Media B.V.

Messner, Steven F., and Robert J. Sampson. 1991. "The Sex Ratio, Family Disruption, and Rates of Violent Crime: The Paradox of Demographic Structure," *Social Forces* 69, 3: 693–713.

Michael, Marc Lawrence King, Liang Guo, Martin McKee, Erica Richardson, and David Stuckler. 2013. "The Mystery of Missing Female Children in the Caucasus: An Analysis of Sex Ratios by Birth Order," *International Perspectives on Sexual and Reproductive Health* 39, 2: 97–102.

Milan, Anne. 2013a. *Marital Status: Overview, 2011*. Component of Statistics Canada Cat. no. 91-209-X, Report on the Demographic Situation in Canada. Ottawa: Minister of Industry.

———. 2013b. *Fertility: Overview, 2009 to 2011*. Component of Statistics Canada Cat. no. 91-902-X, Report on the Demographic Situation in Canada. Ottawa: Ministry of Industry.

———. 2011. *Fertility: Overview, 2008*. Component of Statistics Canada Cat. no. 91-209-X, Report on the Demographic Situation in Canada. Ottawa: Minister of Industry.

———. 2003. "Would You Live in Common-Law?" *Canadian Social Trends* (Autumn): 2–6.

———. 2000. "One Hundred Years of Families," *Canadian Social Trends* 56: 2–12. Cat. no. 11-008. Ottawa: Statistics Canada.

Miller, Warren B. 1986. "Proception: An Important Fertility Behavior," *Demography* 23, 4: 579–94.

———, and R. Kenneth Godwin. 1977. *Psyche and Demos: Individual Psychology and the Issues of Population*. New York: Oxford University Press.

———, Lawrence J. Severy, and David J. Pasta. 2004. "A Framework for Modelling Fertility Motivation in Couples," *Population Studies* 58, 2: 193–206.

Milligan, Kevin. 2002. "Quebec's Baby Bonus: Can Public Policy Affect Fertility?" Toronto: C.D. Howe Institute.

Mills, Edward J., Sonal Singh, Brett D. Nelson, and Jean B. Nachega. 2006. "The Impact of Conflict on HIV/AIDS in Sub-Saharan Africa," *International Journal of Sexually Transmitted Diseases & AIDS* 17: 713–17.

Mincer, Jacob. 1978. "Family Migration Decisions," *Journal of Political Economy* 86: 749–73.

Mishra, Vionod, T.K. Roy, and Robert D. Retherford. 2004. "Sex Differentials in Childhood Feeding, Health Care, and Nutritional Status in India," *Population and Development Review* 30, 2: 269–96.

Mitchell, Barbara A. 2006. *The Boomerang Age: Transitions to Adulthood in Families.* New Brunswick, NJ: Aldine Transactions.

Mitchinson, Wendy. 2002. *Giving Birth in Canada: 1900–1950.* Toronto: University of Toronto Press.

Mokdad, Ali H., James S. Marks, Donna F. Stroup, and Julie L. Gerberding. 2004. "Actual Causes of Death in the United States, 2000," *Journal of the American Medical Association* (10 March) 291, 10: 1238–45.

Moore, Jim. 2004. "The Puzzling Origins of AIDS," *American Scientist* 92 (November–December): 540–7.

Moore, Lorna G., Peter W. Van Arsdale, Jo Ann E. Glittenberg, and Robert A. Aldrich. 1987. *The Biocultural Basis of Health.* Prospect Heights, IL: Wavelength.

Moore, Wilbert E. 1974. *Social Change,* 2nd edn. Englewood Cliffs, NJ: Prentice Hall.

Moran, Michael, and Michael Stevenson. 2014. "Partnerships and the Millennium Development Goals: The Challenges of Reforming Global Health Governance," in Garrett W. Brown, Gavin Yamey, and Satah Wamala, eds, *The Handbook of Global Health Policy,* 519–35. New York: John Wiley & Sons.

Morgan, Philip S. 2003. "Baby Boom, Post-World War II," in Paul Demeny and Geoffrey McNicoll, eds, *Encyclopedia of Population,* 73–7. New York: Macmillan Reference USA/Thompson Gale.

———, and R.B. King. 2001. "Why Have Children in the 21st Century? Biological Predisposition, Social Coercion, Rational Choice," *European Journal of Population* 17, 1: 3–20.

Morris, Ian. 2013. *The Measure of Civilization: How Social Development Decides the Fate of Nations.* Princeton: Princeton University Press.

———. 2010. *Why the West Rules: The Patterns of History and What They Reveal about the Future.* New York: McClelland & Stewart.

Morrison, P.A., and J.P. Wheeler. 1976. "Rural Renaissance in America?" *Population Bulletin* 31, 3. Washington: Population Reference Bureau.

———, Thomas M. Bryan, and David A. Swanson. 2004. "Internal Migration and Short-Distance Mobility," in Jacob A. Siegel and David A. Swanson, eds, *The Methods and Materials of Demography,* 2nd edn, 493–51. Amsterdam: Elsevier.

Moscovitch, Alan. 2013. "Welfare State," *The Canadian Encyclopedia* online. www.thecanadianencyclopedia.com/articles/welfare-state (accessed 14 October 2013).

Moses, Jonathon W. 2006. *International Migration: Globalization's Last Frontier.* London: Zed Books.

Mosher, William D. 1980. "Demographic Responses and Demographic Transitions: A Case Study of Sweden," *Demography* 17: 395–412.

Moyo, Dambisa. 2009. *Dead Aid: Why Aid Is Not Working and How There Is a Better Way for Africa.* New York: Ferrar, Strauss and Giroux.

Muir, C.S., and A.J. Sasco. 1990. "Prospects for Cancer Control in the 1990s," *Annual Review of Public Health* 11: 143–63.

Mumford, Lewis. 1961. *The City in History: Its Origins, Its Transformations, and Its Prospects.* New York: Harcourt (Harbinger Book).

Murphy, Michael. 1993. "The Contraceptive Pill and Women's Employment as Factors in Fertility Change in Britain 1963–1980: A Challenge to the Conventional View," *Population Studies* 47, 2: 221–44.

Myrdal, Gunnar. 1957. *Economic Theory and Under-Developed Regions.* London: Duckworth.

Myrskyla, Mikko, Johsua R. Goldstein, and Yen-Hsin Alice Cheng. 2013. "New Cohort Fertility Forecasts for the Developed World: Rises, Falls, and Reversals," *Population and Development Review* 39, 1: 31–56.

———, Hans-Peter Kohler, and Francesco C. Billari. 2009a. "Advances in Development Reverse Fertility Declines," *Nature* 460 (6 August): 741–3.

———, ———, and ———. 2009b. "Advances in Development Reverse Fertility Declines." United Nations, Expert Group Meeting on Recent and Future Trends in Fertility, 2–4 December 2009. New York: UN.

Nadarajah, T. 1983. "The Transition from Higher Female to Higher Male Mortality in Sri Lanka," *Population and Development Review* 9, 2: 317–25.

Nagnur, Dhruva. 1986a. *Longevity and Historical Life Tables: 1921–1981* (abridged): *Canada and the Provinces.* Cat. no. 89-506. Ottawa: Minister of Supply and Services Canada.

———. 1986b. "Rectangularization of the Survival Curve and Entropy: The Canadian Experience," *Canadian Studies in Population* 13, 1: 83–102.

———, and M. Nagrodski. 1990. "Epidemiological Transition in the Context of Demographic Change: The Evolution of Canadian Mortality Patterns," *Canadian Studies in Population* 17, 1: 1–24.

Narayan, K.M. 1997. "Diabetes Mellitus in Native Americans: The Problem and Its Implications," *Population Research and Policy Review* 16: 169–92.

Nathanson, Constance. 1996. "Disease Prevention and Social Change," *Population and Development Review* 22, 4: 609–38.

———. 1995. "The Position of Women in and Mortality in Developed Countries," in Allan Lopez, Graziella

Caselli, and Tapani Valkonen, eds, *Adult Mortality in Developed Countries: From Description to Explanation*, 135–57. Oxford: Oxford University Press.

National Geographic. 2013. "On World Population Day, Unpacking 9.6 Billion by 2050," (11 July). http://news. nationalgeographic.com/news/2013/13/1307011-population-census-united-nations-un-demographics-world-population-day-birthrate/ (accessed 30 April 2014).

National Research Council. 2003. *Cities Transformed: Demographic Change and Its Implications in the Developing World*. M.R. Montgomery, R. Stren, B. Cohen, and H.E. Reed, eds. Panel on Urban Population. Washington, DC: National Academies Press.

———. 1986. *Population Growth and Economic Development: Policy Questions*. Committee on Population and Working Group on Population Growth and Economic Development. Washington, DC: National Academies Press.

———, and Institute of Medicine. 2005. *Growing Up Global: The Changing Transitions to Adulthood in Developing Countries*. Cynthia B. Lloyd, ed. Panel on Transition to Adulthood in Developing Countries. Washington, DC: National Academies Press.

Nelson, Charles A., Nathan A. Fox, and Charles H. Zeanah. 2013. *Romania's Abandoned Children: Deprivation, Brain Development, and the Struggle for Recovery*. Cambridge, MA: Harvard University Press.

Nelson, S.M., E.E. Telfer, and R.A. Anderson. 2013. "The Ageing Ovary and Uterus: New Biological Insights," *Human Reproduction Update* 19, 1: 67–83.

Newbold, Bruce K. 2011. "Migration Up and Down Canada's Urban Hierarchy," *Canadian Journal of Urban Research* 20, 1: 131–49.

———. 1996. "The Ghettoization of Quebec: Interprovincial Migration and Its Demographic Effects," *Canadian Studies in Population* 23, 1: 1–21.

Newell, Colin. 1998. *Methods and Models in Demography*. London: Belhaven.

Newman, Anne B. and Joanne M. Murabito. 2013. "The Epidemiology of Longevity and Exceptional Survival," *Epidemiologic Reviews* 35, 1: 181–97.

Ng, Edward. 1996. "Disability among Canada's Aboriginal Peoples in 1991," *Health Reports* 8, 1: 25–32.

Ngoma, Abubakar Lawan, and Normaz Wana Ismail. 2013. "Do Migrant Remittances Promote Human Capital Formation? Evidence from 89 Developing Countries," *Migration and Development* 2, 1: 106–16.

Nierenberg, Danielle. 2013. "Agriculture: Growing Food—and Solutions," in The Worldwatch Institute, *State of the World 2013. Is Sustainability Still Possible?* 190–200. Washington: Island Press.

———. 2005. "The Challenge of Uncertainty: The Unexpected Occurrence." *Genus* LXI, 3–4: 91–109.

Norman, Wendy V. 2012. "Induced Abortion in Canada 1974–2005: Trends over the First Generation with Legal Access," *Contraception* 85: 185–91.

Norris, Mary Jane. 1996. "Contemporary Demography of Aboriginal Peoples in Canada," in David Alan Long and Olive Patricia Dickason, eds, *Visions of the Heart: Canadian Aboriginal Issues*, 179–237. Toronto: Harcourt.

———. 1990. "The Demography of Aboriginal People in Canada," in Shiva S. Halli, Frank Trovato, and Leo Driedger, eds, *Ethnic Demography: Canadian Immigrant, Racial and Cultural Variations*, 33–59. Ottawa: Carleton University Press.

———, and Stewart Clatworthy. 2003. "Aboriginal Mobility and Migration within Urban Canada: Outcomes, Factors and Implications." Paper presented at the Annual Meetings of the Population Association of America. Minneapolis, Minnesota, 1–3 May 2003.

———, and ———. 2002. "Aboriginal Mobility and Migration within Urban Canada: Outcomes, Factors and Implications," in David Newhouse and Evelyne Peters, eds, *No Strangers in These Parts: Urban Aboriginal Peoples*, 51–78 Ottawa: Policy Research Initiative.

———, Martin Cooke, Daniel Beavon, et al. 2004. "Registered Indian Mobility and Migration in Canada," in John Taylor and Martin Bell, eds, *Population Mobility and Indigenous Peoples in Australasia and North America*, 136–60. London: Routledge.

Northcott, Herbert C. 1988. *Changing Residence: The Geographic Mobility of Elderly Canadians*. Toronto: Butterworths.

Notestein, Frank W. 1953. "Economic Problems and Population Change," in *Proceedings of the Eighth International Conference of Agricultural Economists*, 13–31. London: Oxford University Press.

———. 1945. "Population: The Long View," in Theodore W. Schultz, ed., *Food for the World*, 36–57. Chicago: University of Chicago Press.

Notkola, Veijo, Ian M. Timaeus, and Harri Siiskonen. 2000. "Mortality Transition in the Ovamboland Region of Namibia, 1930–1990," *Population Studies* 54, 2: 153–67.

Noymer, Andrew, and Michel Garenne. 2000. "The 1918 Influenza Epidemic's Effects on Sex Differentials in Mortality in the United States," *Population and Development Review* 26, 3: 565–81.

Nsiah-Gyabaah, Kwasi. 2004. "Urbanization Processes: Environmental and Health Effects in Africa." Paper produced for a Population-Environment Research Network cyberseminar, 29 November–15 December 2004. www.populationenvironmentresearch.org.

Nuovo Mondo, ii. 1995. "Record di Nascite A Sarjevo Assediata," 18, 3 (February).

O'Connor, Joe. 2012. "Trend of Couples Not Having Children Just Plain Selfish," *National Post* (September 20). http://fullcomment.nationalpost.com/2012/09/19/joe-oconnor-selfishness-behind-growing-trend-for-couples-to-not-have-children/ (accessed 5 September 2013).

OECD (Organisation for Economic Co-operation and Development). 2009. *Society at a Glance 2009: OECD Social Indicators*. OECD Publishing. doi: 10.1787/soc_glance-2008-en.

Oeppen, Jim, and James W. Vaupel. 2002. "Broken Limits to Life Expectancy," *Science* 296 (10 May): 1029–31.

Ogawa, Naohiro, and Quilin Chen. 2013. "End of the First Demographic Dividend and Possible Labor Market Response in China and Other Asian Countries," *China and World Economy* 21, 2: 78–96.

Ohlsson-Wijk, Sofi. 2011. "Sweden's Marriage Revival: An Analysis of the New-Millennium Switch from Long-Term Decline to Increasing Popularity," *Population Studies* 65, 2: 183–200.

Okun, Bernard. 1960. "Comment on Becker's Theory," in National Bureau of Economic Research, *Demographic and Economic Change in Developed Countries*, 235–40. A Conference of the Universities—National Bureau Committed for Economic Research. Princeton: Princeton University Press.

Olshansky, S. Jay, and Brian A. Ault. 1986. "The Fourth Stage of the Epidemiological Transition: The Age of Delayed Degenerative Diseases," *The Milbank Quarterly* 64: 355–91.

——, and Bruce A. Carnes. 2001. *The Quest for Immortality*. New York: W.W. Norton.

——, ——, and C. Cassel. 1990. "In Search of Methuselah: Estimating the Upper Limits to Human Longevity," *Science* 250: 634–40.

——, ——, and Leonard Hayflick. 2004. "No Truth to the Fountain of Youth," in *Scientific American* (special edition), *The Science of Staying Young* 14, 2: 98–102.

——, Douglas J. Passaro, Ronald C. Hershow, et al. 2005. "A Potential Decline in Life Expectancy in the United States in the 21st Century," *The New England Journal of Medicine* 352, 1: 1138–45.

Omran, Abdel R. 1971. "The Epidemiological Transition: A Theory of Epidemiology of Population Change," *The Milbank Quarterly/Health and Society* 49: 507–37.

——, and Farzaneh Roudi. 1993. "The Middle East Population Puzzle," *Population Bulletin* 48, 1. Washington: The Population Reference Bureau.

Ono, H. 1998. "Husbands' and Wives' Resources and Marital Dissolution," *Journal of Marriage and the Family* 60: 674–9.

Opie, Christopher, Quentin D. Atkinson, Robin I.M. Dunbar, and Susanne Shultz. 2013. "Male Infanticide Leads to Social Monogamy in Primates," *Proceedings of the National Academies of Science* 110, 33: 13328–32.

Oppenheimer, Valerie Kincade. 1997. "Women's Employment and the Gain to Marriage: The Specialization and Trading Model," *Annual Review of Sociology* 23: 431–53.

——. 1994. "Women's Rising Employment and the Future of Family in Industrial Societies," *Population and Development Review* 20, 2: 293–337.

——. 1988. "A Theory of Marriage Timing," *American Journal of Sociology* 94, 3: 563–91.

O'Rourke, Kevin H., and Jeffrey G. Williamson. 2002. "When Did Globalisation Begin?" *European Review of Economic History* 6, 1: 23–50.

Ouellette, Nadine, Magali Barbieri, and John R. Wilmoth. 2014. "Period-based Mortality Change: Turning Points in Trends since 1950," *Population and Development Review* 40, 1: 77–106.

Ouyang, Yadan. 2013. "China Relaxes Its One-Child Policy," *Lancet* 382 (30 November): e28.

Overbeek, Johannes. 1974. *History of Population Theories*. Rotterdam: Rotterdam University Press.

Owen, Ian P.F. 2002. "Sex Differences in Mortality Rate," *Science* 297 (20 September): 2008–9.

Owram, Doug. 1996. *Born at the Right Time: A History of the Baby Boom Generation*. Toronto: University of Toronto Press.

Oziewicz, Estanislao. 2005. "Indonesia Prepares for Baby Boom," *Globe and Mail* (25 April): A11.

Pampel, Fred C. 2003. "Declining Sex Differences in Mortality from Lung Cancer in High-Income Nations," *Demography* 40, 1: 45–65.

——. 2002. "Cigarette Use and the Narrowing Sex Differential in Mortality," *Population and Development Review* 28, 1: 77–104.

——. 1998. "Nation, Social Change, and Sex Differences in Suicide Rates," *American Sociological Review* 63, 5: 744–58.

——. 1996. "Cohort Size and Age-specific Suicide Rates: A Contingent Relationship," *Demography* 33, 3: 341–55.

——, and Elizabeth H. Peters. 1995. "The Easterlin Effect," *Annual Review of Sociology* 21: 163–94.

Pang, Henry, and Sue Mary Hanson. 1968. "Higher Divorce Rates in Western United States," *Sociology and Social Research* 52: 228–36.

Panter-Brick, Catherine. 1996. "Proximate Determinants of Birth Seasonality and Conception Failure in Nepal," *Population Studies* 50: 203–21.

Paquet, Gilles. 2010. "Immigration and the Solidarity-Diversity-Security Nexus," *Optimum Online: The*

Journal of Public Sector Management 40, 4: 1–16. www.socialsciences.uottawa.ca/grei-rgei/eng/documents/ (accessed 18 October 2013).

Park, Robert E. 1929 [1959]. *Human Communities.* New York: Free Press.

———. 1916. "The City: Suggestions for the Investigation of Human Behaviour in the Urban Environment," *American Journal of Sociology* 20: 577–612.

Parsons, Craig A., and Timothy M. Smeeding. 2006. "What's Unique about Immigration in Europe?" in Craig A. Parsons and Timothy M. Smeeding, eds, *Immigration and the Transformation of Europe*, 1–29. Cambridge: Cambridge University Press.

Partridge, Linda, Janet Thornton, and Gillian Bates. 2011. "The New Science of Aging," *Philosophical Transactions of the Royal Society B* 366: 6–8.

Partridge, Mark, M. Rose Olfert, and Alessandro Alasia. 2007. "Canadian Cities as Regional Engines of Growth: Agglomeration and Amenities," *Canadian Journal of Economics* 40, 1: 39–68.

Paul Murphy, Annie. 2011. *Origins: How the Nine Months before Birth Shape the Rest of Our Lives.* New York: Free Press.

Pearl, Raymond. 1927. *The Biology of Population Growth.* New York: Knopf.

———, and Lowell J. Reed. 1920. "On the Rate of Growth of the Population of the United States since 1790 and Its Mathematical Representation," *Proceedings of the National Academy of Sciences* 6: 275–88.

Pebley, Anne R. 2003. "Infant and Child Mortality," in Paul Demeny and Geoffrey McNicoll, eds, *Encyclopedia of Population*, 533–6. New York: Macmillan Reference USA/Thompson Gale.

———. 1998. "Demography and the Environment," *Demography* 35, 4: 377–89.

Pelletier, Francois, Jacques Legare, and Robert Bourbeau. 1997. "Mortality in Quebec during the Nineteenth Century: From the State to the Cities," *Population Studies* 51, 1: 93–103.

Pepin, Jacques. 2011. *The Origins of AIDS.* Cambridge: Cambridge University Press.

Perelli-Harris, Brienna, and Nora Sánchez Gassen. 2012. "How Similar Are Cohabitation and Marriage? Legal Approaches to Cohabitation across Western Europe," *Population and Development Review* 38, 3: 435–67.

Perenboom, R.J.M., L.M. Van Herten, H.C. Boshuizen, et al. 2004. "Trends in Disability-Free Life Expectancy," *Disability and Rehabilitation* 26, 7: 377–86.

Peressini, Tracy. 2005. "Urban Inequality: Poverty in Canadian Cities," in Harry H. Hiller, ed., *Urban Canada: Sociological Perspectives*, pp. 169–89. Don Mills, ON: Oxford University Press.

Perkins, Dwight H, Steven Radelet, and David L. Lindauer. 2006. *Economics of Development*, 6th edn. New York: W.W. Norton.

Perls, Thomas T., and Ruth C. Fretts. 2002. "Why Women Live Longer than Men," in Frank Trovato, ed., *Population and Society: Essential Readings*, 101–6. Don Mills, ON: Oxford University Press.

———, and Margery Hutter Silver. 1999. *Living to 100.* New York: Basic Books.

Péron, Yves, and Claude Strohmenger. 1985. *Demography and Health Indicators: Presentation and Interpretation.* Cat. no. 82- 543E. Ottawa: Minister of Supply and Services Canada.

Petersen, William. 2003. "Condorcet, Marquis De," in Paul Demeny and Geoffrey McNicoll, eds, *Encyclopedia of Population*, 167–8. New York: Macmillan Reference USA/Thomson Gale.

———. 2000. *From Birth to Death: A Consumer's Guide to Population Studies.* New Brunswick, NJ and London: Transaction.

———. 1979. *Malthus.* Cambridge, MA: Harvard University Press.

———. 1975. *Population*, 3rd edn. New York: Macmillan.

———. 1958. "A General Typology of Migration," *American Sociological Review* 23: 256–65.

Peterson, Herbert B., Gary L. Darmstadt, and John Bongaarts. 2013. "Meeting the Unmet Need for Family Planning: Now Is the Time," *Lancet* 381 (18 May): 1696–9.

Petrov, Andrey N. 2007. "Revising the Harris-Todaro Framework to Model Labour Migration from the Canadian Northern Frontier," *Journal of Population Research* 24, 2: 185–206.

Pfeff, Margo. 2003. "Out of Davis Inlet," *Canadian Geographic* 123, 1 (January/February): 42–52.

Philip, A.G. 1995. "Neonatal Mortality Rate: Is Further Improvement Possible?" *Journal of Pediatrics* 126: 427–33.

Philosophical Transactions of the Royal Society B. 2009. *The World in 2050: The Impact of Population Growth on Tomorrow's World.* Theme issue edited by Roger V. Short and Malcolm Potts, vol. 364, 1532 (27 October).

Piché, Victor. 2013. "Contemporary Migration Theories as Reflected in Their Founding Texts," *Population-E* 68, 1: 141–64.

Picketty, Thomas. 2014. *Capital in the Twenty-First Century.* Arthur Goldhammer, trans. Cambridge, MA: Harvard University Press.

Picot, Garnett, Feng Hou, and Simon Coulombe. 2007. *Chronic Low Income and Low-Income Dynamics among Recent Immigrants.* Analytical Studies Branch Research Paper Series 11F0019MIE, vol. 2007, no. 294. Ottawa: Statistics Canada.

Pido-Lopez, J., N. Imami, and R. Aspinall. 2001. "Both Age and Gender Affect Thymes Output: More Recent Thymes Migrants in Females than Males as They Age," *Clinical Experimental Immunology* 125: 409–13.

Piore, Michael. 1979. *Birds of Passage: Migrant Labor in Industrial Societies*. Cambridge: Cambridge University Press.

Pison, Giles. 2014. "1914–2014: A Century of Change in the French Population Pyramid," *Population and Societies* 509 (March): 1–4.

———. 2001. "The Population of France in 2000," *Population and Societies* 366 (March): 3.

Plane, David A. 2004. "Population Distribution: Geographic Areas," in Jacob B. Siegel and David A. Swanson, eds, *The Methods and Materials of Demography*, 2nd edn, 81–104. Amsterdam: Elsevier.

———, and Peter A. Rogerson. 1994. *The Geographical Analysis of Population with Applications to Planning and Business*. New York: Academic Press.

Polian, Pavel. 2004. *Against Their Will: The History and Geography of Forced Migrations in the USSR*. Budapest and New York: Central European University Press.

Pollard, A.H., Farhat Yusuf, and G.N. Pollard. 1981. *Demographic Techniques*, 2nd edn. Sydney: Pergamon.

Pool, Ian. 1994. "Cross-Comparative Perspectives on New Zealand's Health," in John Spicer, Andrew Trlin, and Jo Ann Walton, eds, *Social Dimensions of Health and Disease: New Zealand Perspectives*, 16–49. Palmerston North: Dunmore.

———. 1991. *Te Iwi Maori: A New Zealand Population Past, Present and Projected*. Auckland, NZ: Aukland University Press.

Pop-Eleches, Cristian. 2006. "The Impact of an Abortion Ban on Socioeconomic Outcomes of Children: Evidence from Romania," *Journal of Political Economy* 114, 4: 744–73.

Population Reference Bureau. 2014. 2014 *World Population Data Sheet*. Washington, DC: PRB.

Population Reference Bureau. Various years. *World Population Data Sheets*. Washington, DC: Population Reference Bureau.

Porter, John. 1965. *The Vertical Mosaic*. Toronto: University of Toronto Press.

Porter, Roy. 1997. *The Greatest Benefit to Mankind: A Medical History of Humanity from Antiquity to the Present*. London: HarperCollins.

Poston, Dudley L., Jr, and Leon F. Bouvier. 2010. *Population and Society: An Introduction to Demography*. Cambridge: Cambridge University Press.

———, and Richard G. Rogers. 1985. "Toward a Reformulation of the Neonatal Mortality Rate," *Social Biology* 32, (1–2): 1–12.

Potts, Malcolm. 2014. "Getting Family Planning Back on Track," *Global Health: Science and Practice*, 2, 2: 145–51.

———. 2006. "China's One-Child Policy," *British Medical Journal* 333: 361–2.

———, and Martha Campbell. 2008. "The Origins and Future of Patriarchy: The Biological Background of Gender Politics," *Journal of Family Planning and Reproductive Health Care* 34, 3: 171–4.

———, and Peter Selman. 1978. *Society and Fertility*. London: Macdonald and Evans.

———, and Roger Short. 1999. *Ever Since Adam and Eve: The Evolution of Human Sexuality*. Cambridge: Cambridge University Press.

Power, Chris, Diana Kuh, and Susan Morton. 2013. "From Developmental Origins of Adult Disease to Life Course Research on Adult Disease and Aging: Insights from Birth Cohort Studies," *Annual Review of Public Health* 34: 7–28.

Prata, Ndola. 2009. "Making Family Planning Accessible in Resource-Poor Settings." *Philosophical Transactions of the Royal Society B* 363, 1532: 3093-3099.

Pressat, Roland. 1985. *A Dictionary of Demography*, ed. Christopher Wilson. Oxford: Basil Blackwell.

Preston, Samuel H. 1998. "Population and the Environment: Scientific Evidence," in Paul Demeny and Geoffrey McNicoll, eds, *The Earthscan Reader*, 257–63. London: Earthscan.

———. 1986a. "Mortality and Development Revisited," *Population Bulletin of the United Nations* 18: 34–40.

———. 1986b. "Changing Values and Falling Birth Rates," in Mickail Kingsley Davis, S. Bernstam, and Rita Ricardo-Campbell, eds, *Below-Replacement Fertility in Industrial Societies: Causes, Consequences, Policies*, 176–95, supp. to *Population and Development Review* 12, 1986.

———. 1980. "Causes and Consequences of Mortality in Less Developed Countries during the Twentieth Century," in Richard Easterlin, ed., *Population and Economic Change in Developing Countries*, 289–341, 353–60. New York: National Bureau of Economic Research.

———. 1979. "Urban Growth in Developing Countries: A Demographic Reappraisal," *Population and Development Review* 5, 2: 195–216.

———. 1977. 'Mortality Trends," *Annual Review of Sociology* 3: 163–78.

———. 1976. *Mortality Patterns in National Populations: With Special Reference to Recorded Causes of Death*. New York: Academic Press.

———. 1975. "The Changing Relation between Mortality and Economic Development," *Population Studies* 29: 231–48.

———, and Michael R. Haines. 1991. *Fatal Years: Child Mortality in Late Nineteenth-Century America*. Princeton, NJ: Princeton University Press.

———, Patrick Heuveline, and Michel Guillot. 2001. *Demography: Measuring and Modeling Population Processes*. Malden, MA: Blackwell.

————, and Alan Thomas Richards. 1975. "The Influence of Women's Work Opportunities on Marriage Rates," *Demography* 12, 2: 209–22.

————, and Andrew Stokes. 2012. "Sources of Population Aging in More and Less Developed Countries," *Population and Development Review* 38, 12: 221–36.

Priest, Lisa, and Katherine Harding. 2006. "Hours After Birth, Xander Received a New Heart," *Globe and Mail* (Saturday, February 18). A1 and A5.

Prioux, France. 2006. "Cohabitation, Marriage and Separation: Contrasts in Europe," *Population and Societies* 422 (April). Paris: INED.

Pritchett, Lant, and Lawrence H. Summers. 1996. "Wealthier Is Healthier," *The Journal of Human Resources* 31, 4: 841–68.

Proceedings of the Royal Society. 2012. *People and the Planet*. London: The Royal Society. https://royalsociety.org/policy/projects/people-planet/report/ (accessed 2 July 2014).

Proskouriakoff, Tatiana. 1955 [1973]. "The Death of a Civilization," *Readings from Scientific American*, in Kingsley Davis, ed., *Cities: Their Origin, Growth and Human Impact*, pp. 93–7. New York: W.H. Freeman.

Prothero, Mansel R., and M. Chapman, eds. 1984. *Circulation in Third World Countries*. London: Routledge and Kagan Paul.

Ram, Bali. 2004. "New Estimates of Aboriginal Fertility, 1966–1971 to 1996–2001," *Canadian Studies in Population* 31, 2: 179–96.

————. 2000. "Current Issues in Family Demography: Canadian Examples," *Canadian Studies in Population* 27, 1: 1–14.

————, Mary Jane Norris, and K. Skof. 1989. *The Inner City in Transition*. Ottawa: Statistics Canada.

————, and Abdur Rahim. 1993. "Enduring Effects of Women's Early Employment Experiences on Child-Spacing: The Canadian Evidence," *Population Studies* 47, 2: 307–18.

————, and Y. Edward Shin. 2007. "Education Selectivity of Out-migration in Canada: 1976–1981 to 1996–2001," *Canadian Studies in Population* 34, 2: 129–48.

————, ————, and M. Pouliot. 1994. *Canadians on the Move*. Focus on Canada Series, 1991 Census of Canada. Statistics Canada and Prentice Hall.

Randers, Jørgen. 2012. *2052: A Global Forecast for the Next Forty Years*. White River Junction, VT: Chelsea Green Publishing.

Rao, Mohan, and Sarah Sexton, eds. 2010. *Markets and Malthus: Population, Gender, and Health in Neoliberal Times*. Los Angeles: Sage.

Rathor, Anupurna. 2004. *Family Planning Practices in Third World Countries*. Delhi: Adhyayan.

Ravanera, Zenaida R., Fernando Rajulton, and Thomas K. Burch. 1998. "Early Life Transitions of Canadian Women: A Cohort Analysis of Timing, Sequences, and Variations," *European Journal of Population* 14: 179–204.

Ravenstein, Ernst Georg. 1889. "The Laws of Migration," Paper II, *Journal of the Statistics Society* 52, 2: 167–235 (with commentary). Reprinted, 1976, Arno.

————. 1885. "The Laws of Migration," Paper I, *Journal of the Statistics Society* 48, 2: 167–235 (with commentary). Reprinted, 1976, Arno.

Ray, Rebecca, Janet C. Gornick, and John Schmitt. 2008. *Parental Leave Policies in 21 Countries: Assessing Generosity and Gender Equality*. Washington, DC: Center for Economic and Policy Research (CEPR). www.cepr.net/documents/publications/parental_2008_09.pdf.

Razzel, P.E. 1974. "An Interpretation of the Modern Rise of Population in Europe," *Population Studies* 28: 5–17.

Redman, Charles L., and Nancy S. Jones. 2004. "The Environmental, Social, and Health Dimensions of Urban Expansion." Paper produced for a Population-Environment Research Network cyberseminar, 29 November–15 December 2004. www.populationenvironment research.org.

Reed, Campbell B. 1988. "Zipf's Law," in Samuel Kotz, Norman L. Jonson, and Campbell B. Reed, eds, *Encyclopedia of Statistical Sciences*, 674–6. New York: John Wiley & Sons.

Rees, Philip, Martin Bell, Oliver Duke-Williams, and Marcus Blake. 2000. "Problems and Solutions in the Measurement of Migration Intensities: Australia and Britain Compared," *Population Studies* 54: 207–22.

Remer, Bill. 2005. "Rural and Urban: Differences and Common Ground," in Harry H. Hiller, ed., *Urban Canada: Sociological Perspectives*, 71–94. Don Mills, ON: Oxford University Press.

Rice, Dorothy P., and Norman Fineman. 2004. "Economic Implications of Increased Longevity in the United States," *Annual Review of Public Health* 25: 457–73.

Richter, K. 1985 [1996]. "Nonmetropolitian Growth in the Late 1970s: The End of the Turnaround?" in H.S. Geyer and T.M. Kontuly, eds, *Differential Urbanization: Integrating Spatial Models*, 47–66. London: Edward Arnold.

Ricklef, Robert E. 1990. *Ecology*, 3rd edn. New York: W.H. Freeman.

Riley, James C. 2005a. "Estimates of Regional Global Life Expectancy, 1800–2001," *Population and Development Review* 31, 3: 537–43.

————. 2005b. "The Timing and Pace of Health Transitions around the World," *Population and Development Review* 31, 4: 741–64.

———. 2001. *Rising Life Expectancy: A Global History.* Cambridge: Cambridge University Press.

Riley, Matilda White. 1987. "On the Significance of Age in Sociology," *American Sociological Review* 52, 1: 1–14.

Riley, Nancy E. 2005. "Demography of Gender," in Dudley L. Poston and Michael Micklin, eds, *Handbook of Population*, 109–41. New York: Kluwer Academic Publishers/Plenum.

———. 1999. "Challenging Demography: Contributions from Feminist Theory," *Sociological Forum* 14, 3: 369–97.

Rindfuss, Ronald R. 1991. "The Young Adult Years: Diversity, Structural Change, and Fertility," *Demography* 28, 4: 493–512.

———, Minja Kim Choe, Maria Midea, M. Kabamalan, Noriko O. Tsuya, and Larry L. Bumpass. 2010. "Order Amidst Change: Work and Family Trajectories in Japan," *Advances in Life Course Research* 15: 76–88.

———, Karen Benjamin Guzzo, and Philip S. Morgan. 2003. "The Changing Institutional Context of Low Fertility," *Population Research and Policy* Review 22: 411–38.

———, and A. Vandenheuvel. 1990. "Cohabitation: A Precursor to Marriage or an Alternative to Being Single," *Population and Development Review* 16, 4: 703–26.

Risman, B.J., and D. Johnson-Sumerford. 1998. "Doing It Fairly: A Study of Postgender Marriages," *Journal of Marriage and the Family* 60: 23–40.

Ritchey, Neil P. 1976. "Explanations of Migration," *Annual Review of Sociology* 2: 363–404.

Robey, Bryant, Shea O. Rutstein, and Leo Morris. 1993. "The Fertility Decline in Developing Countries," *Scientific American* 269, 6: 60–7.

Robine, Jean-Marie. 2001. "Redefining the Stages of the Epidemiological Transition by a Study of the Dispersion of Life Spans: The Case of France," *Population: An English Selection* 13, 1: 173–94.

Robinson, Warren. 1997. "The Economic Theory of Fertility over Three Decades," *Population Studies* 51, 1: 63–75.

Rockström, Johan, and Mattias Klum. 2013. *The Human Quest: Prospering within Planetary Boundaries.* Stockholm: Langenskiolds.

———, Will Steffen, Kevin Noone, A. Persson, et al. 2009. "A Safe Operating Space for Humanity," *Nature* 461: 472–5.

Rodgers, Joseph Lee, Craig A. St John, and Ronnie Coleman. 2005. "Fertility after the Oklahoma City Bombing," *Demography* 42, 4: 675–92.

Rogers, Andrei. 1992a. "Elderly Migration and Population Redistribution in the United States," in Andrei Rogers, ed., with W.H. Frey, A. Speare Jr., P. Rees, and A.M. Warnes, *Elderly Migration and Population Redistribution: A Comparative Study,* 226–48. London: Belhaven.

———, ed. 1992b. *Elderly Migration and Population Redistribution: A Comparative Study.* London: Belhaven.

———. 1984. *Migration, Urbanization, and Spatial Population Dynamics.* Boulder, CO: Westview.

———, and Luis J. Castro. 1986. "Migration," in Andrei Rogers and Frans J. Willkens, eds, *Migration and Settlement: A Multiregional Comparative Study.* Boston and Dordrecht: D. Reidel.

———, ———, and Megan Lea. 2005. "Model Migration Schedules: Three Alternative Linear Parameter Estimation Methods," *Mathematical Population Studies* 12: 17–38.

Rogers, Richard G., Bethany G. Everett, Jarron M. Saint Onge, and Patrick M. Krueger. 2010. "Social, Behavioral, and Biological Factors, and Sex Differences in Mortality," *Demography* 47, 3: 555–78.

———, and R. Hackenberg. 1987. "Extending Epidemiologic Transition Theory: A New Stage," *Social Biology* 34, 3–4: 234–43.

———, Robert A. Hummer, and Charles B. Nam. 2000. "Family Composition and Mortality," in *Living and Dying in the USA: Behavioral, Health, and Social Differentials of Adult Mortality,* 77–93. New York: Academic Press.

Rogers, Stacy J. 2004. "Dollars, Dependency, and Divorce: Four Perspectives on the Role of Wife's Income," *Journal of Marriage and the Family* 66: 59–74.

Rojansky, N., A. Brzezinski, and J.G. Schenker. 1992. "Seasonality in Human Reproduction: An Update," *Human Reproduction* 7, 6: 735–45.

Romaniuk, Anatole. 2012. "Stationary Population as a Policy Vision," *Optimum Online: The Journal of Public Sector Management* 42, 1: 1–21. www.optimumonline. ca/article.phtml?e=mesokurj&id=405 (accessed 18 October 2013).

———. 2011. "Persistence of High Fertility in Tropical Africa: The Case of the Democratic Republic of Congo," *Population and Development Review* 37, 1: 1–28.

———. 2008. "History-based Explanatory Framework for Procreative Behaviour of Aboriginal People of Canada," *Canadian Studies in Population* 35, 1: 159–186.

———. 1984. *Fertility in Canada: From Baby-boom to Baby-bust.* Cat. no. 91-524E. Ottawa: Statistics Canada.

———. 1980. "Increase in Natural Fertility during the Early Stages of Modernization: Evidence from an African Case Study," *Population Studies* 34, 2: 293–310.

Romellón, Jorge Santibanez. 2001. "Should Frontiers Be Opened to International Migration?" *International Union for the Scientific Study of Population General Conference.* San Salvador de Bahia, Brazil, 24 August 2001.

Rosenbaum, Harry. 1988. "Return Inter-provincial Migration: Canada, 1966–1971," *Canadian Studies in Population* 15, 1: 51–65.

Ross, John A., and W. Parker Mauldin. 1996. "Family Planning Programs: Efforts and Results, 1972–94," *Studies in Family Planning* 27, 3: 137–47.

Ross, Kate, and John Taylor. 2002. "Improving Life Expectancy and Health Status: A Comparison of Indigenous Australians and New Zealand Maori," *Journal of Population Research* and *New Zealand Population Review*, ed. Gordon A. Carmichael, with A. Dharmalingam: 219–38.

Roterman, Michelle. 2006. "Seniors' Health Care Use," *Statistics Canada Health Reports*, supp. to vol. 16: 33–45.

Rothenberg, Richard B., and Jeffrey P. Koplan. 1990. "Chronic Diseases in the 1990s," *Annual Review of Public Health* 11: 267–96.

Rotz, Dana. 2011. "Why Have Divorce Rates Fallen? TheRole of Women's Age at Marriage," (20 December). SSRN discussion paper. http://ssrn.com/abstract=1960017.

Roussel, Louis. 1985. "Le Cycle de la vie familiale dans la societe post-industrielle," in *International Population Conference*, vol. 3, 221–35. Florence, Italy: International Union for the Scientific Study of Population.

Rowland, Donald T. 2003. *Demographic Methods and Concepts*. Oxford: Oxford University Press.

Royal Commission on Aboriginal Peoples. 1995. *Choosing Life: Special Report on Suicide among Aboriginal People*. Ottawa: Minister of Supply and Services Canada.

Ruggles, Steven. 2007. "The Decline of Intergenerational Coresidence in the United States, 1850 to 2000," *American Sociological Review* 72: 964–89.

Rusmich, Ladislav, and Stephen M. Sachs. 2003. *Lessons from the Failure of the Communist Economic System*. Lanham, MD: Lexington Books.

Ryder, Norman B. 1980. *The Cohort Approach: Essays in the Measurement of Temporal Variations in Demographic Behavior*. New York: Arno.

———. 1972. "Cohort Analysis," in D.E. Sills, ed., *International Encyclopedia of the Social Sciences*, 546–50. New York: Macmillan/Free Press.

———. 1965. "The Emergence of a Modern Fertility Pattern: United States, 1917–66," in S.J. Behrman, Leslie Corsa Jr, and Ronald Freedman, eds, *Fertility and Family Planning: A World View*, 99–123. Ann Arbor, Michigan: University of Michigan Press.

Sachs, Jeffrey D. 2008. *Common Wealth: Economics for a Crowded Planet*. New York: Penguin Press.

———. 2007. "Breaking the Poverty Trap," *Scientific American* (19 August). www.sciam.com/article.cfm?id=65077B1D-E7F2-99DF-3D5F60313BBC5668& print=true.

———. 2005. *The End of Poverty: Economic Possibilities in Our Time*. New York: Penguin.

———, and J.W. McArthur. 2005. "The Millennium Project: A Plan for Meeting the Millennium Development Goals," *The Lancet* 365 (22 January): 347–53.

———, Andrew D. Mellinger, and John L. Gallup. 2001. "The Geography of Poverty and Wealth," *Scientific American* 284 (March): 70–5.

Sai, Fred T. 2002. "The Cairo Imperative: How ICPD Forged a New Population Agenda for the Coming Decades," in Sadik Nafis, ed., *An Agenda for People: The UNFPA Through Three Decades*, 113–35. New York and London: New York University Press.

Salomon, Joshua A., and Christopher J.L. Murray. 2002. "The Epidemiologic Transition Revisited: Compositional Models for Causes of Death by Age and Sex," *Population and Development Review* 28, 2: 05–28.

Samuel, John T. 1987. *Immigration and Visible Minorities in the Year 2001: A Projection*. Ottawa: Carleton University Press.

Sandefur, Gary D., Ronald R. Rindfuss, and Barney Cohen, eds. 1996. *Changing Numbers, Changing Needs: American Indian Demography and Public Health*. Washington: National Academies Press.

Sanderson, Warren C. and Sergei Scherbov. 2010. "Remeasuring Aging," *Science* 329, 10 (September): 1287–8.

Sardon, Jean-Paul. 2006. "Recent Demographic Trends in the Developed Countries," *Population* 61, 3: 197–266.

———, 2002. "Recent Demographic Trends in the Developed Countries," *Population* (Eng. edn) 57, 1: 111–56.

Sargent, Michael. 2010. "The Whole Nine Months," *Nature* 468 (4 November): 34.

Sarin, Radhika. 2003. "Rich-Poor Divide Growing," in *Vital Signs 2003*, 88–9. Worldwatch Institute. New York: W.W. Norton.

Sartorius, Gideon A., and Eberhard Nieschlag. 2010. "Paternal Age and Reproduction," *Human Reproduction Update* 16, 1: 65–79.

Sassen, Saskia. 2001a. *The Global City: New York, London, Tokyo*, 2nd edn. Princeton, NJ: Princeton University Press.

———. 2001b. "Cities in the Global Economy," in Ronan Paddison, ed., *Handbook of Urban Studies*, 256–72. London: Sage.

———. 2000. *Cities in a World Economy*. Thousand Oaks, CA: Pine Forge Press.

Satzewich, Vic, and Lloyd Wong, eds. 2006. *Transnational Identities and Practices in Canada*. Toronto: University of Toronto Press.

Schmidt, L., T. Sobotka, J.G. Bentzen, and A. Nyboe Andersen, on behalf of the ESHRE Reproduction and Society Task Force. 2012. "Demographic and Medical Consequences of the Postponement of Parenthood," *Human Reproduction Update*, 18, 1: 29–43.

Schneider, Edward L. 1999. "Aging in the Third Millennium," *Science* 283 (5 February): 796–7.

Schoen, Robert. 2004. "Timing Effects and the Interpretation of Period Fertility," *Demography* 41, 4: 801–19.

———. 1983. "Measuring the Tightness of a Marriage Squeeze," *Demography* 20: 61–78.

Schofield, R., D. Reher, and A. Bideau, eds. 1991. *The Decline of Mortality in Europe*. Oxford: Clarendon.

Schuck, Nathalie. 2007. "Contested French Immigration ill Passes," AP *Associated Press* http://news.yahoo.com.

Schultz, Laura C. 2010. "The Dutch Hunger Winter and the Developmental Origins of Health and Disease," *Proceedings of the National Academies of Science* 107, 39: 16757–8.

Schultz, Paul T. 1993. "Mortality Decline in the Low-Income World: Causes and Consequences," *American Economic Association Papers and Proceedings* 83, 2: 337–42.

Schumacher, E.F. 1974. *Small Is Beautiful: A Study of Economics as if People Mattered*. London: Abacus Books.

Scientific American. 2002. "Science Defends Itself against *The Skeptical Environmentalist*," (January).

Scott, Allen J. 1988. *Metropolis: From the Division of Labor to Urban Form*. Berkeley, CA: University of California Press.

Scott J. South and K.M. Lloyd. 1995. "Spousal Alternatives and Marital Dissolution", *American Sociological Review* 60 (1): 21-35.

Scott, Susan, and Christopher J. Duncan. 2001. *Biology of Plagues: Evidence from Historical Populations*. Cambridge: Cambridge University Press.

Scrimshaw, Susan C. M. 1984. "Infanticide in Human Populations: Societal and Individual Concerns," in Glenn Hausfater and Sarah Blaffer Hrdy eds, *Infanticide: Comparative and Evolutionary Perspectives*, 439–62. New York: Aldine.

———. 1978. "Infant Mortality and Behavior in the Regulation of Family Size," *Population and Development Review* 4, 3: 383–403.

Seiver, Daniel A. 1985. "Trend and Variation in the Seasonality of U.S. Fertility: 1947–1976," *Demography* 22, 1: 79–100.

Seltzer, Judith A., Christine A. Bacharach, Suzanne M. Bianchi, et al. 2005. "Explaining Family Change and Variation: Challenges for Family Demographers," *Journal of Marriage and the Family* 67: 908–25.

Semyonov, Moshe, Rebeca Rijman, and Anastasia Gorodezeisky. 2006. "The Rise of Anti-foreigner Sentiment in European Societies, 1988–2000," *American Sociological Review* 71: 426–49.

Sen, Ragini. 2003. *We the Billion: A Social Psychological Perspective on India's Population*. New Delhi: Sage.

Sennett, Richard, ed. 1969. *Classic Essays on the Culture of Cities*. Englewood Cliffs, NJ: Prentice Hall.

Serow, W.J. 1987. "Determinants of Interstate Migration: Differences between Elderly and Nonelderly Movers," *Journal of Gerontology* 42: 95–100.

Seward, Shirley. 1986. "More and Younger?" *Policy Options/Options Politiques* (January): 16–19.

Shaw, Clifford, and Henry D. McKay. 1942. *Juvenile Delinquency and Urban Areas*. Chicago: University of Chicago Press.

Shaw, R. Paul. 1985. *Intermetropolitan Migration in Canada: Changing Determinants over Three Decades*. Toronto: New Canada Publications.

———. 1975. *Migration Theory and Fact: A Review and Bibliography of Current Literature*. Philadelphia: Regional Science Research Institute.

Sheffer, Gabriel. 2003. *Diaspora Politics: At Home and Abroad*. Cambridge: Cambridge University Press.

Shenk, Mary K., Mary C. Towner, Howard C. Kress, and Nurul Alam. 2013. "A Model Comparison Approach Shows Stronger Support for Economic Models of Fertility Decline," *Proceedings of the National Academies of Sciences* 110, 20: 8045–50.

Shihadeh, Edward S. 1991. "The Prevalence of Husband-Centered Migration: Employment Consequences for Married Mothers," *Journal of Marriage and the Family* 43: 432–44.

Shin, Y. Edward, and Bali Ram. 2008. "Does It Pay to Migrate? The Canadian Evidence," *Canadian Studies in Population* 35, 1: 103–17.

Shorter, Edward. 1975. *The Making of the Modern Family*. New York: McGraw-Hill.

Shryock, Henry S., Jacob Siegel, and associates. 1976. *The Methods and Materials of Demography* (condensed edn by Edward G. Stockwell). San Diego, CA: Academic Press.

———, and ———. 1972. *The Methods and Materials of Demography* Washington, DC: US Bureau of the Census.

Sibly, Richard M., and Jim Hone. 2002. "Population Growth Rate and Its Determinants: An Overview," *Philosophical Transactions of the Royal Society of London B*, 357: 1153–70.

Siegel, Jacob S. 2002. *Applied Demography*. San Diego: Academic Press.

———, and David A. Swanson, eds. 2004. *The Methods and Materials of Demography*, 2nd edn. Amsterdam: Academic Press.

Silverstein, Merril. 1995. "Stability and Change in Temporal Distance between the Elderly and Their Children," *Demography* 32, 1: 29–46.

Simmel, George. 1903 [1969]. "The Metropolis and Mental Life," reprinted in Richard Sennett, ed., *Classic Essays on the Culture of Cities*, 47–60. Englewood Cliffs, NJ: Prentice Hall.

Simmons, Alan B. 2010. *Immigration and Canada: Global and Transnational Perspectives*. Toronto: Canadian Scholars Press.

———. 1999. "Immigration Policy: Imagined Futures," in Shiva S. Halli and Leo Dridger, eds, *Immigrant Canada: Demographic, Economic, and Cultural Challenges*. Toronto: University of Toronto Press.

Simmons, James W. 1982. "The Stability of Migration Patterns: Canada 1966–1971," *Urban Geography* 3: 166–78.

Simon, Julian L. 1996. *The Ultimate Resource 2*. Princeton, NJ: Princeton University Press.

———. 1995. *The State of Humanity*. Cambridge, MA: Blackwell.

Simons, John. 1980. "Reproductive Behaviour as Religious Sacrifice," in Charlotte Hohn and Rainer Mackensen, eds, *Determinants of Fertility Trends: Theories Re-examined* 131–46. Liege, Belgium: Ordina Editions.

Simpson, Jeffrey. 2007. "We Have Seen the Future, and It's Sprawl and Emissions," *Globe and Mail* (17 March): A12.

Singer, Alison. 2013. "State of the World: A Year in Review," in the Worldwatch Institute, *State of the World 2013: Is Sustainability Still Possible?* xxvi–xvii. Washington: Island Press.

Singer, Fred S. 1971. *Is There an Optimum Level of Population?* New York: McGraw-Hill/Population Council Book.

Singh, Susheela, and Renee Samara. 1996. "Early Marriage among Women in Developing Countries," *International Family Planning Perspectives* 22: 148–57, 175.

Sitwell, O.F.G., and N.R.M Seifried. 1984. *The Regional Structure of the Canadian Economy*. Toronto: Methuen.

Sjaastadt, Larry A. 1962. "The Costs and Returns to Human Migration," *Journal of Political Economy* 705: 80–93.

Sjoberg, Gideon. 1960. *The Preindustrial City: Past and Present*. New York: Free Press.

———. 1965 [1973]. "The Origins and Evolution of Cities," in Kingsley Davis ed., *Cities: Their Origins, Growth and Human Impact*, 19–27. *Readings from Scientific American*. San Francisco: W.H. Freeman.

Skartein, Rune. 1997. *Development Theory: A Guide to Some Unfashionable Perspectives*. Delhi: Oxford University Press.

Skorecki, Karl, and Doron M. Behara. 2013. "North Africans Traveling North," *Proceedings of the National Academies of Science* 119, 29: 11668–9.

Small, John, and Michael Witherick. 1995. *A Modern Dictionary of Geography*, 3rd edn. London: EdwardArnold.

———, and ———. 1986. *A Modern Dictionary of Geography*, 3rd edn. London: Edward Arnold.

Smil, Vaclav. 2012. *Harvesting the Biosphere: What We Have Taken from Nature*. Cambridge, MA: MIT Press.

———. 2008. *Global Catastrophes and Trends: The Next Fifty Years*. Cambridge, MA: MIT Press.

Smith, Adam. 1776 [1904]. *An Inquiry into the Nature and Causes of the Wealth of Nations*, 5th edn, ed. Edwin Cannan. London: Methuen

Smith, David W.E. 1993. *Human Longevity*. New York: Oxford University Press.

Smith, Kirsten P., and Nicholas A. Christakis. 2008. "Social Networks and Health," *Annual Review of Sociology* 34: 405–29.

Smith, Peter J. 2000. "Suburbs," in Trudy Bunting and Pierre Filion, eds, *Canadian Cities in Transition: The Twenty-First Century*, 2nd edn, 303–32. Don Mills, ON: Oxford University Press.

Smith, Stanley K., Jeff Tayman, and David A. Swanson. 2001. *State and Local Population Projections: Methodology and Analysis*. New York: Kluwer Academic Publishers/Plenum.

Smith, T.E. 1960. "The Cocos-Keeling Islands: A Demographic Laboratory," *Population Studies* 24: 94–130.

Smith, Vaughn P. 2006. "Rose-Tinted Spectacles" (letter), *British Medical Journal* 333 (22 August).

Smuts, Barbara. 1995. "The Evolutionary Origins of Human Patriarchy," *Human Nature* 6: 1–32.

Socken, Paul. 1997. "*Maria Chapdelaine*," in Eugene Benson and William Toye, eds, *The Oxford Companion to Canadian Literature*, 728–9. Don Mills, ON: Oxford University Press.

Soja, W. Edward. 2000. *Postmetropolis: Critical Studies of Cities and Regions*. Oxford: Blackwell.

Scott J. South and K.M. Lloyd. 1995. "Spousal Alternatives and Marital Dissolution", *American Sociological Review* 60 (1): 21–35.

———, and ———. 1992. "Marriage Opportunities and Family Formation: Further Implications of Unbalanced Sex Ratios," *Journal of Marriage and the Family* 54: 440–51.

Sowards, Kathryn A. 1997. "Premature Birth and the Changing Composition of Newborn Infectious Disease Mortality: Reconsidering 'Exogenous' Mortality," *Demography* 34, 4: 399–409.

Spaar, Debora L. 2006. *The Baby Business: How Money, Science, and Politics Drive the Commerce of Conception*. Boston: Harvard Business School Press.

Speare, Alden Jr. 1972. "Residential Satisfaction as an Intervening Variable in Residential Mobility," *Demography* 11, 2: 173–88.

Spengler, Joseph. 1974. *Population Change, Modernization, and Welfare*. Englewood Cliffs, NJ: Prentice Hall.

Spirelli, Angela, Irene Figá Talamanca, L. Lauria, and the European Study Group on Infertility and Subfecundity. 2000. "Patterns of Contraceptive Use in 5 European Countries," *American Journal of Public Health* 90: 1403–8.

Sreter, Simon. 2002. "The McKeown Thesis. Rethinking McKeown: The Relationship between Public Health and Social Change," *American Journal of Public Health* 92, 5: 722–5.

——. 1988. "The Importance of Social Intervention in Britain's Mortality Decline *c.* 1850–1914: A Re-interpretation of the Role of Public Health," *Social History of Medicine* 1: 1–38.

Stack, Steven. 2000a. "Suicide: A 15-year Review of the Sociological Literature. Part I: Cultural and Economic Factors," *Suicide and Life-Threatening Behavior* 30, 2: 145–62.

——. 2000b. "Suicide: A 15-year Review of the Sociological Literature. Part II: Modernization and Social Integration Perspectives," *Suicide and Life-Threatening Behavior* 30, 2: 163–176.

Stangeland, Charles E. 1904. *Pre-Malthusian Doctrines of Population: A Study in the History of Economic Theory*. New York: Columbia University Press.

Stark, Oded. 1997. *The Migration of Labor*. Cambridge, MA: Basil Blackwell.

Statistics Canada. 2014a. *National Household Survey: Final Response rates for Canada, Provinces and Territories, 2011*. CANSIM (database) www12.statcan.gc.ca/nhs-enm/2011/ref/about-apropos/nhs-enm_r012.cfm?Lang=E (accessed 16 July 2014).

——. 2014b. *Table 102-0122 Health-Adjusted Life Expectancy, at Birth and at Age 65, by Sex and Income, Canada and Provinces*. CANSIM (database) www5.statcan.gc.ca/cansim/a26 (accessed 19 June 2014).

——. 2013a. *Table 102-0529 Deaths, by Cause, Chapter IX: Diseases of the Circulatory System (I00 to I99), Age Group and Sex, Canada, Annual (number)*. CANSIM (database) www5.statcan.gc.ca/cansim/a26?lang=eng&retrLang=eng&id=1020529&tabMode=dataTable&srchLan=-1&p1=-1&p2=9 (accessed 30 June 2013).

——. 2013b. *Table 051-0001 Estimates of Population, by Age Group and Sex for July 1, Canada, Provinces and Territories, Annual (persons unless otherwise noted)*. CANSIM (database) www5.statcan.gc.ca/cansim/a26?lang=eng&retrLang=eng&id=0510001&tabMode=dataTable&srchLan=-1&p1=-1&p2=9 (accessed 30 June 2013).

——. 2013c. *Table 051-0004 Components of Population Growth, Canada, Provinces and Territories, Annual (persons)*. CANSIM (database) www5.statcan.gc.ca/cansim/a26?lang=eng&retrLang=eng&id=0510004&paSer=&pattern=&stByVal=1&p1=1&p2=50&tabMode=dataTable&csid= (Accessed 30 June 2013).

——. 2013d. *History of the Census of Canada*. www12.statcan.gc.ca/census-recensement/2011/ref/about-apropos/history-histoire-eng.cfm (accessed 9 July 2013).

——. 2013e. *Legal Marital Status, Common-law Status, Age Groups and Sex for the Population 15 Years and over of Canada, Provinces, Territories, Census Metropolitan Areas and Census Agglomerations, 2011 Census-based Tabulations. 2006 and 2011 Censuses*. www12.statcan.gc.ca/census-recensement/2011/dp-pd/tbt-tt/Rp-eng.cfm?TABID=1&LANG=E&APATH=3&DETAIL=0&DIM=0&FL=A&FREE=0&GC=0&GK=0&GRP=1&PID=102092&PRID=0&PTYPE=101955&S=0&SHOWALL=0&SUB=0&Temporal=2011&THEME=89&VID=0&VNAMEE=&VNAMEF= (accessed 29 July 2013).

——. 2013f. *Population by Marital Status and Sex Summary Table*. www.statcan.gc.ca/tables-tableaux/sum-som/101/cst01/famil01-eng.htm (accessed 8 August 2013).

——. 2013g. *Table 051-0042 Estimates of Population, by Marital Status or Legal Marital Status, Age and Sex for July 1, Canada, Provinces and Territories, Annual (Persons)*. CANSIM (database) www5.statcan.gc.ca/cansim/a26?lang=eng&retrLang=eng&id=0510042&paSer=&pattern=&stByVal=1&p1=1&p2=50&tabMode=dataTable&csid= (accessed 8 August 2013).

——. 2013h. *Table 102-4503 Live Births, by Age of Mother, Canada, Provinces, and Territories, Annual*. CANSIM (database)www5.statcan.gc.ca/cansim/a26?lang=eng&retrLang=eng&id=1024503&paSer=&pattern=&stByVal=1&p1=1&p2=-1&tabMode=dataTable&csid= (accessed 26 June 2014).

——. 2013i. *Life Tables, Canada, Provinces and Territories, 2009 to 2011*. Cat. no. 84-537-X, no. 005. Ottawa: Minister of Industry.

——. 2013j. *Table 102-4505 Crude Birth Rate, Age-specific and Total Fertility Rates (Live Births), Canada, Provinces and Territories Annual (Rate)*. CANSIM (database) www5.statcan.gc.ca/cansim/a26?lang=eng&retrLang=eng&id=1024505&paSer=&pattern=&stByVal=1&p1=1&p2=-1&tabMode=dataTable&csid= (accessed 28 August 2013).

——. 2013k. *Table 051-0002 Estimates of Deaths, by Sex and Age Group, Canada, Provinces and Territories, Annual (Persons)*. CANSIM (database) www5.statcan.gc.ca/cansim/a26?lang=eng&retrLang=eng&id=0510002&paSer=&pattern=&stByVal=1&p1=1&p2=-1&tabMode=dataTable&csid= (accessed 14 September 2013).

——. 2013l. *Table 102-0506 Infant Deaths and Mortality Rates, by Age Group and Sex, Canada (Annual)*. CANSIM (database) www5.statcan.gc.ca/cansim/a26?lang=eng&retrLang=eng&id=1020506&paSer=&pattern=&stByVal=1&p1=1&p2=-1&tabMode=dataTable&csid= (accessed 2 July 2014).

——. 2013m. *Table 111-0029 In-, Out-, and Net Migration Estimates, by Provincial Regions, Migration Type and Sex, Annual (Number)*. CANSIM (database) www5.statcan.gc.ca/cansim/a26?lang=eng&retrLang=eng&id=1110029&paSer=&pattern=&stByVal=1&p1=

1&p2=-1&tabMode=dataTable&csid= (accessed 19 September 2013).

——. 2013n. *Table 111-0030 In-, Out-, and Net Migration Estimates, by Geographical Region of Origin and Destination, Annual (number)*. CANSIM (database) www5.statcan.gc.ca/cansim/results/cansim-1110030-eng-2528541078779579014.csv (accessed 16 October 2013).

——. 2013o. *Table 051-0020 Number of Non-Permanent Residents, Canada, Provinces and Territories, Quarterly*. CANSIM (database) www5.statcan.gc.ca/cansim/pick-choisir?lang=eng&p2=33&id=0510020 (accessed 26 June 2014).

——. 2013p. *Immigration and Ethnocultural Diversity in Canada*. National Household Survey. Ottawa: Minister of Industry (Catalogue no. 99-010-X2011001).

——. 2013q. *Ethnic Origin, Single and Multiple Ethnic Origin Responses, Generation Status, Age Groups and Sex for the Population in Private Households of Canada, Provinces, Territories, Census Metropolitan Areas and Census Agglomerations. 2011 National Household Survey* 2011 National Household Survey, Statistics Canada Cat. no. 99-010-X2011028 www12.statcan.gc.ca/nhs-enm/2011/dp-pc/dt-td/Rp-eng.cfm?LANG=E&APATH=3&DETAIL=0&DIM=0&FL=A&FREE=0&GC=0&GID=0&GK=0&GRP=1&PID=105396&PRID=0&PTYPE=105277&S=0&SHOWALL=0&SUB=0&Temporal=2013&THEME=95&VID=0&VNAMEE=&VNAMEF (accessed 30 September 2013).

——. 2013r. *Aboriginal Peoples in Canada: First Nations People, Métis and Inuit*. Analytical Document National Household Survey, 2011. Cat. no. 99-011-X2011001. Ottawa: Minister of Industry.

——. 2013s. *Population, Urban and Rural*. Summary Table. www.statcan.gc.ca/tables-tab-eaux/sum-som/l01/cst01/demo62a-eng.htm (accessed 4 July 2014).

——. 2103t. *Table 051-0046 Estimates of Population by Census Metropolitan Area, Sex and Age Group for July 1, based on the Standard Geographical Classification (SGC) 2006*. CANSIM (database) www5.statcan.gc.ca/cansim/a26?lang=eng&retrLang=eng&id=0510046&paSer=&pattern=&stByVal=1&p1=1&p2=37&tabMode=dataTable&csid=#customizeTab (accessed 5 October 2013).

——. 2013u. *Population Counts, for Census Metropolitan Areas, Census Agglomerations, Population Centres and Rural Areas, 2011 Census*. www12.statcan.gc.ca/census-recensement/2011/dp-pd/hlt-fst/pd-pl/Table-Tableau.cfm?LANG=eng&T=209&CMA=825&S=0&O=D&RPP=25 (accessed 4 July 2014).

——. 2013v. *Population Counts, for Census Metropolitan Areas and Census Agglomerations by Urban Core, Urban Fringe, Rural Fringe and Urban Areas, 2006 Census*. www12.statcan.

gc.ca/census-recensement/2006/dp-pd/hlt/97-550/Index.cfm?TPL=P1C&Page=RETR&LANG=Eng&T=207&S-R=1&S=0&O=D&RPP=25&PR=0&CMA=933 (accessed 4 July 2014).

——. 2012a. *Canada Year Book, 2012*. Table 24.5: Components of Population Growth, 1861 to 2011. Cat. no. 11-402-X. www.statcan.gc.ca/pub/11-402-x/2012000/chap/pop/tbl/tbl05-eng.htm (accessed 11 February 2014).

——. 2012b. *Census Briefs: Fifty Years of Families in Canada: 1961–2011*. Families, Households and Marital Status, 2011 Census of Population. Cat. no. 98312X2011003. Ottawa: Minister of Industry.

——. 2012c. *Portrait of Families and Living Arrangements in Canada*. Families, Households and Marital Status, 2011 Census of Population. Ottawa: Minister of Industry (cat. no. 98-312-X2011001).

——. 2012d. *Deaths 2009*. Ottawa: Minister of Industry (cat. no. 84F0211X), 13.

——. 2011a. *Census Dictionary: Census Year, 2011*. Cat. no. 98-301-X2011001. Ottawa. www12.statcan.gc.ca/census-recensement/2011/ref/dict/98-301-X2011001-eng.pdf (accessed 21 April 2014).

——. 2011b. *Census Family Status, Age Groups and Sex for the Population in Private Households of Canada, Provinces, Territories, Census Metropolitan Areas and Census Agglomerations, 2011 Census*. www12.statcan.gc.ca/census-recensement/2011/dp-pd/tbt-tt/Rp-eng.cfm?LANG=E&APATH=3&DETAIL=0&DIM=0&FL=A&FREE=0&GC=0&GID=0&GK=0&GRP=1&PID=102116&PRID=0&PTYPE=101955&S=0&SHOWALL=0&SUB=0&Temporal=2011&THEME=89&VID=0&VNAMEE=&VNAMEF (accessed 2 July 2014).

——. 2011c. *Census Family Status, Age Groups and Sex for Population in Private Households, for Canada, Provinces, Territories, Census Metropolitan Areas and Census Agglomerations, 2001 Census—20% Sample Data*. www12.statcan.gc.ca/english/census01/products/standard/themes/Ap-eng.cfm?LANG=E&APATH=3&DETAIL=0&DIM=0&FL=A&FREE=0&GC=0&GID=0&GK=0&GRP=1&PID=59147&PRID=0&PTYPE=55430,53293 55440,55496,71090&S=0&SHOWALL=0&SUB=0&Temporal=2001&THEME=39&VID=0&VNAMEE=&VNAMEF= (accessed 2 July 2014).

——. 2011d. *Province or Territory of Residence 5 Years Ago (14), Mother Tongue (8), Age Groups (16) and Sex (3) for the Interprovincial Migrants Aged 5 Years and Over in Private Households of Canada, Provinces and Territories, 2011 National Household Survey* National Household Survey. Cat. no. 99-013-X2011026. www12.statcan.gc.ca/nhs-enm/2011/dp-pd/dt-td/Rp-eng.cfm?LANG=E&APATH=3&DETAIL=0&DIM=0&FL=A&FREE=0&GC=0&GID=0&GK=0&GRP=1&PID=105631&PRID=0&PTYPE=105277&S=0&SHOWALL=0&SUB=0&Temporal=2013&T

HEME=97&VID=0&VNAMEE=&VNAMEF (accessed 17 September 2013).

———. 2011e. *From Urban Areas to Population Centres.* www12.statcan.gc.ca/census-recensement/2011/dp-pd/hlt-fst/pd-pl/Table-Tableau.cfm?LANG=eng&T=206&SR=1&S=5&O=D&RPP=999 (7 February 2011).

———. 2010. *Projections of the Diversity of the Canadian Population 2006 to 2031.* Ottawa: Minister of Industry (Catalogue no. 91-551-X).

———. 2008a. *Canadian Demographics at a Glance.* Cat. no. 91-003-XIE. Ottawa: Minister of Industry.

———. 2008b. *Aboriginal Peoples in Canada in 2006: Inuit, Métis and First Nations,* 2006 Census. www12.statcan.ca/english/census06/analysis/aboriginal/index.cfm.

———. 2007a. *Portrait of the Canadian Population in 2006, Population and Dwelling Counts.* 2006 Census. Cat. no. 97-550-XIE. Ottawa.

———. 2007b. *Age and Sex, 2006 Counts for Both Sexes, for Canada and Census Metropolitan Areas and Census Agglomerations: 100% Data (table).* Age and Sex Highlight Tables. 2006 Census. Cat. no. 97-551-XWE2006002. Released 17 July 2007.

———. 2007c. *Table 053-0001 Marriages by Provinces and Territory.* CANSIM (database) http://www40.statcan.ca/ 101/famil04.htm.

———. 2007d. *Annual Demographic Estimates. Census Metropolitan, Economic Regions and Census Divisions, Age and Sex, 2001 to 2006.* Cat. no. 91-214-XIE. Table 1.1–1, p. 20.

———. 2007e. *Family Portrait: Continuity and Change in Canadian Families and Households in 2006.* Cat no. 97-553-XIE.

———. 2007f. *Population 5 Years and over by Mobility Status, by Province and Territory.* 2006 Census. www.40.statcan.ca/l01/cst01/demo57g.htm (12 December 2007).

———. 2007g. *The Evolving Linguistic Portrait.* 2006 Census. Cat. no. 97-555-XIE. Ottawa: Minister of Industry. Statistics Canada Demography Division. 2007a. *Annual Demographic Estimates.*

———. 2007h. *Portrait of the Canadian Population in 2006, by Age and Sex.* 2006 Census. Cat. no. 97-551-XIE.

———. 2006a. *Births: Live Births 2004.* Cat. no. 84F0210XIE. Ottawa.

———. 2006b. *Annual Demographic Statistics 2005.* Cat. no. 91-213-XIB.

———. 2006c. *Births, 2004. Shelf Tables.* Cat. no. 84-F0210XPB. Ottawa: Minister of Industry.

———. 2005a. www.statcan.ca/english/freepub/95F0303XIE/tables/html/agpop1303.htm (accessed 16 January 2005).

———. 2005b. http://www.statcan.ca/ english/freepub/82-221-XIE00502/tables/html/44.htm (accessed 16 January 2005).

———. 2005c. *Population Counts, for Census Metropolitan Areas and Census Agglomerations, by Urban Core,* Urban Fringe and Rural Fringe: 100% data. 2001 Census. www12.statcan.ca/english/census01/products/standard/popdwell/Table-CMA-UR.cfm?T=1&SR=126&S=1&O=A (14 January 2005).

———. 2004a. *Population 5 Years and over by Mobility Status, Provinces and Territories.* 1996 and 2001 Censuses. http://www.statcan.ca/english/Pgdb/demo58a.htm (12 September 2004).

———. 2004b. *Migrants 5 Years and over by Components of Migration, Census Metropolitan Areas.* 1996 Census. www.statcan.ca/english.pgdb/demo59a.htm (12 September 2004).

———. 2003a. *Population and Growth Components.* 1851–2001 Censuses. http://www.statcan.ca/english/ Pgdb/demo03.htm (9 September 2003).

———. 2003b. *Annual Demographic Statistics: 2002.* Cat. no. 91-213-XIB.

———. 2003c. *Marriages, 2000.* Cat. no. 84F0212XPB.

———. 2003d. *Canada's Ethnocultural Portrait: The Changing Mosaic.* Cat. no. 96F0030XIE2001008.

———. 2003e. *2001 Census Analysis Series: Profile of Canadian Families and Households: Diversification Continues.* Cat. no. 96F0030XIE2001003. Ottawa.

———. 2002a. *Age and Sex for the Population of Canada.* 2001 Census. Cat. no. 95F0300XCB01004.

———. 2002b. *Divorces, 2000.* Cat. no. 84F0213XZPB.

———. 2002c. *2001 Census Analysis Series: A Profile of Canadian Families and Households: Diversification Continues.* Cat. no. 96F0030XIE2001003. Ottawa.

———. 2002d. *Births: Live Births, 2000.* Cat. No. 84-F0210XIE. Ottawa: Minister of Industry.

———. 2002e. *2001 Census Analysis Series: A Profile of the Canadian Population by Mobility Status: Canada, a Nation on the Move.* Statistics Canada Census Operations Division. Cat. no. 96F0030XIE2001006. Ottawa: Minister of Industry.

———. 2002f. *Changing Conjugal Life in Canada. General Social Survey: Cycle 15.* Cat. no. 89-576-XIE. Ottawa: Minister of Industry.

———. 1999. *Five-Year Mobility Data.* 1996 Census on CD-ROM.

———. 1997. *Births and Deaths, 1995.* Cat. no. 84-210-XMB. Ottawa: Minister of Industry.

———. 1993. *Selected Birth and Fertility Statistics, Canada, 1921–1990.* Cat. no. 82-553. Ottawa: Minister of Industry Science and Technology.

———. 1992. *Urban Areas.* 1991 Census of Canada. Cat. 93-305. Ottawa.

———. 1990. "Causes of Death 1988," *Health Reports* 2, 1 (supp. 11). Cat. no. 82-03S. Otttawa: Canadian Centre for Health Information.

———. 1983. *Vital Statistics,* vol. 2: *Marriages and Divorces, 1981.* Cat. no. 84-205.

———. 1982. *Geographic Distribution. Census Divisions, Urban Size Groups and Rural, CMAs and CAs, Urbanized*

Core and Fringe with Components, Census Subdivisions. 1981 Census of Canada. Cat. 93-901. Ottawa.

———. 1979. *Vital Statistics,* vol. 2: *Marriages and Divorces, 1977.* Cat. no. 84-205 (annual).

———. 1974. *Life Tables, Canada and Provinces 1970–1972.* Cat. no. 84-532. Ottawa.

———. 1973. *Cities Towns, Villages, CMAs and CAs.* 1971 Census of Canada. Cat. no. 92-708.

Statistics Canada Census Operations Division. 2003a. *2001 Census Handbook Reference.* Cat. no. 92-379-XIE. Ottawa Minister of Industry.

———. 2003b. *Annual Demographic Statistics 2002.* Cat. no. 91-213-XPB. Ottawa: Ministry of Industry.

———. 1997. *1996 Census Handbook: Reference.* Cat. no. 92-352-XPE. Ottawa: Statistics Canada Minister of Industry.

Statistics Canada Communications Division. 2013. *Canada at a Glance 2013.* www.statcan.gc.ca/pub/12-581-x/12-581-x2013000-eng.pdf (accessed 23 July 2013).

———. 2012. *Canada at a Glance 2012.* www.statcan.gc.ca/pub/12-581-x/2012000/pop-eng.htm (accessed 23 July 2013).

Statistics Canada Demography Division. 2013a. *Quarterly Demographic Estimates, January to March 2013.* Cat. no. 91-002-X. Ottawa: Minister responsible for Statistics Canada.

———. 2013b. *Life Tables, Canada, Provinces and Territories, 2009 to 2011.* Cat. no. 84-537-X. Ottawa: Minister of Industry.

———. 2012. *Annual Demographic Estimates: Canada, Provinces and Territories 2012.* Cat. no. 91-215-X, p. 48. Ottawa: Minister of Industry.

———. 2010. *Population Projections for Canada, Provinces and Territories 2009 to 2036.* Cat. no. 91-520-X. Ottawa: Minister of Industry.

———. 2007a. *Population and Family Estimation Methods at Statistics Canada.* Cat. no. 91-528-XIE. Ottawa: Minister of Industry.

———. 2007b. *Annual Demographic Estimates: Canada, Provinces and Territories, 2007.* Cat. no. 91-215-XIE. Ottawa: Minister of Industry.

———. 2007c. *Quarterly Demographic Estimates. July to September 2007, Preliminary* 21, 3. Cat. no. 91-002-X. Ottawa: Minister of Industry.

———. 2003. *Population and Family Estimation Methods at Statistics Canada.* Cat. no. 91-528-XIE. Ottawa: Minister of Industry.

Statistics Canada Health Statistics Division. 2003. *Marriages, 2001.* Cat. no. 84F0212XPB.

———. 1999. *Vital Statistics Compendium 1996.* Cat. no. 84-214-XPE. Ottawa: Minister of Industry.

———., *Deaths* (various years).

Statistics Canada, *The Daily.* 2011. (28 September).

———. 2005a. "Induced Abortions 2002" (11 February).

———. 2005b. "Study: Canada's Visible Minority Population in 2017" (22 March).

———. 2004. "Migration, 2002/2003" (29 September).

———. 2003. (25 September).

———. 1995. *Life Tables, Canada and Provinces, 1990–1992.* Ottawa: Minister of Industry (Cat. No. 84-537).

———. 1979. *Life Tables, Canada and Provinces, 1970–972.* Ottawa: Minister of Supply and Services Canada Cat. No. 84-532).

Statistik Austria. 2005. *Statistisches Jahrbuch 2005.* Vienna.

Steffensmeir, Darrell, Cathy Streifel, and Edward S. Shihadeh. 1992. "Cohort Size and Arrest Rates over the Life Course: Easterlin Reconsidered," *American Sociological Review* 57, 3: 305–14.

Steinhauer, David A. 2013. "Influenza: Pathways to Human Adaptation," *Nature* 499, 7459: 412–13.

Steptoe, Andrew, Aparna Shankar, Panayotes Demakakos, and Jane Wardle. 2013. "Social Isolation, Loneliness, and All-Cause Mortality in Older Men and Women," *Proceedings of the National Academies of Science* 110, 15: 5797–801.

Stern, Michael. 2007. *The Economics of Climate Change: The Stern Review.* Cambridge: Cambridge University Press.

Stiglitz, Joseph. 2003. "Special Contribution: Poverty, Globalization and Growth: Perspectives on Some of the Statistical Links," *United Nations Population Development Program, Human Development Report,* 80. New York: Oxford University Press.

———. 2002. *Globalization and Its Discontents.* New York: W.W. Norton.

Stilwell, J. M. Bell, M. Blake, et al. 2001. "Net Migration and Migration Effectiveness: A Comparison between Australia and the United Kingdom, 1976–96. Part II: Age-related Migration Patterns," *Journal of Population Research* 18, 1: 19–39.

———, ———, ———, et al. 2000. "Net Migration and Migration Effectiveness: A Comparison between Australia and the United Kingdom, 1976–96. Part I: Total Migration Patterns," *Journal of Population Research* 17, 1: 17–38.

Stockholm Resilience Research Centre. n.d. *What Is Resilience? An Introduction to Social-ecological Research.* Stockholm. www.stockholmresilience.org/21/about.html (accessed 11 October 2013).

Stolnitz, George J. 1955. "A Century of International Mortality Trends," *Population Studies* 9 and 10: 24–55, 17–52.

Stone, Elizabeth C., and Paul Zimansky. 2005. "The Tapestry of Power in a Mesopotamian City," *Scientific American* 15, 1: 60–7.

Stone, Leroy O. 1978. *The Frequency of Geographic Mobility in the Population of Canada.* Census Analytical Study. Cat. no. 99-751F. Ottawa: Minister of Supply and Services.

———. 1974. "What We Know about Migration within Canada: A Selective Review and Agenda for Future Research," *International Migration Review* 8, 2: 267–81.

———. 1969. "Migration in Canada: Regional Aspects," *1961 Census Monograph*. Ottawa: Dominion Bureau of Statistics.

Stoufer, Samuel A. 1960. "Intervening Opportunities and Competing Migrants," *Journal of Regional Science* 2: 1–26.

———. 1940. "Intervening Opportunities: A Theory Relating Mobility and Distance," *American Sociological Review* 5: 845–67.

Stringer, Chris. 2012. "What Makes a Modern Human?" *Nature* 485: 33–5.

Stuckler, David. 2008. "Population Causes and Consequences of Leading Chronic Diseases: A Comparative Analysis of Prevailing Explanations," *The Milbank Quarterly* 86, 2: 273–326.

———, Lawrence King, and Martin McKee. 2009. "Mass Privatisation and the Post-Communist Mortality Crisis: A Cross-National Analysis," *Lancet* 373: 399–407.

———, and Karen Seigel, eds. 2011. *Sick Societies: Responding to the Global Challenge of Chronic Disease*. Oxford: Oxford University Press.

Sullivan, D.A. 1985. "The Ties that Bind: Differentials between Seasonal and Permanent Migrants to Retirement Communities," *Research on Aging* 7: 235–50.

———, and S.A. Stevens. 1982. "Snowbirds: Seasonal Migrants to the Sunbelt," *Research on Aging* 4: 159–67.

Sutcliffe, Bob. 2001. *100 Ways of Seeing an Unequal World*. London and New York: Zed Books.

Syme, Leonard, and Lisa F. Berkman. 1976. "Social Class, Susceptibility and Sickness," *American Journal of Epidemiology* 104, 1: 1–8.

Taft, Donald R. 1936. *Human Migration: A Study of International Movements*. New York: Ronald Press.

Tang, Zongli. 2006. "Immigration and Chinese Reproductive Behavior in Canada," *Social Biology*, 51, 1–2: 37–53.

Taylor, J. Edward. 2003. "Migration Models," in Paul Demeny and Geoffrey McNicoll, eds, *Encyclopedia of Population*, vol. 2, 644–9. Macmillan Reference USA/ Thomson Gale.

Taylor, John, and Martin Bell. 2004. "Continuity and Change in Indigenous Australian Population Mobility," in John Taylor and Martin Bell, eds, *Population Mobility and Indigenous Peoples in Australasia and North America*, 13–43. London: Routledge.

Taylor, Peter J. 2012. "Historical World City Networks," in Ben Derudder, Michael Hoyler, Peter J. Taylor, and Frank Witlox, eds, *International Handbook of Globalization and World Cities*, 9–21. Cheltenham, UK: Edward Elgar.

Taylor, Richard, Dale Bampton, and Alan D. Lopez. 2005. "Contemporary Patterns of Pacific Island Mortality," *International Journal of Epidemiology* 34, 1: 207–14.

Teicher, Martin H. 2003. "Scars that Won't Heal: The Neurobiology of Child Abuse," *Scientific American* (March): 68–75.

Teitelbaum, Michael S. 1975. "Relevance of Demographic Transition Theory for Developing Countries," *Science* 188 (2 May): 420–5.

———. 1972. "Factors Associated with the Sex Ratio in Human Populations," in G.A. Harrison and A.J. Boyce, eds, *The Structure of Human Populations*, 90–109. Oxford: Clarendon.

———, and Jay M. Winter. 1985. *The Fear of Population Decline*. San Diego, CA: Academic Press.

Tellier, Luc-Normand. 2009. *Urban World History: An Economic and Geographical Perspective*. Quebec: Presses de L'Université du Québéc.

Ten, Steven. 2010. "The Relative Importance of the Husband's and Wife's Characteristics in Family Migration, 1960–2000," *Journal of Population Economics* 23: 1319–37.

Thandani, Veena N. 1978. "The Logic of Sentiment: The Family and Social Change," *Population and Development Review* 4, 3: 457–500.

Therborn, Goran. 2006. "Meaning, Mechanisms, Patterns, and Forces: An Introduction," in Goran Therborn, ed., *Inequalities of the World: New Theoretical Frameworks, Multiple Empirical Approaches*, 1–60. London: Verso.

———. 2004. *Between Sex and Power: Family in the World, 1900–2000*. London: Routledge.

———. 1987. "Migration and Western Europe: The Old World Turning New," *Science* 237: 1183–8.

Thévenon, Oliver. 2011. "Family Policies in OECD Countries: A Comparative Analysis," *Population and Development Review* 37, 1: 57–87.

Thom, Thomas J. 1989. "International Mortality from Heart Disease: Rates and Trends," *International Journal of Epidemiology* 18, 3 (supp. 1): S20–8.

Thomas, Brinley. 1954. *Migration and Economic Growth*. Cambridge: Cambridge University Press.

Thomas, Dorothy S. 1941. *Social and Economic Aspects of Swedish Population Movements: 1750–1933*. New York: Macmillan.

———. 1938. *Research Memorandum on Migration Differentials*. New York: Social Science Research Council.

Thompson, Bryan. 1983. "Social Ties and Ethnic Settlement Patterns," in William C. McCready, ed., *Culture, Ethnicity and Identity: Current Issues in Research*, 341–56. New York: Academic Press.

Thompson, Warren S. 1944. *Plenty of People*. Lancaster: Jacques Cattel.

———. 1929. "Population," *American Journal of Sociology* 34: 959–75.

Thornton, Arland, and Dimiter Philipov. 2009. "Sweeping Changes in Marriage, Cohabitation and Childbearing in Central and Eastern Europe: New Insights from the Developmental Idealism Framework," *European Journal of Population* 25: 123–56.

Thornton, Russell. 2000. "Population History of Native North Americas," in Michael R. Haines and Richard H. Steckel, eds, *A Population History of North America*, 9–50. Cambridge: Cambridge University Press.

Tjepkema, M., R. Wilkins, S. Senecal, E. Guimond ,and C. Penney. 2010. "Mortality of Urban Aboriginal Adults in Canada, 1991–2001," *Chronic Diseases in Canada* 31, 1: 4–38.

Tobler, Waldo. 1995. "Migration: Ravenstein, Thornthwaite, and Beyond," *Urban Geography* 16, 4: 327–43.

Todaro, Michael P. 1969. "A Model of Labor Migration and Urban Unemployment in Less Developed Countries," *The American Economic Review* 59: 138–48.

Todd, Emanuel. 1985. *Explanation of Ideology: Family Structure and Social System*. London: Blackwell Publishers.

Tönnies, Ferdinand. 1883 [1995]. *Community and Society*. New York: Harper and Row.

Torche, Florencia, and Karine Kleinhaus. 2012. "Prenatal Stress, Gestational Age and Secondary Sex Ratio: The Sex-specific Effects of Exposure to a Natural Disaster in Early Pregnancy," *Human Reproduction* 27, 2: 558–67

Torr, Berna Miller, and Susan E. Short. 2004. "Second Births and the Second Shift: A Research Note on Gender Equity and Fertility," *Population and Development Review* 30, 1: 109–30.

Torrey, Barbara Boyle, and Carl Haub. 2004. "A Comparison of US and Canadian Mortality in 1998," *Population and Development Review* 30, 3: 519–30.

Tracey, W.R. 1941. *Fertility of the Population of Canada*. Eighth Census of Canada, 1931 Census, vol. 12, monographs 99–109. Ottawa: King's Printer.

Trewartha, Glenn T. 1969. *A Geography of Population: World Patterns*. New York: John Wiley & Sons.

Trivers, R.L., and Willard, D.E., 1973. "Natural Selection of Parental Ability to Vary the Sex Ratio of Offspring," *Science* 179: 90–2.

Trovato, Frank. 2010. "Fertility in Alberta in a Context of Rapid Economic Growth, 1997–2007," *Canadian Studies in Population* 37, 3/4: 497–524.

———. 2001. "Comparative Analysis of Aboriginal Mortality in Canada, the United States and New Zealand," *Journal of Biosocial Science* 33: 67–86.

———. 1994. "Mortality Trends in Canada," in B. Singh Bolaria and Harely D. Dickinson, eds, *Health, Illness,* and Health Care in Canada, 2nd edn, 22–64. Toronto: Harcourt Brace & Company.

———. 1992. "An Ecological Analysis of Suicide: Canadian CMAs," *International Review of Modern Sociology* 22: 57–72.

———. 1988. "The Interurban Mobility of the Foreign Born in Canada: 1976–1981," *International Migration Review* 22, 3: 59–86.

———. 1987. "A Macrosociological Analysis of Native Indian Fertility in Canada, 1961, 1971, and 1981," *Social Forces*, 66, 2: 463–85.

———. 1986a. "The Relationship between Migration and the Provincial Divorce Rate in Canada, 1971 and 1978: A Reassessment," *Journal of Marriage and the Family* 48: 207–16.

———. 1986b. "Interprovincial Migration and Suicide in Canada," *International Journal of Social Psychiatry* 32, 1: 14–21.

———. 1981. "Canadian Ethnic Fertility," *Sociological Focus* 14, 1: 57–74.

———, and Carl F. Grindstaff. 1980. "Decomposing the Urban-Rural Fertility Differential: Canada 1971," *Rural Sociology* 45, 3: 448–68.

———, and Nils B. Heyen. 2006. "A Varied Pattern of Change of the Sex Differential in Survival in the G7 Countries," *Journal of Biosocial Science* 38, 3: 301–401.

———, and N.M. Lalu. 2007. "From Divergence to Convergence: The Sex Differential in Life Expectancy in Canada, 1971–2000," *Canadian Review of Sociology and Anthropology* 44, 1: 101–22.

———, and ———. 1996. "Narrowing Sex Differentials in Life Expectancy in the Industrialized World: Early 1970s to Early 1990s," *Social Biology* 43, 1–2: 20–37.

———, and Dave Odynak. 1993. "The Seasonality of Births in Canada and the Provinces, 1881–1989: Theory and Analysis," *Canadian Studies in Population* 20, 1: 1–41.

———, Anatole Romaniuc, and Isaac Addai. 1994. *Aboriginal On and Off Reserve Migration in Canada*. Ottawa: Department of Indian and Northern Affairs.

Trudel, Marcel. 1973. *La Population du Canada en 1663*. Montreal: FIDES.

Trussell, James. 2003. "Fecundity," in Paul Demeny and Geoffrey McNicoll, eds, *Encyclopedia of Population*, 397–9. New York: Macmillan Reference USA/ Thompson Gale.

———, and Chris Wilson. 1985. "Sterility in a Population with Natural Fertility," *Population Studies* 39: 269–86.

Tsui, Amy Ong. 2001. "Population Policies, Family Planning Programs, and Fertility: The Record," in Rudofo A. Bulatao and John B. Casterline, eds, *Global Fertility Transition*, 184–203, supp. to *Population and*

Development Review 27. New York: The Population Council.

Tucker, Catherine, and Jennifer Van Hook. 2013. "Surplus Chinese Men: Demographic Determinants of the Sex Ratio at Marriageable Ages in China," *Population and Development Review* 39, 2: 209–29.

Tuljapurkar, Shripad, Nan Li, and Marcus W. Feldman. 1995. "High Sex Ratios in China's Future," *Science* 10 (February): 874–6.

Turchin, Peter. 2003. *Complex Population Dynamics: A Theoretical/Empirical Synthesis.* Princeton: Princeton University Press.

———, Thomas E. Currie, Edward A.L. Turner, and Sergey Gavrilets. 2013. "War, Space, and the Evolution of Old World Complex Societies," *Proceedings of the National Academies of Science* 110, 41: 16384–9.

Turner, Jonathan H. 1995. *Macrodynamics: Toward a Theory on the Organization of Human Populations.* New Brunswick, NJ: Rutgers University Press.

Turshen, Meredeth. 2010. "What Has Happened in Africa since Cairo?" in Mohan Rao and Sarah Sexton, eds, *Markets and Malthus: Population, Gender, and Health in Neo-liberal Times,* 245–64. Los Angeles: Sage.

Tyrell, Toby. 2013. *On Gaia: A Critical Investigation of the Relationship between Life and Earth.* Princeton: Princeton University Press.

Udry, Richard, and R.L. Cliquet. 1982. "A Cross-cultural Examination of the Relationship between Ages at Menarche, Marriage, and First Birth," *Demography* 19, 1: 53–64.

Uhlenberg, Peter. 1996. "Mutual Attraction: Demography and Life-course Analysis," *The Gerontologist* 36, 2: 226–9.

———. 1980. "Death and the Family," *Journal of Family History* 5, 3: 313–20.

Umberson, Debra. 1987. "Family Status and Health Behaviors: Social Control as a Dimension of Social Integration," *Journal of Health and Social Behaviour* 28, 3: 306–19.

———, Robert Crosnoe, and Corinne Reczek. 2010. "Social Relationships and Health Behavior across the Life Course," *Annual Review of Sociology* 36: 139–57.

UNAIDS. 2012. *Report on the Global AIDS Epidemic.* New York: Joint United Nations Programme on HIV/AIDS (UNAIDS).

Unal, Belgin, Julia A. Critcheley, Dogan Fidan, and S. Capewell. 2005. "Life-years Gained from Modern Cardiological Treatments and Population Risk Factor Changes in England and Wales, 1981–2000," *American Journal of Public Health* 95, 1: 103–8.

UNData. 2010. "Healthy Life Expectancy (HALE) at Birth (Years)." WHO data, World Health Organization. http://data.un.org/Data.aspx?q=life+expectancy&d-=WHO&f=MEASURE_CODE%3AWHOSIS_000002 (accessed 14 September 2013).

United Nations. 2013a. *The Millennium Development Goals Report 2013.* E.13.I.9 (June). New York: UN.

———. 2013b. *A New Global Partnership: Eradicate Poverty and Transform Economies through Sustainable Development.* The Report of the High-level Panel of Eminent Persons on the Post-2015 Development Agenda. E/2012/33. NewYork: UN. www.slideshare.net/andrewwilliamsjr/united-nations-post2015-new-global-partnership-development-agenda-by-high-level-panel-of-eminent-persons# (accessed 11 July 2014).

———. 2007. *The Millennium Development Goals Report 2007,* pp. 6–7. New York: UN. http://mdgs.un.org/unsd/mdg/Resources/Static/Products/Progress2007/UNSD_MDG_Report_2007e.pdf.

———. 1998. *Universal Declaration of Human Rights.* New York: United Nations, Department of Public Information.

United Nations Department of Economic and Social Affairs Population Division. 2013a. *World Population Prospects: The 2012 Revision, Key Findings and Advance Tables.* ESA/P/WP.228. New York: UN.

———. 2013b. *World Population Prospects: The 2012 Revision,* on CD-ROM. New York: UN.

———. 2013c. *World Marriage Data 2012* (POP/DB/Marr/Rev2012). www.un.org/en/development/desa/population/publications/dataset/marriage/wmd2012/MainFrame.html (accessed 2 July 2014).

———. 2013d. *International Migration 2013 Wallchart.* http://esa.un.org/unmigration/documents/WallChart2013.pdf (accessed 26 September 2013).

———. 2013e. *Trends in International Migrant Stock: The 2013 Revision—Migrants by Sex and Age.* http://esa.un.org/unmigration/migrantstocks2013.htm?mtotals (accessed 26 June 2014).

———. 2013f. *World Population Policies Report 2011.* ST/ESA/SER.A/327. New York: UN.

———. 2013g. *International Migration Report 2013.* ST/ESA/SER.A/346. New York: UN.

———. 2012a. *World Mortality Report 2011.* ST/ESA/SER.A/324. New York: UN.

———. 2012b. *World Urbanization Prospects: The 2011 Revision.* ST/ESA/SER.A/322. New York: UN.

———. 2012c. *World Urbanization Prospects. The 2011 Revision. Highlights.* ESA/P/WP/224. New York: UN.

———. 2011. *World Fertility Report, 2009.* T/ESA/SER.A/304. New York: UN.

———. 2007. *World Population Prospects: The 2006 Revision.*

———. 2006a. *World Population Prospects: The 2004 Revision,* vols 1–3. ST/ESA/SER.A/246. New York: UN.

———. 2006b. *World Urbanization Prospects. The 2005 Revision.* (Executive Summary; Fact Sheets; Data Tables). ESA/P/WP/200 (October). New York: UN.

———. 2005. *World Fertility Report: 2003*. ESA/P/WP.189. New York: UN.

———. 2004a. *World Population to 2300*. ST/ESA/SER.A/236. New York: UN.

———. 2004b. *World Urbanization Prospects. The 2003 Revision*. (Data Tables and Highlights). ESA/P/WP.190 (24 March). New York: UN.

———. 2003. *Partnership and Reproductive Behaviour in Low-Fertility Countries*. Revised version for the web. ESA/P/WP.177. New York: UN.

———. 2002. *2000 Demographic Yearbook*. E/F.02.XIII.1. New York: UN.

———. 2001. *Population, Environment and Development: The Concise Report*. ST/ESA/SER.A/202. New York: UN.

———. 2000. *Replacement Migration: Is It a Solution to Declining and Ageing Populations?* ESA/P/WP.160. New York: UN.

———. 1973. *The Determinants and Consequences of Population Trends*, vol. 1. ST/SOA/SER.A/50. Population Studies no. 50. New York: UN.

———. Various years. *UN Demographic Yearbook*. E/F.02. XIII.1. New York: UN.

United Nations Department of International and Social Affairs. 1983. *Manual X. Indirect Techniques for Demographic Estimation*. ST/ESA/SER.A/81. New York: UN.

United Nations Development Programme. 2013. *Human Development Report 2013*. New York: Oxford University Press.

———. 2005. *Human Development Report 2005*. New York: Oxford University Press.

———. 2003a. *Arab Human Development Report 2003*. New York: Oxford University Press.

———. 2003b. *Human Development Report for 2003*. New York: Oxford University Press.

———. 2002. *Human Development Report 2002*. New York: Oxford University Press.

United Nations High Commissioner for Refugees (UNHCR). 2013. *Populations of Concerns to UNHCR, Wallchart*. www.unhcr.org/50a9f81b27.html.

———. 2007. *The 1951 Refugee Convention: Questions and Answers*. New York: UN.

United Nations Human Settlement Programme UN-Habitat. 2013. *State of the World's Cities 2012/2013: Prosperity of Cities*. New York: Routledge.

United Nations Statistics Division. 2002. *Handbook on Training in Civil Registration and Vital Statistics Systems*. Studies in Methods Series F, no. 84, ST/ESA/STAT/SER.F/84. New York: UN.

Urdal, Urkik. 2012. "Youth Bulges and Violence," in Jack A. Goldstone, Eric P. Kaufmann, and Monica Duffy Toft, eds, *Political Demography: How Population Changes Are Reshaping International Security and National Politics*, 117–32. Boulder, CO: Paradigm Publishers.

Urquhart, M.C. 1983. *Historical Statistics of Canada*, 2nd edn. Ottawa: Statistics Canada and Social Sciences Federation of Canada.

Valente, Enza Maria, Patrick M. Abou-Sleiman, Viviana Caputo, et al. 2004. "Hereditary Early-Onset Parkinson's Disease Caused by Mutations in PINK1," *Science* 304 (21 May): 1158–50.

Valente, Paolo. 2010. "Census Taking in Europe: How Are Populations Counted in 2010?" *Population and Societies* 46 (May). Paris: Institut National d'Étude Demographiques.

Vallin, Jacques. 2006. "Europe's Demographic Transition, 1740–1940," in Graziella Caselli, Jacques Vallin, and Guillaume Wunsch, eds, *Demography, Analysis and Synthesis: A Treatise in Population Studies*, 41–66. Amsterdam: Elsevier.

———. 1983. "Sex Patterns of Mortality: A Comparative Study of Model Life Tables and Actual Situations with Special Reference to the Case of Algeria and France," in Alan D. Lopez and Lado T. Ruzicka, eds, *Sex Differentials in Mortality: Trends, Determinants and Consequences*, 376–443. Canberra: Department of Demography, Australian National University.

———, and France Meslé. 2010. "Will Life Expectancy Increase Indefinitely by Three Months Every Year?" *Population and Societies* 473 (December). Paris: INED.

———, and ———. 2009. "The Segmented Trend Line of Highest Life Expectancies," *Population and Development Review* 35, 1: 159–87.

———, ———, and Tapani Valkonen. 2001. "Trends in Mortality and Differential Mortality," *Population Studies* 36. Strasbourg: Council of Europe Publishing.

Van Bavel, Jan, and David S. Reher. 2013. "The Baby Boom and Its Causes: What We Know and What We Need to Know," *Population and Development Review* 39, 2: 257–88.

van de Kaa, Dirk. 2004a. "Is the Second Demographic Transition a Useful Research Concept: Questions and Answers," *Vienna Yearbook of Population Research*. Vienna Institute of Demography. Vienna: Austrian Academy of Sciences.

———. 2004b. "The True Commonality: In Reflexive Modern Societies Fertility Is a Derivative," *Population Studies* 58, 1: 77–92. Discussion of the paper by John Caldwell and Thomas Schindlmayr in *Population Studies* 57, 3 (2003).

———. 2003. "Second Demographic Transition," in Paul Demeny and Geoffrey McNicoll, eds, *Encyclopedia of Population*, 872–3. New York: Macmillan Reference USA/Thompson Gale.

———. 1999. "Europe and Its Population: The Long View," in Dirk J. van de Kaa, Henri Lerido, Giuseppe Gesano, and Marek Okolski, eds, *European Populations: Unite in Diversity*. Dordrecht: Kluwer Academic Publishers.

———. 1987. "Europe's Second Demographic Transition," *Population Bulletin* 42, 1. Washington: Population Reference Bureau.

van de Walle, Etienne. 1992. "Fertility Transition, Conscious Choice and Numeracy," *Demography* 29, 4: 487–502.

Van Heek, F. 1956. "Roman Catholicism and Fertility in the Netherlands," *Population Studies* 10: 125–38.

Vanderkamp, John. 1971. "Migration Flows, Their Determinants and the Effects of Return Migration," *Journal of Political Economy* 79: 1012–31.

———. 1968. "Interregional Mobility in Canada: A Study of the Time Pattern of Migration," *Canadian Journal of Economics* 1: 595–608.

Vaupel, James W. 2010. "Biodemography of Human Ageing," *Nature* 464: 536–42. Published online 24 March 2010. doi:10.1038/nature08984.

———, James R. Carey, Kaare Kristensen, et al. 1998. "Biodemographic Trajectories of Longevity," *Science* 280 (8 May): 855–60.

———, and Elke Lochinger. 2006. "Redistributing Work in Aging Europe," *Science* 312 (30 June): 1911–13.

Veevers, Jane E. 1994. "The 'Real' Marriage Squeeze: Mate Selection, Mortality, and the Mating Gradient," in Frank Trovato and Carl F. Grindstaff, eds, *Perspectives on Canada's Population: An Introduction to Concepts and Issues*, 260–76. Don Mills, ON: Oxford University Press.

———, and Ellen M. Gee. 1986. "Playing It Safe: Accident Mortality and Gender Roles," *Sociological Focus* 19, 4: 349–60.

Verbrugge, Lois M. 1989. "The Twain Meet: Empirical Explanations of Sex Differences in Health and Mortality," *Journal of Health and Social Behavior* 30: 282–304.

———. 1982. "Sex Differentials in Health," *Public Health Reports* 97, 5: 417–37.

———. 1976. "Sex Differentials in Morbidity and Mortality in the United States," *Social Biology* 34, 4: 275–96.

Verhulst, Pierre-Francoise. 1838. "Notice sur la loi que la population suit dans son accroissement," *Correspondence in Mathematics and Physics* 10: 113–21.

Verma, Ravi B.P. 2006. Estimates of Annual Number of Emigrants from Canada, 1971 to 2004. Personal communication.

———, Margaret Michalowski, and Pierre Gauvin. 2004. "Abridged Life Tables for Registered Indians in Canada, 1976–1980 to 1996–2000," *Canadian Studies in Population* 31, 2: 197–235.

Véron, Jacques. 2008. "Alfred J. Lotka and the Mathematics of Population," *Electronic Journal for History of Probability and Statistics* 4, 1: 1–10.

Vining, D.R. Jr, and T.M. Kontuly. 1978 [1996]. "Population Dispersal from Major Metropolitan Regions: An International Comparison," in H.S. Geyer and T.M. Kontuly, eds, *Differential Urbanization: Integrating Spatial Models*, 67–89. London: Edward Arnold.

———, and R. Pallone. 1982. "Migration between Core and Peripheral Regions: A Description and Tentative Explanation of the Patterns in 22 Countries," *Geoforum* 13: 339–410.

———, and A. Strauss. 1977 [1996]. "A Demonstration that the Current Deconcentration of Population in the United States Is a Clean Break with the Past," in H.S. Geyer and T.M. Kontuly, eds, *Differential Urbanization: Integrating Spatial Models*, 28–37. London: Edward Arnold.

Volterra, Vito. 1926. "Fluctuations in the Abundance of a Species Considered Mathematically," *Nature* 118, 558–60.

Wackernagel, Mathis, and William Rees. 1996. *Our Ecological Footprint: Reducing Human Impact on the Earth*. Gabriola Island, BC: New Society Publishers.

Wadhera, Surinder, and Jill Strachan. 1994. *Selected Mortality Statistics, Canada, 1921–1990*. Cat. no. 82-548. Ottawa: Statistics Canada (Canadian Centre for Health Information).

———, and ———. 1993. *Selected Birth and Fertility Statistics, Canada, 1921–1990*. Cat. no. 82-553. Ottawa: Statistics Canada (Canadian Centre for Health Information).

———, and ———. 1992. *Selected Marriage Statistics, 1921–1990*. Cat. no. 82-552. Ottawa: Statistics Canada.

Waldron, Ingrid. 2000. "Trends in Gender Differences in Mortality: Relationships to Changing Gender Differences in Behavior and Other Causal Factors," in E. Annandale and K. Hung, eds, *Gender Inequalities in Health*, 150–81. Buckingham: Open University Press.

———. 1993. "Recent Trends in Sex Mortality Ratios for Adults in Developed Countries," *Social Science and Medicine* 36, 4: 451–62.

———. 1986. "The Contribution of Smoking to Sex Differences in Mortality," *Public Health Reports* 101, 2: 163–73.

———. 1983. "Sex Differences in Human Mortality: The Role of Genetic Factors," *Social Science and Medicine* 17, 6: 321–33.

———. 1976. "Why Do Women Live Longer than Men?" *Social Science and Medicine* 10: 349–62.

Wallace, Iain. 2002. *A Geography of the Canadian Economy*. Don Mills, ON: Oxford University Press.

Wallerstein, Immanuel. 1980. *The Modern World-System II: Mercantilism and the Consolidation of the European World-Economy, 1600–1750*. New York: Academic Press.

———. 1974. *The Modern World-System I: Capitalist Agriculture and the Origins of the European World-Economy in the Sixteenth Century*. New York: Academic Press.

Walmsley, D.J., and G.J. Lewis. 1993. *People and Environment: Behavioral Approaches in Human Geography*, 2nd edn. New York: John Wiley.

Walton, Dawn. 2013. "How Is the Earth Faring on World Environment Day?" *Globe and Mail* (5 June) www.theglobeandmail.com/technology/science/how-is-the-earth-faring-on-world-environment-day/article12355894/?page=all (accessed 19 April 2014).

Walzer, M. 1992. *Spheres of Justice*. New York: Basic Books.

Ward, D. 1971 *Cities and Immigrants: Geography of Change in Nineteenth Century America*. New York: Oxford University Press

Wardwell, J.M. 1977. "Equilibrium and Change in Non-metropolitan Growth," *Rural Sociology* 42: 156–79.

Wargon, Sylvia T. 2002. *Demography in Canada in the Twentieth Century*. Vancouver: University of British Columbia Press.

Warkentin, John. 1999. "Canada and Its Major Regions: Bouchette, Parkin, Rogers, Innis, Hutchison," *The Canadian Geographer* 43, 3: 244–68.

Warnes, Anthony M. 1992. "Age-related Variation and Temporal Change in Elderly Migration," in Andrei Rogers, ed., with W.H. Frey, A. Speare Jr., P. Rees, and A.M. Warnes, *Elderly Migration and Population Redistribution: A Comparative Study*, 35–55. London: Belhaven.

Watkins, Melville H. 1963. "A Staple Theory of Economic Growth," *Canadian Journal of Economics and Political Science* 29, 2: 141–58.

Watkins, Susan Cotts. 1993. "If All We Knew about Women Was What We Read in Demography, What Would We Know?" *Demography* 30: 551–77.

———. 1989. "The Fertility Transition: Europe and the Third World Compared," in J. Mayone Stycos, ed., *Demography as an Interdiscipline*, 27–55. New Brunswick and Oxford: Transaction Publishers.

———, Jane A. Menken, and John Bongaarts. 1987. "Demographic Foundations of Family Change," *American Sociological Review* 52: 346–58.

Weber, Max. 1905 [1958]. *The City*. London: Heinemann.

Weil, David N. 2009. *Economic Growth*, 2nd edn. Boston: Pearson Addison Wesley.

Weindruch R., R.L., Walford, S. Fligiel and D. Guthrie. 1986. "The Retardation of Aging in Mice by Dietary Restriction: Longevity, Cancer, Immunity and Lifetime Energy Intake," *Journal of Nutrition* 116: 641–54.

Weiseman, Alan. 2013. *Countdown: Our Last, Best Hope for a Future on Earth?* London: Little, Brown.

Werlin, Herbert H. 2009. "The Poverty of Nations: The Impact of Foreign Aid," *The Journal of Social, Political, and Economic Studies* 34, 4: 480–510.

Westermarck, Edward, 1891. *The History of Marriage*. New York: Macmillan and Co.

Westoff, Charles F. 2003. "Trends in Marriage and Early Childbearing in Developing Countries," *DHS Comparative Reports* 5: 2–3, 25. Calverton, MD: ORC Macro.

———. 1990. "Reproductive Intentions and Fertility Rates," *International Family Planning Perspectives* 16, 3: 84–9.

———. 1986. "Perspectives on Nuptiality and Fertility," in Kingsley Davis, David Bernstam, and Ricardo Campbell, eds, *Below-Replacement Fertility in Industrialized Societies: Causes, Consequences, Policies*. 155–75, supp. to *Population and Development Review* 12.

———. 1983. "Fertility Decline in the West: Causes and Prospects," *Population and Development Review* 9: 99–104.

———. 1978. "Some Speculations on the Future of Marriage and Fertility," *Family Planning Perspectives* 10: 79–83.

White, Kevin M. 2002. "Longevity Advances in High-Income Countries, 1955–96," *Population and Development Review* 28, 1: 59–76.

———, and Samuel H. Preston. 1996. "How Many Americans Are Alive Because of Twentieth-Century Improvements in Mortality?" *Population and Development Review* 22, 3: 415–30.

Whitehead, Paul C., and Michael J. Hayes. 1998. *The Insanity of Alcohol: Social Problems in Canadian First Nations Communities*. Toronto: Canadian Scholars' Press.

Wigle, Donald T., Yang Mao, Robert Semenciw, and Hoard I. Morrison. 1986. "Cancer Patterns in Canada," *Canadian Medical Association Journal* 134 (1 February): 231–5.

Wilcox, Allen J. 2010. *Fertility and Pregnancy: An Epidemiologic Perspective*. Oxford: Oxford University Press.

Wilkes, Rima, Neil Guppy, and Lily Farris. 2007. "Right-wing Parties and Anti-foreigner Sentiment in Europe," *American Sociological Review* 72: 831–40.

Wilkins, Russell. 1980. *Health Status in Canada, 1926–1976*. Occasional Paper no. 13. Ottawa: Institute for Research on Public Policy.

———, Jean-Marie Berthelot, and Edward Ng. 2002. "Trends in Mortality by Neighbourhood Income in

Urban Canada from 1971 to 1996," *Health Reports* (supp.) vols 1–28.

———, Sharanjit Uppal, Philippe Finès, Sacha Senécal, Éric Guimond, and Rene Dion. 2008. "Life Expectancy in the Inuit-inhabited Areas of Canada, 1989 to 2003," *Health Reports* 19, 1: 7–19.

Wilkinson, Kenneth, P., R.R. Reynolds, Jr., J.G. Thompson, and L.M. Ostrech. 1983. "Divorce and Recent Net Migration in the Old West," *Journal of Marriage and the Family* 45: 437–45.

Wilkinson, Richard G. 2005. *The Impact of Inequality.* New York: New Press.

———. 1996. *Unhealthy Societies: The Afflictions of Inequality.* London: Routledge.

———, and Michael Marmot, eds. 2003. *The Solid Facts: Social Determinants of Health,* 2nd edn. Copenhagen, Denmark: World Health Organization Regional Office for Europe.

———, and Kate Pickett. 2009. *The Spirit Level: Why More Equal Societies Almost Always Do Better.* London: Alan Lane.

Williams, Cara. 2005. "The Sandwich Generation," *Canadian Social Trends* (summer): 16–21. Cat. no. 11-008. Ottawa: Statistics Canada.

Williamson, Jeffrey G. 2006. *Globalization and the Poor Periphery Before 1950.* Cambridge, MA: MIT Press.

———. 1965. "Regional Inequality and the Process of National Development: A Description of the Patterns," *Economic Development and Cultural Change* 13: 3–84.

Willis, Robert J. 1987. "What Have We Learned from the Economics of the Family?' *American Economic Review* 77, 2: 68–81.

———. 1973a. "New Approach to the Economic Theory of Fertility Behavior," *Journal of Political Economy* 81, 2: S14–S64.

———. 1973b. "Economic Theory of Fertility Behavior," in Theodore W. Schultz, ed., *Economics of the Family: Marriage, Children, and Human Capital,* 25–75. Chicago: The University of Chicago Press.

Wilmoth, Jane T., and Kenneth F. Ferraro, eds. 2007. *Gerontology: Perspectives and Issues,* 3rd edn. New York: Springer.

Wilmoth, John R. 2003. "Mortality Decline," in Paul Demeny and Geoffrey McNicoll, eds, *Encyclopedia of Population,* vol. 2, pp. 654–62. New York: Macmillan Reference USA, Thomson/Gale.

———, L.J. Deegan, H. Lundstrom, and S. Horiuchi. 2002. "Increase of Maximum Life-span in Sweden, 1861–1999," *Science* 289 (29 September): 2366–8.

Wilson, Chris. 2013. "Thinking about Post-transitional Demographic Regimes: A Reflection," *Demographic Research* 28, 46: 1373–88.

———. 2011. "Understanding Global Demographic Convergence since 1950," *Population and Development Review* 37, 2: 375–88.

———, Tomas Sobotka, Lee Williamson, and Paul Boyle. 2013. "Migration and Intergenerational Replacement in Europe," *Population and Development Review* 39, 1: 131–57.

Wilson, Leonard S. 2003. "Equalization, Efficiency and Migration: Watson Revisited," *Canadian Public Policy* 29, 4: 385–96.

Wimberley, Dale W. 1990. "Investment Dependence and Alternative Explanations of Third World Mortality," *American Sociological Review* 55, 1: 75–91.

Winch, Donald. 2003. "Darwin, Charles," in Paul Demeny and Geoffrey McNicoll, eds, *Encyclopedia of Population,* 189–90. New York: Macmillan Reference USA/Thomson Gale.

Winckler, Edwin A. 2002. "Chinese Reproductive Policy at the Turn of the Millennium: Dynamic Stability," *Population and Development Review* 28, 3: 379–418.

Wingard, Deborah L. 1982. "The Sex Differential in Mortality Rates: Demographic and Behavioral Factors," *American Journal of Epidemiology* 1, 15: 205–16.

Winsborough, Halliman H. 1978. "Statistical Histories of the Life Cycle of Birth Cohorts," in Karl E. Taeuber, Larry L. Bumpass, and James A. Sweet, eds, *Social Demography,* pp. 231–59. New York: Academic Press.

Wirth, Luis. 1938. "Urbanism as a Way of Life," *American Journal of Sociology* 44: 2–24.

Wise, Paul. 2003. "The Anatomy of a Disparity," *Annual Review of Public Health* 24: 341–62.

Wister, Andrew. 2005. *Baby Boomer Health Dynamics: How Are We Aging?* Toronto: University of Toronto Press.

Woldemicael, Gebremariam, and Roderic Beaujot. 2010. "Fertility Behavior of Immigrants in Canada: Converging Trends," *PSC Discussion Papers Series* 24, 5, art. 1. http://ir.lib.uwo.ca/pscpapers/vol24/iss5/.

Wolfe, Barbara L. 2003. "Fertility, Nonmarital," in Paul Demeny and Geoffrey McNicoll, eds, *Encyclopedia of Population,* vol. 1, 409–12. New York: Macmillan Reference USA/Thomson Gale.

Wolfson, Michael C. 1996. "Health Adjusted Life Expectancy," *Health Reports* 1: 41–6.

Wolpert, John. 1965a. "Behavioral Aspects of the Decision to Migrate," *Papers of the Regional Science Association* 15: 159–69.

———. 1965b. "Migration as an Adjustment to Environmental Stress," *Journal of Social Issues* 22: 92–102.

Wood, James W. 1994. *Dynamics of Human Reproduction: Biology, Biometry, Demography.* Hawthorne, NY: Aldine De Gruyter.

Woods, Robert. 2009. *Death before Birth: Fetal Health and Mortality in Historical Perspective.* Oxford: Oxford University Press.

———. 1982. *Theoretical Population Geography.* London: Longman.

Woolmington, Eric. 1985. "Small May Be Inevitable," *Australian Geographical Studies* 23 (October): 195–207.

World Bank. 2013. "Health Expenditure, Total (% of GDP)," World Health Organization National Health Account Database. http://data.worldbank.org/indicator/SH.XPD.TOTL.ZS (accessed 14 September 2013)

———. 2012. *World Development Report 2013.* Washington, DC: World Bank.

———. 1993. *The East Asian Miracle: Economic Growth and Public Policy.* Oxford: Oxford University Press.

———. 1992. *World Development Report 1992: Development and the Environment.* New York: Oxford University Press.

World Health Organization. 2014. *World Health Statistics 2014.* Geneva: WHO.

———. 2013. *Map Library.* Geneva: WHO. http://gamapserver.who.int/mapLibrary/app/searchResults.aspx (accessed 12 September 2013).

———. 2007. *World Health Statistics 2007.* Geneva: WHO.

———. 2006a. *Number and Rates of Registered Deaths: Canada.* www3.who.int/whosis/mort/table1_process.cfm (28 February 2006).

———. 2006b. *Infant Mortality Database.* Geneva: WHO. www3.who.int/whosis/mort/table2_process.cfm (20 April 2005).

———. 2005a. *Preventing Chronic Diseases: A Vital Investment.* Geneva: WHO. www.who.int/chp/chronic_disease_report/contents/en/index.html.

———. 2005b. *Health and the Millennium Development Goals.* Geneva: WHO.

———. 1998. *World Health Statistics Annual, 1996.* Geneva: WHO.

World Wildlife Fund and Global Footprint Network. 2012. *Living Planet Report 2012.* Summary. http://awsassets.panda.org/downloads/lpr_2012_summary_booklet_final_120505_2_pdf (accessed 15 May 2014).

Wrigley, E.A. 1969. *Population and History.* New York: McGraw-Hill.

———, R.S. Davies, J.E. Oeppen, and R.S. Schofield. 1997. *English Population History from Family Reconstitution, 1580–1837.* Cambridge: Cambridge University Press.

———, and R.S. Schofield. 1981. *The Population History of England 1581–1871: A Reconstruction.* London: Edward Arnold.

———, and David Souden, eds. 1986. *The Works of Thomas Robert Malthus,* vol. 1: *An Essay on the Principle of Population.* London: William Pickering.

Wu, Zhen. 2000 *Cohabitation: A New Form of Family Living.* Don Mills, ON: Oxford University Press.

———, and Christoph Schimmele. 2005. "Divorce and Repartnering," in Maureen Baker, ed., *Families: Changing Trends in Canada,* 202–28. Toronto: McGraw-Hill.

Xu Lei. 2011. "Inter-metropolitan Migration of the Newly Landed Immigrants in Canada: 1991–1996 and 1996–2001," *GeoJournal* 76: 501–24.

Yancey, W.L., E.P. Ericksen, and R.N. Juliani. 1976. "Emergent Ethnicity: A Review and Reformulation," *American Sociological Review* 41: 391–403.

Yano, Keiji, Tomoki Nakay, A. Stewart Rotheringham, S. Openshaw, and Y. Ishikawa. 2003. "A Comparison of Migration Behaviour in Japan and Britain Using Spatial Interaction Models," *International Journal of Population Geography* 9: 419–31.

Yaukey, David. 1985. *Demography: The Study of Human Population.* New York: St Martin's Press.

———. 1969. "Theorizing about Fertility," *The American Sociologist* 4 (May): 100–4.

———, Douglas L. Anderton, and Jennifer Hickes Lundquist. 2007. *Demography: The Study of Human Population,* 3rd edn. Long Grove, IL: Waveland Press.

Yen, I.H., and S.L. Syme. 1999. "The Social Environment and Health: A Discussion of the Epidemiologic Literature," *Annual Review of Public Health* 20: 287–308.

Yongping, Li, and Xizhe Peng. 2000. "Age and Sex Structures," in Xizhe Peng and Zhigang Guo, eds, *The Changing Population of China,* 64–76. Oxford: Blackwell.

Young, E.A. 1995. *Third World in the First: Development and Indigenous Peoples.* London: Routledge.

Young, T. Kue. 1999. *Population Health: Concepts and Methods.* New York: Oxford University Press.

———. 1997. "Recent Health Trends in the Native American Population," *Population Research and Policy Review* 16, 1–2: 147–67.

———. 1994. *The Health of Native Americans: Towards a Biocultural Epidemiology.* New York: Oxford University Press.

———. 1988a. *Health Care and Cultural Change: The Indian Experience in the Central Subarctic.* Toronto: University of Toronto Press.

———. 1988b. "Are Subarctic Indians Undergoing the Epidemiologic Transition?" *Social Science and Medicine* 26, 6: 659–71.

Yount, Kathryn M. 2001. "Excess Mortality of Girls in the Middle East in the 1970s and 1980s: Patterns, Correlates and Gaps in Research," *Population Studies* 55, 3: 291–308.

Zaridze, David, Paul Brennan, Jillian Boreham, et al. 2009. "Alcohol and Cause-specific Mortality in Russia: A Retrospective Case—Control Study of 48 557 Adult Deaths," *Lancet* 373, 9682: 2201–14.

Zatonski, W.A., and N. Bhala. 2012. "Changing Trends of Diseases in Eastern Europe: Closing the Gap," *Public Health* 126: 248–52.

Zavodny, M. 1999. "Determinants of Recent Immigrants' Locational Choices," *International Migration Review* 33, 4: 1014–30.

Zelinsky, Wilbur. 1979. "The Demographic Transition: Changing Patterns of Migration," in *International Union for the Scientific Study of Population*, 165–89. Liege, Belgium: IUSSP.

——. 1978. "Is Nonmetropolitan America Being Repopulated? The Evidence from Pennsylvania's Minor Civil Divisions," *Demography* 15, 1: 13–39.

——. 1971. "The Hypothesis of the Mobility Transition," *Geographical Review* 61, 2: 219–49.

——. 1966. *A Prologue to Population Geography*. Englewood Cliffs, NJ: Prentice Hall.

Zimmer, Zachary, and Susan A. McDaniel. 2013. "Global Ageing in the Twenty-First Century: An Introduction," in Susan A. McDaniel and Zachary Zimmer, eds, *Global Ageing in the Twenty-First Century: Challenges, Opportunities and Implications*, pp. 1–12. Surrey, UK: Ashgate.

Zimmerman, Klaus F., ed. 1989. *Economic Theory of Optimal Population*. London: Springer.

Zipf, George Kingsley. 1949. *Human Behavior and the Principle of Least Effort*. Cambridge, MA: Addison-Wesley.

——. 1946. "The P_1P_2/D Hypothesis: On the Intercity Movement of Persons," *American Sociological Review* 11: 677–86.

Zlotnik, Hania. 2013. "Population: Crowd Control," *Nature* 501 (5 September): 30–31.

——. 2006. "Theories of International Migration," in Graziella Caselli, Jacques Vallin, and Guillaume Wunsch, eds, *Demography: Analysis and Synthesis*, vol. 2, 293–306. Amsterdam: Elsevier.

Zolberg, Aristide R. 1981. "International Migrations in Political Perspective," in Mary M. Kritz, Charles B. Keely, and Silvano M. Tomasi, eds, *Global Trends in Migration: Theory and Research on International Population Movements*, 3–27. Staten Island, New York: Center for Migration Studies.

Zolnik, Edmund J. 2004. "The North American City Revisited: Urban Quality of Life in Canada and the United States," *Urban Geography* 25, 3: 217–40.

Zuberi, Tukufu, Amson Sibanda, Ayaga Bawah, and Amadou Noumbissi. 2003. "Population and African Society," *Annual Review of Sociology* 29: 465–86.